DATE DUE			

Mass Communication Review Yearbook

Editorial Board

Mass Communication Review Yearbook

Volume 2

1981

G. Cleveland Wilhoit
Editor

Harold de Bock
Associate Editor

SAGE
PUBLICATIONS

302.23
M 38
/44/5/
may 1988

For information address:

SAGE Publications, Inc.
275 South Beverly Drive
Beverly Hills, California 90212

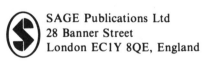

SAGE Publications Ltd
28 Banner Street
London EC1Y 8QE, England

Printed in the United States of America

International Standard Book Number 0-8039-1187-4

International Standard Series Number 0196-8017

FIRST PRINTING

Contents

About the Editors

G. CLEVELAND WILHOIT is Professor of Journalism and Associate Director of the Bureau of Media Research at Indiana University. A member of the editorial board of *Journalism Quarterly*, he is also a member of the News Research Committee of the American Newspaper Publishers Association. A former chairman of the Standing Committee on Research of the Association for Education in Journalism (AEJ), Wilhoit is a past Head of the Theory and Methodology Division of AEJ. He is also a member of the International Association for Mass Communication Research (IAMCR). Wilhoit has published in communication and political science journals and is a contributing author of *Handbook of Reporting Methods*. The editor of Volume 1 of *Mass Communication Review Yearbook*, Wilhoit is co-author of *Newsroom Guide to Polls and Surveys*, *A Computerized Bibliography of Mass Communication Research, 1944-1964*, and *News Media Coverage of U.S. Senators in Four Congresses, 1953-1974*. In 1975 Wilhoit was a visiting research fellow at the Audience Research Department, Netherlands Broadcasting Corporation. He received his Ph.D. in mass communication research and political science at the University of North Carolina at Chapel Hill in 1967.

HAROLD de BOCK is Director of Audience Research at the Netherlands Broadcasting Corporation (NOS), Hilversum. He has published in mass communication research journals in Europe and the United States and was associate editor of Volume 1 of the *Mass Communication Review Yearbook*. De Bock received his Kandidaats and Doctoraat degrees in political science and mass communications from the University of Amsterdam, and his Ph.D. in mass communications from Indiana University in 1973. De Bock is a member of the International Association of Mass Communication Researchers and of the Group of European Audience Researchers (GEAR).

Preface

A chief goal of the Sage *Mass Communication Review Yearbook* series is to produce an enduring volume that is international in scope, concentrating particularly on mass communication research in North America and Europe. With this book we have expanded our range to include work from Japan. Future volumes will, no doubt, seek to cover other emerging world centers of research.

An international editorial board of 40 scholars, whose names are printed in the front matter of the *Yearbook,* has assisted in finding material for this book. These scholars, from 13 countries, examined journals and unpublished sources for the best recent research in their areas.

Hundreds of articles and manuscripts were evaluated for Volume Two. A primary criterion for selection was the extent to which an article synthesized a particular area of inquiry or attempted to define the field in a provocative way. Other work that was representative of significant approaches or that addressed important communication problems was included.

This second volume contains much material that is complementary to the first book in our series. New subject headings include a section on the nature of news and reporters and another on information processing. The standard sections, dealing with theory, methodology, political communication, mass media impact, and comparative research, have been continued in this volume.

For the second year, Harold de Bock has served admirably as associate editor for Europe. The tasks of arranging for translations, ironing out difficulties with copyright clearance, and evaluating manuscripts have been made much easier by his competency. His facility with languages and knowledge of European work have, again, been invaluable.

Richard G. Gray, director of the School of Journalism, gave much encouragement and support to this project. David H. Weaver, Director of the Bureau of Media Research at Indiana University, assisted with critical judgment at crucial times and provided administrative support for the book. Frances Goins Wilhoit, head of the Indiana University journalism library, and her library associate, Gwen Pershing, provided bibliographic assistance in preparation of the volume.

11

Inez Woodley, administrative secretary of the Bureau of Media Research, was again indispensable. Her enthusiasm, eye for detail, and talent as a writer and copy editor improved the volume markedly. Jeff Black, a Bureau assistant, did much to make the clerical work for the book accurate and fun.

—G. Cleveland Wilhoit
Bloomington, Indiana

INTRODUCTION

G. Cleveland Wilhoit

Deep concern about the directions, depth, and philosophy of mass communication research that emerged in the first volume of the *Yearbook* continues here. American researchers appear to have responded to European criticism by taking a closer look at early work on both sides of the Atlantic to get a sharper view of the field's genesis and growth. In the meantime, many prominent Europeans, while still critical of American work, are calling for greater collaboration.

Despite argument about assumptions and approaches that continues—both between and within scholarly groups throughout the world—there is much less discordance of research than the public debate suggests. This volume will show considerable homogeneity of basic research objectives and approaches in mass communication study around the world.

Of course, there are enriching, individual directions in research, and this book reflects this diversity while identifying areas of shared interest. Work is used here from research centers in Eastern and Western Europe, Asia, and the United States—work that indicates there is ample common ground for collaboration.

PURPOSE OF THE BOOK

The second volume of the *Yearbook* continues the main objectives set forth when the series was begun. The first is to publish in a single volume the most durable work in mass communication research of the past year. Articles that integrate ongoing work, that chart new directions, or that are typical studies in an important area have priority. Second, the book attempts to nurture the developing collaboration between European and American researchers and to encourage exchange between Western scholars and research centers in other parts of the world.

A significant portion of this volume contains European and Japanese work that has not come to the widespread attention of American scholars. Also, this volume seeks to acquaint scholars throughout the world with studies of

TABLE 1   Classification of Mass Communication Research Articles by Research
Method Employed

Method	Percentage 1944 - 1964[a]	Percentage 1978 - 1980
Content analysis	10.4	9.2
Critical analysis	35.3	31.7
Experimental	29.8	24.7
Historical analysis	6.6	5.3
Survey	17.9	21.3
Observation	—	1.7
Legal	—	1.6
Multi-methods	—	4.5
N = 2,284 100%		N = 815 100%

a. These data are from Wayne A. Danielson and G. Cleveland Wilhoit, *A Computerized Bibliography of Mass Communication Research, 1944-1964*. New York: Magazine Publishers Association, 1967, p. xvii.

which they may not be aware, especially by younger, emerging researchers in the field.

For this volume, a distinguished editorial board of 40 scholars surveyed their fields of expertise for the best recent work and recommended hundreds of articles. From those recommendations and from extensive searches by the editor and associate editor, 42 articles were selected for publication.

MAJOR TRENDS IN THE FIELD

Review of the literature in preparation for Volume Two of the *Yearbook* suggests that many of the trends noted in the first book persist. Expanded international contacts among researchers; criticism of American work by influential European scholars; reanalysis of the "limited effects" interpretation; increasing numbers of studies in areas such as the agenda-setting function; and a greater concern for long-term studies, all are reflected in contemporary work. In addition, a resurgence of interest in studies of journalists at work, and recently developing research on the audience processing of broadcast news, will be displayed in Volume Two.

To get a more definitive picture of subject-matter trends in the field, an analysis of *Communication Abstracts*—the indispensable abstracting service begun in 1978 by Sage Publications—was conducted. A systematic random sample of 815 entries from the three existing volumes of the *Abstracts* were classified by methodology and subject matter, using subject headings from a similar analysis conducted two decades ago.

The results show remarkably similar patterns of methodology and broad subject matter in the late 1970s as compared to the field in the 1950s. There are some notable differences, however. (See Tables 1 and 2.) Observation,

TABLE 2   Classification of Research Articles by Broad Subject Matter of Mass
            Communication

Mass Communication Category	Percentage 1944 - 1964	Percentage 1978 - 1980
Audiences	7.0	10.2
Communication Process	23.3	26.0
Content	23.5	19.0
Control and Support	5.6	6.6
Development	7.4	7.5
Effects	16.5	12.0
Research Methods	13.9	5.4
Responsibility	2.4	4.3
Miscellaneous	.4	9.0[a]
TOTAL	N = 2,287 100%	N =815 100%[b]

a   This relatively high percentage in miscellaneous suggests, of course, that the broad subject headings used
are no longer completely adequate for the range of subject matter in the modern period. The categories were
adapted originally from Wilbur Schramm (ed.) *Mass Communications* (Urbana: University of Illinois Press,
1959), pp. ix-xi.

b.   Examples of the coding: Uses and gratifications studies were coded as *communication process*. Studies
of media professionalism were coded under *responsibility*. Agenda-setting research was classified as *effects*.
Studies of newspaper and television audiences, and market studies in involving media were placed in
audiences.

legal, and multi methodological studies are a small percentage of the
approaches used today, but they did not appear at all in the 1950s. Critical
analysis and experimentation appear in slightly lesser percentages and
survey research in a slightly higher percentage than in the earlier period. In
addition, a smaller percentage of studies *about* research methods are
published now than two decades ago.

Effects and content studies appear in lesser percentages, and audience and
communication process studies appear in slightly greater percentages than in
the 1950s. Most dramatic is the drop in percentage of studies dealing with
attitudes and attitude change, which declined from about 11% in the 1950s to
a little less than 3% in *Communication Abstracts*.

The most striking finding, though, is in the amount of research being
produced. From 1944 to 1964, using 48 social science journals published in
English, 2287 titles were found to be about mass communication. In the last
three years, *Communication Abstracts* has summarized about 2400 journal
articles, abstracted from 100 academic journals. Even though the journal
population base and the definitions of communication research used by the
compilers are somewhat different in the two sets of data, the comparative
evidence suggests dramatic growth in the field's literature during the last
quarter century.[1]

SCOPE OF THE YEARBOOK

Organized in seven sections, this volume contains both original and reprinted work. The original papers published here are, in most cases, highly significant reports presented at conferences. Several European pieces in the *Yearbook* are translated into English for the first time.

About one half of the 60 authors represented in the volume are young scholars, and this new generation of scholars signals continuing vitality in the field. Several pioneering leaders, such as Wilbur Schramm, Kurt Lang, and Gladys Engel Lang, contribute important articles. Other leading scholars, several of whom are represented in the first volume, appear again here, indicating that the field has marked stability and maturity.

Considerable continuity between the first and second volumes of this series is apparent. Many of the pieces extend and complement material from the first book. The first section, "Theoretical Perspectives," leads off with a refinement of the comparison of European and American work that began Volume One. The section takes a deep look at social theories of the mass media, ending with a delightful essay on communication history.

Highlighting Part II, "Research Strategies and Methodology," is a special symposium on agenda-setting research methods. There is a thorough review of methodological requirements for valid effects studies and a proposal for longitudinal inquiry into life-span media use. A challenge to the validity of news bias analyses and an essay on applying quantitative techniques to journalism history conclude Part II.

A new section, "Nature of News and Reporting," was developed as Part III for this edition of the *Yearbook*. An inquiry into predictors of journalists' professional and organizational commitment sets the stage for three analyses of journalists at work.

Another new section reports on studies of the process of news comprehension. Part IV, "Information Processing and the Mass Media," ends with a claim for the "script" as a common unit of analysis in communication research.

The fifth section, "Political Communication," features a landmark analysis of the mass media and the Watergate scandal that places agenda-setting within the larger framework of the public opinion process. Two analyses with implications for the knowledge-gap hypothesis are also presented in Part V.

"Impact of Mass Communication," Part VI, contains two pieces at the heart of a major scholarly debate concerning the cultivation effects of television. Following these articles is an important integrative work that synthesizes—with a comparative perspective—thousands of studies on the impact of television. Two analyses of the effects of the television series *Holocaust* on European audiences, and a test of selective exposure in a heart disease information campaign in California, conclude the section.

A special symposium on the *informationalized societies* approach to comparative communication research by the Japanese leads Part VII, "International and Comparative Research." From Sweden, a preliminary report on a mass media cultural indicators project is presented. Exciting research on the changing and expanding role of mass communication in China complements work on the same subject published in the first *Yearbook*. Concluding the volume is an unusual study from an Eastern European research center that compares Eastern and Western European press coverage of Polish newsmakers.

PART I: THEORETICAL PERSPECTIVES

Heightening our sensitivity to the effects of cultural and industrial settings on the questions and methods of mass communication research, the work in Part I is a stirring accompaniment to that in the 1980 *Yearbook*. Jay G. Blumler provides a nice bridge between the two books with a second installment of his transatlantic views of the field (Blumler, 1980).

Blumler still sees much greater focus among European than American scholars, but he says that more attention to long-term effects studies would benefit the Europeans and a more critical focus on public policy would aid the Americans. Both sides could gain from greater attempts to link audience-effects work to analyses of the nature of media systems.

Simplistic propositions about mass media maintenance of the status quo—particularly prevalent among European critical theorists, but common among American scholars as well—are challenged in Blumler's critique. He shows that surveillance of violations of political and social norms and values can just as easily be upsetting as supportive of the established order, with the Watergate scandal in the United States a sterling example.

It is in Blumler's effort to frame a conciliatory agenda for world scholars that the most telling points come through. Scholars on both continents share philosophical differences as much within them as between them. The divergencies between British critical theorists such as James Halloran and scholars such as Blumler appear as considerable as those between a James Carey and a Jack McLeod in the United States.

That the differences between the academies of the two continents may be more apparent than real need not be seen as dulling Blumler's point that the continents and various schools have a lot to gain from each other. His suggestion that a research agenda in the United States, organized around the conceptual potential of agenda setting, would provide "plenty to talk to Europeans about" is already being partly realized, as articles in this volume will show.

The review in Part I of the traditional Marxist position by Nicholas Garnham at first glance suggests a larger gap than exists between mainstream American scholarship and the sturdy, if minority, Marxist tradition in

Europe. Garnham's call for a shift in focus from a concern with the ideological content of the mass media to the analysis of the industrial base of culture represented by the media, strikes a responsive chord with the concern among American scholars for economic analyses of media structure (Weaver and Gray, 1980). While the approach to economics by most mainstream U.S. scholars is not Marxist, Garnham's questions about multinational corporate media ownership, labor strife, and the introduction of new communication technologies, are significant to American researchers as well as to others elsewhere in the world.

In pointing out in volume one of the *Yearbook* that good empirical research is *critical,* Kurt Lang (1980) also reminded us that many major questions dominating American work in this century had been anticipated, if not articulated, at the turn of the century by classical German scholars who are so influential in the European critical tradition. Hanno Hardt, in an excerpt from his book on social theories of the press, describes the post-World War II impact of the American functionalist-empirical tradition on German scholarship. It was not until the early 1960s that a reflective tradition in Germany began to argue that empirical techniques were incapable of leading to a theory of society that encompasses mass communication. Hardt sees weaknesses in both approaches, with critical theory seldom leading to practice and empirical-administrative research suffering a sterile preoccupation with methods. There is a contrast between utopia and realism, he says, with each obviously needing a bit of the other. Hardt reminds us, too, that the scholarship of the Hutchins Commission on Freedom of the Press during the 1940s is a good example of American inquiry that combined the critical and empirical moods (Commission on Freedom of the Press, 1947).

Classic examples of American work of an administrative mold, particularly in the eyes of Europeans, are the panel studies of the 1940s and 1950s by Paul F. Lazarsfeld and associates at Columbia University (Lazarsfeld, 1944). The two-step flow and later multi-step flow theories of communication and influence justifiably had impact on American mass communication research, although the theories were being questioned by mass communications scholars as early as the late 1950s (Danielson, 1956; Deutschmann, 1960). Sociologists, political scientists, and other allied researchers often considered the personal influence work as definitive, and felt little else remained to be done there. Thus, in Part I Todd Gitlin is justified in calling multi-step flow theory the "dominant paradigm" of media sociology.

Gitlin, who scrutinizes Lazarsfeld's work in voluminous detail, footnotes and all, links the thesis of minimal media effects (and the dominance of personal influence) to the "administrative" research setting that produced it. He sees Lazarsfeld as so tied to the rapidly expanding mass media institutions—both through grants and philosophical bent—that alternative conclusions about the emerging corporate empires of mass media were impossible. C. Wright Mills, who organized the field work for Katz and Lazarsfeld's *Personal Influence* (1955), apparently attempted a radical analysis of the data—pointing out the pyramidal influence of the mass media, particularly in politics—but none of his conclusions ever emerged in the published work. The marketing orientation, equating buying soap with voting, was dominant, not because of a conspiracy, but as a result of the convergence of the administrative context of the research and Lazarsfeld's philosophical roots in Austrian social democracy.

A broader view of the influence of cultural context on communication theory is portrayed by Lawrence Grossberg, who claims that a variety of philosophies have dominated communication theory, even in the United States. The effects research tradition, typified in the work of Wilbur Schramm, evolved from American liberal ideas that ignorance can be eradicated by scientific information. A second American strain, nurtured by John Dewey and the Chicago school, was rooted in pragmatism and a concern for the role of communication in creating community. Thus, Grossberg's article challenges Gitlin's thesis of the monolithic influence of the administrative paradigm.

Dethronement of positivism in mass media research is to be celebrated, but rigorous, appropriate research by Third World scholars is what is needed now, says James Halloran. Major research questions of the use and societal impact of rapidly changing communication technologies are vital. Halloran calls for critical, sociological, policy-oriented research that will speak to the intelligent use of mass media technology to guard against swamping traditional cultures with the homogenizing, commercial matter of Western media.

Another research query posed by Halloran—whether there is a clear and present risk that information overload may paralyze future societies—is handled in a delightful and unusual essay by Wilbur Schramm. The mind of one of the most resourceful of American mass media scholars, who in Grossberg's piece epitomized the stream of scientism in communication research, takes a historical sweep through communication history to speak to Halloran's question. Schramm shows that the mass media make up an infinitely small part of communication history, but that they were the harbingers of an information flow acceleration that has been overwhelming. He sees hope, though, that rapidly developing communication technology will significantly increase individual control over the huge quantities of data pouring from the new systems. Halloran—and no doubt Garnham—will reject Schramm's thesis, but Schramm's essay is an appropriate reminder that much of the key research inquiry of our time should be subjected to historical analysis.

The final two pieces in Part I deal with specific theories of communication. Sven Windahl's treatment of the uses and gratifications approach is additional evidence that Europeans and Americans share research interests.

Windahl proposes a synthesis of the uses and effects paradigms of mass communication. The merging of the approaches points to a greater balance in the research concerns for both media content and basic individual motives, leading to a new research term: *conseffects,* a notion that combines, as a single variable, media dependency and use with content effects.

That a basic unit of nonverbal communication analysis is likely to emerge from neurophysiological theory rather than linguistics is the basic assumption of the concluding piece in Part I. This state-of-the-art review of the neurophysiological literature by Peter Andersen, John P. Garrison, and Janis F. Andersen has implications for content analysis of visual material and more general work in interpersonal communication.

PART II: RESEARCH STRATEGIES AND METHODOLOGY

Even though mass communication research is a relatively small discipline, the research strategies and methods used in the field have varied considerably. Of the several main directions that are developing, one such, particularly in the United States, is an agenda-setting functional approach.

This section contains five papers that tackle conceptual and methodological problems of agenda-setting research. Maxwell McCombs and his associates, Chaim H. Eyal, James P. Winter, and William F. DeGeorge, see agenda-setting theory as a conceptual link between the mass media effects tradition and the uses and gratifications approach to research. To realize that conceptual link requires greater comparability of methods among the many agenda-setting studies being done now throughout the world.

In separate articles, the agenda-setting group argues that differences in the definitions of the time frames and agenda measurements render many agenda-setting studies incomparable. In addition, failure to consider media audience differences and insensitivity to the *nature* of actual issues that emerge in media coverage limit the theory-building potential of agenda-setting research.

The McCombs group outlines the conditions under which certain methodological approaches—such as the awareness, priorities, or salience models of agenda measurement—should be used. They also anticipate, particularly in the Winter piece on the contingent conditions of agenda-setting, the conceptual development of what Gladys Engel Lang and Kurt Lang call the *agenda-building* process in their article on the Watergate scandal, published in Part V of this volume.

For some forty years, the study of attitude change dominated media effects research. In last year's volume, Steven Chaffee (1980) outlined some new research perspectives that have emerged from improvements in longitudinal methods and conceptually broadened hypotheses that consider contextual factors such as family and community. In a complementary piece in Part V of this volume, Jack McLeod and Byron Reeves review the complexity of evidence required to logically show mass media effects. They outline four elements required in effects designs: (1) assessing media content with high validity; (2) controlling audience exposure to the content; (3) assessing which observed effects are functionally related to the message; and (4) elaborating on conditional processes that may have been stimulated by the message exposure.

McLeod and Reeves also point out that an assessment of the media effects literature requires an understanding of the history of mass communication research as an applied field. They see its history as roughly parallel to the development of political science, with late emergence of a communication academic discipline that focuses on a class of variables rather than on concepts. Furthermore, there exists great potential for productive policy research in mass communication as an applied field with ties to media institutions. McLeod and Reeves caution that ties to the media often constrain the research questions to the range of action in which the media are already engaged, a criticism writ large in Todd Gitlin's earlier analysis of the Lazarsfeld era.

Typical of recent developments in longitudinal designs, John W. Dimmick, Thomas A. McCain, and Theodore Bolton develop a plan for long-term analysis of media use, applying some of the ideas sketched by F. Gerald Kline's (1980) piece on time in communication research in Volume One of the *Yearbook*. Dimmick and associates outline a design for specifying the change functions of uses and gratifications over entire life-spans. They illustrate use of longitudinal panels, cohort analysis, and mixed designs in testing the hypothesis that life-span media use is curvilinear.

Following Karl Erik Rosengren's (1980) outline of methods and concepts in measuring news bias published in the first *Yearbook*, Digby C. Anderson and W.W. Sharrock work from a similar assumption—that the mass media should not be expected to be impartial—and raise serious questions about the validity of content analysis of news. Neither journalists nor audiences are impartial, and by failing to distinguish between journalistic form and content, it is often the investigator's bias that emerges in content analysis.

Supplementing Wilbur Schramm's historical perspective from Part I, Carolyn Stewart Dyer concludes the methods section of the *Yearbook* with a description of quantitative analysis of journalism history. Cluster and regression analysis may be used to test propositions from traditional narrative histories such as these: Newspapers were among the first institutions established in frontier settlements; and they were begun with second-hand equipment. Dyer's work suggests neither of these propositions is supported. In spite of the problem of missing data that always plagues the historian, Dyer concludes that the methods are particularly useful when a seminar, or several historians working together, can divide the labor of sifting masses of data from archival materials.

PART III: NATURE OF NEWS AND REPORTING

One of the most visible developments during the last decade has been the rediscovery of journalists and mass communication by other disciplines, such as sociology and political science. After Warren Breed's early work on social control in the newsroom, at least two decades passed before journalists were to appear regularly in published work in allied disciplines. New research by sociologists and political scientists is enriching the work of mass communication researchers in the area.[2] Part III of the *Yearbook* presents the work of several productive young mass communication scholars as evidence of fresh research relating the institutional setting of journalists to news and professional values.

Using the massive data set from a national sample of professional journalists collected by the Johnstone group (Lee B. Becker, Idowu A. Sobowale, and Robin E. Cobbe) they applied discriminant analysis to look at news organizational and professional commitment. They found job satisfaction to be a significant predictor of both. Journalistic training and background were significant only for professional allegiance, which was also associated with married journalists having families, a larger number of professional involvements, a less critical stance on the media in general, and nonguild status.

The three remaining articles are observations of journalists at work. Sharon Dunwoody uses content analysis, observation, and interviews of science journalists covering the 1977 convention of the American Association for the Advancement of Science. Dunwoody combined several levels of analysis of one of the largest scientific meetings in America to show both the positive and negative aspects of the tendency of groups of reporters to "cooperate" with each other in coverage of such an event. The emphasis on cooperation rather than competition appeared to enhance news story accuracy and to validate event newsworthiness, but it may have constrained the variety of reports about the meeting.

David H. Ostroff scrutinizes TV reporting of state and local politics during the 1978 gubernatorial race in Ohio. Using observation and interviews, Ostroff found the news staffs of the three TV stations in the capital city of Columbus striving for independent news judgment, consciously resisting staged events, and relying much less on visuals than Ostroff had expected. He speculates that the findings may reflect a reaction to widespread criticism of television news.

The concluding piece by Charles R. Bantz, Suzanne McCorkle, and Roberta C. Baade provides a contrasting picture of an unidentified TV news operation in the Western United States. Team observation and interviews of the general news coverage of the station found news at the station reduced to a routine, hence the analogy of the news factory. A lack of journalistic flexibility, little personal investment in the edited broadcast news stories, and a mismatch between news executives and staff led the authors to speculate that TV news may be much more routinized than newspapers. Although Ostroff's research differs from this study in crucial ways, the contrasting findings suggest the need for more organizational analysis that is comparable in method and design.

PART IV: INFORMATION PROCESSING AND THE MASS MEDIA

As broadcast news matures into a popular and powerful force throughout the world, the perceptual processes of audiences using the medium are becoming a subject of wide study. In this field, it appears that industrial researchers have taken the lead. Researchers at Swedish Radio, a state-operated broadcast service, have been looking at this problem for the last decade.

In the lead article, Olle Findahl and Birgitta Hoïjer describe innovative studies that use large random samples. Q-segmentation technique—a computerized matching procedure—produced five experimental groups whose members were similar on patterns of knowledge and retention. When the experimental groups were shown televised news with still photos emphasizing the causal *consequence* of the event (the principals in the resulting milieu of the event's outcome), news story recall was significantly greater than when still photos illustrated the news as an isolated collection of journalistic facts. A subsequent content analysis of Swedish television revealed that few broadcast stories actually contained information about the causal consequence. This finding led the Swedish investigators to conclude that TV news is designed for the "initiated," those persons with sufficient knowledge to supply the causal consequences themselves.

With literally thousands of studies on the response of children to televised violence conducted over the years, it is an unfortunate comment on the field that so few careful studies of TV news acquisition by children exist. Dan G. Drew and Byron Reeves report in Part IV on an experiment with Wisconsin school children, who were observed and tested as they watched "In the News," a CBS news show for children. They found that believability, liking the story, and understanding the news story *function* were significant predictors of news learning. If the children perceived that the purpose of the news item was to inform rather than entertain, their recall was greater, suggesting that children could be taught to consume TV news intelligently.

A different approach to television news processing is taken in experiments by Thomas A. McCain and Mark G. Ross. They use a combination of computerized monitoring and manual content analysis of open-ended questionnaires to test Richard Carter's signalled stopping theory on TV news. Their results provide support for the idea that adults respond to TV news, regardless of specific content, with different cognitive switching styles. The functional elements of the cognitive switching process, however, are standardized. That is, the viewer switches among agreement, disagreement, thinking, or questioning states—the pattern suggested by Carter—at various points during a TV newscast. The results indicated the pattern of switching had little to do with news content, but an obvious next step would be to look at both production and content variables of TV news as possible predictors of switching patterns.

The final piece in this section—an attempt to link interpersonal and mass media "scripts"—easily could have been placed under several of the topics in the *Yearbook*. Michael Roloff hypothesizes that humans make sense of their environments through scripts learned from both interpersonal and mass media situations. The idea that media messages are processed as scripts—coherent projections of actual or perceived vignettes of human actions in response to a situation or problem—is as intriguing as it is elusive. It may be that the notion of script as used by Roloff will illuminate the element of causal consequence that is so effective in increasing news comprehension in the Swedish news experiments reported above. At any rate, the piece is a worthwhile attempt to establish the script as a common factor that binds all forms of communication.

PART V: POLITICAL COMMUNICATION

Agenda-setting theory has provided a much-needed connectivity to the area of political communication and has generated considerable research around the world. A rekindled interest of political scientists and sociologists has led to collaborative work in the area.[3]

Earlier articles in this volume by McCombs and associates review the problems of conceptual and methodological comparability in the emerging field of agenda-setting. They also point out that a great deal more thought is needed on the contingent conditions of agenda-setting. In the lead article in this section, Gladys Engel Lang and Kurt Lang conceptualize agenda-setting as a prominent component of the larger landscape of political communication and public opinion. The Langs see agenda-setting as crucial, but one among many forces, in the *agenda-building* process.

Using the Watergate political scandal as a focal subject and time period, the Langs place the agenda-setting function of mass media in a larger agenda-building process. They develop a concept of *issues* as something more than just topics or concerns covered by mass media. They see issues as having different thresholds of mass sensitivity. Economic matters such as inflation and employment rates are generally *low*-threshold issues readily identified with by almost everyone. More discrete problems, such as the plight of Vietnam refugees, are *high*-threshold problems recognized by relatively few. The Langs see Watergate as a high-threshold issue, and they address this question: How was Watergate transformed into an issue of great salience? Mere frequency of mass media coverage was not enough. The essential facts of Watergate were published in the mass media prior to the Nixon presidential election, but they were met with incredulity on the part of the press and the mass of Americans. It was not until the *content* of the mass media reports reflected a certification of legal and political sources that presidential wrongdoing was a possibility, that both media and public incredulity were overcome. Mass media coverage was certainly a necessary condition, but clearly not a sufficient one to make Watergate salient as an issue. The content of press coverage had to combine with the reciprocal acts of other social institutions to topple, first, the President's credibility and, ultimately, the Nixon Presidency.

Another area of interest in the field is the knowledge-gap hypothesis. Although not limited to a political setting, some of the most rewarding studies on the topic have involved political communication. Two such articles are published here.

The initial work looks at the televised presidential debates of 1976 to analyze the knowledge-gap question. The first volume of the *Yearbook* published a synthesis of some thirty articles on this topic, in which Steven Chaffee (1980) concluded that the debates were clearly useful to prospective voters. The present study by Jack M. McLeod, Carl R. Bybee, and Jean A. Durall examines the contribution of the debates to the quality and quantity of political participation among all segments of the electorate. Analyzing a sample of eligible voters in Wisconsin, McLeod and associates found the effects of the debate on involvement and voting to be roughly equivalent for all segments of the electorate, even though less politically concerned persons spent less time watching the debates than others. The implications are that while the information-rich may gain an additional advantage in *informed* participation through mass media, they are *not* able to use the advantage more effectively in the political system than the less active, information-poorer groups.

Critics are sure to challenge the McLeod findings on the grounds that it is in the political process *between* elections that most public policy is affected to a greater extent by the information-rich than the information-poor, thus enhancing the systemic importance of knowledge-gap findings. However, a second work here offers evidence that the knowledge-gap phenomenon is more clearly related to *motivation* than to class structure. B.K.L. Genova and Bradley S. Greenberg look at *interest* as a factor in the knowledge gap and mass communication.

Genova and Greenberg use a panel design with a large sample of mid-Michigan respondents to chart mass media consumption and information acquisition about the Nixon impeachment controversy and a National Football League strike. In addition to testing education level, they measured social and self-interest in the news topics, and factual and structural knowledge. Social interest was a stronger predictor of structural knowledge than was education level; social interest was equal to education as a predictor of factual knowledge. Their results, like McLeod and associates', suggest that the political system implications of the knowledge-gap phenomenon are more complex than, and possibly not as dire as, heretofore believed.

PART VI: IMPACT OF MASS COMMUNICATION

A sign of maturity in the field of mass communication research is the comment and research that has resulted from the cultural indicators-cultivation analysis project at the Annenberg School. (Volume One of the *Yearbook* had six articles on the subject.) George Gerbner and his associates have produced reports for more than a decade that consistently argue that television is a cultural armada that has no precedent. The overwhelming message of crime, violence, and sexual and racial stereotypes has been analyzed by the Gerbner team not only as a force of social control and legitimization of police and political authority; it creates as well the perception in "heavy" viewers of a world of exaggerated risk and distorted social relations.

The Violence Profile No. 11 that is published here is no exception. Although it documents a slight decline in the sheer amount of violence and victimization on network television, the report maintains the cultivation hypothesis in even stronger terms. Responding to challenges to their findings, most directly to work published in Volume One of the *Yearbook* (Doob and MacDonald, 1980), the Gerbner team of Larry Gross, Michael Morgan, and Nancy Signorielli present new supporting analyses. They compare low-income, urban dwellers with high-income urbanites in a national sample survey of data collected by Opinion Research Corporation. Assuming that the low-income persons are likely to live in high-crime areas and that the high-income urban dwellers are apt to live in less crime-ridden neighborhoods, the Gerbner team compares the groups on a perception-of-danger index. They find a positive, slight correlation between "heavy" television watching and high scores on perceptions of danger among the low-income urbanites, which they interpret—with additional longitudinal data—as supporting cultivation theory.

Gerbner and associates introduce two very elusive notions to explain puzzling findings they and their critics have disclosed. Mainstreaming and resonance, they argue, are refinements of cultivation theory.

Mainstreaming implies that conspicuous evidence of cultivation effects of television may be expected only among groups who are *out* of the *mainstream* of commonality cultivated by television, such as middle- and upper-income groups (but not lower-income persons who are *in* the mainstream). Resonance suggests that evidence for television effects may be greater among certain groups, such as women, who actually experience a greater likelihood of being victims of crime; television, then, resonates with real-life circumstances for these groups.

The logic of mainstreaming is not easily understood at this point, so the debate is just beginning.

Paul Hirsch, in the second article in Part VI, replicates the cultivation analysis on some of the same data sets used by the Gerbner group and interprets the results as not supporting the cultivation hypothesis. Hirsch uses multiple controls simultaneously on age, sex, and education and finds the strength of most of the correlations greatly attenuated between "heavy" viewing and perceptions of danger. More importantly he focuses on *non-viewers* and *extreme* viewers (eight or more hours of viewing per day) to find: nonviewers are *more* frequently fearful, alienated, and favorable to suicide than are light viewers; extreme viewers are *less* likely to be fearful than heavy viewers.

Hirsch is puzzled by the fact that so little replication has been done on Gerbner's work and cites other hypotheses, particularly in sociology, that are of no greater importance but which have received extensive replication and reanalysis. The answer, in part, is simple. Until recently, the number of persons working in mass communication research has been relatively small, making replication unlikely. It is encouraging that the Gerbner work and studies in other significant areas such as agenda-setting, are now being replicated.

In last year's volume, George Comstock (1980) distilled the findings of the RAND Corporation report on *Television and Human Behavior* and pointed out that the conclusion of minimal effects had been erroneously applied to television, primarily because of the failure to show a major independent impact of TV on viewers. He noted that the RAND report showed that even though the independent effects of television seem small because they interact with a host of other factors, their social importance may be great. John P. Murray and Susan Kippax have conducted an ambitious synthesis and review of more than 1000 studies conducted around the world on the role and effects of television. Their piece is an excellent complement to Comstock's analysis.

In general, Murray and Kippax find corroboration for the thrust of the RAND report: that television influences viewers at a variety of levels, ranging from changing attitudes and values to affecting interpersonal behavior. In addition to the synthesis of voluminous studies, Murray and Kippax analyze the findings within a comparative-cultural framework. They begin with a description of world television systems and attempt to place the findings in context. For example, they conclude that the presence of advertising in television systems is associated with high violence content. Further, they note that most of the studies of the effects of televised violence have been conducted in the United States.

Two reports on an historic television event of 1979, the worldwide broadcasting of the American five-part *Holocaust* series, follow the Murray and Kippax summary of the comparative impact of TV. In the first article, Harold de Bock and Jan van Lil write about a major field experimental-panel design conducted in the Netherlands. Following that piece is a sample survey study involving several time-points of response to *Holocaust* in Austria, conducted by Peter Diem. The two works compare significantly, in spite of methodological differences. Holland was occupied by the Nazis during World War II, while Austria was one of the Axis countries and the birthplace of Adolph Hitler.

The Dutch study offers evidence of a coordinated mass media and interpersonal educational campaign that worked. It may become a classic case. All the elements for success were present. The target audience for the *Holocaust* broadcasts (shown on the national television system) was Dutch young people, primarily of secondary and high school age, who were likely to be receptive to the program but whose knowledge of the atrocities and the historical period was limited. Second, an imaginative interpersonal campaign was employed involving seven Jewish and educational organizations and the Dutch school system. Third, supplementary television and radio broadcasts attempted to prepare the population for the program and focused on public reaction after the program series. The results were dramatic, suggesting that both the television series and the interpersonal educational "environment" that accompanied the programs had significant long-term effects in increasing both the knowledge of World War II atrocities and disapproval of anti-Semitism.

Peter Diem's study of Austrians' response to *Holocaust* (which was broadcast two months earlier than in Holland) found little evidence of cognitive change in the adult samples questioned. The results indicate that the small minority who doubted the essential facts of mass extermination of the Jews before the broadcasts were only marginally affected by the broadcasts in the long term. A major finding of the Austrian study, however, involved the unique content analysis of newspaper editorials, columns, and letters to the editor, and phone calls and mail from viewers. This part of the study showed that a majority of the editorials and columns were favorable to *Holocaust.* Letters to the editor, phone calls, and mail to the Austrian Radio were less likely to be favorable. The more spontaneous the viewer communication, the less likely was the respondent to be sympathetic to the broadcast.

Concluding Part VI is a California study of a major heart disease information campaign through the mass media. Michael A. Milburn used a panel design in several California communities in the 1970, subjecting the data to cross-lagged correlation and regressional analysis. He found minimal selective exposure and fairly strong evidence that campaign media exposure increased health knowledge, which resulted in significant attitude change.

PART VII: INTERNATIONAL AND COMPARATIVE RESEARCH

For years many scholars have accepted the argument that little true mass communication theory, or social theory that encompasses mass communication, can emerge without the field becoming more comparative in approach, moving beyond description. Valuable though description is, what is needed now is comparative study of mass communication across cultural boundaries with common units of analysis. Part VII leads off with a symposium of studies that promise a comparative direction based on joint work now developing between Japanese and Americans.

In the first article, Alex Edelstein introduces the concept of *johoka shakai,* or informationalized societies, that is at the source of a vigorous stream of Japanese communication research. Edelstein argues that the approach fosters fundamentally comparative work and requires a complete redefinition of communication research. Edelstein sees the term *mass* as changing to mean interacting collectivities; *public opinion* must be shifted to mean, essentially, communication.

Youichi Ito's article is one of the first explanations of the information-alized societies approach by a Japanese in English. The term *johoka shakai* means the study of the process of societal change toward information saturation and abundance that the Japanese claim is typical of postindustrialized societies. The basic measures of the approach are the information ratio and the *johoka* index.

The information ratio is the ratio of household expenditure for information-related activities, to total household expenditures. The *johoka* index, a macro-level measure, is the mean value of these: (1) amount of information (such as newspaper circulation per 100 persons); (2) distribution of communication media (television sets per 100 households, for example); (3) quality of information activities (such as the population of information service workers in the total labor population); and (4) the information ratio. (It is apparent that amount and distribution overlap in the measure.)

Using the measures, Ito presents comparative data showing the top three informationalized societies to be the United States, Britain, and Japan. The data also produced predictions that Japan and the United States would increase their rate of *johoka* faster than the European nations considered in the analysis.

An even bolder technique was conceived by the Japanese to measure information flow within and among nations, with the word as the basic unit. Conversion rates are used for nonverbal information. A still photograph is equal to 80 words (determined by experiments showing that 80 words could be written on a still photo of standard size and read at normal distance). A minute of black and white television or motion picture is equal to 800 words, with color given a value of 1200 words per minute. Conversion rates are established for various major media, based on a variety of experiments to determine information equivalence.

The information-flow measure enables the Japanese to compare information supply and consumption. In 1960, a little less than half of the information supplied in Japan was being consumed. A decade and a half later, less than 10% of the information supply was being consumed, suggesting that information "overload" had increased nearly five times over a period of 16 years.

The symposium continues with John Bowes's penetrating analysis of the Japanese approach, which he calls a laudable attempt to examine information as the core element of life quality. Their basic method is descriptive, with imaginative application of econometric techniques to aggregate data, but Bowes argues that the conceptual basis for their model-building is often taken for granted or arbitrary. He sees great potential for collaboration between Japanese and American scholars, combining the American concern for social-behavioral effects with the Japanese interest in macroscopic examination of objective information flow within and between countries.

The *johoka shakai* perspective may provide data that will enrich a cultural approach to mass communication theory, in the view of Sheldon Harsel, in the concluding piece of the symposium. Harsel sees the possibility of crafting a natural history of information, analogous to the classic work of Robert Park. He says that the Japanese research may shed light on how the changing forms of information in societies alter, in part, the meaning and form of such things as crime and deviance; in addition, the comparative data collected by the approach may stimulate thought on the cultural sense of such terms as data, information, knowledge, and communication.

Using a typology of social structure and culture he developed in Volume One of the *Yearbook,* Karl Erik Rosengren describes the theoretical development and the first results of the Swedish cultural indicators project (see Rosengren, 1980). Unlike the Japanese work previously described, the cultural indicators research, although quantitative, is closely tied to social-political theory. For example, the Swedish project attempts to test the extent to which patterns of radicalism, internationalism, and activism are both reflected in (and, to some extent, affected by) the mass media. The objective is to establish a data-base of cultural indicators comparable to the vast banks of economic indicators that exist.

Data from various subsections of the Swedish project—ranging from values of freedom and equality in leading newspaper editorials to the proportion of employed women portrayed in advertisements—are published here in English for the first time. Most of the indicators show change in expected directions—a major exception being decline in the proportion of employed women in advertisements since World War II, contrary to the actual employment statistics. The preliminary analysis lends support to the argument that cultural indicators data from mass media are an important new element in the study of social change.

Continuing a concern for analysis of communication in China that was begun in Volume One, Godwin Chu presents his latest work on the current functions of the mass media in China (Chu, 1980). Chu documents stunning changes that have occurred in post-Mao China, altering the relative importance of four basic functions: mobilization, information, power struggle, and ideological reform.

An extensive mass media system—comprised of the New China News Agency, the Party magazine *Red Flag,* the *People's Daily,* provincial newspapers, and radio and television—carries similar official messages, supervised by the Communist Party's Central Committee (or provincial committees) through the Department of Propaganda. Until recent times, objective reality for the Chinese media was not description of what happened, according to Chu. Instead, reality was the final outcome of an arduous process of moving through the Party's "ideological lens." Following a year-long public debate about the mass media and "truth," an editorial in a July 1979 issue of the official *People's Daily* signalled a move toward more factual reporting in the Chinese press. Human-interest features and entertainment returned to Chinese newspapers. Chu concludes that the mass media in post-Mao China now emphasize factual reporting to a greater extent than ideological indoctrination, giving greater weight to the mobilization and information functions than in previous times.

In the concluding article in the *Yearbook,* Walery Pisarek analyzes all issues in 1978 of selected prestige newspapers of East and West. The research looks at coverage of Polish newsmakers in *Nues Deutschland* (German Democratic Republic), *Pravda* (USSR), *Rude Pravo* (Czechoslovakia), *Le Monde* (France), *Frankfurter Allgemeine Zeitung* (Federal Republic of Germany), and the *International Herald Tribune* (United States). Pisarek shows that both socialist and nonsocialist newspapers emphasize coverage of political leadership in news about Poland. Beyond that, dramatic differences emerge. The Western newspapers gave considerable visibility to Church leaders and to opposition-dissenting leadership in Poland. No coverage of Polish Church leaders or political dissenters appeared in the socialist press. This fascinating work, by a well-known Polish scholar, provides evidence for the long-standing proposition that the press is primarily a reflection of the political system in which it operates.

CONCLUSIONS

In *War and Remembrance,* Herman Wouk's novel about World War II, Captain "Pug" Henry, a naval attaché in the American embassy in Moscow and informal adviser to President Roosevelt, accompanies a Russian general and a famous British journalist to the battle front. Witnessing a powerful German attack from which he has just escaped unharmed, Henry listens to the breathless journalist describe the event. Henry ponders the journalist's version and realizes he has always been puzzled by the considerable gap between journalism and the war. The relevance of this episode to a serious book about mass communication research may seem distant, but in many ways it portrays a basic concern of the field. The search for ways to narrow the gaps between mass media performance and society's needs, and between the mass media view of the larger society and its existence, vexes a great many scholars.

A glance at this book makes it evident that the mass communication field throughout the world draws from many sources. But the force of eclecticism is not centrifugal, as it might have appeared to be a few years ago, but rather centripetal. It is this concern about the gap between "journalism and war" that has begun to draw *once again,* into the study of mass communication, researchers from the allied social science disciplines, so that replication, intense scholarly debates, and interdisciplinary and intercontinental collaboration are now becoming matter-of-fact occurrences. Unlike most of the traditional fields, ours is much less hemmed in by the insular boundaries of disciplinary lines. There is far less preoccupation with methodology than there was a quarter century ago.

Above all, the domain of classical thought is now firmly established in the field. More papers today are drawing on the great social thinkers, such as Dewey or Marx, than might have been expected just a decade ago. The field is eclectic, true, but the realization that the mass media now act—and are likely to do so for some time to come—as touchstones of existence is both a binding and a directional force.

CONTENT OF FUTURE VOLUMES

As this second volume of the *Yearbook* goes to press, some emphases of Volume Three are apparent. Many analyses of international news flow have been completed, but, because of proprietary obligations, many were not available for use here. Some of the omitted studies are pertinent to the continuing debate about a new world information order, so Volume Three will devote generous space to them. Secondly, much economic-technological policy research of benchmark significance is underway, and undoubtedly a number of such emerging studies will be used in the next book. The best of the several agenda-setting studies that are now in press will be sought for inclusion. Finally, major investigations of journalists at work are likely to be a focal subject for Volume Three.

NOTES

1. *Communication Abstracts,* edited by Thomas F. Gordon and Robert G. Roberts at Temple University, includes studies broadly related to communication. About one in three of the articles would not have been included in the Danielson and Wilhoit study of the earlier period. Even so, the number of studies that are completely comparable to those of the earlier volume is still quite large in the *Abstracts.* A small random sample of items was subjected to a test of inter-coder reliability. Simple percentage of agreement on method was 91%; agreement on broad subject heading was 73%. (The fairly large number of categories made chance agreement a negligible factor.)

2. For example, see: John W.C. Johnstone, Edward J. Slawski, and William W. Bowman, *The News People: A Sociological Portrait of American Journalists and Their Work* (Urbana: University of Illinois Press); Herbert J. Gans, *Deciding What's News: A Study of CBS Evening News, NBC Nightly News, Newsweek and Time* (New York: Vintage Books of Random House, 1980); and Doris A. Graber, *Mass Media and American Politics* (Washington, D.C.: Congressional Quarterly Press, 1980).

3. For example, see: David H. Weaver, Doris A. Graber, Maxwell E. McCombs, and Chaim H. Eyal, *Media Agenda-Setting in a Presidential Election: Issues, Images, Interest* (New York: Praeger, in press).

REFERENCES

BLUMLER, J. (1980) "Purposes of mass communications research: a transatlantic perspective." Mass Communication Rev. Yearbook 1: 33-44. Beverly Hills, CA: Sage.

BREED, W. (1955) "Social control in the newsroom: a functional analysis." Social Forces 33: 326-335.

CHAFFEE, S. H. (1980) "Mass media effects: new research perspectives." Mass Communication Rev. Yearbook 1: 77-108. Beverly Hills, CA: Sage.

CHU, G. C. (1980) "Revolutionary language and Chinese cognitive processes." Mass Communication Rev. Yearbook 1: 628-637. Beverly Hills, CA: Sage.

Commission on Freedom of the Press (1947) A Free and Responsible Press. Chicago: Univ. of Chicago Press.

COMSTOCK, G. (1980) "Television and its viewers: what social science sees." Mass Communication Rev. Yearbook 1: 491-507. Beverly Hills, CA: Sage.

DANIELSON, W. A. (1956) "Eisenhower's February decision: a study of news impact." Journ. Q. 33: 433-441.

DEUTSCHMANN, P. J. and W. A. DANIELSON (1960) "Diffusion of knowledge of the major news story." Journ. Q. 33: 345-355.

DOOB, A. and G. MACDONALD (1980) "Television viewing and fear of victimization: is the relationship causal?" Mass Communication Rev. Yearbook 1: 479-488. Beverly Hills, CA: Sage.

JOHNSTONE, J.W.C., E. J. SLAWSKI, and W. W. BOWMAN (1976) The News People: A Sociological Portrait of American Journalists and Their Work. Urbana: Univ. of Illinois Press.

KATZ, E. and P. LAZARSFELD (1955) Personal Influence: The Part Played by People in the Flow of Mass Communications. New York: Macmillan.

KLINE, F. G. (1980) "Time in communication research." Mass Communication Rev. Yearbook 1: 183-200. Beverly Hills, CA: Sage.

LANG, K. (1980) "The critical functions of empirical communication research: observations on German-American influences." Mass Communication Rev. Yearbook 1: 45-58. Beverly Hills, CA: Sage.

LAZARSFELD, P., B. BERELSON, and H. GAUDET (1944) The People's Choice. New York: Columbia Univ. Press.

ROSENGREN, K. E. (1980) "Mass media and social change: some current approaches." Mass Communication Rev. Yearbook 1: 168-180. Beverly Hills, CA: Sage.

WEAVER, D. H. and R. G. GRAY (1980) "Journalism and mass communication research in the United States: past, present, and future." Mass Communication Rev. Yearbook 1: 124-151. Beverly Hills, CA: Sage.

PART I

THEORETICAL PERSPECTIVES

Contrasts of European and American research on mass communication presented in the first volume of the *Yearbook* are refined in this volume. Some of the historical details explaining differences between work from the two continents are sketched here.

European and American scholars in this section offer widely differing thought. They not only trace the roots of mass communication research to early German thinkers who predate U.S. scholars, but also show that differences in the work coming out of the two continents may partly result from each group of scholars having grown up under different media systems, one a commercial and the other a public-commercial mix.

The Marxist element of the European tradition, clearly a minority point of view among the published scholars, comes under scrutiny and criticism for having been preoccupied with the ideology of media systems and having ignored the economic framework of the culture industry of modern mass media. A similar theme is struck elsewhere in this section as Third World scholars are called to arms to wage in their own lands scholarly battle that will permanently rid them of the old paradigm and the "bad" scholarship resulting, in part, from Western influence.

The section closes with an attempt by a European scholar to merge the uses and gratifications and effects theoretical traditions, an effort that demonstrates considerable harmony among many European and American researchers. Accompanying this piece is a state-of-the-art review of neurophysiological research and its implications for the study of nonverbal communication, a growing emphasis in the field.

Concluding this section is a delightful look at the development of communication in terms of anthropological history. It is clear that mass communication research has focused on an infinitesimally small slice of human history, and that some of the major research questions facing us are historical in nature.

First delivered as a plenary lecture at the 1980 International Communication Association meeting in Acapulco, Mexico, this piece by Jay Blumler continues the penetrating comparative analysis of European-American research traditions that he began in Volume One. Blumler sounds the familiar criticism that American work lacks the focus of the European scene but that the Europeans badly need to attend more to the kinds of long-term audience/effects study that have been a major strength of American work. Further, he notes the contrast in historical context of the American and European work. American research emerged within a commercial media system, while European study grew up at a time when television was the predominant medium, organized along public service, or state-operated, lines. This, he says, explains much of the European interest in critical research and public policy. In addition, an adversary relationship between groups of scholars, who want "to get it together," is a factor present in Europe and missing in America. He concludes the article with several recommendations for scholars on both sides of the Atlantic, whom he thinks should do a good deal more talking to each other. Dr. Blumler is Director of the Centre for Television Research at the University of Leeds, England.

1

MASS COMMUNICATION RESEARCH IN EUROPE

Some Origins and Prospects

Jay G. Blumler

In recent years mass communication research has gradually come of age in many countries of Western Europe. Signs of this development are not only quantitative—such as increases in the number of university centers and appointments devoted to the field, expanded research activity, and the growing publication of books, articles, and specialist journals—but also qualitative—including gains in European scholars' sense of distinctive identity, self-confidence, and even sheer enjoyment of a path-breaking spirit as new research directions are explored. In this talk I shall pose and offer provisional answers to two questions that naturally arise in the minds of many observers of these striking trends.

AUTHOR'S NOTE: This is a revised version of a lecture delivered to the plenary session of the 30th Annual Convention of the International Communication Association, Acapulco, Mexico, May 18-23, 1980.

From Jay G. Blumler, "Mass Communication Research in Europe: Some Origins and Prospects," original manuscript.

One question has to do with origins and sources: How exactly did European mass communication research "get that way"? Or rather, what features of historical time and societal space help to explain the emergence of certain outstanding tendencies of communication research in Western Europe—in contrast, say, to certain equivalent characteristics of American work?

The second question is related to the complex sense that many of us have of operating in a philosophically polarized field—although it is almost impossible succinctly to distinguish the rival camps without indulging in stereotypes, and it is increasingly difficult to equate our philosophic differences with geographic ones. It is still true that, "Europe is providing a congenial proving ground for . . . much critically grounded mass communications enquiry."[1] Yet some major European figures do not regard themselves as critical researchers; and inside the critical school, some quite exciting disputes of analytical standpoint and approach to evidence are coming ever more insistently to the fore. Moreover, the mass communication literature also includes a conciliatory strand, one that seeks to throw bridges across the divisive gulfs. Recent expressions of that outlook include the Katz report for the BBC[2] and Kurt Lang's claim, "There is no inherent incompatibility between the 'positivism' of administrative communication research and the critical approach associated with the Frankfurt school."[3] In lineage, however, this conciliatory note is traceable to Robert Merton's early postwar plea for a consolidation of European sociology of knowledge with American studies of public opinion and mass communication, "aiming towards that happy combination of the two, which possesses the scientific virtues of both and the superfluous vices of neither."[4] Arising from all this, my second question is: What constructive steps can be taken by divergent research traditions in our field to bring them to easier speaking terms with one another?

ORIGINS OF EUROPEAN AND AMERICAN MASS COMMUNICATION RESEARCH

As I have implied, answers to the first question can be pursued along dimensions of time and space. Taking that of *time* first, the fact that Europe began to find its own mass communication research feet in approximately the mid-1960s is doubly significant. The European research surge originated shortly after the publication of Joseph Klapper's then seemingly authoritative account of the American state of the art as outlined in *The Effects of Mass Communication*.[5] Dominant impressions formed by many Europeans were that Americans had mainly concentrated on audience-level enquiries, effects research, and questions open to quantitative treatment by survey or experimental designs; and that as a result they had marched up a blind alley. Some Europeans attracted to communication study for the first time found little appeal in continuing to plough that furrow and began to suspect that they might have to define the field afresh.[6] For another thing, as Karl Erik Rosengren has pointed out, the middle of the 1960s was a time when European social science, after much prewar speculation over issues of theory of knowledge and an early postwar period of immersion in American quantitative techniques, was hit by a wave of revived interest in Marxism, as well as hosting certain other specialized schools of thought, such as semiotics, structuralism, interactionism, sociolinguistics, contemporary cultural studies, and others.[7]

The conjunction of these temporal influences helps to explain three prominent features of European work. One is the characteristically "holistic approach of European communication science,"[8] or the conviction that mass communication institutions and processes must be studied especially in their linkages to surrounding social orders. Of course, such a broadly societal perspective is grist to a Marxist's mill. As Golding and Murdock have urged in this vein, "we do not need a theory of mass communications but a theory of society to generate guiding propositions and research. . . ."[9] But in Europe Marxists hold no monopoly over holism. A similarly comprehensive thrust can be found, for example, in Elisabeth Noelle-Neumann's spiral of silence theory (which postulates that media journalists, when emphasizing certain societal trends, manage to convey impressions of standpoints that are winning and losing ground to audience members, to create climates in which people feeling in the ascendant are more prepared to voice their views and so to enlist the powerful engine of interpersonal communication in the molding of public opinion).[10] It also can be seen in the efforts of Rosengren and his colleagues to interrelate media content data and extramedia trend data so as to chart sources of change over the postwar period in the symbolic environment of Swedish society.[11] And it can be found in Gurevitch and Blumler's identification of diverse entry points into the analysis of political communication systems, the chief components of which they define as:

1. Political institutions in their communication aspects;
2. Media institutions in their political aspects;
3. Audience orientations to political communication; and
4. Communication-relevant aspects of political culture.[12]

This holistic impulse leads to a second European trait. Put negatively, methodological boundary lines are not always strictly respected. Put positively, research questions are often tackled by mixed methods. Noelle-Neumann's work, for example, relies on a combination of content analysis, panel research, and synchronized investigation of the opinions and perceptions held on certain matters by strategically placed communicators, such as journalists and ordinary members of the public.[13] Another example, from which publications are now emerging, is a project of cross-national research into the role of broadcasting in the 1979 elections to the European Parliament that was designed by a consortium of political communication scholars based in each of the nine member states of the European Community. This combined interviews with political party publicists; interviews with broadcasting executives and journalists; a content analysis of the themes of campaign programs; postelection surveys; and, in some countries, before-and-after electoral panels as well—organized on comparative lines.[14]

Third, except perhaps for a few specialized subfields, such as research on election campaigns, the uses and gratifications approach, studies of children's responses to television, and research into the structure of adult viewing patterns,[15] there are relatively few coherently cumulative traditions of audience-level inquiry in Europe. It is as if, among critical researchers especially, the systematic attempt, empirically and quantitatively, to measure the impact on audience members' ideas of the flow of mass communicated messages has been given a "bad name." Effects research in particular is treated in some quarters as the brothel of media studies: the "madam" rather than the "queen" of our science.

The *spatial* origins of European mass communication research are particularly interesting, only two examples of which I will consider. First, in contrast to the United States, where mass communication research grew up alongside a commercially dominated media system, in Europe the pre-dominant medium at the time when researchers were cutting their teeth was television, organized along public service lines. This meant that its programs would be provided by public service corporations, which were enjoined to serve social interests impartially and were to some extent divorced from direct political control, although they were ultimately accountable to organs of the state. Now, such a system inevitably propels broadcasting right into the heart of the political arena, even in a country like Britain, where many safeguards of media autonomy have been carefully devised. For one thing, just because broadcasters are supposed to be impartial and serve the public interest, they are correspondingly and readily open to accusations of impropriety, bias, and neglect of duty, some sincerely voiced, others mounted to cloak the more naked pursuit of partisan advantage. For another, broadcasters are neces-sarily dependent on governments of the day for decisions vital to their continuing survival and welfare—to raise the level of its license fee, as in the case of the BBC in Britain, or for authorization to open an additional television channel, as in the case of ITV. For yet another, public service broadcasting organizations are singularly lacking in self-sufficiency. They badly need outside support, much of it political, to keep afloat in turbulent societal seas. It is true that in the crises and rows that periodically erupt over TV's social role, broadcasters sometimes can exploit a lack of unity among surrounding political forces. In such circumstances, however, broadcasters can also be undermined by arguments, even from their political friends, that if they do not toe the line, it may be impossible to curb the wilder politicians who are clamoring for more control over television. It is for such reasons that the late Sir Charles Curran, former Director-General of the BBC, proclaimed a need for senior broadcasters continually to engage in "the politics of broadcasting." As he put it, "The broadcaster's life has to be one of continuous political ingenuity."[16]

Three further features of the work of many European mass communication researchers are traceable to the centrality of public service television in the communication systems of their societies. One is their preoccupation with the role of the mass media (and especially broadcasting) in politics and, more specifically, with the tensions that arise between the supposed neutrality and independence of television on one hand and its many ties to prevailing political structures, values, and interests on the other. Another is a frequent tendency to analyze mass media functioning through the concept of "constraints." Although I have not encountered an explicit definition of that important term in its application to our field, I suppose that "constraints" might be conceived as institutionalized practices and patterned relationships, internal or external to media organizations, which serve to narrow, limit, or closely circumscribe their ability to realize their own professed social purposes. Yet another European characteristic which springs in part from this source is a keenness to address issues of media policy.[17] Compared with some Americans, many Europeans are less anxious about the purity and self-sufficiency of their professional research roles and are more ready, even eager, to mix in some way their professional with their civic roles. It is true that Europeans are internally split over how best to relate policy positions to empirical findings. Marxists ignore the positivistic gap between "the is" and "the ought," implying that it can be bridged by sensitivity to the class struggle and to history, while non-Marxists typically aim to draw a clearer boundary line between what they are saying on normative and empirical wave-lengths, respectively. Nevertheless, Europeans often strive to express the policy relevance of their work—for example, in concluding chapters to the books they write, in giving evidence to public bodies with media responsibilities, and in contributions to conferences often convened on policy issues with joint broadcaster/academic participation.

A second major contrast of societal space may help to explain why Europeans and Americans tend to focus on different relationships between mass communication systems and social structures. It was historically true that in many European societies, fundamentally opposed ideological and political options were not only conceivable in principle but were translated into organized partisan cleavages, including radical challenges to prevailing distributions of wealth and power, as in the case of socialist and communist movements. Yet, over the postwar period, the reality of sociopolitical advance toward greater equality has seemed negligible, leaving as if unmodified the traditionally unyielding patterns of social stratification. In contrast, the United States is a country where historically the clash of fundamentally opposed ideological and political options has seemed muted if not inconceivable, while in the postwar period one societal subsector after another has been disturbed by unpredictable currents of social change. I was recently struck in this connection by the readiness of Samuel Becker and Elmer Lower, when comparing social conditions at the time of the Kennedy-Nixon debates in 1960 with those that prevailed when the Carter-Ford exchanges were staged in 1976, to refer to the intervening period as a time of "America in political and social *transition.*"[18] In illustrating that theme, they noted a number of changes that had taken place during those 16 years: the decline of the cities; the nation's involvement in and later extrication from the Vietnam war; the emergence of unconventional lifestyles and sexual mores; and an ever-deepening loss of confidence in government. Had they wished, they could have additionally mentioned higher rates of geographical mobility; the dramatic erosion of voters' partisan identifications; the increasing incidence of marital instability; and a greater recognition of the formerly neglected civil rights of women, blacks, and other minorities.

Different formulations of the social role of mass communications do seem to arise from this contrast. In Europe, academics of a Marxist and critical bent especially regard the mass media chiefly as agencies of social control, blocking pathways of radical social change and propping up the status quo. Golding and Murdock manifest such a standpoint quite clearly when specifying their "basic departure point" as a "recognition that social relations within and between modern societies are radically, though variably, inegalitarian." This causes them to focus in turn, they say, on "the relations between the unequal distribution of control over systems of communications and wider patterns of inequality in the distribution of wealth and power" as well as on "relations between the mass media and the central axis of stratification—the class structure."[19]

In the United States, however, such formulations permeate the literature less pervasively, and the mass media are more often seen either as partial cause agents in social change, or as tools that would-be political actors can use to gain publicity and impetus for their pet projects of change, or as authoritative information sources on which people have become more dependent as the complexities of social differentiation and the pressures of a rapidly changing world threaten to become too much for them (as in De Fleur and Ball-Rokeach's hypothesis that "audience dependency on media information increases as the level of structural instability [societal conflict and change] increases").[20]

PROSPECTUS FOR CONCILIATION
AND FUTURE RESEARCH

Although the second question I posed at the outset referred to prospects of research camp reconciliation, it would be naive to expect certain deep-seated differences of outlook between rival approaches ever to be completely overcome. Take, for example, these ways of writing about mass media effects on audiences. On one side we have Gaye Tuchman's reference to media-constructed news "as a 'frame' organizing 'strips' of everyday reality and imposing order on it";[21] as well as George Gerbner's view of television as a "medium of the socialization of most people into standardized roles and behaviors," the chief function of which "is to spread and stabilize social patterns."[22] On the other side we have Jack McLeod and Byron Reeves' opinion that "it is from the unravelling of conditional and interactive relationships that the most interesting communication theory will come and not from simple assertions that the media set public agendas or that children learn from television";[23] as well as the view, recently expressed by Robert Hawkins and Suzanne Pingree, that the influence of television on viewers' construction of social reality should vary according to a whole host of intervening variables, including their information-processing abilities, critical awareness of television, direct experience of other sources providing confirmation or disconfirmation of TV messages, their place in the social structure, and their patronage of different forms of program content.[24] In one case, the mass media are regarded as imposing categories through which reality is perceived, by-passing potential neutralizing factors and engulfing the audience in a new symbolic environment.[25] In the other, mass media influence is conceived as *essentially differentiated,* filtered through and reflected by the diverse backgrounds, cultures, affiliations, and lifestyles of individual audience members. Ultimately, this division reflects a conflict of political philosophy between those who see society as governed by a more or less unified economic or power elite and those who still adhere to a pluralist vision of society.[26]

Even so, it is curious how the holders of certain positions in our field tend to restrict their appeal to already convinced devotees by arbitrarily narrowing the range of phenomena they study or by turning a blind eye to their own philosophic soft spots. Cross-camp debate could become more mutually enlightening, at least, if attempts were made to break down some of these unnecessary barriers. Let me conclude, therefore, by considering how such a prescription might be followed on both sides of the Atlantic, as it were.

A brisk diagnosis of the American field offered in this spirit might start by noting how it compares with the European scene—where, despite a wide scatter of work, much of it seems to get pulled toward a few focal points of theoretical and policy gravity by the presence of scholars who in their different ways are each trying "to get it together." In contrast, the American scene appears nowadays (as distinct from its pioneering era) to lack such a synthetic and binding quality, resembling more a boxing gym in which each individual is doing his own thing, so that some people are skipping rope, some are punching bags, some lifting weights, some sparring, some taking showers, and some are just having a rest!

Perhaps two ways forward from this state of affairs could be proposed. First, there should be more attempts to push already vigorous traditions of audience-level enquiry back not only to analyses of recurring patterns of media content, but also to those features of media organization that help to generate such systematically structured forms of output. Agenda-setting research is a striking case in point. As Steven Chaffee once remarked, "Agenda-setting is [truly] one of the two or three best research ideas this field has seen in recent years."[27] So far it has been pursued only in a truncated version, however, dealing over and over again with just the media content/ audience reception interface. Yet you cannot properly talk about agenda-*setting* without also considering who or what managed to lay out the agenda in a certain way, so that the issue agendas which audiences may take over are then seen to have derived from weights and meanings, given to news events, that arise in turn from certain abiding features of news-media gatekeeping and story construction. This is not just a matter of looking at media organizations as processors of issue material; it is also one of expanding the range of actors whom we are prepared regularly to take into account when conducting research into mass communication as a social process. That is, we should increasingly be treating mass communication as a "three-legged stool," involving not only audiences and journalists but also all those political and other interest groups that strive to reach audiences by developing strategies for influencing journalists.[28] So a more full and rounded version of agenda-setting still waits in the wings to be called onto the research stage, though its terms were already well stated in 1976 by Becker, McCombs, and McLeod when they pointed out that an agenda-setting framework

> specifies a set of relationships, beginning with the impact of the social system on media institutions, and, then, on their members, particularly reporters and editors. These media operatives make decisions which, the evidence shows, have impact on the cognitions of the media audience members. Those cognitions, for example, have been shown to affect voter turnout and election choice. Both behaviors can be seen as central to the political and social system. So the model takes us full circle.[29]

Follow up *that* prospectus and you really will have plenty to talk to the Europeans about!

Second, Americans should look again—and hard—at those four theories of the press, and particularly at the social responsibility variant among them, that were so influentially propounded by Wilbur Schramm and his colleagues nearly a quarter-century ago.[30] Searchingly realistic attention should be directed especially at the faith that was then pinned on the development of a sense of responsibility among mass media executives and staff communicators to ensure that standards of public service are adequately met. Unfortunately, that expectation seems at odds with the findings of many recent sociological studies of mass media organization, from which one more often receives an impression of institutions that are too hemmed in by externally and internally operative constraints for self-initiated reforms to yield significant results. Of course, I cannot recommend some particular way out of this impasse here; I am only urging scholars who consider that the mass media can and should serve worthier ends than the aggrandizement, through publicity, of dominant power interests to address themselves more closely to it. (Perhaps I may add, however, that in recent years my own response to this impasse in the news and political broadcasting field has taken the form of proposing policies that might act on the fabric of constraints themselves, hoping by pushing them back to give the media more elbow room for promoting more mature understandings of civic affairs in the electorate at large.)[31]

But should not Europeans also be asked to mend some of their ways in this spirit of research detente? Two thoughts occur to me here. One is that those Europeans who are hostile to or suspicious of audience effects research should give up their prejudices. It is a shocking indictment of the state of the field in Europe that it has so few cumulative traditions of effects research that can stand comparison with American work on, for example, agenda-setting, trust in government, and the social construction of reality. Such neglect should no longer be tolerated, for the study of mass communication as a process without systematic investigation of audience response is like a sexology that ignores the orgasm!

Second, it is high time those European radicals and critical thinkers who so repeatedly proclaim that mass communication only bolsters the status quo attended to some vital distinctions which so far they have tended to smudge. One is the distinction between *norm upholding* and *institutional support*. In itself, the critical school's assertion that much mass media content reflects a society's widely shared cultural norms and values is incontestable, first because that is one way in which large and heterogeneous audiences can be simultaneously addressed, and, second because in the field of news the operationalization of "objectivity" cannot be wholly culture-free. It is therefore not at all difficult to accept the statement in *Bad News* (by the Glasgow Media Group) that "the notion of cultural neutrality can never be achieved,"[32] as well as the claim of Stuart Hall et al. in *Policing the Crisis* that much journalism presupposes that "as members of one society . . . we share a common stock of cultural knowledge with our fellow men: we have access to the same 'maps of meaning.' "[33] But the projection of such meanings does not automatically entail the legitimation of a particular institutional order. That equation is sustainable only in press systems where the prevailing institutions are regarded as near-perfect embodiments of the authoritative and shared norms. And that is certainly *not* the case in any straightforward sense in the media systems of liberal-democratic societies. It is fascinating to recall in this connection Lazarsfeld and Merton's classic definition of "the enforcement of social norms" as one of three main functions of mass communication. "The mass media," they said, "may initiate social action by 'exposing' conditions which are at variance with public morality."[34] In short, norm enforcement can undercut as well as prop up particular institutions and the leaders who run them, a possibility that members of the critical school have so far ignored in their analyses.

Of course, in order to counter such criticisms they might reply in effect: Yes, but look at the heavy and regular coverage elite political actors can count on receiving in the news media of all societies. And it is again indisputable that such coverage tends to enhance the perceived status of such actors in the eyes of audience members. Even so, another crucial distinction needs to be made. Perceived status is one thing, but the inculcation of positive affect, respect, and a disposition to trust the actors concerned is quite another and does not automatically accompany the former. Recent experience in Britain of the regular sound broadcasting of Prime Minister's Question Time in Parliament provides an intriguing case in point. Many MPs were so horrified by the unfavorable impressions of politicians' behavior in the House of Commons, which they feared this implanted in listeners' minds, that they exerted pressure on the BBC to take it off the air.[35]

Nevertheless, critical theorists might counterargue that media coverage tends to treat unorthodox approaches to the conduct of politics as if out of court and beyond the pale of the cultural consensus.[36] And once again it cannot be denied that radical minority opinions often do get short shrift from the mass media in this sense. Even so, yet another distinction has to be taken into account when assessing this tendency: It is one thing to shut off an option; it is quite another to legitimate the remaining ones. It is equally possible, after all, for the one to be blocked out while the others are *run down*. Such, at least, is the claim of those American scholars who regard the news media as implicated in some way in the generation of political malaise.[37]

Finally, it might be claimed that news is really the same the whole world over—that newsmen engage in essentially the same organizational routines and are locked in essentially the same way into the predominant values and power structures of their societies, wherever they may be operating. This is the essence of a position taken in a gem of a recent book by Golding and Elliott, entitled *Making the News,* which compares broadcast news bulletin content and newsroom procedures in the three societies of Ireland, Sweden, and Nigeria. In their words, the study shows that "even in highly varied cultural and organizational settings broadcast news emerges with surprisingly similar forms and contents." It is intriguing to realize when reading the book in detail, however, how such a provocative position can be sustained only by taking a very high analytical line. For it turns out that the position is valid only in the *abstract* sense that "news is largely an artefact of the supply of information made available to the newsroom," constraints on which then arise outside the broadcasting sphere "in the state, culture and economy of each country." True enough very likely, but in *concrete* forms (still another neglected distinction) the constraints operative in individual countries may bear down quite differently on the newsmaking process. In fact, Golding and

Elliott give the game away in a comment tucked into a short paragraph that is devoted to the topic of "Drama as news value." Dramatic structure, they say, can often be achieved by the presentation of conflict, as in the matching of opposed viewpoints drawn from spokesmen of both sides of the question. Because of limited resources for film interviews, this technique is less available to poor newsrooms, and "in Nigeria it is almost entirely absent because of the severe authority of government departments."[38] To many of us, of course, there is no sense in which news systems which do give access to opposition voices can be equated with those that provide outlets for government sources only.

These remarks conclude my "conciliatory" contributions to the second theme of this talk. I hope you do not feel that here at the end I have only "regressed to the mean"!

NOTES

1. Blumler, Jay G., "Purposes of Mass Communications Research: A Transatlantic Perspective," First Founders' Lecture, delivered at the Annual Conference of the Association for Education in Journalism, Madison, Wisconsin, August, 1977 and published in *Journalism Quarterly,* Vol. 55, No. 2, 1978, pp. 219-230.

2. Katz, Elihu, *Social Research on Broadcasting: Proposals for Further Development,* BBC, London, 1977.

3. Lang, Kurt, "The Critical Functions of Empirical Communication Research: Observations on German-American Influences," *Media Culture and Society,* Vol. 1, No. 1, Jan. 1979, pp. 83-96.

4. Merton, Robert, *Social Theory and Social Structure: Toward the Codification of Theory and Research,* Free Press, New York, 1951.

5. Klapper, Joseph T., *The Effects of Mass Communication,* Free Press, New York, 1960.

6. The sense of being involved in a crisis of mass communication research, the means of resolving which must be discovered by Europeans drawing on their own intellectual resources, is well conveyed in a paper by Roberto Grandi, "Some Aspects of the Studies and Research Conducted in Italy Concerning Mass Communication," which was prepared for presentation to a seminar at The Annenberg School of Communication, University of Pennsylvania.

7. Rosengren, Karl-Erik (Ed.), *Advances in Content Analysis,* Sage, Beverly Hills, 1981.

8. Nordenstreng, Kaarle, "Recent Developments in European Communication Theory," in Fischer, Heinz-Dietrich and Merrill, John C. (Eds.), *International and Intercultural Communication,* Hastings House, New York, 1976.

9. Golding, Peter and Murdock, Graham, "Theories of Communication and Theories of Society," *Communication Research,* Vol. 5, No. 3, July 1978, pp. 339-356.

10. Noelle-Neumann, Elisabeth, *Die Schweige-spirale: Öffentliche Meinung unsere soziale Haut,* Piper, Munich, 1980.

11. Rosengren, Karl-Erik, "Cultural Indicators: Sweden, 1945-1975," paper presented to the 30th Annual Convention of the International Communication Association, Acapulco, Mexico, May 1980.

12. Gurevitch, Michael and Blumler, Jay G., "Mass Media and Political Institutions: The Systems Approach," in Gerbner, George (Ed.), *Mass Media Policies in Changing Cultures,* John Wiley and Sons, New York, 1977.

13. Noelle-Neumann, Elisabeth, "Mass Media and Social Change in Developed Societies," in Wilhoit, G. Cleveland and de Bock, Harold (Eds.), *Mass Communication Review Yearbook, Vol. 1,* Sage, Beverly Hills, 1980, pp. 657-678.

14. See Blumler, Jay G., "Communication in the European Elections: The Case of British Broadcasting," *Government and Opposition,* Vol. 14, No. 4, 1979, pp. 508-530; and Blumler, Jay G. and Fox, Tony, "The Involvement of Voters in the European Elections of 1979," *European Journal of Political Research* (forthcoming).

15. Examples of recent work in these subfields may be found, respectively, in Blumler, Jay G., Cayrol, Roland, and Thoveron, Gabriel, *La Television fait-elle L'election?,* Presses de la Fondation Nationale des Sciences Politiques, Paris, 1978; Blumler, Jay G. and Katz, Elihu, *The Uses of Mass Communications,* Sage, Beverly Hills, 1974; von Feilitzen, Cecilia, Filipson, Leni, and Schyller, Ingela, *Open Your Eyes to Children's Viewing,* Sveriges Radio, Stockholm, 1979; and Goodhardt, G.J., Ehrenberg, A.S.C., and Collins, M.A., *The Television Audience: Patterns of Viewing,* Saxon House, Westmead, 1975.

16. Curran, Charles, *A Seamless Robe,* Collins, London, 1979.

17. Nordenstreng, Kaarle, op. cit.

18. Becker, Samuel L. and Lower, Elmer W., "Broadcasting in Presidential Campaigns, 1960-1976," in Kraus, Sidney (Ed.), *The Great Debates: Carter vs. Ford, 1976,* Indiana University Press, Bloomington, 1979.

19. Golding and Murdock, op. cit.

20. De Fleur, Melvin L. and Ball-Rokeach, Sandra, *Theories of Mass Communication,* Longman, London, 1975.

21. Tuchman, Gaye, "Myth and the Consciousness Industry," paper presented to the Congress of the International Sociological Association, August 1978.

22. Gerbner, George and Gross, Larry, "Living with Television: The Violence Profile," *Journal of Communication,* Vol. 26, No. 2, 1976, pp. 173-199.

23. McLeod, J.M. and Reeves, Byron, "On the Nature of Mass Media Effects," in Withey, S. B. and Abeles, R. (Eds.), *Television and Social Behavior: Beyond Violence and Children,* Lawrence Erlbaum and Associates, New Jersey, 1980.

24. Hawkins, Robert P. and Pingree, Suzanne, "Television Influence on Constructions of Social Reality," a review prepared for *Television and Behavior: Ten Years of Scientific Progress and Implications for the 80's,* National Institute of Mental Health, forthcoming.

25. Katz, Elihu, "On Conceptualising Media Effects," in *25 Jaar Televisie in Vlaanderen,* Centrum voor Communicatiewetenschappen, Catholic University of Leuven, 1979.

26. Blumler, Jay G., "Models of Mass Media Effects," in *25 Jaar Televisie in Vlaanderen,* Centrum voor Communicatiewetenschappen, Catholic University of Leuven, 1979.

27. Chaffee, Steven H., book review of *The Emergence of American Political Issues: The Agenda-Setting Function of the Press* (by Donald L. Shaw and Maxwell E. McCombs, West, St. Paul, 1977), *Political Communication Review,* Vol. 3, No. 1, 1978, pp. 25-28.

28. Blumler, Jay G. and Gurevitch, Michael, "The Reform of Election Broadcasting: A Reply to Nicholas Garnham," *Media, Culture and Society,* Vol. I, No. 2, pp. 211-219, 1979.

29. Becker, Lee B., McCombs, Maxwell E., and McLeod, Jack M., "The Development of Political Cognitions" in Chaffee, Steven H. (Ed.), *Political Communication: Issues and Strategies for Research,* Sage, Beverly Hills, 1975, pp. 21-64.

30. Siebert, F.S., Peterson, T., and Schramm, W., *Four Theories of the Press,* University of Illinois Press, Illinois, 1956.

31. Blumler, Jay G., "The Intervention of Television in British Politics," research paper commissioned by the Annan Committee, *Report of the Committee on the Future of Broadcasting,* Cmnd. 6753-I, Her Majesty's Stationery Office, London, 1977.

32. Glasgow Media Group, *Bad News,* Routledge and Kegan Paul, London, 1976.

33. Hall, Stuart, Critcher, Chas., Jefferson, Tony, Clarke, John and Roberts, Brian, *Policing the Crisis: Mugging, the State, and Law and Order,* Macmillan Press Ltd., London, 1978.

34. Lazarsfeld, Paul and Merton, Robert, "Mass Communication, Popular Taste and Organized Social Action," in Rosenberg, Bernard, and White, David Manning (Eds.), *Mass Culture,* Free Press, New York, 1957, pp. 457-473.

35. Unpublished research into "Innovation in Political Communication: The Sound Broadcasting of Parliamentary Proceedings," currently being jointly undertaken by the Centre for Television Research, University of Leeds, and The Hansard Society for Parliamentary Government.

36. Hall, Stuart, "Media Power: The Double Bind," *Journal of Communication,* Vol. 24, No. 4, pp. 19-26.

37. Robinson, Michael J., "American Political Legitimacy in an Era of Electronic Journalism," in Cater, D. and Adler, R. (Eds.), *Television as a Social Force: New Approaches to TV Criticism,* Martin Robertson, 1976.

38. Golding, Peter and Elliott, Philip, *Making the News,* Longman, London, 1979.

In the first chapter (reprinted here) of Hanno Hardt's important book on the social theories of the press, Hardt compares the historical roots of the German and American traditions of mass communication scholarship. The much older German tradition—based in critical philosophy and broadly concerned with the political, cultural, and economic bases of the press—saw the press as an uncertain institution, whose consequences for the social order were far from clear. The newer American tradition, although rooted in a generation of men educated or influenced in large measure by German universities, emerged as more pragmatic and functionalist. Hardt caricatures the differences as those between utopia and realism; at the same time he commands, rightly, our serious attention to the strengths and weaknesses of both traditions. He concludes that the study of mass communication must be done in the context of a theory of society, and sees the work of the Hutchins Commission on a Free and Responsible Press of the 1940s as an example of how such work might proceed. Dr. Hardt is a professor of journalism at the University of Iowa.

2

INTRODUCTION TO
SOCIAL THEORIES OF THE PRESS

Hanno Hardt

THE HISTORICAL DIMENSION

The coming of age of a field of study is accompanied by questions about its past to help establish its identity and to secure its position among the arts and sciences. The history of communication and mass communication theory in the United States emerges as a chapter in the history of philosophical, social, and political thought in Europe and North America during the last hundred years. The present account concentrates on aspects which deal with the reflections of early American sociologists and their German colleagues or teachers who may have contributed to the development of communication and mass communication studies in this country and elsewhere. At the same time, the following pages are intended as a suggestion and a reminder that the intellectual history of this field may also yield theoretical insights concerning the relationship between communication and the advancement of society which may have consequences for the development of communication and mass communication research today.

Based upon the contributions of individual scholars during the late nineteenth and early twentieth centuries rather than on major themes of German or European intellectual history of that time, this has been a subjective and rather intuitive selection, guided in part by explanations of academic kinship, theoretical proximity, commonality of interests, and social-political involvement in contemporary issues.

From Hanno Hardt, "Introduction," pp. 17-39 in *Social Theories of the Press: Early German & American Perspectives.* Copyright 1979 by Sage Publications, Inc.

The social thought of this age was dominated by the writings of Spencer, Comte, and Marx, in particular, which shaped the work of others or prompted a response to their theoretical propositions. By the time the nineteenth century came to a close, the spirit of social criticism had been firmly established. The observation of social life had led to the Spencerian view of freedom through competing religious or philosophical doctrines, the Comtean realization that religion had to be replaced by a new scientific philosophy which would help organize the political and economic conditions, and a Marxian position which foresaw the growth of science and technology and the rise of an egalitarian society as a reaction to capitalistic forces. The work of these theorists was supported by others who engaged in closer observations of specific conditions, who conducted surveys and reported the failures of society in a scientific manner, e.g., in objective descriptions. They were not always dispassionate, and they were often supported by socialist thought and reformist ideas that surfaced in the journalism of the day. At times, social science theory and social criticism appeared to flow simultaneously from the work of committed intellectuals. While it was mainly an ideological force that dominated the social criticism of German scholars, it was an engagement in social reform which provided the focal point for the American social sciences. This means that sociology and the study of mass communication as a social phenomenon came into being in the United States as part of an expressed need for the improvement of social conditions and in Germany as a variation of philosophical and political thought. In both instances, however, the developments were caused, at least in part, also by the rapid transformation of society which had resulted in economic and political inequality. Most important for this study, however, was another recurrent notion throughout this period: the tracing of the development of social consciousness through communication as a definition and explanation of the rise of modern society. It was Marx who formulated the idea that the social structure must evolve out of the life-process of individuals, suggesting a way for the social sciences to investigate the workings of society:

> The production of ideas, of conceptions, of consciousness, is at first directly interwoven with the material activity and the material intercourse of men, the language of real life. Conceiving, thinking, the mental intercourse of men, appear at this stage as the direct efflux of their material behaviour. The same applies to mental production as expressed in the language of politics, law, morality, religion, metaphysics, etc.—real, active men, as they are conditioned by a definite development of their productive forces and of the intercourse corresponding to these, up to the furthest forms. Consciousness can never be anything else than conscious existence, and the existence of men is their actual life-process.[1]

This meant that the study of history must include language, public opinion, and the press as necessary elements in any explanation of the material or intellectual and spiritual growth of society. As a matter of fact, they provide central themes for the discussion of those social, economic, and political processes that help shape the human environment.

One of the strongest suggestions that emerges from the work of these early social scientists is that a theory of society, or any attempt to explain the coming of the modern age, must be based upon some understanding of communication as a basic social process involving individuals. In fact, communication becomes the sine qua non of human existence and the growth of society. Consequently, considerable attention is paid to the role and function of language as a socializing and integrating mechanism, as a tool or instrument for the construction of everyday realities as well as for scientific or political world views.

The production of symbols is crucial for the exchange of ideas; without language, man's ability to function as a social being is impaired, he is abandoned to live in a state of ignorance and isolation. Language, then, is the foundation of knowledge, it functions to preserve traditions, and it marks the beginning of civilization.

Communication implies the presence of language and the existence of dialogical relationships; it also fosters the idea of exchange. At the same time, language and communication are effective instruments or tools for individuals or groups; their use involves manipulation of different symbolic forms to effect individual or public opinions.

Therefore, any understanding or human progress from communal relationships to urban societies must be predicated upon an appreciation of the fundamental role of communication in this life-process of society.

The communication of ideas, the importance of preserving and transmitting knowledge as prerequisite for the growth and survival of society called for the creation of communication media that were not only accurate and efficient, but also fast and durable and therefore superior to oral modes of communication. These results were achieved almost instantaneously with the invention of the printing press, the publication of books and pamphlets, and the circulation of newspapers in modern times. The expression of facts and opinions on a large scale had the potential, if not the effect, of social and political integration through democratizing access to knowledge and to the media of dissemination.

The newspaper press rises to a powerful institution in the development of Western civilization: it is the medium for the exchange of ideas and it facilitates the time- and space-binding activities of society. The press as a technological invention or a political medium plays a major role in the definition of reality for the individual as well as for a nation; it supplies identification and formulates public opinions; and it supplements industrial and economic progress as an indispensible organizer of public sentiments.

The history of the modern press reflects the rise of liberalism, the reign of democracy and capitalism, and the growth of urban society. The daily press is a child of the city, and the process of public communication must necessarily be filtered through the economic and political interests that are identified with the concerns for urban development.

Throughout this period the work of political economists supplies a strong bias; thus, the role and function of the press receives a critical treatment that stresses economic aspects. These views range from an interpretation of the press reminiscent of Harold Innis' later work which produced a unique communication and mass communication perspective of world history, to assessments of the traditional, and unavoidable, ties between politics and business that effect the workings of the modern newspaper.

The press is central to any discussion of the production and dissemination of symbols, either in the form of political facts or opinions or in commercial messages. Newspapers sell either information or space for appropriate messages; in all cases there are economic interests at stake that cannot be ignored. As a capitalistic enterprise, the press not only serves other businesses, but by itself represents a capitalistic concern. Thus, the press helps coordinate production, transportation, and exchange of wealth; it aids in the search for ways of disposing of surplus and of promoting territorial divisions of labor; but it also promotes knowledge and education and provides political information.

Press criticism, therefore, focuses upon the real or potential conflict between these functions of newspapers: as an independent institution of society that produces and disseminates information, and as a medium of special interest groups that serves particular business and political segments of society. The difficulties of this position that characterizes the modern press are described in terms of the problems of a journalistic work ethic, the ideas of political as opposed to commercial newspapers, or the consequences of a press system that is recognized for what it is: the effective protection of an economic status quo.

This latter position can be explained also in terms of ideological differences regarding the treatment of leadership, the press, and public opinion. Specifically, the German position frequently reflects an elitist-aristocratic view which upholds the leader-masses dichotomy in the discussion of social, political, or cultural developments. Thus, it extols the intellectual qualities of a minority and delivers a rationale for its position vis-à-vis the masses which are capable of understanding and reflecting the ideas of their leaders but unfit to assume a creative and innovative role in the rise of modern society. The idea prevails that newspapers serve social and cultural elites in their communication with the masses. Even journalists are often reduced in their functions to mere objects through which the transmission of knowledge and information occurs without distortion. Although the press may reflect the opinions of the masses, it is not independent thought or creative insight, but more frequently a reaction to the opinions of the leaders that is reported. In this sense, the press assumes a rather fixed role in its relationship with society. The idea of the "average man" as a participant in the process of social communication is seriously reduced to that of a cooperating consumer of information in the context of describing the forces of history and the distribution of decision-making powers in society.

The views represented by the American position as it evolves in this study reveal the tendency to treat the press as a forum for the review of *all* ideas. Although the concept of authority may appear and suggest expert knowledge or special interest that will make itself felt in the communication process, there is no suggestion here that this precludes others from gaining similar access to the society through the newspapers, for instance. The press offers access to all kinds of commercial or political thoughts; and despite its economic interests, it is basically seen in the context of a classless society. This approach also suggests a concept of communication that fits the idea of a participatory democracy; in what is really a political process, all information is considered equally important, with the result that anyone may advance propositions which either support or oppose individual or special interest group goals.

Since newspapers do not just present windows on the world, but make or affect the opinions of their readers, the uses of the press by intellectual, political, or capitalistic elites present a serious problem. Indeed, control over the media of dissemination may suggest control over the mind of society.

Throughout the history of the press, criticism has assumed an inherent power in newspapers to change attitudes and to corrupt minds and has treated it as a particularly alarming aspect of a mass medium. Indeed, the workings of cultural and political forces in society are said to become transparent in the process of public communication where the communicator's purpose and intent are revealed and expose the nature of his ideology. The suggestive power of the press lies in its position as an institution *and* in the content of its messages. Thus, readers will follow the dictates of the press, because newspapers have gained their respect, are credible, and deliver facts and opinions convincingly. For this reason, newspapers are thought of as even more powerful instruments of communication than conversation, although, generally, greater effectiveness is attributed to face-to-face communication. Specifically, communicator effectiveness is also related to types of communication; the use of pictures (or films), for instance, offers still another argument for the persuasive power of the media.

But even the possibility of corruptive influences of mass communication does not result in an advocacy of drastic changes; instead, there is an implicit belief in the corrective influence of other types of communication which allows for comparison and intelligent choice. This position, in particular, is close to a definition of man as an educated, intelligent individual who participates in the societal process. The effects of the press are described, then, at a societal level where newspapers as institutions of society contribute to the political decision-making process, and at an individual level, where the press may change attitudes and the perception of reality. How this is accomplished and what the long-range effects would be for society were key questions that stimulated the suggestions for empirical research.

Thus, the origins of a modern study of the press are bound up with the rise of social criticism. It seems appropriate, especially in the light of the problems of contemporary communication and mass communication theory and research, to point to these beginnings and to renew the effort to embark upon a critical assessment of the role and function of the mass media in society.

This is so despite the fact that it could be argued, as Stuart Hughes has suggested, that social thinkers following Marx "were haunted by a sense of living in an age of merely derivative philosophy and scholarship"; and that their major contributions lay in the fact that they "narrowed the range through which such general theorizing might operate and cast doubt on the future usefulness of intellectual operations of this type."[2]

THE AMERICAN TRADITION

Specifically, today the tradition of American mass communication research is confronted by the crisis of the social sciences and the emergence of a critical approach to a theory of society. This situation is reflected not only in reactions to specific theoretical and methodological suggestions as they are being formulated and discussed by other disciplines, notably sociology, but also in acts of self-reflection and in a reappraisal of mass communication studies after a generation of research activities has had a profound effect upon the views about media activities and the way in which research is defined and executed.

The current dilemma of mass communication research is neither new nor unique; rather, it is the result of a historical development of a social-scientific enterprise that grew rapidly as a reaction to a number of social problems and as an attempt to treat specific conditions of society in a historical setting. This development also suggests the strength and weakness of the field. The immediacy of mass communication, its relevancy in everyday life, and the promise of research activities to help solve considerable social and political problems, provided the reasons for its prominence and initial success in academic and commercial contexts. Thus, mass communication studies received attention and built a strong rationale for their position among other disciplines and fields of study, particularly after World War II. At the same time, however, they neglected the larger, more meaningful contextual relationship that exists among media, communication and society, namely, the role and function of communication and mass communication in the process of civilization and the growth of society.[3]

Questions about the role and function of the mass media in American society are as old as the press itself. However, the interest in the phenomenon and the necessity for a systematic treatment of mass communication are relatively new. They seem to coincide with two major recent events, the invention of broadcasting technologies and the outbreak of wars. Both created specific demands for the social sciences: to summarize the effects of new technologies and to provide knowledge about the relationship of communicators and their audiences, about messages, and about the effects upon the political and economic lifestyles of society. The introduction of new types of media was accompanied by what Paul Lazarsfeld once called unanticipated consequences[4] which had to be identified and taken into account systematically for a complete understanding of real or potential uses of the mass media.

Not only did broadcasting cross continents and bridge oceans, but it was also envisioned as penetrating the minds of people more than other, older media and, therefore, expanding its influence as a tool of mass persuasion in the service of commercial or political interests. As a result, questions concerning the effects of mass communication were legitimized through economic and political support of research activities.

Similarly, the outbreak of a major conflict like World War II focused attention upon communication as a means of organizing national defenses, and also as an offensive weapon, in the field of psychological warfare, for instance. Consequently, the study of communication techniques received attention and continued encouragement—from government, in particular.

Lazarsfeld concluded quite correctly some years ago that communication research is a legitimate task of the social sciences and, although new, "it is, so to speak, the academic and intellectual shadow of the great changes which have come about in the world."[5] Thus, society became the laboratory and much of the initial research concentrated upon how to reach large numbers of individuals efficiently and effectively through the mass media. This was quite consistent with one of the prevailing definitions of mass communication as an activity directed towards a relatively large, heterogeneous, and anonymous audience.[6] Furthermore, much of the work that was completed treated society as potential or actual consumer of commercial or political messages at the expense of considering other, perhaps more critical perspectives on communication as a societal force.

There is still another reason for this development of the field. As we know, modern mass communication research has its roots primarily in the work of Harold Lasswell, Paul Lazarsfeld, Kurt Lewin, and Carl Hovland. Their interests in political power, audience effects, small group communication, and psychological analyses of communication effects, respectively, have been shaped by their disciplines. Their work provided important points of departure since the 1930s for several generations of communication and mass communication researchers. Nevertheless, this period of innovative ideas and the implementation of research designs was relatively short; it remained identified with the work of these principals in the field whose concerns with communication or mass communication phenomena, by the way, were rather peripheral to their major professional interests. Their students and followers, as is often the case, were less successful in generating and advancing new ideas; they were more successful in sustaining interest in those approaches with their particular methodologies and disciplinary frames of reference. There have been some exceptions, perhaps, but even so, the continuity of mass communication research often suffered, since little attention was paid to potential contributions to a mass communication theory. Instead, the collection of information became a preoccupation that raised some questions about the accumulation of unintegrated data that soon flooded the mass communication research field.

Nevertheless, a definitive perspective for an inquiry into mass communication activities was established and emerged from the early encounters with empirical communication research as a dominant way of looking at the world of the media and society. There was always an economic or political context, however, which mass communication research shared in the United States and which affected the investigation of media behavior. Specifically, the work was frequently conducted in an environment that was highly sensitive to the expert criticism of social scientists. Lazarsfeld observed as early as the late 1940s that "we academic people always have a certain sense of tight-rope walking: at what point will the commercial partners find some necessary conclusion too hard to take and at what point will they shut us off from the indispensable sources of funds and data?"[7] Not much has changed since that time; it is safe to assume that many of the most recent mass communication research projects have been sponsored by official or private sources rather than by academic institutions.

The shaping of a research perspective, then, rested upon the influence of economic and political environments as well as upon the theoretical and methodological orientations of a number of academic disciplines. Sociology, psychology, and political science, in particular, played a major role in the formation of research questions. They also introduced intra- and interpersonal communication aspects as part of a necessary condition to help explain causes and effects of mass communication, to understand differences between oral and written modes of communication, and to define traditional and modern systems of communication and society.

Most important, however, was the fact that mass communication research continued to operate within the prevailing philosophical mode of social-scientific research. Veikko Pietilä identified and described the influence of empiricism, behaviorism, and psychologism in the development of American communication research, for instance.[8] Consequently, not only was the search for mass communication causes and effects generally conducted with methodologies that generated knowledge based upon the interpretation of quantitative data, but also the search for an understanding of the consequences of mass communication activities was based upon various models of communication which provided a schematic diagram that identified major components like communicator, message, and audience as focal points, if not agendas for research.

The encounter with functionalism in its sociological and anthropological approaches, which postulate a system of society with stable relationships among its individual elements, meant that mass communication phenomena were treated as sources of information about the current state of exchange of information within a social system. Thus, functional analysis of mass communication suggested guidelines for the study of mass communication as an activity that contributed to the support and maintenance of the social system.

Functionalism as it emerged from its psychological roots provided mass communication research with its stimulus-response model; based upon a behavioristic theory, the approach led to a view of the mass media as deterministic stimuli with direct, cumulative effects upon the members of society.

THE GERMAN EXPERIENCE

The history of mass communication as a field of scholarly study is considerably older in Germany than in the United States. Recent encounters with the tradition of the American social sciences may help illustrate the pervasive influence of mass communication theory and research in Germany. The following reaction against unreflected adoption of theoretical or methodological premises may help define a framework for criticism.

The "discovery" of empirical social research for mass communication studies in Germany roughly coincided with the return of members of the Frankfurt Institute from the United States who began to promote the use of empirical techniques in the early 1950s. Thus, Adorno argued in 1952 for abandoning the idea of sociology as a *Geisteswissenschaft* and suggested the study of social phenomena with the methods of administrative research.[9] A few years later the widespread use of social science research methods resulted in a polarization of empirical and dialectical methodologists. The latter ones were represented by members of the Frankfurt Institute and Jürgen Habermas, who now exposed the dangers of a strictly empirical approach to the study of society. Adorno's warning that empirical social research is not "a magic mirror that reflects the future, no science-oriented astrology" did not prevent a *Positivismusstreit* among German sociologists. The clash occurred over the meta-theoretical foundation of sociology as science and involved representatives of critical theory (Adorno, Habermas) and critical rationalism (Karl Popper, Hans Albert). The outcome was not clear, not even to some participants; but the problem of the dialectical position focused on "how to integrate those techniques [of empirical social research] with a truly critical approach stressing the primacy of theory."[10]

It was not only Habermas' *Strukturwandel der Öffentlichkeit*, published in 1962, that focused the attention of *Publizistikwissenschaft* on the problem of critical theory, but also the availability of most of the American mass communication and communication literature, and the rise of a postwar generation of young social scientists whose commitments were to the development of a contemporary theory of mass communication which brought about a drastic change in the direction of *Publizistikwissenschaft*.

The introduction of functionalism as an American contribution to the development of postwar studies of communication and mass communication at various institutes of *Publizistik* also included a particular view of society. Based upon a sociological tradition represented at that time by Parsons, Merton, and Davis in the United States, the functional or structural-functional approach suggested a view which describes a tendency of society towards stability, value consensus, and equilibrium. The problems of sudden and profound changes, conflict and revolution, for instance, could be taken into account only in terms of "deviations," "variances," or "dysfunctions," that is to say, without departing from a "static" picture of society. Although critics, like Ralph Dahrendorf,[11] pointed out the necessity of studying social change in postwar German society and, therefore, the need for rejecting the functional model of society, their ideas remained largely ineffective, particularly with respect to the work on communication and mass communication problems.

At another level, functionalism could be seen as a conscious alternative to Marxism. Without characterizing it as a political ideology that rose from the structure of American capitalism, it was, nevertheless, a product of modern American social thought. Specifically, the activities of a group of Harvard scholars, among them George Homans, Parsons, and L. J. Henderson, perhaps described how sociology in the United States searched for "a theoretical defense against Marxism"[12] in the 1930s when it became a new perspective brought into sharp focus by the collapse of the American economy. Functionalism projected a politically and ideologically neutral image, while it supported values of order and stability. Thus, supporting change within the context of a status quo did not alter its position vis-à-vis social criticism or efforts of radical social changes.

In addition, the end of World War II also brought along a new style of scientific inquiry described as "abstract empiricism." It provided social scientists in postwar Western Europe with a powerful and compelling description of their function and added to their definition of sociology at the same time. Paul Lazarsfeld, in a paper delivered in 1948 to a group of social scientists in Sweden who wanted to set up research institutions, explained the work of the sociologist as the methodologist of the social sciences. He said,

> This then is the first function of the sociologist, which we can make fairly explicit. He is so to say the *pathfinder* of the advancing army of social scientists, when a new sector of human affairs is about to become an object of empirical scientific investigations. It is the sociologist who takes the first steps. He is the bridge between the social philospher, the individual observer and commentator on the one hand and the organized team work of the empirical investigators and analysers on the other. . . . Historically speaking we then have to distinguish three major ways of looking at social subject matters: social analysis as practiced by the individual observer; organized full-fledged empirical sciences; and a transitory phase which we call the sociology of any special area of social behavior.[13]

The promise of empirical methods as they had been developed in the United States was turned into a stream of mass communication studies at a number of institutes in West Germany. The method, it seemed, gave status and respectability to the field of mass communication research by providing an instrument for the collection of data and by supplying the scientific context for the interpretation of communication phenomena in modern society. The results were less than encouraging, however, because German mass communication researchers missed asking relevant or significant questions from the point of view of aiding society in its new beginning, politically as well as morally. When Dröge and Lerg observed a lack of theory development in American mass communication research as it had developed up to 1965, they failed to comment on an identical trend then visible in West German social science research.[14]

What Hans Bohrmann and Rolf Sülzer have called the "reformed" *Publizistikwissenschaft*[15] was now in a position of legitimizing its own role in the context of the university, but also vis-à-vis the professions and industry through a close identification with a respected empirical research tradition.

It is more than a coincidence that the end of World War II marked the beginning of a process of reorientation that has led to the exploration of other fields, including sociology, social psychology, philosophy, and political science as related areas and as fields of study that have recognized the importance of mass communication in their definitions of social and political processes. The challenges of contemporary life could be met only after understanding the relationship among various social forces in society; there was a need for a comprehensive view of society in order to develop a theoretical base for the study of social phenomena. Therefore, the process of democratization of postwar Germany resulted also in a breakdown of the traditional barriers around *Zeitungswissenschaft* through the introduction and acceptance of theoretical and methodological frameworks suggested by other disciplines.

Finally, since the late 1960s *Publizistikwissenschaft* has entered what could be called a critical or reflective phase in its approach to problems of social research as well as to questions of its own position in society. The controversies in sociology as well as the demands of students and faculty for relevance of research and teaching helped accelerate the process of internal debates and forced discussions into the open. In addition, there was the realization that the mounting number of independent, empirical studies could neither solve the problems of Germany's mass communication system with respect to questions of monopolization and freedom of the press, for instance, nor satisfy the demands for a comprehensive theory that would bring about the necessary or desired social or political changes in the mass media system. It was never so much a question of whether to reject empirical methods or not as it was a problem of interpretation of what empirical social research could and should do *within* a theoretical framework. The limitations of empirical techniques became more obvious: empirical methods provided a mirror for the curious mass media researcher; they satisfied the demands for an accurate picture of a particular media situation and thus provided immediate feedback; they were unable, however, to suggest a theory of society that takes into account the mass media behavior.

The critical approach to the study of mass communication as a social phenomenon has received support from writers like Hans Magnus Enzensberger, Horst Holzer, Friedrich Knilli, Dieter Prokop, and Franz Dröge. They seem to agree with Dröge's remark that "it cannot be the task of science in a late capitalist, alienated society to deal with single social phenomena."[16] And there is general agreement that communication research must develop methodologies that will allow drawing conclusions about the interdependence of communication phenomena and society.

It may be well, however, to remember Adorno's words that "the applicability of a science to society depends in an essential way on the state of society itself. There is no general social issue which some scientific method of therapy could treat universally."[17] Thus, a critical communication theory must not rely on speculations but be based on the condition of society and knowledge about communication in society.

REALISM AND UTOPIA

The current dilemma of mass communication studies is a result of
these developments in the social sciences; although variations or
adjustments to these perspectives exist, there prevails a spirit
of realism which continues to dominate and control the field. Its
major characteristics are an emphasis upon facts combined with
the search for causes and an explanation of their consequences
for the social system. At the individual level this approach
translates into the exploration of communication as a process
of adaptation to the irresistible forces of the social system.
Such a perspective is opposed by what could be called a utopian
outlook that views the role of communication and mass communication in terms of creating a possible or desirable social
environment; it is based upon theories or visions of a better
society in which mass communication performs a major task.

The antithesis of utopia and reality, so to speak, reveals
itself in a division between a critical-intellectual and an administrative-bureaucratic view of mass communication. The critical
position seeks to make practice conform to theory; it is more
interested in general principles and based upon certain human
values. Lazarsfeld's description of critical research is quite
useful as an explanation of this view. He said that critical research
"develops a theory of the prevailing trends in our times, general
trends which yet require consideration in any concrete research
problem; and it seems to imply ideas of basic human values
according to which all actual or desired effects should be ap-
praised."[18] The administrative view, on the other hand, is characterized by its empirical basis. Practice, or action, is more important than any consideration of theoretical propositions; there
are strong ties with the existing economic and political powers
in society and with those forces which support the established
order. This perspective also aims to provide a meticulous account
for mass communication phenomena, their role and function in
the dominant social and political system, and it tends to lead
to conclusions about adaption rather than conflict or revolution.

There is a tendency for the critical-intellectual position also to coincide with a politically liberal or radical perspective, whereas the administrative-bureaucratic position tends to lean toward a more conservative view concerning mass communication and its role in society.

Both positions contain unsatisfactory elements, however. The critical approach fails to translate theory into practice and, although intellectually convincing in its arguments, it remains relatively ineffective as an alternative to the present mode of thinking about mass communication research. It is an idea that is based upon what Lazarsfeld described as the need "to do and think what we consider true and not to adjust ourselves to the seemingly inescapable."[19] This task is demanding, however, and it may seem easier to follow the lead of an administrative approach that supports routinized research activities instead of sharing the fascination of new theories and the flow of ideas. The force of the latter position may produce undesirable results in the long run, however, and it may help to introduce a critical dimension to mass communication studies in order to provoke ideas hitherto neglected or undiscovered in the discourse about mass communication in contemporary society.

One of the best examples of recent years and a source of challenging ideas has been the work of the Commission on Freedom of the Press. Based upon notions of democracy, freedom of expression, and freedom of the press, the authors embarked upon a vigorous critique of the American media. They demonstrated by their work how the academic community can bring to bear upon society its expert observations concerning one of the most important institutions in a democracy. The commission concluded in its report, about 30 years ago, that the mass media were the single, most powerful influence in modern society. The document also noted the failure of other agencies of society suggesting that "if the schools did a better job of educating our people, the responsibility of the press to raise the level of American culture, or even to supply our citizens with correct and full political, economic, and social information would be materially altered."[20] The commission was particularly interested in the flow of ideas; it stated that a "civilized society is a working system of ideas. Therefore, it must make sure that as many as possible of the ideas which its members have are available for its examination"; because of the great influence of the media it is "imperative that the great agencies of mass communication show hospitality to ideas which their owners do not share."[21]

Specifically, the study of mass communication can make sense only in the context of a theory of society; thus, questions of freedom and control of expression, of private and public spheres of communication, and of a democratic system of mass communication must be raised as part of an attempt to define the position of individuals in contemporary industrialized Western societies. It is vital for an understanding of the importance of mass media research as a social and political force to comprehend the relationship between economic and political powers in society, their use of communication research as a source of knowledge, and the effect of this relationship upon defining the role of the media. It is equally important to address individual concerns for identity and self-respect in the process of societal communication.

This approach also implies that the study of communication and of the institutions of societal communication must be placed in the realm of a cultural and intellectual history of society. The mass media play a major role in the creation and perpetuation of cultural and social-political traditions. At the same time, they can be understood and explained only in relation to other social institutions, particularly education and religion, and in the context of economic-technological patterns of control.

Concerns about the press as a societal institution had a place in the writings of American sociologists who acknowledged not only the importance of communication, but who were equally involved in discussing the role of the press as it emerged as a powerful agent for the collection and dissemination of information in society. The following chapters may help contribute to the writing of a more complete history of communication and mass communication theory and research as it emerged from the works of sociologists in the United States and in Germany, whose universities provided in many cases a cultural and intellectual environment for American scholars at the beginning of their careers. It seemd important for that reason to deal more extensively with the contributions of German scholars who are among the major sources of a German tradition of *Zeitungswissenschaft*, to demonstrate the nature of their arguments, and to illustrate the character of their work as it concerned questions of communication and the role and function of the press in society.

The contributions of Albert Schaffle, Karl Knies, Karl Bücher, Ferdinand Tönnies, and Max Weber as they relate to the field of communication and mass communication studies are synonymous with the rise of the social sciences that included the first theoretical discussions of the mass media. Although primarily known for their scholarship in economic and sociological thought, their ideas concerning communication and the press appear as integral parts of any contemplation of societal issues; they suggest the need for a study of communication and mass communication in social and economic contexts, and they reflect, in an autobiographical sense, their own knowledge and experience with the press and public opinion as political and economic forces in the Germany of their own times. As teachers, colleagues, or contemporaries of American sociologists, they are among the most important sources of communication and mass communication theories emerging from German scholarship. The following chapters may provide some insights into the richness and originality of their thought. Since little is known about these individuals, with the exception of Weber and Tönnies brief biographical introductions will focus on their major contributions and their backgrounds as they relate to the issues under discussion. Most of the original material will appear for the first time in translation.

Among American scholars whose ideas appeared to be similar to those of their German colleagues are Albion Small, Edward A. Ross, and William Graham Sumner. They stand as representatives of a number of early American sociologists whose training

or background included encounters with the German tradition of
the social sciences and whose scholarship, labeled "American
science" in Germany, included similar notions concerning the
importance of communication and mass communication in a
modern society. Not only does their work reflect the influence
of German or European social thought, but it also represents a
first attempt to integrate some foreign ideas into uniquely
American social, economic, and political conditions. There are
long-standing and recognized differences in the social thought
of the United States and Germany, for instance, based upon the
nature of political and cultural movements that created different
premises for arguments concerning the role and function of
societal institutions, including the press. Hawthorn characterized
these differences when he concluded that "philosophical, social
and political thinking has proceeded within what are by comparison with Europe extremely narrow bounds, the bounds of an
established liberalism. In Europe, liberalism was at first a critical
principle, and no sooner had it been established . . . than it
itself began to be undermined by what has there generally been
understood as socialism. In the United States, on the other
hand, liberalism was only ever a critical principle in arguments
against Europe. It was established with the new republic, ideologically, if not in fact, and criticisms of the progress, or not,
of that republic have always been in its own terms."[22]

A review and comparison of these critical approaches to the
study of communication and mass communication should
include an awareness of these roots of sociological thought.
In this sense, the tradition of social criticism in the United
States, particularly as it includes the role and function of the
press, has never been a strong one, because it never overcame
the limitations of its own peculiar development as an intellectual
exercise within an established social and political system. The
following pages, finally, may suggest that turning towards a
critical-intellectual tradition in the study of communication
and mass communication must begin with an understanding of its
history.

NOTES

1. Karl Marx and Friedrich Engels, *The German Ideology*, edited by C. J. Arthur. (New York: International Publishers, New World Paperbacks, 1970), 47.

2. As quoted in T. B. Bottomore, *Critics of Society: Radical Thought in North America* (New York: Pantheon Books, 1968), 132.

3. This is a point at which historical and sociological interests meet to form a necessary alliance of shared research questions. The debate concerning the relationship between history and sociology has continued for some years. See, for instance, H. Stuart Hughes, "The Historian and the Social Scientist," *American Historical Review* 66 (1960), 20-46; A. S. Eisenstadt, "American History and Social Science," *The Centennial Review* 7 (1963), 255-272; C. Vann Woodward, "History and the Third Culture," *Journal of Contemporary History* 3:2 (1968), 23-35.

4. "Mass Media of Communication in Modern Society," reprinted in *Qualitative Analysis. Historical and Critical Essays* (Boston: Allyn and Bacon, 1972), 110.

5. Ibid., 112.

6. Charles R. Wright, *Mass Communication. A Sociological Perspective* (New York: Random House, 1975), 8.

7. "The Role of Criticism in the Management of Mass Media," in *Qualitative Analysis*, 124.

8. *On the Scientific Status and Position of Communication Research* (Tampere; Institute of Journalism and Mass Communication, Monograph No. 35, 1977), 34-44.

9. Martin Jay, *The Dialectical Imagination. A History of the Frankfurt School and the Institute of Social Research, 1923-50* (Boston: Little, Brown, 1973), 346.

10. Ibid., 251.

11. *Pfade aus Utopia: Arbeiten zur Theorie und Methode der Soziologie* (München: Piper, 1967), 263-277.

12. For a discussion of these developments, see Alvin Gouldner, *The Coming Crisis of Western Sociology* (New York: Basic Books, 1970), 149.

13. Lazarsfeld's paper is discussed by C. Wright Mills, *The Sociological Imagination* (Harmondsworth, England: Penguin Books, 1970), 70.

14. Franz W. Dröge and Winfried B. Lerg, *Kritik der Kommunikationswissenschaft* (Bremen: B. C. Heye, 1965); reprinted from *Publizistik* 10:3 (1965), 251-284.

15. "Massenkommunikationsforschung in der BRD. Deutschsprachige Veröffentlichungen nach 1960. Kommentar und Bibliographie," in Jörg Aufermann, Hans Bohrmann, and Rolf Sülzer, eds., *Gesellschaftliche Kommunikation und Information*, Band 1 (Frankfurt: Athenäum, 1973), 101.

16. *Wissen ohne Bewusstsein—Materialien zur Medienanalyse* (Frankfurt: Athenäum, 1972), 1. Also, Horst Holzer, *Gescheiterte Aufklärung? Politik, Ökonomie und Kommunikation in der Bundesrepublik Deutschland* (München: Piper, 1971); Hans Magnus Enzensberger, *Einzelheiten I. Bewusstseins Industrie* (Frankfurt: Suhrkamp, 1962); Friedrich Knilli, *Deutsche Lautsprecher. Versuch zu einer Semiotik des Radios* (Stuttgart: Metzler, 1970); Dieter Prokop, *Materialien zur Theorie des Films* (München: Hanser, 1971).

17. Frankfurt Institute for Social Research, *Aspects of Sociology* (Boston: Beacon Press, 1972), 126.

    18. "Administrative and Critical Communication Research," in *Qualitative Analysis*, 160.
    19. Ibid., 161.
    20. Robert D. Leigh, ed., *A Free and Responsible Press. A General Report on Mass Communication: Newspapers, Radio, Motion Pictures, Magazines, and Books By the Commission on Freedom of the Press* (Chicago: University of Chicago Press: Midway Reprints, 1974), vii.
    21. Ibid.
    22. Geoffrey Hawthorn, *Enlightenment & Despair. A History of Sociology*. (Cambridge: Cambridge University Press, 1976), 194-195.

Although widely questioned by mass communication scholars for nearly two decades, it is undeniable that the two-step, multistep flow theory of communication and influence had a major impact on the field. Its greatest impact has been on how related fields—such as sociology, political science, and psychology—have treated mass media within their own purview of study. Todd Gitlin, a sociologist at the University of California at Berkeley, does a thorough analysis of the major works of the Lazarsfeld school, finding contradictions and variant interpretations of the "theory" in footnotes and other sources. Like many of the contemporary European critics of American work, Gitlin traces the bankruptcy of the personal influence theory to the administrative research environment and model that produced it. Lazarsfeld was an institution man, a resourceful grant-getter who was blind to the pyramidal influence of the expanding media corporations because he sought to maintain harmony between institutions and the people, thereby legitimizing through research the very institutions he served. It was not a conspiracy, says Gitlin, but was a powerful convergence of the capitalist context with Lazarsfeld's roots in Austrian social democracy.

3

MEDIA SOCIOLOGY
The Dominant Paradigm

Todd Gitlin

Since the Second World War, as mass media in the United States have become more concentrated in ownership, more centralized in operations, more national in reach, more pervasive in presence, sociological study of the media has been dominated by the theme of the relative powerlessness of the broadcasters. Just as the national television networks — the first in history — were going to work, American sociology was turning away from the study of propaganda. In this essay I argue that such a strange conjunction of events is not without its logic. I argue that because of intellectual, ideological and institutional commitments sociologists have not put the critical questions; that behind the idea of the relative unimportance of mass media lies a skewed, faulty concept of "importance," similar to the faulty concept of "power" also maintained by political sociologists, specifically those of the pluralist persuasion, during the same period; and that, like pluralism, the dominant sociology of mass communication has been unable to grasp certain fundamental features of its subject. More than that: it has obscured them, scanted them, at times defined them out of existence, and therefore it has had the effect of justifying the existing system of mass media ownership, control, and purpose.

The dominant paradigm in media sociology, what Daniel Bell has called the "received knowledge" of "personal influence,"[1] has drained attention from the power of the media to define normal and abnormal social and political activity, to say what is politically real and legitimate and what is not; to justify the two-party political structure; to establish certain political agendas for social attention and to contain, channel, and exclude others; and to shape the images of opposition movements. By its methodology, media sociology has highlighted the recalcitrance of audiences, their resistance to media-

From Todd Gitlin, "Media Sociology: The Dominant Paradigm," *Theory and Society* 6 (1978) 205-253. Copyright 1978 by Elsevier Scientific Publishing Company, Amsterdam. Reprinted by permission.

generated messages, and not their dependency, their acquiescence, their gulli-
bility. It has looked to "effects" of broadcast programming in a specifically
behaviorist fashion, defining "effects" so narrowly, microscopically, and
directly as to make it very likely that survey studies could show only slight
effects at most. It has enshrined short-run "effects" as "measures" of
"importance" largely because these "effects" are measurable in a strict, repli-
cable behavioral sense, thereby deflecting attention from larger social meanings
of mass media production. It has tended to seek "hard data," often enough
with results so mixed as to satisfy anyone and no one, when it might have
more fruitfully sought hard questions. By studying only the "effects" that
could be "measured" experimentally or in surveys, it has put the methodological cart ahead of the theoretical horse. Or rather: it has procured a horse
that could pull its particular cart. Is it any wonder, then, that thirty years of
methodical research on "effects" of mass media have produced little theory
and few coherent findings? The main result, in marvelous paradox, is the
beginning of the decomposition of the going paradigm itself.[2]

In the process of amassing its impressive bulk of empirical findings, the field
of mass media research has also perforce been certifying as normal precisely
what it might have been investigating as problematic, namely the vast reach
and scope of the instruments of mass broadcasting, especially television. By
emphasizing precise effects on "attitudes" and microscopically defined
"behavior," the field has conspicuously failed to attend to the significance of
the fact that mass broadcasting exists in the first place, in a corporate housing
and under a certain degree of State regulation. For during most of civilized
history there has been no such thing. Who wanted broadcasting, and toward
what ends? Which institutional configurations have been generated because of
mass broadcasting, and which going institutions — politics, family, schooling,
sports — have been altered in structure, goals, social meaning, and how have
they reached back into broadcasting to shape its products? How has the prevalence of broadcasting changed the conduct of politics, the texture of political life, hopes, expectations? How does it bear on social structure? Which
popular epistemologies have made their way across the broadcasting societies?
How does the routine reach of certain hierarchies into millions of living rooms
on any given day affect the common language and concepts and symbols? By
skirting these questions, by taking for granted the existing institutional order,
the field has also been able to skirt the substantive questions of valuation:
Does the television apparatus as it exists fulfill or frustrate human needs and
the social interest? But of course by failing to ask such questions, it has made
itself useful to the networks, to the market research firms, to the political
candidates.

I. THE DOMINANT PARADIGM AND ITS DEFECTS

The dominant paradigm in the field since World War II has been, clearly, the cluster of ideas, methods, and findings associated with Paul F. Lazarsfeld and his school: the search for specific, measurable, short-term, individual, attitudinal and behavioral "effects" of media content, and the conclusion that media are not very important in the formation of public opinion. Within this whole configuration, the most influential single theory has been, most likely, "the two-step flow of communications": the idea that media messages reach people not so much directly as through the selective, partisan, complicating interpolation of "opinion leaders." In the subtitle of *Personal Influence*, their famous and influential study of the diffusion of opinion in Decatur, Illinois in the mid-Forties, Elihu Katz and Lazarsfeld were concerned with "the part played by people in the flow of mass communications."[3] One technical commentator comments with due and transparent qualification: "It may be that few formulations in the behavioral sciences have had more impact than the two-step flow model."[4] Daniel Bell, with his characteristic sweep, calls *Personal Influence* "the standard work."[5]

As in all sociology, the questions asked and the field of attention define the paradigm even before the results are recorded. In the tradition staked out by Lazarsfeld and his associates, researchers pay most attention to those "variables" that intervene between message-producers and message-receivers, especially to the "variable" of interpersonal relations. They conceptualize the audience as a tissue of interrelated individuals rather than as isolated point-targets in a mass society. They see mass media as only one of several "variables" that influence "attitudes" or voting choices, and they are interested in the measurable "effects" of media especially in comparison with other "variables" like "personal contact." They measure "effects" as *changes* over time in respondents' attitudes or discrete behaviors, as these are reported in surveys. In a sequence of studies beginning with *The People's Choice*,[6] Lazarsfeld and his associates developed a methodology (emphasizing panel studies and sociometry) commensurate with their concern for mediating "variables" like social status, age, and gregariousness. But in what sense does their total apparatus constitute a "paradigm," and in what sense has it been "dominant"?

I want to use the word loosely only, without history-of-science baggage, to indicate a tendency of thought that (a) identifies as important certain *areas* of investigation in a field, (b) exploits a certain *methodology*, more or less distinctive, and (c) produces a set of *results* which are distinctive and, more important, come to be recognized as such. In this sense, a paradigm is established as such not only by its producers but by its consumers, the profession that accords it standing as a primary outlook.

Within the paradigm, Katz's and Lazarsfeld's specific theory of "the two-step flow of communication," the idea that "opinion leaders" mediate decisively between mass communicators and audiences, has occupied the center of scholarly attention. In any discussion of mass media effects, citations of *Personal Influence* remain virtually obligatory. As the first extended exploration of the idea — "the two-step flow" appears only as an afterthought, and without much elaboration, at the end of the earlier *The People's Choice* — *Personal Influence* can be read as the founding document of an entire field of inquiry. If the theory has recently been contested with great force on empirical grounds,[7] the paradigm as a whole continues to be the central idea-configuration that cannot be overlooked by critics. Joseph T. Klapper's *The Effects of Mass Communication* (1960) is the definitive compilation of the field's early stages; but the Decatur study, spread out as it is in detail, seems to me a better testing-ground for a reexamination of the whole paradigm. By having the power to call forth citations and critiques at its own level of generality, it remains central to the field. For twenty years replicating studies have proliferated, complicating and multiplying the categories of the Decatur study, looking at different types of behavior, different types of "news function" ("relay," "information," and so on), some of them confirming the two-step flow on a small scale,[8] but most of them disconfirming or severely qualifying it.[9] All these studies proceed from the introduction into an isolated social system of a single artifact — a product, an "attitude," an image. The "effect" is always that of a controlled experiment (such, at least, is the aspiration), but the tendency is to extrapolate, without warrant, from the study of a single artifact's "effect" to the vastly more general and significant "effect" of broadcasting under corporate and State auspices. Whatever the particular findings, the general issues of structural impact and institutional change are lost in the aura, the reputation of the "two-step flow."

Perhaps Paul Lazarsfeld's looming presence throughout recent sociology is a "personal influence" that helps account for the dominance of his paradigm, even beyond what were at times his own relatively modest claims for it. But one man's charisma, however routinized, cannot be the whole story. It cannot explain, for example, how the "personal influence" paradigm finds its way, uncritically accepted, into a critical book like Anthony Giddens's *The Class Structure of the Advanced Societies*:[10]

> The influence of the mass media, and the diffusion of "mass culture" generally, is usually pointed to as a primary source of the supposed "homogenisation" of patterns of consumption, and of needs and tastes.

But research on the "two-step flow of communication" shows that formally identical content, as disseminated in the mass media, may be interpreted and responded to in quite different ways. Far from being eradicated by the uniform content of the media, existing forms of differentiation in social structure may be actively reinforced by it, as a consequence of such selectivity of perception and response.

Of course the issue for class structure may be neither its eradication (a straw man) nor its "simple" reinforcement (as if reinforcement were simple), but its transformation *in a patterned way* through the possibility of alternate, and hierachically preferred, "readings" of any given media material.[11] But my point is that the Katz-Lazarsfeld theory still in 1973 had the power to compel enthusiasm in a theorist otherwise unsympathetic to their approach.

As Melvin L. DeFleur[12] and Roger L. Brown[13] have stressed, the course of mass media theory has to be understood as a historical process, in which theorists confront not only social reality but also the theories extant. Theorists, of course, respond to the going theories in the languages of social research then current, that is, within a social scientific worldview now "normal," or becoming "normal," or contesting for "normalcy." They respond, explicitly or not, in the light or darkness of history — of new, salient forces in the world, social, political, and technological. There are thus three metatheoretical conditions shaping any given theoretical perspective: the nature of the theory or theories preceding (in this case, the "hypodermic" theory); the "normal" sociological worldview now current, or contesting the ideological field (in this case, behaviorism); and actual social, political, technological conditions in the world. The theory of the two-step flow, and the specific approach to "effects" in which the theory is embedded, are generated by a behaviorist worldview which makes itself decisive — and invisible — in the form of methodological microassumptions. The dominant paradigm has to be understood as an intersection of all these factors.

In the critique that follows, throughout Part I, I am concerned with *Personal Influence* as both buttress and instance of the larger, more general "normal" approach to questions of mass media "effects"; I want to identify the flaws in one particular theory, but more, to inquire into what they might imply for the whole field of communications research. In Part II, I probe for the roots of the whole intellectual enterprise.

The "Hypodermic" Theory

The "personal influence" paradigm is itself located within a critique of the earlier "hypodermic" theory, which is in turn both a theory of society and a theory of the workings of mass media within it.[14] In the "hypodermic" model, society is mass society, and mass communications "inject" ideas, attitudes, and dispositions towards behavior into passive, atomized, extremely vulnerable individuals. Katz and Lazarsfeld, who first named the "personal influence" paradigm, codified it, and brought it to the center of the field, were explicitly aiming to dethrone the "hypodermic" theory:[15]

> ...the media of communication were looked upon as a new kind of unifying force — a simple kind of nervous system — reaching out to every eye and ear, in a society characterized by an amorphous social organization and a paucity of interpersonal relations.

> This was the "model" — of society and of the processes of communication — which mass media research seems to have had in mind when it first began, shortly after the introduction of radio, in the 1920s. Partly, the "model" developed from an image of the potency of the mass media which was in the popular mind. At the same time, it also found support in the thought of certain schools of social and psychological theory. Thus, classical sociology of the late 19th century European schools emphasized the breakdown of interpersonal relations in urban, industrial society and the emergence of new forms of remote, impersonal social control.

During the Twenties, the "popular mind" of which Katz and Lazarsfeld spoke was recoiling from the unprecedented barrage of nation-state propaganda during the First World War, and the first wide-scale use of radio. The "schools of social and psychological theory" to which they referred were those governed by the relatively simple stimulus-response psychology.[16] It was this "hypodermic" model which Katz and Lazarsfeld proposed to dislodge by drawing attention to the social milieux within which audiences received media messages. As a corrective to overdrawn "hypodermic" notions, as a reinstatement of society within the study of social communication, the new insistence on the complexity of the mediation process made good sense.

Behaviorist Assumptions and Damaged Findings

But the "personal influence" theory was founded on limiting assumptions, so that its solid claims would be misleading even if substantial. Indeed, as it happens, the theory does not even hold up in its own terms; the Decatur study, taken on its face, fails in important ways to confirm the theory it claims to be confirming. Moreover, the anomalies themselves help us grasp the theory's social context; the anomalies mean something. For now I want to isolate the theoretical assumptions of the entire paradigm, and to see how they were applied in *Personal Influence*. In the discussion that follows, I center on the theory's limiting *assumptions*, some empirical *discrepancies*, and — a larger matter even if we set these aside — the theory's *limits in time*.

It is worth stressing again that the theory was rooted in a strict behaviorism. "Effects" of mass media lay on the surface; they were to be sought as short-term "effects" on precisely measurable changes in "attitude" or in discrete behavior. Whether in Lazarsfeld's surveys or the laboratory experiments of Carl Hovland and associates, the purpose was to generate *predictive* theories of audience response, which are necessarily — intentionally or not — consonant with an administrative point of view, with which centrally located administrators who possess adequate information can make decisions that affect their entire domain with a good idea of the consequences of their choices.

Now it is true that in a number of footnotes, Katz and Lazarsfeld did note (the word is apt) the self-imposed limitations of their study and their concept. Later developers, users, and promoters of the theory were not always so careful to specify the boundaries of their work. As "received knowledge," the notion of "two-step flow" and "opinion leaders" tends not to be qualified.[17] In one footnote, Katz and Lazarsfeld classified four types of "effects" "along a rough time dimension": "immediate response, short term effects, long term effects and institutional change."[18] On the next page, again in a footnote, they wrote:[19]

> It is important to note that some of these longer range effects which have barely been looked into promise to reveal the potency of the mass media much more than do "campaign" effects [i. e., effects of a single, short-run promotional or electoral campaign]. The latter, as we shall note below, give the impression that the media are quite ineffectual as far as persuasion in social and political [i. e., non-marketing] matters is concerned.

A few pages later, they cautioned again:[20]

> It would be a mistake...to generalize from the role of the mass media in... direct, short-run effects to the degree of media potency which would be revealed if some longer-run, more indirect effects were conceptualized and subjected to study.

And as the last word of their theoretical Part One, they concluded with a reminder that is as forceful as a footnote can be:[21]

It is perhaps worth reiterating what was said at the very opening: Mass media research has been concerned almost exclusively with the study of only one kind of effect – the effect of short-run attempts ("campaigns") to change opinions and attitudes....What should not be lost in all of this, however, is the idea that there are other kinds of mass media effects – which have not been much studied – where the impact of the mass media on society may be very much greater. Thus, the mass media surely lend themselves to all kinds of psychological gratifications and social "uses"; they seem to have visible effects on the character of personal "participation" in a variety of cultural and political activities; they have often been credited with being the primary agencies for the transmission of cultural values, etc. These chapters have not been explicitly concerned with these (predominantly long-range) matters. But our prescription – that communications research must take full account of the interpersonal contexts into which the mass media are injected – may hold good, too, for the much needed research on these less apparent, but perhaps more potent, effects of mass communications.

Finally, to avert any possible misunderstanding, they inserted a statement in the text to locate the personal influence analysis, "short-range changes and face-to-face influences," in any more ambitious program of inquiry:[22]

We hope that as time goes on, more and more links in the general influence chains permeating our society will be studied....No reader should confuse the modesty of our present enterprise with a blindness to broader and more complex problems. But these problems will forever be out of reach if we lose patience with very specific investigations such as the present one.

This last sentence must mean that personal influence analysis is *necessary* to a general analysis of mass media effects and *commensurate* with it.

But all disclaimers aside, the method of the *Personal Influence* study, and that of its precursors and successors, stands as a perspective of its own. Not only did a generation of successors work with the personal influence model, but Katz himself[23] and many later commentators wrote on it as a self-contained hypothesis. The model by itself is meant to be more than preliminary; it is of a piece; it stands separate from the wished-for general model that never materialized. It demands its own critique, beginning with its taken-for-granted assumptions.

Assumption 1. *Commensurability of the Modes of Influence: The exercise of power through mass media is presumed to be comparable to the exercise of power in face-to-face situations.* "People" "play a part" in the "flow of mass communications." The links in "the general influence chain" are all of the same order; the relations between their influences can be characterized as "greater" or "lesser." This was assumed rather than explicitly stated in *Personal Influence*, although there are points in the text (for example, p. 96) where the assumption lay relatively close to the surface. Discussing the two "forms of influence" in the same breath, as functional equivalents or commensurables, is what made for the general effect.

This reduction of structurally distinct social processes to commensurables can be recognized as a cardinal operation in the behaviorist canon. But what is distinct about the two processes, of course, is that everyone has the opportunity to exercise "personal influence" directly on someone else, albeit informally, and generally the relation is reciprocal, whereas the direct influence of mass media belongs routinely and professionally to the hierarchically organized handful who have access to it. The very image of a chain is reminiscent of the medieval Great Chain of Being, in which everyone, indeed everything, is in its duly and divinely appointed place. Language of this sort reveals the silent premise of the work.

Assumption 2, *Power as Distinct Occasions: Power is to be assessed in case studies of discrete incidents.* Katz and Lazarsfeld discussed and rejected two other possible criteria of influence: The reputational method, for one, (a) fails to reveal the frequency of influences, and (b) may elicit the names of prestigious individuals who have not actually directly influenced the respondent. Second, the counting of face-to-face contacts might let the decisive encounters through the sieve. Instead of these alternatives, they decided to ask respondents to recall "incidents of influence exchange," and the specific influentials involved therein.[24] In particular, they would ask respondents how they had changed their minds in each of four issue areas; then they would interview the next link in the chain. The occasion of influence was the face-to-face encounter in which individual A commended attitude *a* or behavior *b* to individual B. Those who exercised influence on such occasions were defined as "opinion leaders."

Notice that this behavioralization of power is identical to that achieved and insisted upon by the pluralist school of community political analysts who also came to prominence and began to dominate their field in the 1950s.[25] Here too the revolt against an earlier paradigm which emphasized the power of elites (the hypodermic model on the one hand, vulgar Marxism or elite theory on the other). Here too the tacit denial of patterns of structurally maintained power, or what will later be called "nondecisions."[26] Here too the insistence on studying discrete episodes of the exercise of influence, as if power were a kind of freely flowing marketplace commodity in a situation of equality, more or less; whence, as we shall see below, the discovery that opinion leadership, like the pluralist concept of influence, is issue-specific and "non-pyramiding."[27] "Opinion leaders" in one sphere did not have influence over other spheres, just as Dahl's New Haven influentials did not "pyramid" their influence. The structural homology of the two paradigms, personal influence and pluralism reveals something more significant than a coincidental similarity in the shape of their results; it reveals the similarity of problematics and methodologies, the common thrusts of the two fields.

Assumption 3. The Commensurability of Buying and Politics: The unit of influence is a short-term "attitude change" or a discrete behavior; or, more exactly, the report of such "change" or behavior by a respondent, and one which the respondent can attribute to some specific intervention from outside. Katz and Lazarsfeld were concerned with "four arenas of everyday decisions: marketing, fashions, public affairs and movie-going."[28] *These areas were assumed to be assimilable within a single theory.*

The domain of their interest is most accurately conveyed with a look at the relevant questionnaire items:[29]

With regard to marketing:

During the last month or so, have you bought any new product or brand that you don't usually buy? (I don't mean something you had to buy because it was the only one available.) Yes... No... (If no) On which of these have you tried a new brand most recently? a. breakfast cereals... b. soap flakes or chips... c. coffee... d. None of these.

With regard to fashions:

Have you recently changed anything about your hairdo, type of clothing, cosmetics, make-up, or made any other change to something more fashionable? Yes... No... (If so) What sort of change did you make?

With regard to movies, "our starting point was to ask the respondent to tell us the name of the last movie that she saw." (The respondents were women. For the reason, see p. 236.)

And on public affairs, the interviewers asked a number of recent poll questions, then asked if the respondent had recently changed her mind about any "like" them.

So in two of the four issue-areas, the concern was explicitly with changes in consumer behavior; in the third, with another discrete behavior in the realm of consumer choice; and in the fourth, with change in the opinion expressed. These issue-areas were taken to be comparable, and the presumed comparability of political ideas and product preferences distorted some of the actual findings. But more: the blithe assumption of the commensurability of buying and politics, never explicitly justified, never opened up to question, hung over the entire argument of *Personal Influence* like an ideological smog.

Assumption 4. *"Attitude Change" as the Dependent Variable: More deeply, more tellingly, the microscopic attention to "attitude change" was built on a confining approach to the nature of power.* In *Personal Influence*, power was the power to compel a certain behavior, namely buying, or, in the case of "public affairs," it was the power to compel a change in "attitude" on some current issue. Respondents were asked if they had recently changed their attitudes on a current issue; if they had, they were asked who had influenced them.[30] *If they had not changed their attitudes, they were assumed not to have been influenced.*

Now there are two ways in which this sense of influence is inadequate. First, its is possible that a respondent had begun to "change her mind" on a given issue, only to be persuaded back to the original position by personal influences or, directly, by mass media. More important still are the ways in which attitudes failed to change at all. If one does not take invariance for granted, but as something to be explained, how are we to understand the resulting "nondecisions?" For there is no compelling reason why constancy of attitude, in the capitalist age, must be taken for granted. Indeed, what in the modern age is called a constancy of attitude would have been inconstancy itself in previous times. Fickleness of loyalties is a prerequisite of capitalist society, where private property routinely yields to the claims of wealth and accumulation.[31] In the phase of high-consumption capitalism especially, when "new" is the symbolic affirmation of positive value and "old-fashioned" an emblem of backwardness, "changing one's mind" about products is a routine event. And in the realm of public life generally, one is frequently confronted with new political agendas (ecology, say), not to mention technological inventions, social "trends," celebrities and cultural artifacts, on which one is provoked into having opinions in the first place. Shifting policies of state routinely call for the mobilization and shift of public opinion.

In this historical situation, to take a constancy of attitude for granted amounts to a choice, and a fundamental one, to ignore the question of the sources of the very opinions which remain constant throughout shifting circumstances. Limiting their investigation thus, Katz and Lazarsfeld could not possibly explore the institutional power of mass media: the degree of their power to shape public agendas, to mobilize networks of support for the policies of state and party, to condition public support for these institutional arrangements themselves. Nor could they even crack open the questions of the sources of these powers.

And this absence is not rectified by the presence of another major term in the Lazarsfeld canon: *reinforcement*. For Lazarsfeld and his school, especially Joseph T. Klapper, reinforcement is the way in which media influence makes itself felt. The media are taken only to "reinforce existing opinions" rather than to change minds. Klapper's summary book, *The Effects of Mass Communication*,[32] remains the *locus classicus* of this argument, which comes forward to void criticism of the more general argument about the ineffectuality of media. Klapper and others who write in this vein think of reinforcement as a lower order affair compared to persuasion or mobilization. Yet reinforcement of opinion is an indispensable link between attitudes and actions. If media "only" reinforce "existing opinions," they may well be readying action, or anchoring opinion in newly routine behavior. Moreover, "reinforcement" can be understood as the crucial solidifying of attitude into *ideology*, a relatively enduring configuration of consciousness which importantly determines how people may perceive and respond to new situations. But "ideology" and "consciousness" are concepts that fall through the sieves of both behaviorism and stimulus-response psychology. They have no ontological standing in the constraining conceptual world of mainstream media research.[33]

Though he missed these points in his earlier work, Klapper has more recently compensated with a proposition that effectively demolishes the old theoretical apparatus:[34]

Reinforcement and conversion can, of course, occur only where there is an opinion to reinforce or oppose. It cannot occur in the absence of opinion. *Although there has been relatively little research on the subject, the media appear to be extremely effective in creating opinions.* By way of a commonsense example, a few months before Fidel Castro came to power, probably less than 2 per cent of the American people so much as knew his name, let alone his political leanings. A year thereafter, however, the American public knew a great deal about him and his political behavior and were rather homogeneous in their opinions about him. The source of their knowledge and the bases of their opinions were obviously restricted, for all practical purposes, to the mass media.

And of course such situations are routine in national and international political life: people are constantly expected to know something about situations they barely knew existed the day before. The issues presented in this way are among the most momentous: issues of war and peace, of international stance and alignment, of economic policy. A media sociology severed from a sense of the political importance of such issues systematically misses the point.

Without raising such points, Klapper, the head of research for CBS Television and one of Lazarsfeld's foremost students, goes on:

> It is not difficult to see why the mass media are extremely effective in creating opinion on new issues. In such a situation the audiences have no existing opinions to be guarded by the conscious or subconscious play of selective exposure, selective retention, or selective perception. Their reference groups are likewise without opinion, and opinion leaders are not yet ready to lead. In short, the factors that ordinarily render mass communications an agent of reinforcement are inoperative, and the media are thus able to work directly upon their audiences.

Now of course even this exclusion does not suffice as a statement of the conditions for media impact, since it does not discuss the source of whatever "existing opinion" do "ordinarily" prevail. And it does not address the substratum of belief that underlies discrete "opinions." Klapper is holding on to the personal influence paradigm. But his remark does show it is impossible to ground a theory of media impact in data collected on self-attributed sources of opinion *change*. And further: although Lazarsfeld and his students did seek to show that attitudes may be rooted in social position (socio-economic status, etc.), their practice of taking attitudes as discrete and disconnected units does not address their location in ideational structure: that is, in ideology.

Assumption 5. *Followers as "Opinion Leaders": Katz and Lazarsfeld took as given, definitive, and fundamental the structure and content of the media.* The close attention they paid to "opinion leaders" not only automatically distracted from the central importance of the broadcast networks and wire services, *it defined "opinion leading" as an act of following* without the awareness — indeed, the amusement — that such confusion should have occasioned. They were looking at the process of ideas moving through society through the wrong end of the telescope.

Specifically, the Decatur women were asked to nominate "opinion leaders" *in relation to the externally defined news.* To tell who was an "opinion leader," Katz and Lazarsfeld asked them "for their opinions on a variety of domestic and international problems *then current in the news*, e. g., on Truman's foreign policy, on demobilization policy for the army, etc." Then the women were asked if they had "recently changed their opinions" and whether they had been asked for advice.[35] "Experts," meanwhile — those whose general public-affairs influence overflowed the boundaries between issues — were defined as those nominated in response to this question: "Do you know anyone around here who keeps up with the news and whom you can trust to let you know what is really going on?"[36] In what sense, then, did an "opinion leader" actually lead? What was an "expert" expert in, and who decided the content of certified expertise?

The problem, to use the official language of sociology, is that the administrative mentality exaggerates the importance of "independent variables" that are located closest in time and space to the "dependent variables" under investigation.[37] Only their administrative point of view prevented Katz and Lazarsfeld from taking seriously the obvious: that their "experts" were dependent for their expertise on a "variable" explicitly ruled out of the scope of analysis. Respondents were being asked to name as influentials those individuals who they thought were most tuned in to the mass media. Katz and Lazarsfeld were taking for granted the power of mass media to define news; and they were therefore discovering not "the part played by people in the flow of mass communications," but the nature of the *channels* of that flow.[38] Vague language (indeed, a vague concept of power, as we shall see) masked a crucial distinction. It is as if one were studying the influence of streets on mortality rates during an enormous flood. A street is a conduit, not a cause of drowning. But the distinction is lost in bland language. When they came to address the issue, Katz and Lazarsfeld skirted the issue of institutionalized news this way:[39]

> Compared with the realm of fashions at any rate, one is led to suspect that the chain of interpersonal influence is longer in the realm of public affairs and that "inside dope" as well as influencing in specific influence episodes is much more a person-to-person affair.

The suspicion of a "longer chain of influence" is an evasion of institutionalized relations between broadcasters and audiences.

But an administrative point of view is likely, from the outset, to confuse a report of a certain sort of influence with originating power, since the institutional origin, by being more distant both conceptually and in time and space, will inevitably "leak" in transmission. In the process of asking *how* decisions are made at the bottom of the influence structure, it cannot ask *why* the occasion for deciding exists in the first place. It asks, in other words, the questions an administrator asks, or, in this case, the questions a marketer asks. (In fact it was a marketer, Macfadden Publications, who commissioned the Decatur study in the first place. On the roots of Lazarsfeld's work in marketing research, see pp. 233–40.)

Empirical Failings and Discrepancies

Even if we accepted the behaviorist premises embedded in the plan of *Personal Influence*, we would still have to confront the specific ways in which the theory fails of its *intended* purposes. Because of the sweep of their claim to have discovered a general principle of social interaction, Katz and Lazarsfeld blurred some of the interesting discrepancies in their findings. That is, they *reported* discrepancies but failed to *interpret* them, to give them proper weight in their theorizing.

The most striking discrepancy between finding and theory comes where Katz and Lazarsfeld reported the results of their survey of the sources of whatever "attitude change" on public affairs showed up between the two interview periods, June and August. Even if we permit the questionable assumption that people can reliably testify to the sources of their "attitude changes," there is a peculiar anomaly. How is one to make sense of the following result?[40]

> Not every [public affairs] opinion change [between June and August] involved a personal contact. Fifty-eight per cent (of the *changes*, not the *changers*) were apparently made without involving any remembered personal contact, and were, very often, dependent upon the mass media.

On the face of it, this extraordinary finding discredits the theory of the two-step flow; it is, in fact, consistent with the old "hypodermic" notion. "Not every opinion change" indeed![41] The general theoretical conclusion, that "ideas often flow *from* radio and print to the opinion leaders and *from* them to the less active sections of the population,"[42] is now seen to be more wrong than right. How did this disconfirmation fail to enter into Katz's and Lazarsfeld's theoretical conclusion? I can only conjecture that the failure to incorporate the empirical disconfirmation into the theory – that is, the discrepancy was mentioned at one point in the book, but not when the general theory was being stated – flows from the study's construction of a false commensurability among the four areas of fashion, marketing, movies and public affairs. If one regards these areas as equally significant and comparable, and the theory is constructed to apply to all of them indiscriminately, then a serious disconformation in *only* one of the areas does not weigh so heavily. If, on the other hand, one is investigating the impact of mass communications on political attitudes, the disconfirmation is decisive. Thus the extrinsic choice of four issue-areas (see p. 236) ends up permitting the authors to push a serious discrepancy off to one side.

There is another instance where the Decatur data pointed away from the two-step flow theory, and in which Katz and Lazarsfeld failed to take the empirical lapse into account in formulating their theory. People named as influentials or influencees in the area of public affairs were far less likely to confirm that status — to confirm, in other words, that they had in fact made an attempt to influence, or that they had in fact been influenced — than people named in the areas of marketing and fashions.[43] Fifty-seven percent of the designated marketing influencees acknowledged that role; 56 percent of the fashion influencees; but 38 percent of the public affairs influencees. For designated influentials, the confirmations were 71 percent for marketing, 61 percent for influencees; but only 38 percent of the public affairs influencees. For designated influentials, the confirmations were 71 percent for marketing, 61 percent for fashions, but only 37 percent for public affairs. In other words, in the area of discrepancy,[44] Katz and Lazarsfeld mentioned the possibility that the *men* who were disproportionately the public-affairs influencers may have been poor informants on these matters; they did not mention the possibility that specific influence on one's "public affairs attitude changes" was so hard to trace as to cast discredit on the idea of a two-step flow operating at all, or any other decisive interpersonal process of influence. Data like these are entirely consistent with the "hypodermic" theory: with the hypothesis that, in the area of public affairs, media work directly upon public consciousness. Although this marked failure of confirmation bankrupts the public-affairs variant of the theory, certainly one of the major extrapolations from their work in later years, Katz and Lazarsfeld passed over any such implication by calling for "much more study" and by labeling their study "exploratory."

The Theory's Limits in Time

Even if we accepted the behaviorist assumptions of *Personal Influence*, and limited the theory's claims in order to be true to the empirical discrepancies, we would still have to confront its barely suggested historical boundaries.

Often enough footnotes are the burial grounds of anticipated criticism; they are also, therefore, good sites to begin the archaeological digs of critical investigation. So it is that, after hundreds of pages of generalization about mass communications, it was in a footnote that Katz and Lazarsfeld reminded the reader: "The study was completed before the general introduction of

television."[45] And then they darted back to their discussion without noticeably adulterating the generality of their conclusions about "the flow of mass
communications."

It is hard to know what to make of this, and the authors did not afford us
any assistance. But to begin with it is not obvious, to say the least, that what
went for radio and print in 1945 should go for the more intrusive, more
immediate, more "credible" medium of television later on. It would rather
seem, *a priori*, that television would have, or at least could have, a more direct
impact than radio or print. In other words, even if the findings of *Personal
Influence* were persuasive on their face (which they are not), and even if the
theory embodied there were compelling rather than weak (which it is not),
we would still not be in a position to say anything cogent about the era after
1945, about the force of television in the domain of political consciousness
and political conduct.

But a larger question arises here too, of the confusion between synchronic
and diachronic dimensions. As their rhetoric makes clear, Katz and Lazarsfeld
did not intend simply to make assertions about the relations between more
and less media-exposed women in Decatur, Illinois, in the summer of 1945;
they intended general statements, valid across the boundaries of time. Because
of the methodological difficulties that would be entailed in studying long-run
effects in a positivist fashion, they and their followers constructed a paradigm
which would then be taken as valid over the historical long haul. From the
snapshot, they proposed the inferences one could only make about a film.
But the transposition was not justifiable. C. Wright Mills, who had supervised
the field work in Decatur and then drafted the original analysis of the data in
1946, made one critical point very clearly:[46]

> Many problems with which [abstracted empiricism's] practitioners do try
> to deal — effects of the mass media, for example — cannot be adequately
> stated without some structural setting. Can one hope to understand the
> effects of these media — much less their combined meaning for the devel-
> opment of a mass society — if one studies, with whatever precision, only a
> population that has been "saturated" by these media for almost a genera-
> tion? The attempt to sort out individuals "less exposed" from those "more
> exposed" to one or another medium may well be of great concern to
> advertising interests, but it is not an adequate basis for the development of
> a theory of the social meaning of the mass media.

Of course it was precisely what Mills considered "a theory of the social
meaning of the mass media," necessarily a theory of the mass media *in history*,

that Katz and Lazarsfeld would discount as vague, unscientific, and impracticable. Indeed, Lazarsfeld did so in no uncertain terms in the midst of his most critical essay (written with Robert K. Merton):[47]

> What role can be assigned to the mass media by virtue of the fact that they exist? What are the implications of a Hollywood, a Radio City, and a Time-Life-Fortune enterprise for our society? These questions can, of course, be discussed only in grossly speculative terms, since no experimentation or rigorous comparative study is possible. Comparisons with other societies lacking these mass media would be too crude to yield decisive results, and comparisons with an earlier day in American society would still involve gross assertions rather than precise demonstrations. In such an instance, brevity is clearly indicated. And opinions should be leavened with caution.

And yet Lazarsfeld's cleanly positivist approach in *Personal Influence* is "grossly speculative" in its own way, by elevating the findings of a single study, themselves dubious, to the status of timeless theory. A four-hundred page book found a one-line footnote sufficient notice that its general propositions did not take account of a central feature of the reality they claimed to be uncovering; or, to put it technically, the central "independent variable" was grossly incomplete. Such brevity was plainly indicative of a lapse in caution. And if it were to be claimed that the positivist propositions of *Personal Influence*, however couched in the ordinary language of timeless truths, could in principle be discredited by future replications, and therefore remain scientific in the Popperian sense, it would have to be granted in return that general historical statements are in principle equally refutable, and are therefore equally capable of validation by the criteria of Karl Popper. Failing to admit straightforward historical speculation (and why could there not be *fine* speculation?), rejecting it as "gross assertion rather than precise demonstration," Lazarsfeld let "gross assertion" in through the back door.

If the alternatives are "gross assertion" and "precise demonstration," we seem to be left with the overly elaborated categories of microscopic technique, or what Alfred North Whitehead called "misplaced concretism." But a multiplication of categories is not necessarily a clarification of reality. Confusing the two is the occupational hazard of the positivist tradition. Later generations of scholars inherit and perpetuate the main outlines of the pioneering and misleading study, according it paradigm-founding status, and usually failing to examine it critically. It is so easy, especially in the press of one's own studies, to ignore or to override the cautions and contradictions of the founding work, especially when they are located obscurely in the text. The shape of the social science that results is nicely grasped in the memoir of a former Columbia graduate student, Maurice Stein:[48]

One of my favorite fantasies is a dialogue between Mills and Lazarsfeld in which the former reads to the latter the first sentence of *The Sociological Imagination*: "Nowadays men often feel that their private lives are a series of traps." Lazarsfeld immediately replies: "How many men, which men, how long have they felt this way, which aspects of their private lives bother them, do their public lives bother them, when do they feel free rather than trapped, what kinds of traps do they experience, etc., etc., etc." If Mills succumbed, the two of them would have to apply to the National Institute of Mental Health for a million-dollar grant to check out and elaborate that first sentence. They would need a staff of hundreds, and when finished they would have written *Americans View Their Mental Health* rather than *The Sociological Imagination*, provided that they finished at all, and provided that either of them cared enough at the end to bother writing anything

One should ponder well the actual uses of the studies Stein mocks; for the absurdity of their pretensions and the trivialization of their language do not halt them. Indeed, the web of assumptions that stands behind *Personal Influence* persists, albeit contested now by structural and radical critiques. Not surprisingly, this pattern of theoretical assumptions bears a strong resemblance to the assumptions of corporate broadcasting itself. The two enterprises share in a fetishism of facts, facts which by their raw muscularity, their indisputability, their very "hardness," take on the authority of coherent theory. The fact in social science becomes a sort of commodity, the common currency of discourse, to be compared with, exchanged for, and supplanted by others, just as the fact as it is presented through mass media becomes authority itself, an orientation to the bewildering world that lies outside one's milieu and outside one's control. The society of the crisp, authoritative radio and TV voice, of objective journalism, and of abstract empiricism, is the society of the instant replay, of microscopically interesting sports records, of the Guinness Book of World Records — and of body counts and megaton nuances. *Dragnet's* Sgt. Friday and mainstream sociology both demand "Just the facts, ma'am." T. W. Adorno has traced this sociological orientation to "Durkheim's rule that one should treat social facts like objects, should first and foremost renounce any effort to 'understand' them," and this in turn to the reality of "relationships between men which have grown increasingly independent of them, opaque, now standing off against human beings like some different substance."[49] The practice of making a fetish of the "hard" behavioral fact in sociology grows along with the use of "hard news," of the mediated fact as "technological propaganda," or in "a propaganda of facts," which functions to discourage reflectiveness. These phrases emanate, by the way, from an excellent analysis of the phenomenon, first published in 1943 by – Robert K. Merton and Paul F. Lazarsfeld.[50] The fetishism of facts as a practice proves stronger than the ironic theoretical understanding of its rise.[51]

II. ROOTS OF THE PARADIGM

Why did the *Personal Influence* study start by assuming that mass media influence is comparable to face-to-face influence, and that power exists as discrete occasions of short-term "attitude change" or behavioral choice? How may we account for the theory's thin sampling of reality, for its discrepancies and their absence from the summary theory? And why did the field that grew from these beginnings preserve that thinness and those discrepancies in both theory and methodology? If we step back from the Decatur study and its successors to the general style of thought they embody, to their sociological tenor, we find a whole and interwoven fabric of ideological predispositions and orientations. We find, in particular, an *administrative point of view* rooted in academic sociology's ideological assimilation into modern capitalism and its institutional rapprochement with major foundations and corporations in an oligopolistic high-consumption society; we find a concordant *marketing orientation*, in which the emphasis on commercially useful audience research flourishes; and we find, curiously, a justifying *social democratic ideology*. The administrative point of view, the marketing orientation, and the Austro-Marxist variant of social-democratic ideology are a constellation that arose together but are (at least) analytically separable, and I will treat them one at a time.

One further prefatory note: *in the whole of the discussion that follows, I want to stress that I will be looking at roots of the paradigm as a whole – the search for specific, measurable, short-term, individual "effects," and not beyond them – and not solely at sources of the specific two-step flow theory within it.* It is the whole scope of the paradigm – its methodological individualism, its market assumptions, its structural naivete – that is at issue. The "two-step flow" might be a sound theory, and questions would remain about the prevalence of its premises throughout the field.

And lest this search for general origins be seen as unjustifiably contextual, reductionist, or perhaps *ad hominem*, it seems only proper to quote an illustrious predecessor. Paul F. Lazarsfeld himself wrote that the "ideological component," "the intellectual climate," and "the personal equation" were "probable roots" of his "new research style," and that his ideological, intellectual, and personal origins permitted him "structural fit" with the emerging sociological scene in America.[52]

The Administrative Point of View

When I say that the Lazarsfeld point of view is administrative, I mean that in general it poses questions from the vantage of the command-posts of institutions that seek to improve or rationalize their control over social sectors in social functions. The sociologist, from this point of view, is an expert who addresses problems that are formulated, directly or indirectly, by those command-posts, who are concerned, in essence, with managing the expansion, stability, and legitimacy of their enterprises, and with controlling potential challenges to them. In the development of media research in particular, as in the whole of postwar positivist surge in social science, the search is for models of mass media effects that are *predictive*, which in the context can mean only that results can be predicted from, or for, the commanding heights of the media. The "variables" are to be varied by those in charge of mass media production, and only by them; therefore they tend to be short-run in time-span and behavioral rather than structural in focus. From the administrator's point of view, the mass media system in its structural organization is of course not at issue; it is the very premise of the inquiry. Thus, the administrative theorist (the term is Lazarsfeld's own self-characterization)[53] is not concerned, for example, with the corporate decision to produce radio and television receivers as household commodities rather than, say, public ones, although this fundamental choice had serious consequences for the social uses, power, and meaning of mass media.[54] The administrative theorist is not concerned with the corporate structure of ownership and control at all, or with the corporate criteria for media content that follow from it: he or she begins with the existing order and considers the effects of a certain use of it. What C. Wright Mills called abstracted empiricism is not at all abstracted from a concrete social order, a concrete system of power.

It stands to reason that the administrative point of view comes most easily to the mind of one who is himself or herself an administrator, or comfortably *en route* to that position, especially of an intellectual enterprise developed under corporate or State auspices, set up with its financial backing, and in its organizational image, able to capitalize on its legitimacy to open research doors and to recruit a skilled staff. For the administrative point of view is an angle of theory intimately connected with a practice, and best nurtured within it. Point of view and institutional position select for one another. Lazarsfeld was himself, of course, one of the pioneers in the bureaucratic approach to sociological research, by his own account an "institution man,"[55] indeed an administrative and entrepreneurial wizard. At first with the Office of Radio Research at Princeton he took charge of in 1937, then with its reincarnation as the Bureau of Applied Social Research at Columbia University, he "developed," in his own words, "the image of the managerial scholar."[56] He presided there over any number of research projects in marketing and media, over the training of successors, and over the reputation gathered by both projects and successors. His skill in gathering research funds was legendary; he knew how to shift them with aplomb from project to project, raising money here from foundations and companies for narrow, specific purposes, and then using the money, there, often for wider purposes. (Such was the case, indeed, with the Decatur study. See p. 236.) As a bureau director he was able "to take reasonable risks, to try deviant innovations without coming into too much conflict with prevailing norms."[57]

The time of his ascendancy in American academic life was, as he pointed out, a fortuitous one. It was a time when administered politics, administered markets, administered culture, administered education were each coming into its own, each becoming legitimate, each developing tight interlocks with the others. Their mutual gravitational pulls were gradually forming them into a fixed and rising constellation, a recognizable life-world with distinct and dominant, though flexible, norms and practices. Universities, corporations and foundations were finding themselves in sometimes uneasy but mutually indispensable partnerships; and they were meeting under the sign of behaviorism.

In 1929, the new head of Social Sciences for the Rockefeller Foundation, Edmund E. Day, had begun his tenure with these words:[58]

> Practically all the sciences have sprung initially from philosophy. The introduction of laboratory methods enabled the natural sciences to make a rather complete separation, and the medical sciences made the same break later. The social sciences are still in the process of establishing their independence.....*We have thus virtually to break an academic pattern. We have to establish a new academic mold.*

Within the next fifteen years, and with no small boost from the Rockefeller Foundation, that new academic mold was forming. A man like Paul Lazarsfeld, a serious and skilled theoretician and bargainer among theories as well as among men, a practitioner of positivism as well as an "institution man," could become central to the whole developing process, in all its intellectual and organizational aspects. But it makes little sense to ask exactly which particular institutions led, and which followed, in the vast social and cultural transformation into oligopolistic capitalism. Men like Lazarsfeld, coming to intellectual maturity under the political star of European social democracy, inventive with mathematical tools, able to put sociological methods at the service of a brash, expanding consumer capitalism, were looking for institutions to embody their approach to the world. Foundations and corporations, having learned the uses of quantification in the rise of engineering (especially in Taylorist production) and in the model-changing, price-increasing mass marketing pioneered by Alfred E. Sloan at General Motors, wanted to rationalize the social sciences and make them practical. The State was interested in knowing the conditions for effective propaganda. Universities wanted to establish new financial bases, to integrate themselves into the postwar boom and the new hegemonic culture, although they would have to be convinced that the new research style was legitimate, that it would not threaten the position of the entrenched academic mandarins. All these interests and strategies were converging, and a farsighted and adventuresome and skilled thinker like Paul Lazarsfeld was one to insist on the *common* interest, with great success.

In the crystallization of the new intellectual force, the Rockefeller Foundation did in fact play a substantial role, and never more effectively than in putting Paul F. Lazarsfeld on the American map. Lazarsfeld recalled much later that the pioneering study he organized, in 1930, of unemployment in the village of Marienthal, was suggested to him originally by Otto Bauer, a leader of the Socialist Party of Austria.[59] That study, a statistically rich prefiguring of his later work,

> brought me to the attention of the Paris representative of the Rockefeller Foundation, and in 1932 I obtained a traveling fellowship to the United States, where I arrived in September 1933.

In a footnote to his memoir, Lazarsfeld added:[60]

> The way I received my fellowship has its own interest. The Rockefeller representative gave me an application form. Living in the pessimistic climate of Vienna at the time, I was sure I would not get the fellowship, and did not apply. In November 1932 I got a cable from the Paris Rockefeller office informing me that my application had been misfiled, and that they wanted another copy. They had obviously decided to grant me the fellowship on the recommendation of their representative and it had never occurred to them that I had not applied. I mailed a "duplicate," and the fellowship was granted.

The Foundation continued to care assiduously for "establishing the independence" of social science from primitive, non-instrumental philosophy. When, in 1937, the Foundation bestowed upon Hadley Cantril of Princeton and Frank Stanton of CBS the money for an Office of Radio Research, Robert Lynd at Columbia convinced Cantril to hire Lazarsfeld as Director. Within a few years the Office "had acquired an institutional life of its own," and was able to procure grants from other sources.[61] But the Foundation remained its major buttress.[62] In Lazarsfeld the Foundation had found a superlative organization man who could bring the "new research style" inside reluctant universities, and make the positivist spirit prevail against the backwardness of of philosophy. The second edition of *The People's Choice* records: "This study was made financially possible by drawing upon a general grant from the Rockefeller Foundation, the income of the Consulting Division of Columbia University's Office of Radio Research, and by special contributions from *Life* magazine and Elmo Roper."[63] Here is what the former President of the Rockefeller Foundation has written about the Foundation's support:[64]

> An undertaking of perhaps deeper promise was the support given to the School of Public and International Affairs of Princeton University toward a study of the role that radio plays in the lives of the listeners. Organized under Dr. Paul F. Lazarsfeld, it attempted to answer such questions as these: What individuals and social groups listen to the radio? How much do they listen and why? In what ways are they affected by their listening? The radio industry had, of course, been concerned with determining the size and distribution of its audience as prospective purchasers for products advertised over the air. To learn what it could of the listener as an individual and as a member of society, the Princeton study, quite literally, began where the industry left off. This same type of study was later supported at Columbia University, also under Dr. Lazarsfeld. The research by the two institutions not only gave a detailed and accurate portrait of the American listening public, but also developed new methods of inquiry applicable to forecasting and testing the response of untried programs; and *the reports which grew out of the studies having been widely used in the radio industry, Dr. Lazarsfeld's office was increasingly consulted as a source of expert and impartial advice.*

Lazarsfeld, for his part, was not worried by his dependence on the Foundation. "The liberal formulation of the Rockefeller program," he wrote later, "permitted me to do any kind of specific study as long as I gave it some nominal connection with radio problems...."[65] But not quite. The Rockefeller program insisted on underwriting only studies that were consonant with the empiricist program, and in at least one instance Lazarsfeld described, the hand that paid the piper did actually and .directly, and apparently despite Lazarsfeld's hesitation, call the proverbial tune. In 1938 Lazarsfeld, along with Max Horkheimer, now at Columbia, invited T. W. Adorno to the United States, to direct the music division of Lazarsfeld's Office of Radio Research. One would have to speculate on the full complexity of Lazarsfeld's motives: the humanitarian wish to aid a fellow refugee; Lazarsfeld's affinity for some of the Frankfurt Institut's early empirical studies; his desire, perhaps, to give more active expression to his suppressed critical underside. By his own account, Lazarsfeld wanted "to see whether I could induce Adorno to try to link his ideas with empirical research." In his own manner, fitfully, reluctantly, and critically, Adorno did try: during his time with Lazarsfeld he wrote a number of concrete studies of what he would later call "the culture industry."[66] Writing about the same period, Adorno did not criticize Lazarsfeld directly; instead he wrote this:[67]

> Naturally there appeared to be little room for...critical social research in the framework of the Princeton Project. *Its charter, which came from the Rockefeller Foundation, expressly stipulated that the investigations must be performed within the limits of the commercial radio system prevailing in the United States.* It was thereby implied that the system itself, its cultural and sociological consequences and its social and economic presuppositions were not to be analyzed.

Adorno added dryly: "I cannot say that I strictly obeyed the charter." After a year of tension over the proper domain of curtural research, Lazarsfeld, to his credit, tried in a long letter to convince Adorno to abandon his own fetishism of language and his "disrespect" for empirical procedures, but to no avail.[68] Again according to Lazarsfeld,[69] John Marshall of the Rockefeller Foundation "probably felt that my efforts to bring Adorno's type of critical research into the communications field were a failure," and in the fall of 1939 the Foundation refused to renew the music project.

Lazarsfeld would argue in the Frankfurt Institut's own journal that "critical" and "administrative" research were in fact compatible;[70] he wanted empirical research to answer the questions put by critical theory. Adorno himself insisted that he objected not to empirical research as such but to its primacy *over* — and finally *instead of* — theory.[71] But however conflicted Lazarsfeld's position on critical theory, and however personally-grounded his difficulties with Adorno, the Foundation evidently did not want to come even this close to retrograde, offending "philosophy." "Expertise and impartiality" finally meant attentiveness to the practical problems of the culture industry; it required strict adherence to an administrative point of view.[72]

Lazarsfeld's administrative theory and his close relations with the cultural industry, in the person of Frank Stanton, proceeded apace. It was in 1935 that Lazarsfeld established what was to be a long working partnership — "friendly relations," Lazarsfeld called them — with Stanton, "then a junior staff member of the Columbia Broadcasting System."[73] Of course Stanton's corporate standing does not automatically establish that, in any simple sense, Lazarsfeld was beholden to the narrowly construed corporate interests of CBS, as opposed to, say, NBC or *The New York Times*. In fact, their affinity was considerably more profound than an immediate interest. Lazarsfeld's relations with Stanton, and Stanton's successful career, personify the rising estate of administrative social science just before, during and after the Second World War, and its tight links with the apparatus of corporation and State. The two men shared a common interest in positivist research, especially in the measurement of audiences and the "effects" of particular media messages, which would enable centralized institutions (broadcasters, advertisers, the State) to predict public reactions to institutional choices. Stanton himself had been hired by CBS in 1935 because the network was impressed with his Ph. D. psychology dissertation on audience research. Stanton had invented "the first automatic recording device designed to be placed inside home radio receivers";[74] thus he anticipated A. C. Neilsen's lucrative little polling box. By 1938, Stanton was research director of CBS, and at the same time an Assistant Director of the Princeton project. Much was at stake for Lazarsfeld in such a relationship. He could become legitimate in the eyes of the media establishment, just as, in his associations with such sociologists as Robert Lynd and Hadley Cantril, he could strive for intellectual legitimacy. As a "marginal man" who understood himself as such, and more-over as a refugee Jew in the anti-Semitic academy, Lazarsfeld would have to secure both flanks.[75] With direct corporate connections, he could gain access not only to research money, but to the data without which administrative-type research was unimaginable. Stanton, meanwhile, would become President of CBS Inc. in 1946, and remain there until 1971, presiding over the decisive early years of television. The convergence of research interests between Lazarsfeld and Stanton, their lengthy collaboration in directing first the Office of Radio Research and then the Bureau of Applied Social Research, and in editing the intermittent Radio Research series from 1940 on, traced an emblematic success story: the two careers succeeded together, harnessed to the social science they brought to both commercial utility and academic legitimacy. It was a stunning instance of being in the right place at the right time, or what Lazarsfeld later called "structural fit": the convergence of a refugee sociologist's worldview with "some nascent trends in the American community."[76] One of his fellow immigrants recently said of Paul Lazarsfeld: "He was very American — the most successful of us all."[77]

A man of political, ethnic, and ideological marginality, Lazarsfeld became what he called an "institution man," precisely what empiricist social research in the United States needed to embody the new academic style in an autonomous but academically affiliated base.[78] His own training in both social science and mathematical methods, and his Viennese-Machian philosophical bent, made him valuable to the new commercial and social-scientific establishments. "It seems plausible," Lazarsfeld wrote with characteristic insight and bluntness, "that such a configuration would lead to a career detoured through an institutional innovation rather than routed directly toward individual mobility."[79] The institution builder, a marginal man by his own account, needed the firmest possible affiliations with the determining institutions, affiliated and indispensable to all yet independent of every particular interest.

No conspiracy here, but a powerful convergence of commitments. The crucial point is that the administrative mentality of Lazarsfeld and Stanton harmonized with the corporate interest of CBS *and* with the practical program of the Rockefeller Foundation *and* with the swelling positivist mode of American social science. Where there was friction, as with Adorno, Lazarsfeld was willing to sacrifice the putative critical edge of his thought. To understand Paul Lazarsfeld's orientation, the force and reach of the theory and method of *Personal Influence*, it is not so important to know the exact identity of the signature of any given paycheck (though that is important too) as to understand the thematic unity of the administrative worldview in whatever institution it arises. With all the pressures working toward it, with all its utility for so many coordinating interests, some requisite signature almost certainly, sooner or later, would have turned up. The worldview and its research methods went seeking sponsors perhaps even more industriously than the sponsors went seeking techniques. So does ideology, shrewd and flexible, often hunt up the support of the interest it defends.

In his fascinating — and fascinatingly incomplete — memoir, Lazarsfeld discussed some of the difficulties he faced in negotiating the lingering differences between the institutional interests of the mass media and the methodological requirements of behaviorist research. And what he did not say directly, he implied. "Communications research was, at the time," he wrote, "a new enterprise, and I gave speeches about it to rather high-level audiences such as the National Association of Broadcasters and the Association of American Newspaper Editors. On such occasions I faced a very difficult problem: the relation with the industry." He continued:[80]

In one of those speeches, later published in *The Journalism Quarterly*,[81] I formulated the issue as follows: "Those of us social scientists who are

especially interested in communications research depend upon the industry for much of our data. Actually most publishers and broadcasters have
been very generous and cooperative in this recent period during which
*communications research had developed as a kind of joint enterprise
between industries and universities.* But we academic people always have
a certain sense of tightrope walking: at what point will the commercial
partners find some necessary conclusion too hard to take and at what
point will they shut us off from the indispensable sources of funds and
data?"

It is interesting that in this speech Lazarsfeld did not worry about his relationship with universities; his commercial audience might have been assured
to know that the tightrope had more than one edge. But, in any case,
Lazarsfeld went on:[82]

I finally thought of a compromise formula. In a speech on "The Role of
Criticism in the Management of Mass Media," I started out by saying that
the mass media were overly sensitive to the criticism of intellectuals,
while the latter were too strict in their overall indictment; *there ought to
be a way of making criticism more useful and manageable for those who
offer it and those who receive it.*

And he moved on in that speech to propose that journalism schools train
students in criticism — presumably "useful," "manageable" criticism, not
the unruly, contextual, structural, radical mode of an Adorno.

A delicate business indeed. What sort of "independence" is it that occupies
the interstices of universities, foundations, media corporations, and the
State? The "institution man" can negotiate differences among them, interpret each to the others, highlight and consolidate the common interest in
the form of shared ideological symbols. As he "walks the tightrope," he
safeguards the stability, the frequently delicate mutual dependence of the
"joint enterprise." As an arbiter and go-between, the sociological administrator-
expert avoids becoming beholden to any *particular* interest: a limited "independence" indeed. In a period of rapprochement among the political,
economic, and cultural sectors, in this converging social vision of a rationalized
oligopolistic capitalism, Lazarsfeld would seek the widest possible domain
of institutional amity. He would take an interest, not surprisingly, in that
sector of the State which coordinated and regulated corporate operations.
So it was that, immediately after he finished discussing his speech to the
media elite, without visible sign of conclusion or transition, or any grammatical
justification for the subject, he continued in the following vein:[83]

In all of the work of the Princeton Office I tried to relate to public controversies, *but usually thought of our office as serving a mediating function*. Thus, for example, we served as a channel for a project of the progressive chairman of the Federal Communications Commission, Clifford Durr. He had commissioned Charles Siepmann to develop ideas on how the FCC could better work for higher broadcasting standards. This assignment resulted in two documents, the FCC's "blue book" promulgating stricter licensing standards, and Siepmann's *Radio: Second Chance*. To both publications the industry reacted with violent antagonism, and I prevailed upon John Marshall of the Rockefeller Foundation to provide a special budget so that I could organize a two-day conference among the industry, the FCC, and prominent scholars in the research field to discuss the issues.

As we see, this was no change of subject at all.

The administrative mentality, in sum, is a bargaining mentality, desiring harmonious relations among the commanding institutions, within a common, hegemonic ideological frame: in this case, that established through the legitimacy of a commercial culture industry. In the academy it is "interdisciplinary," in the government it is "interbureau," in the Pentagon it is "interservice," in the economy it is "labor-management." It is always coordinating, mediating, stabilizing, harmonizing. In the process, it manages external reality as data, and it prefers to work within and along with the main institutions, those which have the capacity to make the world sit still and become data, or to imagine it that way. Its *modus operandi* is, above all, the contact and connection of "personal influence."

The Marketing Orientation

An administrative mentality is compatible with a range of societies, totalitarian as well as liberal; to each of these corresponds a theoretical orientation in social science. By itself, the administrative mentality cannot account for the appeal of the search for "personal influence," or the peculiar stress on narrowly construed behavioral or attitudinal "effects" in social investigation. We are closer to understanding American media sociology when we look to the particular variant of administrative thought that Paul Lazarsfeld brought into the American academy: the marketing orientation. Only with a search for the relevant history — in particular, the history of mass media in the United States — can we begin to grasp the significance of Lazarsfeld's work. For it is an *oeuvre* that is unimaginable apart from the emergence of the

practice and theory of a mass-consuming society in the twentieth century.

It is no secret that mass communications research descends directly from the development of sophisticated marketing techniques. The theory of "effects" was first developed for the direct, explicit use of broadcasters and advertisers, and continues to be used mostly in those circles, to grow more sophisticated there. With admirable brevity, Robert K. Merton has summarized the logical and historical line of descent:[84]

> As Lazarsfeld and others have pointed out, mass communications research developed very largely in response to market requirements. The severe competition for advertising among the several mass media and among agencies within each medium has provoked an economic demand for objective measures of size, composition and responses of audiences (of newspapers, magazine, radio and television). And in their quest for the largest possible share of the advertising dollar, each mass medium and each agency becomes alerted to possible deficiences in the audience yardsticks employed by competitors, thus introducing a considerable pressure for evolving rigorous and objective measures not easily vulnerable to criticism.[85]

As Paul Lazarsfeld arrived in the United States, marketing and advertising had just begun to come into their own. Through the Twenties, as Stuart Ewen has shown,[86] the oligopolies were emplacing the advertising and sales techniques for the consumer society that would emerge after 1945 in full flush. Mass consumer markets were already looming; advertising was shifting over the thin but noticeable line from the provision of information to meet existing, traditional demands, to the glorification of commodities and the manufacture of demands and, more important, the demanding consumer. (The all-black, single-model, no-options, Model T was replaced with a complex variety of automobiles rising in price, beginning in the 1930s.)[87] National brands were multiplying and taking over larger shares of their markets, and, inseparably, corporations were resorting to national advertising campaigns. They needed a marketing "science" to tell them what to say, how often, over which channels, to whom. The actual markets contracted during the Depression, but the technical infrastructure for a full-blown consumer society was steadily being developed under the surface, awaiting the explosion of consumer demand in 1945.

Broadcasting was in some ways the leading edge of the new, though now deferred, consumer society, and the Thirties, the time of Paul Lazarsfeld's settlement in the United States, were a pivotal time not only in American social science but in the history of American broadcasting. Despite the

Depression, or partly because of it (with the great hunger for cheap entertainment), the mass market in broadcasting was in the making: it was one of
the few mass markets that could penetrate an impoverished population.
Television was not yet in mass production, and the market for radio receivers
was on its way to saturation. The simple figures are suggestive. In 1925 there
were 4,000,000 sets in the United States, or 0.15 per household; in 1930,
13,000,000 sets, or 0.43 per household; in 1935, 30,500,000 sets, or 0.96
per household; in 1940, 51,000,000 sets, or 1.45 per household.[88] Accordingly,
as Merton says, competition was heating up. It would become more important to stations, and then to networks, to increase their shares of the existing
audience, and to find their profits in selling advertising time more than in
manufacturing radio sets. (When David Sarnoff had first imagined the possibility of a mass broadcasting industry in 1915, he had envisioned enormous
sales of "Radio Music Boxes," but he had not even dreamed of commercial
advertising on the airwaves.)[89] NBC was organized in late 1926, and CBS first
became a serious threat in 1928, with William S. Paley's assumption to the
presidency. Competition between CBS and NBC radio intensified through the
Thirties.[90] In 1940, the Federal Communications Commission directed NBC
to divest itself of one of its two radio networks, and in 1943 NBC did sell one
to the newly formed American Broadcasting Company.[91] Between market
saturation for radio sets and increasing network growth and competition for
advertising, corporate developments were coming to require precise audience
research on a grand scale.

CBS had hired Lazarsfeld's collaborator-to-be Frank Stanton from Ohio State
University in 1935, to give its new research apparatus the necessary rigor.[92]
Henceforward, audience research (on the *marketing* of commodities) would
be as important as "hardware" research (on the *production* of commodities).[93]
In order to increase the price they could charge advertisers for network time,
the networks would have to develop reliable knowledge of the size and composition ("demographics") of audiences. The kind of research Stanton and
Lazarsfeld were equipped and eager to do was going to come into greater and
greater demand over the years — from the major retailers, from broadcasting
networks, from publishers, from the conglomerates that would accumulate
control over the means of mass communications, and finally from the academic
world.[94] The Princeton Office of Radio Research was the first research
institution on radio in America — a measure of the new importance of radio
in the cultural life of the society and in the thinking of its economic-political
managers. The stereotyped commercial, "Amos 'n' Andy," the Fireside Chat,
and the Office of Radio Research were shoots of a common plant. Radio
had arrived now. It was not only necessary, but legitimate.

So its should not be surprising that, in one of Lazarsfeld's "strategic fits," a specific marketing need and an academic interest could fuse, in the early Forties, to provide the backing for the Decatur study. When the first edition of *The People's Choice* appeared in 1944, with its first broaching of the "two-step flow" and "opinion leader" ideas, Macfadden Publications became interested in the theory of opinion leaders, hoping that a "two-step flow" could help improve the circulation, and therefore the advertising rates, of its *True Story* magazine.[95] Bernarr Macfadden, the founder, published *Physical Culture, Liberty, Graphic, True Story, True Confessions,* and *True Detective Mysteries,* and he had long been interested in boosting their circulation with broadcast techniques. In 1925 he had become the first commercial sponsor on radio station WOR in Newark, advertising on a morning calisthenics show.[96] In 1927 he nearly bought the network that was soon to become CBS under Paley.[97] Now his company was eager to use the research techniques of broadcasting to see if working-class readers would come to *True Story* "horizontally," through word-of-mouth from working-class "opinion leaders," rather than "vertically," from higher-class readers. For his part, Lazarsfeld had wanted for years to follow up the 1940 Erie County, Ohio study (written up in *The People's Choice*), to pursue the hypothesis of the two-step flow. He arranged the grant from Macfadden, and the Decatur study was ready to go.

It seems reasonable to suppose that Macfadden's sponsorship of the study directly influenced both the selection of the respondents and the questions asked of them. There seems no other plausible explanation for limiting the study to female respondents: women were, after all, the readers of *True Story*. And it seems highly likely too that Macfadden's sponsorship shaped the choice of the issue-areas of product buying, fashions, and movies; information about the process by which products, fashions, and movies were chosen by potential *True Story* readers would be useful to Macfadden advertisers. (Presumably the questions about political attitudes were added by Lazarsfeld.) Thus the ungainly and crudely ideological quality of much of *Personal Influence*, as it struggled to view political attitudes as commensurate with instant coffee preferences, may be attributed directly to the Macfadden sponsorship, though there is also, as we shall see below (pp. 243–5), a deeper meaning to this questionnaire symmetry: the *actual* convergence of political choices and consumer choices, in social fact as well as in theory. Again, it would be simple-minded and misleading to reduce this convergence to the Macfadden influence *in particular*. Long before he had heard of Bernarr Macfadden, indeed as a youthful socialist, Lazarsfeld had been struck by "the methodological equivalence of socialist voting and the buying of soap,"[98] and he was inclined on theoretical grounds, as we shall see below, to view political and consumer choices as structurally similar commensurables. That *Personal Influence* and its successors were soaked in the values of consumer society — with consumer choice taken as the *ne plus ultra* of freedom — cannot be laid at Macfadden's door. But it would be naive to say that the study's sponsorship had nothing to do with its theoretical shape, and its failings.

Whether underwritten by Macfadden or McCann-Erikson, by Columbia University or the Columbia Broadcasting System, the marketing orientation takes the consumerist frame for granted, asks questions that arise within it, questions about "how," and stubbornly does not ask others. It is interested in how the mass media may increase their reach, and in how ordinary social life presents obstacles to the extension of media power. It is not interested, overall, in whether the reach of mass media is a social good, and in which circumstances. It is not interested in the structural and cultural consequences of different models of communication ownership. It is not interested in the construction of a worldview through media techniques, nor — except polemically — in the historical precursors of mass media. Nor does it take as problematic the consumer culture itself. It cannot imagine a living political discourse that would be affected for better or worse by media representations of politics. Questions of this sort are not "practical" for the institutions that define what is practical, and so, as Merton has concluded,[99]

> the categories of [mass communications] research have, until the recent past, been shaped not so much by the needs of sociological or psychological theory as by the practical needs of those groups and agencies which have created the demand for audience research. Under direct market pressures and military needs, definite research techniques are developed and these techniques initially bear the marks of their origin; they are strongly conditioned by the practical uses to which they are first to be put.

But then what was the alternative for media research? Is the critique necessarily abstract, a retrospective wish in the name of an unrealizable, Platonic ideal of social research? Critique always confronts this possibility when it cannot point to an actual choice-point when actual actors prefer one proposed course to others. In the present case, however, a conceptual alternative was actually put forward. Its fate and its limits tell us something of the grip of the marketing orientation. As a sidelight in the recent history of social research, it casts a distinct shadow.

As Katz and Lazarsfeld tell us in their Acknowledgments, the actual field work in Decatur, Illinois, was organized by none other than C. Wright Mills, then attached to the Bureau of Applied Social Research at Columbia. We will know more about how Mills proceeded through methodological orthodoxy to a radical break when the historian Richard Gillam publishes his pending biography of Mills; for now, it will have to suffice if we note that it was the ambitious young Mills who had gone to Decatur for the two waves of interviewing in June and August 1945. By the middle of 1946 Mills had drafted, for discussion, an analysis of the data. In this lengthy unpublished document, according to Richard Gillam, who has studied it in the University of Texas archives, Mills wrote "not just of 'influence' and 'opinion' but also more boldly of 'ideology'...and relates it to institutional and class structure. Mills finds some evidence for the two-step theory of horizontal influence, but he also argues the importance of vertical or 'pyramidal' influence, especially in politics." Mills speculated that the United States exists midway between the extreme models of "simple, democratic society" and "mass authoritarian society."[100] Mills' draft was actually a blurry document of divided loyalties, according to Gillam; Mills was immersed in the particularities of positivist analysis while trying to pay at least lip service to a sort of populist radicalism.[101] But he did propose a very different framework for the Decatur data. He proposed to read back from the sociometric data on political attitudes to infer a structure of political decision-making; and he proposed the beginnings of a theory of political communication as the foundation of a theory of American ideology in society. As Mills put it, guardedly, in a paper he read to the December 29, 1946 meeting of the American Association for the Advancement of Science in Boston, the "chain of political leadership is definitely a vertical affair."[102]

Although he did not challenge Mills' work in gathering and presenting the data, Lazarsfeld was evidently alarmed at the reach and the populist edge of Mills' rhetoric, at his "handling and interpretation of information already gathered"; and consequently he decided to take the analysis of the Decatur data back from Mills.[103] But oddly, as late as 1950 Mills still had hopes of joining as a co-author in the Decatur study.[104] In that same year he wrote a paper endorsing the Lazarsfeld point of view.[105] Here, in a State Department publication for a Russian audience, of all things, he riproaringly endorsed that pluralist vision he was to repudiate so roundly in *The Power Elite*, published in 1956.

But Mills' alternative of 1946 did not yet grasp, or was pretending not to grasp, that postwar America was already moving toward a new form of high-technology corporate capitalism with a tightening political culture based on consumption, in which bipartisan consensus would prevail and class opposition would be defeated and deflected and then — for a time — would peter out. Perhaps Mills' failure stemmed from his affiliation with Lazarsfeld's Bureau of Applied Social Research, or his own lingering illusions about the American labor movement; perhaps there were other reasons as well. In any event, the emergence of a high-consumption society was not yet grasped – as Mills was to grasp it in *The Power Elite* – as a new condition. Which is another way of saying that, with a few exceptions in the margins of American sociology,[106] the marketing orientation of Paul F. Lazarsfeld was for the moment uncontested, indeed hegemonic. The moment stretched into a sociological era; the orientation and the paradigms attending it established themselves as normal sociological opinion.

A deeper alternative, both in theory and practice, might have begun, and might still proceed, by noticing the productivity gains that capital could accrue with the "scientific" organization of work, gains that made possible a consumer society in the first place. This distinct approach would notice and analyze whatever more-or-less autonomous political culture could be detected beneath the gelid surface of the consumer culture. It might approach consumer culture as a displacement into the private, individual sphere of impulses toward freedom and happiness unrealizable in everyday life as both condition and consequence of the failure of a radical political alternative that could speak to the prevailing unhappiness.[107] A counter-paradigm could scrutinize the "culture industry" as both social control and failed, muddled, privatized revolt against the exploitative conditions of work and family in the world of organized capitalism. Empirically, it could then pay attention to the degeneration of authentic, bottom-up political life in the twentieth century, and to the fate of counter-movements; it could note the multiplication of means for the engineering of public consent, especially for Cold War policies. It could study the decision-making processes of soap manufacturers and soap-ad propagators and soap-opera producers as well as that of soap consumers. It could look into the origins of political issues as into the origins of "political attitudes." It could look at the consequences of broadcasting not only for individuals but for collective formations like social movements.[108] At the level of theory, it could grasp the compatibility of elitist structures and pluralist procedures in a "totality" of domination. With a complex methodology including life-histories and participant observation, it could inquire into the degree of *actual* convergence of consumer choice and political knowing, of voting and soap-buying in the lives of citizens, and inquire into the origins of this convergence instead of taking it methodologically for granted. Beginning with a sense of political structure, a media sociology could work toward what Dave Morley has called an "ethnography of audiences,"[109] showing how distinct class, ethnic, age and other audiences distinctly "decode" (and ignore, and assimilate) the patterns in media messages over time. (Then some of the specific Lazarsfeldian findings might be integrated into a larger social analysis.) It could work, in other words, to show a dynamic but determinate media process articulated with the whole of political culture.

Some of this, perhaps, was what Mills was driving at, obliquely, in 1946. In any case, it remained undone. Most of it remains still undone, and to be done. Instead, the marketing orientation *became* media sociology.

The Ideological Field: Social Democracy

Theorists do not live by theory alone. Abstract empiricism is no exception. Just as facts do not stand by themselves, neither do the theorists of abstract empiricism motivate themselves for sheer love of endlessly accumulated small facts, or for the advantage that is gained by the possession and exchange of them. Abstracted empiricism is not only concretely founded on the prevailing political and commercial culture, it is also, for the most part, justified by an ideological position. Such a position may be more or less conscious and, if conscious, more or less public. It is generally considered bad taste to assert that ideology matters in this setting, unless it is radical; the genetic fallacy is adduced as a free ticket to the weightless, interest-less, empyrean realm of science, where all ideas are born equal and with equal opportunity to prove their merit through good (empirical) works. In practice, the genetic fallacy is less common than the fallacy of immaculate conception.

I said before that social democracy was an ideological frame that surrounded and served to justify the whole of the dominant media sociology paradigm. Here I want to open up some territory for this "outrageous hypothesis," hoping that some of the leads that follow may be pursued by scholars whose critical temper and large spirit are matched by a long reach and vast patience. My sketch is concerned with two types of linkage between social democracy and the work of Paul Lazarsfeld: the biographical and the theoretical. A survey of the first will carry us toward the second, the interface of social democratic ideology and the theory of high-consumption society, where some implications of the biographical facts will speak.

The biographical facts linking Paul Lazarsfeld with Austro-Marxist social democracy are plain enough.[110] In his own memoir, Lazarsfeld teasingly — and self-teasingly — pointed to the linkages himself: they are at least methodological. But more, by his own account, social democracy was part of the ideological climate that gave rise, sometimes by indirection, to his interests. Lazarsfeld did not develop his theories in post-Hapsburg Vienna, did not come to his conclusions there, but he *did* define his lifelong problematic there, and the roots of his approach to it. The facts will require a slight historical commentary — enough, I hope, to outline a context and feeling-tone.

In his youth, Lazarsfeld was a leader of the Association of Socialist High School Students in Austria.[111] In 1916, he was, for reasons unexplained, "living in the custody of Rudolf Hilferding," one of the great theorists of Austro-Marxism.[112] He credited the Social Democratic leader Otto Bauer with giving him the idea of studying unemployment, the subject of his first major social-survey work.[113] He attributed the general interest in decision-making in the Viennese academy to the Austro-Marxist emphasis on electoral strategy, and credited this "political climate" in turn with his own academic interest.[114] When preparing his very first study (of occupational choices among Austrian youth), Lazarsfeld was able to overcome certain analytical obstacles by collaborating with an unnamed student who had been trained in early American market research techniques. She was subsequently to be his "main collaborator" in the field work for the even more ambitious study of the unemployed village of Marienthal, and the inspiration for Lazarsfeld's own market research studies in Vienna. Writing of this happy collaboration, Lazarsfeld remarked, as we have already had reason to notice, on "the methodological equivalence of socialist voting and the buying of soap."[115] I take it that, with this deadpan statement, Lazarsfeld meant to neutralize the rhetoric of his critics precisely by indulging in it to show its harmlessness. Yes of course, he seemed to be saying, they are equivalent, *methodologically* equivalent; I make no larger claims, though this one is large enough; and so what? Quiet and ironic, he disarmed the kind of critique that charges in to find that its territory is already occupied. Such bluntness was mordant.

But other sorts of mordant commentary have come down on Austrian Social Democracy, not always so quietly. Leon Trotsky, who spent seven pre-war years in Vienna, looked the prominent Austro-Marxists over and saw, in their political marginality, something imperious:[116]

> In the old imperial, hierarchic, vain and futile Vienna, the academic Marxists would refer to each other with a sort of sensuous delight as "Herr Doktor."

They were incapable of speaking easily with social democratic workers, Trotsky wrote: they were knowledgeable but provincial, philistine, chauvinistic. "These people prided themselves on being realists and on being businesslike," Trotsky wrote scornfully; but despite their ambition, they were possessed of a "ridiculous mandarin attitude."[117] That an administrative point of view might emerge from such a crucible, as a way of maintaining elite status and a sense of pride in an unfavorable situation, should not be surprising. What Trotsky did not appreciate, though, were some of the real grounds for Austro-Marxism's marginality: socially, the isolation of the Viennese working class in Austria-Hungary (and later Austria) as a whole,

and the isolation of Jews in an anti-Semitic culture;[118] politically, the failure
of the 1918 revolution in Germany, compounding Austro-Marxism's isolation.

Trotsky summed up the pre-war Austro-Marxist stance as "self-satisfaction."
By the end of World War I, though, Paul Lazarsfeld, active in the Socialist
Student Movement, saw not self-satisfaction but what follows from the
failure of it: defensiveness. The social democratic ideology which "proved to
be decisive" for Lazarsfeld's later intellectual life was "on the defensive
before the growing nationalistic wave."[119] And with the collapse of the
Second International in 1914, and the success of Leninism in Russia in 1917,
social democracy now had a Left to ward off internationally, as well as a
nationalist, revanchist Right. In Vienna, though Leninism was never as significant as in Germany, social democracy still found it necessary both to pay lip
service to the Marxist revolutionary ideal and to differentiate itself from
Leninism; it remained, then, doubly defensive. Yet this embattled Austro-
Marxism was also a major intellectual force. It monopolized sociology in the
University, and it could claim serious psychological credentials in the anti-
Freudian environmentalist socialism of Alfred Adler.[120] Adler's circle was,
in fact, Lazarsfeld's "social reference group," and he was influenced by
Adler's emphasis on socialist education for workers.[121] In all, though, the
intellectual prestige of social democracy did not overcome the insecurity
which Trotsky astutely recognized. Lazarsfeld summed it up this way:[122]

> We were concerned with why our propaganda was unsuccessful, and
> wanted to conduct psychological studies to explain it. I remember a
> formula I created at the time: a fighting revolution requires economics
> (Marx); a victorious revolution requires engineers (Russia); a defeated
> revolution calls for psychology (Vienna).

And here is one link, though only one, between the Austrian social democratic
ideology and positivist social science.[123] But while social democracy was
failing cataclysmically in Europe, an uncontested capitalism in America was
needing *its* engineers: it was also a revolution of a sort, against traditional
social relations. From the meeting of the engineer and the psychologist, the
new sociology of administration and marketing came forth.

But of course the affinity between socialist voting and the buying of soap is
not only methodological. It is built into corporate capitalist society as well as
into Lazarsfeld's later theoretical formulations, and into the whole thought-
structure of American media research. Media ideology too is implicitly social-
democratic, and that is one reason, parenthetically, why socialists are alter-
nately repelled by and defensive about mass culture.

The marketing orientation and at least one important variant of European social democracy share a common conception of "the people," and it is at first appearance paradoxical: they are both sovereign and passive. Indeed high-consumption capitalism justifies itself in the terms of mass satisfaction, and insists that the market is the true measure of democratic expression. The people are, in a word, consumers. They choose from among the major possibilities available, whether brand names, occupations, or political parties. When the consumers choose, they confirm the legitimacy of the suppliers. It seems that Paul Lazarsfeld's marketing orientation coincided with his interest in the larger legitimacy that might be found in a social democratic future. To put it another way, social democracy would *require* a marketing orientation, a rigorous procedure for "giving people what they want." This would be true for the actual marketing of goods, and it would be true for all the domains of freedom, including the question of occupational choice, on which Lazarsfeld had done his earliest work.

Social democracy would require not only a marketing orientation but an administrative point of view, for the choices would be prepared from above. It would be the responsibility of the centralized, hierarchical supplier to know what the consumers want; this is the difference, after all, between tyranny and democracy. Thus Lazarsfeld spoke of "the implications for a planned society" of his study of *Jugend und Beruf*:[124]

> most young people do not have decided occupational plans and therefore would not mind being guided — as a matter of fact might like to be guided — to an occupational choice; it should, consequently, be easy to fill the occupational quotas established through a central economic plan.

In this logic, when people do not know what they want, they *therefore* "would not mind being guided — as a matter of fact might like to be guided." The premise is that when people do not know, they do not object to domination: this is one of the ubiquitous ideological premises of the twentieth century. One starts out assuming that people might be sheep, and ends up working for the woolens industry. From the hypothetical social democratic state, which would know what young people want to do with their lives, to the giant broadcasting network, which insists it is giving people what they want, is not a great distance.[125] The transport is especially comfortable for a social science sponsored by foundations and corporations. The same model of research is required in both cases.

But in the late twenties, the time of *Jugend und Beruf*, what was probably not anticipated by Paul Lazarsfeld, nor by Marxist theory, was that a form of capitalist society would arise that could promise to deliver — and to some degree actually deliver — a simulacrum of the pleasure and ease that all forms of socialist ideology promised: a privatized, class-bound, mutilated version, but a version nonetheless. The United States was, and remains, the most advanced homeland of that consumer society. "The commercial culture of the twenties," as Stuart Ewen writes, "draped itself with 'social democratic' ideals, channeled toward the maintenance of capitalist power. The commercial culture strove to leave corporate domination of the productive process intact and at the same time speak to the demand for a richer social life."[126] So Paul Lazarsfeld's transition to American social science was not as difficult as that of other refugees, especially those of the Frankfurt Institut. American consumerism was only the transposing of the essential social-democratic theme to a new key. The invariant *Leitmotif* was the limitation of alternatives to the handful provided by authority. Again Ewen:[127]

> Within the political ideology of consumption, *democracy* emerged as a natural expression of American industrial production — if not a by-product of the commodity system. The equation of the consumption of goods with political freedom made such a configuration possible.

> One business theorist of that time spoke of "mass citizenship" predicated on "the process of 'fact-finding' — acquainting oneself with the variety of goods." Another spoke of business determining "for a people what they consider worth consuming."

> Yet within each of these notions of political democracy [Ewen continues], there was an implicit acceptance of the centralization of the political process. Democracy was never treated as something that flowed out of people's needs or desires, but was rather an expression of people's ability to participate in and emulate the "pluralism of values" [the phrase is Max Horkheimer's] which were paraded before people and which filtered downward from the directors of business enterprise.

And as actual political sovereignty waned, consumer sovereignty loomed larger, in fact as well as in theory. Thus the American Socialist Party of Eugene Debs, which had gotten about six percent of the popular vote in the Presidential election of 1912, sank into futile sectarianism by the end of that decade, and a combination of repression and internal weakness did away with the syndicalist Industrial Workers of the World around the same time. Populism was already dead. Simultaneously, the United States came out of World War I dominating the world economy, particularly in the consumer-good industries of automobiles and electronics (radio and film).[128] The multiplication of such spectacular consumer goods, along with the advertising apparatus that made it possible, conjured up what Marcus Raskin has called "the dream colony," a new orientation toward freedom itself.[129] Again Ewen lucidly suggests the process by which the new conception may have developed:[130]

> The consumer culture grew in response to [social] crisis [in the Twenties] and to the monumental growth of productive capacity with which it was interlaced. As production changed and as the social character of work became even more routinized and monotonous, the consumer culture presented itself as the realm within which gratification and excitement might be had — an alternative to more radical and anti-authoritarian prescriptions....The aim was the consolidation of a new "national character" keyed to the exigencies of expanding capitalism....
>
> The rise of advertising and consumerism in the twenties was part of a broader change in the character of capitalist society. Commercial propaganda didn't act as the determinant of change, but was in many ways *both* a reflection and agent of transformation. Advertising raised the banner of *consumable social democracy* in a world where monumental corporate development was eclipsing and redefining much of the space in which critical alternatives might be effectively developed....

Over the course of the twentieth century, using strategies that Ewen elaborates schematically, capitalism would work to present consumer sovereignty as the equivalent of freedom, in the common view and the common parlance. ("If you don't like TV, turn it off." "If you don't like cars, don't drive them." "If you don't like it here, go back to Russia." "If you don't like Crest, buy Gleem." "If you don't like Republicans, vote Democratic.") The assumption that choice among the givens amounts to freedom then becomes the root of the worldwide rationale of the global corporations, what Richard Barnet and Ronald Müller have called the vision of "the global shopping center."[131] Thus it is that a society develops in which voting and soap-buying, movie choice and political opinion, become more than methodological equivalents as objects of study; they become similarly manipulable and marginal acts that promise much while they deliver mostly preservative-stuffed "goods" that flatten the ability to taste. By ignoring the systemic and institutionalized nature of these processes, and by fusing its administrative, commercial, and social-democratic impulses, the mainstream of American media sociology has done its share to consolidate and legitimize the cornucopian regime of mid-century capitalism. That the dominant paradigm is now proving vulnerable to critique at many levels is a measure of the decline of capitalist legitimacy, commercial values, and the political self-confidence of the rulers. But that is another story.

Acknowledgement

Thanks for conversation and both substantive and bibliographical advice
(though not necessarily consent) to Richard Gillam, David Horowitz, Leo
Lowenthal, David Matza, and James Mulherin. I learned especially from the
interested criticism and elaboration of an earlier draft, by Arlie Hochschild,
Michael Paul Rogin, Alan Wolfe, Martin Jay, and Tim Haight. Most of all, I
could not imagine having attempted this work without the encouragement
and challenging guidance of William Kornhauser.

NOTES

1. Daniel Bell, "The End of American Exceptionalism," *The Public Interest* Fall 1975, p. 218.
2. Some recent American departures from the dominant paradigm are the papers in Steven H. Chaffee, ed., *Political Communication* (Beverly Hills: Sage, 1975); and, more basically, Oscar H. Gandy, "The Economics and Structure of Bias in Mass Media Research," paper delivered to the Leipzig meeting of the International Association for Mass Communications Research, 1976. Against the Lazarsfeldian emphasis on the limited and mediated influence of the mass media, the wide-spread interest in agenda-setting functions of the media (following Maxwell E. McCombs and Donald L. Shaw, "The Agenda-Setting Function of the Mass Media," *Public Opinion Quarterly* XXXVI [Summer 1972], pp. 176–187) is promising, but still too narrow and ahistorical: analytically it abstracts both media and audiences from their social and historical matrix. In England, the alternative approach of cultural studies, influenced by Marxist cultural theory and semiological "readings" of content, seems to me the most promising angle of analysis. For a fine example, see Stanley Cohen, *Folk Devils and Moral Panics* (London: MacGibbon & Kee, 1972); the papers gathered in Cohen and Jock Young, eds., *The Manufacture of News* (London Constable, and Beverly Hills: Sage, 1973), and Stuart Hall's essays, gathered in a forthcoming collection from Macmillan in London. See also the discussion of the field in Todd Gitlin, "'The Whole World is Watching': Mass Media and the New Left, 1965–70," unpublished Ph. D. dissertation, Sociology Department, University of California, Berkeley, 1977, pp. 15–23 and Ch. 10. The Lazarsfeld paradigm retains considerable force and prestige despite all this: for a recent study in that tradition, see Thomas E. Patterson and Robert D. McClure, *The Unseeing Eye: The Myth of Television Power in National Elections* (New York: Putnam, 1976).
3. Elihu Katz and Paul F. Lazarsfeld, *Personal Influence: The Part Played by People in the Flow of Mass Communications* (New York: Free Press, 1955).
4. J. Arndt, "A Test of the Two-Step Flow in Diffusion of a New Product," *Journalism Quarterly* 47 (Autumn 1968), pp. 457–465.
5. Bell, loc. cit.
6. Paul F. Lazarsfeld, Bernard Berelson, and Hazel Gaudet, *The People's Choice*, Second Edition (New York: Columbia University Press, 1948).
7. See the following studies: Paul J. Deutschman and Wayne A. Danielson, "Diffusion of Knowledge of the Major News Story," *Journalism Quarterly* 37 (Summer 1960), pp. 345–355; V. C. Troldahl and R. Van Dam, "Face to Face Communication about Major Topics in the News," *Public Opinion Quarterly* 29 (1965), p. 634;

V. C. Troldahl, "A Field Test of a Modified 'Two-Step Flow of Communication' Model," *Public Opinion Quarterly* 30 (Winter 1966–67), pp. 609–623; Arndt, op. cit.; I. L. Allen, "Social Relations and the Two-Step Flow: A Defense of the Tradition," *Journalism Quarterly* 46 (Autumn 1969), pp. 492–498; L. R. Bostian, "The Two-Step Flow Theory: Cross-Cultural Implications," *Journalism Quarterly* 47 (Spring 1970), pp. 109–117; and Nan Lin, "Information Flow, Influence Flow and the Decision-Making Process," *Journalism Quarterly* 48 (Spring 1971), pp. 33–40. In the Chaffee volume cited in note 2 above, Lee B. Becker, Maxwell E. McCombs and Jack M. McLeod ("Development of Political Cognitions," pp. 29–31) reinterpret data from Lazarsfeld's own *The People's Choice* and its successor, *Voting*, to show that the media are more influential than Lazarsfeld concluded. For a collation of empirical criticisms of the two-step flow, citing later studies that tend to show direct media impact especially on the poor, the isolated, and the highly anomic, see Morris Janowitz, "Mass Communication: Study," *International Encyclopedia of the Social Sciences* (New York: Macmillan and The Free Press, 1968), Vol. 10, p. 51.

8. F. Z. Rosario, "The Leader in Family Planning and the Two-Step Flow Model," *Journalism Quarterly* 48 (Summer 1971), pp. 288–297, in particular.

9. See all the other studies cited in note 7.

10. Anthony Giddens, *The Class Structure of the Advanced Societies* (New York: Harper Torchbooks, 1975), p. 222.

11. Stuart Hall, "Encoding and Decoding in the Television Discourse," mimeographed paper, Centre for Cultural Studies, University of Birmingham, 1973; and Raymond Williams, *Marxism and Literature* (New York: Oxford University Press, 1977) pp. 121–127.

12. Melvin L. DeFleur, *Theories of Mass Communication*, Second Edition (New York: McKay, 1970), pp. 112–154.

13. Roger L. Brown, "Approaches to the Historical Development of Mass Media Studies," in Jeremy Tunstall, ed., *Media Sociology: A Reader* (Urbana: University of Illinois Press, 1970), pp. 41–57.

14. For more on "personal influence" theory as a critique of the earlier "hypodermic" theory, see Elihu Katz, "Communication Research and the Image of Society: Convergence of Two Traditions," *American Journal of Sociology* 65 (March 1960), p. 113, and DeFleur, op. cit., pp. 112–117.

15. Katz and Lazarsfeld, op. cit. pp. 16–17.

16. See DeFleur, loc. cit.

17. For example, Raymond Bauer, "The Communicator and the Audience," *Journal of Conflict Resolution* 2 (March 1958), p. 67: "...attempts to establish the effects of mass communication forced Lazarsfeld and his asociates...to accord a larger role to informal personal influences."

18. Katz and Lazarsfeld, op. cit., p. 18, n. 5.

19. Ibid., p. 19, n. 6.

20. Ibid., p. 24, n. 16.

21. Ibid., p. 133, n. 20.

22. Ibid., p. 163.

23. Elihu Katz, "The Two-Step Flow of Communication: An Up-to-Date Report on an Hypothesis," *Public Opinion Quarterly* XXI (Spring 1957), pp. 61–78.

24. Katz and Lazarsfeld, op. cit., p. 146.

25. See especially Robert Dahl, *Who Governs?* (New Haven: Yale University Press, 1961), and Nelson Polsby, *Community Power and Political Theory* (New Haven: Yale University Press, 1963). Of course the literature on pluralism and elite theory is vast. For an earlier critique of pluralist theory along the present lines, see Todd Gitlin, "Local Pluralism as Theory and Ideology," *Studies on the Left* 5 (Summer 1965) pp. 21–45. For an interesting critique of both pluralism and its

"nondecision" critique, culminating in a proposal for a "three-dimensional" approach which integrates the strengths of each, see Steven Lukes, *Power: A Radical View* (London: Macmillan, 1974). There arises the question of whether the structural homology between pluralism and the two-step flow reflects an actual homology in their subject matters as well as, or rather than, in the respective theoretical problematics. In other words: Is there, or was there in the Fifties, an actual plurality of communication influence-sources parallel to an actual plurality of power sources? I cannot defend my answer to this question at length within the confines of the present essay, but I do want to put it forth: the answer is a qualified No. The actual plurality of sources in both communities and media chains was actually drying up as both were becoming centralized and homogenized in the Fifties. The networks and the huge national security state were major national features of that decade: *prima facie* evidence of the growing weight of nationalizing forces and therefore of the ideological nature of the two paradigms.

26. Peter Bachrach and Morton S. Baratz, "The Two Faces of Power," *American Political Science Review* 56 (1962), pp. 947–952, and their *Power and Poverty: Theory and Practice* (New York: Oxford University Press, 1970).

27. Katz and Lazarsfeld, op. cit., pp. 107–8, 332–334.

28. Ibid., p. 138.

29. Ibid., p. 341.

30. Ibid., p. 271, n. 2.

31. See Hannah Arendt, *The Human Condition* (Garden City: Anchor, 1958).

32. Joseph T. Klapper, *The Effects of Mass Communication* (New York: The Free Press, 1960).

33. Thanks to William Kornhauser for pointing this out to me in conversation.

34. Joseph T. Klapper, "Mass Communication: Effects," in *International Encyclopedia of the Social Sciences*" (New York: Macmillan and The Free Press, 1968), p. 85. Emphasis added.

35. Katz and Lazarsfeld, op. cit., p. 271n. Emphasis added.

36. Ibid., p. 276n.

37. Thanks to David Matza for putting this point to me in conversation.

38. Even at that, as we shall see on pages 219–20, the Katz-Lazarsfeld findings on "public affairs influence" are the weakest in the book *on their face*, and do not warrant the exorbitant claims later made in their name. Nor did Katz and Lazarsfeld seem interested in the distinction between marketing and public affairs "flows." The differences might have spoken to the difference between consuming and politics.

39. Ibid., p. 319.

40. Ibid., p. 142. Emphasis in original.

41. If the 58 percent of changes involved personal contacts that took place and were later forgotten – a logical possibility, but a claim Katz and Lazarsfeld did not make, by the way – the same assumption would have to be made about other findings, therefore making hash of the theoretical conclusions drawn from these data.

42. Ibid., p. 309, quoting Lazarsfeld, Berelson, and Gaudet, op. cit., p. 151.

43. See Katz and Lazarsfeld, op. cit., p. 159.

44. Ibid., p. 160.

45. Ibid., p. 312, n. 4.

46. C. Wright Mills, *The Sociological Imagination* (New York: Oxford University Press, 1959), p. 52.

47. Paul F. Lazarsfeld and Robert K. Merton, "Mass Communications, Popular Taste, and Organized Social Action," reprinted in Bernard Rosenberg and David Manning White, eds., *Mass Culture* (New York: Free Press, 1957), p. 459.

48. Maurice Stein, "The Eclipse of Community: Some Glances at the Education of a

Sociologist," in Arthur Vidich, Joseph Bensman, and Maurice Stein, eds., *Reflections on Community Power* (New York: John Wiley & Sons, 1964), pp. 215-6. Thanks to Richard Gillam for alerting me to this quotation.

49. T. W. Adorno, "Scientific Experiences of a European Scholar in America," in Donald Fleming and Bernard Bailyn, eds., *The Intellectual Migration: Europe and America, 1930–1960* (Cambridge, Mass.: Harvard University Press, 1969), p. 147.

50. In Robert K. Merton, *Social Theory and Social Structure*, Revised Edition (New York: The Free Press, 1968), pp. 578–582.

51. I discuss the fetishism of facts, and formal and technical ways of accomplishing it in mass media, in my "Spotlights and Shadows: Television and the Culture of Politics," *College English* 38 (April 1977), pp. 793–4. For origins of "a new world of facts" in consumerist ideology of the Twenties, see Stuart Ewen, *Captains of Consciousness: Advertising and the Social Roots of the Consumer Culture* (New York: McGraw-Hill, 1976), pp. 51–59, 69–70. On the origins of the concept in the Frankfurt Institut's critique of positivism, see Martin Jay, *The Dialectical Imagination* (Boston: Little, Brown, 1973), pp. 189–190.

52. Paul F. Lazarsfeld, "An Episode in the History of Social Research: A Memoir," in Fleming and Bailyn, eds., op. cit., pp. 277, 299.

53. In Lazarsfeld, "Remarks on Administrative and Critical Communications Research," *Studies in Philosophy and Social Science* IX (1941), pp. 2–16.

54. This was an actual historical decision, first proposed for RCA, the first mass broadcasting apparatus, by the young David Sarnoff in 1915. See Eugene Lyons, *David Sarnoff* (New York: Harper and Row, 1966), pp. 71–73, and Eric Barnouw, *A Tower in Babel (A History of Broadcasting in the United States,* Vol. 1) (New York: Oxford University Press, 1966), pp. 78–79.

55. Lazarsfeld, "Memoir," pp. 302–3.

56. Ibid., p. 310.

57. Ibid., p. 303.

58. Quoted in Raymond Fosdick, *The Story of the Rockefeller Foundation* (New York: Harper, 1952), p. 202. Emphasis added.

59. Lazarsfeld, "Memoir," pp. 275–6. I discuss this tantalizing fact further on p. 245.

60. Ibid., p. 276, n. 10.

61. Ibid., pp. 305, 309.

62. Ibid., p. 329.

63. Lazarsfeld, Berelson, and Gaudet, op. cit., p. xxix.

64. Fosdick, op. cit., pp. 246–7. Emphasis added.

65. Lazarsfeld, "Memoir," p. 308.

66. See Jay, op. cit., pp. 191–3.

67. Adorno, op.cit., p. 343. Emphasis added.

68. Lazarsfeld's letter to Adorno is excerpted in Jay, op. cit., pp. 222–3.

69. Lazarsfeld, "Memoir," pp. 322, 324.

70. Lazarsfeld, "Remarks on Administrative and Critical Communications Research."

71. Adorno wrote (op. cit., p. 353): "My own position in the controversy between empirical and theoretical sociology, so often misrepresented, particularly in Europe, I may sum up by saying that empirical investigations are not only legitimate but essential, even in the realm of cultural phenomena. But one must not confer autonomy upon them or regard them as a universal key. Above all, they must themselves terminate in theoretical knowledge." It was not empirical work he opposed, in principle, but *empiricism*, though earlier in the same essay (p. 348) he wrote: "No continuum exists between critical theorems and the empirical procedures of natural science. They have entirely different historical origins and can be integrated only with the greatest effort." But elsewhere, in the early Fifties, Horkheimer and Adorno wrote that "administrative" and "critical" research "do

not...stand in such a direct opposition. The reproduction of life under contemporary conditions does not appear to be possible at all, unless the central organs of administration are fed those precise informations about the most varied social conditions, which can be gained only by applying the techniques of empirical social research....The cult of technical specialization cannot be overcome by abstract and irrelevant humanistic demands added by way of complementary addenda. The path of true humanism leads through the midst of the specialized and technical problems, insofar as one succeeds in gaining insight into their significance within the societal whole and in drawing conclusions from this." (Frankfurt Institute for Social Research, *Aspects of Sociology* [Boston: Beacon Press, 1972], p. 127). It must be said, then, that Adorno's position in these matters was fluid, developing, and conflicted. His formulations were abstract enough to protect his claim to the privileges of "objective insight," but in his actual engagement with Lazarsfeld he was unwilling to bend as far as Lazarsfeld's synthesis required — at least far enough to make the project palatable to the Rockefeller Foundation.

72. Adorno wrote (op. cit., pp. 342–3) that the Princeton group's work "was concerned with the collection of data, which were supposed to benefit the planning departments in the field of the mass media, whether in industry itself or in cultural advisory boards and similar bodies. For the first time, I saw 'administrative research' before me. I don't now recall whether Lazarsfeld coined this phrase, or I myself in my astonishment at a practically oriented kind of science, so entirely unknown to me...."

73. Lazarsfeld, "Memoir," p. 304.

74. *Current Biography*, "Frank Stanton," 1965 Edition, pp. 402–4.

75. Lazarsfeld's insecurity about being Jewish in America was well grounded in the reality of academic anti-Semitism. His memoir (pp. 300–1) gives evidence of some of the social bases of his sense of marginality. It is worth noting that John Marshall of the Rockefeller Foundation, Stanton, Lynd, and Cantril were all white Anglo-Saxon Protestants: the most reliable sponsors to accumulate.

76. Ibid., p. 299.

77. Interview, Leo Lowenthal, June 4, 1976. Professor Lowenthal told me that, after publishing his justly famous critical study "Biographies in Popular Magazines" in the *Radio Research* annual of 1943, Lazarsfeld told him: "Now, Leo, you should write a book on how to write a *good* biography. You always tear down.... Show how to make it better!" Very American indeed!

78. Lazarsfeld, "Memoir," p. 302.

79. Ibid., p. 303.

80. Ibid., pp. 314–5. Emphasis added.

81. Lazarsfeld, "Some Notes on the Relationships Between Radio and the Press." *Journalism Quarterly* 18 (1941), pp. 10–13.

82. Lazarsfeld, "Memoir," p. 315. Emphasis added.

83. Ibid., p. 316. Emphasis added.

84. Merton, op. cit., pp. 504–5.

85. The details of Lazarsfeld's institutional involvement with advertising research appear in his "Memoir," pp. 297–299.

86. Ewen, op. cit.

87. See Emma Rothschild, *Paradise Lost: The Decline of the Auto-Industrial Age* (New York: Random House, 1973), pp. 37–40.

88. DeFleur, op. cit., p. 66.

89. See Barnouw, op. cit., pp. 78–9.

90. Ibid., pp. 224, 272–3.

91. Barnouw, *The Golden Web (A History of Broadcasting in the United States, Vol. II)* (New York: Oxford University Press, 1968), pp. 170–1, 190.

92. The convergence of the "new academic style" and the new corporate strategy is conspicuous in the memoir of one of Stanton's famous contemporaries. Peter C. Goldmark, the inventor of long-playing records and of several major color TV processes for CBS, was hired by the same CBS Vice President who hired Stanton, at around the same time, and wrote of him: "Kesten came across Stanton, as he had me, through reading a monograph in a scientific journal. The future of CBS, he felt, belonged to the scientific method. A serious student who was used to the careful methodology of academia, Stanton added a scholarly formulation to Kesten's lightning intuitions, and eventually brought respectability to the flashy side of show business. In 1936 the spirit of research rode high at CBS." Peter C. Goldmark, with Lee Edson, *Maverick Inventor: My Turbulent Years at CBS* (New York: Saturday Review Press, 1973), pp. 39–40.

93. For the comparable case of the automobile industry, see again Emma Rothschild's analysis (op. cit.) of the simultaneous development of "Fordism" (production efficiency) and "Sloanism" (new marketing practices) in the Thirties.

94. Lazarsfeld had, in fact, first come to the United States thinking he had a job at the Retail Research Institute at the University of Pittsburgh. See Lazarsfeld, "Memoir," p. 303.

95. Katz and Lazarsfeld, op. cit., p. 3; Richard Gillam, "C. Wright Mills, 1916–1948: An Intellectual Biography," unpublished Ph. D. dissertation, History Department, Stanford University, 1972, p. 300.

96. Barnouw, *A Tower in Babel*. pp. 167–8.

97. Ibid., p. 220.

98. Lazarsfeld, "Memoir," p. 279.

99. Merton, op. cit., pp. 505–6.

100. Gillam, op. cit., pp. 302–3.

101. Interview, Richard Gillam, June 21, 1976.

102. I was able to read this paper thanks to Richard Gillam and his files.

103. Gillam, op. cit., p. 304.

104. Ibid., p. 307n.

105. C. Wright Mills, "Mass Media and Public Opinion," reprinted in Irving Louis Horowitz, ed., *Power, Politics and People* (New York: Ballantine Books, 1963), pp. 577–598.

106. For example, Robert Lynd, as cited in Ewen, op. cit., pp. 37, 56, 136.

107. This is the approach of Stuart Ewen's recent book, op. cit. and of some of the Frankfurt arguments; it lies latent in the historiography of Herbert Gutman (*Work, Culture and Society in Industrializing America* [New York: Knopf, 1976]), following from the work of E. P. Thompson and others in England. Ewen's argument is stronger on assertion than on evidence for the content of working-class consciousness around the turn of the century, and he is selective in citing corporate strategists. The counter-paradigm I am advocating here will need to dive deeper and stay longer in historical materials.

108. Scarcely any studies have been published on the impacts and meanings of mass media for political and social movements and parties. For a brief discussion and citation of a few studies, see W. Phillips Davison, "Functions of Mass Communication for the Collectivity," in Davison and Frederick T. C. Yu, eds., *Mass Communication Research: Major Issues and Future Directions* (New York: Praeger, 1974), pp. 66–82. British work on the terrain of cultural studies does not draw a sharp line between mass media "effects" and the careers of social formations including movements, and therefore is open to considering broad social constraints and consequences. For a fine example, see Stanley Cohen, op. cit. More recently, see my own "'The Whole World is Watching,'" and, on the feminist movement, Jo Freeman, *The Politics of Women's Liberation* (New York: McKay, 1975), and Gaye Tuchman, "Ridicule, Advocacy and Professionalism: Newspaper

Reporting About a Social Movement," paper delivered at the American Sociological Association meetings. New York, August 1976.

109. Dave Morley, "Reconceptualising the Media Audience: Towards an Ethnography of Audiences," mimeographed paper, Centre for Contemporary Cultural Studies, University of Birmingham, 1974.

110. But of course they are very fragmentary. I regret that Professor Lazarsfeld died in August 1976, before I had a chance to interview him on these matters.

111. Joseph Buttinger, *In the Twilight of Socialism: A History of the Revolutionary Socialists of Austria* (New York: Praeger, 1953), p. 83.

112. Lazarsfeld, "Memoir," p. 285n.

113. Ibid., p. 275n.

114. Ibid., p. 279.

115. Ibid.

116. Leon Trotsky, *My Life* (New York: Pathfinder Press, 1970), p. 209. First published 1929.

117. Ibid., pp. 210, 212. He includes Otto Bauer in this category. For some equally critical remarks on the Austrian Social Democrats, also see Victor Serge, *Memoirs of a Revolutionary* (New York: Oxford University Press, 1963), pp. 188–9: "If only the Social-Democrats of Austria had had a little of the impassioned energy of the Bolsheviks of Russia! All they ever did was to sip sweet white wine in the operetta-land of the Blue Danube...." But Serge is also more sympathetic to the Austro-Marxists' plight in isolated Vienna within an Austria still more isolated in Europe.

118. William M. Johnston, an intellectual historian of Austria, suggests that Jewish self-hatred was central to the politics of Viktor Adler, "the father of socialism in Austria." Johnston, *The Austrian Mind: An Intellectual and Social History, 1848–1939* (Berkeley: University of California Press, 1972), p. 99. The fascinating and thick relations of Jews, anti-Semitism and socialism in Austria await a deeper history.

119. Lazarsfeld, "Memoir," p. 272.

120. No relation to Viktor Adler. On Alfred Adler's meliorist psychology, see Russell Jacoby, *Social Amnesia* (Boston: Beacon Press, 1975).

121. Lazarsfeld, "Memoir," p. 272.

122. Ibid.

123. Because of the constraints of space, I cannot discuss here the great influence the psychological work of the Bühlers exerted on Lazarsfeld ("Memoir," pp. 208–3), nor the impact of the positivist current (including the passion for classification) that circulated around Mach and his circle (ibid., p. 273). Of the latter, Lazarsfeld wrote: "I was impressed by the idea that mere 'clarification' was a road to discovery." But "clarification" is a concept itself needing clarification, especially in its relations to historical understanding.

124. Lazarsfeld, "Memoir," p. 280.

125. It is worth noting, in passing, that the social democratic State was able to achieve some standing in quasi-Marxian futurology because it had the prophetic field to itself. The Marxian taboo on specifying the future organization of socialism left a vacuum that could be filled by administrative models, both Leninist and social-democratic. See the excellent discussion of this point in Carl Landauer, in collaboration with Elizabeth Kridl Valkenier and Hilde Stein Landauer, *European Socialism: A History of Ideas and Movements*, Vol. I (Berkeley: University of California Press, 1959), pp. 205–6.

126. Ewen, op. cit., p. 197.

127. Ibid., p. 89. Emphasis in original.

128. For the history of the American success in radio development from 1900 on, see Barnouw, *A Tower in Babel*, and the reviews of the same material in Todd

Gitlin, "Sixteen Notes on Television and the Movement," in George A. White and Charles Newman, eds., *Literature in Revolution* (New York: Holt, Rinehart & Winston, 1972), pp. 336—7, and Raymond Williams, *Television: Technology and Cultural Form* (New York: Schocken, 1975), pp. 14—41.

129.   Marcus Raskin, *Being and Doing* (New York: Random House, 1971).

130.   Ewen, op. cit., pp. 189—90. Ewen goes on (pp. 190--1): "While the contours of commercial culture were taking on a decided modernity by the 1920s, it was decades before the commodified 'good life' took hold to the degree only dreamed of in the twenties. In the period between 1920 and the end of the Second World War, American capitalism's ability to expand markets commensurate with its growing productive capacity was severely limited....With the entry of the U. S. into World War II, however, things began to change. War industries created jobs and reinvigorated domestic markets....It was in the period of postwar boom that the social policies postulated and initiated in the twenties began to make their most effective inroads upon the social landscape of American society." Media research had a roughly comparable history. The behaviorist theoretical orientation first propounded in general terms in media sociology before World War II came to flourish only in the Forties and Fifties. During the war, Carl Hovland and associates were granted the funds for their elaborate empirical studies of media "effects," and only after the war did Lazarsfeld and associates develop specific theoretical propositions like that of the "two step flow."

131.   Barnet and Müller, *Global Reach* (New York: Simon & Schuster, 1974).

Growing prominence of Marxist analysis of mass communication heightens the need for understanding the assumptions and approaches of Marxist scholars. In this article, Nicholas Garnham outlines traditional Marxist assumptions and calls for a major revision of Marxist cultural theory. Dr. Garnham, a senior lecturer at the School of Communication of the Polytechnic of Central London, argues that Marxist analysis must discontinue its focus on the ideological content of the mass media. Instead, he urges a concentration upon the industrialization of culture. This industrialization is marked by growing media control by multinational corporations, labor strife within the mass media, efforts in Western Europe to commercialize broadcasting, and attempts to create new world markets through the introduction of new communication technologies. Garnham points to the need to separate analytically the processes of material production in mass media from the media as a locus of ideological struggle.

4

CONTRIBUTION TO A
POLITICAL ECONOMY OF
MASS-COMMUNICATION

Nicholas Garnham

Introduction

'The major modern communication systems are now so evidently key institutions in advanced capitalist societies that they require the same kind of attention, at least initially, that is given to the institutions of industrial production and distribution. Studies of the ownership and control of the capitalist press, the capitalist cinema, and capitalist and state capitalist radio and television interlock, historically and theoretically, with wider analysis of capitalist society, capitalist economy and the neo-capitalist state. Further, many of the same institutions require analysis in the context of modern imperialism and neo-colonialism, to which they are crucially relevant.

Over and above their empirical results, these analyses force theoretical revision of the formula of base and superstructure and of the definition of productive forces, in a social area in which large scale capitalist economic activity and cultural production are now inseparable. Unless this theoretical revision is made, even the best work of the radical and anti-capitalist empiricists is in the end overlaid or absorbed by the specific theoretical structures of bourgeois cultural sociology' (R. Williams, 1977: 136).

The purpose of this article is to support this call for a major revision within cultural theory, to explain why such a revision is necessary and to begin to explore some of its consequences.

The fact that Williams's own call for this theoretical revision is hidden, gnomically, in a book of literary theory, and has thus not received the attention it deserves within mass-media research, is itself symptomatic of the existing ideological resistances to such a revision, not only within 'bourgeois cultural theory', but also within what pass for Marxist alternatives. Indeed, I will go on to argue that in his effort to break with this all pervasive idealism, Williams, in formulating his own 'cultural materialism', has reacted by taking too materialist a stance.

What this article calls for, therefore, is the elaboration of a political economy of culture with a political economy of mass-communication taking its subsidiary place within that wider framework as the analysis of an important, but historically specific mode of the wider process of cultural production and reproduction. The need to elaborate such a political economy is intensely practical. It stems from actual changes in the structure of contemporary capitalism as they effect what has been dubbed 'The Culture Industry' and the relationship of that industry to the State. Symptoms

From Nicholas Garnham, "Contribution to a political economy of mass-communication," *Media, Culture and Society* I (1979) 123-146. Copyright 1979 by Academic Press Inc. (London) Limited. Reprinted by permission.

of the urgent political problems raised by these changes can be observed throughout
the developed, capitalist world. They can be seen in a whole range of Government
Reports and interventions of which, in Britain, the most obvious recent examples are
the Royal Commission on the Press, the Annan Committee Report and the subsequent
White Paper on Broadcasting, the Prime Minister's Working Party on the Film
Industry and its proposals for a British Film Authority. They can be seen underlying
the present dispute at Times Newspapers, the debate over the allocation of the
fourth TV channel and the present financial problems of the BBC. Parallels to these
reports, problems and debates can be found in all the member countries of OECD.
At an international level, recent debates in UNESCO and the continuing diplomatic
activity surrounding the concept of a New World Information Order can only be
properly understood in this context. In the face of such developments most current
mass-media research and theorizing is demonstrably inadequate.

Before moving on to examine some of the theoretical problems raised by this shift
in research emphasis, let me give just one concrete example of the kind of information
to which it gives privileged attention and why. During the last few weeks in Britain
we have witnessed the failure of the Government to provide the BBC with adequate
finance, a matter of great and ill-understood strategic significance in the whole
development of British broadcasting and a subject that will repay substantive analysis
from the perspective I am here outlining in a future edition of this journal. We have
also witnessed the reactivation of the debate on TV and Violence by the publication
of Dr Belson's study, a matter of undoubted importance to anyone concerned with
mass-media research in Britain. Nonetheless, in my view the most significant development of the period was hidden away on the financial pages, namely the take-over
of British Relay Wireless by the Electronic Rental Group, making ERG the second
largest TV rental group in the UK. The significance of this take-over is that it was
financed by a £10 million loan from ERG's controlling share-holder **Philips** Electronic. Now **Philips** is one of the firms involved in the audio-visual sector of the
culture industry, in terms of total sales the world's third largest after General Electric
and ITT and in terms of the proportion of its business related to electronic audio-
visual manufacture and production it is the world leader by some way. The next
phase of development of the culture industry will involve the attempt to develop and
exploit the domestic entertainment market, particularly through video. Control of
a rental network will be one of the keys to success in the competitive struggle for this
market for two reasons: firstly, as has been true for domestic TV receivers, because
the necessary hardware can only be sold in sufficient quantity on credit, but secondly,
and here we have a crucial distinction between the new developments and the rental
of TV receivers, because there is no internationally agreed technical standard for
video recorders and players (whether of cassettes or discs) with the result that the
decision on the choice of hardware limits the consumers subsequent choice of software. Now since, of all the world's major electronic companies, only **Philips** is
already in a position to develop co-ordinated software production (through such
subsidiaries as Polygram and Phonogram) control of tied rental outlets for their
hardware would give them a vertically integrated international cultural monopoly
of a scale and type not yet seen in this sector and with cultural consequences over the
medium term (10 to 20 years) that make our petty domestic disputes over the allocation
of the fourth channel pale into insignificance (see *Financial Times*, 19 December
1978).

A necessary return to fundamentals

Before returning to further concrete examples of the problems a political economy of mass-communication tries to analyse, it is necessary, precisely because of the dominance of idealism within the analysis of culture and of the mass-media, to make an unavoidable theoretical digression in order to base subsequent discussion firmly within the necessary historical materialist perspective. In asking for a shift within mass-media research towards historical materialism, one is asserting an order of priorities which is both a hierarchy of concrete historical and material determinants in the real world as well as an order of research priorities. That is to say, we are faced with the problem of understanding an actual historical process which itself concretely exhibits structurally ordered determinants within which material production is ultimately determinant, which is what makes our theory materialist, while at the same time there are a limited number of researchers with limited material resources among which I include time, who must thus choose, from within the complex totality of the historical social process, to examine those aspects of the process which are likely to lead to the clearest understanding of the dynamics of that process and through that understanding to its human control. It is this question of choice which underlies Marx's own mode of abstraction. Thus, in opposition to that post-Althusserian Lacanian current which has been dangerously dominant within recent British Marxist research in the area of mass-media, a current of which *Screen* is a representative example, one asserts, not that the problem of subjectivity for instance is of no interest, but that it is of less interest than that of class or capital accumulation. Moreover, one is not asserting that such a hierarchy of historical determinants of research concerns is universal, that there is A theory of mass-media, but that they correspond to the actual historically specific hierarchy of a particular social formation. Or as Marx himself put it,

my analytical method . . . does not start out from man, but from the analytically given social period.[1]

That is to say the economic is determinant under capitalism, because capitalism is a mode of social organization characterized by the domination of an abstract system of exchange relations. Further the particular relationship between the abstract and the concrete or between 'phenomenal forms' and 'real relations' or between ideas and matter, which is appropriate to historical materialism as a mode of analysis of capitalism, stems from the real relation between the abstract (exchange relations) and the concrete (individual lived experience, real labour etc.) within the social formation itself. In a social formation in which social relations were not abstracted into a relation of exchange a different theoretical relationship between the abstract and the concrete would hold.

Moreover, the abstract should not be opposed to the concrete, just as the phenomenal forms should not be opposed to the real relations. One is precisely a form of the other. That is to say, the exchange relation has a concrete material reality in the form of money, bills of exchange, credit cards, banks etc., but its mode of operation and with it the reproduction of the capitalist social formation depends upon its abstraction, the fact that it works 'behind men's backs' and thus 'can be determined with the

[1] See Marx, 'Notes on Adolph Wagner' in Marx (1975). Quoted in Corrigan and Singer (1978). Here Corrigan and Singer present an extended version of this methodological argument. See also Sayer (forthcoming).

precision of natural science'. It can only be determined with such precision so long as it is a supra-individual social process. This is both a methodological and historical postulate. That is to say, the necessary condition for a capitalist social formation is the existence of a more or less universal domination of social relations by the exchange relation, i.e. a market economy. Wherever such domination is challenged (and we do not and never have seen, in this sense, an 'ideal' capitalist social formation) by explicit political action, by human will and reason, the logic of capital is challenged. It is for this reason that the State is a necessarily contradictory form.

This leads us to the concept of ideology which so dominates our field of study and to the central problem within cultural theory, namely the base/superstructure relationship. The central postulate of historical materialism is that man as a biological organism must undertake a constant material exchange with nature and it is this exchange that is named labour. Within history the labour/nature relationship has become increasingly mediated through specific modes of production, thus making the links more difficult to analyse. Because of this difficulty the possibility of error and thus of ideology enters. But it remains a material fact that, ultimately, material production in this direct sense is determinate in that it is only the surplus produced by this labour that enables other forms of human activity to be pursued. Thus the superstructure remains dependent upon and determined by the base of material production in that very fundamental sense.

Clearly the greater the surplus to immediate physical reproductive needs the greater the autonomy of the superstructure and indeed the greater the possible variation and diversity within superstructural organization, always providing of course that the mode of material production is such as to guarantee the necessary surplus. In this important sense the superstructure/culture is and remains subordinate and secondary and the crucial questions are the relationship between, on the one hand, the mode of extraction and distribution of the material surplus, e.g. class relations and, on the other, the allocation of this material surplus within the superstructure, for instance, the problem of public expenditure among others. But while, historically, the superstructure has become more autonomous, there still remain direct, narrow material constraints upon individuals even within developed, industrial societies. Everyone has to eat and sleep and be maintained at a given body temperature in determinate temporal cycles. Thus, as Marx himself noted, every economy is an economy of time (Marx, 1973), which is why labour-time is so crucial an analytical concept. Cultural reproduction is still directly governed by these material determinants in the sense that the time and resources available to those who have to sell their labour power to capital, within labour-time constraints largely imposed by capital, remain limited and they still use the most significant proportion of their available time and material resources in order to ensure material, biological reproduction.

It is at this primary level both theoretically and actually that social being determines social consciousness. Thus economism, the concern for immediate physical survival and reproduction within the dominant relations of exchange is an immediate and rational response to the determinants of social being. What E. P. Thompson has recently dubbed 'lumped bourgeois intellectuals' (Thompson, 1978) too easily forget this, both because their material conditions of existence are often less immediately determinate and also because of a guilty conscience concerning the subjective relationship of exploitation in which they stand *vis-à-vis* productive material labour.

The material, the economic and the ideological

No political economy of culture can avoid discussion of the base/superstructure relationship, but in so doing it needs to avoid the twin traps of economic reductionism and of the idealist autonomization of the ideological level. The central problem with the base/superstructure metaphor as with the related culture/society dichotomy is that being a metaphor of polarity, essentially binary in form, it is unable adequately to deal with the number of distinctions that are necessary, in this instance between the material, the economic and the ideological. These should be seen not as three levels, but as analytically distinct, but coterminous moments both of concrete social practices and of concrete analysis. Furthermore, any political economy needs to hold constantly to the historicity of the specific articulations between these moments. There is a sense in which the base/superstructure metaphor always does imply a notion of expressive totality, a totality in which either the superstructure is expressive of an economic base (under capitalism of a capitalist economic base) or, on the other hand, a tautological sense of expressive totality by which all phenomena of a social formation are expressive of that social formation. That is to say, the notion of expressive totality can be used either deterministically or relationally. For me at least it is clear that the analysis in *Capital* is of the latter type. That is to say what is being analysed is not, as Mandel (1975) has stressed, a social formation in equilibrium but in disequilibrium; an uncompleted at the time Marx wrote, and still incomplete, process of capitalist development, a development which was marked not by the total domination and determinacy of capitalist economic forms, an expressive totality in that sense, but on the contrary by a series of shifting relationships between the economic and other instances each interacting with the other in a process of uneven and contradictory development, so that the totality of the social formation at any historic moment was only expressive of the actual state of those shifting interrelationships.

Thus the pertinence or meaning of any analytical category, such as base and superstructure, expressing as it does a relationship, will shift as the historical reality it is used to explain shifts. Similarly, we could say that the purpose of a political economy of culture is to elucidate what Marx and Engels meant in the German Ideology by 'control of the means of mental production', while stressing that the meaning that they gave to the term was quite clearly historical and therefore shifting and was never meant to be frozen into some simple dichotomy as it has so often been in subsequent Marxist writing. Further the political economy of mass-media is the analysis of a specific historical phase of this general development linked to historically distinct modalities of cultural production and reproduction.

In his discussion of base and superstructure in *Marxism and Literature*, Williams points out that, although, in stressing the determinacy of the base against bourgeois idealism, one version of Marxist cultural theory has been accused, both by bourgeois and Marxist critics, of 'vulgar materialism', 'the truth is that it was never materialist enough'. And he continues:

What any notion of a 'self-subsistent order' suppresses is the material character of the productive forces which produce such a version of production. Indeed it is often a way of suppressing full consciousness of the very nature of such a society. If 'production', in capitalist society, is the production of commodities for a market, then different but misleading terms are found for every other kind of production and productive force. What is most often suppressed is the direct material production of 'politics'. Yet any ruling class devotes a significant part of material production to establishing a political order. The social and political order which maintains a capitalist market, like the social and political struggle that created it, is necessarily a material production. From castles and palaces and churches to prisons and workhouses and schools; from weapons of war to a controlled press: any ruling class, in variable ways though always materially, produces a social and political order. These are never superstructural activities. They are the necessary material production within which an apparently self-subsistent mode of production can alone be carried on. The complexity of the process is especially remarkable in advanced capitalist societies, where it is wholly beside the point to isolate 'production' and 'industry' from the comparable material production of 'defence', 'law and order', 'welfare', 'entertainment' and 'public opinion'. In failing to grasp the material character of the production of a social and political order, this specialised (and bourgeois) materialism failed also, but even more conspicuously, to understand the material character of the production of a cultural order. The concept of the superstructure was then not a reduction but an evasion (Williams, 1977: 92–93).

Williams's stress here on the materiality of the cultural process is a necessary correction to both bourgeois idealism and its post-Althusserian Marxist variants. But this formulation also suffers from a misleading reductionism by failing to distinguish between the material and the economic. It is in fact a materialist rather than a historical materialist formulation. The absence of this necessary distinction is contained in the apparently insignificant but crucial phrase 'in variable ways though always materially', for it is precisely the specific articulations of these variable ways that characterize various stages of pre-capitalist and capitalist development, that characterize the shifting meaning of what Marx and Engels called 'control of the means of mental production', shifts which it is the central purpose of a political economy of mass-communication to map and analyse. Certainly a licensed press and a commercial, 'free' press are both material, but the economic differences between these two forms of 'political' control are precisely what differentiates a capitalist from a pre-capitalist form. Similarly, the difference between the economic structure of private and public education constitutes within the same materiality, the substance of 'political' struggle. While the materiality of politics, i.e. its maintenance out of the total social surplus of material production, is a general, universal phenomenon, the ways in which that surplus is extracted and distributed and the relation of that economic form to the political are historically distinct and specific, so that, at present, the matter of subsidies to political parties or to the Press becomes an object of 'political' struggle to change economic forms and by so doing to change 'political' structures.

Similarly, while Williams is correct to stress the materiality of all social practices it cannot be said, from an economic perspective, that it is wholly beside the point to isolate 'production' and 'industry' from the material production of 'defence', etc., when what is often in question when considering the relation between these various social practices is not their shared materiality, but on the contrary their significantly different economic articulation, for instance the variance between those practices carried on by private capital for profit, the publication of a newspaper for instance, and those practices carried on by the State outside direct commodity production, e.g. the BBC or the State education system. To collapse all this into a general category of 'material' production is precisely an 'evasion', both of the differing and developing economic articulations between various forms of material production and also of the amount of cultural production and reproduction that takes place within the industrial sphere as narrowly defined, in the organizations of the labour process with its industrial psychologists, its labour relations experts, its time and motion study experts, its production engineers and its personnel managers, in the structures of employer paternalism, in the organization of the market itself, etc. To take one example of such an articulation one might hypothesize that the relationship between the male predominance in newspaper readership compared with TV was not unconnected with the contrast between the culture of work as against the culture of home and has important political consequences.

This confusion between the material and the economic is common and it is worth dwelling briefly on the nature of the distinction. Insofar as historical materialism is materialist, it is based upon the postulates that Williams outlines. But insofar as it is historical, it is concerned to analyse the specific and shifting modes of this fundamental material relation, all of which are forms of that relation. In particular, it is postulated that any form of extended social relationship depends upon the extraction and distribution of material surplus and the means by which this is achieved is thus the central determining characteristic of any social formation. Such modes of social production and exchange are cultural, hence the very real problem of making a society/culture differentiation without narrowing the definition of culture to include only those elements of social interaction which involve a secondary level of abstraction, namely the representation of concrete, material relations in *symbolic* forms. Thus we must distinguish two types of form, a social form which is a series of material relations that, insofar as they operate unconsciously, can be abstractly analysed and determined with the precision of natural science, and a cultural form which, while it entails a material support, is not itself material and which has an essentially mediated relationship with the material reality it represents. Indeed, there is an essential divide between these distinct formal realms, the existence of which allows ideology to enter, because it allows denial and the lie, both of which depend upon a relationship which is not determinant. However, this autonomy is bought at the cost of a loss of real or material effectivity. Cultural forms only become effective when they are translated into social forms which do have material effectivity. Thus there is a constant dialectic at the cultural level between autonomy and effectivity and it is at the level of social effectivity that material production is ultimately determinant.

However, to return to the level of social forms, the economic is a specific historical form of the social relations of production and distribution. It is the form these relations take in a social formation within which commodity exchange is dominant. Thus, it is possible to argue that the economic is superstructural in relation to the material base or structure, that it could in fact be seen as the dominant level of the superstructure. For what Marx argues in *Capital* is that the real historical transition to capitalism involves a move from a system of social relations and domination based upon the direct physical control of landed property and people to one based upon the increasingly indirect control through commodity exchange and, in particular, through the exchange of the commodity of labour power, and that this real historical process is a real process of social abstraction which thus requires appropriate theoretical abstraction for its analysis. It is because the economic is the most abstract and fundamental form of the social relation within capitalism that it is primary both theoretically and actually, but as a historically specific representation of a predeterminate material relationship.

It is the real existence of this abstract economic level of extended commodity production that allows for the development of an increasing division of labour and thus for the development of the specific superstructural forms of capitalism. Thus the relative autonomy of the superstructure is a real and increasingly central characteristic of capitalism, but it is itself determined at the level of the economic and ultimately it is a form, at two levels of mediation, of a material relation which also remains determinant in and through the economic.

The inadequacies of existing Marxist theory

From this perspective available historical materialist theories are inadequate to deal with the real practical challenges they face largely because they offer reductionist explanations which favour either a simple economic determinism or an ideological autonomy, thus failing to analyse and explain precisely that which makes the object of analysis centrally significant, namely the relationship between the economic and the ideological. Thus we are offered the following.

(a) An unproblematic acceptance of the base/superstructure model drawn from a partial reading of the German Ideology which, unargued, simply states that the mass-media are ideological tools of ruling-class domination either through direct ownership or, as in the case of broadcasting, via ruling class control of the State. Such a position neglects both the specific effects of subordinating cultural production and reproduction to the general logic of capitalist commodity production and the specificities of the varying and shifting relationships between economic, ideological and political levels within actual concrete historical moments. Milliband in *Marxism and Politics* expresses a classic version of this theory:

Whatever else the immense output of the mass media is intended to achieve, it is *also* intended to help prevent the development of class-consciousness in the working class and to reduce as much as possible any hankering it might have for a radical alternative to capitalism. The ways in which this is attempted are endlessly different; and the degree of success achieved varies considerably from country to country and from one period to another—there are other influences at work. But the fact remains that 'the class which has the means of material production at its disposal' does have, 'control at the same time of the means of mental production': and that it does seek to use them for the weakening of opposition to the established order. Nor is the point much affected by the fact that the state in almost all capitalist countries 'owns' the radio and television—its purpose is identical (Milliband, 1977: 50).

It should be noted here that for all its philosophical sophistication the Althusserian position on ISA represents little if any advance on this position, as indeed Simon Clarke (1977) has correctly noted with respect to the Milliband/Poulantzas controversy.

(b) Secondly, and in partial reaction against this classic Marxist explanation of the role of the mass-media, we are offered an elaboration of the relative autonomy of the superstructure and within the superstructure of the ideological and political levels. All such theories in their effort to reject economism or, as Althusser puts it, 'the idea of a "pure and simple" non-overdetermined contradiction', to a greater or lesser extent have also removed economic determinacy, i.e. as Althusser again puts it, in such theories 'the lonely hour of the "last instance" never comes' (Althusser, 1969: 113). This general position has rightly developed the insights of the Frankfurt School into the importance of the superstructure and of mediation, while damagingly neglecting a crucial component of the Frankfurt School's original position, namely the fact that under monopoly capitalism the superstructure becomes precisely industrialized; it is invaded by the base and the base/superstructure distinction breaks down but via a collapse into the base rather than, as is the tendency with the post-Althusserian position, via the transformation of the base into another autonomous superstructural discourse.

In our age the objective social tendency is incarnate in the hidden subjective purpose of company directors, the foremost among whom are in the most powerful sectors of industry—

steel, petroleum, electricity and chemicals. Culture monopolies are weak and dependant in comparison. They cannot afford to neglect their appeasement of the real holders of power if their sphere of activity in mass-society is not to undergo a series of purges (Adorno and Hork-heimer, 1977: 351).

The truth of this original insight is demonstrated monthly as firms in the cultural sector are absorbed into large industrial conglomerates and brought under the sway of their business logic. Indeed, the real weakness of the Frankfurt School's original position was not their failure to realize the importance of the base or the economic, but insufficiently to take account of the economically contradictory nature of the process they observed and thus to see the industrialization of culture as unproblematic and irresistible. Those who have come after, while rightly criticizing the Frankfurt School for its absence of concrete class analysis, an absence stemming precisely from their insufficiently nuanced analysis of the economic level, in developing their theories of the effectivity of the superstructure have, ironically, massively compounded the original error.

The most distinguished exponent of the post-Althusserian position in Britain, Stuart Hall, in his essay 'Culture, the Media and the Ideological Effect' (Curran et al., 1977), recognizes that there is a decisive relationship between the growth of the mass-media and 'everything that we now understand as characterizing "monopoly capitalism" ', but at the same time refuses an analysis of this decisive relationship claiming that 'these aspects of the growth and expansion of the media historically have to be left to one side by the exclusive attention given here to media as "ideo-logical apparatuses".' Murdoch and Golding (1979) rightly criticize Hall and claim that 'on the contrary the ways in which the mass-media function as "ideological apparatuses" can only be adequately understood when they are systematically related to their position as large scale commercial enterprises in a capitalist economic system and if these relations are examined historically'. Hall's failure to do this leads him to explain the ideological effect in terms of pre-existent and ideologically predetermined communicators or encoders choosing from a pre-existent and ideologically pre-determined set of codes so that there is a systematic tendency of the media to re-produce the ideological field of society in such a way as to reproduce also its structure of domination. That is to say he offers the description of an ideological process, but not an explanation of why or how it takes place, except in tautological terms.

Moreover, he is led by his mode of analysis, as again Murdoch and Golding rightly point out, to favour a specific and atypical instance of media practice, namely public service broadcasting and indeed within that, an atypical form, namely informational broadcasting. While stressing that the production of the ideological effect requires work and struggle, his mode of analysis does not allow him to deal, for instance, with an important and developing moment in that struggle within the Press caused by a contradiction between the crucial underpinning idea of a 'free press' and the economic pressures towards monopoly or the relationship precisely between the ideological effect of broadcasting and the fact that it is perceived by its audience to be under State control as opposed to the biased privately owned press.

(c) A further elaboration of the post-Althusserian position, popular within film studies leads in its elaboration of a theory of autonomous discourses effectively to an evacuation of the field of historical materialism, whatever its materialistic rhetoric, placing its determinacy in the last instance on the unconscious as theorized within an essentially idealist, indeed Platonist, problematic. Such idiocies need detain us no further.[2]

(d) Finally, Dallas Smythe, identifying the excessive stress on the autonomy of the ideological level within Western Marxism as its 'Blind-spot', rightly redirects our attention away from the mass-media as ideological apparatuses and back to their economic function within capitalism. But in so doing, he proposes an extreme reductionist theory. For Smythe, any political economy of mass-media must be based upon an analysis of its commodity form and for him the commodity form specific to the mass-media is the Audience, that is to say, for Smythe, the crucial function of the mass-media is not to sell packages of ideology to consumers, but audiences to advertisers. Now it is undoubtedly important to focus attention upon the ways in which the mass-media manufacture and sell audiences as one moment in the complex circuit of capital that structures the operation of the mass-media economically. Moreover, to stress this moment as the crucial one and to concentrate on the mass-media's directly functional role for capital as advertising vehicles is undoubtedly a more plausible reflection of reality in the North American context than it would be in Europe. However, Smythe's theory misunderstands the function of the commodity form as an abstraction within Marxist economic theory and thus neglects the relationship between specific forms of the commodity, in this case the audience, and the commodity form in general. As a result, his theory lacks any sense of contradiction, failing to account for the function of those cultural commodities directly exchanged, failing to account for the role of the State, failing sufficiently to elaborate the function for capital of advertising itself and, perhaps most crucially of all, failing to relate the process of audience production by the mass-media to determinants of class and to class-struggle.[3]

The ideological level

What problems is it, then, that a political economy of mass-communication attempts to analyse. The research perspective, whose theoretical and historical basis I have briefly outlined, attempts to shift attention away from the conception of the mass-media as ISAs and sees them first as economic entities with both a direct economic role as creators of surplus value through commodity production and exchange and an indirect role, through advertising, in the creation of surplus value within other sectors of commodity production. Indeed, a political economy of mass-communication in part chooses its object of study precisely because it offers a challenge to the Althusser/Poulantzas theorization of the social formation as structured into the relatively autonomous levels of the economic, the ideological and the political. For the major institutions of mass-communication, the press and broadcasting, although, as will be analysed later, displaying notable differences of articulation, both at the same time display the close inter-weaving within concrete institutions and within their specific commodity forms of the economic, the ideological and the political. When we buy a newspaper we participate simultaneously in an economic exchange, in subjection to or reaction against an ideological formation and often in a quite specific act of political identification or at least involvement. We also know from historical

[2] We intend to publish a detailed critique of this position in a forthcoming issue. In the meantime, see Thompson (1978), Williams (1977) and Corrigan and Singer (1978) [Eds].

[3] See Smythe (1977), Murdoch (1978), Smythe (1978) and Levant (1978).

analysis of the development of the press that the nature of the political involvement is quite specifically economically conditioned. Similarly, TV news is economically determined within commodity production in general, performs an ideological function and explicitly operates within politics, in terms of balance, etc.

While accepting that the mass media can be and are politically and ideologically over-determined within many specific conjunctures, a political economy, as I understand it, rests upon ultimate determination by the economic (a level that itself always remains problematic and to be defined in the process of analysis).

Indeed, one of the key features of the mass media within monopoly capitalism has been the exercise of political, and ideological domination through the economic.[4] What concerns us in fact is firstly to stress, from the analytical perspective, the validity of the base/superstructure model while at the same time pointing to and analysing the ways in which the development of monopoly capitalism has industrialized the superstructure. Indeed Marx's own central insight into the capitalist mode of production stressed its generalizing, abstracting drive; the pressure to reduce everything to the equivalence of exchange value.

Before going on to examine the economic level and its specific articulations within the cultural sphere, let us look at the relationship between the material conditions of production (not, as we have seen, to be confused with the economic far less the capitalist modes of such production, which are specific forms) on the one hand and ideological forms on the other. That is to say how do we relate Williams's correct stress, within the limits indicated, upon the materiality of cultural production, to Marx's famous distinction 'between the material transformations of the economic conditions of production, which can be determined with the precision of natural science, and the legal, political, aesthetic or philosophic—in short—ideological—forms in which men become conscious of this conflict and fight it out' (Marx, 1859).

What the quotation from Marx underlines is the importance of the distinction between the two levels, a distinction focused upon the difference between the *unconscious* forces governing material production 'beyond our will', etc. and the conscious form of ideology. If we follow the Althusserians and make ideology an unconscious process this crucial distinction is lost.

As far as the mass-media specifically are concerned this distinction points to the need to distinguish between the media as processes of material production (whether capitalist or not is precisely a question for analysis) on the one hand, and as sites of ideological struggle on the other and the relationship between those two levels or instances.

There are here two distinctions to be made. I think we can liken ideological practice to what Marx called the 'real labour process'.

Looking at the process of production from its real side, i.e. as a process which creates new use-values by performing useful labour with existing use values, we find it to be a *real labour process*. As such its element, its conceptually specific components, are those of the labour process itself, of any labour process, irrespective of the mode of production or the stage of economic development in which they find themselves (Marx, 1976).

That is to say the process of consciousness and of representation, for instance, language, are real processes by which human beings socially appropriate their environment (nature) which pre-exist and continue to exist within specifically

4 See J. Curran, 'Capitalism and Control of the Press 1800–1979', in Curran *et al.* (1977).

capitalist modes of ideological production and indeed upon which these capitalist modes rest.

The materiality of such ideological production *qua* ideology rests upon the fact that consciousness is a human transformation of 'real' experience, it is in that sense 'practical knowledge'. Clearly therefore, the relationship of any particular instance of ideological production to the totality of social experience will depend upon an analysis of the experiential position of the human consciousness in question, e.g. the conventional and simple definition of class consciousness as based upon the direct experience of a given position within the capital/labour relationship. Of course in any complex society such direct experience becomes highly mediated both diachronically and synchronically. But its translation into forms of representation is nonetheless a process of consciousness which is different from and in its forms has no necessary correspondence with, the economic processes to which it relates or of which it is a representation. Indeed as a representation it is precisely by definition distinct from those processes which it represents.

Moreover ideological forms can never be simply collapsed into a system of exchange values, i.e. the specifically capitalist mode of production, precisely because ideological forms, forms of consciousness, are concerned with difference, with distinction; they are by definition heterogeneous (as Marx himself remarked when discussing the limited possibilities for the subsumption of ideological production under capitalism, 'I want the doctor and not his errand boy'). Whereas exchange value is precisely the realm of equivalence.[5]

Material and mental production

In order to study the connection between intellectual and material production it is above all essential to conceive the latter in its determined historical form and not as a general category. For example, there corresponds to the capitalist mode of production a type of intellectual production quite different from that which corresponded to the mediaeval mode of production. Unless material production itself is understood in its specific historical form, it is impossible to grasp the characteristics of the intellectual production which corresponds to it or the reciprocal action between the two (Marx, 1963: 96–97).

We need to lay stress on and distinguish two distinct but related moments in a historical materialist analysis of intellectual production.

(a) Culture as a superstructural phenomenon in relation to non-cultural modes of material production, i.e. on the one hand, the dominant or hegemonic cultural production paid for out of capitalist *revenue* and, on the other, a subordinate working class or oppositional culture paid for out of wages. Cultural production in this sense and its articulations with the sphere of material production involves one specific interpretation of the meaning in The German Ideology of 'control of the means of mental production', i.e. through the direct payment of ideologists and the necessary maintenance of the physical instruments of their ideological production. It is within that analytical perspective that we need to analyse the historical development of the 'historically specific needs' of the working class and their sustenance of 'organic intellectuals' and of specific instruments of cultural production such as trade-unions.

(b) Culture as part of material production itself, directly subordinate to or at least in a closely determined articulation with the laws of development of capital. This is both a latter historical phase, part of developing monopoly capitalism, the pheno-

---

[5] For a detailed discussion of this problem see Baudrillard (1972, 1975).

menon dubbed 'the industrialization of culture', but it also lives alongside the other moment and in specific instances we need to analyse the interrelationship between these two distinct modes of intellectual production within intellectual production (Culture in its narrow sense) in general.

What, in general, has been lost in Marxist studies of the mass media is the precise historical elaboration of what Marx and Engels meant in The German Ideology by 'control of the means of mental production'.

In general it is clear, I think, in The German Ideology that, reflecting the contemporary stage of capitalist development, Marx and Engels were concerned with the payment of ideologists, of intellectuals, out of capitalist revenue. It is this perspective that Raymond Williams picks up in the passage already cited. That is to say they rightly saw that superstructural activities require a cohort of mental workers who were not directly economically or materially productive and thus whose price of reproduction must be borne by the sphere of material production. Since under capitalism it was capitalists who were extracting this surplus, it was they who could redistribute this surplus into superstructural activities of their choosing and by so doing exert direct economic pressures on the ideologists who were their hired servants.

The creation of surplus labour on the one side corresponds to the creation of minus labour, relative idleness (or non-productive labour at best) on the other. This goes without saying as regards capital itself; but holds then also for the classes with which it shares; hence of paupers, flunkeys, lick-spittles, etc. living from the surplus product, in short, the whole train of retainers; the part of the *servant* class which lives not from capital but from revenue (Marx, 1973: 401).

This direct relationship remains important and should not be forgotten. That is to say the working class also developed, out of its wages, a subordinate or counter culture with its own 'organic intellectuals' such as paid trade-union officials, co-operative organizers, journalists, etc., but the surplus available for this purpose was exiguous both really and comparatively, so that this direct ideological power was decisively weighted in favour of capital and remains so. Compare a small organisation like Counter Information Services with the public relations and research investment of a major company. Look at the way in which large companies manipulate the legal system by their ability to sustain expensive, long drawn out actions (e.g. the Thalidomide case). Look at the way media research itself has been and is significantly influenced by the flow of funds from vested commercial interests.

There now exists of course, as the division of labour has developed further, a more mediated version of this employment of ideologists out of revenue, namely, as Bourdieu has analysed, the creation of a subordinate fraction of the capitalist class who possess cultural capital (Bourdieu and Passeron, 1977). Just as younger sons of the aristocracy went into Church and army, so now a section of the capitalist class occupies key positions in the cultural sector. The class origins of ideological workers remains an important but neglected aspect of media analysis. This does not of course mean that such people necessarily reproduce ruling class ideology (see Engels and William Morris for obvious counter examples). It does mean that there is a structural tendency so to do.

Neglect of this aspect of direct economic control of ideologists is reflected in current discussion of the ideological role of the media where there is much sophisticated discussion of professionalization, of heirarchies of discourse, of hegemonic and subordinate codes, etc. discussions which often serve to mask a reality which is ever present to those actually working in the media, namely the possibility of losing one's job. This economic reality is of course often internalized by both employee and employer in the form of the ideologies of professionalism or managerialism but it remains nonetheless potent for that, indeed is the underpinning which professionalism requires. Once again, this was a fact that Adorno and Horkheimer did not make the mistake of forgetting:

Under the private culture monopoly it is a fact that 'tyranny leaves the body free and directs its attack at the soul'. The ruler no longer says, 'You must think as I do, or die'. He says, 'You are free not to think as I do, your life, your property, everything shall remain yours, but from this day on you are a stranger among us'. Not to conform means to be rendered powerless, economically and therefore, spiritually—to be 'self-employed'. When the outsider is excluded from the concern, he can only too easily be accused of incompetence. Whereas today in material production the mechanism of supply and demand is disintegrating in the superstructure it still operates as a check in the ruler's favour.[6]

The second moment, upon which of course increasingly in the actual historical development the former moment has come to depend, is the actual control by capital within the process of commodity production of the means of cultural production. This moment was clearly under-developed at the time when The German Ideology was written but, while not entirely superceding the other moment as I have indicated, it is this moment that has become crucial for an analysis of cultural reproduction under monopoly capitalism.[7] Within the sphere of cultural production the development of specifically economic, industrial forms was in part possible precisely because of the effect of the other moment, i.e. working class powers of cultural resistance were weakened. A good example of this is R. Williams' suggestion that the popular success of ITV and of the general invasion of American commercialized cultural forms was a reaction on the part of the working class to the liberating overthrow of a particular hegemonic cultural formation represented by the BBC. It is in particular on the implications of this second moment that I wish to concentrate, i.e. the effects of the imposition of capital logic upon cultural production.

As I have indicated there has been a tendency to see such an imposition as ideologically non-contradictory. One must stress at the outset that this is not so. Because capital controls the means of cultural production in the sense that the production and exchange of cultural commodities becomes the dominant forms of cultural relationship, it does not follow that these cultural commodities will necessarily support, either in their explicit content or in their mode of cultural appropriation, the dominant ideology. Indeed as Terry Lovell has recently stressed and as, once again, Adorno and Horkheimer made clear, the cultural commodity possesses an inherent contradiction, a contradiction which, as with the other contradictions within the capitalist mode of production, may be profoundly subversive.[8] Whether

[6] Adorno and Horkheimer, 'The Dialectic of Enlightenment', in Curran et al. (1977: 133, 358–359).

[7] But note Marx's own comments in the Grundrisse, p. 532:

The highest development of capital exists when the general conditions of the process of social production are not paid out of deduction from the social revenue, the state's taxes—where revenue and not capital appears as the labour fund, and where the worker, although he is a free wage worker like any other, nevertheless stands economically in a different relation—but rather out of capital as capital. This shows the degree to which capital has subjugated all conditions of social production to itself, on the one side; and, on the other side, hence, the extent to which social reproduction wealth has been capitalised and all needs are satisfied through the exchange form (Marx's italics).

[8] See T. Lovell (1979) and Adorno and Horkheimer:

Nevertheless the culture industry remains the entertainment business. Its influence over the consumer is established by entertainment; that will ultimately be broken not by an outright decree, but by the hostility inherent in the principle of entertainment to what is greater than itself (in Curran et al., 1977: 361).

it is or not depends upon a concrete analysis of a specific conjuncture. Before turning
to the general implications of the proposition that one definition of the control of the
means of mental production is the take-over of large areas of cultural production and
reproduction by capitalist commodity production, what the proposition leads one to
question is that stress on intentionality which we find in theories such as that of
Milliband. It is quite clear in Marx's analysis of *Capital* that he wished to distinguish
firmly between the logic of capital and the intention of individual capitalists, even
at the economic, let alone the ideological, level:

The fact that baking, shoemaking, etc. are only just being put on a capitalist basis in England
is entirely due to the circumstances that English capital cherished feudal preconceptions of
'respectability'. It was 'respectable' to sell Negroes into slavery, but it was not respectable to
make sausages, shoes or bread (Marx, 1976: 1014, footnote).

It is perhaps worth noting in passing that this characteristic of British capital still
operates with respect to the media, which still carry a certain bohemian, mountebank
and marginal reputation. Hence the characteristics of the particular capitals who
started ITV for instance or who developed the British film industry in the 1930s or
the role of colonial capital via Beaverbrook and Murdoch in the British Press. Such
attitudes still affect the Tory party in its ambivalent relation to commercial broadcasting.

The function fulfilled by the capitalist is no more than the function of capital viz. the
valorization of value by absorbing living labour—executed *consciously* and *willingly*. The
capitalist functions only as personified capital, capital as a person, just as the worker is no more
than *labour* personified (Marx, 1976: 989).

What this quotation points to is the importance of not viewing capitalists, for
analytical purposes, as unified subjects. That is to say a given person or group can
only be described as capitalist in those moments when s/he or they are acting in
conscious and willed accord with the logic of capital accumulation. Thus there may
well be many such conscious, willed actions, never mind unconscious actions, that
are contradictory to the logic of capital, of course always within determinate limits.
There may be therefore a clear divergence between the functions of capital within the
material process of mental production and the conscious, willed intentions of the
capitalist or of their ideologues. We cannot predict *a priori* which at any time will be
predominant, e.g. how long a Harmsworth, a Beaverbrook or a Thomson will keep a
loss-making newspaper going for reasons of social prestige or political power, although
clearly the outer limits of such possibilities of deviation by the individual capitalist
will be determined by the norms of capital's logic.

There is then, and this cannot be sufficiently stressed, no necessary coincidence
between the effects of the capitalist process proper and the ideological needs of the
dominant class. On the contrary the entire thesis of capital points to the opposite
conclusion.

This, for instance, effects assumptions concerning the relationship between
capital and the State. To take one example, the proportion of the budget of the COI
that has to be devoted to paid access to the media, i.e. the use of paid advertising for
Government propaganda or information, has risen in the last decade from 20% to
50%. Such evidence can be interpreted in two ways. Either there is an observable
conflict between the ideological needs of the State and the accumulation process
within the media sector (leaving aside the question of whether the State is in fact the
representative of capital or of the dominant class and therefore whether such a

conflict would represent a contradiction between the economic and ideological needs of that class in general or whether it represents a contradiction between the ideological needs of capital in general versus the economic needs of a class fraction who control the media sector). Alternatively, this evidence can be interpreted to show the increasing sway of capitalist logic over the political and ideological level, i.e. forcing it to work increasingly through direct exchange relations within the economic.

This question of intentionality within ideological production is, of course, central to the media debate, within both the bourgeois and Marxist problematic. That is to say one argument runs, for instance the Frankfurt School tradition, that the mass media are important because monopoly capitalism has moved from direct coercion of the working class, for instance within the labour process, to ideological coercion as its preferred method of domination and the mass-media or ISA's are crucial in this process.

But do we in fact require this shift onto the terrain of ideology in order to explain the absence of direct coercion. Marx himself on the contrary saw the avoidance of such coercion as central to the economic mechanism of capitalism. That is to say the abstraction of exchange value, the wage-form, etc. were in themselves quite powerful enough to explain the dominance of capital and indeed that this non-coercive dominance was both historically necessary and progressive. Bourdieu has developed this general proposition.[9]

Thus at the level of material production, of the life process in the realm of the social—for that is what the process of production is—we find the *same* situation that we find in *religion* at the ideological level, namely the inversion of subject into object and vice-versa. Viewed *historically* this inversion is the indispensable transition without which wealth as such, i.e. the relentless productive forces of social labour, which alone can form the material base of a free human society, could not possibly be created by force at the expense of the majority (Marx, 1976: 990).

Mental production and capitalist commodity production

Let us now turn back to look at mental production, of which the mass media are an example, as processes of capitalist production and at the implications for our modes of social communication of the subsumption by capital of the real forms of ideological production.

This needs to be looked at historically, i.e. unlike the capital logic or capital derivation school we must not see capitalism as a mode of production which arrives *sui generis* and then sprouts a social formation like dragon's teeth. It is rather a specific form which grew within a pre-existing social formation and is involved in a process of expansion and conquest of non-capitalist sectors, a process which is incomplete and contradictory. This process of expansion involves both the subsumption of other areas of material production and pre-capitalist forms of economic organisation and also of non-economic activity under the sway of the economic in its capitalist form.

[9] See Bourdieu (1971: 183–197):
It is in the degree of objectification of the accumulated social capital that one finds the basis of all pertinent differences between the modes of domination . . . Objectification guarantees the permanence and cumulativity of material and symbolic acquisition which can thus subsist without agents having to recreate them continuously and in their entirety by deliberate action; but, because the profits of their institutions are the object of differential appropriation, objectification also and inseparably ensures the reproduction of the structure of distribution of the capital which, in its various forms, is the precondition for such appropriation, and in so doing, reproduces the structure of the relation of dominance and dependence (p. 184).

When examining mass communication within predominantly capitalist social formations we must not make the mistake of assuming that they are therefore necessarily capitalist, i.e. we cannot make the easy ellision Milliband makes between those sectors controlled by private capital and those controlled by the State. Nor can we assume that all non-State sectors are in fact capitalist. Indeed the relationship between pre-capitalist and capitalist forms within the media sector is a significant feature both economically and ideologically, i.e. the relationship between notions of creative freedom, freedom of the Press, the Fourth Channel debate, community communication, etc. This relationship significantly determines the forms of the struggle within the media over the labour process.

Thus artisanal modes of labour organization ranging from individual craft production, i.e. the authorship of a book, to the small group, i.e. the independent film company or record producer, remain common and important within the cultural sphere. Such residues have been the focus for struggle against the logic of capital and have produced a powerful anti-economic cultural ideology (see the whole culture/ society tradition). Nonetheless in certain instances such artisanal organization may be functional for capital so long as capital controls the means of mass reproduction of the authorial product and of the means of mass distribution, because it ensures the necessary production of a range of heterogeneous cultural artefacts from which capital can choose for further exploitation without capital having to bear the risks and overheads for this production which are born directly by labour. Indeed, the ideology of creative freedom can be used by capital to keep their labour force divided and weak and with no control over the strategic moments of the total labour process. Thus, for instance, while the Open Broadcasting Authority will be fought for by cultural workers under the banner of creative freedom and against the apparent interests of capital in the form of ITV, such a structure of small-scale freelance production, if it were to be realized, would be more functional for capital in general than an extension of the present structure, because it would open British broadcasting more fully both to advertising and to the pressures of the international market.[10]

Nor must we make the mistake of assuming an easy equation between private ownership and capitalism.

Where capital still appears only in its elementary forms such as commodities . . . or money, the capitalist manifests himself in the already familiar character of the owner of money or commodities. But such a person is no more a capitalist in himself than money or commodities are capital in themselves. They become translated into capital only in certain specific circumstances and their owners likewise become capitalist only when these circumstances obtain (Marx, 1976: 976).

What then are these circumstances? The central characteristic of capital is growth or accumulation.

In itself the sum of money may only be defined as capital if it is employed, spent, with the aim of increasing it, if it is spent expressly in order to increase it. In the case of the sum of value or money this phenomenon is its destiny, its inner law, its tendency, while to the capitalist, i.e. the owner of the sum of money, in whose hands it shall acquire its function, it appears as intention, purpose (Marx, 1976: 976).

Thus to examine the specifically capitalist mode of media production we need to see the ways in which capital uses the real process of media production in order to increase its value, in order to grow, and the barriers which are placed in the way of

[10] For a fuller elaboration of the modes of labour organization within capitalist cultural industries, see Huet *et al.* (1978).

this process either by the inherent contradictions of the process itself or by external forces.

At a minimum in order to accumulate capital must bring living labour into the production process by exchanging in the sphere of circulation through the wage bargain. It must combine this living labour in a determinate manner with objectified labour as means of production (raw materials and instruments) in the production of a commodity in the exchange of which surplus value will be realized.

In a fully constituted capitalist mode based upon relative surplus value and competition between capitals this process of growth requires ever increased productivity and ever widening markets.

Historically the sphere of mental production or non-material production presented and continues to present important barriers to this process and the forms and dynamics of the mass media can in part be understood as resulting from a continuous attempt to surmount those barriers and from the concretely various successes and failures of this attempt.

We thus start from the historical materialist assumption that the development of capitalism or the capitalist mode of production is:

(a) a contradictory process;
(b) not yet complete.

The contradictory nature of the process is in part intrinsic, i.e. the conflict between capital and labour, the conflict between capital accumulation and the socialization of the forces and relations of production, the conflict between the drive to accumulate through the extraction of relative surplus value and labour power as the creator of surplus value, a contradiction expressed in the tendency of the rate of profit to fall.

In part the contradictions are extrinsic, that is to say related precisely to the relationship between developing capitalism and the non-capitalist areas of the social formation. The necessary expansion of the valorization process is not a process of automatic expansion; it comes up against social and political barriers; it needs to conquer physical barriers, e.g. communication and transport; it requires the necessary accumulation of capital, etc.

We see these contradictions in the field of mass-media:

(a) in resistances both actual and ideological to the industrialization of the artisanal modes of cultural production;
(b) in the conflicts between national and international capitals, sometimes mediated through the State and sometimes direct, e.g. the split in the Tory party over the original introduction of commercial broadcasting—or the developing struggle over national versus supra-national control of European satellite broadcasting— or the existence of quotas on the importation of foreign film and TV material;
(c) growing Third World demand for a New World Information Order.

The problem with cultural and informational goods is that, because their use value is almost limitless, i.e. cannot be destroyed or consumed by use, it is extremely difficult to attach an exchange value to them. They are in fact, in general, classic public goods. What we are considering is what Marx called 'non-material production'. Marx discusses such production in the context of a discussion of the distinction between productive and non-productive labour (whether such a distinction can be maintained and, if so, its analytical significance, is a matter of general importance within the field of the political economy of culture which we cannot pursue further here). In brief, Marx clearly foresaw difficulties in subsuming non-material production under capitalism. He identified two possible forms of such production:

(1) It results in commodities which exist separately from the producer, i.e. they can circulate in the interval between production and consumption as commodities, e.g. books, paintings and all products of art as distinct from the artistic achievement of the practising artist. Here capitalist production is possible only within very narrow limits. Apart from such cases as, say, sculptors who employ assistants, these people (where they are not independent) mainly work for merchants capital, e.g. booksellers, a pattern that is only transitional in itself and can only lead to a capitalist mode of production in the formal sense. Nor is the position altered by the fact that exploitation is at its greatest precisely in these transitional forms.

(2) The product is not separable from the act of producing. Here too the capitalist mode of production occurs only on a limited scale and in the nature of the case it can only operate in certain areas (I want the doctor not his errand boy). For example, in teaching institutions the teacher can be no more than wage-labour for the entrepreneur of the learning factory. Such peripheral phenomena can be ignored when considering capitalist production as a whole.

(Marx, 1976: 1047–1048).

This passage would be worth lengthy analysis. At this stage I would only like to point to the following.

(a) The relevance of example (1) for the debate between Marcuse and Benjamin concerning the role of the aura of a work of art and the effect on that aura of the attempt to subject culture production to at least the forces of capitalist production.[11]

(b) The need to look, with reference to the observation concerning the degree of exploitation in this field, at the evidence of the persistent low pay of cultural workers and the extent to which even the most advanced sectors of capitalist cultural production depend upon drawing relative surplus value from sectors which still operate a pre-capitalist artisanal mode of economic organization.[12]

(c) The above relates to the need to examine the relationship between Marx's belief that capitalist production of cultural goods was possible only within very narrow limits, the phenomenon of Baumol's disease (Baumol and Bowen, 1976) and the ever increasing pressure on the State to intervene in the cultural sector.

(d) Similar considerations are raised by Marx's second example where the product is not separable from the act of producing, thus raising strict limits to productivity and thus raising relative costs.

The economic contradictions that arise from the nature of cultural commodities takes different forms within different sectors of the media and at different historical moments.

Five main ways have been adopted in an attempt to circumvent the problem.

(a) Copyright. This is in effect an attempt to commoditize information via the uniqueness of authorship or by turning the author into a commodity. But this only works if you either then make the commodity scarce, i.e. stress its uniqueness. We see this in the economics of the art market. Or if you control supply, i.e. control access to the means of reproduction such as printing presses and film laboratories. However, if such control is used to over-price it will encourage the development of pirating alternatives. This is now a major problem internationally for the cultural industries in records, books, films and even TV programmes.

(b) Control of access to consumption through a box-office mechanism at the point of sale and/or through economic control of the channels of distribution, i.e. newspapers and cinema.

The problem here is that such control is resistant to economies of scale and as the

[11] See Benjamin (1977) for the positive view and Marcuse (1972) for the negative view.

[12] See Huet et al. (1978) for theoretical elaboration and Krust (1977) for data. See also discussion in Owen, Beebe and Manning (1974), which shows, from a neo-classical perspective that the so-called economic efficiency of US TV depends upon high unemployment in Hollywood.

theatre found when faced by the cinema and the cinema when faced by broadcasting, is highly susceptible to competition from more efficient technologies of reproduction and distribution. However, as broadcasting demonstrates, the massive economies of scale produced by these more efficient means of distribution by destroying the box office, i.e. by making access open, create major problems of creating the necessary moment of exchange.

(c) Built-in obsolescence through the manipulation of time. This was the great achievement of the newspaper which, by creating rapidly decaying information, created thereby a constant need to re-consume. But this manipulation of time has its limits since consumption time is physically limited. (The central importance of time within the economics of the mass-media is a subject to which I intend to give substantive treatment in a subsequent article.)

(d) The creation, packaging and sale, not of cultural and informational goods to direct consumers, but of audiences to advertisers (Smythe, 1977).

(e) State patronage.

The inherent tendency towards the socialization of cultural and informational goods has always given the State an important role in this field from the days of direct patronage of cultural workers by King, Aristocracy and Church via the early subsidy of newspapers by governments and political parties, through public libraries and public education, to the key contemporary example of broadcasting.

In brief therefore, the specific nature of the commodity form within cultural production leads to a constant problem of realization and thus to a two-way pressure either towards advertising finance or towards State finance. We find these pressures quite clearly at the moment in the growing controversy over sponsorship in sport and the arts.[13]

The questions these pressures raise is in what ways (a) advertising and (b) State intervention in this sphere is functional or disfunctional for capitalism in general on the one hand and on the other the effect of such pressures upon cultural production itself.

The modes of extraction and distribution of the cultural surplus

Since all cultural forms are material in the sense that they take time which will only be available after the needs of physical reproduction are satisfied, the material requirements of the cultural process must be extracted as surplus from direct material production. As we have seen this can be done by paying for cultural production directly out of revenue. But as Marx remarked of capitalism in general, it has found it more efficient as a means of control to extract surpluses directly by means of economic processes. Thus the developments of the capitalist mode of production and its associated division of mental and manual labour has lead to the development of the extraction of the necessary surplus for the maintenance of cultural production and reproduction directly via the commodity and exchange form. But this process will only take place to the extent that:

(a) there is surplus capital searching for opportunities for valorization;
(b) the anticipated rate of profit in the chosen sphere of cultural production is at least as high as that available elsewhere.

[13] See, for instance, P. Harland (1978) and recent correspondence in the *Times* concerning the Arts Council's expression of disapproval of its grant recipients giving too large a billing to commercial sponsors at the expense of itself.

Where these conditions do not exist cultural processes will have to continue to be undertaken by the direct transfer of resources, i.e. by the expenditure of surplus. This may take place under the following conditions.

(a) By capitalist as individuals or groups funding such activities, e.g. the classic model of arts patronage. Such a form may be sustained within the contemporary capitalist social formation by means of tax concessions. It may be channelled through charitable foundations, etc.

Such funding leads to direct ideological control, legitimated as the cultural extension of private property, namely personal taste. This sphere can give rise to significant political battles, e.g. the wealth tax/national heritage debate.

But examples within the media field are the direct subsidy of newspapers by political parties or by politically ambitious individuals, e.g. Beaverbrook, Goldsmith and possibly now Broakes and Matthews, the new owners of the *Express* Group and Morgan-Grampian.

(b) Via the State. Here electronic communication is the key case. The exact mix in the field of both telephonic and broadcast communication between the State and capital needs examination state by state. As any superficial examination will show, key differences between Western Europe and the United States give the lie to any simple capital logic explanation of how the particular economic and institutional forms, within which electronic communication has developed, have arisen.

The explanation of such differences and the present conjunctural relations between national capitals and the State, between states and between international capital and states in this area would have to take account of the following.

(1) The structures of national capitals.

(2) The existing State structure, i.e. federal structure of US and Germany as opposed to centralized structure of Britain and even more, France.

(3) The strategic requirements of the State, e.g. the State-inspired creation of RCA as the first step in a long history of the US government's explicit geo political involvement in communication, the clearest case of which is satellites, such a policy requiring intervention to restructure national capitals.

(4) The balance of forces between sections of capital and the relations of that balance of force to the State's assessment of both economic and strategic requirements, e.g. the foundation of the BBC in which we see an interaction between the needs of the nascent British electronic industry, which the State wished to foster both for strategic and economic reasons, but which was only interested in the sales of hardware and was able to shift the expense and ideological problems of programme production onto the State, because the State needed also to take account both of the economically and politically powerful British press, which was opposed to competition for advertising and of a culturally conservative and elitist ruling class fraction.[14]

To sum up, historically the development of the material process known as the superstructure depended upon the availability of a surplus in the sphere of direct material production, i.e. the sphere of the extraction, shaping and consumption of nature. Historically the shape of that superstructure is determined by the social relations of production, because it is these social relations that determine the distribution of that surplus. For example, Athenian democracy as a form of political practice depends directly materially upon the slave economy that supported it by making time

---

[14] For a discussion of the relationship between the French State and private capital in the development of the electronic audio-visual field in general, see Flichy (1978) and Huet *et al.* (1978).

available for political activity to a non-productive class. Such directly material considerations remain important, i.e. in a planned economy like the Soviet Union direct choices have to be made between for instance producing more shoes or the paper for more newspapers. Such considerations may be acute in the planning of media systems in Third World countries and indeed it is the influencing of such decisions in the interest not of the indigenous economy or social formation but of a foreign high surplus economy that is one of the matters at issue in the media imperialism debate. It is a less obvious form of the starvation caused in some countries by the development of industrialized agriculture serving a world market. Under developing capitalism the means of cultural production may be provided either in commodity form as part of the accumulation process, e.g. records or as part of the realization process of other sectors of the capitalist economy, e.g. advertising or directly out of capitalist revenue, e.g. arts patronage or the Thomson family and *The Times* or through the State.

Each of the above means of surplus distribution to the cultural sphere will differentially affect the ways in which the dominant class controls the means of cultural production. Different contradictions will come into play, contradictions which need to be specifically analysed in each conjunctural case. Not only are these contradictions intrinsic to each subsidiary mode of cultural production but there are also contradictions which arise because of conflicts between them, e.g. between broadcasting whether state or private and the press, a conflict in its turn differentially mediated through competition for readers/viewers and through competition for advertising.

The industrialization of culture

While drawing different conclusions as to the significance of the phenomenon both bourgeois and Marxist economists agree that the current phase of capitalist development is characterized by the following.

    (a) Unprecedented capital concentration in all the key traditional manufacturing sectors accompanied in general by a rising surplus.

    (b) A resulting problem of valorization which drives surplus capital in search of other areas of investment.

    (c) An associated development of the so-called service sector characterized by the industrialization of sectors which were either more primitively organised or, as in the sphere of domestic labour, altogether outside the market.

These tendencies are now rapidly affecting the whole cultural, mass-media sector. This has been extensively documented by A. Mattelart in his recent 'Multi-nationales et systeme de communication' and, for France, by A. Huet *et al.* in their 'Capitalisme et industries culturelles'. So all I wish to do here, is point out certain key aspects and examples of this tendency.

This absorption of the sphere of reproduction into full-scale commodity production is characterized by the following.

    (a) Increased international competition and the resulting take-over of domestic, national publishing companies, advertising agencies, private broadcasting stations etc. by multinational companies. See, for instance, the example of Phillips given at the start of this piece. This competition also leads to increasing penetration by international media products, particularly Anglo-Saxon.[15]

[15] It should be noted that from this point of view the UK is in a privileged position since it is second only to the USA as a media exporter.

(b) A sharpening struggle within cultural production over the labour process in an attempt by capital to increase productivity in a sector which is notoriously resistant to such increases. This struggle has been most marked recently in the newspaper industry with the present dispute at Times Newspapers being the most notorious and current example in Britain.

(c) Increasingly persistent attempts to open up new markets in order to absorb excess capital. The most obvious example of this is the increasing pressure throughout Western Europe to privatize public broadcasting. See, for instance, the case of Italy, but the current crisis in the financing of the BBC and Annan's proposals for an advertising financed O.B.A. must be seen in this light.

(d) Attempts to open up new markets for both cultural hard-ware and soft-ware by introducing new communication technologies, such as cable TV, satellites, Teletext, etc. Because of the huge infrastructural investments involved and the comparatively low rate of return on such investments these moves involve close alliances between capital and the State in an attempt to get the tax-payer to carry the cost of the distribution system, while private capital takes the profits from the sale of hardware and from the subsequent development of a consumer durable market in such items as teletex decoders and of a software market, e.g. Pay TV. The full development of this push into new technologies has undoubtedly been slowed down significantly by the current recession in the Western economies, but the long-term implications for national cultures, for class cultures and for freedom of expression of all these trends, not only in the Third World where the problem is dramatized as media imperialism, but in the capitalist heartlands, are profoundly significant.

Thus I return to where I started by reiterating that the development of political economy in the cultural sphere is not a mere matter of theoretical interest but of urgent practical political priority. So long as Marxist analysis concentrates on the ideological content of the mass media it will be difficult to develop coherent political strategies for resisting the underlying dynamics of development in the cultural sphere in general which rest firmly and increasingly upon the logic of generalized commodity production. In order to understand the structure of our culture, its production, consumption and reproduction and of the role of the mass media in that process, we increasingly need to confront some of the central questions of political economy in general, the problem of productive and non-productive labour, the relation between the private and public sectors and the role of the State in capitalist accumulation, the role of advertising within late capitalism, etc.

As long ago as 1960, Asa Briggs wrote in his Fisher Memorial Lecture:

The provision of entertainment has never been a subject of great interest either to economists or to economic historians—at least in their working hours. Yet in 20th century conditions it is proper to talk of a highly organized entertainment industry, to distinguish within it between production and distribution, to examine forces making for competition, integration, concentration and control and to relate such study to the statistics of national income and output, the development of advertising, international economic relations and—not least—to the central economic concept of the market which, in the 20th century, is as much concerned with leisure as it is with work (Briggs, 1960).

Nearly two decades later that research gap remains and there has been little coherent effort to understand the process known as 'the industrialization of culture', a process by which, as Briggs put it, 'Massive market interests have come to dominate an area of life which, until recently, was dominated by individuals themselves' (Briggs, 1960).

Bibliography

ADORNO, T. and HORKHEIMER, M. (1977). The culture industry (abridged), in J. Curran *et al.*, (eds), *Mass Communication and Society*, Edward Arnold, London

ALTHUSSER, L. (1969). *Contradiction and Over-determination*, Allen Lane, London

BAUDRILLARD, J. (1972). *Pour une Critique de l'Economic Politique du Signe*, Gallimard, Paris

BAUDRILLARD, J. (1975). *The Mirror of Production*, Tela Press, St. Louis

BAUMOL, W. J. and BOURAN, W. G. (1976). On the performing arts: the anatomy of their economic problems, in M. Blang, (ed.), *The Economics of the Arts*, Martin Robertson, London

BENJAMIN, W. (1977). The work of art in the age of mechanical reproduction, in Curran *et al.*, op. cit.

BOTTOMORE, T. and RUBEL, M. (1963). Theories of surplus value, in *K. Marx on Sociology and Social Philosophy*, pp. 96, 97, Pelican

BOURDIEU, P. (1971). *Outline of a Theory of Practice*, CUP

BOURDIEU, P. and PASSERON, J. L. (1977). *Reproduction*, Sage, London

BRIGGS, A. (1960). Fisher Memorial Lecture, University of Adelaide

CLARKE, S. (1977). Marxism, sociology and Poulantzas's theory of the state, *Capital and Class*, no. 2, Summer

CORRIGAN, P. and SINGER, D. (1978). Hindess and Hirst: a critical review, *Socialist Register*, Merlin, London

CURRAN, J. *et al.*, (eds) (1977). *Mass-Communication and Society*, Edward Arnold, London

Financial Times (1978). Electronic Rentals ups its ratings, 19 December

FLICHY, P. (1978). *Contribution à une Étude du Industries de l'Audiovisual*, Institut National de l'Audiovisual

HARLAND, P. (1978). Enter the money men, stage right, *Sunday Times*, 11 June

HUET, A. *et al.* (1978). *Capitalisme et Industries Culturelles*, University of Grenoble Press

KRUST, M. (1977). *Droit au Travail et Problems d'Emploi du Travailleur Culturels du Spectacle et de l'Interpretation Musicale dans la Communante Economique Europeene*, CCE

LEVANT, P. (1978). The audience commodity: on the blindspot debate, *Canadian Journal of Political and Social Theory*

LOVELL, T. (1979). *Realism, Ideology and Film*, British Film Institute, London (forthcoming)

MANDEL, E. (1975). *Late Capitalism*, ch. 1, NLB, London

MARCUSE, H. (1972). Art as a form of reality, *New Left Review* 74

MARX, K. (1859). Preface to a contribution to a critique of political economy, in Marx, K. and Engels, F., (eds), *Selected Works*, vol. 1, p. 364, Lawrence and Wishart, London (1962)

MARX, K. (1973). *Grundrisse*, Pelican, London

MARX, K. (1975). Notes on Adolph Wagner, in T. Carver, (ed.), *Texts on Method*, p. 201, Blackwell, Oxford

MARX, K. (1976). Results of the immediate process of production, in *Capital*, vol. 1, Pelican

MILLIBAND, R. R. (1977). *Marxism and Politics*, p. 50, OUP

MURDOCH, G. (1978). Blindspots about Western Marxism: a reply to Dallas Smythe, *Canadian Journal of Political and Social Theory*, vol. 2, no. 2

MURDOCH, G. and GOLDING, P. (1979). Ideology and the mass media: the question of determination, in M. Barrett *et al.* (eds) *Ideology and Cultural Production*, Croom-Helm, London

OWEN, B., BEEBE, J. and MANNING, W. (1974). *TV Economics*, D. C. Heath, London

SAYER, D. (1979). *Marx's Method*, Harvester Press, forthcoming

SMYTHE, D. (1977). Communication: blindspot of Western Marxism, *Canadian Journal of Political and Social Theory*, vol. 1, no. 3

SMYTHE, D. (1978). Rejoinder to Graham Murdoch, *Canadian Journal of Political and Social Theory*, vol. 2, no. 2

THOMPSON, E. P. (1978). *The Poverty of Theory*, Merlin, London

WILLIAMS, R. (1977). *Marxism and Literature*, OUP

Prevailing views about the "crisis" to culture (caused by modernization) affect communication theories and philosophies, says Lawrence Grossberg in this provocative essay. Grossberg sees informational, subjective, interactional, transcendental, and representational images of culture and modernization in contemporary thought. The effects research tradition, epitomized by Wilbur Schramm, sprang from American liberal thought that saw ignorance being eradicated by scientific information. A second strain in America, nurtured by John Dewey and the Chicago school, was rooted in pragmatism and a concern for the role of communication in creating community. Cultural theorists—such as James Carey in the United States, Harold Innis in Canada, Raymond Williams in Britain, and Jurgen Habermas in Germany—seek to remove the scientism from communication theory but assume a variety of stances on the symbolic environment of mass media and its role in culture.

5

INTERPRETING THE "CRISIS" OF CULTURE IN COMMUNICATION THEORY

Lawrence Grossberg

The tradition of mass media effects research and the work of Innis, McLuhan, Dewey, Carey, Williams, and Habermas are explored through their images of the cultural crisis and how they conceive of communication.

As the number of different theories and approaches to mass communication grows, it becomes more obvious that a way is needed to talk about the relationships among them and to identify their similarities and differences. One approach that I propose to explore in this article is to compare the work of several theorists in terms of their visions of the "crisis,"[1] brought on by the processes of modernization, which faces contemporary culture.

[1] The term "crisis" may be inappropriate to describe this idea, as Professor Richard Grabau of Purdue has pointed out to me, since the "crisis of culture" is too long-term and in fact, seems to have become normality. Perhaps the notion would be better captured as "the threat of culture which is also a threat to culture." I will, however, use the term because of its long-standing presence within the literature.

Lawrence Grossberg is Assistant Professor in the Department of Speech Communication, University of Illinois at Urbana-Champaign.

Reprinted from "Interpreting the 'Crisis' of Culture in Communication Theory" by Lawrence Grossberg in the JOURNAL OF COMMUNICATION (Winter 1979). Copyright 1979 by the Annenberg School of Communications.

Relating mass communication theory to the idea of a cultural crisis is not without precedent. Alan Blum, 15 years ago, suggested that there may be a strong connection between researchers' assumptions about the inherent failures of modern society and their findings about how communication functions within it (4). Blum, however, fails to take into account that researchers' assumptions about the nature of the failure of modern society may differ from each other, and instead assimilated all of them under "mass society theory." By examining particular theorists' underlying assumptions concerning the principal danger confronting modern society, we may be able to better understand the diversity of views offered of the nature and function of communication in society.

To begin we must identify the variety of images of the cultural crisis operative in contemporary thought. I have distinguished six views of the crisis: informational, subjective, structural, interactional, transcendental and representational.[2] The first, a view of the crisis as one of information, is perhaps the most prevalent in our scientifically oriented culture. In this view the crisis is not located in the social changes that have taken place but rather, in our failure to respond properly to these changes. To know what would constitute a proper response, one must have accurate, descriptive information about the world. Thus, the crisis is located in our inadequate knowledge and in those attitudes which interfere with the acquisition of this information. This view is closely tied to an understanding of communication as a process of transmission, the movement of "pieces" of information from one place to another; it is through such a process as well that the attitudes and behaviors of individuals can be appropriately modified. Thus, we find the "informational" view often conjoined with a second view of communication, as a process of persuasion.

The "subjective" view of the cultural crisis is not very influential in mass communication theory, although its influence is strong in general discussions of modern culture. Basically, according to this position, the crisis lies in the loss of "true" subjectivity or individuality in the face of some claim of commonality and equality. The great achievements, values, virtues and creative potential of Western civilization are losing the battle (a metaphor quite common in such writers, e.g., Ortega y Gasset) to the masses gathered under the banner of democracy and "mass culture." It is not difficult to see why such a position would contribute little to mass communication theory—it unambiguously defines it as the enemy. Nevertheless, such a view embodies a commonly held view of communication: communication is the process of transmitting or sharing essentially private and subjective thoughts or meanings.

The third or "structural" view of the crisis of culture is built upon theories of symbolic structures or systems. These systems act as filters or mediating screens located between man and the world, and are the source of the meanings and interpretations we give to our experiences. Thus, the crisis of modern culture is understood as the domination of some particular symbolic structure and the subsequent control that structure has over our world view. Communication, in

---

[2] This typology of views is derived from Grossberg (12). In that work, I have attempted to construct a typology of philosophies of meaning and language.

such a view, belongs to the symbolic structures or codes rather than to the individuals who appear to use them. It is the system rather than the speaker which is the source of meaning.

Perhaps the most common understanding of the cultural crisis is what can be described as the "interactional" view. In its simplest form, this view points to a lack of shared values, norms, and meanings underlying interpersonal relationships, and is closely tied to the idea that modern society involves a loss of community. Deriving from Tonnies' distinction between *Gemeinschaft* and *Gesellschaft*, this idea characterizes two forms of social organization—community and society. In community, people who are essentially alike and homogeneous in beliefs, values, and experiences are united by "reciprocal binding sentiments." The means of social control are informal and the individual is subsidiary to the social totality. On the other hand, society is built upon a formal, i.e., contractual, system of social control, and is unified not by sharedness but through a mutual dependence necessitated by an increased division of labor. Consequently, relationships become increasingly competitive and impersonal, the individual is isolated, increasingly insecure, and "alienated." In this view communication is conceived as an ongoing process of situated, symbolic interactions through which shared meanings are reciprocally negotiated and created, thus maintaining the fabric of social life.

The fifth or "transcendental" view of the crisis lays the blame squarely on the shoulders of our contemporary beliefs about the nature of being human. Insofar as we have increasingly come to think of ourselves as the masters of the universe and of our own existence, we have lost a sense of our rootedness, of our grounding in or dependence upon something outside of our understanding and control. Because we conceive of knowledge and language as tools for our projects, we use them to define the real as that which is amenable to our manipulations and control. Consequently, we cut ourselves off from that other domain which has traditionally served as a wellspring or foundation on which we may ground our sense of ourselves and the world. A "transcendental" view, not surprisingly, will try to reinsert the "transcendental" (grounding) nature of communication. Communication is not merely a tool to be used for some human purpose, whether that purpose is transmitting information or creating shared meanings. Instead, communication is seen as the source of social life, "a living process in which a community of life is lived out" (10, p. 404). Almost like a deity existing outside human existence as its cause, communication is posited as a given rather than a human creation. It is the source of the possibility of social life and shared meaning, for it is only within communication that intersubjectivity becomes possible. A "transcendental" view points to communication as having already opened up the space in which interaction can occur before we can attempt to manipulate it as a medium for our projects.

The final, "representational" view of the cultural crisis has not yet entered into discussions of mass communication, but deserves to be mentioned because of its increasing exposure through the work of Roland Barthes and Michel Foucault (2, 9). Basically, in such a view, the contemporary crisis is the result of the enduring power of a number of "myths," in particular the myth of the subject and the myth of meaning. While we have increasingly lost faith in the ability of signs to carry meaning (either as a subjective reference back to a subject or an objective reference to a world), we find ourselves unable to accept the consequences of the loss of these myths. Because these theories are relatively recent, however, it is difficult to project their possible implications for communication theory.

> *Using these six views of the cultural crisis,*
> *I shall next identify how they operate*
> *in a number of current theories, beginning*
> *with the so-called mainstream or effects research.*

The roots of communication "effects" research are in the liberal *Weltanschauung*. Liberalism, it has often been noted, is historically connected with the various processes of modernization: the growth of democracy, of science, and of industrialization. It is not surprising, therefore, that its staunchest supporters have arisen within the United States. Liberalism can be characterized in terms of three basic assumptions: individualism, science and progress.

The assumption of the absolute value and primacy of the individual is most obvious in the liberal theory of political freedom which granted rights to the individual based upon the laws of nature. This belief in the autonomous self was expressed in an atomistic theory of society, i.e., the view that society is created through the free agreement of individuals. Faith in science is grounded in the autonomy and ability of human (i.e., individual) reason, and involves a unique combination of rationalism and empiricism. It was assumed that the individual mind could discover the laws governing the machinery of the universe through scientific observation and objective reason. Consequently, ignorance replaced sin as the great evil, salvation was information, and power the reward. A belief in progress, the inherent forward motion of human history, was necessary as an argument against both pessimistic interpretations of history and views of man which challenged his autonomy (e.g., Freud, Darwin). It is this optimistic vision of the future, built upon a metaphysical individualism and an epistemological scientism, which gave American social thought in general, and communication theory in particular, its own unique flavor.

The liberal view of the cultural crisis serves to define significant aspects of contemporary mass communication research.[3] Although most contemporary mainstream researchers no longer recognize their debt to the liberal *Weltanschauung*, that does not lessen its foundational significance for this tradition.

The liberal definition of the crisis, then, would be most closely related to the "informational" view, through a belief in the efficacy of knowledge. Historically, liberals acknowledged a crisis brought on by the processes of modernization, but they tended to ascribe it to ignorance rather than social change. The crisis for them was merely a new form of a problem that has existed throughout human history: ignorance, ideology, and the tyranny of authority. It was in-

[3] The works of Daniel Bell, Edward Shils, and David M. White provide good examples of the liberal response to mass society.

appropriate to locate the crisis in a new form of social organization or new modes of communication. On the contrary, for the liberal the new forms of social organization and of communications opened up, perhaps for the first time, the possibility of a society built on the free exchange of ideas and information between rational individuals. Community has not been destroyed; instead, patterns of interpersonal association have become more rational and open to choice. The real crisis was located in the need for objective (i.e., non-ideological) information on which to base decisions; once scientific research had gathered this information, ways of disseminating it would have to be found. The result of this would be the creation of a democracy built upon a process of rational decision making and scientific problem solving.

> *Therefore, in the liberal view, the study of*
> *the role and effects of the new mass media*
> *was essentially to fight the crisis of ignorance*
> *and ideology under the banner of individualism and science.*

The commitments to individualism and science characterize the commonality of contemporary mainstream communication research. As a result of the commitment to individualism, communication was seen in terms of its relationship to individuals rather than to social forces or institutions,[4] and mass communication theorists turned to psychology and social psychology. Behaviorism, as the dominant psychology of that time, defined much of the early research. Newer psychological theories were gradually adopted by communication theorists, but the commitment to individualism and psychology has remained.

The study of communication was seen from its very beginnings as a scientific endeavor. This was a natural outgrowth of the liberal's view of the crisis as involving a loss of certainty and a lack of objective knowledge, conditions which intensified the threat of irrationality. Science provided both the model of successful rational thinking and the means for assuring its attainment by the masses (see 1, p. 431). Thus, for example, Lasswell argued that the function of science was to facilitate "efficient communication" where efficiency is understood as "the degree that rational judgments are facilitated" (18, p. 93).

More importantly, however, the faith in science required that researchers be able to objectively measure the concepts they used and to manipulate them experimentally. Consequently, the notion of communication itself had to be quantifiable and was defined in terms of its informational and influential value to provide the field with its necessary tools. For instance, Schramm, one of the leaders in the emergence of mass communication as an organized field of study, defines communication "simply by saying that it is the sharing of an orientation toward a set of informational signs" (19). While expressing the sentiment that information should be defined broadly, he nevertheless goes on to limit it to terms amenable to direct quantification: "It is any content that reduces uncertainty or the number of alternative possibilities in a situation" (19, p. 13). This

---

[4] This separates Dewey as well as Gerbner (11) from mainstream communication research.

supported the liberal's view that what needed to be communicated were scientifically derived descriptions of the environment.

There is, however, another side of communication which had to be considered. Communication was and continued to be used to manipulate the opinions and actions of individuals. Therefore the persuasive possibilities of communication required scientific investigation as well. Such investigations would potentially inoculate people against manipulation, and, in the right hands, this knowledge could be used to help construct a more rational society, one in which manipulation via communication would no longer be required.

Thus, mainstream mass communication theory can be directly related to the liberal interpretation of the modern crisis as essentially an informational one. The connection resulted in a series of methodological, normative and definitional decisions which still ground the mainstream tradition of theory and research.

> *Cultural theories, while united in their opposition*
> *to mainstream research, differ in their understanding*
> *of communication and the cultural crisis.*

Harold Innis was one of the first to include the relationship of communication and culture as a key element in his world view. Innis saw the crisis of culture, in this case for Canada, in terms of the threat of cultural domination. As has been perusasively argued by both Theall (20) and Carey (6, pp. 28–29), Innis saw Canada as poised between the then two largest empires—Britain and America. In addition to the socioeconomic ties with Britain and America which dated back to Canadian origins, the time at which Innis wrote was marked by the increasing effectiveness and sophistication of American communication systems. Built upon an economically based technology, the U.S. communications, he felt, struck "at the heart of cultural life in Canada" (17, p. 19). It is not surprising, therefore, that Innis articulated an interpretation of the role of communication in cultural life built upon the central images of empire and bias.

His reading of economic history led him to focus on the role of communication (and transportation) through the lens of a technological determinism. Culture came to be seen as dependent upon, derived from, even "epiphenomenal of" (see 6) communication technology. Concerned with understanding the significance of the threats represented by the two empires, Innis looked to the "biases" of communication in its various technological forms. He argued that particular biases of communication were partly determinative of particular forms of social organization; the forms of social organization themselves, in turn, could be interpreted as distributions of political power based upon technologically determined "monopolies of knowledge."

Innis identifies two forms of bias: time-binding and space-binding. The British empire, with its great burden of tradition and history, was seen as embodying a time bias, and the American empire, so conscious of its spatial freedom and so committed to control and unity across that space, as embodying a space bias. As Canada was precariously located between two empires and between these two biases, it was natural to interpret the uniqueness of the Canadian experience in the possibility of mediating between these two. Innis clearly believes that the ideal culture would be one in which the two biases are balanced (see 16, p. 85). Innis, thus, provides a striking example of the way in which a theory of communication can be understood in the context of a perceived crisis at the heart of cultural life.

It is but a short step from Innis' rich and complex theory of communication to McLuhan's global observations.

McLuhan inherited from Innis a view of technological determinism, but he places it within the context of a global crisis of the alienation of consciousness and perception. McLuhan defines culture using three terms: oral, print, and electronic media. The first two correspond generally to Innis' time and space biases. But while Innis sees the idea as a mediation between opposing forces of technological determinism, McLuhan tends to see it as a return to many of the characteristics of the oral culture—the recreation of the whole human and community life. McLuhan's solution rests upon a concept of communication defined solely in terms of technology. The crisis results from the inability or unwillingness of contemporary cultures to flow with the historical forces of technological communications. The decreasing influence of McLuhan in communication theory may in part be due to his essentially passive rendering of the role of the individual in the crisis of culture.

Both Innis and McLuhan, then, hold a variation of a "structural" view of the crisis of modern culture. Communication is seen as a filter which organizes and interprets our social existence. The meaningfulness of our experience is not within our control, but is determined by the structure of a particular (in this case, technological) system. And for both, the crisis of culture is understood in terms of the domination of one system over other potential systems.

The Chicago school of social thought, rooted in pragmatism, is another uniquely American tradition, best represented in the works of John Dewey.

For Dewey and all the members of the Chicago school, the crisis of contemporary culture was at the very core of the American experience. Responding to Turner's "frontier thesis," Dewey argues that the true source of the American promise was embodied in the creation of communities in the Midwest and New England. It was here that the very spirit of democracy was made active in both political and everyday life. The crisis for Dewey was the eclipse of community and democracy resulting from the forces of modernization. Thus, the problem of community became central; his work focused on the role of language and communication in the creation of community.

Belman has argued that the work of the Chicago school, and of Dewey in particular, can be seen as three distinct but interrelated projects (3). First, like his colleague George Herbert Mead, Dewey was concerned with articulating a philosophical anthropology built upon the perception that language is the distinctively humanizing element: language gives humans the capacities of empathy and foresight. Second, he interpreted the social changes wrought by technological advances in communication and transportation as a move away from the shared experiences of community. These social changes meant that we could no longer have knowledge of the world and our fellow citizens from face-to-face interaction required for foresight and empathic understanding. Instead, technology had made individuals dependent upon strangers who were separated from them by space and cultural experience. And for Dewey the idea of community life defines democracy; it is the political face of the community, the idea born of association. The new communication technology, then, caused the demise of face-to-face communication and with it, the demise of community and democracy.

Dewey is not content, however, to conclude on such a pessimistic note. His third project dealt with the viability of democracy in the modern eye. Ironically, it is the technology of communication which provides Dewey with hope for a rebirth of democracy. Although the new media elided face-to-face communication, they also could create a new kind of empathic understanding among all citizens and present the public with the information it needed to make rational decisions once again. The new technology, wedded to an unfettered social science, provided the remedy for the disease it had spawned.

This tension in Dewey's work—communication is both the cause of and the cure for the loss of social community and political democracy—is characteristic of the Chicago school. Communication is understood simultaneously as technology and the process of communication. Within the context of this "interactional" view of the crisis, Dewey refused to accept the possibility that these defined antagonistic views. The liberalism of pragmatism gave him a fundamental faith in both communication and science, while his own historical interpretations showed that these were the enemy.

> *Although their faith in science has often linked*
> *the Chicago school to the mainstream effects tradition,*
> *there has been a recent attempt to purge*
> *the scientism from their theory by James Carey.*

In Carey's interpretation, the meaningfulness of language is no longer seen in terms of foresight and consequences. He focuses instead on its symbolic content. Consequently, the problem of interpreting the meaning of symbols and cultural rituals becomes central. However, like Dewey, Carey draws an indivisible link between communication and community. The crisis of the age is still the decline of community, but Carey resists making technology the villain. Although he accepts Dewey's historical arguments, Carey asserts that community and democracy are in eclipse because of the models of communication we assume in our lives. In other words, as a result of conceiving of communication in particular ways, we have created forms of social relationships precluding the possibility of community life. Carey seeks to articulate a theory of communication allowing us "to enlarge the 'human conversation' by comprehending what others are saying" (7, p. 189).

Carey sees communication as the process whereby "we first produce the world by symbolic work and then take up residence in the world we have produced" (5, p. 16). Thus, Carey avoids the tension, within pragmatism, of seeing language and communication both in scientific/technological terms and in terms of the symbolic construction of reality. On the other hand, his commitment to social democracy as the political form of community life and his perception that "problems of communication are linked to problems of community, to problems of the kinds of communities we create and in which we live," are clearly built upon a vision of the crisis he shares with Dewey (5, p. 19). By purging communication of its scientistic overtones, Carey avoids the potential reduction of communication to technology. This move is necessary if only because Dewey's faith in the processes of communication technology and science proved to be unwarranted. If viewing the cultural crisis as the eclipse of community is not to result in pessimism, Carey's attempt to unite communication and community in a theory of the symbolic creation of reality is indispensable. It also makes clear the connection between an interactional view of the crisis and a particular way of talking about the process of communication.

> *The work of Raymond Williams, like that*
> *of Dewey, can be seen as a direct response*
> *to the experience of modernization (25).*

Williams also experienced modernity in terms of mobility and recognized the problem of community as central. "What community is, what it has been, what it might be . . . these related themes are the dominant bearing. For this is a period in which what it means to live in a community is more uncertain, more critical, more disturbing as a question both to societies and to persons than ever before in history" (24, p. 12).

But Williams never experienced, as did Dewey, the *loss* of community life, the slow and invisible destruction of the community under the constant pressure of the forces of modernization. Rather, he found his life dislocated, existing between *two* communities, between cultures in a "border country . . . between custom and education, between work and ideas, between love of place and an experience of change," and we might add, between intelligence and fellow-feeling, between education and class (25, p. 197). The questions he asked were drawn from his own experience of existing between two communities, the working-class culture of his family and the middle-class intellectual community of the university, and being unable to belong to either because the cultures defining them were so far removed from one another.

As a result, Williams sees the crisis of contemporary culture in terms of the "knowable community" and a "common culture." It is increasingly difficult for us to understand the concrete experience of community life, he argues, for we must move between communities. Each has its own social relationships and language; each has its own way of seeing the world. As long as one remains outside of a culture, one can not fully participate in the community life. The problem of the knowable community is that of "finding a position, a position convincingly experienced, from which community can begin to be known" (24, p. 17). For Williams, the crisis of culture is not the absence of community but the absense of understanding and of appropriate ways to share that understanding. This points to the need for a "common culture" as a "position" or grounding process from which communication and understanding between cultures is possible (22, pp. 316–317).

But a common culture could not merely be another way of seeing the world, imposing itself upon the cultures of existing classes and communities. Williams' view of a common culture would not reduce cultural diversity. Instead, he sees it as "a common process of participation in the creation of meanings and values" (23, p. 34). Culture is, then, simultaneously the particular structure of experience defining a particular community ("the structure of feeling") and the general activity of offering, evaluating, and sharing new meanings and experiences within the context of already shared meanings (the "community of process"). Seen in this way, the problem of common culture is identifiable as a "transcendental" view of communication.

The crisis of contemporary culture then resides in precisely the fact that such a common culture does not exist. There is no point (or process) outside of particular communities which allows us to communicate. Williams finds the reasons for this absence in an analysis of the actual conditions of communication and culture. As a Marxist, he finds that community is also "a social system containing radical inequalities and conflicts of interests" (26, p. 149). The interests of one group dominate those of others—defining their own forms of experience and social relations as the only legitimate ones. We must, therefore, attend to "the interests and agencies of communication" (26, p. 120).

Insofar as culture is dominative, communicative forms and practices will embody relationships of inequality and passivity; the possibility of participation in the process of culture is denied by the hegemony of the dominant culture. Communication, then, must be studied in the context of its role in the processes of culture and domination. To the extent that communication is a creative act of individuals, it cannot be reduced to technology, objects, or structures. It must be seen as forms of activity which define the possibilities of community. To the extent that the contemporary forms of communication exclude people from participation in the cultural process and inhibit the creation of a common culture, they are in the service of some dominative culture. And the problem of communication becomes "the problem of revolutionary politics" (23, p. 297). It is this "long revolution" leading towards a "transcendental" common culture which underlies the entire theoretical structure of Williams' view of communication.

Like Williams, Jürgen Habermas sees the crisis of contemporary culture in terms of domination and communication.

At the social level, Habermas sees the contemporary crisis within the sphere of motivation and culture. The crisis has been displaced, he argues, from the social spheres of economics and politics to the individual domain of social interaction. The crisis of capitalism in the modern world results from its demand for and lack of legitimation as it increasingly fails to meet the needs of the members of society. This "legitimation crisis" has been transformed into a crisis of motivation, in which the individual can no longer find norms and values to sustain his everyday decisions. According to Habermas, the solution preferred by the state is to demand loyalty by restricting the possible criteria of truth.

In one of his early works, Habermas identified three "quasi-transcendental" interests underlying human knowledge and activity (13). The *technical* interest underlies material labor as purposive-rational activity, the *practical* interest underlies communicative interaction, and the *emancipatory* interest underlies critical reflection and revolutionary praxis. Each is conceptually tied to a particular form of knowledge and truth. The capitalist solution to the crisis of the modern age, Habermas argues, has been to attempt to make technical rationality the only acceptable form of truth, thus denying the possibility of the practical and critical conceptions. Rational life, on the other hand, requires the recognition that each of the three interests has a legitimate place in human affairs, and that each provides a check on the claims of the others by providing the grounds for a particular set of activities and social relations.

Habermas' discussions of communication are an attempt to justify the demands of these alternative conceptions of truth. He has attempted to do this by developing a "theory of communicative competence" (14) in which he demonstrates that communication presupposes claims of truth and validity outside the conventions of technical rationality. Rationality within human affairs assumes the possibility of an ideal speech situation, that is, of an interaction within a structure of undistorted communication. Communication will be undistorted when all participants have the abilities to engage in the various forms of communicative action equally.

On a first reading of Habermas, it seems that he holds a "structural" view of the crisis—modern society is characterized by the domination of a scientific world view and rationality. A closer examination, however, reveals that the three interests serve as necessary grounds from which communication is possible. It is not merely a question of one system dominating others, but of one "quasi-transcendental" interest negating the other two.

> *In this article I have tried to suggest that there is*
> *a close connection between how a theorist conceives of*
> *communication and his image of the crisis of culture.*

This relationship between communication and culture has implications for the ethical dimensions of communications study. Numerous writers reject the notion of a value-free social science, and raise instead the possibility of evaluating and discussing various theories on the basis of their ethical implications. For example, Carey has argued persuasively that "the wide-spread social interest in communication derives from a derangement in our models of communication and community. . . . Our existing models of communication are less an analysis than a contribution to the chaos of modern culture" (5, p. 20). For

Carey, the study of communication must not only attempt to describe and analyze the processes of communication in everyday life, but must also locate itself in a broadly based ethical concern to find "a way in which to rebuild a model of and for communication of some restorative value in reshaping our common culture" (5, p. 21).

In fact, the study of communication seems to have obvious ethical dimensions as soon as the researchers face questions of policy and normative concerns. But it is often difficult to draw the ethical implications of theoretical positions directly out of the more descriptive writings. The notion of cultural crisis, however, allows us to look at the ethical dimensions of theories less directly. It accomplishes this in two ways. First, it locates the notion of culture at the heart of communication theory; and the concept of culture includes a moral dimension at its very core. Williams has demonstrated this in his attempt to trace the historical development of the meaning of the term. The concept of culture, in his view, originally pointed at an attempt by a literary elite to argue that the new forces of change have been divorced from the critical processes of critical and moral evaluation. Consequently, they sought to find some criterion, source, or locus of value which could serve to render judgment on the rapidly expanding forces of modernization. Thus, in Williams' analysis, the very idea of culture represents "a general reaction to a general and major change in the conditions of our common life. Its basic element is its effort at total qualitative assessment" (22, p. 295). The continuing presence of this normative dimension of culture is still obvious in the complexity of meanings surrounding the concept.

Second, the question of the crisis facing modern man and culture raises a normative question in terms of the future survival of human and humane existence. The notion of a cultural crisis implies some image of an ideal culture, or at least of a culture not in crisis. And since culture is, broadly speaking, the framework within which an individual lives, the notion of a cultural crisis must have a conception of an ideal form of human existence underlying its judgment. Of course, this is not to say that such an ideal must or even can be explicitly articulated. Thus, an understanding of the relationship of communication and cultural crisis raises the ethical question in terms of the ethical foundations rather than implications of communication theories.

Moreover, there is also a theoretical reason making the identification of such normative dimensions desirable, namely, that of raising the possibility of making comparative evaluations of alternative perspectives. Such evaluations are difficult, if not impossible, on the basis of the epistemological, methodological, and metaphysical assumptions of theories. One is no more likely to gain agreement on the criteria to be used in judging such assumptions than on those used to judge the theories themselves. Similarly, comparisons on the basis of the ethical implications of theoretical positions do not fare much better. The notion of a cultural crisis, however, might provide a partial solution to this problem. One could reasonably attempt to compare and evaluate alternative conceptions of the cultural crisis. Such conceptions are neither purely normative nor descriptive. Certainly, their descriptive claims are open to question. We can inquire into (a) the adequacy and accuracy of the description of the modern age and (b) the comprehensiveness of the description. For each theory we can ask whether there are good reasons to accept or reject its characterization of the crisis and whether its characterization can be encompassed by or can encompass other conceptions of the threat to culture.[5] The very possibility of such critical comparisons is a potential contribution to our reflections on communication theory.

REFERENCES

1. Albig, William. *Public Opinion*. New York. McGraw-Hill, 1939.
2. Barthes, Roland. *Mythologies* (Translated by Annette Lavers). New York. Hill and Wang, 1972.
3. Belman, Lary S. "John Dewey's Concept of Communication." *Journal of Communication* 27(1), Winter 1977, pp. 29–37.
4. Blum, Alan F. "Popular Culture and the Image of the *Gesellschaft.*" *Studies in Public Communication* 3, Summer 1961, pp. 145–158.
5. Carey, James W. "A Cultural Approach to Communication." *Communication* 2, 1975, pp. 1–22.
6. Carey, James W. "Canadian Communication Theory: Extensions and Interpretations of Harold Innis." In Gertrude J. Robinson and Donald F. Theall (Eds.) *Studies in Canadian Communications*. Montreal: McGill University, 1975, pp. 27–60.
7. Carey, James W. "Communication and Culture." *Communication Research* 2, 1975, pp. 173–191.
8. Foucault, Michel. *The Order of Things*. New York: Pantheon Books, 1970.
9. Gadamer, Hans-George. *Truth and Method*. New York: Seabury Press, 1975.
10. Gerbner, George. "Communication and Social Environment." In *Communication: A Scientific American Book*. San Francisco, Cal.: W. H. Freeman, 1972, pp. 111–120.
11. Grossberg, Lawrence. "Language and Theorizing in the Human Sciences." In Norman K. Denzin (Ed.) *Studies in Symbolic Interaction*, Volume 2. Greenwich, Conn.: J. A. I. Press, in press.
12. Habermas, Jurgen. *Knowledge and Human Interests* (Translated by Jeremy J. Shapiro). Boston, Mass.: Beacon, 1968.
13. Habermas, Jurgen. "Towards a Theory of Communicative Competence." In Hans Peter Dreitzel (Ed.) *Recent Sociology 2*. New York: MacMillan, 1970, pp. 114–148.
14. Innis, Harold A. *The Bias of Communication*. Toronto: University of Toronto, 1951.
15. Innis, Harold A. *Changing Concepts of Time*. Toronto: University of Toronto, 1952.
16. Lasswell, Harold D. "The Structure and Function of Communication in Society." In Wilbur Schramm and Donald F. Roberts (Eds.) *The Processes and Effects of Mass Communication* (rev. ed.). Urbana, Ill.: University of Illinois, 1971, pp. 84–99.
17. Schramm, Wilbur. "The Nature of Communication Between Humans." In Wilbur Schramm and Donald F. Roberts (Eds.) *The Processes and Effects of Mass Communication* (rev. ed.). Urbana, Ill.: University of Illinois, 1971, pp. 3–53.
18. Theall, Donald F. "Communication Theory and the Marginal Culture: The Socio-aesthetic Dimensions of Communication Study." In Gertrude J. Robinson and Donald F. Theall (Eds.) *Studies in Canadian Communications*. Montreal: McGill University, 1975, pp. 7–26.
19. Williams, Raymond. *Culture and Society 1780–1950*. New York: Harper and Row, 1966.
20. Williams, Raymond. "Culture and Revolution." In Terry Eagleton and Brian Wicker (Eds.) *From Culture to Revolution*. London: Sheed and Ward, 1968.
21. Williams, Raymond. *The English Novel From Dickens to Lawrence*. New York: Oxford University, 1970.
22. Williams, Raymond. *The Country and the City*. New York: Oxford University, 1973.
23. Williams, Raymond. *Television: Technology and Cultural Form*. New York: Schocken, 1975.

[5] My own inclination would be to argue that each of the six views is broader than the previous ones and attempts to incorporate and account for previous ones as limited cases.

Many argue that much of the research on the Third World is bankrupt because of the use of the Western model. Just plain bad research and bad social science are the real reasons for the bankruptcy, according to James Halloran. This is a beginning proposition in his hard-hitting critique of past research done by outsiders in the Third World. He contends that future research must be carried out by Third World scholars, with a critical perspective, and must provide the basis for intelligent communication policies. The research must be rigorous in more than method, focusing on and contributing to a theory of society. Celebration of the dethronement of positivism is not enough, says Halloran. Critical, sociological, policy-oriented research is what is needed. Halloran fears that the emergence of "warring" schools, bound by dogma rather than rigorous research, may dominate unless disciplined scholars are willing to reflect honestly on their work and to devote allegiance to independent scholarship that challenges the imbalance and inequities of existing social order. He outlines 15 basic research questions and priorities for the field. Dr. Halloran is president of the International Association for Mass Communication Research (IAMCR) and director of the Centre for Mass Communication Research, University of Leicester. This paper was first delivered at the inauguration of CIESPAL's new headquarters in Quito, Ecuador, in May 1979.

6

THE NEED FOR COMMUNICATION RESEARCH IN DEVELOPING SOCIETIES

James D. Halloran

Whatever part of the world we come from, we are all concerned with *development* in some way or other. As mass communication researchers, we examine, amongst other things, the relationships between means and ends: between social systems, institutional forms, and organizational structures, and declared communication policy, goals, and objectives. We seek answers to such questions as What institutional forms are most likely to help us attain the objectives of our communication policies? What structural changes will be required for the effective execution of our policy? How might media potential be used to satisfy basic communication needs? Despite clearly recognizable differences, these sorts of questions are common to all of us.

Of course, there are different conceptions and definitions of development, and different approaches to the use of communication in pursuing developmental goals. One can argue that it is not particularly useful to talk about

From James D. Halloran, "The Need for Communication Research in Developing Societies," original manuscript.

development, developing countries, or even communication as such. The history, development, and operation of media and other institutions within national frameworks means that research and analysis, if they are to be meaningful, must be designed and carried out within such frameworks.

One way of presenting this chapter would be to look at the communication/ development relationship in different national settings and see if some general principles could be extrapolated. However, here I shall look at the general developments and achievements of communication research over the past twenty years or so, and attempt to establish why communication research (more specifically, a certain type of communication research) is necessary in any country, irrespective of the stage of development.

I shall do this fully conscious of the implications and dangers of the method. I recognize (despite the important national differences within regions, to say nothing of the differences between regions—say Africa and Latin America) that most developing countries have something in common, particularly with regard to the various forms of imperialism and colonialism, the current implications of these, and a continuing economic/cultural dependency. This I take for granted, and in no circumstances would I wish to underplay it.

I also know that if my approach draws heavily on research experience in Western industrialized nations—as it inevitably does—I lay myself open to accusations of exporting Western research concepts, models, and methods that are not appropriate to Third World developmental problems. However, I take this point without fully accepting it. I think that here we have an issue that is frequently characterized by false conceptualizations and confusion. There is a problem—make no mistake about this—but it is not always well defined and, as a result, the right lessons are not always learned. Research on media and development has been and is being carried out in the Third World using developmental criteria and an overall approach that are totally inappropriate. But this is not because it is "Western research," whatever this may be; *it is because it is bad research, and bad social science.* As I hope to show, this research, with its inadequate models of society and limited notions of the communication process, is and always has been equally inapplicable and equally unsatisfactory in the industrialized nations where it was conceived.

A further difficulty arises because of the misunderstanding of this problem. The understandable concern about what is seen as research imperialism often takes the form of a demand that research in the developing countries be carried out by researchers from those countries. Up to a point, at practical and educational levels, there is something to be said for this. But it by no means solves the problem. In fact it may exacerbate it, if the native researchers have been trained (as they so often have) by those researchers from the industrialized nations who favor the inadequate approaches I have just mentioned. As Antonio Pasquali (1978) reminds us (although in another context), we need to beware of the "local collaborator" who tends to be more "obtuse," more "inflexible," and more "antinationalist" than his "principal."

I readily and happily recognize that there is some excellent research being carried out in developing societies, particularly here in Latin America, by home-based scholars. I fully appreciate that the critical exposure of the implications of the existing international information order and the interesting initiatives with regard to the development of a new order owe much to these scholars. But my point is that this research has more in common with "good critical research" in the West than with much of the conventional research still being carried out in the developing countries, irrespective of the country or region of origin of the researcher. There is a problem, then—a problem all researchers must face—but let us define it correctly. Accurate diagnoses are the sine qua non of effective remedies.

One final point on this matter: If we make the mistake of overemphasizing the distinctions between research in developing countries and research in the so-called developed countries, we play into the hands of those in my own and similar countries (and there are plenty of them) who are unable or unwilling to think in terms of communication policies and planning. "Communication policies may be needed in developing countries, but not in England or Europe" is not an uncommon attitude.

After working in mass communication research in many countries for many years, my firm belief (and an underlying principle of this chapter) is that, in any country, whatever the level of development, enlightened and intelligent communication policies depend on the information that only research can provide. Of course, the provision of such information is no guarantee that an intelligent policy (however this may be defined) will be formulated and executed. Still, let me emphasize that the provision of research data, even if not sufficient, is an absolute necessity.

However, as will be clear from what I have said already, I do not mean *any* research data, nor do I favor research at any cost or research for its own sake. Some research may hinder development, and much conventional research is implicitly or explicitly geared to serve the establishment and maintain the status quo.

In broad, general terms, I use "conventional research" with a mainly value-free, positivistic, empiricist, behavioristic, psychological emphasis. In saying this, however, I do not want to be seen as throwing the baby out with the bath water. Of course, there is much useful work that might fall under the above-mentioned headings. I must also emphasize that I am not opposed to rigorous methods, experimental work, quantification, and the like; but I am against an approach where "scientific" is defined solely in terms of method, and where little or no attention is given to theory, concepts, or the nature of the relevant substantive issues and their relationship to wider societal concerns.

This problem is not confined to communication research; it is central to the whole of social science. I have not the time here to deal with it at length, but I shall return to it briefly later in the chapter. For the time being, let me remind you that although many of us rightly welcome the dethronement of the type of positivism and abstract empiricism that ruled for so long, dethronement is not enough in itself. Something else has to be elevated and put in its place. Unfortunately, we have to admit that in recent years there have been some very strange claimants for the throne, most of which, whatever else may be said about them, can certainly not be accused of an obsession with (even an interest in) a rigorous, disciplined, systematic approach to communication problems.

PROSPECTUS FOR RESEARCH
IN THE THIRD WORLD

The type of research I think we require in all countries is what I would term critical, problem, and policy-oriented research, with a primarily sociological perspective. It is worth noting here that I make a distinction between policy-oriented research and policy research. The latter is frequently of the variety that seeks to bring about the efficient execution of policy and thereby make the existing system more efficient. On the whole, it is not concerned with asking questions about the validity of the system or challenging predominant values or suggesting alternatives. Policy-oriented research, on the other hand, ideally addresses itself to the major issues of our time, and is concerned with, amongst other things, questioning the values and claims of the system, applying independent criteria, suggesting alternatives with regard to both means and ends, and exploring the possibility of new forms and structures. It is not necessary to make an either/or issue out of these different approaches. We are not talking about incompatibilities, but about the different implications for policy and society of approaches that prevailed in the past (and that up to a point are still with us) and those that are now emerging. Put crudely, the conventional approaches of the past which characterized so much communication research served and supported rather than criticized or challenged.

I appreciate that it may be argued that to talk in terms of a critical, problem, and policy-oriented sociological approach may beg more questions than it answers. There are different sociological approaches, and it might be said, for example, that sociological functionalism may have more in common with psychological functionalism than it has with other, more critical sociological approaches. There is some truth in this, but even so I would still maintain that there is something meaningful and distinctive about the emerging critical sociological perspective referred to above, and most definitely something that marks it off from the approaches that prevailed in the past.

To summarize and perhaps oversimplify, the main characteristics of this emerging approach are, first, that it deals with communication as a social process; second, that it studies media institutions not in isolation but as, and together with, other institutions, and within the wider social context (nationally and internationally); and third, that it conceptualizes research in terms of structure, organization, professionalization, socialization, participation, and so on.

One of the clear implications of this is that all aspects of the communication process should be studied. The factors (historical, economic, political, organizational, technological, professional, personal, and so on) that impinge on the production process and determine what is produced demand close scrutiny. In addition, we should examine those factors that influence the use of that product. Previously, the emphasis in research was on use, reaction, effects, influence, and the like—not on ownership, control, structure, organization, and production relationships.

We have been emphasizing the need to carry out this type of research in Europe and, to a much lesser degree, in developing countries for the past fifteen years, and in view of what I said earlier about "good" and "bad" approaches to research it is most interesting for me to read that Antonio Pasquali, a prominent Venezuelan scholar, in his article "Mass Media and National Culture," makes the same general points, giving particular attention to the international/developmental context. The same basic principles and questions are relevant, *mutatis mutandis,* wherever the research is carried out. Moreover, this approach also shows the futility of studying communication in isolation, or of studying communication policies without reference to other related policies (educational, cultural, economic, social, and so on). The relationship between media policies and education policies and the implications and consequences of such relationships in different countries would make an excellent subject for comparative international research.

Research might also address itself with some benefit to some of the other problems to which Pasquali refers in his article. Simple categorizations or classifications in terms of media systems of institutions may tell us little beyond the superficial and the obvious, and may even obscure important differences at a more fundamental, cultural level. Pasquali advises us not to make hasty inferences about the nature of the relationships between media and culture and the overall social implications of these relationships from superficial structural data. It used to be common (and it still happens in some fields) to infer effects from an analysis of media content. More recently there has been an equally erroneous tendency to make statements about content, influence, consciousness, and social consequences generally, solely from studies of ownership and control. As Pasquali states, the researcher has to be very careful here, for there is nothing automatic or mechanical about these linking processes. This is another area calling for careful, systematic, disciplined, comparative research, and where we need to be on our guard lest we uncritically accept attractive slogans and ready-made, oversimplified formulae.

Earlier I referred to the critical, questioning nature of the type of research I so obviously favor. The questioning of basic assumptions, conventional wisdom, media myths, and the accepted ways of doing things, together with the suggestions that the media should be demystified and the call for an exploration of alternatives, are bound to be seen as a threat and a challenge by those who nationally and internationally own or control the media, who regulate the global flow of communication, who will benefit from the maintenance of the status quo, and who stand to lose from any changes.

We need to remember that on the whole the medium is the system, that it tends to be elitist, primarily one-way, operating from the top downwards, and serving the interests of those in power. I suggest that although there are important differences from country to country, this basic pattern is well nigh universal, and that a similar pattern prevails internationally.

If this is disputed, then systematic comparative research based on an agreed operationalization of such concepts as participation, access, manipulation should give the correct answer, but this is easier said than done. However, if we really wish to understand the full human and social implications of different forms and arrangements, if we wish to see what participation actually means in terms of human behavior and involvement, and then explore the possibility of alternatives, this is the sort of research we must be prepared to do. Knowledge derived from such work might also help us to challenge the myths and false claims, and eliminate some of the cant and hypocrisy that all too frequently characterize the debate on these and related issues.

We are not playing at games—we are not dilettante or remote academics engaged in research for the sake of research. Once we adopt the critical stance, once we accept our responsibilities as independent researchers, scholars, and intellectuals, we shall inevitably find ourselves in conflict with extremely powerful national and international forces convinced that they (and the world at large) have nothing whatsoever to gain from the critical investigations we propose. They know all they want to know about communication and the media. The current situation suits them fine and its maintenance or extension is what they seek. Alternative forms of thinking are not welcome because they might lead to alternative systems. What is more, they are in a most favorable position, because they set the agenda and control the discourse.

In passing, it is worth remembering the massive, well-orchestrated counterattack mounted by the international media establishment against the UNESCO-supported and -related research that exposed the nature and inequity of the international information order and suggested, inter alia, how the imbalance might be redressed.[1] It is also worth noting, particularly in view of what I said earlier about the differences between conventional and critical research, that this was the first time that UNESCO-related research had ever attracted the attention of the established media powers. But then, this is not surprising, for the conventional research approaches that prevailed at UNESCO, at least until the end of the 1960s, tended to serve the existing system rather than challenge it.[2]

We have, then, clear responsibilities as intellectuals and scholars to continue to probe, to question and to challenge. But just as we rightly question and seek to change the lack of balance in the international information order, so we ought to do our utmost to ensure that we are not open to attack from the international media establishment because of the lack of balance in our own research activities, or because we have failed to define the problems or apply our critical criteria within a universal context.

Of course, we cannot do everything at once. We have to select from many areas of possible enquiry, and it is perfectly legitimate to establish research priorities and make choices accordingly. But it is neither legitimate nor responsible for the researcher to be partial, blind, or perhaps just simply naive to such a degree that an outsider might assume that there are parts of the world so perfect that critical criteria—say with regard to access, participation, and manipulation—need never be applied. Neither is it very wise tactically to adopt such a stance or to slip unsuspectingly into such a position. As we have already seen, any challenge to the established order will lead to counterattacks from the powers that be—and they are powerful. We should do our utmost to ensure that there are no unnecessary loopholes in our defense. We should not leave ourselves open to criticism of imbalance in one area (our research) when we seek to condemn it in another.

DIFFERENCES BETWEEN OLD AND NEW
RESEARCH APPROACHES

I shall deal now with some more specific aspects of communication research in an attempt to illustrate some differences between the new and the old approaches. I have already mentioned some of the essential features of the critical sociological approach. I have also suggested that the emphasis by the conventional researcher in media and development research, within the unquestioned framework of the Protestant ethic, on such psychological or individualistic concepts as empathy, psychic mobility, development consciousness, imitation, and attitude change, reflected an inadequate understanding of both the concept of development and society and the nature of the communication process.

We now know that to restrict our understanding of media influence to that which can be assessed by way of attitude change, imitation, or identification presents a very misleading picture of the part played by the media in society. It is not possible in this short chapter to dwell at length on the question of influence or effects, but over the past few years we have moved to a position where we now think of media influence in terms of association, amplification, legitimation, agenda setting, and so on. We also take into account units other than the individual as we attempt to assess the influence of the media on other institutions, in defining social reality, and on culture and society more generally. Of course, these phenomena are not so easily susceptible to what passes for scientific measurement as are attitude change and imitation, and in one way this is what has caused a problem. The issues deemed worthy of investigation have tended to be those which could be measured by the *approved* available techniques. I would argue for a more flexible, imaginative, insightful, adventurous, less hidebound approach to the study of media influence than we have had in the past. But in doing this I must emphasize that I am neither seeking an easy way out nor offering support for some of the sloppy, unsystematic, impressionistic, soft options that have appeared in recent years. This challenging situation calls for more ability, more imagination, more insight, more discipline, more dedication, more effort—not less.

We may also find evidence of another hangover from the past when we examine communication and information (Halloran, 1979). There are many examples across a wide range of communication issues (such as development, health education, family planning, agricultural innovation and adoption, social action, and social policy) where one still has the impression that those responsible for information campaigns and educational programs work on the assumption that their main, perhaps even their sole, task is to provide information, and all will be well.

Yet research shows this is not the case. The adoption of a sociological perspective where the information process and the relevant individuals and groups are studied in the appropriate historical and social contexts illustrates the importance of many other nonmedia factors. People may possess the necessary information on any given issue, but may not possess the social skills to translate the information into the appropriate social action. Others may possess the information too, but they might also have conflicting information or opposing attitudes or experiences from the past that act as obstacles and get in the way of the translation. The effective conversion and utilization of information may also depend on other institutional arrangements and support factors in the social structure generally. All these intervening factors are extremely important in any analysis of communication information problems. An analysis may indicate, for example, that in any given campaign it would be more fruitful to concentrate on the transfer, the obstacles, the intervening factors, the conversion and utilization of information, and so on, than on its provision. Generally, we may say that information is a necessary but never a sufficient cause of social action, although there are even some instances when it may be used as a substitute for action.

MASS COMMUNICATION RESEARCH PRIORITIES

I referred earlier to research priorities, and I also suggested that as far as research problems were concerned, despite the differences stemming mainly from dependency relationships, both developing countries and the so-called developed countries have many things in common. Several years ago I listed my own research priorities—the sort of questions I felt we ought to be asking, nationally and internationally, about the role of the media and the nature of the communication process (Halloran, 1974). In general, the list still holds, although more progress has been made in some areas than in others. It should be noted, of course, that the questions, as listed, are not mutually exclusive.

The questions I asked were as follows:

(1) In what way, to what extent, and over what time period will the new developments in media technology render existing communication technology obsolete?

(2) Does the "communications revolution" represent an entirely new factor in the socialization process and, if so, how?

(3) Does the new technology demand an entirely new institutional and organizational structure, or can existing structures be suitably adapted?

(4) How should one decide between (a) private interests and public control? (b) public accountability and freedom of speech?

(5) Many decisions in media policy are made in the name of "the public good" and "the national interest." But what do these terms really mean, and who decides what is good?

(6) Granted existing structures of newsgathering, selection, and presentation, is it not inevitable that the "free flow of information" will work to the advantage of those who possess the information and the means to disseminate it?

(7) Is it not time that the media were demystified, and that we began to question the restrictions and the possible tyranny of professionalism? Must we always have the few talking about the many to the many?

(8) Will the multiplicity of channels made possible by the new technology lead to cultural diversity and better opportunities for minority interests? In any case, who will control the software, the input, or the programs?

(9) Is public monopoly the only real guarantee of diversity?

(10) Granted existing systems of ownership and control and the prevalence of Western news values, are the media ever likely to provide the amount and quality of information necessary for people to act intelligently in a participatory democracy?

(11) Is there not a grave risk that we shall become paralyzed by an overload of information? How much can we tolerate? How much can we understand?

(12) Internationally, will the "communications revolution" lead to an increase or a decrease in the gap between the haves and the have-nots?

(13) As far as the developing countries are concerned, is not the main, perhaps even the sole, concern, how to use the media in the interests of national identity and development? Never mind objectivity, impartiality, or balance.

How can one harness the new technology for national as distinct from sectional objectives?

(14) How can we guard against the possible homogenizing influence of the new technology as traditional cultures may become swamped by the commercial off-loading of cheap alien material?

(15) What do we know about the processes of media influence?

At this stage, with the benefit of many years work in the field, I would now want to develop the point about cultural homogeneity and pose some additional questions about the Media and National Culture. I would also wish to give more attention to the very important question of participation.

Antonio Pasquali (1978), in calling for a redefinition of the concept of national culture as an operational aim, recognizes the dangers of extremism (Nazism, apartheid, and so on) but nonetheless feels that the concept is "sane and operative," the "positive nature" of which must be strongly defended against erosion by the mass media.

I share Pasquali's concern about the present position, particularly in "dependent" areas, and about the homogenizing influence of international mass media that have no respect for national cultures. But I am less optimistic than he is about arriving at a working definition—"the synthesis of the spiritual legacy of a national community"—that may be easily accepted, made meaningful, operationalized, and defended without bringing several other problems in its wake.

These differences undoubtedly reflect our different experiences in countries with different histories, at different stages of development, and differently placed with regard to dependency on international mass media. Differences in our interpretations of recent attempts to defend or recreate national culture may also be relevant. My interpretation leads me to look with some suspicion on what, in some countries, might be defended in the name of national culture—what will be promoted, what will be excluded, and the reasons behind these decisions and policies. Pasquali is not unaware of the problems involved in his approach, but What is a nation? and What is the identifiable unit of national culture? are questions which would appear to spring more readily to my lips than to Pasquali's.

I am also concerned about chauvinism, about narrow, inward-looking parochialism, about in-group solidarity being the other side of the coin or even a cause of out-group hostility, and about Gordan Zahn's feeling some years ago, after his study of German Catholics and Hitler's wars, that probably nationalism and patriotism were the only sins we still needed to worry about.

As will be clear, I have some reservations about the principles involved in the creation or maintenance of national culture, but this apart, I wonder if Pasquali's aims are realistic or if his objectives are capable of being attained.

It is not just a matter of changing the international media system and relying on the goodwill and high ideals of those who are so liberated from the alienating media. The problems associated with nationalism, and therefore related to national culture, were with us long before the establishment of the present international information order, and seem likely to outlive it. Of course, it need not always be like this; at several institutional levels appropriate changes could be made which might lead to radical changes elsewhere. Certainly the monitoring and evaluation of these changes and their consequences in different national contexts should now be high on the list of our research priorities. There may be differences of opinion, interpretation, emphasis, and optimism about some of the points just covered, but there is clear agreement on the importance of the subjects and on the need for research.

Participation is a key concept in this debate at both national and international levels, but it is not always precisely defined, uniformly interpreted, or consistently applied. There is plenty of lip service to the notion, but this is often little more than a thinly disguised coverup for the arrogance and intolerance of the media professionals and political technocrats who are likely to be impatient of experimentation and resistant to radical change. Efficiency is their watchword, and in their terms participation is not likely to be efficient or professional. A form of professional tyranny is never far from the surface.

Ideally we should be working toward situations wherein people will have the opportunity, and be encouraged, to participate at all levels in their own development by means of discussion, decision-making, involvement, and the like.

Unfortunately, the media systems of the world are not geared to this form of participation. The technology that might facilitate greater participation is available, but this availability is being countered by an increasing reluctance on the part of the communication establishment to share their powers in any meaningful way. So-called experiments in participation often serve little more than an alibi function. Moreover, it is not always appreciated that access and participation do not necessarily work in the same direction but often need to be balanced one against the other.

MASS COMMUNICATION RESEARCH AND
CULTURAL LIBERATION

It also needs to be emphasized that both national and international structural changes, although absolutely essential, can never be sufficient in themselves. Structural, organizational, and institutional changes should not be regarded as ends in themselves, but as means toward the achievement of the goals of individual development. We must have independent criteria relating to the human being that go beyond mere structure. Structural changes must be evaluated in terms of their contribution to the fulfillment of human communication needs, which we must be prepared to identify and spell out. Again, this is not an either/or situation, but we must pay attention to types of individuals *as well as* to types of society. We are in danger of forgetting this and seem to assume that a given type of society and set of institutional arrangements will inevitably be in the best interests of all individuals in that society. We should know, both from history and from the contemporary situation, that there is no guaranteed or automatic relationship between any given structure, on the one hand, and individual freedom and human development, on the other. Pasquali reminds us of this as he also reminds researchers of their responsibilities. Here is another vitally important area, calling for systematic comparative research. This is a real challenge to communication researchers, for they must continue to expose the imbalance and inequities of the existing order, seeking at the same time a more just order which itself must be evaluated in terms of the type of independent criteria just mentioned. Genuine, critical research is a continuing process; it must be applied without fear or favor to the new as well as to the old. We must be careful not to jump out of the frying pan into the fire by replacing the old, imbalanced system with one that rests more on slogans, tautologies, wishful thinking, and self-fulfilling prophecies than on substantiated achievements judged according to consistently applied criteria.

The reasons for these remarks may not be immediately obvious to Third World scholars, who are quite rightly preoccupied with changing a system that has exploited them for so long, and with achieving cultural liberation. I must emphasize that my warning does not stem from any judgment of Latin American research. But it does stem from my experience of recent trends and troubles in European research, and it would not be the first time the problems and prejudices of Europe found their way across the Atlantic. Briefly, the last twenty years or so have seen changes in mass communication research reflecting changes in social science generally. One of the outcomes, more apparent in Europe and Britain than in the United States, has been the development of a critical sociological approach that has challenged not only the supremacy of earlier, mainly positivistic, research approaches, but also the service and administrative functions of these approaches and the claims and presumptions of the media systems they serve. In more recent years similar challenges, perhaps representing an interesting fusion between regional initiatives in Latin America and the aforementioned critical approach, have also developed in this part of the world.

So far, so good. But there are those who now see a crisis in sociology that is bound to be reflected in some way or other in our own field of research. John Rex (1961) has argued that we have gone astray. He welcomed the dethroning of the old approaches but is not very happy with the new claimants and usurpers. Instead of the considered and thoughtful development of plural paradigms that enjoy complementary relationships, he fears that a situation has developed not of complementarity, but of conflict between "warring" schools. As he sees it, this situation is not marked by speculative and reflective approaches or by careful examination, consideration of alternatives, or the caution and tolerance that one might expect from social science, but by dogma, doctrinaire statements, selective use of evidence, unsubstantiated assertions, and, at times, a hostile intolerance. He likens the situation to the religious wars of the past. The firmly held positions brook no contradictions, and evidence must not be allowed to get in the way of faith. Like others who claim to be social scientists, he is more than a little worried about a situation where, if one hundred hypotheses derived from a theory or set of beliefs were invalidated in research, the theory might still remain inviolate. This certainly has little in common with the "rational, moderate and democratic" approach advocated by Pasquali.

I do not pretend to know the answers to all these problems, and I do not propose here to attempt to come to grips with the question of the relationships between ideology and social science. Suffice it to say that I share some of Rex's anxieties. I am afraid that the aims and objectives that I am sure we all share will never be attained if the atmosphere of intolerant warring schools prevails.

Several years ago that prominent European communication scholar, Kaarle Nordenstreng (1976), referred to the conventional research which at that time dominated the North American mass communication research scene as concerned with doing rather than with thinking. He was right to do this, and helped to promote a more thoughtful, critical approach to the communication problems of society. But we must not stop thinking now, just because we have made some progress. We must not fall into the trap of automatically, repetitively doing research without constantly reviewing our principles, premises, and assumptions. There is always the danger that we shall develop our own conventional wisdom, myths, and rigidities, which might become just as disabling as those which, with some success, we fought to replace. We must guard against this, engage more in self-examination, and hope for greater self-awareness. After all, these are the marks of scholarly enterprise.

It could be that my fears are exaggerated, and it might also be argued that what I have said is more appropriate to the European scene than to Latin America, where the very real practical problems related to dependency have still to be overcome. I accept this, and would also stress that I am basically optimistic. I look forward to change, to a new economic order, to a new information order, and to a situation where every researcher in any country will always be willing to examine alternatives and where he or she will always have the opportunity to do this. One of our main tasks should be to encourage the pursuit of these objectives in a rational, moderate, and balanced way. We rightly call for more balance in the international flow of information; let us apply the same principle to the development of our research activities and the dissemination of our results.

NOTES

1. See, for example *Mass Media in Society: The Need of Research,* Reports and Papers in Mass Communications 54, UNESCO, Paris, 1970. K. Nordenstreng and T. Varis, "Television Traffic: A One-Way Street," in *A Survey and Analysis of the International Flow of Television Material,* Reports and Papers in Mass Communications 70, UNESCO, Paris, 1974. *Proposals for an International Programme of Communication Research,* COM/MD/20, UNESCO, Paris, 1971. J. D. Halloran, *The Context of Mass Communication Research,* International Commissions of the Study of Communication Problems 78, UNESCO, Paris, 1980. K. Nordenstreng and H. I. Schiller (eds.), *National Sovereignty and International Communication,* Ablex Publishing Corporation, New Jersey 1979 (see bibliography and references). Righter, *Whose News? Politics, the Press and the Third World,* IPI, 1979.

2. See, for example, almost any of UNESCO Reports and Papers in Mass Communications before 1970, and also the works of Lerner and William Schramm, particularly Schramm's *Mass Media and National Development,* Harvard University Press, 1964.

REFERENCES

HALLORAN, James D. (1979) "Information and communication." ASLIP Proceedings 31, 1: 21-28, London, England.

——(1974) Mass Media and Society: The Challenge of Research. Leicester, England: Leicester University Press.

NORDENSTRENG, Kaarle (1976) "Recent developments in European Communications theory," in Heinz-Dietrich Fischer and John C. Merrill (eds.) International and Intercultural Communication. New York: Hastings House.

PASQUALI, Antonio (1978) "Mass media and national culture." Media Asia 5, 2: 62-67.

REX, John (1961) Problems of Sociological Theory. London: Routledge & Kegan Paul.

In this critical review of research, Sven Windahl proposes a synthesis of uses and effects models of mass communication. Windahl's model leads to a new research term, "conseffects," a synthesis of "medium content effects" and "gratification process consequences." His approach aims at minimizing the notion of basic needs as sources of media use. His model also pays more attention to media content and source motives than have previous uses and gratifications approaches. Windahl has a joint appointment as mass communication researcher in the Department of Information Techniques at Vaxjo University College and the Department of Sociology at the University of Lund in Sweden. This paper was originally presented at the Acapulco, Mexico, conference of the International Communication Association in 1980.

7

USES AND GRATIFICATIONS AT THE CROSSROADS

Sven Windahl

It has often been said that some of the criticisms of uses and gratification research are misleading because critics treat the approach as a single theory, when it is more correct to regard it as an umbrella under which several uses and gratifications theories and models may be found (Blumler, 1979). Criticisms of questionable points in what really are different models are then lumped together as if concerning a single uses and gratifications theory.

Even so, uses and gratifications theorists have so much in common that they seem to understand each other fairly well, and most of them would not reject a basic model such as this one by Linné and von Feilitzen (1972), shown in Figure 7.1. Here, the basic elements—needs, motives, media use, and media functions—are related in such a way that human needs, formed by social and individual characteristics, lead up to motives for need fulfillment. Some needs are perceived by the individual as possible to satisfy by means of mass media consumption or by some functional alternative. The uses made of the media content will have consequences on different levels. This model may be used as a point of departure when discussing the research efforts of the approach.

From Sven Windahl, "Uses and Gratifications at the Crossroads," original manuscript.

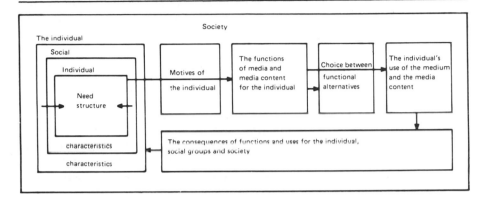

Figure 7.1: The Linné and von Feilitzen Uses and Gratifications Model

This kind of reasoning has resulted in several types of criticism. McQuail (1979) has summarized the criticism most commonly expressed like this:

(a) The approach is often said to be too individualistic in method and conception, which makes it difficult to tie to larger structures.

(b) The empirical research relies to a high degree on subjective reports of mental states and is therefore regarded as too "mentalistic."

(c) The models depict the audience as fairly active. They picture the audience as choosing selectively and freely among different media contents. The notion of such an active audience may be regarded as inconsistent with another assumption of this approach—namely, that motives for media use are determined by basic needs, social experience, and conditions.

(d) The approach assumes that media behavior is based on conscious or rational choice, which goes against research results saying that media use is habitual and nonselective.

(e) The approach shows little or no sensitivity to the substance and nuances of the media content itself.

To this may be added the criticism of the functionalistic character of the approach and its alleged conservatism.

Some of this criticism has been answered; some has not. But, let us ask, if the state of uses and gratifications research and theory is unsatisfying, is there a satisfactory solution?

This paper argues for a merger between two research traditions, that of uses and gratifications and that of effects. Depending on how one looks at this effort, it may either be regarded as a synthesis between the two traditions (a view that I prefer) or a stressing of the effect/consequence part of existing uses and gratification models. The uses and effects model which I propose could be seen either as a uses and gratification model with effect elements or an effects model, containing some uses and gratifications elements.

This is by no means the only possible merger. Uses and gratifications may also be tied to theories of socialization, and an orientation toward studies of culture will surely give other opportunities.

TOWARD A SYNTHESIS:
A USES AND EFFECTS MODEL

Probably a majority of communication researchers find the effects tradition and the uses and gratifications approach in opposition to each other. Swanson's (1979) description of the latter approach as "a dramatic break with the effects tradition of the past" is rather typical in this respect. Blumler (1979) describes its appearance as a reaction to the shortcomings in the study of short-term effects.

What, then, is different and new in the uses and gratifications tradition compared with effects research? (See Figure 7.2.)

One difference is that often expressed in the catchword that the effects tradition is interested in "what media do with people," whereas the gratifications tradition pays attention to "what people do with the media." There is supposed to be a difference between the two approaches in their view of the audience, a difference which could be summarized as that between action and reaction.

The concept of the active audience, stemming "from liberal-rational beliefs in human dignity and the potential of the individual for self-realization" (Blumler, 1977), plays an important role in the debate over the approach. Some power researchers earlier had attributed to the communicator and the media was transferred to the audience.

The term "active" is often used vaguely, although some attempts have been made to clarify it (Blumler, 1979). It may be remarked that the element of "activeness" is usually more strongly stressed in debates than in actual research. The notion of activeness leads to a picture of the audience as superrational and very selective, a tendency which invites criticism. Yet, no one would deny the existence of at least fairly active audience members. Indeed, this notion has been incorporated in most general mass communication models of today, and it has no doubt contributed considerably to a better understanding of audience behavior. The effects researcher most often looks at the mass communication process from the communicator's end, whereas his fellow colleague, using a uses and gratifications paradigm, starts at the other end, taking the audience member as a point of departure. One can easily verify this if one studies graphic models of the mass communication process, drawn by advocates for the different traditions.

In a strict sense, a uses and gratifications model is not a model of the mass communication process, but a model of the receiving process. This is an important characteristic of the approach compared with most effect models. In the gratifications tradition the stimulus side is more or less nonexistent,

	Effects approach	Uses and gratifications approach
Advantages	Social relevance Takes the whole communication process into account Interest in stimuli characteristics	Gives dynamic and nuanced description of the audience Audience member not completely passive Explains media use
Drawbacks	Audience member often depicted as completely passive and manipulated Mechanistic view of communication process common Explains effect too much in terms of stimuli	Stimuli disregarded Merely a receiver process model Exaggeration of audience member's rationality and activeness Uses mental factors (e.g. motives for explanation)

Figure 7.2: Advantages and Drawbacks of Two Approaches

which makes elements such as needs and motives too dominant in the process and may lead the researcher and the student to neglect the impact of elements such as communicator, intent, and media characteristics. This may be part of an explanation why mass media content itself gets so little attention by researchers of the "uses" school (McQuail, 1979).

The two approaches differ, finally, in their approach to the outcomes of the processes they describe. Effects researchers discuss the *effects of media content* on the audience, whereas the uses and gratifications researcher looks for *consequences of media use.* At first glance this may seem a rather trivial and obvious thought, but, keeping this distinction in mind, we may more easily discuss the nature of outcomes from mass communication processes.

To exemplify: The traditional effects researcher may be more interested in behavioral and attitudinal change. His fellow colleague, working within the gratifications approach, directs his attention to the question of whether a sought gratification is obtained or not or if an audience becomes dependent on a special medium. From now on in this article, the term "effect" will be used to denote outcomes of mass communication processes primarily caused by the media material itself or by factors tied to it, such as, say, trustworthiness of source. The term "consequence" will be reserved for outcomes where the *media use* and factors tied to it in themselves are the primary cause.

When aiming at some sort of synthesis between two scientific perspectives, it seems reasonable to look for similarities rather than differences. In this case the similarities are not difficult to find. Although the two traditions may be interested in different types of outcome, it is a fact that *both deal with outcomes* of the processes they describe.

Most gratifications researchers would include some kind of consequence in their paradigms, even if far from all of them take the step to do any empirical research about possible consequences (Katz et al., 1974). However, there are a number of consequences that should be of interest to the gratifications researcher, some of which have already been empirically demonstrated.

The fact that you get or do not get an expected gratification may be an important kind of consequence, which in turn may *influence* your *need structure.* Nordlund (1976) and Hvitfelt (1977) both discuss how the media consumer may become *dependent* on a special medium or on a special media content as a result of media use.

McQuail (Windahl and McQuail, 1979) stresses that media use may have consequences such as *dependency on a medium* or a communicator as well as on the formation of new needs and preferences, outcomes of the communication process which have hardly been systematically investigated.

The notion that differential mass media use may have consequences on higher, for example societal, levels, seems promising and interesting. This theme has been developed by, among others, Nordlund (1976), who maintains that preferences systematically distributed in a population may contribute to *widening gaps of knowledge and information.*

It has often been pointed out that the mere use of mass media and their content may lead to change of behavioral as well as cultural patterns. For example, TV-viewing replaces real interaction and that consumption of one medium gives less time for other cultural activities. Results obtained by Rosengren and Windahl (1977) indicate that for some categories mass media use as a substitute for interaction may lead to an increased degree of neuroticism.

Sometimes, consequences like these are treated as "effects," and it may be discussed as if these outcomes really are "consequences" as defined earlier. There are other "borderline studies" in which you have only to change "exposure" to "media use" to make an effect study into a uses and gratifications one and to do the reverse to make a claimed gratifications study into an effect one.

A USES AND EFFECTS MODEL

The model presented in this section will regard the uses and gratifications process, partly as a bundle of intervening variables—as argued by Klapper in 1963—partly as a system of independent variables. The model is eclectic. It has borrowed more elements from the "uses" tradition than from the effects one, but in the end it may look more of an effects model.

A natural starting point in the uses and gratifications tradition is the concept of need. Elliott (1974) argues that the use of need "is the source of most of the difficulties to be found in uses and gratifications research in general." He maintains that it easily gives rise to circular explanations and that, from a methodological point of view, it is difficult to measure. In my model, need is given a less dominant role. Needs may in some cases be externally imposed, sometimes as result of environmental factors (such as the need for escape originating in an unsatisfactory work situation). Nordlund's (1976) distinction between basic and derived needs is pertinent.

The audience member is guided by his expectations and by his perception of the media and their content, which is another way of saying that the communication process to a large extent contains subjective choices and interpretations. Naturally, however, no one in an audience has the possibility of making a complete choice among all kinds of media content. For one thing, access is a limiting factor.

As in many uses and gratifications studies, media use may be seen as a functional alternative to other activities. Rosengren and Windahl (1972) demonstrate, for example, that certain kinds of mass media consumption may serve as functional alternatives to interaction.

THE "USE" CONCEPT

Uses and gratifications researchers have often been accused of lack of precision in their vocabulary. Especially with respect to the concept of "use," this criticism is warranted. I have tried to specify the denotations of "use," as can be seen below. It would be of great interest to further discuss possible interpretations of the concept and their operationalizations in much the same way as Salomon and Cohen (1978) treat the concept of "television viewing." (See Figure 7.3.)

All these aspects of media use are relevant for predicting and explaining the outcomes of the receiving/consumption process. It seems as though especially the third aspect could be further developed. For example, one could add variables such as degree of perceived reality and of motivation (Werner, 1975).

Probably the three aspects of use could be supplemented with variables tapping the circumstances under which the media use takes place (alone/in company, media use as a primary/secondary activity, etc.). Different combinations of values on the three levels may be systematized, allowing 27 different combinations.

Differential combinations of values from such a table will probably lead up to differential outcomes. For example: A given amount of "use" of violent drama looked at by someone strongly identifying with the aggressors of the

Use 1: Amount of media use (for example TV-viewing)	Low	Medium	High
Use 2: Proportion of total amount of use being of specific type of content (e.g. entertainment)	Low	Medium	High
Use 3: Relation (for example identication) to specific type of content	None	Weak	Strong

Figure 7.3: Example of a "Use" Table

plays is probably more likely to result in an overt aggression than the same amount of use without the relation in question. Individuals could, hence, be qualitatively characterized by means of their location in a typology. Another possibility would be to build a composite index based upon the three types of use suggested here, and to characterize the individual quantitatively by means of his value in such an index.

I think that media use, defined as above, will serve as an important and useful intervening factor in the study of most effect processes.

EFFECTS, CONSEQUENCES, AND "CONSEFFECTS"

In our model we find three types of outcomes of communication/receiving processes, but it may sometimes be difficult to tell whether a certain outcome belongs to one type or another. First, there are *effects* of media content with media use as an intervening variable (in "use" the elements leading up to the media use such as needs, expectations, interests and motives are also included). Second, there are the *consequences* of processes where media use in itself is the most important cause of the outcome. Third, there are what may be called *"conseffects"* which are partly results of content mediated by use and partly results of media use in itself, thus a combination of the two types mentioned above. (See Figure 7.4.)

(1) Effects. In the model proposed here, the cause of the outcome is elements or characteristics of the media content and factors related to that content. The role of media *use* is to either reinforce or weaken the influence of media content as stimulus. Kline et al. (1974) argue:

> The uses and gratifications model suggests that the individual use of media content acts as an intervening variable: mitigating or enhancing the ultimate effects of a media message.

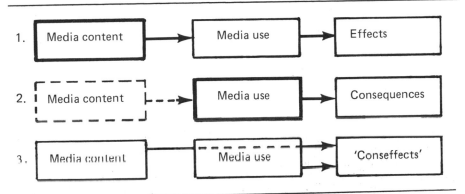

Figure 7.4: Three Possible Relations Among Media Content, Media Use, and Outcomes

Klapper (1963) is an early advocate of this thought. Blumler (1979) exemplifies with cases in which gratifications reasoning may contribute to a better understanding of the emergence of media effects:

(a) Media consumption for purposes of diversion and escape will favor audience acceptance of perceptions of social situations in line with portrayals frequently found in entertainment materials (this kind of media consumption often means that the audience member's perceptual guard is lowered, which in turn may mean that he is more easily persuaded and influenced).

(b) Involvement in media materials for personal identity reasons is likely to promote reinforcement effects (many people select media content which reinforces their attitudes and values). In these cases, the uses and gratifications process constitutes a bundle of intervening variables in the mass communication process.

(2) Consequences.   Where media use in itself is the primary cause may be of the following types:

(a) Cases when media use excludes, prevents, or reduces other activities, as when TV-viewing is said to decrease the amount of "real" interaction between people. Use of one type of content—for example, entertainment—may mean nonuse of other types of content—for example, information. In this way, political ignorance may be said to be a consequence of a certain type of media use.

(b) Mass media use provides material which is stored and structured, for example, for forming a view of the world. The outcome that one gets from such a world view is a consequence of media use, whereas the fact that you get a *specific* world view may be considered as an effect.

(c) Psychological outcomes of some sorts are consequences of use. If an expected gratification from media use is obtained, it seems reasonable to call this a consequence. If much TV-viewing makes you dependent on watching TV every evening, this is, I think, a consequence as well. These consequences affect the individual as a media consumer and occur in the media system itself.

(3) Conseffects.   When one effect process (type 1, above) and one consequence process (type 2) more or less simultaneously work toward the same outcome, we may label that outcome a "conseffect." Educational content often results in "conseffects"; part of the content is designed to encourage learning and gives effects through use, part of it is the material to be learned itself and is stored by help of use. Dependency on *specific* content may also be of "conseffect" type.

An important question is whether this tricotomy includes all possible types of outcome. Another question deals with the relations among the three types of outcomes, if they tend to reinforce each other, and so on.

So far, we have dealt only with consequences/effects on the individual level. We can, however, easily take a further step and identify outcomes on the societal level. For example, dependency on media for parasocial interaction may contribute to changes in the way of life of large strata of the population of a society. Systematic differential media use may also cause information and knowledge gaps. A widespread dependency on media for information may give rise to "spirals of silence" (Noelle-Neumann, 1974) as well as to effects on society, media systems, and audience, as pictured by Ball-Rokeach and De Fleur (1976).

We have here categorized outcomes in terms of their causes. A natural further step will be to try to relate this typology to one where outcomes are defined by the way they manifest themselves. I think, for example, that attitude change may be the result of at least two of the processes described, but that there must be tendencies that certain types of attitude change may relate to certain outcome processes. Still, already an elaborate cause-based typology may be worthwhile in giving us useful information about how to analyze, predict, and modify outcomes of the mass communication process.

A uses and gratifications model is not a model of the entire communication process, but rather a model of how mass media content is received and used and of the outcomes of this process. In order to underline one essential point in the model, that the uses and gratifications process serves as an important group of intervening variables, we may add the traditional elements communicator, message, and media. The communicator is guided by the perception of alternative messages, of the media, and of the audience. The communicator's behavior consists of a choice of form and content. (See Figure 7.5.)

In summary, this paper argues that linking uses and effects thinking in a single model avoids some of the pitfalls of the original uses and gratifications approaches:

— it does not stress the "basic need" factor, allowing for other sources of media use;

— it gives more attention to the media content than is usually the case;

— it does not regard the audience member as the only active part of the process—it recognizes intent and activity on part of the sender;

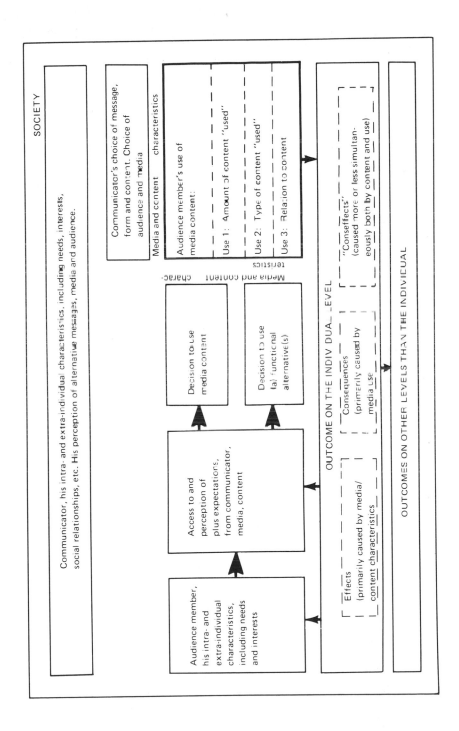

SOCIETY

Communicator, his intra- and extra-individual characteristics, including needs, interests, social relationships, etc. His perception of alternative messages, media and audience.

Communicator's choice of message, form and content. Choice of audience and media

Media and content   characteristics

Audience member's use of media content:

Use 1: Amount of content "used"

Use 2: Type of content "used"

Use 3: Relation to content

Media and content charac-
teristics

Decision to use media content

Decision to use (a) functional alternative(s)

Access to and perception of plus expectations, from communicator, media, content

Audience member, his intra- and extra-individual characteristics, including needs and interests

OUTCOME ON THE INDIVIDUAL LEVEL

"Conseffects" (caused "more or less simultan-eously both by content and use)

Consequences (primarily caused by media use

Effects (primarily caused by media/ content characteristics

OUTCOMES ON OTHER LEVELS THAN THE INDIVIDUAL

— the weight given to "use" may be of value for those reluctant to consider the rest of the uses and gratification concepts. "Use" may add considerably to ordinary effects models.

But there is certainly a great deal of work left between this proposed model and day-to-day research. As usual, further development may show that some of the aspects which here seem obvious are more complicated and those which are thought of as problems may not be problems at all.

REFERENCES

Ball-Rokeach, S. and DeFleur, M. (1976) "A dependency model of mass media effects." Communication Research 3: 3-21.

Blumler, J.G. (1977) "The role of theory in uses and gratifications studies." Paper to ICA Conference, Berlin, 1977.

Blumler, J.G. (1979) "The role of theory in uses and gratifications studies." Communication Research 6: 9-36.

Blumler, J.G. and Katz, E. [eds.] (1974) The Uses of Mass Communications. Beverly Hills: Sage.

DeFleur, M. (1966) Theories of Mass Communication. New York: David McKay.

Elliott, P. (1974) "Uses and gratifications research: a critique and a sociological alternative"; in J. G. Blumler and E. Katz (eds.) The Uses of Mass Communications. Beverly Hills: Sage.

Greenberg, B.S. and Reeves, B. (1976) "Children and the perceived reality of television." Journal of Social Issues 32: 86-97.

Hvitfelt, H. (1977) Verklighetsförträngning. Lund: CWK Gleerup.

Höst, S. (1979) "Moderne bruksstudier—snarvei eller blindspor?" Institute for Mass Communication Research, University of Oslo. (mimeo)

Katz, E. (1959) "Mass communication research and the study of popular culture." Studies in Public Communication 2: 1-6.

Katz, E. et al. (1974) "Utilization of mass communication by the individual," in J. G. Blumler and E. Katz (eds.) The Uses of Mass Communications. Beverly Hills: Sage.

Kline, F. G. et al. (1974) "Adolescents and family planning information," in J. G. Blumler and E. Katz (eds.) The Uses of Mass Communications. Beverly Hills: Sage.

Klapper, J. T. (1963) "Mass communication research: an old road resurveyed." Public Opinion Quarterly 27: 516-527.

Langenbucher, W. R., Räder, G. and Weiss, H. J. (1978) "Zur Notwendigkeit einer Neukonzeption der Massenkommunikationforschung in der Bundesrepublik"; in K. Berg and L. Kiefer (eds.) Massenkommunikation. Hase & Koehler: Mainz.

McQuail, D. (1979) "The uses and gratifications approach: origins, present troubles and future applications." University of Amsterdam. (mimeo)

McQuail, D. and Gurevitch, M. (1974) "Explaining audience behavior: three approaches considered," in J. G. Blumler and E. Katz (eds.) The Uses of Mass Communications. Beverly Hills: Sage.

Noble, G. (1975) Children in Front of the Small Screen. London: Constable.

Noelle-Neuman, E. (1974) "The spiral of silence, a theory of public opinion." Journal of Communication 24: 43-51.

Nördlund, J. E. (1976) Mediaumgänge—en explorativ studie. Lund: Studentlitteratur.

Rosengren, K. E. (1974) "Uses and gratifications: a paradigm outlined," in J. G. Blumler and E. Katz (eds.) The Uses of Mass Communications. Beverly Hills: Sage.

Rosengren, K. E. and Windahl, S. (1972) "Mass media consumption as a functional alternative," in D. McQuail (ed.) Sociology of Mass Communications. Harmondsworth: Penguin.

Rosengren, K. E. and Windahl, S. (1977) Mass media use: causes and effects. Bulletin of the Institute for Communications Research. Keio University, Tokyo.

Rosengren, K. E. and Windahl, S. (1978) Media Panel: A Presentation of a Program. Media Panel Report Series No. 4, Lund. (mimeo)

Salomon, G. and Cohen, A. A. (1978) "On the meaning and validity of television viewing." Human Communication Research 4: 256-270.

Swanson, D. L. (1979) "The continuing evolution of the uses and gratifications approach." Communication Research 6: 3-7.

Werner, A. (1975) "Massmediernes rolle i sosialiseringsprocessen." Paper to Nordic Conference for Mass Communication Research, Bjerringbro, Danmark.

Windahl, S. and McQuail, D. (1979) Kommunikationsmodeller. Lund: Studentlitteratur.

Content analysis of photography and broadcasting are areas of increasing emphasis in the field as visual data archives begin to emerge, such as the Vanderbilt Television Archive. Development of units of analysis will require sophisticated knowledge of the growing body of work on "non-linguistic" communication, as the field is labeled in the following article by Peter A. Andersen, John P. Garrison, and Janis F. Andersen. Their state-of-the-art piece summarizes the neurophysiological literature and concludes that a basic unit of nonverbal analysis is not likely to be found by using models that are based on linguistic assumptions. Drs. Peter Andersen and Janis F. Andersen are assistant professors of speech communication at West Virginia University. The late Dr. John P. Garrison was assistant professor of speech communication at Auburn University.

8

IMPLICATIONS OF A NEUROPHYSIOLOGICAL APPROACH FOR THE STUDY OF A NONVERBAL COMMUNICATION

Peter A. Andersen, John P. Garrison, and Janis F. Andersen

Research on the human brain has produced considerable knowledge useful to communication scholars in understanding the basis of the human communication system. One of the most important areas of brain research has involved the functions of the right and left brain hemispheres of the cerebral cortex. Speech pathologists have been cognizant of the communication functions of the brain for some time (e.g., Eisenson, 1971a, 1971b; Head, 1926), but it is only recently that writers and researchers investigating nonverbal communication have begun to examine the role of the brain (cf. Andersen, Garrison, & Andersen, 1975; Burgoon & Saine, 1978; Jaffe, 1978; Knapp, 1978).

Medical researchers have examined the neurophysiological systems which underlie nonverbal communication for several decades, yet the results of this research are almost completely absent

Peter A. Andersen (Ph.D., Florida State University, 1975) is assistant professor of speech communication at West Virginia University, Morgantown, West Virginia 26506. *John P. Garrison* (Ph.D., University of Nebraska—Lincoln, 1978) is assistant professor of speech communication at Auburn University, Auburn, Alabama 36830, and president of Learning Research Associates, Inc. of Lincoln, Nebraska 68516. *Janis F. Andersen* (Ed.D., West Virginia University, 1978) is assistant professor of speech communication at West Virginia University, Morgantown, West Virginia 26506. This study accepted for publication July 5, 1979.

from human communication literature. The purpose of this article is to introduce researchers and teachers of human communication to the neurophysiological literature, particularly as it can help them to understand nonverbal communication.

The literature reviewed in this report is published primarily in medical books and journals. Thus, a few comments about the structure of the human nervous system are necessary for a clear understanding of this report. The two sides of the human brain generally serve different functions even though they are connected by the largest set of associative fibers in the brain, the corpus callosum. Usually the language functions are managed by the left hemisphere, which also controls the right side of the body. The right hemisphere governs the left side of the body. Information arriving in either half of the body is immediately transmitted to the opposite hemisphere. Then, if necessary for better information processing, information is transmitted via the corpus callosum to the opposite brain hemisphere with only a slight delay. The ears are primarily connected to the opposite hemisphere, although some auditory pathways connect to the same side. The eyes are unique in that *each* eye is split into two visual hemifields, with little or no overlapping between them. The left visual field of each eye is

Published by permission of Transaction, Inc. from HUMAN COMMUNICATION RESEARCH, Vol. 6, No. 1. Copyright © 1979 by the International Communication Association.

connected to the right hemisphere, and each of the right visual fields is connected to the left brain hemisphere. Consequently, each brain hemisphere controls motor and sensory information functions for the opposite side of the body. Much of the research in this report has been conducted on patients who have had a radical commissurotomy, an operation which severs the corpus callosum. This produces a person with two disconnected and independent brain hemispheres. Thus, researchers are able to determine the primary functions of each hemisphere by feeding verbal or nonverbal information to only one side of the body, one visual field, or one ear in commissurotomy patients and monitoring patient reactions.

Researchers since the time of Broca (1865) have concluded that speech is localized in the left cerebral hemisphere. Recent reports (Eisenson, 1971b; Galin & Ornstein, 1972; Kimura, 1973; Luria, 1966; Milner, 1971; Moscovitch, 1973; Tomlinson-Keasey, Kelly, & Burton, 1978) indicate that verbal, linguistic, and mathematical abilities are located in the left brain hemisphere. The left hemisphere seems to be specialized for dealing with things in sequence, such as causal relations or logical problems. The logical, sequential nature of verbal, linguistic, and mathematical processes predisposes the brain to process these types of information in the part of the brain best suited for such tasks—the left hemisphere. Verbal or linguistic information can be processed in the right brain hemisphere, but it is inefficient to do so. Processing linguistic information in the right brain hemisphere would reduce the linguistic competence of a typical adult to that of a preschooler (cf. Searleman, 1977; Zaidel, 1973). Similarly, nonverbal communication can be processed by the left hemisphere but with little skill or competence. Ornstein (1978) maintains that we do not have a split brain but a whole brain with highly specialized parts.

COMMUNICATION FUNCTIONS OF THE RIGHT HEMISPHERE

The importance of the right hemisphere is examined in the next six sections. In each section, experiments involving three types of persons are reported. First, persons with lateralized lesions of one brain hemisphere are examined with reference to the type of communication deficit resulting from the lesion. Second, persons with surgically separated brain hemispheres are examined to determine which kinds of messages are processed by the left and right hemispheres within the same individual. Finally, since generalization from persons with brain lesions or surgically disconnected brain hemispheres to normal persons is dangerous, research on normal persons is also reported.

Proxemic and Spatial Communication

This section examines evidence on proxemic and spatial messages, including research on visual-spatial relations, environmental perceptions, and interpersonal distance.

Hemispheric damage and space. Studies of persons with unilateral brain damage suggest that the right brain hemisphere is primarily responsible for proxemic and spatial communication. Patients with right hemispheric injuries or diseases frequently experience spatial disorders, including loss of topographic memory and inability to understand topographic concepts (Bogen, 1974; Critchley, 1966; Eisenson, 1971a; Galin & Ornstein, 1972). Milner (1967), in observing patients with right temporal lesions, and Galin and Ornstein (1972), in examining patients with right temporal lobectomies, report patient impairment in negotiating maze tasks. Hecaén (1967) indicates that right-hemispherically damaged patients are able to retain their writing ability, although the shapes of their letters are incorrect and sloppy, indicating a deficiency of spatial orientation but not of verbal ability. Luria (1966) observed Russian patients with right hemispheric injuries who were unable to dress themselves, make their beds, or locate their rooms and who even had trouble differentiating horizontal from vertical directions.

Corresponding left hemispheric damage has little or no effect on the reception of spatial messages. Luria (1966) found no significant visual-spatial problems associated with left hemispheric injuries. Head (1926) found that aphasia—a left hemispheric problem resulting in an inability to use words—did not affect navigational skills. Persons with left temporal lobectomies were entirely normal in their ability to learn maze tasks (Galin & Ornstein, 1972).

Separated hemispheres and space. Research findings based on persons with surgically separated hemispheres also indicate that the right brain hemisphere is responsible for processing spatial information. Bogen (1969) found that in split-brained persons, geometric designs were copied better with the left hand/right hemisphere in both right- and left-handed persons. Gazzaniga, Bogen, and Sperry (1965) and Sperry (1968) have independently indicated that the left hand and left visual field/right hemisphere are superior for block design tasks and for visual perceptions of spatial relations.

Normal persons and space. In a series of experiments on normal subjects, Kimura (1966, 1969, 1973) examined the information-receiving capabilities of the right and left visual fields. Since the visual fields of each eye are connected to the contralateral brain hemisphere, the capacity of each hemisphere to receive information can be independently examined when subjects maintain fixation at a central point. Kimura has found that nonverbal stimuli, including dots and geometric forms, were located more accurately by the left visual field/right hemisphere. Durnford and Kimura (1971) and Kimura (1973) report that the left visual field/right brain hemisphere are better at depth perception tasks than are the right visual field/left brain hemisphere. This indicates that spatial information in the third dimension is processed more accurately by the right hemisphere than by the left.

Durnford and Kimura (1971) also found that slopes and slanted lines were identified more accurately when they were presented to the left visual field/right hemisphere. While the left visual field is superior for identifying and processing visual shapes in spatial relationships, Hermelin and O'Connor (1971) and Durnford and Kimura (1971) report that letters of the alphabet were better identified in the right visual field. This finding is consistent with left hemispheric specialization for linguistic information.

Physiological measures of normal persons also

indicate that the left hemisphere processes verbal information and that the right hemisphere processes nonverbal, spatial information. Galin and Ornstein (1972) recorded significantly higher electroencephalographic (EEG) activity in the left brain hemisphere for verbal tasks and significantly higher EEG activity in the right brain hemisphere for spatial tasks.

Proxemics has been defined as an individual's use of space in "conversational distance, planning, use of interior space, town layout and the like" (Hall, 1976, p. 218). Proxemics, including the location of others' bodies in space, is primarily governed by the right brain hemisphere (Hecaén, 1967). The preceding section leads to the following research generalization:

Generalization 1: The perception of spatial, directional, and proxemic information is processed primarily by the right brain hemisphere.

Tactile Communication

In this section, the capacity of the two brain hemispheres to process tactile communication will be examined.

Hemispheric damage and touch. Research by Corkin (1965) demonstrated that persons with severe right hemispheric damage performed poorly on tactual maze tasks, whereas left hemispheric damage resulted in no impairment of performance. Carmon and Benton (1969) administered a tactile task which required subjects to determine the direction of moving points. Left hemispheric damage failed to reduce the perceptual accuracy of either hand, whereas right hemispheric damage considerably reduced the perceptual accuracy of the left hand. Fontenot and Benton (1971) have also found that right hemispheric lesions caused impairment for both hands in directional perception of tactile stimulation applied to the skin surface. Available research on brain damage is consistent in finding a right hemispheric specialization for spatial perceptions in the touch modality.

Research on form board tasks, administered with subjects blindfolded, showed that right temporal lesions severely impair performance (Teuber & Weinstein, 1954), with no corresponding impairment reported for left hemispheric lesions. Luria (1966) reports that lesions of the right brain hemisphere often lead to tactile agnosia, the inability to recognize a shape or object through touch. DeRenzi and Scotti's (1969) research found that patients with right hemispheric lesions performed worse on visual shape identification tests than those with left hemispheric lesions. Overall, tactile shape recognition and interpretation seem to be processed primarily by the right brain hemisphere.

While the right hemisphere is specialized for tactile perceptions, numerical-tactile tasks seem to require both hemispheres. Carmon and Benton (1969) found that both left and right hemispheric lesions caused deficiencies on tactile point-counting tasks. This finding indicates that tactile counting tasks require the numerical abilities of the left hemisphere *and* the tactile abilities of the right hemisphere.

Separated hemispheres and touch. Evidence collected on subjects with divided hemispheres also supports the right hemispheric localization of tactile perceptions. Sperry (1968) and Gazzaniga (1974) report that the left hand/right brain hemisphere are specialized for determining object size, shape, and texture. The corresponding right hand/left hemisphere, deprived of information from the severed right hemisphere, were unable to perform these same tasks. Milner and Taylor (1972) tested split-brained patients on tactile matching tasks and also found right hemispheric superiority for the recognition of nonmeaningful shapes, while the left hemisphere was somewhat superior for the recognition of meaningful, verbally labeled shapes.

Normal persons and touch. Using normal subjects, Witelson (1974) found that nonsense shapes were more accurately identified by the left hand/right hemisphere than by the right hand/left hemisphere. Weinstein and Sersen (1961) reported that a majority of subjects are more sensitive to touch on their left palms, forearms, and soles than on their right.

Two additional findings indicate the importance of both hemispheres in tactile tasks of a verbal nature. Witelson (1974) has found that linguistic

tactile stimuli, such as letters, were processed equally well by each hand. He indicates that letter shapes must be processed by both brain hemispheres, since analysis requires interpretation of both spatial and linguistic codes. Mountcastle's (1966) studies show that good Braille readers use both hands to read each word. Braille readers apparently do better with two fingers (one from each hand), as if the person summed the information from each brain hemisphere. From the previous discussion of the nonverbal basis of tactile communication, two generalizations can be formulated:

Generalization 2: The perception of tactile information dealing with space, direction, shape, and form is processed primarily by the right brain hemisphere.

Generalization 3: The left and right brain hemispheres together are superior to either hemisphere independently for receiving linguistic or numerical information in the tactile mode.

Bodily Communication

Hemispheric specialization for perceptions of physical appearance and bodily motion (kinesics) are examined in this section.

Hemispheric damage and bodily communication. Damage to the right brain hemisphere impairs one's perception of his/her own body. Persons with right brain lesions often have considerable difficulty locating themselves or the bodies of others in three-dimensional space (Hecaén, 1967). Luria (1966) examined patients with right hemispheric lesions who could not locate motion in their own fingers and manifested no awareness of their disability.

Recognition of others' appearances also seems to be impaired by right hemispheric damage. Luria (1966) found that right hemispheric lesions, but not similar lesions of the left hemisphere, produced a complete inability to recognize familiar faces. Patients with right temporal lobectomies examined by Milner (1967) had difficulty recognizing snapshots of faces examined only two minutes earlier. These patients maintained that all of the faces were basically similar. Critchley (1966) labeled these right hemispheric losses as somatoparaphrenia, a distorted perception of body image.

Separated hemispheres and bodily communication. Sperry and Gazzaniga (1967) found that the right hemisphere triggers facial expressions, including grimacing and wincing. Split-brain patients in experiments by Gazzaniga (1970) and Sperry (1968) were shown nude photographs in the left visual field. Since only their right (nonverbal) hemisphere could receive this information, the subjects verbally denied seeing these photographs but responded nonverbally by giggling and blushing.

Normal persons and bodily communication. In a study of normal male subjects, Rizzolatti, Umilta, and Berlucci (1971) found a left visual field/right hemisphere superiority for face recognition. A right visual field/left hemisphere superiority was found for letter recognition. The researchers concluded that a left hemispheric specialization exists for verbal material, while a right hemispheric specialization exists for spatial configuration, including facial recognition. Based on the previous evidence, the next generalization follows from the existing neurophysiological research.

Generalization 4: The perception of bodily communication, including kinesic cues, facial expressions, and physical appearance, is processed primarily by the right brain hemisphere.

Object Communication

The perception and production of objects and forms in relation to hemispheric specialization will be examined in this section.

Hemispheric damage and objects. Lesions of the right brain hemisphere have been found by Critchley (1966) and Piercy, Hecaén, and Ajuriaguerra (1960) to produce constructional apraxia, a defective execution of construction tasks. Kimura (1963) showed that damage to the right temporal lobe impaired the understanding of geometric designs, drawings, and sculpture. Damage to the right posterior portion of the brain was reported by Kimura (1973) to impair model-building ability. Luria (1966) found that right hemispheric lesions could lead to visual agnosia, the inability to recognize objects by sight. Corresponding left hemispheric disorders do not result in impaired object perception. Luria (1966) found that aphasic patients who were unable to speak or write were able to perform geometric operations and to construct spatial analogies.

Similarly, patients examined by Hecaen (1967) with right hemispheric disease or injury produced disorganized, distorted, and incomplete drawings and paintings. Patients tested by Luria (1966) with right hemispheric lesions lost their ability to draw or copy objects. Similarly, Kimura (1973) reports that injuries to the right parieto-occipital region impaired drawing in her patients. Bogen (1974) observed that right temporal lobectomy patients were severely impaired in picture comprehension. However, injuries to the left hemisphere seem to have little effect on artistic ability. Aphasic painters examined by Alajouanine (1948), although unable to speak, were able to paint without impairment. Hecaén (1967) found that patients with left hemispheric injuries had difficulty following verbal instructions, but they were able to draw and paint very well from a model. While evidence is less extensive regarding color perception, this too seems to be a right hemispheric function (DeRenzi & Spinnler, 1967). This evidence seems to suggest that artistic ability and perception are functions of the right hemisphere.

Separated hemispheres and objects. In a series of studies by Gazzaniga (1974) and Sperry (1973), the left hand/right hemisphere were capable of arranging blocks, distinguishing between object size, shape, and texture, and drawing in three dimensions, while the corresponding right hand/left hemisphere, deprived of instructions from the severed right hemisphere, were unable to perform these tasks.

Normal persons and objects. A limited body of research on normal subjects also substantiates right hemispheric dominance for object recognition.

Durnford and Kimura (1971) found a left visual field/right hemisphere superiority for recognition of shapes and dots. Milner (1971) likewise found superior dot recognition in the left visual field. The following generalization was formulated:

Generalization 5: The perception of object communication, including shape and form, is processed primarily by the right brain hemisphere.

Environmental Sound Communication

Hemispheric specialization for nonspeech sounds will be examined in this section.

Hemispheric damage and sound. Research by Milner (1967) and Shankweiler (1966) found that nonverbal and environmental sounds were selectively impaired by right temporal lobectomies, indicating a right hemispheric specialization for these types of sounds. Conversely, a left temporal lobectomy did not impair nonverbal sounds, but did impair auditory perception of digits.

Normal persons and sound. Most of the research on environmental sound communication has been conducted with normal subjects, and the results are consistent with subjects who have experienced brain injuries. Nonverbal sounds are understood more accurately by the left ear/right hemisphere (Curry, 1967; Gerber & Goldman, 1971), while verbal sounds are understood with greater accuracy by the right ear/left brain hemisphere. Nonverbal signal detection has been shown by Murphy and Venables (1970) to be interpreted more accurately by the left ear/right hemisphere. Experiments by Knox and Kimura (1970) have found a left ear superiority in children for identifying environmental sounds, including pouring water, dishwashing, and toothbrushing. Kimura (1973) reports a distinct left ear/right hemispheric superiority for the perception of human vocal characteristics, such as coughing, laughing, and crying. However, the right ear/left hemisphere are better able to recognize human verbal sounds that are one syllable in length or longer. Kimura (1973) concludes that the right hemisphere is specialized for sound, unless the

sound is a human verbalization, in which case a left hemispheric generalization is observed. Thus, our sixth research generalization follows.

Generalization 6: The right brain hemisphere is primarily responsible for processing nonlinguistic environmental sounds.

Music

The evidence for hemispheric specialization in processing musical information, including singing, is examined in this section. Bogen (1974) builds an extensive case for viewing music, including singing, as a nonverbal, nonlinguistic, primarily right hemispheric function.

Hemispheric damage and music. The right hemisphere plays a primary role in the reception of musical information (Brookshire, 1975). Research on persons with damaged right temporal lobes (Kimura, 1973) and with right temporal lobectomies (Milner, 1967; Shankweiler, 1966) demonstrates impairment of tonal discrimination. Tonal quality, tonal pattern discrimination, melodic patterning, and timbre were all negatively affected. These same researchers found that corresponding left hemispheric injuries have little or no impact on musical ability.

The effects of brain damage on musical ability extend to singing, which involves words but is nonverbal and right hemispheric (cf. Andersen, Andersen, & Garrison, 1978). Evidently words perform little or no linguistic function for the sender when they are sung but are vehicles through which musical tones are carried. Evidence for the location of singing in the right, nonverbal hemisphere is provided by patients with left hemispheric damage, who do not lose their ability to sing. Alajouanine's (1948) patients suffering from aphasia remembered tunes easily and sang them with little or no difficulty. Henschen (1926, p. 117) reports that, in aphasics, "the faculty of singing words is conserved in spite of the complete inability to speak a single word." Head (1926) reports that disorders of speech do not affect the ability to sing the words to a song. Additional evidence is provided by Smith's

(1966) left hemispherectomy patients, who retained little capacity to speak or to write, yet were able to sing with little hesitation and few errors in articulation. Smith (1966, p. 476) concludes that "the ability to recall and sing old songs suggests that the right hemisphere plays an important role in musical memory and in the neuromotor process of singing."

Stutterers and music. Welsbacher (1972) discovered that it is common for a severe stutterer to sing the lyrics of a song perfectly but to be unable to speak the same words apart from their musical context. To these stutterers, like country and western singer Mel Tillis, musical and verbal experiences are of a completely different nature. Welsbacher (1972) maintains that singing is often the first successful communication experience for many children who are stutterers or verbally handicapped. Andrews and Harris (1964) report differential hemispheric activity to be associated with stuttering. They found left hemispheric alpha waves (a sign of mental relaxation) to be excessive for stutterers, although corresponding right brain activity was normal. This evidence links stuttering (a verbal disfluency) with insufficient left hemispheric arousal, but indicates that normal right hemispheric activity explains why singing would not be affected by the disfluency.

Normal persons and music. A series of tests with normal subjects has examined the relative musical ability of each ear and the corresponding opposite brain hemisphere. Several studies have found the right ear/left brain hemisphere to be superior for the perception of digits (Curry, 1967; Darwin, 1971; Kimura, 1964), for vowel sounds (Darwin, 1971), for words (Curry, 1967; Kimura, 1966), and for human speech in general (Knox & Kimura, 1970). The left ear/right brain more accurately perceive *nonverbal* sounds, including music and singing. Kimura (1964, 1967, 1973), Knox and Kimura (1970), and Berlin (1977) found that melodies were better perceived and more easily identified by the left ear/right brain. Spreen, Spellacy, and Reid (1970) found a left ear/right hemispheric advantage for tonal and musical stimuli. Finally, pitch sweeps and orchestrated melodies were perceived more ac-

curately by the left ear/right brain (Darwin, 1971). Kimura (1964, p. 367) summarizes the neurophysiological research in this area: "The differentiation appears to be along the verbal-nonverbal dimension and among nonverbal sounds music may be especially effective in eliciting a left ear effect."

Generalization 7: Both singing and instrumental music are processed primarily by the right brain hemisphere.

QUALIFICATIONS OF A NEUROPHYSIOLOGICAL APPROACH

The conclusion from the previous section is that at least six types of nonverbal communication are primarily governed by the right brain hemisphere. This conclusion needs to be partially qualified in four ways: (1) the brain hemispheres are not entirely functionally independent; (2) some left-handed people have reversed hemispheric function; (3) women are less hemispherically differentiated than men; and (4) the right hemisphere has limited verbal/linguistic ability.

Functional Independence of the Hemispheres

While each brain is specialized for either verbal or nonverbal communication, the two hemispheres are connected by a band of nerve fibers called the corpus callosum. The corpus callosum relays information from one hemisphere to the other in approximately 30 to 40 milliseconds through a complex process that is not fully understood (Filbey & Gazzaniga, 1969). It is unclear whether this information is transmitted through a verbal code, a nonverbal code, or some modality-unspecific neural code (Moscovitch, 1973). It is clear, however, that verbal or nonverbal messages are altered when they are transmitted to the opposite hemisphere. The difficulties of transmitting nonverbal, analogic information into a digital, verbal code are well known (cf. Sousa-Posa & Rohrberg, 1977; Wilden, 1972a, 1972b). While delays and distortions occur in the interhemispheric transmission of information, the brain hemispheres do not function in complete isolation. Moreover, each hemisphere has minor abilities to govern tasks normally accomplished by the hemisphere specialized for the specific task under consideration. To that extent, brain functions related to human communication can be thought of as on a continuum. Nonetheless, a dichotomy between the *primary* function of each brain hemisphere can be empirically demonstrated for verbal and nonverbal communication.

Left-Handed People

Empirical research supports a left hemisphere specialization for verbal tasks and a right hemisphere specialization for nonverbal tasks for right-handed persons (cf. Bogen & Gazzaniga, 1965; Ornstein, 1972, 1974). Left-handed people are somewhat different, as Ornstein (1972, p. 53) points out: "The right left specialization process is based primarily on righthanders. Lefthanders, representing about five percent of the general population are less consistent; some have reversed specialization of the hemispheres, but some have mixed specialization e.g., language in both sides." While 60 to 70 percent of left-handed people process some linguistic and verbal tasks in their left cerebral hemisphere, the remainder (30 to 40 percent) use the right side for language (Hecaén & Sauget, 1971; Herron, 1976; Hines, 1975; Lishman & McMeekan, 1977; Searleman, 1977). This exception to the left-verbal/right-nonverbal distinction, however, applies to only 40 percent of left handed persons, or about 2 percent of the general population. Furthermore, even these 2 percent process one kind of communicated information in one hemisphere and a different kind in the other hemisphere; the functions of each hemisphere are simply reversed.

Hemsiphere Differentiation

Evidence exists that women tend to be more hemispherically integrated and less specialized than men. Bakan (1971) has found that men exhibit more distinct conjugate lateral eye movements than do women, which seems to indicate greater hemispheric specialization for men. Moreover, many researchers have found that the right hemisphere of women can more easily recover language than is the case for men. This indicates not only less specialization for language in women (Eisenson, 1971a; Geschwind, 1966; Lansdell, 1967) but also, as Witelson (1976, p. 426) suggests, that "language functions may transfer more readily to the right hemisphere in females than in males following early damage to the left hemisphere." In fact, for patients with early brain lesions, women show less impairment than men on verbal tasks after neurosurgical removal of the left hemisphere at maturity (Lansdell, 1969). While the research generalizations presented about nonverbal communication in this report are applicable to both sexes, they *may* fit males a bit more neatly than they fit females.

Language Ability of the Right Hemisphere

The final qualification involves the linguistic capacity of the right hemisphere. Moscovitch (1973) indicates that the linguistic capabilities of the normal right hemisphere are approximately equivalent to the language abilities of an average five-year-old. Others (e.g., Kumar, Zaidel, & Bogen, 1976; Sperry & Zaidel, 1973; Zaidel, 1973, 1976a, 1976b) have empirically demonstrated that commissurotomy and left hemispherectomy patients still possess some language ability after surgery. This phenomenon can be explained in at least two ways.

First, as Kotulak (1976) explains, when a diseased or injured left hemisphere is unable to assume linguistic abilities early in a person' life, the right hemisphere assumes these functions. Early in life, the localization of language skills remains "equipotential and transferable" (Searleman, 1977, p. 512). The age at which language and nonverbal functions become permanently lateralized is still in dispute. Gardiner and Walter (1977, p. 482) report from EEG studies that "hemispheric difference in the processing of linguistic and nonlinguistic stimuli may already exist very early in infancy and perhaps at birth." Likewise, Turkewitz (1977) indicates that infants are asymmetric in their response to auditory, tactile, and visual stimulations at 24 hours of age. Another group of researchers argues that permanent lateralization occurs before age five, and another group argues for puberty. Regardless of the specific age when the process is complete, Lansdell (1969) points out that, as age increases, there is a diminishing capacity for the right hemisphere to be involved in language functions.

Second, when the left brain hemisphere becomes seriously injured or diseased later in life, the right brain still assumes some basic linguistic functions. Moscovitch (1973) has even argued that this is possible because the right hemisphere possesses limited linguistic functions that are simply suppressed in normal-functioning humans.

Several alternative explanations of left hemispheric control for language functions can be provided with the acknowledgment that the mechanism is not yet fully understood. However, the presence of a suppressing function for right hemispheric language is not disputed, since clinical cases as well as logical argument point to the difficulty of language being located in two separate and competing hemispheres. Lateralization or specialization of hemispheric functions is the general pattern for normal adults (worldwide), but serious left hemispheric disease or injury may alter this pattern.

IMPLICATIONS OF A
NEUROPHYSIOLOGICAL PERSPECTIVE

The final section of this report examines the neurophysiological model, with implications for: (1) defining nonverbal communication, (2) phylogeny, and (3) researching nonverbal communication.

Defining Nonverbal Communication

Considerable disagreement exists regarding the importance of defining nonverbal communication. Knapp, Wiemann, and Daly (1978) maintain that scholars spend a disproportionate amount of time trying to deduce the nature of the field from the covering label, when their time could be better spent conducting research and developing theory. Rosenfeld and Civikly (1976) suggest that attempts at definition are a "foolhardy venture," since it will shed little light on assignment of meaning to experience, the central concern of their approach. Similarly, Ekman (1976) considers naming and defining

to be an "odd preoccupation for students of nonverbal communication." Instead, his purpose is to better understand facial and body movement.

Several other scholars and writers believe that definitional issues are quite important. Kibler (1970) has stated that a high-priority task facing communication scholars is the definition of key concepts which play an important role in the generation of theory. Koneya (1977) contends that the conceptual framework of nonverbal communication is in sore need of repair. Koneya suggests that researchers need to determine if there are separate and distinct verbal and nonverbal communication domains or if one is a subdivision of the other. This answer has implications for appropriate generalization about human communication processes. Lyons (1972) maintains that research has been slowed because it is not clear whether the term "nonverbal communication," as it is used by many authors, is intended to include linguistic components or not. Similarly, Siegman and Feldstein (1978) contend that defining nonverbal communication has a very practical implication: what to include in a book or course.

While it is not expected that this controversy will be resolved in this paper, or by any other single report, examination and comparison of the various definitions will permit the reader to understand differences and commonalities among them and may help readers to decide if definitions are an important scholarly enterprise. Finally, neurophysiological data presented earlier may aid the reader in selecting an appropriate definition of nonverbal communication.

The social science literature indicates that there are at least six common varying approaches for defining nonverbal communication. The first approach to defining nonverbal communication is really a controversy over how to define communication in general. The essence of this controversy is a disagreement over whether nonverbal communication must have a symbolic referent. Wiener, Devoe, Rubinow, and Geller (1972) suggest that nonverbal communication must be in the form of a symbolic code which bears an arbitrary relationship to its referent. This definition excludes most nonverbal *behavior* from the realm of communication. Siegman and Feldstein (1978, p. 4) argue that definitions of this type are too restrictive, because they employ a purely linguistic model as the prototype for all communication:

> But the concern with nonverbal communication is precisely the result of the increasing realization that there is more to communication than language. Infants communicate before they have even the rudimentary form of language and it is not unreasonable to assume that nonverbal communication predated verbal communication in the history of mankind as well. It will simply not do, therefore, to formulate a model of nonverbal communication based on verbal communication.

At the other extreme of this debate is the position taken by Wilden (1972a) that all behavior is communication. This position may be as unrestrictive as the Wiener et al. (1972) position is overrestrictive. Most definitions of nonverbal communication require that a decoder interpret the behavior for it to constitute communication (cf. Burgoon & Saine, 1978, pp. 9-10). Exline and Fehr (1978, p. 121) express this idea behaviorally: "Our position is that all behavior is potentially communicative. Any given behavior becomes communicative when it produces a change in a receiver."

A second common approach is the "other than words" definition of nonverbal communication (cf. Burgoon & Saine, 1978; Eisenburg & Smith, 1971; Harrison, 1974; Knapp, 1972; Mehrabian, 1972a, 1972b; Rosenfeld & Civikly, 1976). Indeed, this has probably been the *most* common approach. A third definition employs a list of areas or examples that constitute nonverbal communication (cf. Barker & Collins, 1970; Benson & Frandsen, 1976; Brooks, 1974, Harrison, 1973, Leathers, 1976, McCroskey, Larson, & Knapp, 1971). A fourth approach defines nonverbal communication as nonlinguistic and verbal communication as involving language (cf. Appelbaum, Anatol, Hays, Jenson, Porter, & Mandel, 1973; Eisenburg & Smith, 1971; Harrison, 1974). Fifth, some investigators define nonverbal communication as analogic, and verbal communication as digital (cf. Watzlawick, Beavin, & Jackson, 1967). A sixth definition, focusing on neurophysiology, has been introduced (Andersen, Garrison, & Andersen, 1975; Jaffe, 1978) and has been discussed in several nonverbal

textbooks (cf. Burgoon & Saine, 1978; Knapp, 1978; Rosenfeld & Civikly, 1976).

Three of these definitions of nonverbal communication are quite compatible. Analogic, nonlinguistic, and right hemispheric are all ways of describing an underlying nonverbal coding schemata that unites a variety of communication behaviors into one system. Ruesch (1973) described the two primary psychological processes as digital (verbal or logical) and analogic (nonverbal or nondiscursive). The digital/analogic continuum has been consistently recognized by communication scholars (cf Harrison, 1974; McCroskey & Wheeless, 1976) and psychologists (cf. Siegman & Feldstein, 1978). Harrison (1974) explains that the digital code is discrete, arbitrary, and easy to encode as a written or spoken verbal system, while the analogic code is continuous, natural, nonverbal, and easy to decode because of its more direct representation of reality. Bogen (1974) suggests that this dichotomy has pervaded the work of dozens of psychologists. He proposes that the left hemisphere is capable of propositional thought, syntax, semantics, mathematics, and logic, whereas the right hemisphere is appositional and usually capable of only gross or analogic thought. Watzlawick et al. (1967) and Wilden (1972a) suggest that gestures, posture, facial expression, inflection, cadence, and the context in which a human communication occurs are types of analogs or iconic communication, whereas all denotative, linguistic communication is arbitrary and digital.

Advocates of a neurophysiological definition (cf. Andersen, Garrison, & Andersen, 1975) use two lines of reasoning to derive their definition. First, it is generally agreed that proxemics and spatial communication, tactile or haptic communication, bodily appearance and kinesics, object communication, environmental sound, and musical communication are part of the nonverbal domain (cf. Burgoon & Saine, 1978; Knapp, 1978; Rosenfeld & Civikly, 1976). While this should not be construed as an all-encompassing list of various types of nonverbal communication, it is nevertheless representative of what is commonly called *nonverbal* communication. Second, verbal processes (e.g., reading, writing, and speaking) are generally governed by the left brain hemisphere. Since other types of right hemisphere communication discussed in the previous generalizations have been shown to be neurophysiologically separate from verbal processes, it logically follows that these types of communication should be labeled not verbal (nonverbal). Thus, advocates of this position maintain that nonverbal communication can be defined as *a process of sending and receiving messages which is primarily governed by the right brain hemisphere*.

The other three definitions of nonverbal communication share little in common with each other or with the analogic, nonlinguistic, and right hemispheric definitions. The "other than words" approach focuses on the surface structure rather than the underlying system. Words can be used linguistically or nonlinguistically, digitally or analogically, and can originate in the right brain. Finally, the listing approach is simply predefinitional.

The definition of nonverbal communication employed by a given scholar is still a function of personal preference and prior training, since no definition is currently agreed upon as particularly superior or widespread. Perhaps the term "nonlinguistic" is a more accurate label to describe the phenomena than is the term "nonverbal." Knapp, Wiemann, and Daly (1978) indicate that the term "nonverbal" may suggest a conceptually dysfunctional dichotomy for examining human message systems. Moreover, the terms "verbal/nonverbal" are often used as synonyms for "oral/nonoral," as in courts of law, further confusing the issue. Petrovich and Hess (1978) suggest that there are degrees of linguisticness, with the verbal component at the top of the continuum. Similarly, Lyons (1972) suggests that nonverbal and verbal communication can be interpreted as the "less linguistic" and the "more linguistic" aspects of human communication, respectively. Like it or not, however, the term "nonverbal" is popular, widely used, and will not be quickly supplanted by another term.

Phylogenetic Implications

Researchers have suggested that, during the process of human evolution, the two hemispheres of the brain actually developed as efficient processors of face-to-face interaction. A number of studies now seem to suggest that, in face-to-face interaction, a disproportionate share of nonverbal information is projected directly to the right brain hemisphere via the left ear and the left visual field. Jaffe (1978) argues that this division preserves sender/receiver roles and provides a left brain/right ear system which is maximally sensitive to the rapid rhythm of spoken syllables while freeing the receiver's left ear/right brain for nonlinguistic information.

Most illustrators (gestures accompanying speech) are right-handed and controlled by the left hemisphere (Kimura, 1973). Burgoon and Saine (1978) cite this research as an exception to the right hemisphere/nonverbal specialization. This phenomenon, however, is explained by the fact that right-handed gestures are projected into the receiver's left visual field/right hemisphere (Jaffe, 1978). Thus, gestural information can be processed by the receiver's right hemisphere without interfering with the left hemisphere's verbal decoding (Jaffe, 1978; Kimura, 1973).

Considerable research on facial expression indicates that the two halves of the face play a different role in interpersonal communication. Wolff (1933) observed that substantial asymmetries exist in the human face. Moreover, his experiments indicated that composite faces (whole faces constructed of two left or two right halves) are more like the original if they were constructed from two right half-faces. The greater salience of the right side of the face has been replicated and confirmed by several researchers (Gilbert & Bakan, 1973; Lindzey, Prince, & Wright, 1952; McCurdy, 1949). These researchers suggest that asymmetrical recognition patterns are a function of a right hemisphere/left visual field superiority for recognition of faces and facial affect and are not due to handedness or direction of reading (Gilbert & Bakan, 1973; Lindzey, Prince, & Wright, 1952). Recently, Sackeim, Gur, and Saucy (1978) found that emotions were expressed more intensely in left-side composites, again indicating greater right hemispheric involvement in the production of facial expression. The right-side composites conveyed only happiness more accurately, supporting Wolff's (1933) original proposition that the right side of the face is the social side that we present to the world. Collectively, these findings suggest that: (1) the right side of the human face is predominant in social interaction; (2) this predominance exists across culture, indicating a genetic, neurophysiological predisposition to non-verbally communicate with the right side of the body, thereby projecting nonverbal information to the right hemisphere of the receiver.

Implications for Research

The distinction between the verbal/linguistic left brain system and the nonverbal/nonlinguistic right brain system has implications for measurement models and general research models. First, as several authors have suggested (Andersen, Garrison, & Andersen, 1975; Knapp, Wiemann, & Daly, 1978), communication researchers should develop nonverbal methods of measuring nonverbal variables. This procedure will permit more direct assessment of nonverbal communication, reducing extraneous and circuitous information processing by the corpus callosum and left brain hemisphere.

Similarly, basing a program of nonverbal research on a verbal or linguistic model may be problematic. Dittmann (1978) maintains that, in body language or kinesics, there is no organization into larger chunks of meaning comparable to spoken language or sign language. An example of a search for a basic unit or chunk of nonverbal communication is the kinesic research of Birdwhistell (1970), which followed a linguistic model. He attempted to identify the kine as the basic unit of kinesics in the same way the phoneme was used as the basic unit of language. Unfortunately, kinesic communication is analogic and contains no basic unit of meaning (Bogen, 1974; Dittmann, 1978, Ruesch, 1973). Birdwhistell's model has generated little subsequent research, perhaps because he used a linguistic model that is not particularly appropriate for investigating nonverbal communication (cf. Siegman & Feldstein, 1978).

A third area for future research involves the development of techniques to teach the right hemisphere. Several writers have argued that we predominantly teach the left brain hemisphere and should develop methods to teach both hemispheres independently and together (Bogen, 1977; Samples, 1975). A priority for researchers should be the examination of effective teaching strategies that

focus the right brain hemisphere both exclusively and in conjunction with the left brain hemisphere.

Fourth, researchers should examine asymmetries in everyday communication behavior which are a function of brain-sidedness. Since previous research has established that the face and hands behave asymmetrically and that receivers tend to rely on the right side of the body for most information (Kimura, 1973; Sackeim, Gur, & Saucy, 1978), future research should examine the following questions: (1) Are the right half-face, body, eye, and arm consistently more important during interpersonal interaction? (2) Should receivers tune in to the right side, the left side, or both sides in interpersonal interaction? (3) Is one side of the body superior for detecting affect, immediacy, or deception? and (4) Is the left side of the body (which is right hemispherically controlled) more genuine and less subject to manipulation? Examination of these questions may illuminate pragmatic implications of brain-sidedness which are important to our daily interactions.

Fifth, future research should examine how lateralized functions result in coherent, integrated behavior. Knapp, Wiemann, and Daly (1978) state that verbal and nonverbal behaviors are unquestionably part and parcel of the same communication system. The interrelationships of these two modes of communication require considerable future research. Recent articles by Dittmann (1978), Rosenfeld (1978), and Siegman (1978) provide excellent perspectives on integrating research in the verbal and nonverbal modes.

A sixth area for research should examine the impact of the various media on the right brain hemisphere. Recent speculation has linked declines in standardized reading scores with television viewing. Ascertaining the impact of television and other media on the brain hemispheres may shed light on this question. Similarly, studies should examine the impact of various media on the development of verbal and nonverbal communication skills. Finally, research should examine the relative importance of verbal and nonverbal communication in persuasion and information acquisition.

Finally, future research needs to address two important deficiencies existing within the body of literature supportive of a brain-sidedness model of human communication. First, research supporting the application of the brain-sidedness model to communication functions is more extensive for the receiving functions of communicated stimuli than for the sending functions. Future research needs to validate this model for the sending or enactment functions of communication. This research will either extend or limit the brain-sidedness model of human communication and will provide information about the similarities and differences in the communication sending and receiving functions.

Second, the literature suggests a brain-sidedness model of communication for perception of communicated stimuli, but there is little evidence validating the model in ongoing human interaction. Future research needs to examine ongoing human communication and corresponding neural activity. This research will add an important dimension to the understanding and explication of human communication processes.

REFERENCES

ALAJOUANINE, T. Aphasia and artistic realization. *Brain*, 1948, 71, 229-241.

ANDERSEN, P.A., ANDERSEN, J.F., & GARRISON, J.P. Singing apprehension and talking apprehension: The development of two constructs. *Sign Language Studies*, 1978, 19, 155-186.

ANDERSEN, P.A., GARRISON, J.P., & ANDERSEN, J.F. Defining nonverbal communication: A neurophysiological explanation of nonverbal information processing. Paper presented at the annual convention of the Western Speech Communication Association, Seattle, Washington, November 1975.

ANDREWS, G., & HARRIS, M. *The syndrome of stuttering*. London: Heineman, 1964.

APPELBAUM, R.L., ANATOL, K.W., HAYS, E.R., JENSON, O.O., PORTER, R.E., & MANDEL, J.R. *Fundamental concepts in human communication*. New York: Harper & Row, 1973.

BAKAN, P. The eyes have it. *Psychology Today*, 1971, 4(4), 64-67.

BARKER, L.L., & COLLINS, N.B. Nonverbal and kinesic research. In P. Emmert and W.D. Brooks (Eds.), *Methods of research in communication*. New York: Houghton Mifflin, 1970.

BENSON, T.W., & FRANDSEN, K.D. *An orientation to nonverbal communication*. Chicago: Science Research Associates, 1976.

BERLIN, C.J. Hemispheric asymmetry in auditory tasks. In S. Harrad et al. (Eds.), *Lateralization in the nervous system*. New York: Academic Press, 1977.

BIRDWHISTELL, R.L. *Kinesics and context*. Philadelphia: University of Pennsylvania Press, 1970.

BOGEN, J.E. The other side of the brain. I. Dysgraphia and dyscopia following cerebral commissurotomy. *Bulletin of the Los Angeles Neurological Society*, 1969, 34, 73-105.

BOGEN, J.E. The other side of the brain: An appositional mind. In R.E. Ornstein (Ed.), *The nature of human consciousness*. New York: Viking Press, 1974.

BOGEN, J.E. Some educational implications of recent research on the human brain. In M.C. Wittrock (Ed.), *The human brain*. Englewood Cliffs, New Jersey: Prentice-Hall, 1977.

BOGEN, J.E., & GAZZANIGA, M.S. Cerebral commissurotomy in man: Minor hemisphere dominance for certain visuo-spatial functions. *Journal of Neurosurgery*, 1965, 23, 394-399.

BROCA, P. Sur la faculté du language articule. *Bulletin de la Société d'Anthropologie*, 1865, 4, 493-494.

BROOKS, W.D. *Speech communication* (2nd ed.). Dubuque, Iowa: Brown, 1974.

BROOKSHIRE, R.H. Recognition of auditory sequences by aphasic, right-hemisphere-damaged and non-brain-damaged subjects. *Journal of Communication Disorders*, 1975, 8, 51-59.

BURGOON, J.E., & SAINE, T. *The unspoken dialogue*. Boston: Houghton Mifflin, 1978.

CARMON, A., & BENTON, A.L. Tactile perception of direction and number of patients with unilateral cerebral disease. *Neurology*, 1969, 19, 525-532.

CORKIN, S. Tactually guided maze learning in man: Effect of unilateral cortical excision and bilateral hippocampal lesions. *Neuropsychologia*, 1965, 3, 339.

CRITCHLEY, M. *The parietal lobes* (2nd ed.) London: Arnold, 1966.

CURRY, F.K.W. A comparison of left-handed and right-handed subjects on verbal and nonverbal dichotic listening tasks. *Cortex*, 1967, 3, 34.

DARWIN, C.J. Ear differences in the recall of fixatives and vowels. *Quarterly Journal of Experimental Psychology*, 1971, 23, 46.

DeRENZI, E., & SCOTTI, G. The influence of spatial disorders in impairing tactual discrimination of shapes. *Cortex*, 1969, 5, 53-62.

DeRENZI, E., & SPINNLER, H. Impaired performance on color tasks in patients with hemispheric damage. *Cortex*, 1967, 3, 194.

DITTMAN, A.T. The role of body movement in communication. In A.W. Siegman and S. Feldstein (Eds.), *Nonverbal behavior and communication*. Hillsdale, New Jersey: Lawrence Erlbaum Associates, 1978.

DURNFORD, M., & KIMURA, D. Right hemispheric specialization for depth perception reflected in visual field differences. *Nature*, 1971, 231, 394-395.

EISENBURG, A.M., & SMITH, R.R., Jr. *Nonverbal communication*. Indianapolis: Bobbs-Merrill, 1971.

EISENSON, J. Aphasia in adults: Basic considerations. In L.E. Travis (Ed.), *Handbook of speech pathology and audiology*. New York: Appleton-Century-Crofts, 1971. (a)

EISENSON, J. Correlates of aphasia in adults. In L.E. Travis (Ed.), *Handbook of speech pathology and audiology*. New York: Appleton-Century-Crofts, 1971. (b)

EKMAN, P. Movements with precise meanings. *Journal of Communication*, 1976, 26, 14-26.

EXLINE, R.V., & FEHR, B.J. Applications of semiosis to the study of visual interaction. In A.W. Siegman and S. Feldstein (Eds.), *Nonverbal behavior and communication*. Hillsdale, New Jersey: Lawrence Erlbaum Associates, 1978.

FILBEY, R.A., & GAZZANIGA, M.S. Splitting the normal brain with reaction time. *Psychonomic Science*, 1969, 17, 335.

FONTENOT, D.F., & BENTON, A.L. Tactile perception of direction in relation to hemispheric locus of lesion. *Neuropsychologia*, 1971, 9, 83-88.

GALIN, D., & ORNSTEIN, R. Lateral specialization of cognitive mode: an EEG study. *Psychophysiology*, 1972, 9, 412-418.

GARDINER, M.F., & WALTER, D.O. Evidence of hemispheric specialization from infant EEG. In S. Harrad et al. (Eds.), *Lateralization in the nervous system*. New York: Academic Press, 1977.

GAZZANIGA, M.S. *The bisected brain*. New York. Appleton-Century-Crofts, 1970.

GAZZANIGA, M.S. The split brain in man. In R.E. Ornstein (Ed.), *The nature of human consciousness*. New York: Viking Press, 1974.

GAZZANIGA, M.S., BOGEN, J.E., & SPERRY, R.W. Some functional effects of sectioning the cerebral commissures in man. *Proceedings of the National Academy of Sciences*, 1965, 48, 1765-1769.

GERBER, S.E., & GOLDMAN, P. Ear preference for dichotically presented verbal stimuli as a function of report strategy *Journal of the Acoustical Society of America*, 1971, 49, 1163-1168.

GESCHWIND, N. Speech disorders in childhood. In E.C. Carterette (Ed.), *Brain function*. Berkeley: University of California Press, 1966.

GILBERT, C., & BAKAN, P. Visual asymmetry in perception of faces. *Neuropsychologia*, 1973, 11, 355-362.

HALL, E.T. *Beyond culture*. Garden City, New York: Anchor-Doubleday, 1976.

HARRISON, R.P. Nonverbal communication. In I. de Sola Pool, W. Schramm, N. Maccoby, F. Fry, E. Parker, and J.L. Fein (Eds.), *Handbook of communication*. Chicago: Rand McNally, 1973.

HARRISON, R.P. *Beyond words: An introduction to nonverbal communication*. Englewood Cliffs, New Jersey: Prentice-Hall, 1974.

HEAD, H. *Aphasia and kindred disorders of speech*. Cambridge: University Press, 1926.

HECAEN, H. Brain mechanisms suggested by studies of the parietal lobes. In C.H. Millikan and F. Darley (Eds.), *Brain mechanisms underlying speech and language*. New York: Grune and Stratton, 1967.

HECAEN, H., & SAUGET, J. Cerebral dominance in left-handed subjects. *Cortex*, 1971, 7, 19-48.

HENSCHEN, S.E. On the function of the right hemisphere in relation to the left in speech, music, and calculation. *Brain*, 1926, 49, 110-123.

HERMELIN, B., & O'CONNOR, N. Right and left handed reading of Braille. *Nature*, 1971, 231, 470.

HERRON, J. Southpaws: How different are they? *Psychology Today*, 1976, 9(10), 50-56.

HINES, D. Independent functioning of the two cerebral hemispheres for recognizing bilaterally presented visual stimuli. *Cortex*, 1975, 11, 132-143.

JAFFE, J. Parliamentary procedure and the brain. In A.W. Siegman and S. Feldstein (Eds.), *Nonverbal behavior and*

communication. Hillsdale, New Jersey: Lawrence Erlbaum Associates, 1978.

KIBLER, R.J. Basic communication research considerations. In P. Emmert and W.D. Brooks (Eds.), *Methods of research in communication*. New York: Houghton Mifflin, 1970.

KIMURA, D. Right temporal lobe damage. *Archives of Neurology*, 1963, 8, 264.

KIMURA, D. Left-right differences in the perception of melodies. *Quarterly Journal of Experimental Psychology*. 1964, 16, 355-358.

KIMURA, D. Dual functional asymmetry of the brain in visual perception. *Neuropsychologia*, 1966, 4, 275.

KIMURA, D. Functional asymmetry of the brain in dichotic listening. *Cortex*, 1967, 3, 163.

KIMURA, D. Spatial localization in left and right visual fields. *Canadian Journal of Psychology*, 1969, 23, 445-458.

KIMURA, D. The asymmetry of the human brain. *Scientific American*, 1973, 231, 70-76.

KNAPP, M.L. *Nonverbal communication in human interaction*. New York: Holt, Rinehart, and Winston, 1972.

KNAPP, M.L. *Nonverbal communication in human interaction* (2nd ed.). New York: Holt, Rinehart, and Winston, 1978.

KNAPP, M.L., WIEMANN, J.M., & DALY, J.A. Nonverbal communication: Issues and appraisal. *Human Communication Research*, 1978, 4, 271-280.

KNOX, C. & KIMURA, D. Cerebral processing of nonverbal sounds in boys and girls. *Neuropsychologia*, 1970, 8, 227.

KONEYA, M. Query on Ekman: Nonverbal movements or verbal surrogates. *Journal of Communication*, 1977, 27, 235-237.

KOTULAK, R. With half a brain, his IQ is 126, and doctors are dumbfounded. *Chicago Tribune*, November 7, 1976, 6.

KUMAR, S., ZAIDEL, E., & BOGEN, J.E. Muller Lyer illusion in disconnected right and left cerebral hemispheres. *Abstracts of the Society of Neurosciences*, 1976, 2, 1081.

LANSDELL, H.C. Studies in the parietal lobes. In C.H. Millikan and F. Darley (Eds.), *Brain mechanisms underlying speech and language*. New York: Grune and Stratton, 1967.

LANSDELL, H.C. Verbal and nonverbal factors in right-hemisphere speech: Relations to early neurological history. *Journal of Comparative and Physiological Psychology*, 1969, 69, 734-738.

LEATHERS, D.G. *Nonverbal communication systems*. Boston: Allyn and Bacon, 1976.

LINDZEY, G., PRINCE, B., & WRIGHT, H.K. A study of facial asymmetry. *Journal of Personality*, 1952, 21, 68-84.

LISHMAN, W.A., & McMEEKAN, E.R.L. Handedness in relation to direction and degree of cerebral dominance in language. *Cortex*, 1977, 8, 30-43.

LURIA, A.R. *Higher cortical functions in man*. New York: Basic, 1966.

LYONS, J. Human language. In R.A. Hinde (Ed.), *Nonverbal communication*. London: Cambridge University Press, 1972.

McCROSKEY, J.C., LARSON, C.E., & KNAPP, M.L. *An introduction to interpersonal communication*. Englewood Cliffs, New Jersey: Prentice-Hall, 1971.

McCROSKEY, J.C., & WHEELESS, L.R. *Introduction to human communication*. Boston: Allyn and Bacon, 1976.

McCURDY, H.G. Experimental notes on the asymmetry of the human face. *Journal of Abnormal Social Psychology*, 1949, 44, 553-565.

MEHRABIAN, A. *Nonverbal communication*. Chicago: Aldine, 1972. (a)

MEHRABIAN, A. *Silent messages*. Belmont, California: Wadsworth, 1972. (b)

MILNER, B. Brain mechanisms suggested by studies of the temporal lobes. In C.H. Millikan and F. Darley (Eds.), *Brain mechanisms underlying speech and language*. New York: Grune and Stratton, 1967.

MILNER, B. Interhemispheric differences in the localization of psychological processes in man. *British Medical Bulletin*, 1971, 27, 272-277.

MILNER, B., & TAYLOR, L. Right hemisphere superiority in tactile pattern-recognition after cerebral commissurotomy: Evidence for nonverbal memory. *Neuropsychologia*, 1972, 10, 1-15.

MOSCOVITCH, M. Language and the cerebral hemispheres. In P. Pliner, L. Krames, and T. Alloway (Eds.), *Communication and affect: Language and thought*. New York: Academic Press, 1973.

MOUNTCASTLE, V.P. Representation of information. In A. DeReuck and J. Knight (Eds.), *Touch, heat, and pain*. Boston: Little, Brown, 1966.

MURPHY, E.H., & VENABLES, P.H. Ear asymmetry in the threshold of fusion of two clicks: A signal detection analysis. *Quarterly Journal of Experimental Psychology*, 1970, 22, 288.

ORNSTEIN, R.E. *The psychology of consciousness*. San Francisco: Freeman, 1972.

ORNSTEIN, R.E. Introduction: Two modes of consciousness. In R.E. Ornstein (Ed.), *The nature of human consciousness*. New York: Viking Press, 1974.

ORNSTEIN, R.E. The split and whole brain. *Human Nature*, 1978, 1, 76-83.

PETROVICH, S.B., & HESS, E.H. An introduction to animal communication. In A.W. Siegman and S. Feldstein (Eds.), *Nonverbal behavior and communication*. Hillsdale, New Jersey: Lawrence Erlbaum, 1978.

PIERCY, M., HECAÉN, H., & AJURIAGUERRA, J. Constructional apraxia association with unilateral cerebral lesions—left and right sides compared. *Brain*. 1960, 83, 225-242.

RIZZOLATTI, G., UMILTA, C., & BERLUCCI, G. Opposite superiorities of the right and left cerebral hemispheres in discriminative reaction time to physiognomical and alphabetical material. *Brain*, 1971, 94, 431-442.

ROSENFELD, H.M. Conversational control functions of nonverbal behavior. In A.W. Siegman and S. Feldstein (Eds.), *Nonverbal behavior and communication*. Hillsdale, New Jersey: Lawrence Erlbaum, 1978.

ROSENFELD, L.B., & CIVIKLY, J.M. *With words unspoken: The nonverbal experience*. New York: Holt, Rinehart, and Winston, 1976.

RUESCH, J. Nonverbal language. In J. Stewart (Ed.), *Bridges not walls*. Reading, Massachusetts: Addison-Wesley, 1973.

SACKEIM, H.A., GUR, R.C., & SAUCY, M.C. Emotions are expressed more intensely on the left side of the face. *Science*, 1978, 202(27), 434-435.

SAMPLES, R.E. Are you teaching only one side of brain? *Learning*, 1975, February, 25-28.

SEARLEMAN, A. A review of right hemisphere linguistic capabilities. *Psychological Bulletin*, 1977, 84, 503-528.

SHANKWEILER, D. Effects of temporal lobe damage on perception of dichotically presented melodies. *Journal of Comparative Psychological Physiology*, 1966, 62, 115-119.

SIEGMAN, A.W. The telltale voice: Nonverbal messages of verbal communication. In A.W. Siegman and S. Feldstein (Eds.), *Nonverbal behavior and communication*. Hillsdale, New Jersey: Lawrence Erlbaum, 1978.

SIEGMAN, A.W., & FELDSTEIN, S. *Nonverbal behavior and communication*. Hillsdale, New Jersey: Lawrence Erlbaum, 1978.

SMITH, A. Speech and other functions after left (dominant) hemispherectomy. *Journal of Neurological Neurosurgical Psychiatry*, 1966, 29, 467-471.

SOUSA-POSA, J.F., & ROHRBERG, R. Body movement in relation to type of information and cognitive style. *Human Communication Research*, 1977, 4, 19-29.

SPERRY, R.W. Hemisphere deconnection and unity in conscious awareness. *American Psychologist*, 1968, 23, 723-733.

SPERRY, R.W. Lateral specialization of cerebral function in the surgically separated hemispheres. In F.J. McGuigan and R.A. Schoonover (Eds.), *The psychophysiology of thinking: Studies of covert processes*. New York: Academic Press, 1973.

SPERRY, R.W., & GAZZANIGA, M.S. Language following surgical disconnection of the hemispheres. In C.H. Millikan and F. Darley (Eds.), *Brain mechanisms underlying speech and language*. New York: Grune and Stratton, 1967.

SPERRY, R.W., & ZAIDEL, E. Level of consciousness in the surgically disconnected minor hemisphere. *Proceedings of the Psychonomic Society*, 1973, 14, 184.

SPREEN, O., SPELLACY, F.J., & REID, J.R. The effect of interstimulus interval and intensity on ears' asymmetry for nonverbal stimuli in dichotic listening. *Neuropsychologia*, 1970, 8, 245-250.

TEUBER, H., & WEINSTEIN, S. Performance on a form board task after penetrating brain injury. *Journal of Psychology*, 1954, 38, 177-190.

TOMLINSON-KEASEY, C., KELLY, R.R., & BURTON, J.K. Hemispheric changes in information processing during development. *Developmental Psychology*, 1978, 14, 214-223.

TURKEWITZ, G. The development of lateral differences in the human infant. In S. Harrad et al. (Eds.), *Lateralization in the nervous system*. New York: Academic Press, 1977.

WATZLAWICK, P., BEAVIN J.H., & JACKSON, D.D. *Pragmatics of human communication*. New York: Norton, 1967.

WEINSTEIN, S., & SERSEN, E.A. Tactual sensitivity as a function of handedness and laterality. *Journal of Comparative and Physiological Psychology*, 1961, 54, 665-669.

WELSBACHER, B.T. More than a package of bizarre behaviors. *Music Educators Journal*, 1972, 26.

WIENER, M., DEVOE, S., RUBINOW, S., & GELLER, J. Nonverbal behavior and nonverbal communication. *Psychological Review*, 1972, 79, 185-214.

WILDEN, A. Analog and digital communication. *Semiotica*, 1972, 10, 50-82. (a)

WILDEN, A. *System and structure: Essays in communication and exchange*. London: Tavistock, 1972. (b)

WITELSON, S.F. Hemispheric specialization for linguistic and nonlinguistic tactual perception using a dichotomous stimulation technique. *Cortex*, 1974, 10, 1-25.

WITELSON, S.F. Sex and the right hemisphere: Specialization of the right hemisphere for spatial processing. *Science*, 1976, 193, 425-427.

WOLFF, W. The experimental study of forms of expression. *Character and Personality*, 1933, 2, 168-176.

ZAIDEL, E. Linguistic competence and related functions in the right cerebral hemisphere of man following commissurotomy and hemispherectomy (doctoral dissertation, California Institute of Technology, 1973). *Dissertation Abstracts International*, 1973, 34, 2350B (University Microfilms No. 73-26,481).

ZAIDEL, E. Auditory language comprehension in the right hemisphere following cerebral commissurotomy and hemispherectomy: A comparison with child language and aphasia. In E.B. Zurif and A. Caramazza (Eds.), *The acquisition and breakdown of language: Parallels and divergencies*. Baltimore: Johns Hopkins University Press, 1976. (a)

ZAIDEL, E. Language, dichotic listening, and the disconnected hemispheres. In D.O. Walter, L. Rogers, and J.M. Finzi-Fried (Eds.), *Human brain function*. Los Angeles: Brain Information Service/BRI Publications, 1976. (b)

The inventive mind of Wilbur Schramm has turned to the history of communication. This unusual piece uses Carl Sagan's cosmic calendar approach to illustrate the development of human communication in all its forms. Schramm's 24-hour clock for Man's Day on Earth as a communicating being leads to a number of points. First, it illustrates graphically what an infinitely small part of human communication history the mass media (and most of our scholarly concern) make up. Second, the acceleration of the flow of information has been incredible, resulting in increasingly "hurried" media. However, Schramm speculates that rapidly developing new technology will dramatically increase individual control over the vast quantities of information flowing around them. Dr. Schramm was Howard R. Marsh Visiting Professor of Communication at the University of Michigan when he wrote this piece.

9

WHAT IS A LONG TIME?

Wilbur Schramm

My son thinks a long time is an hour waiting to go fishing, and doubtless he is correct. On the other hand, it may be that time moves faster now and parents sleep slower. This is my son's general theory of relativity, and makes quite as much sense as any of his parents' contributions to the problem.

The longest time we can now comprehend is the "Big Bang," which supposedly took place about 15 billion years ago—15 *billion*, not million. Precisely what happened at that time, or how, or why, is in doubt. But whatever happened, the nuclear forces of the universe gathered themselves into an incomprehensible, almost unimaginable explosion that blew everything out in all directions from some central point in the universe at some speed near the pace of light. We are *assuming* this. Whatever happened is so far beyond the human ability to map, and so far beyond the translation capacity of light telescopes and radio telescopes that we really know very little about what happened except that a great event took place, and that the approximate time stick between it and us is about 15 billion years.

So we can begin at least by saying that 15 billion years is a long time, and is, in fact, the longest time we know anything about. But young fellows like my son are unwilling to rest the matter there. If there was a Big Bang, they say, what was going on before *that?*

And if the Big Bang shot everything out in all directions, does that mean that everything will turn around and come back? And if you say that all this happened 15 billion years ago, does that mean that it will come back in 15 billion years? Or more? Or less?

I think that most parents are familiar with the kind of childish question that has no really satisfactory answer except: "Wouldn't you like to go out and throw baseball a little while?"

Yet these simple questions have their own strength and their own challenge. And when you realize that the field we study—human communication—has time as one of its chief dimensions, then you have to force yourself to make some kind of commonsense answer to even such a question as "what is a long time?"

You have to start somewhere. So let's start with the longest time stick we know anything about—15 billion years. Can anyone comprehend even *that* length of time? The only way to start comprehending it is to break it up, conceive it in units which are not themselves completely beyond the comprehension of man. Carl Sagan did this in *The Dragons of Eden*. Rather than trying to make us visualize billions of years, he took familiar measures—the 12-month year, the 31-day month. Then he divided those enormous millions of months into a calendar we might hope to understand in our own terrestrial way.

Let us make a clock for Man's Day on Earth somewhat as Sagan made his calendar for the Universe (see
figure 2). If Man's Day on Earth has been about a million years, then one hour of that day is 41,667 years:
for convenience, let us round it out to 42,000. One
minute of Man's Day on Earth would be about 694
years—round it out to 700. One second would be
about 12 years. This is the imaginary clock we shall be
dealing with.

Start the clock:

Man's Day on Earth: 1 minute after midnight. For
the first half-day there is very little evidence except
fossils and a few tools. Many of these remnants are
very interesting because they indicate a swifter
development of humanoids than had been anticipated. Tools are mostly quite crude—flakes, or
wafer shaped. Sometime after 9:00 p.m. (2100 hours)
of that first day of man an event took place that is so
important we wish we knew far more about it than we
do—when it occurred, where, in how many different
places, through what processes. Of course, I am talking about *language*. Language existed, in a primitive
form, probably by 100,000 B.C. We are guessing at the
time; we have no way other than to guess, because
language leaves no writing behind it. But if you want
to guess at what time on man's million-year clock he
first had language, a good guess would be 9:33 p.m.,—
21 hours and 33 minutes after the dawn of that day.
Let me say again that we know very little precisely
about the birth of human language. We have pic-
turesque and imaginative theories, but they are
theories only. The birth of language, however, was
very probably the most remarkable achievement of
man. And when writing came into use—about 3500
B.C., the equivalent of seven minutes before midnight on Man's Day on Earth—those two developments dwarfed all the other accomplishments of man:
one, his greatest intellectual achievement; the other,
his greatest invention.

I have been spending so much time on prehistoric
man and his communication in order to set communication history, as we know it, in perspective. One
of the noteworthy developments of the study of
human communication during the last several
decades has been the backward stretching of this
history trying to understand more and more clearly
how man learned to communicate and how his life
and his history have been affected by the choices he
has had to make as to how to communicate and to
whom and for what purposes. "What it will prove
most important to remember," said the distinguished historian Jacquetta Hawkes (Mrs. J. B.
Priestley), "is that our species did not only inherit
from the past its bodily equipment, dominated by its
subtly elaborated brain, but also highly charged
emotional centres and all the strange ancient furni-

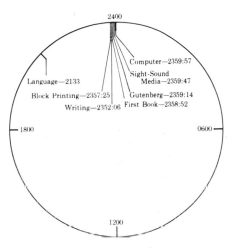

Figure 2   A 24-hour clock for Man's Day on Earth (24
hours = one million years).

ture of the unconscious mind. Man emerged bringing
with him hate, fear, and anger, together with love and
the joy of life in their simple animal form. He also
brought the social heritage of family affection and
group loyalty. Today some of us believe (while others
do not) that among the most elusive and yet the most
precious heirlooms of all were shadowy, deep-seated
memories of the experiences of the evolving animal
line during the vast stretches of its history, memories
which enrich and unite modern man by throwing up
from the unconscious the images and ideas that in-
spire our arts and help to make them universally
evocative. . . . There can be no question, whatever
construction we put upon them, that these mental
and emotional inheritances which man received from
the prehuman past were to provide a most potent
force in the creature of culture."

We have taken such a long road back, therefore, in
order to gather light for the road forward. The history
of our field is a rather young, new history because so
many of our technologies and our institutions are so
new. The questions are: how long can we afford to
write young history, and how soon must we enrich it
with a series of books that have depth as well as fact? I
can say confidently that most of the great books on
the history of human communication have not yet
been written, and I hope they soon will, because we
are entering upon an age in which it is going to be
dangerous not to be able to write them.

Forgive me this homily. Let us turn back to the long road where we find, as usual, that a travelogue usually draws larger audiences than a sermon. We are back now in Man's Day on Earth, his first million years as a human on Earth. The first half-day, so far as we know, must have been taken up largely with learning to live in the rough and challenging Pleistocene period, when four separate sheets of ice swept out of the north and the great mountain ranges of the Earth curled up and uncurled. Man learned how to keep warm with animal skins, to make a home in a cave, to become a quick and skillful hunter. There was communication, of course: how could humanoids live together without communicating? Much of their communication may have been very skillful—the language of the glance or the gesture or the moving position; sign language; group communication; fire on the hillside; tracks in the meadow.

For at least 100,000 years the habitats of man must have resounded with sounds we could certainly call words. The echoes of those words have died. Marks of the words have never existed. What richness of oratory and ritual must have resounded through the caves of Altamira? We have no doubt man was talking in those caves even while he was painting some of the world's fine pictures. That was, say, 25,000 years ago. We can only guess what signs and gestures and expressive movements, what half-animal, half-human grunts and cries preceded the repetitious sounds, gestures, and expressions that grew into the disciplined sounds and movements we call words. Who was it, and how did it happen, that someone got the idea that a certain sound could always refer to an object or an event without having to carry the object in one's hand or point to it? That may have been the most dramatic Everest man climbed on his ascent to humanity. Who got the idea that abstractions as well as specifics could be denoted or connoted by words—not only thunder and animals and rain, but also goodness, badness, danger, happiness, immortality?

If language was man's greatest intellectual achievement, his greatest invention was writing. Greater than the invention of the wheel. Greater than the concept of the number zero by the ingenious Hindus, or the calculus by Leibnitz and Newton. Greater than the invention of the telephone, or the motion picture, or the telegraph. Greater than the computer. Greater because writing presented man a memory, freed him from being able to communicate only so far as his voice would carry or his signal fire could be seen; greater because it built a bridge over which language and picture could be carried measureless distance and endless time.

It is interesting that the chief impetus behind the development of writing should be not so much the impulse to send messages as to preserve information. For many centuries, and in illiterate cultures today, the "memory man" has preserved the ritual, the histories, the sacred genealogies, the holy writings. Writing made it possible to share much of this responsibility so that the skills of writing and reading could be used for other purposes, two of the most important of which were the library and the school.

We have spoken of language and writing, and properly so because they are the foundation for all the human communication that follows. But we have said almost nothing about printing or publishing, about the electric, or photographic, or electronic media, or the computer. One way to look at the years from Altamira to today is in the form of a kind of *déjà vu* drama, a circularity of events that leads us away and then brings us back toward the old familiar path. That is, we learn to interpose communicating machines or process in the basic steps we have already learned to take. We learn to write with beauty and skill, and then find machines that will let us write faster and more efficiently (although no more beautifully) so that we learn to live in an age of reading and duplicating and printing. We learn to paint the bison on the dark wall of the cave, and then find apparatus that will take the brush out of our hand and make more pictures faster. We find a way to construct a huge megaphone that will let us talk not only to the next hill but also the next continent. We find a way to listen without cupping our ears or being alert for the distant drum. As we used to watch the dance against our firelight so now we find a way to watch the dance and the expressions and the events in the distant village. And to *remember* them in all their real color. To *save* them, *preserve* them. Yes, even to the instant replay.

Is this the map we have been following? From the wonderful clarity of the starlight, through the spoken word and the sharp and subtle non-verbal relationships, through the ages when we learn to recognize marks on paper or stone as translations of spoken sounds, through the ages when machines then take over our reading and our writing so that we learn to see the world as lines of symbols, through the ages when machines talk and listen and picture for us, so that the experience of world-living is not quite the same as at Altamira, but in a sense more efficient because once again we can see the world not merely as rows of writing, but also as pictures and sounds, and we can use all our senses again even for very distant communication. Is this the path we have been following?

Let us see what kind of schedule we might make for this long way we have come:

The Basic Skills:

Language—sometime around 100,000 B.C. (On our 24-hour clock this would be about 9:33 p.m., or 21 hours and 33 minutes after the dawn of the day of man.) Writing—about 3500 B.C. (7 minutes, 54 seconds before midnight).

The Age of Reading:

Handcopying—soon after the origin of writing. Block printing, paper, and ink—in use in China between 100 and 300 A.D. (2 minutes, 35 seconds before midnight). First completely preserved block-printed book (Diamond Sutra)—dated from 868 A.D. (1 minute, 8 seconds before midnight)

Rapid development of block printing and even wooden letters.

Printing from movable metal type in Korea—early in 15th century and perhaps earlier. Gutenberg printed indulgences on press at Mainz, Germany, by 1450 (46 seconds before midnight). Thereafter, a flood of printed books, news sheets, newspapers, magazines, business publications, and so forth.

The Age of Sound and Seeing:

Photography usable still pictures—in France in 1839 (13 seconds before midnight).

Telegraph about 1844 (11 seconds before midnight).

Telephone Alexander Graham Bell, 1876 (8 seconds before midnight).

Phonograph Thomas A. Edison, 1878 (8 seconds).

Motion Picture—Edison, 1895 (7 seconds before midnight).

Radio telegraph—Marconi, 1895 (7 seconds), first transmission across the ocean, 1901

Radio speech—Fessenden, 1900 (7 seconds).

Regularly scheduled radio broadcasts—1920 (5 seconds before midnight)

Television—demonstrated by John Baird, in England, 1926 (4 seconds before midnight). First regularly scheduled broadcasts, BBC, 1936 (4 seconds before midnight).

The Age of Electronics:

Communication satellite—Clarke's pioneer article, 1945 (3 seconds before midnight).

High-storage computer—Von Neumann's pioneer article, 1946 (3 seconds before midnight).

Transistor—invented by Bardeen, Brattain, and Schockley, Bell Telephone Laboratories, 1947 (3 seconds before midnight), leading to miniaturization of electronic parts and circuits.

It is a great temptation, of course, to talk about these events and processes in detail, for each one of them has resulted in a significant social change and a significant readjustment of the information system. But those questions are not for today.

However, since we began by asking "What is a long time?"—and, indeed, taking a long time talking about it—perhaps I may be permitted to make a few concluding remarks on the subject of time.

In the first place, such a schedule as we have just presented leads us to consider how typically, how almost exclusively, we deal with very recent elements in the study of human communication. When we study communication in our universities, read about it in our libraries, discuss it with our professional colleagues, we speak almost entirely of events so recent that we can hardly find room for them on the clock of Man's Day on Earth. Take an example: the entire human development from photography, through the telephone, the movies, radio, and television, took place in a little less than ten seconds of our 24-time clock. If you find it easier to read in other time measures, from the first practical photography to the first successfully demonstrated television was about 100 years. If we sign up for a course, let us say, in the history of American journalism, that is likely to begin with *Publick Occurences*, which lasted for one issue in 1690, leaving something less than half a minute on man's 24-hour clock for the development of all the rest of this country's journalism. If one starts with those exciting and productive years of electronics 1945 1946, and 1947—one has left himself only 3 seconds of Man's Day on Earth to develop them. I am not suggesting that there is anything wrong about this, only that it is perhaps worth thinking about how restricted in time our view of human communication has been.

Second, it is impossible to examine such a time schedule as we have been presenting without being impressed by the enormous acceleration of the flow of information since we have any records of it. Here is a homely example:

From language to writing—at least 50 million years

From writing to printing—about 5 thousand years

From printing to the media of photography and sound—about 500 years

From the first of the sight-sound media to the modern computer—fewer than 50 years

The growth of modern media has been even more impressive. In 1946, the year after World War II, about one home out of every 5,000 in the United States had a television receiver. Ten years later, 72 *percent* of all U.S. homes had TV receivers. Now the figure is nearing 100 percent.

Making use of the best figures available, futurists have tried to calculate how much factual information has been available to human beings at various stages of their history. In very rough terms it can be estimated that the increase in bits of information based on vocabulary available to man has risen about one order of magnitude (10 times) from prewriting to preprinting (3100 B.C.-1450 A.D.); still another from 1450 to the beginning of the electronic age (beginning about 1830); and from 1830 to the present time, still another order of magnitude. Or, in rough and ready terms, thanks to writing, printing, electronic gadgetry, libraries, and schools, the average supply of information available to the average human must have risen in 5000 years by at least 1,000 times.

But the significance of these figures is more than the need of storage or study space (libraries that can afford it will double in contents about every 14 years!) or of newsprint or digests or even of computers which are the only electronics that seem to offer a reasonable hope of handling the overload. The bothersome question is learning how to live with such an overload of information and such an exaggerated pace of flow. The exchange of digital information has been doubling every three or four years over the satellite channels, but there is no corresponding residue in what we retain. Our newspapers are crowded, but we skim, just as the newspaper similarly must reduce what comes to it from the wire, and the wire reduces its own input. Beyond the size and pace of flow, however, philosophers and social scientists have been concerned with possible impact on society and personality. Certainly, what our news media decide to cover has an effect on the way we perceive the world around us, the topics we think are worth focusing attention on, and the kind of political and social value questions that concern us.

Television is a hurried medium; the more hurried, the thinner the content. Is it making hurried people, too? Is it encouraging a taste for information rather than a taste for knowledge? Are people using it to get the latest "word" rather than the deepest explanation? These are not questions we can answer here, but they indicate the depth of concern over a flow of information that has become one of the major avenues of exchange in the world.

A few pages ago we talked about a possible circularity in the development of human communication. This is a line McLuhan has sometimes taken: having "detribalized" ourselves by learning the solitary skills of reading and writing, we are now "retribalizing" ourselves by exposure to television. It is an interesting idea and in some ways attractive, but raises almost as many questions as it answers.

For example, what effect can we anticipate from the developments we identified as "The Age of Electronics"—the three remarkable years 1945, 1946, and 1947—which gave us the communication satellite, the modern computer, and the transistor? The satellite, of course, will enormously increase the load of information we can circulate. The computer will enormously increase our ability to file, sort, manipulate, store, and retrieve the information in the world around us. And the transistor, and the developments in solid state physics that have followed it, have made it possible for us to do in miniature what could recently have been done only with instrumentation of great size so that a piece of electronics the size of a fingernail now will do what once required an enormous machine.

Therefore we can look forward to a new constellation of electronic equipment—some that will deliver more information; others that will file, store, and retrieve it with such speed and skill as we have never known before; and finally a new set of machines that will miniaturize the task and make pocket calculators and desk-top computers as common as typewriters.

How is this going to work out? The three remarkable years came only three seconds before midnight of Man's Day on Earth, and therefore we have had very little time to look at new evidence. But this at least we can say: the combination is something new in the history of man's communication. And it seems less likely to suggest a circularity of development than a challenge to move forward into new and imaginative users of the new technology. One development that seems most likely is that individuals are going to have more control than before over the information that flows around them. They will have more power than before to call for the information (of whatever kind) they need, more power to maintain communication with individuals elsewhere, more power to make use of files and databanks and libraries—in other words, more *individual* control over information resources no longer far away, no longer restricted from their use.

So this is a long way, indeed, we have come even though we are not entirely sure what to expect. We have found out what "a long time" is, and that it is not necessarily measured in regular ticks of a clock but rather in terms of where it takes man, and the combination of uncertainty and promise it offers.

PART II

RESEARCH STRATEGIES AND METHODOLOGY

Research on the agenda-setting function of mass media is published widely, confirming the observation of a prominent scholar that the agenda-setting notion is one of the best research ideas of the last couple of decades. Methodological and conceptual differences, however, retard the productivity of the myriad of studies on agenda-setting. An in-depth look at the problems of such research by a group of fresh young scholars highlights this section of the *Yearbook*. The lack of comparability of many agenda-setting analyses is traced to differences in time-frame and measurement of agendas.

Some scholars see agenda-setting as bridging the gap between the effects tradition and the uses-and-gratifications approach. Quite a different view of the effects approach is taken in this section in an article that deals with the perennial difficulty of establishing media effects. This vital discussion outlines the major variable sources and necessary controls for conducting solid effects research. Related work adopts a uses-and-gratifications approach and outlines concepts and methods for studying long-term media use over entire life-spans.

Thoughtful discussions of the validity of content analysis are rare indeed, because most research reports dutifully list reliability statistics and hurry on to the results as if face validity is established. A most irreverent but careful analysis of the validity problem in media-bias studies is presented here, making the section a relevant follow-up on work reported in the first volume of the *Yearbook*.

The final piece in this section discusses the application of quantitative methods to historical questions. When considering these questions, the use of social scientists' methods alone is not enough. Dyer says these techniques must be applied with the historian's unique sense of the problem.

A symposium of papers on the theory and method of agenda-setting research is introduced here by Maxwell McCombs, John Ben Snow professor of newspaper research at the Newhouse School of Communications at Syracuse University. Dr. McCombs sees agenda-setting as a conceptual bridge between the mass media effects tradition and the uses and gratifications approach to mass communication research and theory. These articles were edited especially for the Mass Communication Review Yearbook *from papers originally presented at the annual convention of the American Association for Public Opinion Research in 1979.*

10

SETTING THE AGENDA FOR AGENDA-SETTING RESEARCH

An Assessment of the Priority Ideas and Problems

Maxwell E. McCombs

There clearly is a need for a review of the research literature on the agenda-setting role of mass communication. Since publication of the original McCombs and Shaw article in the Summer 1972 *Public Opinion Quarterly* there has been a steady proliferation of empirical papers on convention programs and in research journals. However, this attractiveness and fruitfulness of the concept of agenda-setting has both advantages and disadvantages.

The advantage has been the attraction of many scholars to this line of research, scholars who have produced more than 50 papers in the past six years. Agenda-setting has achieved an established position in the intellectual tradition of the field. But there also have been disadvantages to this rapid, scattered growth. The idea of agenda-setting has been examined in many different research settings and the components of this idea—the media agenda, the public agenda, and the linkage between them—have been conceptualized and measured in a great variety of ways. As James Winter comments despairingly (Chapter 14, this volume): "the drive for total innovation has overwhelmed the scientific prerequisite of at least partial replication." This lack of replication leaves many alternative explanations for the variations in the empirical findings.

From Maxwell E. McCombs, "Setting the Agenda for Agenda-Setting Research: An Assessment of the Priority Ideas and Problems," original manuscript.

The burgeoning number of subconcepts used to operationalize the public agenda, media agenda, and their relationships define dozens of sub-hypotheses, each detailing the idea of an agenda-setting role of mass communication in a different way. It is this great variety of detail, which one could pessimistically say approaches near chaos, that underscores the appropriateness of a literature review at this stage in the history of agenda-setting research.

So in the fall of 1978 four of us here in the School of Public Communications at Syracuse University began the task of sifting through the accumulated research on an article-by-article basis. Our goal was not the traditional type of literature review.

Rather our goal was to identify the major theoretical elements and methodological problems which should receive priority attention in subsequent research. Our goal was the preparation of the research memoranda presented here, memoranda for interested scholars outlining the major principles and decision points which they should consider in the design of any subsequent research.

Good science is, of necessity, a laissez-faire activity. But good science also is cumulative, with one study building on another. To this point agenda-setting research has been exploratory, not cumulative, discovering fresh applications of the idea and new ways of operationalization. Due to the volume of this research, we now stand on the threshold of a new, cumulative stage where agenda-setting has the potential of important theoretical contribution. However, to realize this potential the ideas and findings of previous research must be systematically organized and applied.

Part of the difficulty in intellectually assimilating the variety of agenda-setting studies now in the literature is that we now have an apples and oranges mix. While some studies test the *basic concept* of an agenda-setting function of mass communication, others assume this relationship and/or go beyond it to link agenda-setting with other variables. These latter studies represent the first connected pieces in a larger jigsaw puzzle that we might label a theory of agenda-setting. So on the one hand, we have a concept of agenda-setting, which is itself a hypothesis, and on the other, we have a larger theory of agenda-setting.

Collectively, these memoranda provide guidelines for the systematic accumulation of knowledge about both the concept and theory of agenda-setting through careful replication and extension.

In numerous ways they also point up the need for a more theoretical approach to agenda-setting research in the place of quick, almost casual, empirical forays. Two quite disparate points illustrate this need for theoretical strategy in place of tactical empiricism.

1. The basic idea of agenda-setting asserts a direct, causal relationship between the content of the media agenda and subsequent public perception of what the important issues of the day are. This is an assertion of direct learning by members of the public from the media agenda. Obviously, people can

learn only from those messages to which they are exposed. Yet few studies bother to insert controls which limit comparisons with a mass medium agenda to the agendas of those members of the public who report exposure to that medium. More commonly, an aggregate measure of public opinion is compared to the aggregate content of all the media included in a particular study. Common sense, and simple theoretical considerations, dictate otherwise!

2. There is another, more basic, theoretical point. Agenda-setting grows out of a general concern with how people organize and structure the world around them. The metaphor of agenda-setting is a macro-description of this process. As developed by McCombs and Shaw and their colleagues, this research rests on some specific assumptions and questions about the kind of cues which people attend to in structuring their world. For example, the typical measure of media agendas, which arrays issues according to frequency of mention, is based on an assumption that the frequency with which an item or topic appears is a major cue used by audiences to evaluate its salience. This assumption that individuals in the audience do seek cues which help order their environment—and, in fact, feel uncomfortable in the absence of such order—is further elaborated in the psychological concept "need for orientation," which has been used in a number of agenda-setting studies. Since these assumptions about the need for, and use of, orienting cues are assumptions about a psychological process, they also explain the major emphasis in agenda setting research on intrapersonal agendas rather than alternative conceptualizations of the public agenda.

However, there are other viewpoints and other assumptions about how people organize and structure the world about them. The fruitfulness of alternative theoretical frameworks needs to be explored, and the loose set of assumptions guiding the research to date needs to be made explicit.

Forming a bridge between the long-dominant effects tradition and the more recently emphasized uses-and-gratification tradition of mass communication research, the idea of an agenda-setting role of mass communication offers a theoretical point of convergence for many long-standing concerns of mass communication scholars.

Many agenda-setting studies appear to be replications but are actually not because of differences in time-frame models. Chaim H. Eyal, James P. Winter, and William F. DeGeorge show how a variety of studies differ on time frame, rendering the results incomparable. Rather than relying on intuition and guesswork to establish time frames, the authors call for designs that allow independent examination of separate media and distinct issues along a variety of time-frame models. Dr. Eyal is on the faculty of Social Sciences of Hebrew University's Communication Institute in Jerusalem. Dr. Winter is an adjunct lecturer in the School of Communications at Syracuse University. Dr. DeGeorge is adjunct lecturer in organizational communication at the University of Houston and is a consultant in corporate communications.

11

THE CONCEPT OF TIME FRAME
IN AGENDA-SETTING

Chaim H. Eyal, James P. Winter, and
William F. DeGeorge

Traditionally, agenda-setting research has involved the construction of media and public measures on the basis of extensive content analyses to determine the former and survey methods for the latter. Since we are measuring and comparing media and public agendas *over time,* intuitively, the temporal variable would appear to be crucial, but a review of the literature indicates it has not been treated as such. The question of the appropriate "time frame" for agenda-setting has yet to be elaborated, much less given serious consideration as a variable in the agenda-setting process. To begin to rectify this situation, this paper will first outline the concept of time frame as it applies to agenda-setting and then compare the various time frames utilized in research to date.

In agenda-setting research five distinct temporal features can be identified (Eyal, 1979). (1) The *time-frame,* which is the total period under consideration, from the beginning to the completion of the data gathering process; (2) the *time-lag,* which refers to the elapsed time between the independent variable (the media agenda) and the dependent variable (the public agenda); (3) the *duration of the media agenda measure,* which is the total interval during which the media measure is collected; (4) the *duration of the public agenda measure,* referring to the overall time span during which the public-

From Chaim H. Eyal, James P. Winter, and William F. DeGeorge, "The Concept of Time Frame in Agenda-Setting," original manuscript.

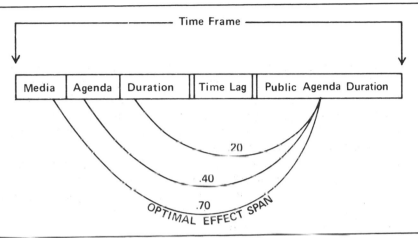

Figure 11.1   The Concept of Time Frame in Agenda-Setting

agenda measure has been gathered; and (5) the *optimal effect span* or peak association between media emphasis and public emphasis of an issue. Figure 11.1 graphically illustrates these features.

Various substantive and methodological questions emerge from this formulation. Two of the substantive questions are: How much time do the media require to bring issues and topics to the public domain (i.e., what is the optimal effect span)? And is there a cumulative media effect over time? Methodologically of interest are such questions as whether the duration of the media and public agenda measures affects the obtained results, how we choose a valid time-lag, and what the overall time-frame should be.

Decisions on appropriate time formulation are difficult to make. The theoretical conceptualization of the agenda-setting phenomenon does not stipulate the nature of the time frame. Consequently, researchers have resorted to intuition and guesswork in designing their investigations.

PREVIOUS RESEARCH

McCombs and Shaw's (1972) agenda-setting study employed a time-frame of three and one-half weeks, consisting of a three-and-a-half-week-long measure of the media agenda and a public agenda measure of two-and-a-half-weeks' duration. An overlap of two and a half weeks of simultaneous media and public agenda data-gathering accounts for the lack of time-lag in that study.

The diffusion of agenda-setting research in recent years has led to a variety of what can only loosely be termed "replications," due to the numerous operationalizations, conceptualizations, and populations employed. Among these are incomparable time-related decisions often based on conjecture and speculation. For example, Cohen (1975) used a time-frame of three years in his study of the Lake Monroe issue in Bloomington, Indiana. Palmgreen and Clarke (1977) adopted a time-frame of only two and a half weeks in their Toledo, Ohio, study of local and national issues. The time-lag has also been inconsistently applied. Frequently, the concepts of "time-frame" and "time-lag" interchangeably recur. Using the above definition of time-lag we find that agenda-setting studies vary extensively along this dimension from a multitude of studies incorporating no time-lag at all (Auh, 1977; Benton and Frazier, 1976; Bowers, 1977; Cohen, 1975; Hilker, 1976; McClure and Patterson, 1976; McCombs and Shaw, 1972; McLeod et al., 1974; Palmgreen and Clarke, 1977; Semlak and Williams, 1977; Shaw and Bowers, 1973; Weaver et al., 1975) to time-lag formulations as long as five months (Gormley, 1975) or nine months (Sohn, 1978).

Variations also abound in the *duration* of the interval used for the construction of the media and public agendas. For instance, Mullins' (1977) Chapel Hill media agenda was the product of a single week of media content analysis, while Gormley (1975) gathered media agenda information for four and a half months. Hilker (1976) collected a public agenda measure in one day of interviewing for her study of agenda-setting in a nonelection year; and McLeod, Becker, and Byrnes (1974) used data collected over four weeks in assembling their public agenda. While most of the examples cited consist of extreme choices, the field of agenda-setting research as a whole offers a wide range of time formulations.

Very few agenda-setting researchers have tackled the methodological problem of time-frame. Without specifically testing the concept, but on the basis of supportive evidence, Shaw and McCombs (1977) suggested that, in general, the agenda-setting influence of newspapers is a three- to five-month process. Stone (1975) and Winter (1979) have carried out more elaborate treatments of the subject.

In the Stone study the agendas of *Time* and *Newsweek* were analyzed for six months prior to, and three months following, the fieldwork of two different public opinion surveys. Using Pearson correlations between each month's media-agenda and the public agenda, the author tested the strength of the relationship in the context of differing "effect spans" (although he did not refer to them as such). In addition, by systematically expanding the media agenda to include more and more months, Stone was able to examine the cumulative agenda-setting effect. With one set of data the analysis yielded a monotonic increase in the correlations as the time-frame was extended backward in time from the field survey period. The findings showed a *dramatic increase* in the correlations from the interview period to the time two months prior to the interviews. As the time-frame was stretched back farther, the correlations continued to increase, but not as rapidly as in the first two months. The results led the author to the conclusion that a four month "optimal effect span" (our term) extending from two to six months prior to the public agenda measure constituted the parameters for the agenda-setting effect.

With a second data set, Stone obtained moderately similar patterns; however, no monotonic relationship was found. He attributed the differences in patterns to the *nature of the social context* involved (a presidential election for the second data set, a nonelection period for the first set.)

Winter (1979) compared Gallup poll data on the importance of the civil rights issue, with front-page stories in the New York *Times,* over a 22-year period. His media agenda consisted of a six-month period prior to each of 27 Gallup polls. His findings, expressed in zero- and partial-order correlations, portrayed a somewhat different picture. Moving backward by months from the interview period resulted in an initially moderate and then dramatic *monotonic decline* in correlations between media and public agendas. While Stone's study emphasized simple cumulative correlations only, Winter's larger sample allowed for techniques of partialling and regression. As a result, Winter (1979) concluded that for the civil rights issue the optimal effect span encompassed the period between zero and eight weeks prior to interviewing.

Thus, what appear to be conflicting findings are in part due to a larger sample and more refined analysis in Winter's study. In fact, the cumulative correlations in the two studies were highly similar. What differences do exist—such as the discrepancy over the importance of media content in the first month prior to interviewing—may be explained by the idiosyncracies of each study. Stone (1974) used magazine information for his media agenda. Since most studies have used newspapers and television, replications are called for. In addition, Stone used an entire set of issues in his analysis, and aggregating issues has an averaging effect which may conceal individual differences (Eyal, 1979).

Winter (1979) used a single issue and correlated its public salience with front-page stories in the New York *Times.* While this effort is revealing and important in terms of time-series analysis and individual examination of issues, it nonetheless used aggregated media content data and, as the author points out, does not take into account antecedent and intervening variables such as media use patterns, demographic data, and other contingent conditions. Despite these limitations, the study provides evidence of a strong agenda-setting effect at the aggregate level. More importantly, it also suggests that a reduced time-frame is appropriate for the civil rights issue.

THE NATURE OF ISSUES

The differences outlined above highlight the need for more precise explications of temporal concepts in agenda-setting. Issues vary in the amount of time necessary to bring them to a position of importance in public opinion. An oil embargo may suddenly thrust the issue of energy shortage and conservation onto public agendas; an oil spill can make pollution rise to importance; whereas it may take years for the honesty in government issue to become prominent in public awareness. Because each issue will have its own temporal history, examining more than one issue at a time can be problematic.

In the "typical" agenda-setting study, media content is analyzed to determine the salience of perhaps seven different issues in a single cross-sectional period, and these findings are then compared to an assessment of the public agenda. Because of the nature of the data that are gathered, nothing short of almost wholesale transferal of the rank-order salience of these issues from media to public will demonstrate agenda-setting effects. With seven issues (or cases), a rank-order correlation of $+.71$ is required for statistical significance at conventional levels (p.$=$.05, 1-tail). Anything short of this will not demonstrate agenda-setting effects. Yet issues vary in the time required to place them on the public agenda, as discussed above. Too, opposite effects of positive correlations for some issues and negative correlations for others may cancel each other out. Aggregate correlations may also conceal other individual relationships, but the point is that there is a clear need for different approaches to agenda-setting research, approaches that will overcome individual issue differences, and the limitations of small samples.

TIME-FRAMES FOR DIFFERENT MEDIA

Earlier it was suggested that on the basis of the discrepant findings by Stone (1974), compared to Winter (1979), the medium used may in part determine the nature of the agenda-setting effect. McCombs (1977) provides evidence to suggest that the agenda-setting potential over time is indeed different for newspapers and television. He found that early in the 1972 presidential campaign, newspapers performed a more effective agenda-setting role than television, and clearly took the role of major public opinion movers. As the election day approaches, however, television appears to "catch up" and become better attuned to the agenda of its audience than are newspapers. While McCombs and Shaw (1977) reject the possibility of agenda-setting within the media, in this respect, their conclusion is that technological and stylistic differences between the media account for different functions during distinct phases over time. The precise operation of different media within the context of varied agenda-setting time-frames has yet to be explored.

SUMMARY

The period within which the agenda-setting function of the media occurs is a critical and complex issue. Traditionally, time formulations have been based on intuition and guesswork, in the absence of established theoretical formulations. The critical components of time-frame in agenda-setting have been identified in this paper and are seen as consisting of four crucial measures: (1) time-lag; (2) duration of the media agenda measure; (3) duration of the public agenda measure; and (4) optimal effect span. A review of the existing literature reveals that agenda-setting research efforts vary widely along these dimensions, rendering results incomparable.

The type of mass medium and the kind and number of issues involved in the process appear to constitute important considerations; each holds the potential of affecting the obtained results and conclusions regarding the agenda-setting process. It is therefore felt that designs which will allow the independent examination of separate media and distinct issues along various time-frame models would, in the future, provide answers to questions about the temporal nature of the agenda-setting function.

REFERENCES

Benton, Marc and P. Jean Frazier (1976) "The Agenda-Setting Function of Mass Media at Three Levels of 'Information Holding'." Pp. 261-274 in *Communication Research*, Vol. 3, No. 3 (July).

Bowers, Thomas A. (1977) "Candidate Advertising: The Agenda is the Message." Pp. 53-67 in D.L. Shaw and M.E. McCombs (Eds.) *The Emergence of American Political Issues: The Agenda-Setting Function of the Press.* St. Paul, Minn.: West Publishing Co.

Eyal, Chaim (1979) Time Frame in Agenda-setting Research: A study of the conceptual and methodological factors affecting the time frame context of the agenda-setting process. Unpublished doctorial dissertation, Syracuse University.

Gormley, William Thomas, Jr. (1975) "Newspaper Agendas and Political Elites." Pp. 304-308 in *Journalism Quarterly*, Vol. 52, No. 2 (Summer).

Hilker, Anne K. (1976) "Agenda-Setting Influence in an Off-Year Election." Pp. 7-10 in the *American Newspaper Publishers Association News Research Bulletin*, No. 4 (November 10).

McClure, Robert D. and Thomas E. Patterson (1976) "Setting the Political Agenda: Print vs. Network News." Pp. 23-28 in the *Journal of Communication*, Vol. 26, No. 2 (Spring).

McCombs, Maxwell E. (1977a) "The Agenda-Setting Function of the Press." Paper prepared for Women and the News (S.T. Olin Conference) Washington University, St. Louis (September).

_____(1977b) "Expanding the Domain of Agenda-Setting Research: Strategies for Theoretical Development." Paper presented to the Mass Communication Div. of the Speech Communication Association, Washington D.C. (December).

_____(1977c) "Newspapers Versus Television: Mass Communication Effects Across Time." Pp. 89-105 in D.L. Shaw and M.E. McCombs (Eds.) *The Emergence of American Political Issues: The Agenda-Setting Function of the Press.* St. Paul, Minn.: West Publishing Co.

McCombs, Maxwell E. and Donald L. Shaw (1972) "The Agenda-Setting Function of the Mass Media." Pp. 176-187 in *Public Opinion Quarterly*, Vol. 36 (Summer).

McLeod, J.M., Lee B. Becker, and J.E. Byrnes (1974) "Another Look at The Agenda-Setting Function of the Press," *Communication Research* 1, Pp. 131-66 (April).

Mullins, L. Edward (1977) "Agenda-Setting and the Younger Voter." Pp. 133-148 in D.L. Shaw and M.E. McCombs (Eds.) *The Emergence of American Political Issues: The Agenda-Setting Function of the Press.* St. Paul, Minn.: West Publishing Co.

Palmgreen, Philip and Peter Clarke (1977) "Agenda-Setting with Local and National Issues." Pp. 435-452 in *Communication Research,* Vol. 4, No. 4 (October).

Shaw, Donald L. and Thomas A. Bowers (1973) "Learning from Commercials: The Influence of TV Advertising on the Voter's Political 'Agenda'." Paper presented to the annual conference of the Association for Education in Journalism, Fort Collins, Colorado.

Sohn, Ardyth Broadrick (1978) "A Longitudinal Analysis of Local Non-Political Agenda-Setting Effects." *Journalism Quarterly.*

Stone, Gerald (1975) "Cumulative Effects of the Media." Paper presented at the conference on Agenda-Setting, Syracuse University, Syracuse, NY.

Weaver, David, Taik Sup Auh, Timothy Stehla, and Cleve Wilhoit (1975) "A Path Analysis of Individual Agenda-Setting During the 1974 Indiana Senatorial Campaign." Paper presented to the Association for Education in Journalism, Annual Convention, Ottawa.

Winter, James P. (1979) "An Agenda-Setting Time Frame for the Civil Rights Issue: 1954-1976." Unpublished paper, Syracuse University (February).

Measuring media and public agendas is, obviously, critical in agenda-setting research. William F. DeGeorge reviews the awareness, priorities (ranking), and salience (high-low importance) approaches to public agenda. He concludes that an awareness model is likely to be most valid with situations involving low media exposure and low influence from intervening factors. The priorities approach may work best in settings of high media exposure and heavy influence of intervening variables. A salience approach is more appropriate for mixed media-intervening variable contexts. Dr. DeGeorge is an adjunct lecturer in organizational communication at the University of Houston and is a consultant in corporate communications.

12

CONCEPTUALIZATION AND MEASUREMENT OF AUDIENCE AGENDA

William F. DeGeorge

Seven years have passed since McCombs and Shaw (1972) published empirical evidence of the agenda-setting effects which mass media exert over public opinion. Although the idea of such an influence had been in the public domain for many years (Lippmann, 1922; Cohen, 1963), this recent attempt to bridge the gap between speculative ideas and a conceptual scheme unleashed a proliferation of related studies.

Under the broad label of "agenda-setting," hypotheses usually have concerned the relationship between topics or issues deemed important by the mass media and the perceived importance of those topics or issues among media users. While there has been general agreement among researchers about an acceptable way to determine media agendas—for example, through appropriate content analysis procedures—there is little concensus about the measurement of audience agendas. The research done to date shows a wide variety in the conceptualization and measurement of these variables.

This paper examines these studies and, with the aid of hindsight, comments on their weaknesses and suggests new areas or extensions of current trends for expanding the domain of agenda-setting theory, insofar as the measurement of audiences agendas is concerned.

THEORETICAL BACKGROUND

The ability of mass media to effect cognitive change is attributed to the ongoing selective process by media gatekeepers who, first, determine which

From William F. DeGeorge, "Conceptualization and Measurement of Audience Agenda," original manuscript.

events are newsworthy and which are not, and then assign different weights in terms of such variables as length (time or space), prominence (headline size, location in the newspaper, frequency of appearance, position in the news flow), and conflict (the manner in which the material is presented) to those items which pass through the gate. Some news items are treated in detail; others are given superfluous attention; still others are completely ignored. In the same way, broadcast media can use a story in the leadoff position or not at all. Media very clearly reveal their assessment of the salience of an item. Agenda-setting posits that audiences adopt these media assessments and, in so doing, incorporate an equal set of weights into their own agendas.

MEASUREMENT OF AGENDAS

Most researchers evaluate media behavior through traditional applications of content analysis, although several different approaches have been used in selecting the media for study. The majority of studies thus far involve a combination of print and broadcast media, either in tandem or distinctively.

A point of greater contention among researchers is the data-collection technique used to obtain the measure of the public agenda. The measurement strategy must ensure that collected observations permit hypothesis-testing and, equally important, that all of the relevant data are obtained. Open-ended questions have frequently been employed (McCombs and Shaw, 1972, 1973; Tipton et al., 1975). This method of data collection is thought to elicit the least bias because of its unobtrusive nature. Respondents are free to identify any issue or topic which comes to mind. For this very reason, however, open-ended questions reduce the comparability across subjects, and their use invites a certain amount of subjectivity in subsequent coding.

Researchers often overcome this problem by providing a list of topics or issues which the respondent is asked to rank-order. While this forced-choice technique assures that respondents use a common vocabulary, it may restrict the respondent from expressing a personal point of view. A respondent may find that his position on a particular subject does not correspond with any of the possible choices. There are several other forced-measurement strategies which appeal to researchers, including Likert scales, paired-comparison scales, and semantic-differential scales. One of the problems associated with the use of these scales, however, may be their association with the measurement of underlying or latent attitude variables. Whenever respondents are required to express judgment in terms of some degree of favorableness toward social objects, they are indeed being forced to form attitudinal or behavioral patterns, with which agenda-setting is *not* directly concerned. To sum up, there is a great need for further conceptual and methodological research—especially comparative research—on the measurement of public agendas.

CONCEPTUALIZATION OF AGENDAS

The decision to operationalize the media agenda by taking each medium individually versus taking all media in the aggregate has not received the attention it deserves. One can attempt to isolate those particular media which exert the most influence upon the public being measured during the period of analysis, or all possible media influences can be grouped and their content measured in the aggregate. Inferences can find support in a totally different direction depending upon the method selected.

In the McCombs and Shaw (1972) study, the reported intercorrelations between the New York *Times* and the local newspapers ranged between .66 and .70; between the *Times* and either network newscast it was .66; and between the *Times* and the newsmagazines it was .51 to .54.

In short, newspapers and other mass media differ somewhat in their choice of which specific issue receives the greatest attention. It follows that if one's agenda is being set by the media, the particular medium attended to is an important variable. Researchers should aggregate the media agenda only when a very high intermedia correlation is attained. The number and nature of the elements within each medium also are critical. Gormley (1975) measured the correlation between the agendas of political elites at the state level and the aggregate of five newspapers normally read by state legislators. He found strong support (.75 correlation) for agenda-setting when his 25 issues were collapsed into seven issue areas, but very weak evidence of support (.20 correlation) when the 25 issues were dealt with specifically and individually. Thus, the level of agreement between media and public agendas may depend to a large degree on how broadly an issue is defined.

Hong and Shemer (1976) considered the public agenda, asking whether "inferences regarding media agenda-setting can be made at the individual level as well as at the aggregate level." Their point, that individuals have different ways of ranking issues, is well taken. Communication theory holds that encoding and decoding is a very individual and personal process, and what one person perceives to be important may be perceived by another to be very unimportant. In the aggregate, these extremes cancel and the true picture may very well be disguised. Hong and Shemer asked respondents to rank-order a set of seven health issues. In order to examine the interpersonal influence on this rank-ordering, each respondent was then asked to identify several "talking partners," who were subsequently interviewed. Thus each individual's agenda could be examined in conjunction with agendas of those who may have exerted interpersonal influence. Unfortunately, they chose a very small and homogeneous sample: "50 target persons drawn from an area . . . located near the University of Minnesota." Their results, which showed little support for agenda-setting, may have suffered from poor sample selection. Nevertheless, their question about individual versus aggregate public agendas as the best focus for research is an important one!

ANALYSIS MODELS

The relationship between media and public agendas is usually described in terms of agenda-setting models. The most basic of these is the *awareness* model. According to the agenda-setting hypothesis, the public is primarily aware of those issues or topics which are reported by the media. If the media choose not to carry a particular event, in most cases the public simply will not be aware of that event. At the other extreme is the *priorities* model. In this version, the media establish a rank-ordering of topics through decisions about coverage and display. In this model the agenda of events, in proper rank-order, will be transferred to the public largely intact.

Midway between these is a third version, the *salience* model. Following the lead of the media, the public assigns high or low importance to topics as held by the media.

There is no clear evidence about which model best exemplifies agenda-setting. It is probable, however, that the *priorities* model will work best—best describe reality—when there is high media emphasis and public exposure to a set of topics or issues *and* high influence of some intervening variable, such as interest or need for orientation. The *awareness* model will best describe the situation when there is both low media exposure and low influence from the intervening variable. Following this reasoning, the *salience* model is logical for use in an environment where there is a combination of high/low or low/high influence between media emphasis and the contingent variable. Perhaps these suggested interactions should be used by researchers as a guide in establishing their measurement designs.

PERSONAL AGENDAS

After the transfer from media to public agenda takes place, the agenda-setting process can be examined from the point of view of what a person *thinks* about (intrapersonal), what he or she *talks* about (interpersonal), or what they think *others are talking* about (perceived community salience). The great majority of work so far has been in the intrapersonal area, what a respondent personally thinks is most important.

McCombs and Shaw (1972) operationalized this concept by asking respondents to "outline the key issues as they saw them, regardless of what the candidates might be saying at the moment." This approach has found considerable favor in the agenda-setting community, with many researchers collecting public opinion data in this manner.

Mullins (1973) asked respondents in an open-ended question to "identify some of the major problems facing the United States today." He then followed with two specific questions:

> Which of these is most important to you, personally?
>
> Which have you talked about most often with others?

The first collects data from the intrapersonal agenda of the respondents, while the second seeks data from the interpersonal agenda.

McLeod et al. (1974) operationalized the perceived community salience agenda by asking respondents what they talk about with others, and what others talk about to them.

Thus, while we have three models (awareness, salience, priorities) and three ways to operationalize the concept (intrapersonal, interpersonal, perceived community), it appears that most researchers are content with employing the priorities model to measure the intrapersonal agenda. Considerable work is necessary to define and examine the environment under which each model and operationalization is most appropriate.

SUMMARY

Research on audience agendas requires a series of key decisions on conceptualization and measurement:

- How will the personal agenda be conceptualized? As an intrapersonal, interpersonal, or perceived community agenda?
- How will the location of an issue on the agenda be measured? By open-ended questions, rating scales, paired-comparisons or rank-order procedures?
- Will the analysis use individual agendas or an aggregate public agenda?
- Will the analysis assume the priorities model or be based on the salience or awareness models?

Only by careful attention to these points will our knowledge of agenda-setting accumulate.

REFERENCES

Cohen, Bernard C. (1963) *The Press, the Public, and Foreign Policy.* Princeton: Princeton University Press.

Gormley, William Thomas, Jr. (1975) "Newspaper Agendas and Political Elites." Pp. 304-308 in *Journalism Quarterly,* Vol. 52, No. 2 (Summer).

Hong, Kisum and Sara Shemer (1976) "Influence of Media and Interpersonal Agendas on Personal Agendas." Paper presented at the annual convention of the Association for Education in Journalism, Madison, Wisc. (August).

Lippmann, Walter (1922) *Public Opinion,* MacMillian, NY.

McCombs, Maxwell E., D. Shaw, and E. Shaw (1972) "The News and Public Response: Three Studies of the Agenda-Setting Power of the Press." Paper presented to the Association for Education in Journalism, Carbondale, IL.

McCombs, Maxwell E. and Donald L. Shaw (1972) "The Agenda-Setting Function of the Mass Media." Pp. 176-187 in *Public Opinion Quarterly,* Vol. 36 (Summer).

McLeod, J.M., Lee B. Becker, and J.E. Byrnes (1974) "Another Look at The Agenda-Setting Function of the Press," *Communication Research* 1, Pp. 131-166 (April).

Mullins, L.E. (1973) "Agenda-Setting on the Campus: The Mass Media and Learning of Issue Importance in the '72 Election." Paper presented to the Association for Education in Journalism, Fort Collins, CO.

Tipton, Leonard P., Roger D. Haney, and John R. Baseheart (1975) "Media Agenda-Setting in City and State Election Campaigns." Pp. 15-22 in *Journalism Quarterly,* Vol. 52, No. 1 (Spring).

Chaim Eyal compares various agenda-setting studies to point out the implications of methodological differences, but his main point in this piece is that agenda-setting researchers should be mindful of audience differences when comparing effects reported in various studies. The newspaper audience behaves differently from TV viewers, in his opinion, possibly accounting for the agenda-setting "superiority" of newspapers. Dr. Eyal is on the faculty of Social Sciences in the Communication Institute of Hebrew University, Jerusalem.

13

THE ROLES OF NEWSPAPERS AND TELEVISION IN AGENDA-SETTING

Chaim H. Eyal

Agenda-setting research investigates the relationship between issues and subjects prominently emphasized in the mass media ("media agenda") and the salience of such topics in the minds of the public ("public agenda"). Since newspapers and television have been viewed as the leading news outlets, they have most often constituted the "media" component in these studies.[1]

McCombs and Shaw's (1972) agenda-setting study indicated no significant differences between the two media, and many researchers have subsequently assumed no differences and used aggregate media agendas (Sanders and Atwood, 1975; Carey, 1976; Hilker, 1976; Hong and Shemer, 1976). In such studies, inferences were drawn from the aggregate media measures following the assumption that the mass media are a homogeneous entity exerting influence on the public.[2]

Other researchers have found that newspapers are more effective than television in their agenda-setting function. Printed agendas have often been found to better match the agenda of the public than did broadcast agendas (Tipton et al., 1975; Benton and Frazier, 1976; McClure and Patterson, 1976; McCombs, 1977c; Weaver, 1977; Mullins, 1977).

But Palmgreen and Clarke (1977) found only limited support for the hypothesis that newspapers manifest a stronger agenda-setting effect than television. They found that on local issues newspapers exerted a strong influence while—as would logically be expected—television networks have no impact at all. On the other hand, and contrary to previous research,

From Chaim H. Eyal, "The Roles of Newspapers and Television in Agenda-Setting," original manuscript.

national network news was superior to newspapers in influencing the public agenda on national issues. These findings may be explained by the fact that, unlike earlier research, the study was *not* conducted during a national political campaign, and by the authors' suggestion that national TV news programs are more efficient than newspapers' presentation of the news.

Finally, other studies only analyzing television content have presented significant agenda-setting effects (Frank, 1973; Shaw and Bowers, 1973; Zucker, 1978).

INCONSISTENCY IN CONCEPTUALIZATION AND MEASUREMENT

Overall, the results have been mixed, and while the viewpoint that the two media have different effects appears to dominate, inconsistency in measurement and problem-formulation plagues this area of research. A large part of the problem is methodological: It is difficult, if not impossible, to cite two studies employing the same methodology. Operational definitions, contingent conditions, and critical variables differ from one study to the next, so much so that true replications and verifications are hard to find.

Despite a strong pattern of support for the "differential effects" proposition, this lack of uniformity in approach and conceptualization prevents conclusive inference about the comparative agenda-setting function of the two media. Current agenda-setting research seems to branch off in new and different directions rather than pursuing replication and clarification. Such expansion might be premature, since the basic difference between newspapers and television has not been clearly established, and the roles of various contextual, antecedent, and intervening variables have not been systematically analyzed.

A comparison of three studies, all resulting in different conclusions, will illustrate the problem. McCombs and Shaw (1972) found no differences between the agenda-setting effects of newspapers and television; Tipton, Haney, and Baseheart (1975) found an agenda-setting role for newspapers but not for television; and Palmgreen and Clarke (1977) obtained only partial support for the hypothesis that newspapers manifest a stronger agenda-setting effect than television. In addition to the differences in their conclusions, the three studies differ in their methodology and conceptualization. Table 13.1 indicates some of the differences among four critical variables.

Time-frame in agenda-setting research is probably the most elusive concept. It refers to the total elapsed time during which the assumed agenda-setting effects take place. Most time-frame choices appear to be motivated by intuition rather than substantiated theory. While McCombs and Shaw's and Palmgreen and Clarke's time frames are somewhat similar, Tipton, Haney, and Baseheart's is nearly doubled in duration. It is plausible that different time-frames might result in different effects. Thus, it is conceivable that

TABLE 13.1   Partial Comparison of Three Agenda-Setting Studies

STUDY	TIME-FRAME	NUMBER AND TYPE OF ISSUES	PUBLIC AGENDA CONCEPTUALI-ZATION
McCombs and Shaw (1972)	3½ weeks	15 various issues	Intrapersonal agendas
Tipton, Haney, and Baseheart (1975)	7 weeks	7 respondent issues 9 media-covered issues	Perceived-community agendas
Palmgreen and Clarke (1977)	2½ weeks	55 local issues 33 national issues	Perceived-community agendas

Tipton et al. measured an aspect of agenda-setting other than those measured in the two other studies.[3]

McCombs and Shaw analyzed 15 issues: Tipton et al. studied seven respondent issues and nine media-covered issues; Palmgreen and Clarke incorporated 55 local and 33 national issues. It is possible that the *number* of issues examined, the *type* of issues, and the manner in which the topics are generated may constitute independent variables affecting the agenda-setting process. Various issues may be treated differently by the two media as a result of specific media characteristics. For example, the issue of the economy may not be treated as extensively on television as the war in Vietnam due to the more highly visual nature of the latter.

The three studies also vary in their definitions of what constitutes the public agenda. McCombs and Shaw examined the "intra-personal agenda," while the others measured what Becker, McCombs, and McLeod (1975) termed the "perceived community agenda," soliciting responses to the question of what the respondents felt were the two or three major issues facing voters. Again, these studies—as well as many others—may well have been measuring different things in varied contexts and with different measuring instruments.

PARTIAL ANALYSIS OF TELEVISION CONTENT

In their study of the 1972 presidential elections, Patterson and McClure (1976) concluded that television news had minimal impact on public awareness of issues and on the perception of candidates' images. Conversely, they discovered that televised political advertising accounted for a significant rise in audience awareness of the candidates' positions on issues.

This conclusion supports Shaw and Bowers' (1973) finding that political commercials on television perform a different agenda-setting role than other televised information. They found that the appearance of issues in the commercials raised the salience of those issues among persons exposed to the commercial.

Bowers (1977) reported the same results, but carried his analysis further. Comparing the agenda of issues reported in the local newspaper (the Charlotte *Observer)* and the candidates' advertising agenda, he found no significant correlation. But a low correlation was discovered between the candidates' advertising agenda and the television news agenda. These findings suggest that, from a methodological point of view, drawing conclusions about television's agenda-setting role on the basis of news alone may be unjustified because televised commercials and the news, while related, appear to exert different effects—sometimes independent of each other. This suggestion is supported by Bowers' finding that "exposure to television is related to exposure to commercials and is probably due a great deal to incidental exposure." In other words, due to the nature of television and to the normal patterns of audience-exposure, incidental attendance to various messages is often unavoidable, yet such exposure is not accounted for in studies employing news content only.

While most TV agenda-setting studies use only the news to define the television agenda, it is clear that the medium provides numerous additional cues and information relating to the issues of the day. Besides political advertising, television provides such information in special programming, brief news summaries, updates and teasers, regular issue-oriented programs (such as *60 Minutes),* talk shows, and even in situation comedies. Many of the cues are received incidentally, while others are consciously attended to. Agenda-setting research frequently fails to take such exposure into consideration. On the other hand, newspaper agendas are usually determined on the basis of rather comprehensive content analyses, often including editorials, letters to the editor, cartoons, and minor news items buried deep in the inside pages.

If, as McCombs (1977c) contends, television news programs are analogous to the newspaper's front page account of the day's events, then it stands to reason that in comparing the two media only the front page of the newspaper should enter the comparison. However, since the front page may be a better indicator of the public agenda than other pages (McCombs and Shaw, 1972; Shaw, 1973) such analysis will probably reveal an even stronger newspaper agenda-setting influence. A more realistic approach would be based on the analysis of *all* relevant content in *both* media. It is recognized that such an approach represents tedious and lengthy coding efforts, but if this route is not taken, research results must explicitly state that differences found between the two mediums' impact are based on the study of newspapers and *television news* rather than on newspapers and television.

ALTERNATIVE EXPLANATIONS

Although he did not directly test the agenda-setting hypothesis, Carey (1976) examined the media agendas of three national television networks, three national magazines, and three national newspapers. In his analysis he found that "press coverage across media (TV, newspapers, and magazines) was remarkably consistent." Thus, within the agenda-setting framework, it appears logical that similar media agendas will have correspondingly similar effects on the audience agendas. To the extent that the effects are not the same — and the bulk of the literature suggests that they are not—the differential influence of the two media might be explained by factors such as the technological nature of newspapers versus television, their dissimilarity in news format, and by the composition of their audiences and the audiences' media-use patterns.[4] The latter proposition suggests that various media might exert separate influence as a result of such audience-related variables as time- and media-use habits, duration of exposure, interest, and differential credibility attached to each news outlet.

In attempting to explain the newspaper-versus-television agenda-setting effects, researchers often resort to the explanation that it is the media per se which create the differences. A *broad* explanation, which might include audience-related variables, seldom has been systematically and consistently pursued.

A number of *specific* explanations have been suggested. Most scholars (McCombs and Shaw, 1972; Glavin, 1976; McClure and Patterson, 1976; McCombs, 1977a, 1977b, 1977c; McCombs and Weaver, 1977) have theorized that because of various characteristics television is not the best teacher of the relative salience of issues. The television viewer is time-bound and is forced to follow a series of reports presented in rapid succession. The newspaper reader, on the other hand, may attend to the newspaper fare in his own time, at his own pace, and can reread and reexamine the information made available by the newspaper. In addition, newspapers have the ability to repeat items more often over time.

On the basis of such differences, according to McCombs (1976: 6):

> newspapers are the prime movers in organizing the public agenda. They largely set the stage of public concern. But television news is not wholly without influence. It has some short-term impact on the composition of the public agenda. Perhaps the best way to describe and contrast these influences is to label the role of the newspaper as agenda-setting and the role of television spotlighting. The basic nature of the agenda seems often to be set by the newspapers, while television primarily reorders or rearranges the top items of the agenda.

Based on data gathered in Charlotte, North Carolina, it was found that as the election date draws nearer (October), the public agenda shows a better match with television than with newspapers. In other words, it appears that for the public, the television agendas "catch up" and adjust to fit the audience's agenda. The television networks thus become better attuned to their public agenda—even more so than newspapers. McCombs (1977c) concludes that two distinct phases seem to exist in the agenda-setting process.

Early in the campaign, newspapers are the initiators and prime movers of public opinion, and television plays a very minor agenda-setting role. The newspaper's characteristics permit coverage of public issues early in their development. But, as time goes on and as the election date approaches, television becomes instrumental in making political issues salient for many voters, especially those not reached by newspapers.

According to this view, the role of television is not merely that of reinforcing the newspaper agenda. Rather, McCombs asserts, "television news cuts into reality at a different angle. It is, for one, more visually oriented. Television news also has a very different style from news stories in the print media. TV news is not newspaper news with pictures" (1977c: 98).

While these formulations appear possible and logical, the point made here is that since television audiences are different from newspaper readers, such differences might account for distinct agenda-setting effects. This audience differential may offer an alternative explanation for the apparent agenda-setting superiority of the newspaper. To advance such an explanation, the roles of the two media should be assessed in light of the nature and behavior of their audiences. Such an approach would be based on the assumption that global, or aggregated media agendas are crude measures that do not account for media-specific audience variables that might prove to be important in the overall agenda-setting process (see the discussion by Winter, Chapter 14 in this volume).

USE AND MISUSE OF
AGENDA-SETTING MODELS

Three distinct models have been conceptualized in agenda-setting research: the awareness, salience, and priority models (McCombs, 1977c; see also DeGeorge's discussion in Chapter 12). Some researchers fail to distinguish among the three models and fall into the trap of including information-acquisition and knowledge-gain processes under the rubric of agenda-setting. The problem afflicts the entire field of study, not only work related to the differential influence of newspapers and television. The problem is discussed here because what is presented as the strongest evidence of television agenda-setting effects may not qualify as agenda-setting at all. Regrettably, studies are still being made using a faulty conceptualization of agenda-setting. For example, Barbic's (1976) finding of a significant positive correlation between the amount of radio and television exposure and political knowledge levels does not fit into the agenda-setting category, although it has been classified as such. Earlier studies, such as the work by Trenaman and McQuail (1961) and by Blumler and McQuail (1969), have been alluded to as agenda-setting work as well, while they actually concerned knowledge gain.

SUMMARY

To arrive at clear and conclusive inferences about the nature of the differential role of newspapers and TV, future research should consider the following points:

(1) Past research lacks uniformity in design. Many of the studies done share few, and often only incidental, common denominators. Almost every study is contaminated by various variables and conditions arising from a diversity of conceptualizations, operational definitions, and measuring schemes. Research on agenda-setting branches off, uncontrolled, in many directions.

(2) Time frame formulations have been mostly intuitive. It is time to draw preliminary conclusions from the multitude of time-schemes tested so far and to begin the development of theoretical time-frame propositions.

(3) It is possible that the *number* of issues examined, as well as the *type* of issues, may constitute independent variables affecting the agenda-setting process. This possibility has not been seriously considered.

(4) There is a mixture of definitions in the literature of the public agenda. Many of the existing studies fail to distinguish among types of public agendas. Intrapersonal, interpersonal, and perceived community agendas have been identified as three public-agenda types; yet, such formulations are often ignored.

(5) The television agenda generally has been based on measures of news and, in a few cases, on political advertising. TV offers many additional cues, and much pertinent information, that has not been considered as a potential influence on the public awareness of issues.

(6) The literature offers very little systematic concern for specific audience variables such as demographic and media-use patterns.

(7) Agenda-setting research, in general, should follow the bounds of the developing theory. Toward the goal of arriving at such a theory, certain models and definitions have been carefully developed and tested. To the extent that such models are not adhered to, the research should not be labeled "agenda-setting," or it should carry the burden of showing that it follows an alternative model that is valid, reliable, and consistent with an established theoretical framework.

NOTES

1. Some researchers have used magazines (Funkhouser, 1973; Stone, 1975; Stroman, 1978) as well as radio (Williams and Larsen, 1977) in their "media-agenda" formulations.

2. Typically, those studied have also failed to control for actual media exposure.

3. For an elaborate discussion of the time-frame issue, see Eyal et al. (Chapter 11).

4. In this context it is interesting to find that the recent trend (1959-1976) in the public choice of news sources is toward increased use of television and decreased preference of radio, newspapers and magazines (Sterling and Haight, 1978).

REFERENCES

Agnir, F. (1976) "Testing New Approaches to Agenda-Setting: A Replication and Extension." In *Studies in Agenda-Setting,* edited by M. McCombs and G. Stone. Syracuse, NY: Newhouse Communication Research Center, Syracuse University.

Atwood, L. Erwin, Ardyth Sohn, and Harold Sohn (1976) "Community Discussion and Newspapers Content." Paper presented at the Annual Convention of the Association for Education in Journalism, University of Maryland (July-August).

Ball-Rokeach, Sandra and Melvin DeFleur (1976) "A Dependency Model of Mass Media Effects," *Communication Research,* January: 3-21.

Barbic, Ana (1976) "Setting the Political Agenda: Participation or Escape?" Pp. 36-42 in the *Journal of Communication,* Vol. 26, No. 2 (Spring).

Benton, Marc and P. Jean Frazier (1976) "The Agenda-Setting Function of Mass Media at Three Levels of 'Information Holding'." Pp. 261-274 in *Communication Research,* Vol. 3, No. 3 (July).

Blumler, Jay G. and Denis McQuail (1969) *Television in Politics.* Chicago: University of Chicago Press.

Bowers, Thomas A. (1974) "Political Advertising: Setting the Candidate's Agenda." Paper presented to the National Conference on tne Agenda-Setting Function of the Press, Syracuse University.

_____(1977) "Candidate Advertising: The Agenda is the Message." Pp. 53-67 in D.L. Shaw and M.E. McCombs (Eds.) *The Emergence of American Political Issues: The Agenda-Setting Function of the Press.* St. Paul, Minn.: West Publishing Co.

Carey, John (1976) "Setting the Political Agenda: How Media Shape Campaigns." Pp. 50-57 in the *Journal of Communication,* Vol. 26, No. 2 (Spring).

Cohen, Bernard C. (1963) *The Press, the Public, and Foreign Policy.* Princeton: Princeton University Press.

Eyal, Chaim (1979) Time Frame in Agenda-setting Research: A study of the conceptual and methodological factors affecting the time frame context of the agenda-setting process. Unpublished doctorial dissertation, Syracuse University.

Frank, R.S. (1973) *Message Dimensions of Televised News.* Lexington, Ma.: Lexington Books.

Funkhouser, G. Ray (1973) "The Issues of the Sixties: An Exploratory Study in the Dynamics of Public Opinion." Pp. 62-75 in *Public Opinion Quarterly,* Vol. XXXVII, No. 1 (Spring).

Glavin, William (1976) "Political Influence of the Press." Pp. 1-6 in the *American Newspaper Publishers Association Research Bulletin,* No. 4 (November 10).

Gormley, William Thomas, Jr. (1975) "Newspaper Agendas and Political Elites." Pp. 304-308 in *Journalism Quarterly,* Vol. 52, No. 2 (Summer).

Hilker, Anne K. (1976) "Agenda-Setting Influence in an Off-Year Election." Pp. 7-10 in the *American Newspaper Publishers Association News Research Bulletin,* No. 4 (November 10).

Hong, Kisum and Sara Shemer (1976) "Influence of Media and Interpersonal Agendas on Personal Agendas." Paper presented at the annual convention of the Association for Education in Journalism, Madison, Wisc. (August).

Kaid, Lynda Lee, Kathy Hale, and Jo Ann Williams (1977) "Media Agenda-Setting of A Specific Political Event." *Journalism Quarterly,* (Summer).

Lippmann, Walter (1922) *Public Opinion,* MacMillan, NY.

McClure, Robert D. and Thomas E. Patterson (1976) "Setting the Political Agenda: Print vs. Network News." Pp. 23-28 in the *Journal of Communication,* Vol. 26, No. 2 (Spring).

McCombs, Maxwell E. (1973) "Working Papers on Agenda-Setting." Series no. 1, School of Journalism, University of North Carolina.

———(1976) "Elaborating the Agenda-Setting Influence of Mass Communication." Paper prepared for the Bulletin of the Institute for Communication Research, Keio University, Tokyo, Japan (Fall).

———(1977a) "The Agenda-Setting Function of the Press." Paper prepared for Women and the News (S.T. Olin Conference) Washington University, St. Louis (September).

———(1977b) "Expanding the Domain of Agenda-Setting Research: Strategies for Theoretical Development." Paper presented to the Mass Communication Div. of the Speech Communication Association, Washington D.C. (December).

———(1977c) "Newspapers Versus Television: Mass Communication Effects Across Time." Pp. 89-105 in D.L. Shaw and M.E. McCombs (Eds.) *The Emergence of American Political Issues: The Agenda-Setting Function of the Press.* St. Paul, Minn.: West Publishing Co.

——— and Donald L. Shaw (1972) "The Agenda-Setting Function of the Mass Media." Pp. 176-187 in *Public Opinion Quarterly,* Vol. 36 (Summer).

——— and E. Shaw (1972) "The News and Public Response: Three Studies of the Agenda-Setting Power of the Press." Paper presented to the Association for Education in Journalism, Carbondale, IL.

McCombs, Maxwell E. and David H. Weaver (1973) "Voters' Need for Orientation and Use of Mass Media." Paper presented to the annual convention of the International Communication Association, Montreal.

———(1977) "Voters and the Mass Media: Information Seeking, Political Interest, and Issue Agendas." Paper presented at the annual convention of the American Association of Public Opinion Research, Buck Hill Falls, Pa.

McLeod, J.M., Lee B. Becker, and J.E. Byrnes (1974) "Another Look at The Agenda-Setting Function of the Press," *Communication Research* 1, Pp. 131-166 (April).

Miller, Arthur, Lutz Erbring, and Edie Goldberg (1976) "Front Page News and Real-World Cues: Another Look at Agenda-Setting by the Media." Paper presented to the American Political Science Association.

Mullins, L.E. (1973) "Agenda-Setting on the Campus: The Mass Media and Learning of Issue Importance in the '72 Election." Paper presented to the Association for Education in Journalism, Fort Collins, Colorado.

———(1977) "Agenda-Setting and the Younger Voter." Pp. 133-148 in D.L. Shaw and M.E. McCombs (Eds.) *The Emergence of American Political Issues: The Agenda-Setting Function of the Press.* St. Paul, Minn.: West Publishing Co.

Noelle-Neumann, Elisabeth (1974) "The Spiral of Silence—A Theory of Public Opinion." Pp. 43-51 in the *Journal of Communication,* Vol. 24, No. 2 (Spring).

———(1977) "Turbulences in the Climate of Opinion: Methodological Applications of the Spiral of Silence Theory." Pp. 143-158 in *Public Opinion Quarterly,* Vol. 41. 2 (Summer).

Palmgreen, Philip and Peter Clarke (1977) "Agenda-Setting with Local and National Issues." Pp. 435-452 in *Communication Research,* Vol. 4, No. 4 (October).

Park, R.E. (1940) "News as a Form of Knowledge," *American Journal of Sociology,* 45: 699-86 (March).

Patterson, Thomas E. and Robert D. McClure (1976) *The Unseeing Eye.* N.Y.: G.P. Putnam's Sons.

Sanders, K.R. and L.E. Atwood (1975) "Communication Exposure and Electoral Decision Making." Paper presented to the annual convention of the Association for Education in Journalism.

Shaw, Donald L. and Thomas A. Bowers (1973) "Learning from Commercials: The influence of TV Advertising on the Voter's Political 'Agenda'." Paper presented to the annual conference of the Association for Education in Journalism, Fort Collins, Colorado.

Shaw, Eugene F. (1973) "Front Page Versus Total Coverage." University of N. Carolina, Chapel Hill: Working Papers on Agenda-Setting, Series no. 1.

———(1974) "Some Interpersonal Dimensions of the Media's Agenda-Setting Function." Paper presented at the Conference on the Agenda-Setting Function of the Press, Syracuse University, Syracuse, N.Y. (October).

Siune, K. and O. Borre (1975) "Setting the Agenda for a Danish Election." *Journal of Communication,* Vol. 25: 65-73. (Winter)

Sohn, Ardyth Broadrick (1978) "A Longitudinal Analysis of Local Non-Political Agenda-Setting Effects." *Journalism Quarterly.*

Sterling, Christopher H. and Timothy R. Haight (1978) *The Mass Media: Aspen Guide to Communication Industry Trends.* N.Y.: Praeger Publishers.

Stone, Gerald (1975) "Cumulative Effects of the Media." Paper presented at the conference on Agenda-Setting, Syracuse University, Syracuse, NY.

Stroman, Carolyn (1978) "Race, Public Opinion and Print Media Coverage." An unpublished doctoral dissertation, Syracuse University, Syracuse, N.Y.

Thurston, Carol M. (1977) "Modification of Judgment Through Increase in Message Length." *Journalism Quarterly.*

Tipton, Leonard P., Roger D. Haney, and John R. Baseheart (1975) "Media Agenda-Setting in City and State Election Campaigns." Pp. 15-22 in *Journalism Quarterly,* Vol. 52, No. 1 (Spring).

Tolman, E. C. (1932) *Purposive Behavior in Animals and Men.* Appleton-Century, N.E.

Trenaman, J. and Denis McQuail (1961) *Television and the Political Image.* London: Methuen.

Weaver, David H. (1977) "Political Issues and Voters Need for Orientation." Pp. 107-119 in D. L. Shaw and M.E. McCombs (Eds.) *The Emergence of American Political Issues: The Agenda-Setting Function of the Press.* St. Paul, Minn.: West Publishing Co.

———, Taik Sup Auh, Timothy Stehla, and Cleve Wilhoit (1975) "A Path Analysis of Individual Agenda-Setting During the 1974 Indiana Senatorial Campaign." Paper presented to the Association for Education in Journalism, Annual Convention, Ottawa.

Weaver, David, Lee Becker, and Maxwell E. McCombs (1976) "Influence of the Mass Media on Issues, Images, and Political Interest: The Agenda-Setting Function of Mass Communication During the 1976 Campaign." Paper presented to the Midwest Association for Public Opinion Research, Annual Convention, Chicago.

Weaver, David H. and Maxwell E. McCombs (1978) "Voters' Need for Orientation and Choice of Candidates: Mass Media and Electoral Decision Making." Paper presented at the Annual Conference of the American Association for Public Opinion Research, Roanoke, Virginia (June).

Weaver, D., M.E. McCombs, and C. Spellman (1975) "Watergate and the Media: A Case Study of Agenda-Setting." *American Politics Quarterly,* Vol.3 (October): 458-472.

Williams, Wenmouth, Jr. and David C. Larsen (1977) "Agenda-Setting in an Off-Election Year." Pp. 444-479 in *Journalism Quarterly,* Vol. 54, No. 4 (Winter).

——— and William D. Semlak (1976) "Campaign 76: The Agenda-Setting Effects of Television Network News and a Local Daily Newspaper on Interpersonal Agendas During the New Hampshire Primary." Paper presented to the Speech Communication Association Convention, San Francisco.

Winter, James P. (1979) "An Agenda-Setting Time Frame for the Civil Rights Issue: 1954-1976." Unpublished paper, Syracuse University (February).

Zucker, Harold G. (1978) "The Variable Nature of News Media Influence." Pp. 225-240 in B.D. Ruben (Ed.) *Communication Yearbook 2,* New Brunswick, N.J.: Transaction Books.

In addition to methodological inconsistencies that plague agenda-setting as a theory-building research area, James Winter reviews a number of contingent conditions that affect agenda-setting. He argues that the nature of the issues *on the agenda, their obtrusiveness and geographic proximity, and the duration of audience exposure to them, combine with the medium and its credibility to influence the agenda-setting process. Dr. Winter is an adjunct lecturer at the Newhouse School of Communications of Syracuse University.*

14

CONTINGENT CONDITIONS IN THE AGENDA-SETTING PROCESS

James P. Winter

Salient and pervasive though media effects on society may be, few communications scholars would argue that the media exert a monolithic influence in any respect. They do not have equal influences on all people in all settings. As the research which led to the primacy of the law of minimal consequences in the late 1950s indicated, the media do not operate in a vacuum: Media and audiences are all integral parts of a larger social system. However, by providing the public with what Lippmann (1922) referred to as "the pictures in our heads," or what Tolman (1932) called our "cognitive maps," the media explain the world beyond our personal experiences.

More recently, Ball-Rokeach and DeFleur (1976) have referred to this process as one of determining "social realities." They argue that it is our social realities which provide frameworks for our receptiveness to information and whether we act on it. It is the relative adequacy of our social realities and our dependency on media information sources which explain and predict media effects on us as individuals. It is therefore thought that the media exercise selected influence based on individual or group differences.

With ideas similar to these in mind, researchers who have tested agenda-setting hypotheses have paid special attention to contingent conditions, or those attributes of the communication situation under which effects are either enhanced or diminished. Especially in survey research, where there are

From James P. Winter, "Contingent Conditions in the Agenda-Setting Process," original manuscript.

numerous uncontrolled variables, it is not sufficient to simply indicate that relationships occurred. It is important to determine the robustness of relationships, and one way to do this is to look at their contingent conditions.

In this discussion contingent conditions have been divided into those which pertain to the stimulus and those related to the audience. An argument can also be made for including as a third category those contingencies related to the responses made by audiences, under agenda-setting conditions. For example, Benton and Frazier (1976) looked at the characteristics of respondents at three different levels of "information holding," or what might be called degree of *knowledge about* issues, and found that education intervened between media content and audience knowledge. But as agenda-setting per se does not address the question of *knowledge about* issues but rather *awareness of* issues—much as Park (1940) distinguished between *acquaintance with* and *knowledge of*—this aspect will not be considered in the present discussion.

STIMULUS ATTRIBUTES

Although most studies have concentrated on audience attributes, a few have explored the relationship between agenda-setting effects and stimulus attributes. For example, Zucker (1978) compared national Gallup Poll data and television news content to determine whether the *obtrusiveness* of issues—the amount of direct public contact with the issue independent of media emphasis—and their terms or duration of exposure in the media play an important part in the degree of influence on subsequent audience agendas. Zucker found an effect only for comparatively unobtrusive issues, and at that, only relatively early in their rise to prominence on the television agenda. Issues would appear to be a variable, with differing effects for relatively unobtrusive events such as international developments, where one would expect maximal media impact, compared to more obtrusive issues such as inflation, unemployment, or crime, where people are more likely to be influenced by firsthand experience. The variable nature of issues is a question that deserves more consideration in the future.

Duration of exposure also appears to be important, with issues rising and falling on both public and media agendas over time. Zucker (1978) looked at pollution, drug abuse, and energy over an eight-year period and found significant agenda-setting effects only relatively early in these issues' rise to prominence in the television medium. Dividing his study period in half, Zucker found effects in the first four-year period but not in the second. This finding suggests that despite continued media coverage of issues, public interest may wax and wane.

If obtrusiveness and duration of issue should be taken into consideration, so, it appears, should the related question of their geographic proximity. Palmgreen and Clarke (1977) found *diminished* mass media effects on the local level, with respect to local issues, compared with national issues. This obviously is closely related to issue obtrusiveness.

In their study of agenda-setting in a Danish election, Siune and Borre (1975) found that the *credibility* of the perceived source of media messages plays an important role in the magnitude of the agenda-setting effect.

A related contingency involves the influence of a particular medium—for example, newspaper versus television (see Eyal, Chapter 13). Others include such influences as the duration, length, amount, and kind of information contained in the message. Some of these contingencies have been examined by Thurston (1977).

In sum, a number of stimulus attributes have been identified and have been the focus of scattered attention, including the nature of the particular issue or its obtrusiveness, geographic proximity, and length or duration of exposure. The medium itself may affect the message, as can the type of information presented, the way in which it is presented, and the perceived source. Future agenda-setting research cannot, in good scientific conscience, treat these conditions in the unsystematic fashion that has characterized past research.

AUDIENCE ATTRIBUTES

By far most of the contingent conditions that have been examined in relation to media agenda-setting have dealt with audience attributes. Perhaps McCombs and Shaw (1972) set the stage for this development when, in their test of the hypothesis, they examined several audience attributes. Most notable was the fact that they included only *undecided voters* in their sample. The argument was, of course, that uncertain voters would be most susceptible to an agenda-setting influence.

Mere exposure. Measuring the amount of exposure to the media is one of two areas (the other being the more complex need for orientation typology discussed below) where research results are consistent. Mullins (1973) for example, found that agenda-setting effect increased with media exposure. Weaver, Auh, Stehla, and Wilhoit (1975) found weak support in the same direction. Weaver, McCombs, and Spellman (1975) found that a higher level of media use was associated with increased perceived salience of the Watergate issue. Similar findings are reported by Agnir (1976) and McClure and Patterson (1976).

In most cases, it is no longer adequate to match aggregate media agendas with aggregate public agendas, as has been done in many studies. Future research should match on specific source of media information as well as level of exposure to that medium.

The potential problems involved in comparing aggregate media and public agendas were indicated in a panel study of the 1976 election undertaken by Weaver, Becker, and McCombs (1976). The authors identified three media types: those who primarily relied on newspapers for political information;

those who relied on television; and those who used both media about equally. The three media types showed distinct differences in issue agendas—a finding which could lead to spurious conclusions were the data analyzed on an aggregate level.

The studies mentioned above are exemplary in that they took this seemingly basic condition, level of exposure to the media, into consideration. Some researchers have not even done that. But these exposure measures are still problematic in that they rely on respondent recall, which may not be overly accurate, and in that they are a simple measure of "how much" respondents read or view rather than precisely "what" it is they attend to.

There is reason to believe that future studies could further improve our understanding of the agenda-setting function through more precise estimates of what viewers and readers attend to. We might do well to differentiate between "regular" readers of the local daily who only read the comic pages and the Ann Landers column and those who read every news item in some detail.

Interpersonal discussion. The nature of the relationship between agenda-setting and respondent involvement in interpersonal communication is a matter of some dispute. Some researchers have argued that interpersonal discussion will tend to filter or reduce media influences, while others argue that it enhances their effect. McCombs and Shaw (1972) for example, found that increased interpersonal communication *reduced* the agenda-setting effect. In a study of students at the University of North Carolina at Chapel Hill during the 1972 election, Mullins (1973) found that increased interpersonal discussion *facilitated* the agenda-setting effect. In their study of 244 Indiana University students during the 1974 Indiana senatorial campaign, Weaver, Auh, Stehla, and Wilhoit (1975) found that the agenda-setting effect *decreased* with increased interpersonal discussion.

Of course, part of the problem may be due to the different populations measured. But even where the populations appear to be comparable, frequency of discussion has been conceptualized and operationalized in different ways. Mullins (1973) and Weaver et al. (1975) surveyed student populations during an election, although one was an election for the senate, the other for the presidency. An important factor is the *topic* of interpersonal discussion involved. Clearly, intense discussions between political campaign workers differ from gossip between office workers over lunch. Also, while Weaver et al. (1975) indexed degree of interpersonal communication via the frequency that respondents mentioned interpersonal sources for the topic they cited, Mullins (1973) measured interpersonal discussion with a five-point scale directed at discussion of politics generally.

In sum, there are at least two apparent problems contributing to the inconsistency in findings. First, we must decide what we mean by interpersonal discussion. Discussion of what, with whom? Do we measure the discussion of specific issues directly, or of politics generally? The former would seem to be better suited to the notions underlying agenda-setting.

The second problem is one of inconsistency in measurement from study to study. It may be preferable to rely on the Likert-type scales, as did Mullins, rather than simple frequency of mention associated with topics, as did Weaver et al.

Hong and Shemer (1976) have argued that the media exert a direct influence on interpersonal discussion, which subsequently affects personal agendas. They argue that interpersonal communication is an intervening variable between media and personal agendas which may subsequently *either* facilitate or reduce the importance of certain issues. Particularly due to the small sample size involved, this study bears replication in an attempt to clarify the nature of the relationships.

Another consideration is the role taken by the individual in interpersonal discussion: Are they an opinion leader or a follower? Clearly, this could be expected to affect the role played by interpersonal discussion in the agenda-setting process.

A related area of research has been investigated by Noelle-Neumann (1974, 1977) who asserted that the fear of isolation is critical to individual judgment of what is important. As part of the overall "Spiral of Silence" theory, she maintains that what individuals view as important and say is important is contingent on the perceived popularity of opinion, their estimate of the current "climate of opinion." Thus the perceived climate of opinion also could be a contingent condition related to interpersonal discussion.

Need for orientation.   Since the study by McCombs and Shaw (1972), the condition of voter uncertainty which they used as a criterion for including respondents has been expanded to include measures of party affiliation, and combined with measures of either interest or relevance and political participation to form an index of "need for orientation" (McCombs, Shaw, and Shaw, 1972; McCombs and Weaver, 1973; Weaver and McCombs, 1978).

As mentioned above, the need for orientation concept is one of only two contingent conditions (the other is simple amount of media exposure) for which there is totally unambiguous evidence. In all of the studies surveyed which reported introducing the concept, high need for orientation led to an enhanced agenda-setting effect compared with lower levels, and usually the relationship was monotonic (McCombs et al., 1972; McCombs and Weaver, 1973; Weaver et al., 1975; Weaver, McCombs, and Spellman, 1975; Cohen, 1975; Weaver, 1977).

However, those studies that have used an interest measure by itself have not shown as consistent results as those measuring need for orientation. Mullins (1973) found no relationship between interest in the campaign and agenda-setting effect. Shaw (1974) found a positive relationship. McLeod,

Becker, and Byrnes (1974) found a negative relationship: Those least interested in the campaign were most likely to show an agenda-setting effect. In her study of the 1974 congressional race in Illinois' 10th District, Hilker (1976) also found that low-interest voters had a slightly better match with the media agenda. This apparent interaction between interest and agenda-setting effect, which is not present when interest is combined with certainty to form need for orientation, deserves future attention as well.

Interest level has also been examined indirectly, by looking at groups with built-in levels of interest. For example, Gormley (1975) studied political elites in the form of state legislators. Mullins (1973) looked at students, who may be thought to hold unique interests with respect to certain issues.

Other contingencies. Several other contingent conditions have been addressed, primarily in single studies. While they are to be congratulated for their innovation, a more systematic approach such as the one taken by Weaver and McCombs in their need for orientation research is preferable.

Atwood, Sohn, and Sohn (1976), for example, found that women and those under 35 were more likely to discuss issues interpersonally, and thus concluded they were more susceptible to media influences. McLeod, Becker, and Byrnes (1974) found no effect for voters under 25, but a positive relationship for those above that age.

Mullins (1977) found differences between young in-college voters compared to young working voters, differences he attributed to the effects of education rather than differing lifestyles.

SUMMARY

A number of stimulus attributes warrant further attention, including: The nature of the issue, its obtrusiveness, geographic proximity and duration of exposure. The particular medium of information, source credibility, type of information and manner of presentation all appear to influence agenda-setting effects. However, there is an urgent need in future research to begin the type of systematic replication which will provide answers to the questions raised above. A similar comment can be made in regard to audience attributes, where seemingly the drive for total innovation has overwhelmed the scientific prerequisite of at least partial replication.

It is clear that at a minimum future studies should include specific measures of need for orientation; amount and preferably kind of exposure to individual rather than aggregate media; and amount of interpersonal discussion. Furthermore, it is hoped that their conceptual and operational lines will be drawn from the above discussion.

The above evidence also points to the need for more social psychological measures, the importance of which is shown by the success of the need for orientation concept. There is an urgent need to explore additional variables such as media credibility—do respondents take a critical approach to the information media or do they trust them as sources? Measures of dogmatism or authoritarianism, innovativeness, and self esteem are examples of measures which would probably enhance our ability to predict the conditions under which media agenda-setting is most and least effective.

REFERENCES

Agnir, F. (1976) "Testing New Approaches to Agenda-Setting: A Replication and Extension." In *Studies in Agenda-Setting,* edited by M. McCombs and G. Stone. Syracuse, NY: Newhouse Communication Research Center, Syracuse University.

Atwood, L. Erwin, Ardyth Sohn, and Harold Sohn (1976) "Community Discussion and Newspaper Content." Paper presented at the Annual Convention of the Association for Education in Journalism, University of Maryland (July-August).

Ball-Rokeach, Sandra and Melvin DeFleur (1976) "A Dependency Model of Mass Media Effects," *Communication Research,* January: 3-21.

Barbic, Ana (1976) "Setting the Political Agenda: Participation or Escape?" Pp. 36-42 in the *Journal of Communication,* Vol. 26, No. 2 (Spring).

Benton, Marc and P. Jean Frazier (1976) "The Agenda-Setting Function of Mass Media at Three Levels of 'Information Holding'." Pp. 261-274 in *Communication Research,* Vol. 3, No. 3 (July).

Blumler, Jay G. and Denis McQuail (1969) *Television in Politics.* Chicago: University of Chicago Press.

Bowers, Thomas A. (1974) "Political Advertising: Setting the Candidate's Agenda." Paper presented to the National Conference on the Agenda-Setting Function of the Press, Syracuse University.

_____ (1977) "Candidate Advertising: The Agenda is the Message." Pp. 53-67 in D.L. Shaw and M.E. McCombs (Eds.) *The Emergence of American Political Issues: The Agenda-Setting Function of the Press.* St. Paul, Minn.: West Publishing Co.

Carey, John (1976) "Setting the Political Agenda: How Media Shape Campaigns." Pp. 50-57 in the *Journal of Communication,* Vol. 26, No. 2 (Spring).

Cohen, Bernard C. (1963) *The Press, the Public, and Foreign Policy.* Princeton: Princeton University Press.

Eyal, Chaim (1979) Time Frame in Agenda-setting Research: A study of the conceptual and methodological factors affecting the time frame context of the agenda-setting process. Unpublished doctorial dissertation, Syracuse University.

Frank, R.S. (1973) *Message Dimensions of Televised News* Lexington, Ma.: Lexington Books.

Funkhouser, G. Ray (1973) "The Issues of the Sixties: An Exploratory Study in the Dynamics of Public Opinion." Pp. 62-75 in *Public Opinion Quarterly,* Vol. XXXVII, No. 1 (Spring).

Glavin, William (1976) "Political Influence of the Press." Pp. 1-6 in the *American Newspaper Publishers Association Research Bulletin,* No. 4 (November 10).

Gormley, William Thomas, Jr. (1975) "Newspaper Agendas and Political Elites." Pp. 304-308 in *Journalism Quarterly,* Vol. 52, No. 2 (Summer).

Hilker, Anne K. (1976) "Agenda-Setting Influence in an Off-Year Election." Pp. 7-10 in the *American Newspaper Publishers Association News Research Bulletin,* No. 4 (November 10).

Hong, Kisum and Sara Shemer (1976) "Influence of Media and Interpersonal Agendas on Personal Agendas." Paper presented at the annual convention of the Association for Education in Journalism, Madison, Wisc. (August).

Kaid, Lynda Lee, Kathy Hale, and Jo Ann Williams (1977) "Media Agenda-Setting of A Specific Political Event." *Journalism Quarterly,* (Summer).

Lippmann, Walter (1922) *Public Opinion,* MacMillan, NY.

McClure, Robert D. and Thomas E. Patterson (1976) "Setting the Political Agenda: Print vs. Network News." Pp. 23-28 in the *Journal of Communication,* Vol. 26, No. 2 (Spring).

McCombs, Maxwell E. (1973) "Working Papers on Agenda-Setting." Series no. 1, School of Journalism, University of North Carolina.

_____(1976) "Elaborating the Agenda-Setting Influence of Mass Communication." Paper prepared for the Bulletin of the Institute for Communication Research, Keio University, Tokyo, Japan (Fall).

_____(1977a) "The Agenda-Setting Function of the Press." Paper prepared for Women and the News (S.T. Olin Conference) Washington University, St. Louis (September).

_____(1977b) "Expanding the Domain of Agenda-Setting Research: Strategies for Theoretical Development." Paper presented to the Mass Communication Div. of the Speech Communication Association, Washington D.C. (December).

_____(1977c) "Newspapers Versus Television: Mass Communication Effects Across Time." Pp. 89-105 in D.L. Shaw and M.E. McCombs (Eds.) *The Emergence of American Political Issues: The Agenda-Setting Function of the Press.* St. Paul, Minn.: West Publishing Co.

_____ and Donald L. Shaw (1972) "The Agenda-Setting Function of the Mass Media." Pp. 176-187 in *Public Opinion Quarterly,* Vol. 36 (Summer).

_____ and E. Shaw (1972) "The News and Public Response: Three Studies of the Agenda-Setting Power of the Press." Paper presented to the Association for Education in Journalism, Carbondale, IL.

McCombs, Maxwell E. and David H. Weaver (1973) "Voters' Need for Orientation and Use of Mass Media." Paper presented to the annual convention of the International Communication Association, Montreal.

_____(1977) "Voters and the Mass Media: Information Seeking, Political Interest, and Issue Agendas." Paper presented at the annual convention of the American Association of Public Opinion Research, Buck Hill Falls, Pa.

McLeod, J.M., Lee B. Becker, and J.E. Byrnes (1974) "Another Look at The Agenda-Setting Function of the Press," *Communication Research* 1, Pp. 131-166 (April).

Miller, Arthur, Lutz Erbring, and Edie Goldberg (1976) "Front Page News and Real-World Cues: Another Look at Agenda-Setting by the Media." Paper presented to the American Political Science Association.

Mullins, L.E. (1973) "Agenda-Setting on the Campus: The Mass Media and Learning of Issue Importance in the '72 Election." Paper presented to the Association for Education in Journalism, Fort Collins, CO.

_____(1977) "Agenda-Setting and the Younger Voter." Pp. 133-148 in D.L. Shaw and M.E. McCombs (Eds.) *The Emergence of American Political Issues: The Agenda-Setting Function of the Press.* St. Paul, Minn.: West Publishing Co.

Noelle-Neumann, Elisabeth (1974) "The Spiral of Silence—A Theory of Public Opinion." Pp. 43-51 in the *Journal of Communication,* Vol. 24, No. 2 (Spring).

_____(1977) "Turbulences in the Climate of Opinion: Methodological Applications of the Spiral of Silence Theory." Pp. 143-158 in *Public Opinion Quarterly,* Vol. 41, No. 2 (Summer).

Palmgreen, Philip and Peter Clarke (1977) "Agenda-Setting with Local and National Issues." Pp. 435-452 in *Communication Research,* Vol. 4, No. 4 (October).

Park, R.E. (1940) "News as a Form of Knowledge," *American Journal of Sociology,* 45: 699-86 (March).

Patterson, Thomas E. and Robert D. McClure (1976) *The Unseeing Eye.* N.Y.: G.P. Putnam's Sons.

Sanders, K.R. and L.E. Atwood (1975) "Communication Exposure and Electoral Decision Making." Paper presented to the annual convention of the Association for Education in Journalism.

Shaw, Donald L. and Thomas A. Bowers (1973) "Learning from Commercials: The influence of TV Advertising on the Voter's Political 'Agenda'." Paper presented to the annual conference of the Association for Education in Journalism, Fort Collins, Colorado.

Shaw, Eugene F. (1973) "Front Page Versus Total Coverage." University of N. Carolina, Chapel Hill: Working Papers on Agenda-Setting, Series no. 1.

———(1974) "Some Interpersonal Dimensions of the Media's Agenda-Setting Function." Paper presented at the Conference on the Agenda-Setting Function of the Press, Syracuse University, Syracuse, N.Y. (October).

Siune, K. and O. Borre (1975) "Setting the Agenda for a Danish Election." *Journal of Communication,* Vol. 25 (Winter): 65-73.

Sohn, Ardyth Broadrick (1978) "A Longitudinal Analysis of Local Non-Political Agenda-Setting Effects." *Journalism Quarterly.*

Sterling, Christopher H. and Timothy R. Haight (1978) *The Mass Media: Aspen Guide to Communication Industry Trends.* N.Y.: Praeger Publishers.

Stone, Gerald (1975) "Cumulative Effects of the Media." Paper presented at the conference on Agenda-Setting, Syracuse University, Syracuse, NY.

Stroman, Carolyn (1978) "Race, Public Opinion and Print Media Coverage." An unpublished doctoral dissertation, Syracuse University, Syracuse, N.Y.

Thurston, Carol M. (1977) "Modification of Judgment Through Increase in Message Length." *Journalism Quarterly.*

Tipton, Leonard P., Roger D. Haney, and John R. Baseheart (1975) "Media Agenda-Setting in City and State Election Campaigns." Pp. 15-22 in *Journalism Quarterly,* Vol. 52, No. 1 (Spring).

Tolman, E.C. (1932) *Purposive Behavior in Animals and Men.* Appleton-Century, N.E.

Trenaman, J. and Denis McQuail (1961) *Television and the Political Image.* London: Methuen.

Weaver, David H. (1977) "Political Issues and Voters Need for Orientation." Pp. 107-119 in D.L. Shaw and M.E. McCombs (Eds.) *The Emergence of American Political Issues: The Agenda-Setting Function of the Press.* St. Paul, Minn.: West Publishing Co.

———, Taik Sup Auh, Timothy Stehla, and Cleve Wilhoit (1975) "A Path Analysis of Individual Agenda-Setting During the 1974 Indiana Senatorial Campaign." Paper presented to the Association for Education in Journalism, Annual Convention, Ottawa.

Weaver, David, Lee Becker, and Maxwell E. McCombs (1976) "Influence of the Mass Media on Issues, Images, and Political Interest: The Agenda-Setting Function of Mass Communication During the 1976 Campaign." Paper presented to the Midwest Association for Public Opinion Research, Annual Convention, Chicago.

Weaver, David H. and Maxwell E. McCombs (1978) "Voters' Need for Orientation and Choice of Candidates: Mass Media and Electoral Decision Making." Paper presented at the Annual Conference of the American Association for Public Opinion Research, Roanoke, Virginia (June).

Weaver, D., M.E. McCombs, and C. Spellman (1975) "Watergate and the Media: A Case Study of Agenda-Setting." *American Politics Quarterly,* Vol. 3 (October): 458-472.

Williams, Wenmouth, Jr. and David C. Larsen (1977) "Agenda-Setting in an Off-Election Year." Pp. 444-479 in *Journalism Quarterly,* Vol. 54, No. 4 (Winter).

——— and William D. Semlak (1976) "Campaign 76: The Agenda-Setting Effects of Television Network News and a Local Daily Newspaper on Interpersonal Agendas During the New Hampshire Primary." Paper presented to the Speech Communication Association Convention, San Francisco.

Winter, James P. (1979) "An Agenda-Setting Time Frame for the Civil Rights Issue: 1954-1976." Unpublished paper, Syracuse University (February).

Zucker, Harold G. (1978) "The Variable Nature of News Media Influence." Pp. 225-240 in B.D. Ruben (Ed.) *Communication Yearbook 2,* New Brunswick, N.J.: Transaction Books.

This encyclopaedic article reviews the complexity of evidence required to generalize about mass media effects. In addition to reviewing a great deal of effects research in the context of a history and structural analysis of the field, the authors argue that full documentation of media effects requires coordinated measurement and codification from four variable sources: media content, audience exposure, effects, and conditional processes. Most studies consider only one or two of these variable sources, leading to unsubstantiated conclusions. They see the history of the field as peculiar, but not unique, to the social sciences. Jack M. McLeod is professor of journalism and mass communication and Byron Reeves is assistant professor of journalism and mass communication at the University of Wisconsin—Madison. Both are active researchers in the Mass Communication Research Center at Wisconsin.

15

ON THE NATURE OF
MASS MEDIA EFFECTS

Jack M. McLeod and Byron Reeves

An uncomfortable question is often asked of those professing expertise in the field of mass communication: "Why, after all this research and public clamor about television effects, can't we say with greater clarity and certainty whether the medium does or does not affect the behavior of children and adults in harmful or beneficial ways?" An adequate answer to that question, as is usual in science, is uncomfortably complex. Even a partial answer must consider the following: the number and types of potential effects; the complexity of media stimuli; the special problems in documenting effects; the varying strategies of making inferences from evidence; and the peculiar history and current structure of the communication research field.

TYPES OF MASS MEDIA EFFECTS

A common idea of a mass media effect is that some aspect of content has a direct and immediate impact on members of the audience. In the vocabulary of the philosophy of science, this implies that the content is viewed as a necessary and sufficient condition for some effect. Unfortunately, such simple models of causation seldom fit the reality of any area of human behavior, and the study of communication is no exception. We are more likely to find media effects if we understand that the consequences of exposure to media content are likely to be varied and complex.

Television particularly seems to be a topic about which we all have opinions. Perhaps as a result of this, literally hundreds of possible effects of television and other media have been suggested, even if few of these assertions

From Jack M. McLeod and Byron Reeves, "On the Nature of Mass Media Effects," *Television and Social Behavior: Beyond Violence and Children,* Stephen B. Withey and Ronald P. Abeles, eds. Copyright by Lawrence Erlbaum Associates, Inc., Publishers. Reprinted by permission.

have been backed by solid research evidence. Lurking within this long list are dimensions along which these supposed effects vary and that illustrate the complexity of what we call effects. We can classify variances according to *who* is affected, *what* is changing, *how* the process takes place, and *when* the impact is evidenced.

Micro vs. Macro

Most experimental studies of communication effects restrict their attention to individual audience members and are often criticized for doing so. At least their data and their inferences are consistently at the micro level. For nonexperimental field studies, however, the "who" of media effects is often ambiguous. Quite often, for example, effects are measured in terms of individual audience members, whereas the inferences from those effects are made with respect to the larger society. That is, the micro data gathered from individuals are simply summed to come to macro societal conclusions. For example, if some members of the audience are found to become more informed by using media content, it is sometimes assumed that such information gain must be functional for the society. But societal consequences cannot be inferred solely from estimates of the number of changes. The social location (e.g., social class) of those gaining information must be considered in assessing system consequences. The same problem applies to the term "public opinion," which is often used as a grand reification of individually measured opinions having little connection to their mode of organization in the community or society.

Certain other potential effects are clearly not identifiable from changes in individual behavior alone. For example, research investigating the hypothesis that the media contribute to a "knowledge gap" between the more advantaged and less advantaged groups depends on an analysis of the *relative* gain in information for each status level (Robinson, 1972; Tichenor et al., 1970, 1973). Two communities might have the same average level of knowledge, but yet be very different in the way information is distributed across subgroups in these communities. Similarly, other assessments of effects such as the diffusion of information through a population become meaningful only when plotted against time and in comparison between two social systems differing in macro characteristics such as population density, degree of stratification, and so on. Still other types of research problems seem to focus entirely on the analysis of effects at the macro level—the effects of concentration of media ownership on the quality of news coverage, for example (Gormley, 1976). Other more whimsical illustrations suggest the depletion of societal resources—for example, the idea that intensive television use drains electrical energy, or that the newspaper industry depletes the wood pulp supply, or that the sudden demands of half-time toilet flushing during the Super Bowl seriously affect the municipal water levels.

Direct vs. Conditional

The popular idea of media impact carries with it an implicit assumption that effects are equally probable for everyone in the audience. The model implies an immediate response without either delay or alteration by the emotional states, cognitive processes, or social behavior of the recipient. Such a simple model of media effects would be considered naive by most investigators of communication effects. The bulk of recent research has indicated that media message effects do not appear to have direct or across the board impact. Rather, the thrust of research has been to identify various conditions under which effects are present or not present or present with varying probabilities. Unfortunately, theoretical development and practical understanding of such complications are hindered by a lack of uniformity and clarity as to the labels and meaning of the role of various third "conditional" variables, as we call them, affecting the relationship between exposure to media and effect of that exposure.

One set of conditional variables influencing the relationships between media exposure and effects are those originating prior to media exposure. If the control for the third variable identifies some subgroup or situation in which the effect does *not* take place, we can say that the conditional variable represents a *contingent* condition. For example, there is evidence that suggests that the highly touted agenda-setting effect of the newspaper in "telling the public not what to think but what to think about" (Cohen, 1963; McCombs & Shaw, 1972) is limited to those who consider newspapers to be their major source of political information (McLeod, Becker, & Byrnes, 1974). Thus, newspaper reading is a necessary condition for the operation of agenda-setting. Another type of prior situation is where the third variable acts as a *contributory* condition making the effect of media exposure more likely. For example, the prior angering of members of an audience can make the instigation of aggressive behavior more likely after they have seen a violent film (Berkowitz, 1962).

Contributory and other types of conditional variables can also have impact *after* exposure to media content. A variety of labels are used for third variables operating in this way: hypothetical construct, intervening variable, and mediating variable among others. In psychology a distinction has been made between a hypothetical construct as a theoretically postulated but unmeasured variable and an intervening variable as the measured and/or experimentally manipulated concept clarifying the relationship between a stimulus and effect (MacCorquodale & Meehl, 1948). The intervening variable is often conceived of and measured at a less abstract level of discourse, as, for example, a physiological state in research at the individual cognitive level or a psychological or cognitive state in studies of communication in social systems. The term "intervening variable" is, however, more loosely used in more sociologically oriented research as an alternative to the term "mediating variable." It is sometimes used to mean a social process set off by communication exposure and at other times simply as a third variable affecting the exposure–effect relationship. An example of its use as a social process is to be found in the recent research on the 1976 presidential debates where greater debate exposure appeared to simulate interpersonal discussion. Discussion, in turn, had much greater impact on the political process than did the initial exposure (McLeod, Durall, Ziemke, & Bybee, in press). A large part of the impact of viewing the debates, therefore, can be said to be an indirect effect operating through the stimulation of discussion. Because discussion effects might be expected to be delayed a day or more after exposure, studies of the immediate direct effect of debate watching might well miss the stronger indirect effect. Other research on the 1976 debates found that the perceptions of who won these encounters were not well formulated until several days afterward, when respondents presumably had a chance to read press evaluations (Lang & Lang, in press; Morrison, Steeper, & Greendale, 1977).

Conditioning third variables may also operate at the same time as the communication variable, or their time order may be undetermined. To the extent that media exposure and the third variable operate independently to produce an effect, we can say that each has a main effect (Kerlinger & Pedhazur, 1973).

An example from recent communication research may help to illustrate the necessity of specifying the way in which conditional variables operate. As one explanation for the rather modest strength of the direct relationship between children's exposure to television and the various effects of television, it has been suggested that the relationship is dependent on or its strength is proportionate to the child's perceived reality of the content (Feshbach, 1972; Greenberg & Reeves, 1976; Hawkins, 1977). Perceiving program content to be realistic is assumed to make television information more socially useful and more likely to be assimilated equitably with information from nontelevision sources. Thus all or most of the impact of television exposure operates through the perception of reality as a conditional variable. There are, however, several different ways of specifying *how* perceived reality operates as a conditional variable, and each of these specifications suggest quite different theoretical interpretations of media effects.

Figure 3.1 shows six examples of how perceived reality may operate as a conditional variable. All of the examples show the relationship between the frequency of exposure to television and the magnitude of effects at two levels of perceived reality (I = high perceived reality; II = low perceived reality). The high reality condition in each of the examples is shown with the same difference in effects at the two levels of exposure (as indicated by the distance "a"). The low reality condition is shown with different changes in the

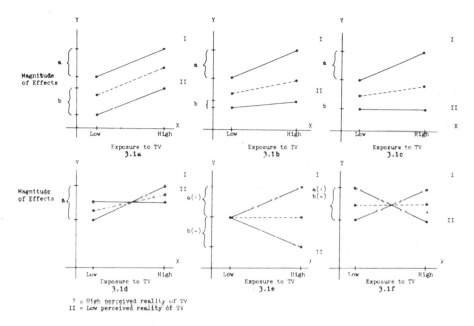

FIG. 3.1. Hypothetical example of the perceived reality of television as a
conditional variable in the relationship between exposure to television (X axis)
and the effects of television (Y axis).

magnitude of effects between low and high exposure (as indicated by the
distance "b") to illustrate changes in the theoretical interpretation of the role
of perceived reality as a conditional variable in each of the examples. The
dotted line in each example indicates the change in effects from low to high
TV exposure that would be found if the conditional variable were ignored.

Figure 3.1a shows perceived reality as a conditional variable that operates
independent of children's exposure to television. Although the high perceived
reality condition results in greater *levels* of effects, there is no difference
between the two conditions in the estimation of the change in effects from low
to high TV exposure (as indicated by the fact that a = b). If perceived reality
were not considered in this case, the estimation of the difference between low
and high exposure would not change (as indicated by the dotted line),
although an estimate of the level of effects at both low and high levels of TV
exposure would not represent either condition. In this case, then, the
conditional variable is additive and noninteractive. It is important to note
that most studies in which conditional variables are hypothesized make the
assumption that the effects of the third variable—that is, perceived reality—
are additive in relation to exposure. This is a mathematical assumption, for

example, of multiple regression techniques in which no interaction term is introduced. Third variables are typically added to a prediction equation as main effects without consideration of possible interactions.

Figure 3.1b shows an interaction between perceived reality and exposure. The high perceived reality condition results in the greatest change in effects from low to high TV exposure (as indicated by a > b). In this case, if perceived reality were not considered as a conditional variable, some difference in effects at the two levels of exposure would likely be found (dotted line); however, that difference would underestimate the differences associated with the high reality conditon and overestimate those in the low reality condition. In this sense, perceived reality could be viewed as a contributory conditional variable. Accounting for perceived reality would *increase* the ability to estimate accurately changes in media effects at different levels of TV exposure.

A similar overestimation of the low reality condition would exist in Fig.3.1c; however, in this example there is no relationship between exposure and effects in the low reality condition (as indicated by the absence of change in the level of effects from low to high exposure). There is a relationship between exposure to television and effects only for those in the high reality condition. In the sense that perceived reality limits the domain of the exposure–effect relationship, perceived reality becomes a contingent variable. If perceived reality were not measured in this case, there might appear to be a slight relationship between exposure and effects (as indicated by the dotted line); however, that relationship might not be significantly different from zero.

It would also be possible to generalize this example to a situation in which several levels of perceived reality were considered. With 10 levels of reality, for example, it could be that a significant positive relationship between exposure and efffects exists only for the 10th or highest level of perceived reality. In this situation, the overall relationship would almost certainly not be significantly different from zero (the average of nine conditions showing no change in effects and one condition showing a change), although a near-perfect relationshp may exist at the 10th level of perceived reality. Overall, this may not be an interesting finding, because the relative number of individuals in the 10th category would be small. However, in cases of significant rare effects of media (e.g., commission of felony crimes such as murder or rape that are modeled from TV portrayals), the conditional variable may be a crucial piece of information in the explanation of effects.

Another version of this contingent condition is shown in Fig. 3.1d. There is still no relationship between exposure and reality for the low reality condition; however, in this case the relationship between the two conditions is disordinal (i.e., the lines for the two conditions intersect). Although the relationship between exposure and effects in this case would be exactly the same as those in Fig. 3.1c (because the dotted line in each example indicates the same change in effects from low to high exposure), the interpretation and use of the data could be very different. In Fig. 3.1d there exists a critical point at which those in the low perceived reality condition are affected more than those in the high reality condition (as indicated by the exact point of intersection). This would mean that for the low level of TV exposure, those who perceived television to be most real would be affected *less* than those in the low reality condition. A similar problem would exist in this example if perceived reality were ignored as a conditional variable. It is possible that the combination of the conditions would make the relationship between exposure and effects appear to be nonexistent or at best uninteresting.

The final examples, Figs. 3.1e and 3.1f, demonstrate that ignoring a conditional variable may actually preclude understanding the relationship between exposure and effects. In Fig. 3.1e the high reality condition produces an increase in the level of effects from low to high exposure (as indicated by the fact that a is positive), and the low reality condition produces a decrease in the magnitude of effects (as indicated by the fact that b is negative). Perceived reality makes a difference as a conditional variable only for the high level of exposure—augmenting the effects in the high reality group and diminishing effects in the low reality group. In Fig. 3.1f, which is the disordinal version of this example, the two conditions again show either a positive or negative change in effects; however, these effects are found in the low reality condition at low exposure *and* in the high reality condition at high exposure. The important point to consider in these final examples is that traditional correlational procedures would totally miss the relationship, *even if the conditional variable was measured and evaluated in the three-variable relationship.* The change in the magnitude of effects in both cases would average to zero (as indicated by the dotted lines). Although it is difficult to imagine these results actually being operative for the perceived reality of television, they are nevertheless possibilities that may fit other conditonal variables.

From these examples it is clear that merely including conditional variables in analyses of media effects is potentially misleading unless the specific relationships of these variables to exposure and effects are also studied. Unfortunately, once conditional variables are identified as important in the effects process, they are often studied only descriptively or as dependent or independent variables. Perceived reality, for example, has been theoretically hypothesized to be an intervening variable; however, most studies using perceived reality have concentrated on the dimensions of perceived reality; levels of perceived reality for various program and character types; or the ability to predict different levels of perceived reality by accounting for variables such as childhood experiences with the real-life counterparts of television, time context of the program, and overall exposure to television

(Reeves, 1978). In studying other conditional variables that may help explain individual or subgroup differences in how media have effects, it seems important at least to measure and simultaneously evaluate all three variables. Studying conditional variables descriptively or as independent and dependent variables in two-variable designs could lead to errors in conclusions about television effects or to a misallocation of effort, should the variable be of little value in explaining effects. Although we explore conditional variables independent of exposure and impact, we should also study them within the process they are expected to have a role in explaining.

Other communication concepts have undergone a transition similar to that of perceived reality in being seen first as conditional variables and then as effects in themselves. The gratifications sought from media were first treated as correctives to a simple exposure to effect model but later came to be treated as important phenomena without specified effects and most often without any cause (Blumler & Katz, 1974).

Conditional variables may be important beyond their role in clarifying media effects. For example, they may prove to be more likely targets for policy change or social action than is the body of content found in the mass media. Parental intervention strategies, educational programs, and warning messages all may be more viable than any direct governmental control over television programming.

Content-Specific vs. Diffuse–General

It is natural to look for media effects that bear a one-to-one relationship to the specific content of the medium. We seek to measure the aggressive responses of children exposed to violent content and to assess the stereotypical cognitions of those paying closest attention to programs portraying biased sex or occupational roles. There is also an unfortunate tendency for many observers to skip the step of actually assessing audience reactions and to infer effects from the content alone. At the time of the Surgeon General's report on effects (Comstock & Rubinstein, 1972) of televised violence, for example, one magazine editor wondered aloud why all that money had been spent to document what was obvious from the content that he could see on his own television screen. From such logic we might see a parallel to the expression "we are what we eat" and assert instead "we become what we see."

The great majority of media effects research also focuses on content-specific effects, albeit with more complicated models than the exposure to effect causation implied by the editor. Not all of the effects attributed to the media, however, are so directly tied to the content. For example, erotic as well as aggressive film content can enhance subsequent aggressive behavior among previously angered subjects (Zillmann, 1972). It is argued that the observed effects may not be so much the consequence of exposure to the content per se as they are the function of the excitatory potential of the communication. Such nonspecific arousal can also enhance more positive effects such as music appreciation (Cantor & Zillmann, 1973). Nonexperimental research has shown that aggressive behavior can be predicted as well from the *form* of a given television program (e.g., unpredictability of audio and visuals, location and characters, mode of presentation) as from the frequency of violent content alone (Watt & Krull, 1977).

A very different set of examples of effects not tied to specific content can be found in the various studies of the displacement effects of media. For example, Parker (1963) found that the advent of television in a community was associated with a decline in the circulation rates of fiction in public libraries but not with the level of use of nonfiction materials. The heavy dosage of fictionalized content of television apparently displaced fiction books in serving whatever needs such materials fulfill, but the effect was not a direct effect of television per se. A host of studies have dealt with either the replacement of one medium with another, or with displacement in terms of lowering the time devoted to the original medium, and some have examined the displacement effect of television on children's play (Himmelweit, Oppenheim, & Vince, 1958, Lyle & Hoffman, 1972; Schramm, Lyle, & Parker, 1961). Speculation about other displacement effects have included more elusive and less researched criteria such as language skills, reading behavior, impaired eyesight, declining college entrance test scores, and general apathy. What these speculations have in common is that they assert that it is the activity of watching television per se and not its specific content that generates the effect. Finally, we should add to this list of proponents of diffuse noncontent effects the name of McLuhan (1964) and his assertion that it is the form of the medium and not its message that is the critical element in understanding the consequences of media use.

Attitudinal vs. Behavioral vs. Cognitive

The history of media effects research is very nearly the history of attitude change research. For 40 years various source, message, personality and situational characteristics have been studied in relation to their effectiveness in shifting audience attitudes. Much less attention has been given to the more natural function of the media in conveying knowledge, changing various types of cognitions, and altering overt forms of behavior. This imbalance would be less serious if we could assume a strong causal flow, say, from media exposure to knowledge gain (or other cognitive change) to attitude shift to behavior change. Unfortunately, none of these links is supported by strong evidence. The last step, from attitude shift to behavior change, has been given close scrutiny in recent years, and it has been concluded that supportive evidence is lacking (Festinger, 1964; Siebold, 1975). It is obvious that much more systematic research into nonattitudinal effects of media exposure is needed along with how such changes relate to attitude change.

Alteration vs. Stabilization

Another basic distinction among types of effects is between the facilitation of change and its prevention or stabilization of existing attitudes or behavior. Although there has been a substantial amount of work done on immunization against persuasive messages (McGuire, 1964; Tannenbaum, 1967), the overwhelming proportion of studies has dealt with enhancing attitude change. Although nonexperimental survey research on media effects has also concentrated on persuasive attitude change, a dominant inference from the research of the past 30 years has been that the major effect of media exposure has been to "reinforce" preexisting attitudes (Berelson, Lazarsfeld, & McPhee, 1954; Hyman & Sheatsley, 1958; Lazarsfeld, Berelson, & Gaudet, 1948; Star & Hughes, 1950). Unfortunately, extremely gross measures of change were used such that only those who showed large shifts (e.g., conversion from one party's candidate to another's) were counted as changing, whereas all other members of the audience were assumed to be "reinforced." More recent research continues to show evidence of stabilization of attitudes, but by using more varied and sensitive measures of effect other more nonreinforcing destabilizing types of changes also have been shown (Becker, McCombs, & McLeod, 1975; Blumler & McLeod, 1974; Chaffee, 1975; Kline, Miller & Morrison, 1974).

Other Dimensions of Effects

In addition to the five foregoing dimensions there are many other ways in which the various alleged effects of the mass media might be classified. For example, most experimental studies deal with relatively short duration of effects following exposure to a message and do not address the long-term consequences of the change directly. This is true more often than not for all types of research strategies, but it is also the case that many proposed media effects such as the diffusion of information through a population require a longer time perspective of effect. Other dimensions include cumulative versus noncumulative effects and learning of novel versus previously learned behaviors.

The basic point is that each of these dimensions represents possible types of effects that can be put together in a complex matrix of possible effects. If each of the five dimensions we have described were to be treated as dichotomies, 2 to the 5th power or 32 possible types of effects are possible. Among these possible effects, however, only a few dominate the existing research of the field. The combination micro-direct-content–specific-attitudinal-alteration occupies the foreground whereas most other types are virtually ignored. Answers to questions of the extent of media effects may depend on which combination of these cells we are referring to. It follows that adequate answers to media effect questions require more systematic attempts to investigate effect combinations other than those that have dominated attention up to this time. The marketplace of ideas, unfortunately, is likely to keep the focus of attention on only certain types of effects. Equally sobering is the realization that many specific effects simply are undetectable given the current crudeness of measurement available within the social sciences.

COMPLEXITY OF EVIDENCE REQUIRED

We have seen that the diversity of potential effects has contributed to the confusion of evaluating mass media impact. Another major reason for the scarcity of definitive answers about media effects is the complexity of evidence needed to document and to make inferences about such effects. These requirements may differ in degree but probably not in form from the necessities for testing any kind of effect in the social sciences or in other scientific fields: knowledge of the stimulus material, control of its application, assessment of effect, and an understanding of the mechanism or process underlying the effects. In the analysis of media effects we need to accomplish the following:

(1) Assess the media *content* in relation to the expectations about how media have an impact. This is often approached by simply analyzing what is most quantifiable or obvious about the media content under study. What is actually needed is a coding scheme whose categories are isomorphic to (have a one-to-one relationship with) the dimensions and categories used to measure the effect on the audience and the process by which the message is received. Put simply, we need evidence that the audience is reacting to the same things as is the content analyst. The problem is no less for the experimental analysis of messages, if the manipulation is to have an effect or at least one that is interpretable.

(2) Control the *exposure* of the audience to the content. In natural settings this is a major problem, for much of media use is done under conditions of low attention. People frequently watch television without much specific motivation or rational choice about content, and their viewing is often lacking in focused attention (Bogart, 1972; Gans, Chapter 4, this volume; Goodhardt, Ehrenberg, & Collins, 1975). This has some serious implications for the conduct of media effects research. First, the lack of conscious selection leads to imperfect recall by audience members about what programs they

watched. Second, the variation in motivation and in attention makes measures of mere exposure frequency relatively weak indicators of the actual strength of the media stimulus. As a result of these problems, the reliability and validity of measurement of exposure may be lessened, and any coefficient may understate the actual strength of the relationship between exposure and effect. Laboratory experiments, of course, do not suffer from these problems, because they manipulate the message content and maximize attention through control of extraneous conditions. They pose the problem not of threats to internal validity from these sources but rather of external validity in generalizing to the less than perfect conditions outside the laboratory.

(3) Assess the *effect* of media content. As discussed earlier, a great number of types of effect are possible. The question is then to determine which of these can be identified as functionally related to the message. The closer the particular effect to various conditional processes as well as to exposure to the specific content of the message, the more fully the relationshp can said to be documented.

(4) Elaborate the *conditional processes* that help interpret and specify the relationship. Research linking media exposure to effects frequently invokes as an explanation for the relationship an unmeasured process that is assumed to have been stimulated by the exposure to the message. If research findings indicate that children who frequently watch situation comedies with highly traditional family roles also have more highly stereotyped views of sex roles than other children, the investigator is apt to assume that the child is learning such views through the process of identification with one of the leading characters. Direct measurement of identification would help to test this inference against various alternative explanations.

There are abundant numbers of other processes and concepts that have been suggested as modifying or interpreting media exposure to effect relationships. Variables such as the gratifications sought from content should be analyzed as both additive increments altering effects beyond those of exposure and as potential factors interacting with exposure to produce nonadditive effects (McLeod & Becker, 1974), not simply as isolated variables. For the most part, the most interesting communication theory results from the unraveling of these conditions and interactive relationships, not from the simple assertion that the media set public agendas or that children learn from television.

An assumption about a conditional process—namely, that children will learn antisocial or prosocial material from television to the extent they perceive the video portrayals as real—serves to illustrate the inadequacies of incomplete evidence for media effects. Because the perception of reality is both measurable and experimentally manipulable, in recent years the concept has been the subject of several studies that have examined its dimensionality (Hawkins, 1977); its antecedents such as age (Lyle & Hoffman, 1972), socioeconomic background (Dominick & Greenberg, 1970), and real life experience (Greenberg & Reeves, 1976); and its consequent effects (Feshbach, 1972). Despite all the research now in print and the theoretical predictions that perceived reality operates as a conditional variable enhancing the effect of exposure to television content, very little research has actually addressed the three-variable question or attempted to integrate two-variable studies into a comprehensive statement about how perceived reality works (Reeves, 1978).

Our basic point is that evidence for full documentation of media effects requires coordinated codification and measurement from all four sources of variables: content, exposure, effect, and conditional processes. A larger proportion of media research examines only one or two of those variable sources, sometimes making unsubstantiated assertions about change. This leads to inaccurate interpretation and to the disparity of current views about media effects.

Nonexperimental studies of media effects face challenges to the validity of their inferences, because media use is an activity embedded in other activities and its presumed effects can be and often are caused by other activities. A simple positive correlation between media exposure and some effect is a necessary but not a sufficient basis for inferring that the media exposure caused the effect. Many other alternative explanations for the correlation can be advanced. These alternatives fall into two classes: third variable causation and reverse causation. Third variable explanations assert that some other antecedent or concurrent factor may have caused both the media exposure and the effect. For example, children of lower social class status may watch more television and also exhibit more aggressive behavior. We are more confident that our inference is not spurious if we can show that controlling for social status does not make our original exposure–effect correlation disappear (McLeod, Atkin, & Chaffee, 1972).

The second alternative explanation, reverse causation, asserts that the proposed effect may actually have caused an increase in media exposure rather than the reverse. This is difficult to test in the usual cross-section study conducted at a single point in time. Longitudinal designs measuring the audience at two or three points in time represent greater opportunities for testing the direction of causation. Cross-lagged correlation analyses that examine the strength of the across-time correlations of one variable with another can be useful to the causal direction problem (Chaffee, 1972a, 1972b; Kenny, 1973). An opportunity to test for media effects with panel designs is provided when the exposure variable is measured in regard to a particular time-bound set of events such as the Watergate hearings (McLeod, Brown,

Becker, & Ziemke, 1977) or the presidential debates (McLeod, Durall, Ziemke, & Bybee, in press). Here the pre-event levels of the effect variable along with prior measures of potential third variable challenges can be entered as preliminary control in regression analyses, and the test of media exposure to the events is made with respect to the remaining variance in the effect variable not accountable to prior levels or to the other prior variables (Kerlinger & Pedhazur, 1973). It forms a stronger measure of change in the effect variable not possible in static, one-time designs.

COMPLEXITY OF MEDIA STIMULI

A good test of effects depends on the presence of strong stimulus conditions. The ideal characteristics of good stimulus conditions include the following: There should be a stimulus unit signifying the nature of the stimuli and their beginning and end; the stimulus measurement should be well specified and precise or its manipulation sufficiently strong such that we can reasonably expect detectable effects; and the stimulus should be independent of other extraneous stimuli so that effects can be properly attributed. Unfortunately, research on media effects in natural field situations seldom meets any of these criteria.

Natural Stimulus Units

With the exception of highly salient events like the media coverage of the Watergate hearings, the presidential debates, or the Super Bowl, media exposure is most easily describable as a habitual ongoing behavior taking place over an extended period of time. We expect that effects will come largely from the viewing of typical content over a relatively long period of time. As a result, both the nature and the level of abstraction used to describe and measure media exposure is varied and uncertain. Time spent with television is the most frequently used measure of exposure, and, unfortunately, it suffers from being unreliably measured (for reasons described earlier) and also from being dependent on a rough correspondence between viewing time and the "typical" content of the media. It is not surprising that few media effects have been uncovered using exposure time or time spent measures. Beyond time, the selection of a unit of time requires a choice among different media, program types, specific programs, characters, the interaction sequence within programs and so forth. At least in part, the selection of a unit of media exposure is an empirical question that can be ascertained through research. But at present there is no standardization of units in the field, a fact that contributes to the disparity of reported media effect findings.

Strength of the Stimulus

There is an old dictum in experimental research that urges the investigator to "start strong" in manipulating the differences between conditions. The nonexperimental counterpart of this dictum is to find sufficient variance in the natural conditions of the stimulus such that significant relationships with effects might be obtained. This is a potential problem for mass media research where the level of exposure is being measured. For example, there might be insufficient variation in the large amount of violent television content viewed by young adolescents. This would markedly lower the likelihood of finding any strong association with effect variables.

It can be argued that customary nonexperimental research designs are weak in that they depend on natural variation in media behavior within a given community or area within a single country. Admittedly, the strongest differences may be found within countries or communities before and after the introduction of television, but studies of these are rare and may be contaminated by the prior availability of radio and other media (Cramond, 1976; Furu, 1971; Harrison & Ekman, 1976; Himmelweit, Oppenheim, & Vince, 1958; Schramm, et al, 1961; Werner, 1971). A more viable possibility exists in designs that intentionally sample and compare communities on the basis of the "richness" of the available media ranging, say, from New York city with three daily newspapers and a multitude of television and radio stations to a small community with only a local weekly and single radio station (Chaffee & Izcaray, 1975; Chaffee & Wilson, 1976; Kraus, Davis, Lang, & Lang, 1975). Apart from the characteristics of individuals in those communities, the context provided by the media systems could well have important consequences. The detection of these consequences, of course, depends on the ability to control the many social factors likely to be associated with the media richness of the community.

There is a potential problem of insufficient stimulus strength even in field experiments in which a set of messages is disseminated differently to experimental and control communities to study effects. If any manipulated set of messages about a topic on which subjects have preexisting attitudes is nonnovel in that they merely add to the customary level of information flow on the topic, then the expected effects may be only an incremental fraction and any effects may escape unnoticed. The alternative is to stay with novel messages about previously unknown or low salient topics; however, in the latter case the dilemma is that it may be impossible to generate enough salience in the topic adequately to test the effect of the message. A final problem of stimulus strength is that it may not bear a one-to-one relationship to the number of repetitions of the message. Density as measured by the number of repeated messages per unit time may be a more appropriate measure where a very dense set of redundant messages may actually lower the effects of mere exposure presumably because of their irritating quality (Becker & Doolittle, 1975).

Independence of Stimuli

It is important to the interpretation of media effects to be able to specify as precisely as possible what aspect of media content led to any effect found in research. This is very difficult to do at the gross level at which most media effects research has been conducted. Perhaps the most basic question is whether the effect is due to something the media added to or subtracted from "reality" or conversely, whether the media simply acted as a conduit in expediting what the audience would have obtained from other sources. If it is the latter, do we wish to label an effect as a media effect or merely as an effect transmitted by the media?

The production of network news and public affairs programming serves to illustrate the wide variation in the amount of discretion and judgment involved in presenting various types of content. At one extreme is the large amount of selectivity involved in producing the approximately 18 news stories contained in the average evening network newscast. A given story has been chosen from among hundreds of possible items, and each has been condensed to fit the tight time average of a bit over 1 minute per story. A voice-over interpretation has been added in most cases. Clearly differences between viewers and nonviewers of such programs might be attributable to the news judgments of the reporters and editors. At the other extreme with much less reportorial discretion are political party conventions and presidential press conferences, which represent live performances with most of the judgment falling to the party managers and political leaders. In the second instance it is debatable just how much of any effect can be attributable to the media. The research on the effectiveness of television versus classroom teaching serves further to illustrate this problem. Schramm (1962) reports that 83 studies showed television to be superior; another 55 studies found the reverse, with classroom teaching better; and another 255 could draw no conclusions. We suspect that not only is the strength of the contrasting teaching conditions likely to have been weak but that the various studies were apt to have been confounded by variables other than the mode of instruction.

Another problem of stimulus specification derives from the fact that much of the natural audience exposure to media content is embedded in a complex of other social and media behaviors. The analytical problem becomes one of controlling these other sources of potential influence in order to evaluate the media exposure of immediate interest. The 1976 presidential debates offer a good example. During the period of the debates, voters were also learning about the campaign from other information sources such as the daily accounts of the campaign, political advertising, and so forth. Any net gains shown in knowledge, vote preference, or other effect variables might be due to debate viewing; but they might also be due to influence from these other sources. Before strong inferences can be made regarding debate effects per se, correlations between debate viewing and an effect variable require control for other information sources that might be correlated with both viewing and effect changes. Examination of the debates relative to the more customary information sources also is needed to assess any *unique* contribution of the debates.

The presidential debates also illustrate another problem in specifying media stimuli. We might analyze the direct impact of debate-viewing by examining the strength of its relationship to various effect variables measured after the debates controlling for predebate levels of these measures. But this may be too narrow a view of the complexity of the debates as stimuli in that it ignores the likelihood of their initiating a diverse set of social processes that themselves may have effects. Because the content of these processes may go well beyond the issues covered in the broadcast debates, it is likely that some of these social-process-induced effects will not be detectable from the content of the debates alone. Investigators taking the narrower view of effects obviously will be likely to come to less strong conclusions about debate impact than will those taking a broader view that includes such processes as discussion of the debates, following accounts of them in the media, and perceiving one or the other candidate as winning the debates. Research taking the broader view has found these subsequent variables to have greater effects than did the level of debate exposure (McLeod et al., in press).

VARYING STRATEGIES OF INFERENCE

Up to this point we have been discussing the consequences that various research decisions have on the nature of evidence regarding mass media effects. Differing criteria and research strategies will produce very different evidence. Even within any particular body of evidence, however, there is considerable room to make very different inferences about the extent of media effects. The strength and nature of the inferences that investigators make depend in turn on what kinds of risks they are willing to take regarding the evidence. We can draw a parallel to the testing of statistical data where the investigator must make a decision based on research evidence whether to reject the null hypothesis of no difference or to decline to reject that hypothesis. Whichever decision is made, the investigator risks making an error. The question is which type of error will be more damaging or costly, given the purpose of the research.

An analogy can be made to the drawing of inferences from evidence. Here it is an even more general problem than in the testing of hypotheses, because research inferences and conclusions are made not only by the investigator conducting the research but even more often by secondary analysts who have their own values and priorities. Historically, public knowledge of mass media effects has been set more by oversimplified summaries (Berelson & Steiner, 1964; Klapper, 1960) than by more detailed research findings. Two quite different images of media effects have emerged from various reviews of research findings, reflecting which type of error the reviewer worries about most. At the risk of oversimplification, we have called these two types of analysts Type One and Type Two worriers.

Type One worriers fear the possibility of making too strong inferences and consequently tend to accept a null position of no media effects. The evidence they cite tends to be from field studies of persuasion using gross measures of both media exposure and attitude change. The lack of major change and the apparent stability are attributed to selective exposure and selective perception, and the major impact is thought to be reinforcement of preexisting attitudes. If they should encounter a correlation coefficient of 0.30 between media exposure and effect, they are likely to point out that (by squaring the coefficient) this accounts for less than 10% of the effect variance. It is interesting that much of the evidence cited was obtained before the advent of television (Berelson et al., 1954; Katz & Lazarsfeld, 1955; Lazarsfeld et al., 1948) and that secondary citation of the original evidence has tended to move toward limited inconsequential effects or no effects at all.

Type Two worriers hold a diametrically opposing set of concerns in making research inferences. They worry most about overlooking any media effect and frequently cite the difficulties that beset attempts to find even "obvious" effects. At worst they are willing to accept any change taking place at the same time as some media event (e.g., debates, sports events) as evidence of media effects. They seek results among a much more diverse set of effects and may overlook the possibility of obtaining chance findings in such a large number of comparisons. They worry less about the proportion of effect that media variables account for, noting that even a small effect—say 2% in an election campaign—can make a very great difference.

Type Two worriers note too that communication variables tend to be less reliably measured than demographic and other variables and hence that correlation coefficients understate considerably their "true" predictive power. They are not likely to hestiate counting as effects the media acting as mere conduits of public events, as discussed earlier. Their interest includes indirect as well as direct effects. Their definition of media as stimuli tends to break down media exposure into fine units and includes motivation to viewing and social processes set off by media exposure as sources of effect. Finally, they seem to assume that the public spends so much time with television and other media that there must be some kind of effect in at least some segment or subpopulation of the audience. Theirs is an almost unbeatable faith.

Our point is that variance in discussion of media effects comes from more than contrary evidence or the level of conservatism in setting statistical alpha levels in testing hypotheses. The disparity relates to the nature of what is evidence and what kinds of errors are most likely to be harmful. Obviously, we have overdrawn the two types of worriers in order to make our point clear. But rather different sets of inferences are apparent in the literature of the field, and anyone wanting to understand more about media effects should be aware of this. Neither type of worry is completely foolish or unwise. Perhaps one way out of the dilemma is to use the broad research strategies of the Type Two worrier in combination with the basic caution of the Type One worrier.

PECULIAR HISTORY AND CURRENT STRUCTURE OF THE FIELD

It is important for anyone who wishes to gain an adequate understanding of mass media effects to learn some of the peculiar history of the communication research field. The history is indeed peculiar but probably not unique in the social sciences. A rough parallel can be seen, for example, between the development of social psychology as a field and similar stages in mass communication research some 15 to 25 years later.

Changing Models of Effects

Polemical writing about the effects of mass media was frequent in the post-World War I era when massive propaganda impact was attributed to the persuasive content of the media. The mass model of society prevailed in these writings, and the dominant influence mechanism was thought to be simple learning through repetitive messages (Bauer & Bauer, 1960). It was in reaction to this view that the so-called "limited effects" model of media influence developed largely through the voting and functional media use studies at Columbia University in the 1940s (Berelson, 1949; Berelson et al., 1954; Lazarsfeld et al., 1948; Wolfe & Fiske, 1949). This view has become the dominant one in reviews of the field in various social science texts despite the lack of methodological sophistication in its original evidence and a dearth of fresh evidence from the posttelevision era. For example, communication was of little concern in the voting studies from 1952 to 1972, but that situation has begun to be corrected in studies such as those of the 1974 and 1976 election campaigns funded by the John and Mary R. Markle Foundation and the National Science Foundation, under the auspices of the Social Science Research Council's Committee on Mass Communication and Political Behavior.

Although the limited effects model still dominates academic reviews of the field, the public, along with many public action groups, holds to a view that is much closer to a mass persuasion model. This split has resulted in a wide gap between the basic academic research and applied concerns. At least until recently, the limited effects view has also discouraged "visitors" from "outside" social science departments from doing research in this area. Gans (1972) reviewed the mass communication research activity within sociology and other standard social science departments and judged that a "famine" existed. The situation has changed recently, particularly in political science where it has become apparent that the standard party affiliation and socioeconomic variables are declining in their power to predict voting behavior. They reason that the potential for television and other media influences may well be growing (Nie, Verba, & Petrocik, 1976).

It is clear that the earlier models of mass media effects did little to stimulate and develop communication research. Although no single model has emerged to replace them, unquestionably much greater attention will be paid to models that include the specification of conditions under which media exposure will produce effects on certain audience members. These are more complicated multivariate models, but they are likely to be much closer to the realities of mass media influence than are simple models overstating or understating effects on the total public.

Emphasis on Applied Research

A second historical factor limiting the integration of mass media effects findings is the fact that the field arose largely from the study of applied problems rather than as a response to intellectual concerns. Evidence-based research began in the 1930s with sample surveys that attempted to identify the audiences of various mass media, but particularly that of radio. World War II provided an unparalleled stimulus to communication research through government sponsorship of experimental studies of the effectiveness of film and other media in persuading audiences. Sample surveys studying problems relevant to the war effort also touched on issues of media effectiveness. The war thereby served as a common meeting ground for social scientists from a variety of academic disciplines who were out of necessity involved in communication research problems. Some of them retained an interest in these problems when they returned to academic settings, but their allegiances tended to return to their previous academic fields. The emergence of communication as a separate discipline did not take place until a decade later.

Applied problems continued to dominate communication research activities after the war. The perception that America's world responsibilities included aiding less developed nations led to a ready acceptance of the idea that the mass media could foster economic growth and political development by disseminating needed information, by stimulating achievement motivation and empathy, and so forth (Lerner, 1958; Schramm, 1964; Rogers, 1972). The empirical difficulties of inducing social change appear to have scaled down this optimistic hope, at least to a point where the mass media are no longer seen as sufficient causes (i.e., media exposure producing change all by itself) of the various forms of national development (Rogers, 1976).

The domination of applied research in the study of mass media effects has continued to the present day. In 1969, for example, pressure from the public and from Congress led to the formation of the Surgeon General's Scientific Advisory Committee on Television and Social Behavior and to the earmarking of about one million dollars for research recommended by this committee. The funding resulted in the publication of 60 reports from investigators representing a wide variety of fields (Comstock & Rubinstein, 1972). Although the major focus was on the possible effects of televised violence on the aggressive behavior of children, the topic did not represent the dominant research interests of most of the investigators. Their tangential interests and the relatively short duration of the research contracts (12 to 18 months) undoubtedly contributed to a lack of theoretical orientation among the reports. The history of communication research is replete with other examples of funding being infused into the field on a short-term basis for the study of a variety of applied problems: health communication (e.g., heart disease, cancer campaigns); dissemination of birth control information; television advertising effects; cable television and other technological advances; and effects of televised courtroom proceedings. No comparable funding is available for basic research, and communication researchers must apply to agencies whose scientific panels are labeled according to established academic fields. The relative adequacy of funding for applied research in combination with the scarcity of support for basic research has helped to make the mass communication area highly relevant to public policy issues but at the same time theoretically impoverished.

Late Emergence as an Academic Discipline

The applied focus has also helped to retain communication research as "an academic crossroad where many have passed, but few have tarried" (Schramm, 1963 p. 2). To the present day, a large share of the research relevant to mass media effects emanates from social scientists with allegiances to a variety of fields other than communication. Few would identify themselves as communication researchers. Not only does this tend to impede theoretical integration of research, but it also makes it very difficult for any given person to locate the scattered studies relevant to mass media effects.

There has been a gradual shift away from the temporary crossroads situation described by Schramm and toward the emergence of communication as an academic discipline. This was seen first in the mid-1950s with the founding of several communication research centers at universities like Illinois, Stanford, Wisconsin, and Michigan State. From these arose academic programs including doctoral training and degrees in communication and mass communication. The resulting research has had major impact on existing academic organizations such as the Association for Education in Journalism and the Speech Communication Association and has probably contributed to the founding of new organizations like the International Communication Association. Not surprisingly, these developments have served to develop orientations that view communication research as a new discipline with unique concepts and styles of theorizing rather than as an applied derivative of existing social science fields. The growing numbers of self-conscious communication researchers helps to account for the birth of several new communication journals within the past few years (e.g., *Communication Research, Human Communication Research*) and the growing amount of evidence-based articles in the older publications of the field.

Communication as a "Variable Field"

Communication research represents what has been termed a "variable field" as opposed to a "level field" (Paisley, 1972). Level fields within the social sciences are those whose concepts and theories tend to operate at a common level of discourse. For example, psychologists study individual systems using appropriate cognitive, affective, and behavior concepts, whereas sociologists examine the structure and processes of various types of social systems (e.g., societies, communities, organizations, primary groups) at a more abstract level. Of course, there are many exceptions among psychologists using physiological variables and sociologists having recourse to psychological concepts and explanations. But in general the consistency in abstraction is much greater in these level fields.

Variable fields, on the other hand, focus on a particular class of variables that have consequences at more than one level of abstraction. Economics and political science are examples of relatively old and established variable fields, but level fields tend to have longer research traditions. Business and educational research are also variable fields, as are the new hybrids of social psychology, cybernetics, and communication research. The older variable fields have tended to resolve their inherent differences in abstraction by coexistence of two traditions such as macroinstitutional versus microbehavioral with different research problems and methodological strategies. These arrangements are still to be worked out in communication research, and the shifting levels of abstraction have implications for what we know and don't know about the effects of the mass media.

Variable fields tend to utilize research strategies that are common to the level field at any given level of abstraction. Experimental research dominates at the less abstract levels, whereas nonexperimental field studies are more common in research in the more abstract social systems level fields. As a result, standards of evidence vary, and there tends to be little agreement about strategies of research. Theoretical development in the newer variable fields tends to be sporadic and characterized by fads and "small islands" of theory rather than by traditional "grand" theories.

Communication research appears to closely fit the model of the variable field. There is little standardization of research approaches. Not only does the field admit both experimental and nonexperimental evidence, but knowledge claims are also based on legal and historical scholarship, literary criticism, and other strategies. In the attempt to study media process and effects at all levels of discourse, communication research has no broad encompassing theories that cover the field. Rather, most theories are borrowed from other level fields, particularly from psychology and sociology and from the more established variable fields. Unfortunately there is often a lag between the prominence of a theory in another field and its appearance in communication research, so that the latter is often in a position of pursuing a dead theory.

The dispersion of communication interest across levels has also led to looking to methodological innovation in lieu of unifying theory. Sequentially, over the past 30 years, various techniques have been seized upon as solutions to communication problems: factor analysis, the authoritarian *f*-scale, the semantic differential, *Q*-methodology, coorientation, smallest-space analysis, path analysis, and gallilean coordinate systems. Although most of these techniques became useful tools in communication as well as in the other social sciences, none proved to be the panacea some hoped for. There remains, however, a tendency to propose technical solutions to substantive and theoretical problems.

Variable fields tend to have as part of their origins a close connection with public or professional institutions. Economics and political science (originally called political economy) have traditional ties to financial institutions and government as have business and education research to their respective institutions. Communication research is no exception to this pattern, at least if we consider those investigators who profess allegiance to the field rather than those from other fields who occasionally do research others might label communication research. Given the already existing tradition of audience research, it was not surprising that communication research found a home in schools of journalism in the post-World War II era. The resulting tie to the professional field of journalism and to the mass media industry has had important consequences for research priorities and questions. The more direct ties to media institutions have maintained the focus on applied problems and reduced the proposition of esoteric research. This contact also may have made even the more basic research more realistic in the sense that the economic and procedural realities of media production constraints are taken into account. On the other hand, much of the research emanating from academic journalism has tended to be too narrowly applied to have much general value. Confusion over whether the client is the media institution or the public also has consequences for research.

Communication research is done today not only in schools of journalism but also in departments of speech communication (or equivalent title). The latter field originates in large part from the humanities rather than from the social sciences and includes such areas as rhetoric–public address, speech correction and audiology, radio–TV and film, interpersonal communication, and sometimes theater and drama. In both journalism schools and speech communication departments, those interested in mass media effects are apt to be a small minority (sometimes one person) at a given school. As a result, investigators are spread thinly across the country and, for quite different reasons, across the rest of the world as well. The isolation of researchers is alleviated only partially by the research divisions within professional associations and more informally by "invisible colleges" of like-minded scholars. Autonomous schools and departments of communication have arisen at Michigan State and Pennsylvania, for example, but the dominant picture is that of isolation with little standardization of definitions, goals, or standards of training. This also tends to spread research findings across the journals of the various fields, although the recent founding of new publications not tied to any one field may lessen their problems.

Media-Centric vs. Effects-Centric
Approaches to Research

In examining the more recent work on mass media effects, we can identify two rather different perspectives guiding research. Individual researchers tend to follow one or the other but not both of these perspectives. The first, a "media-centric" approach (a term coined by Chaffee, 1977), begins with a concern for the structure and content of media and often involves a monitoring of media content. The focus is frequently on the media content and its origins. As a result, communication variables are often treated as dependent on various economic and production factors, whereas effects on the audience are sometimes tacitly assumed from the content. Research within this perspective is more likely to be done by mass communication researchers allied to journalism or speech communication settings than by other social scientists and by others trying to "prove" that the media have effects. Researchers in this mode are in business as long as the content of the media keeps changing or as long as they are able to find new content that could have effects. The tradition of "critical events" analysis (e.g., the Lang and Lang [1960] study of the MacArthur homecoming parade, studies of the Kennedy assassination, presidential debates) illustrates the strengths and weaknesses of the approach. The results of such studies provide rich detail about the operation of the media and their audiences in a particular situation; however, the conditions are so specific as to prevent generalization to other situations. Media-centric research not tied to any critical event has similar strengths and weaknesses. In order to make a lasting contribution to the understanding of media effects, the media-centric perspective must be integrated with other studies to explain effects more fully. This is particularly important in considering the large majority of effects in which the media are likely to be only one among many sources of influence.

The second perspective, which can be called an "effects-centric" approach, is likely to emanate from a concern for the dependent effect rather than for the communication variables. At least prior to the 1970s, research on the relationship between media violence and aggressive behavior showed much more concern with the latter and used filmed violence largely because of experimental convenience of providing a common stimulus to subjects. Research in this tradition is apt to study communication variables relative to other influences on the particular effect of interest. The result may tend to be the opposite of that of the media-centric approach. The effect criterion is well understood and measured, but the mass media stimulus may be overly simplistic. The social context of media use is particularly likely to be ignored in effects-centric research. Although the historic segmentation of the field has tended to produce and continue this dualistic set of research approaches, it is clear that communication research would be improved if the strengths of the media-centric and effects-centric approaches were effectively combined. This might be facilitated through revising graduate training, with programs such that communication students with predominately media-centric orientations would receive more intensive experience regarding particular classes of effects and those with effects-centric orientations would concentrate on gaining greater awareness of the nuances of media perspectives. It also might be useful to mix both media-centric and effects-centric researchers in teams investigating applied problems or developing and evaluating media programs designed for children, the elderly, and other specific audiences.

MEDIA EFFECTS RESEARCH AND PUBLIC POLICY

The foregoing material should convince even the most optimistic reader that identifying or answering questions about media effects is extremely complicated. Several concerns were mentioned that make media effects questions difficult, including the number of different types of possible media effects; the complexity of media stimuli; the special problems in studying and documenting media effects; the varying strategies of making inferences from evidence; and the peculiar history and organization of the field of communication research. Despite these difficulties, however, it is still important to confront the application of research to important social problems. The fact that most media research has a traditionally applied orientation may be a weakness for the development of communication theory, but it may be considered a strength when considering the potential for research to contribute to media policy.

Researchers in the field of communication are not narrowly entrenched in the esoteric concerns of level fields (i.e., psychology and sociology). They are more likely to have ties with the media, perhaps even professional experience, and have a more thorough understanding of the context of media policy. We should not, however, expect immediate answers. The utilization of research is complicated by a very real discrepancy in the understanding of media effects among policy makers, researchers, and the general public.

Public interest in the mass media seems to be guided by an implicit assumption that media have powerful and pervasive effects. Although media researchers have developed through various conceptions of media effects—from direct effect models to limited effects models to concern for the conditional aspects of media effects—it seems that the popular conception of effects has been universally one of undifferentiated concern for the all-powerful media. Current policy related to media, however, does not reflect the popular image of image effects. Policy actions, which are perhaps largely a function of the Constitutional and economic limitations of regulating media, seem unrelated to public concern or evidence from social research. The orientations of the public, policy makers, and the research community are currently very much out of synchrony.

Despite the apparent gap between social research and public policy, most people at least recognize the potential for empirical research as an input to policy. The translation of data into action, however, is possibly more complex and involves more issues than at first appear. To suggest that media research should be an important part of public policy logically assumes that we have answered or at least considered several questions: (a) Is the field of communication research ready to offer policy suggestions based on empirical research? What standards of evidence are appropriate in deciding which research should apply to which problems? (b) Do we know what the goal of media policy should be? Should policy guide media in the direction of social change, or should media be encouraged to reflect reality as closely as possible, or should media be left to serve commercial interests at whatever cost to the quality of content? (c) Do we know where we want to direct policy? Should we consider only the content of media and those people responsible for the content, or are there other elements in the process of communication effects that would make appropriate targets for social policy? (d) What role and amount of responsibility should researchers, policy makers, or other intermediaries be willing to assume in the translation of research into public policy?

How Should We Evaluate Communication Research?

A first policy consideration asks what communication researchers are able to say about media policy, given the complexity of the process they are trying to explain. A careful analysis of the many different types of media effects, and especially of the problems in designing empirical tests that identify unique media effects, could lead to an unnecessarily dismal view of the policy potential of media research. We do have persistent evidence that media have some effects on audiences that at least justifies the consideration of research in the formulation of policy. There is overwhelming evidence, for example, that children can learn from television and that voters at least partially depend on media for political information. Although there is a great deal of variance in the confidence we place in the documentation of several other media effects, there is a corresponding variance in the risk of enacting the policy counterparts to research.

Two considerations seem important in first determining the need for policy action: (1) the magnitude of the impact of media and (2) the costs involved in originating and applying policy related to the effects. First, the media issues addressed by research involve effects that could vary greatly in terms of social significance. The potential of media to influence elections, alter the crime rate, or narrow the knowledge gap between disadvantaged and advantaged children may be of greater significance than media effects on adolescent dating behavior or audience knowledge of sports activities. Although setting an agenda of the importance of various media effects involves value judgments as much as examination of data, media messages do vary according to the negative threat or potential positive gain they may cause. Unfortunately, this is difficult to infer from either experimental studies that show that media are sufficient conditions for effects or from correlational studies that examine the degree of relationship between exposure to media and media effects. It is still unclear how much change in criterion behaviors (e.g., cutting the incidence of violence) is to be gained from a given amount of change in media content.

A second criterion that could determine the appropriateness of policy is the cost of originating and applying the policy solutions. Policy will require various degrees of change from current standards both in direction and in relation to the regulatory group assigned to monitor its progress. Certainly policy decisions that require tampering with constitutional guarantees will involve greater risks than those included in voluntary codes. Similarly, government regulation of media, whether by congressional action or through federal commissions, could involve greater costs than policy that is initiated and controlled through industry self-regulation, public action groups, or educational systems.

The standards of evidence required to evaluate a research input into policy need not be any more consistent than the costs of various policy solutions.

Perhaps we should not be willing to become *either* Type One *or* Type Two worriers but rather be willing to adopt a degree of conservatism in evaluating research that corresponds to the amount of changes and costs required to enact policy. Type One standards should apply to high cost policy, for example, requiring by law that networks cut the amount of violence on television by 50% over the next five years. Adopting an addition to a self-regulating voluntary code that suggests the elimination of gratuitous violence between 7 and 9 p.m., however, could more appropriately be based on a Type Two approach to research.

Policy to What End? What Is the Goal?

Despite the attempts by social scientists to be guided to the greatest extent possible by standards of objectivity, it is often difficult, especially for researchers dealing with media effects, totally to ignore personal biases and outside pressures in designing and conducting social research. Even by the selection of certain media effects questions to the exclusion of others, we are making statements that at least identify the effects we feel are most important. It is, however, much easier to *conduct* social research without subjective evaluations of the system being studied than it is to *translate* research into social policy. The necessity for media policy logically assumes a goal for the system, and if research is to be utilized in policy, its application must be with respect to the standards and goals of the system.

Frequently, however, the goals of different groups involved in policy decisions are in conflict. When confrontations between television networks and public pressure groups take place, for example, the two groups may conceive of the social function of media very differently, although their conceptions are seldom a major part of their arguments. One group may believe media should operate to promote social change whereas the other may feel media exist mostly as a commercial venture. In formulating policy, research would be applied very differently to policy questions in these two systems, and therefore it seems essential that we consider the end goal of policy before attempting to translate research into viable policy solutions. Identical evidence could be used in opposing ways, depending on the values of the system. This would apply to different values within the American media system and especially to systems in different countries.

If we consider, for example, the policy translation of a recent finding about the effects of television on children's perceptions of occupational sex roles, the difficulties in utilizing research become clear. The study found that the frequency of portrayals of women in various occupations traditionally held by men (e.g., police officer) was related to children's perceptions of the ratio of men and women who held these jobs in real life (Miller & Reeves, 1976). Imagine now that we have been asked to determine, in a policy statement, the number of females that must be portrayed as doctors and lawyers on prime-time television. Should we say that television has a responsibility in social change and insist that 50% of the portrayals include women? Or should we insist that television portrayals reflect real occupational statistics so that media do not become responsible for creating a falsely reassuring picture of the world for young people? Or should we say that as a commercial venture, media have the responsibility to attract the largest possible audience despite incidental effects of their programs. Several other alternatives are probably also possible. The major point is that the same data could support several policy alternatives. We must agree on policy or at least be aware of the differences in our conceptions of media systems before research can be meaningfully applied to policy actions.

Policy About What?

The first objects of social policy that most people consider are the sources of media messages. Furthermore, most policy proposals usually include laws, regulations, rulings, and codes. Although policy could effectively deal with communication sources, we should not consider them the only outlet for solutions, no more that we should consider their messages the only required piece of evidence to document media effects. Policy could especially consider the conditional aspects of the effects process and focus on those variables that determine when and for whom media effects will occur. This would include, for example, teaching children about unreal aspects of television and educating voters about the role of media in elections.

There could be several advantages to focusing policy on conditional variables. First, those people most affected by the media would be the primary objects of the policy. If it is true that several of the media effects we are most concerned about are operative only for certain subgroups of the audience, then policy directed primarily at those subgroups would preserve the content for those not affected. For example, those who approach television drama with a willing suspension of belief would not be penalized by policy that attempted to educate those who perceive television drama to reflect the real world. Policy related to conditional variables may also require less risk, because most of the complex legal and economic questions surface only when control of media content is suggested. Finally, by not having to control content, we could be more assured that content changes would not invoke a new set of incidental effects.

There are also different aspects of the type of media research that is used for policy that may determine what policy is about and the risks that policy-makers are willing to take. Utilization of effects-centric research may be less likely to suggest high cost policy, because media effects would be reported in relation to other information sources that could be as responsible—and in many cases more responsible—for the effects. Given the complexity of the process by which media have effects, reliance on only effects-centric research for policy may also result in a less precise description of the portion of the effects that can be uniquely attributed to media. Media-centric research, although more limited in its coverage of the causes of effects, may actually provide more useful information that could be translated into policy. A tolerance for less comprehensive but more detailed research, whether oriented toward media or toward effects, may ultimately result in more accurate and beneficial policy directives.

It may even be reasonable to suggest that there should be media- and effects-centric policy-makers, just as there are media- and effects-centric researchers. Consider, for example, two government commissions that have both examined the violence issue. The Eisenhower Commission on Violence, operating from an effects-centric perspective, approached the general issue of violence and considered several possible causes of violence. The Surgeon General's Scientific Advisory Committee on Television and Violence, operating from a media-centric perspective, considered only a single possible cause of violence—television. From a reading of both reports, it would seem much easier to derive policy directives concerning the media from the surgeon general's report. However, the more general conclusions of the Eisenhower Commission offer important information about other aspects of violence that may be crucial to an understanding of the social context of the effects of televised violence. The major point here is that although both perspectives are useful, policy may to some extent be determined by the orientation of the research that is used in its formulation. Rather than relying on a random matchup, we should make a deliberate effort to correlate policy goals and research perspectives.

Policy by Whom?

Even a sketchy introduction to media effects research suggests to most people several possible linkages between research and policy. If this is so, what role and amount of responsibility should policy-makers and researchers take in the translation process? This has traditionally been a problem of policy-makers mixing in the objectivity of research versus researchers mixing in the subjectivity of policy. Both must recognize, however, that at least to some extent their roles are not mutually exclusive. Researchers, especially those interested in applied research, must depend on policy makers to define problems accurately and issue priorities, and policy-makers must rely on researchers to insure that results are interpreted correctly and accurately applied to policy concerns.

There are at least two aspects of the current organization of the communication field that may contribute to the gap between research and policy. A major problem may be simply geographical. A substantial portion of the research in communication and in media effects is conducted in the Midwest, far from the administrative headquarters of media in the East and the production facilities in the West. There are few established communication links between universities, Hollywood, and New York. Second, as the brief history of the development of communication as a unique area of theory and research indicated, we are a new field, unknown even to many academicians. Certainly a majority of the communication research currently being done comes from new departments of communication, from communication and mass communication research centers, or from schools of journalism and departments of speech. Many policy-makers view communication only within the context of psychology and sociology, which is probably correct as far as the content of most communication research is concerned; however, this view ignores the rather peculiar organization of the communication field.

There is at least one other important consideration in determining the role of researchers and policy-makers in this process. Although policy decisions should be based on evidence from social research, this should not be done in isolation from other considerations or expertise from other information sources. The violence issue, for example, is to a large extent a legal and economic concern. From a policy perspective, the constitutionality of legislative action should be considered in relation to research evidence about the effect. Why should we expend large efforts relating media research to policy issues only to find afterward that control is legally or economically impossible? All information that is relevant to policy should be collated and considered in the appropriate sequence.

The roles of persons with various types of input and evidence relating to policy questions, however, should not be confused. Scientists attempting to translate systematically collected data into policy should not be confused with experts offering a legal opinion. To some extent, legal standards of evidence, which are currently responsible for most policy decisions, may be incompatible with what media researchers have to offer to policy. Although different types of input need simultaneous consideration, we should recognize the uniqueness of each input and attempt to weight the various policy formulas to maximize the benefit from each source.

In addition to differences between contributions of social, legal, and economic information to the formation of policy, there are important differences in the roles that individual researchers play in the translation of social research into policy. Recognizing these differences illustrates the number of unique ways in which research can be utilized and also points out that although an attempt is made to conduct research under the highest possible standards of objectivity, the use of research in policy necessarily implies a consideration of values that may determine and shape final policy as much as or more than the research itself.

Before considering the different roles that researchers can play and have played in the translation of media research into policy, it is important to note that the *type* of information supplied in each of these roles can vary as much as the situation in which the information has been offered. Each type of information requires a different amount of commitment to issues by the researcher and also draws on different forms of evidence. First, researchers are likely to make data-based contributions either by generating original data or summarizing data already available. The Surgeon General's Commission on Television and Violence, for example, required researchers to propose and carry out original research that would recommend policy. Reviews of research, however, are just as likely to have contributed to policy decisions; a good example is the recent review of research on the effects of television advertising on children compiled for the National Science Foundation for the purpose of providing research information to policy-makers as well as for guiding future policy-related research (Adler, 1977). The problem with such literature reviews is that there is considerable slippage in precision in moving from the original work. Findings and qualifications are often rounded off to fit an overly simple and consistent summary of research results.

A second type of contribution is opinion. Regarding researchers' expertise in certain areas, policy-makers are often anxious to have these experts help resolve policy conflicts by offering opinions based on a unique perspective on an issue. A frequent recipient of this type of information, for example, is the Federal Trade Commission, which is increasingly soliciting opinions from researchers as well as consumers on the public's probable understanding of potentially deceptive advertising (Brandt & Preston, 1977). The transition from presenting evidence to giving opinion is a particularly abrupt one for both the researcher and the policy-maker. Hearings are conducted in a quasi-legal format that dictates opinion about a specific case whereas the researcher is accustomed to dealing with research findings aggregated across a large number of cases. The researcher is nervous about extrapolating to a specific case and policy, and the policy-maker or commission attorney is impatient to be rid of all the qualifications and timidities of the social scientist.

Regardless of the type of information researchers bring to the formation of policy, the nature of the interaction between researchers and policy-makers has a great potential to determine how research will be used. We have identified seven researcher roles that could affect the use of research in policy (Broom & Smith, 1978).

First, researchers often find themselves in the role of *legitimizer*. In this situation, researchers and research are typically used to confirm an already established position or policy. Regardless of the type of evidence submitted, the researcher in this role serves to enhance the credibility of current practices by selectively linking evidence with policy after the policy has been established. Reviews of research defending network policies on the portrayals of violence, for example, often fall within this perspective.

In what is often their most influential role, researchers may contribute information via a one-to-one relationship with the highest sources of policy-making authority within an organization or agency. This is sometimes referred to as the *Merlin* role (Sussman, 1966). In this case, researchers offer information without the restrictions often imposed by formal decision-making processes and the complexities of bureaucracies. The potential for more accurate translations of research may actually be increased in this role because of the absence of political and legal constraints and by the fact that consensus may not be as important because both parties have relatively little to lose within their private relationship.

Researchers also play the role of *information broker*, relating the concerns of the research community to institutions and policy-makers. Although single individuals are seldom placed in this role, organizations have been created and are often staffed by individuals from the research community for the purpose of providing a clearinghouse of research information. To some extent, this role is played by the professional associations within the general field of communication research (e.g., the International Communication Association, the Association for Education in Journalism, and the Speech Communication Association); however, this role is the prime focus of private nonprofit agencies such as the Aspen Institute.

Very often researchers are called on after a policy conflict has already been identified. In these situations the researchers can act either as mediator or arbitrator. A researcher as *mediator* will typically make contributions aimed at resolving a policy conflict, while at the same time relying on the policy-makers themselves to make the final policy decisions. It is even possible in this situation for the researcher to initiate the interaction between policy-makers and to make empirical research the focus of that interaction. This role is exemplified by a recent joint effort by British political parties, media representatives, and political communication researchers to restructure British political campaigns (Blumler, Gurevitch, & Ives, 1977).

The researcher as *arbitrator* is usually presented with a policy conflict and then asked, on the basis of data or expertise, to select the right alternative. One of two outcomes is almost inevitable in this situation: Either the researcher will alienate one of the two sides or the research contributions and policy recommendations will be compromised with the goal of pleasing both sides and with the risk of making the policy too innocuous to be effective. The dilemma posed to the arbitrator is exemplified by requests of researchers to decide who is right concerning the question of television and violence—the networks or those interested in stricter regulation.

One of the more difficult roles for researchers is *policy-maker*. There are several instances in which researchers have been a part of commissions or other decision-making groups that are ultimately responsible for policy. Although researchers are typically part of this group because of familiarity with empirical evidence relating to policy, it becomes very difficult to make contributions to decision-making based on social research while at the same time having to consider politics, law, economics, and personal and system values that are also relevant to the final decisions. Separating the roles of researcher and policy-maker, especially within a single individual, is very difficult and could involve serious conflicts of interest.

A final role involves the researcher as a *passive participant* in policy. In this role, researchers maintain that the objectivity of research would be tarnished if the researcher were involved in any way in the translation process. Researchers are often anxious to operate in this role, especially in situations in which the translation of research into policy obviously involves taking a stand on an issue based on subjective values. Although it is somewhat difficult to imagine "no role" as a role, it is just this orientation to policy that critics frequently accuse researchers of playing—with policy the likely loser, because it will be based on factors that are possibly less appropriate than social research.

Comparing these roles, it is evident that the role of researchers in policy formation may differ along the following important dimensions: the type of information contributed to policy; access to policy-makers; the stage of the decision-making process in which researchers are consulted; researchers' concern for the process of decision-making versus the content of policy decisions; the degree of advocacy required; and the ownership of ideas. What is important to remember in the context of the larger discussion of media effects research is that finding logical conclusions for research, even if the research is formulated and designed as applied research, very much depends on the type of information and type of role relationships that are structured to link the research community with policy-makers.

Although the optimal arrangement of communication researcher roles with respect to policy is not yet clear, it is evident that present arrangements should be readjusted in at least two major ways. First, more sensitive communication policy decisions are likely to be made to the extent that research findings can be introduced more quickly into the planning process. This means that research must play a more central role in the actual formulation of policy, not just in evaluating decisions or programs after the fact. This has been referred to as formative as opposed to summative use of research evidence (Scriven, 1967). The production of "Sesame Street" serves as a model for this approach (Lesser, 1975).

A second imbalance, arising from the origins of communication research as an applied field, is an overly narrow view of policy research. If research investigates variation only within the mass media constraints currently operating on a given media system, research may only ameliorate present limitations. If policy-makers alone have the responsibility of deciding what questions to ask about media effects, this is likely to be the case. Increased attention to the support of basic communication research to some extent independent of the directness of the apparent linkages between the research question and the social problem would seem appropriate to encourage creative solutions to policy issues.

REFERENCES

Adler, R. P. *Research on the effects of television advertising on children.* Washington, D.C.: U.S. Government Printing Office, 1977.

Bauer, R. A., & Bauer, A. America, "mass society" and mass media. *Journal of Social Issues,* 1960, *16,* 3–66.

Becker, L. B., & Doolittle, J. C. How repetition affects evaluations of and information seeking about candidates. *Journalism Quarterly,* 1975, *52,* 611–617.

Becker, L. B., McCombs, M. E., & McLeod, J. M. The development of political cognitions. In S. H. Chaffee (Ed.), *Political communications: Issues and strategies for research.* Sage Annual Reviews of Communication Research, Vol. IV. Beverly Hills: Sage, 1975.

Berelson, B. What "missing the newspaper" means. In P. F. Lazarsfeld & F. N. Stanton (Eds.), *Communication Research 1948–49.* New York: Duell, Sloan & Pearce, 1949.

Berelson, B. R., Lazarsfeld, P. F., & McPhee, W. N. *Voting: A study of opinion formation in a presidential campaign.* Chicago: University of Chicago Press, 1954.

Berelson, B., & Steiner, G. A. *Human Behavior: An inventory of research findings.* New York: Harcourt, Brace, 1964.

Berkowitz, L. Violence in the mass media. In L. Berkowitz (Ed.), *Aggression: A social psychological analysis.* New York: McGraw-Hill, 1962.

Blumler, J. G., Gurevitch, M. & Ives, J. The challenge of election broadcasting. Leeds, Centre for Television Research, University of Leeds, LS2 9JT, 1977.

Blumler, J. G., & Katz, E. (Eds.). *The uses of mass communication.* Sage Annual Reviews of Communication Research, Vol. III. Beverly Hills: Sage, 1974.

Blumler, J. G., & McLeod, J. M. Communication and voter turnout in Britain. In T. Leggatt (Ed.), *Sociological theory and survey research.* London: Sage, 1974.

Bogart, L. *The age of television.* New York: Ungar, 1972.

Brandt, M. T., & Preston, I. L. The Federal Trade Commission's use of evidence to determine deception. *Journal of Marketing,* January, 1977, *41,* 54–62.

Broom, G. M., & Smith, G. C. *Toward an understanding of public relations roles: An empirical test of five role models' impact on clients.* Paper presented at the meeting of the Association for Education in Journalism, Seattle, August, 1978.

Cantor, J. R., & Zillmann, D. The effect of affective state and emotional arousal on music appreciation. *Journal of General Psychology,* 1973, *89,* 97–108.

Chaffee, S. H. Memorandum to the Committee on Mass Communication and Political Behavior, Social Science Research Council, August 30, 1977.

Chaffee, S. H. *Longitudinal designs for communication research: Cross-lagged correlation.* Paper presented at the meeting of the Association for Education in Journalism, Carbondale, August 1972.(a).

Chaffee, S. H. Television and adolescent aggressiveness. In G. A. Comstock & E. A. Rubinstein (Eds.), *Television and social behavior. Vol. 3. Television and adolescent aggressiveness.* Washington, D. C.: U.S. Government Printing Office, 1972. (b)

Chaffee, S. H. (Ed.). *Political communication: Issues and strategies for research.* Beverly Hills: Sage, 1975.

Chaffee, S. H., & Izcaray, F. Mass communication functions in a media-rich developing society. *Communication Research,* 1975, *2,* 367–395.

Chaffee, S. H., & Wilson, D. *Media rich, media poor: Two studies of diversity in agenda-holding.* Paper presented at the meeting of the Association for Education in Journalism, College Park, Md., August 1976.

Cohen, B. C. *The press, the public and foreign policy.* Princeton: Princeton University Press, 1963.

Comstock, G. A., & Rubinstein, E. A. *Television and social behavior* (Vols. 1-4), Washington, D.C.: U.S. Government Printing Office, 1972.

Cramond, J. Introduction of TV and effects upon children's daily lives. In R. Brown (Ed.), *Children and television.* Beverly Hills: Sage, 1976.

Dominick, J., & Greenberg, B. S. Mass media functions among low-income adolescents. In B. S. Greenberg & B. Dervin (Eds.), *Use of the mass media by the urban poor.* New York: Praeger, 1970.

Feshbach, S. Reality and fantasy in filmed violence. In J. P. Murray, E. A. Rubinstein, & G. A. Comstock (Eds.), *Television and social behavior* (Vol. 2). *Television and social learning.* Washington, D.C.: U.S. Government Printing Office, 1972.

Festinger, L. Behavioral support for opinion change. *Public Opinion Quarterly,* 1964, *28,* 404-417.

Furu, T. *The function of television for children and adolescents.* Tokyo: Sophia University Press, 1971.

Gans, H. J. The famine in American mass-communications research: Comments on Hirsch, Tuchman, and Gecas. *American Journal of Sociology,* 1972, *77,* 697-705.

Goodhardt, G. J., Ehrenberg, A. S. C., & Collins, M. A. *The television audience: Patterns of viewing.* London: Saxon House, 1975.

Gormley, W. T. *The effects of newspaper-television cross-ownership on news homogeneity.* Chapel Hill: Institute for Research in Social Science, University of North Carolina, 1976.

Greenberg, B. S., & Reeves, B. Children and the perceived reality of television. *Journal of Social Issues,* 1976, *32* (4), 86-97.

Harrison, R., & Ekman, P. TV's last frontier: South Africa. *Journal of Communication,* 1976, *26,* 102-109.

Hawkins, R. P. The dimensional structure of children's perceptions of television reality. *Communication Research,* 1977, *3,* 299-320.

Himmelweit, H. T., Oppenheim, A. N., & Vince, P. *Television and the child.* London: Oxford University Press, 1958.

Hyman, H. H., & Sheatsley, P. B. Some reasons why information campaigns fail. In E. E. Maccoby, T. M. Newcomb, & E. L. Hartley (Eds), *Readings in social psychology.* New York: Holt, 1958.

Katz, E., & Lazarsfeld, P. F. *Personal influence.* Glencoe: Free Press, 1955.

Kenny, D. A. Cross-lagged and synchronous common factors in panel data. In A. S. Goldberger & O. D. Duncan (Eds.), *Structural equation models in the social sciences.* New York: Seminar Press, 1973.

Kerlinger, F., & Pedhazur, E. *Multiple regression in behavioral research.* New York: Holt, 1973.

Klapper, J. T. *The effects of mass communication.* New York: Free Press, 1960.

Kline, F. G., Miller, P. V., & Morrison, A. J. Adolescents and family planning information: An Exploration of audience needs and media effects. In J. G. Blumler & E. Katz (Eds.), *The uses of mass communication.* Beverly Hills, Sage, 1974.

Kraus, S., Davis, D., Lang, G. E., & Lang, K. Critical events analysis. In S. H. Chaffee (Ed.), *Political communication issues and strategies for research.* Sage Annual Reviews of Communication Research, Vol IV. Beverly Hills: Sage, 1975.

Lang, K., & Lang, G. E. The unique perspective of television and its effect: A pilot study. In W. Schramm (Ed.), *Mass communications.* Urbana: University of Illinois Press, 1960.

Lang, G. E., & Lang, K. Immediate and mediated responses: First debate. In S. Kraus (Eds.), *Great Debates, 1976—Ford vs. Carter.* Bloomington: Indiana University Press, in press.

Lazarsfeld, P. F., Berelson, B., & Gaudet, H. *The people's choice.* New York: Columbia University Press, 1948.

Lerner, D. *The passing of traditional society.* New York: Free Press, 1958.

Lesser, G. S. *Children and television.* New York: Vintage, 1975.

Lyle, J., & Hoffman, H. R. Children's use of television and other media. In E. H. Rubinstein, G. A. Comstock, & J. P. Murray (Eds.), *Television and social behavior. Vol. 4. Television in day-to-day life: Patterns of use.* Washington, D.C.: U.S. Government Printing Office, 1972.

MacCorquodale, K., & Meehl, P. E. On a distinction between hypothetical constructs and intervening variables. *Psychological Review,* 1948, *55,* 95–107.

McCombs, M. E., & Shaw, D. C. The agenda-setting function of mass media. *Public Opinion Quarterly,* 1972, *36,* 176–187.

McGuire, W. J. Inducing resistance to persuasion. In L. Berkowitz (Ed.), *Advances in experimental social psychology* (Vol. 1) New York: Academic Press, 1964.

McLeod, J., Atkin, C., & Chaffee, S. Adolescents, parents and television use: Adolescent self-report measures from Maryland and Wisconsin samples. In G. A. Comstock & E. A. Rubinstein (Eds.), *Television and social behavior. Vol. 3. Television and adolescent aggresiveness.* Washington D.C.: U.S. Government Printing Office, 1972.

McLeod, J. M., & Becker, L. B. Testing the validity of gratification measures through political effects analysis In J. G. Blumler & E. Katz (Eds.), *The uses of mass communication.* Beverly Hills: Sage, 1974.

McLeod, J. M., Becker, L. B., & Byrnes, J. E. Another look at the agenda-setting function of the press. *Communication Research,* 1974, *1,* 131–166.

McLeod, J. M., Brown, J. D., Becker, L. B., & Ziemke, D. A. Decline and fall at the White House: A longitudinal analysis of communication effects. *Communication Research,* 1977, *4,* 3–20, 35–39.

McLeod, J. M., Durall, J. A., Ziemke, D. A., & Bybee, C. R. Reactions of young and older voters: Expanding the context of debate effects. In S. Kraus (Ed.), *Great Debates, 1976— Ford vs. Carter.* Bloomington: Indiana University Press, in press.

McLuhan, M. *Understanding media.* New York: McGraw-Hill, 1964.

Miller, M. M., & Reeves, B. Linking dramatic TV content to children's occupational sex-role stereotypes. *Journal of Broadcasting,* 1976, *20,* 35–50.

Morrison, A. J., Steeper, F., & Greendale, S. The first 1976 presidential debate: The votes win. Paper presented at the meeting of the American Association for Public Opinion Research, Buck Hills Falls, May 1977.

Nie, N. H., Verba, S., & Petrocik, J. R. *The changing American voter.* Cambridge: Harvard University Press, 1976.

Paisley, W. *Communication research as a behavioral discipline.* Stanford: Institute for Communication Research, 1972. (mimeographed)

Parker, E. B. The effects of television on library circulation. *Public Opinion Quarterly,* 1963, *27,* 578–589.

Reeves, b. Perceived TV reality as a predictor of children's social behavior. *Journalism Quarterly,* 1978, *55,* 682–689, 695.

Robinson, J. P. Mass communication and information diffusion. In F J. Kline & P. F. Tichenor (Eds.), *Current perspectives in mass communication research.* Beverly Hills: Sage, 1972.

Rogers, E. M. *The communication of innovations.* New York: Free Press, 1972.

Rogers, E. M. Communication and development: Critical perspectives. *Communication Research,* 1976, *3,* 99–106, 213–240.

Schramm, W. Mass communication. *Annual Review of Psychology,* 1962, *13,* 251–284.

Schramm, W. Communication research in the United States. In W. Schramm (Ed.), *The science of human communication.* New York: Basic Books, 1963.

Schramm, W. *Mass media and national development.* Stanford: Stanford University Press, 1964.

Schramm, W., Lyle, J., & Parker, E. B. *Television in the lives of our children.* Stanford: Stanford University Press, 1961.

Scriven, M. The methodology of evaluation. In S. Tyler, R. M. Gagne, & M. Scriven (Eds.), *Perceptives on curriculum education.* Chicago: Rand, 1967.

Siebold, D. T. Communication research and the attitude-verbal report—overt behavior relationship: A critique and theoretical reformulation. *Human Communication Research,* 1975, *2,* 2–32.

Star, S. A., & Hughes, H. M. Report of an educational campaign: The Cincinnati plan for the United Nations. *American Journal of Sociology,* 1950, *55,* 389–400.

Sussman, M. The sociologist as a tool of social action. In Arthur B. Shostak (Ed.), *Sociology in action.* Homewood, Ill.:Dorsey Press, 1966.

Tannenbaum, P. H. The congruity principle revisited: Studies in the reduction, induction, and generalization of persuasion. In L. Berkowitz (Ed.), *Advances in experimental social psychology,* (Vol. 3). New York: Academic Press, 1967.

Tichenor, P. J., Donohue, G. A., & Olien, D. N. Mass media and differential growth in knowledge. *Public Opinion Quarterly,* 1970, *34,* 158–170.

Tichenor, P. J., Rodenkirchen, J. M., Olien, C. N., & Donohue, G. A. Community issues, conflict and public affairs knowledge. In P. Clarke (Ed.), *New models for mass communication research.* Beverly Hills: Sage, 1973.

Watt, J. H., & Krull, R. An examination of three models of television viewing and aggression. *Human Communication Research,* 1977, *3,* 99–112.

Werner, A. Children and television in Norway. *Gazette,* XVII (3), 1971.

Wolfe, K. M., & Fiske, M. The children talk about comics. In P. F. Lazarsfeld & F. N. Stanton (Eds.), *Communication research, 1948–49.* New York: Harper, 1949.

Zillmann, D. The role of excitation in aggressive behavior. *Proceedings of the Seventeenth International Congress of Applied Psychology, 1971.* Brussels: Editest, 1972.

Development of sophisticated longitudinal design and analysis has prompted interest in long-term media-use research. This article outlines hypotheses and research strategies that may be used in researching media use throughout the life cycle. John Dimmick, Thomas A. McCain, and W. Theodore Bolton hypothesize that media informational use over the life span is curvilinear: low in childhood, rising in adolescence and young adulthood, peaking in preretirement years, and declining thereafter. They discuss application of time-based designs and data archives appropriate for testing the hypothesis. Drs. Dimmick and McCain are associate professors in the department of communication at Ohio State University, where Theodore Bolton is a doctoral student.

16

MEDIA USE AND THE LIFE SPAN
Notes on Theory and Method

*John W. Dimmick, Thomas A. McCain, and
W. Theodore Bolton*

This article is about change: specifically, the changes over the life course which are associated with changes in the uses and gratifications which individuals derive from the media of mass communication. The uses and gratifications approach has been the subject of much scholarly discussion and debate (Elliott, 1974; Carey and Kreiling, 1974; Swanson, 1979; Katz, 1979), and it is the dominant paradigm guiding the study of the audiences of mass communication. One of the unique virtues of the approach is its ability to reach out "effectively to a wide range of new theoretical developments in other disciplines" (Blumler and Katz, 1974: 15).

In the following pages we will, first, provide a brief overview of the uses and gratifications paradigm. Second, we will offer a tentative view of the process by which the gratifications derived from the media and other activities change as a result of the alterations in need structure of the individual. Third, we will present a crude stage-theory which is an attempt to chart the points and regions in the life course at which changes in the need structure are prompted by alterations in biophysical and

From John W. Dimmick, Thomas A. McCain, and W. Theodore Bolton, "Media Use and the Life Span: Notes on Theory and Method," *American Behavioral Scientist* 23, 1 (1979) 7-31. Copyright 1979 by Sage Publications, Inc.

sociopsychological states. Finally, we will illustrate the formation and testing of hypotheses concerning media use in the life span by focusing on the concept of the change function.

THE USES AND GRATIFICATIONS PARADIGM

Katz, Blumler, and Gurevitch (1974: 20) have summarized the uses and gratifications paradigm approach to the study of media audiences as being "concerned with (1) the social and psychological origins of (2) needs, which generate (3) expectations of (4) the mass media and other sources, which lead to (5) differential patterns of media exposure (or engagement in other activities), resulting in (6) need gratifications and (7) other consequences, perhaps mostly unintended ones." It is important to note that while this terse description of the paradigm seems to imply a linear process, the gratifications derived from media and other sources affect the individual's life satisfaction, one important dimension of sociopsychological state (see Swank, in this issue).

Studies which have attempted to operationalize all or most of the seven elements of the paradigm are conspicuous by their paucity in the research literature. Blumler (1979) is one of the few researchers who has measured more than a handful of variables indexing sociopsychological state. Despite McGuire's (1974) classification of need or motives, few studies have attempted to measure need states independently of the gratifications derived from the media. Similarly, Katz, Gurevitch, and Haas's (1973) study of Israeli adults is an exception to the rule that uses and gratifications research is unremittingly "media-centric" in focusing solely on media as sources of gratification. The majority of the research literature is composed of studies concerned only with gratifications derived from the media by their audiences. Hence, we know a great deal more about media-based gratifications than about the antecedents of need gratification or the role of media in the larger process of need satisfaction.

One crucial task of research and theory in media use and the life span is to ascertain how changes in the antecedents of need satisfaction—sociopsychological state, needs, and available gratification alternatives—are associated with changes in gratifications across the life course. In the following two sections of the article, we will offer a tentative conceptualization of changes in need structure and how these may be prompted by changes in the sociopsychological or biophysical state of the individual.

CHANGE IN NEED STRUCTURE AND GRATIFICATION ALTERNATIVES

The uses and gratifications paradigm implies that changes in the patterns of uses and gratifications could derive from either (a) changes in sociopsychological or biophysical states which result in alterations in the individual's need structure or (b) changes in the available media and nonmedia sources of need satisfaction. The following section will portray stages in the life span which serve to outline the changes in sociopsychological and biophysical states. The task of this section is to offer a perspective on changes in need structure and the sources of need satisfaction.

One hypothesis which emerges from both the uses and gratification research and the life-span literature concerns change in the need hierarchy over the life span. Uses and gratifications researchers have used various terms to describe the property which we will term need salience. For example, Greenberg (1974: 89) noted that the motivation structure which emerged from his study of television viewing by children and adolescents might well appear in studies of other audience groups "differing only in emphasis and salience for adults." Katz et al. (1974: 24) have pointed out the necessity of "sorting out different levels of need," and Brown et al. (1974: 109) have called for studies to assess whether "dominant need states change over time." However, only one known study (Swank, 1977) has actually employed a measure of need salience. In the life-span literature, Veroff and Veroff (1971) have presented a theoretical view of the development and change of the power motive over the life span. Although the empirical evidence bearing on this point is sparse, a study by Rubin (1977) of the gratifications derived from television by three groups of children and adolescents aged nine, thirteen, and seventeen found that while such gratification factors as viewing to learn, pass the time, or relax were constant across groups the relative importance or salience of the factors across the three groups was significantly different. Hence, we would expect the salience or importance of needs to change over the life span in response to changes in sociopsychological states and that the changes in need structure would eventuate in a reorganization of need-satisfying activities including the mass media.

Changes in the salience of needs imply that the relatively stable patterns of uses of the media and other activities which were associated with the former need structure are no longer perceived as providing an adequate level of satisfaction or gratification. This lack of satisfaction prompts a reorganization of need-satisfying activities. Such a reorganization might well proceed by a process which March and Simon (1958) have termed "problemistic search" in order to match newly salient needs with available sources of gratification. "Search" is used to mean both discovering and defining alternatives as well as "testing" the alternatives for "fit" in an adaptive trial-and-error fashion.

Problemistic search is characterized by what March and Simon (1958) have termed "satisficing" behavior; choice proceeds by seeking and choosing alternatives which are satisfactory rather than optimal. "An example is the difference between searching a haystack to find the *sharpest* needle in it and searching the haystack to find the a needle sharp enough to sew with" (March and Simon, 1958: 141). The search process is terminated once a desired level of satisfaction or gratification (defined by the individual) is achieved. Satisficing rather than optimizing behavior results not only from the limitations on the search process imposed by limited time and energy but also from the tendency for expectations of satisfaction or gratification to adjust to achievement. Faced with the fact that "optimal" alternatives which are perceived as too expensive, too distant, or not attainable for other reasons, the individual may "settle for" a less than maximally gratifying activity by adjusting downward the initially high expectation.

Although there is no existing evidence known to the authors to support the hypothesis that problemistic search follows a restructuring of the need hierarchy, there is evidence in the media literature which is consistent with the satisficing concept. Blumler (1979) has used the term *compensatory* to indicate uses of the media as substitutes for presumably more satisfying but unavailable sources of gratification. Studies have shown, for example, that people who phone radio talk shows in large metropolitan areas are "satisficing" by substituting the contact with the talk show host for the face-to-face contact of which they are deprived (Turow, 1974; Bierig and Dimmick, 1979). Similarly, Wenner (1976) found that one type of elderly television viewer used the medium as a substitute for interpersonal interactions. This may be quite similar to Horton and Wohl's (1956) finding that some viewers used television to perform a parasocial companionship function.

The satisficing concept and the notion of substitute activities raise the question of the number and kind of gratification alternatives available to the individual over the life span. Changes which occur in the life course influence the availability of media and other activities to satisfy needs. For example, the evolving cognitive abilities of the child and adolescent make possible new uses of the media (see Wartella, in this issue). Similarly, legal constraints and the lack of familial and economic autonomy limit the availability of some alternatives to children and teen-agers, although adults are largely free of the same constraints (Morrison, in this issue). For older people, changes in occupational status such as retirement may remove a major source of gratification (Swank, in this issue). Data reported by Brown, Cramond, and Wilde (1974) suggest that the addition and, perhaps, the deletion of gratification alternatives to individuals' lives may trigger a total reorganization of need-gratifying activities.

THE AGE VARIABLE AND CHANGES
IN THE LIFE CYCLE

The following section of the article will present an overview of the positions in the life cycle at which changes in the biophysical and sociopsychological state of the individual will eventuate in changes in need salience and, in consequence, in changes in media uses and gratifications. It might seem that chronological age is the most obvious predictor of changes in biophysical and socio-psychological state. However, recent developments in the study of the life span as well as mass communication suggest that this is not the case.

Wohlwill (1970) argued that age is not an independent variable in studis of the life span, but rather is the temporal dimension along which change is mapped. Wohlwill's position, as Overton and Reese (1973) have shown, is based on assumptions stemming from an organismic model of man and the types of causation accepted by those who employ the model. It will suffice to say that Wohlwill's position, based as it is on what Overton and Reese call the organismic model, is consistent with the assumptions about the active nature of the audience which underlie the uses and gratifications approach. Hence, Wohlwill's argument is persuasive on grounds of the consistency of the pretheoretical assumptions of the uses and gratifications approach with his proposal.

While, as Chaffee and Wilson (1975) point out, age occupies a venerable status in mass communication research, Danowski (1975) has questioned the usefulness of the variable in research concerning media and the life cycle. His data indicate that a variable he terms informational aging is of more importance in the life cycle than chronological age. This concept is based on a view of life-cycle change which "assumes that individuals age at different rates along different psychological and social dimensions" (Danowski, 1975: 4).

Nevertheless, age has been fruitfully employed at some stages of the life cycle as a "marker" variable. For example, the strong relationship between age and the emergence of cognitive and communicative abilities in the developing child (see Wartella, 1979) makes the age variable useful in this respect. However, as one moves from childhood to later stages of the life cycle, it is apparent that the strong relationship between age and critical life events weakens considerably. The age at which the individual enters the job market, marries, and/or becomes a parent, for example, varies so greatly that the utility of age even as a marker variable for these life events weakens considerably. Hence, in the following sections of the article, we will use the terms *life cycle* or *life-span position* to locate individuals in life space, or we will use terms such as childhood as adulthood rather than chronological age.

CHANGE POINTS IN THE LIFE CYCLE

In order to put our concern for understanding people's mass media use in the life cycle in some perspective, a cursory examination of development through the life cycle is presented below. Our view generally includes those aspects of the socialization perspective which has been articulated by McLeod and O'Keefe, and assumes that "to understand human behavior, we must specify its social origins and the processes by which it is learned and maintained" (1972: 127-128). In addition, the biological and physical development of individuals must be taken into account, especially at the extremes of the life cycle. The notion of chronological age, which is often used as the sole indicator of life-span development, has been previously set aside in this article as perhaps a too convenient and sometimes misleading marker of stages in a person's life.

The reader should be aware that the data upon which most theory of life-span change is based are often problematic. As can be observed from the other articles in this issue, research in various life-span positions relies on differing kinds of indicators to generate explanations about a particular stage. Sparse data are available which have tracked individuals across time, or followed the socialization processes through on various levels. The seminal works have been interested in either one aspect of development, such as personality (Kagan and Moss, 1962) or in a particular type of individual, such as the mentally gifted (Terman and Oden, 1959). This has resulted in a patch-work picture of what it is we know about progression through the life cycle.

A STAGE THEORY APPROACH

The most widely held views of life-span development are often referred to as stage theories, among the most notable accounts being those of Freud, Erikson, Piaget, and Kübler-Ross. Kastenbaum (1975: 37) notes that "stage theories are characterized by emphasis upon qualitative differences that are thought to appear in a relatively fixed sequence." The qualitative differences occur at critical change points in a person's development. Although stage theories have been appropriately criticized on a number of grounds (Kastenbaum, 1975), a crude stage theory is presented here in the hope that it will illuminate some of the important changes which occur in the life span with regard to media use.

A variety of authors and scholars have attempted to indicate the dimensions upon which people develop from infancy to old age. Kimmel's (1974) category scheme seems to encompass most other accounts. He noted that the human organism develops along: (1) the inner-biological, (2) the individual-psychological, (3) the cultural-sociological, and (4) the outer-physical. Riegel (1975) points out that these four aspects should be viewed as planes of progression along which people and society change. For example, a person's progression through the life cycle could be independently traced in terms of the cell structure growing and dying (biological), the development of attitudes, feelings, and learning ability (psychological), the communicative competence and peer relationships (sociological), or the outward appearance and size (physical). Any one of these accounts by itself would, however, give an incomplete and misleading picture of the life-span change in an individual. These four broad planes seem to account for the "eight stages of man" proposed by Erikson (1963) as well as the notion of individuals' styles of progression noted by Buhler (1968) and elaborated by Kuhlen (1964). They also subsume the dual systems of the environmental structural forms and the internal structural forms suggested by Danowski (1976). Different theorists have emphasized varying aspects of the interaction among these four "planes of progression."

For our purposes, Riegel's (1975) planes of progression have been relied upon quite heavily. He argues that since so little is known in adult development concerning the inner-biological, treating outer and inner together as a biophysical plane is appropriate. He further collapses the other two factors into a psychological plane for purposes of parsimony.

SPIRALS OF PROGRESSION

We prefer to view these two planes of progression as three-dimensional spirals rather than two-dimensional planes. Spirals must be understood in terms of three dominant features: length, breadth, and twist. These three characteristics of any spiral are analogous to the three major concerns of understanding development in the life cycle: life-span position, cohort (shared life event), and period (history). Uses and gratifications of media in the life cycle is a function of these three factors working on each spiral of progression—the biophysical spiral and the psychosocial spiral. The life-span position of a person does in some respect mark his/her progression in the psychosocial spiral, for at various ages society "expects" certain types of behavior. Likewise, when a person was born (birth cohort) determines to a great degree how an individual interprets the changing environment—an eighteen year old during the depression years is different from an eighteen-year-old in the early 1970s. Finally, the social milieu (period) of the times influences the choices people make in their progression along the life-cycle spirals of progression. Each of these three factors—life-span position, cohort, and period—is a necessary though not sufficient condition for describing the development of either of the spirals of progression.

POSITION IN THE LIFE CYCLE
AND USES OF THE MASS MEDIA

Following Riegel (1975), Table 1 divides the life course into nine positions or stages. The first three stages—childhood, middle-childhood, and adolescence—are demarcated on the basis of the chronological-age ranges associated with Piaget's stages of development within which age is a fairly reliable marker of the emerging abilities of the developing individual. However, the age ranges and life events associated with the later stages of the life span, although loosely based on normative expectations, are somewhat arbitrary and should be considered heuristic rather than definitive. Life experiences listed in the columns headed biophysical and sociopsychological states are potential change points—junctures at which changes in need salience and a consequent re-organization of media and nonmedia sources of need satisfaction may occur. In the following paragraphs we will briefly review the evidence from the media literature which bears on the alterations in media use which are associated with the change points in Table 1.

While the ability to communicate symbolically grows out of earlier attempts to represent the world kinesthetically and iconically (Bruner, 1966), the emergence of language facilitates the child's first contacts with the media—bedtime stories read by parents, *Mister Rogers' Neighborhood* story records or popular music, and the obligatory movies produced by the Walt Disney Studios. In the later stages of childhood, the ability to read opens up new opportunities for gratification, although at what point or by what process the child becomes truly "active" in gratifying needs is, at present, problematic. Childhood is characterized by family dependence, and this is reflected in media use. Freidson (1953) found that children—whose primary group allegiance is to the family—preferred viewing television to other media activities because it provided contact with the family. In this period, television is the dominant medium (see Wartella et al., in this issue), and use of the medium peaks around age twelve, the threshold of adolescence.

TABLE 1
Positions and Events in the Life Cycle

Life Span-Position	Psychosocial	Biophysical
Level I: Childhood-Egocentric (1-7 years)	cognitive development non-symbolic communication skills family dependence sex-role identification begins	cognitive development neural patterning motor coordination crawling walking talking
Level II: Middle Childhood-Concrete Operational (7-12 years)	peer relationships important hobbies and Interests explored conforming behavior development of multiple roles daughter/son student friend sister/brother	eye-hand coordination growth spurts complex memory system
Level III. Adolescence-Formal Operations (12-18 years)	attraction to others attempts to independence testing of physical capabilities rebellion career plans egocentric	physical maturation sexual maturation conceptual/abstract ability
Level IV: Pre Adults (18-25 years)	college/first job marriage first child	first child (F)*
Level V: Early Adults (25-30 years)	second job/loss of job (F) other children children In pre-school first home	other children (F)
Level VI: Early-Middle Adults (30-35 years)	move promotion children to school	
Level VII: Middle Adults (35-50 years)	second home promotion/second career (F) departure of children	notice loss of stamina
Level VIII: Older Adults (50-65 years)	unemployment/retirement isolation grandparenting parents die friends die head of kin	menopause (F) illness
Level IX: Elderly Adults (65+ years)	loss of partner deprivation	sensory-motor deficiencies

NOTE: Adapted from Riegel (1975).
*(F) = female only or predominantly.

In adolescence, peers become a valued social group, and a medium such as movies which facilitates contact with friends assumes greater importance (Freidson, 1953). The onset of puberty in this stage of the life span predisposes the adolescent to be receptive to information about sexually related matters as family planning, especially when such information is presented through a medium congenial to adolescent tastes, such as radio (Kline, Miller, and Morrison, 1974). Faber, Brown, and McLeod (1979) have suggested that entertainment programs on television may provide the material for the adolescent's development of a favorable body image by conveying the society's standards of attractiveness. In relationships with the opposite sex, television programs may provide behavioral repertoires for use in dating. These authors also suggest that entertainment series on television may assist the adolescent in attempts at achieving affective and economic independence from the family by providing young role models who are "on their own." Similarly, television may provide information about future career options by portraying a wider range of occupational roles than adolescents would personally encounter in their daily lives. Avery's review of the research and theory (in this issue) provides a more comprehensive and complete discussion of this stage in the life span.

As Table 1 suggests, the onset of independence and maturity may be marked by the first full-time job or leaving home to attend college. Beyond the entry into adulthood, however, both the life-span literature and the uses and gratifications literature are silent on the question of the relationship of the life events of adulthood and the uses and gratifications derived from the media. Compared with the research which has accumulated on the life stages of childhood, adolescence, and the elderly, few studies have focused on media use by adults and the references to adult uses of the media in the life-span literature are almost non-existent. Morrison (in this issue) views adulthood as a life stage relatively free of the legal and economic limitations on media use which characterize earlier periods of life and as a stage which is marked by the constraints imposed on leisure time by the life events shown in Table 1, such as the demands of occupation or job and/or family.

As Table 1 indicates, in the latter stages of adulthood, possibly the central life event is retirement. Since individuals may gratify a number of needs through their jobs or occupations (see Swank, in this issue), this change point in the life cycle is particularly significant. In this region of the life span, the use of television increases and reading may decrease because of impaired eyesight (Chaffee and Wilson, 1975). Young's review of the literature in mass communication and social gerontology indicates that, like their younger counterparts, the elderly are an active audience.

MEDIA USE IN THE LIFE CYCLE:
HYPOTHESES AND RESEARCH STRATEGIES

Research which seeks to examine media uses and gratifications across the life span is, by definition, concerned with change across time. However, as Kline (1977) observes, the concept of time has not often been an explicit consideration in research design in the field of communication. Hence, in this section we will illustrate the hypothesis-formation process and provide an overview of the research strategies appropriate to studying media use in the life span and attempt to assess the potential of various strategies for contributing to our knowledge.

THE CHANGE FUNCTION

The primary task in the design of research is to specify the change function—the form of the relationship between positions in the life span and the uses and gratifications derived from the media. While it is a common research procedure to investigate intragroup and intergroup differences, in life-span research it is the curve described by these differences, parsimoniously expressed as the change function, which carries the essential information.

The change function for qualitative variables might take the form of statements which specify the order or sequence of changes. An example of a qualitative change function may be drawn from a study by Jeffres (1975) which classified respondents' media use as media seeking (e.g., watching television to pass the time) and content seeking (watching a newscast for information about a specific event). In this study, individuals in the early stages of the life span tended to display media-seeking patterns. In contrast, those in the middle of the life cycle tended toward a mixed pattern of use composed of both media seeking and content seeking, while those in the latter stages of the life span exhibited a content-seeking pattern.

In the case of quantitative variables, the change function might range from specifying the general form of the function (e.g., convex or concave) to a more precise statement in the form of a mathematical equation (Wohlwill, 1970). Bower (1973) reports an example of a quantitative change function. He found a U-shaped relationship between attitudes toward television and a respondent's position in the life span. The respondents occupying earlier and later positions in the life span were more positive in their ratings of the medium than those in the middle of the life span.

Whether qualitative or quantitative, change functions are important both as hypotheses and, ultimately, as descriptions of a relationship. Since research in this area is still in the formative stages, this discussion will concentrate on the phase of inquiry which begins with change functions as hypotheses and eventuates in valid descriptions of the media uses and gratifications in the life cycle.

SPECIFYING THE FORM
OF THE CHANGE FUNCTION

While the theoretical perspective developed in the previous section enumerates possible points in the life cycle at which we would expect media uses and gratifications to change, it does not provide any basis for predicting the form of the changes. In other words, in specifying the hypothesized change function for a specific medium on any given need dimension, it is not possible to predict—for any given pair of change points—whether the slope of the line connecting them is positive or negative. Hence, in order to illustrate the process of developing hypotheses in the form of change functions, we will utilize scattered findings from research concerning media use in the life span. This strategy seems efficient in light of the rich accumulation of studies dealing with media use. A central problem in this approach, however, is that since research findings have almost invariably been reported in terms of chronological age it will not be possible to relate changes in media use to the specific change points discussed in the previous section. As an approximation, we will use descriptive terms such as "childhood," "adolescence," or "middle adulthood." The substantive life-span hypothesis developed in this section is the apparent increase in the use of "serious" or informational media content such as news and public affairs programs on television and the hard news content in the daily paper.

In the early stages of life, use of the informational content of the media is apparently rare or nonexistent. In Lyle and Hoffman's (1971) study, TV news programs were not mentioned at all by first graders, and were nominated as favorites by only one percent of the sixth and tenth graders. As might be expected, first graders preferred cartoons and situation comedies, while the proportion nominating adventure programs increases across the three grade-levels. While these young viewers differed in the types of television entertainment they preferred, it is clear that they evinced little interest in television news.

In adolescence, however, the beginnings of an apparent awakening of interest in the informational aspects of media content emerges. For example, one study of teen-age newspaper readership (reported in Bush, 1968) found that while these young people did read the major news stories of the day, such reading ranked lower than the readership of such items as "action line" and the TV listings. Meine (1941) reports that the percentage of respondents who read stories of a more serious nature in the newspaper such as political news and foreign news increased substantially from the seventh grade through the senior year in high school. Similarly, Rubin (1977) found an increase in preference for television news and public affairs programs from childhood to adolescence.

At least one study shows that the increase in using the media for information which seems to emerge in adolescence is continued into young adulthood. A study of newspaper readership (reported in Rarick, 1971) shows that a higher percentage of college students, both male and female, read the major news stories of the day, along with political news and editorials, than do high school students.

Several studies suggest that this increase in the serious content of the media continues to build through the later stages of adulthood. Zukin, for example, in a study of the uses and gratifications derived by voters in the 1976 presidential campaign, found a negative relationship ($r = -.30$) between age and a "play" factor among viewers of the televised debates. In Bower's (1973) national sample, the amount of viewing of television news and public affairs programs was higher for those in middle-adulthood (35-54) than for younger adults (under 35), whereas older adults (55+) viewed more than those in the middle years. Chaffee and Wilson's (1975) data show a similar pattern for the amount of news viewing.

The available evidence suggests that the interest in informational media may persist into the post retirement period. Davis et al. (1976) report that consistently across several measures news and public affairs programs are the most preferred programs among the elderly. This is consistent with Danowski's (1975) finding that television news is the most frequently watched of seven program categories. Similarly, one viewer type which emerged from Wenner's (1976) Q-sort analysis valued television for the medium's information content. These findings must be balanced, however, by Chaffee and Wilson's (1975) data, which show that all reading, including newspaper reading, declines after the age of 73 because, they speculate, of sensory decay. At the same time, general TV viewing increases while TV news viewing declines.

In summary, the available evidence suggests that the use of television and newspapers for their information content is very low in childhood, rises somewhat in adolescence and young adulthood, and reaches its peak in the years just before retirement age, after which the change may become decremental. Therefore, the hypothesized change function relating media use to life-cycle position is curvilinear in form. Such a pattern might be attributable to the changing salience of information needs over the life course.

STRATEGIES FOR ESTIMATING
THE CHANGE FUNCTION

In the previous section, we formulated a hypothesis—in the form of a change function—that the use of the media over the life span for information was curvilinear in form. The purpose here is to review the available research strategies for their suitability in assessing whether such a change function accurately describes the relationship. If a hypothesized change function has been developed on the basis of previous research produced by cross-sectional designs (i.e., data comparing persons at different stages of the life span based on a sample drawn at a single point in time) then no matter how voluminous the research literature or how consistent the findings across studies, the change function thus derived must still be treated as hypothesis. The reason is that cross-sectional studies simultaneously vary position in the life-span position and cohort membership (generation) and therefore necessarily confound life-span and cohort differences. Hence, the results of cross-sectional studies must be treated as tentative until they can be verified, refuted, or modified by time-based designs. The time-based methods which might be used to assess the accuracy of the change function we formulated earlier are: (a) longitudinal panel designs, (b) cohort analysis, and (c) mixed designs. (More comprehensive overviews of time-based methods may be found in introductory form in Glenn, 1977, and Baltes,

1977, which more advanced treatments in Goulet and Baltes, 1970, and Nesselroade and Reese, 1973.) These time-based designs are fraught with methodological problems, but perhaps the most serious obstacles to their implementation in media research in the life span is their expense in time and money.

The longitudinal panel design has been suggested as a research tool to study changes in uses and gratifications across time by Brown, Cramond, and Wilde (1974: 11). Panel designs, which measure the same individuals at two or more points in time, are likely to be most efficiently employed when the time span over which the changes under investigation evolve is rather short. For example, panel designs could be used to measure changes in need structure and gratifications at such predictable change points as entry into college or retirement. Panel designs would be less efficient in terms of the expenditure of time and money if the time scale of the changes is rather long or if the sheer number of repeated measurements is large.

As a form of secondary analysis, cohort analysis generally requires the analyst to employ archive data. An example of cohort analysis which bears on the hypothesis of increasing use of the media for information over the life span is shown in Table 2. The data in Table 2 were gathered by the University of Michigan Institute of Social Research Election Studies. Codebooks provided by the ISR Survey Data Archive were searched for media-related questions. The question—"How many television programs about the campaigns would you say you watched: a good many, several, or just one or two?"—remained constant in the national election years from 1960 through 1976 and was selected for analysis.

A standard cohort table, such as Table 2, contains columns which represent data from independent random samples in which the life-span positions are arrayed in descending order from early to late. Thus, each column compares different life-cycle positions at the same point in time, each row compares the same life-span position at different points in time, and each diagonal compares those occupying a life-span position at successively later points in time (see Glenn, 1977). While Danowski (1975) and Danowski

TABLE 2
Percentage of Respondents Who Reported that They Watched "A Good Many" Television Programs About the Campaign

		1960 (N=1098)	1964 (N=1668)	1968 (N=1442)	1972* (N=918)	1976 (N=1585)
Pre Adults	21-24	55.6	27.9	25.1	27.8	25.8
Early Adults	25-29	44.2	32.8	39.1	27.0	27.4
Early Middle Adults	30-34	40.3	35.5	27.7	27.8	33.5
Middle Adults	35-39	47.2	42.0	41.3	27.3	30.9
	40-44	46.4	42.7	43.3	39.3	41.2
	45-49	47.5	41.9	50.3	24.3	39.3
Older Adults	50-54	51.3	46.7	43.6	35.8	43.4
	55-59	44.4	48.8	38.5	37.7	43.0
	60-64	54.3	51.9	63.0	40.6	57.1
Elderly Adults	65-69	58.3	54.8	54.5	40.7	49.5
	70-74	55.9	55.6	35.8	60.4	61.2
	75-79	44.1	41.7	36.6	35.1	53.3

*Postelection survey.

and Cutler (1977) have employed archive data in cohort analyses, the archival data on media use currently available are rather sparse.

The data shown in Table 2 are consistent with the hypothesis developed earlier that the use of the media for information over the life course follows a curvilinear pattern. The table shows that an increasing percentage of the respondents across the life span report that they watched "a good many" programs about the campaign, with the peak occurring in the later stages of older adulthood or among elderly adults. An alternative explanation, which cannot be ruled out by the available evidence, is that the pattern in the table simply reflects an increasing exposure to television over the life span, that people in the later stages of the life cycle are watching more programs about the political campaigns because they are watching more television (see Bower, 1973).

As noted earlier, one major problem with time-based designs is their expense in time, money, or both. Since archive data suitable for testing hypotheses in the form of change functions are not likely to be available in great quantity in the near future, cohort analysis has rather limited utility. Likewise, the longitudinal panel design is of limited appeal since a single investigation could well extend over the life span of the researcher. A way around this impasse has been suggested by Nunnally (1973) who proposed a "mixed" design which combines the economy in time and money of the cross-sectional design with the ability of the longitudinal design to provide accurate descriptions of change. At minimum, the design requires measurements performed on two or more life-span positions at two points in time.

Figure 1 shows how this design might be applied to the change function regarding informational uses of the media developed earlier. In the hypothetical study depicted in Figure 1, data on media use have been collected from five life-span cohorts—children, adolescents, and young, middle, and older adults—at two points in time. The figure illustrates an outcome of the data collection which would confirm the hypothesis which specified a curvilinear relationship between use of the media for information and positions in the life span.

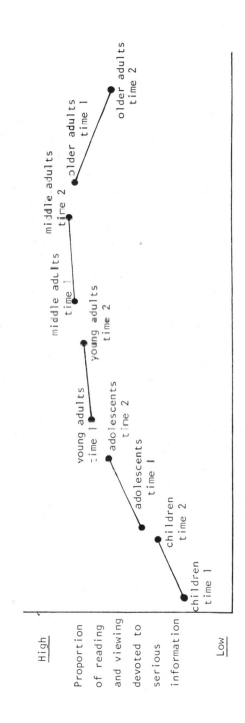

Figure 1: Position in the Life Span

FUTURE RESEARCH

The current state of our knowledge of the uses and gratifications derived by people across the life course is rather uneven;
we know the most about children and adolescents, somewhat less
about the elderly, and certainly the least about adults. While
further studies in the life stages of children, adolescents and elderly
adults are clearly needed, the middle regions of the life-course
also deserve the attention of researchers.

One of the essential tasks of future research and theory is to
identify the change points and change regions, those elements of
the biophysical state of the individual which prompt changes in
need structure. Another essential task is to map the changing
salience of needs across the life stages in relation to the changes
in the patterns of gratification derived from the media and other
sources of satisfaction.

Despite the earlier emphasis on time-based designs, cross-
sectional studies will continue to be important in providing the
information necessary to formulate hypotheses in the form of
change functions. In the previous section, one hypothesized
change function was derived from the extant research, and other
hypotheses could doubtless be distilled from existing studies. As
further cross-sectional research accumulates, such studies will
provide the basis for additional life-span hypotheses.

If change points (e.g., retirement) or change regions (e.g.,
occupational choice) have been isolated, panel designs in which
measurements bracket the change points could be utilized to test
hypotheses concerning such short-term changes in need structure
and gratification. The extensive use of cohort analysis, on the
other hand, will have to await the establishment of a uses and
gratifications or life-span archive. Finally, the mixed design
discussed in the previous section would be reserved for testing
life-span change functions which have evolved from the findings
of cross-sectional or panel studies.

REFERENCES

ATCHLEY, R. C. (1975) "The life course, age grading, and age-linked demands for decision making," pp. 261-278 in N. Datan and L. H. Ginsburg (eds.) Life-Span Development Psychology: Normative Life Crises. New York: Academic Press.

BALTES, P. B., H. W. REESE, and J. R. NESSELROADE (1977) Life-Span Developmental Psychology: Introduction to Research Methods. Belmont, CA: Wadsworth.

BIERIG, J. and J. DIMMICK (1979) "The late night radio talk show as interpersonal communication." Journalism Q. (Spring): 92-96.

BLUMLER, J. G. (1979) "The role of theory in uses and gratifications studies." Communication Research 6: 9-36.

——— and E. KATZ [eds.] (1974) The Uses of Mass Communications. Beverly Hills: Sage.

BOWER, R. T. (1973) Television and the Public. New York: Holt, Rinehart & Winston.

BROWN, J. R., J. K. CRAMOND, and J. R. WILDE (1974) "Displacement effects of television and the child's functional orientations to media," pp. 93-112 in J. G. Blumler and E. Katz (eds.) The Uses of Mass Communications. Beverly Hills: Sage.

BRUNER, J., R. R. OLVER, et al. (1966) Studies in Cognitive Growth. New York: John Wiley.

BUHLER, C. (1968) "The developmental structure of goal setting in group and individual studies," pp. 27-54 in C. Buhler and F. Massarik (eds.) The Course of Human Life. New York: Springer-Verlag.

BUSH, C. R. [ed.] (1967) News Research for Better Newspapers, Vol. 2. Washington, DC: American Newspaper Publishers Assn. Foundation.

CAREY, J. and A. KREILING (1974) "Popular culture and uses and gratifications: notes toward an accommodation," pp. 224-248 in J. Blumler and E. Katz (eds.) The Uses of Mass Communication. Beverly Hills: Sage.

CHAFFEE, S. H. and D. WILSON (1975) "Adult life cycle changes in mass media use." Presented at the Association for Education in Journalism Convention. Ottawa, Ontario.

DANOWSKI, J. (1976) "Environmental uncertainty and communication network complexity: a cross-system, cross-cultural test." Presented at the annual conference of the International Communication Association, Portland, Oregon.

——— (1975) "Informational aging: implications for alternative futures of societal information systems." Presented at the International Communication Association Convention, Chicago, Illinois.

——— and N. E. CUTLER (1977) "Political information, mass media use in early adulthood, and political socialization: seeking clarity through cohort curves," pp. 205-230 in P.M. Hirsch, P.V. Miller, and F.G. Kline (eds.) Strategies for Communication Research. Beverly Hills
Research. Beverly Hills: Sage.

DATAN, N. and L. H. GINSBURG [eds.] (1975) Life-Span Developmental Psychology: Normative Life Crises. New York: Academic Press.

DAVIS, R. H., A. E. EDWARDS, D. J. BARTEL, and D. MARTIN (1976) "Assessing television viewing behavior of older adults." J. of Broadcasting 20: 69-77.

ELLIOTT, P. (1974) "Uses and gratifications research: a critique and a sociological alternative," pp. 249-268 in J. G. Blumler and E. Katz (eds.) The Uses of Mass Communications. Beverly Hills: Sage.

ERIKSON, E. H. (1963) Childhood and Society. New York: Norton.

FABER, R. J., J. D. BROWN, and J. M. McLEOD (1979) "Coming of age in the global village: television and adolescence," pp. 215-250 in E. Wartella (ed.) Children Communicating. Beverly Hills: Sage.

FREIDSON, E. (1953) "The relation of the social situation of contact to the media in mass communications." Public Opinion Q. 17: 230-238.

GLENN, N. D. (1977) Cohort Analysis. Sage University Series Paper on Quantitative Applications in the Social Sciences, 07-005. Beverly Hills: Sage.

GOULET, L. R. and P. B. BALTES (1970) Life-Span Developmental Psychology: Research and Theory. New York: Academic Press.

GREENBERG, B. (1974) "Gratification of television viewing and their correlates for British children," pp. 71-92 in J. Blumler and E. Katz (eds.) The Uses of Mass Communications. Beverly Hills: Sage.

HORTON, D. and R. WOHL (1976) "Mass communication and parasocial interaction." Psychiatry 19: 216-225.

JEFFRES, L. W. (1975) "Functions of media behaviors." Communication Research 2: 137-160.

KAGAN, J. and H. MOSS (1962) Birth to Maturity: A Study in Psychological Development. New York: John Wiley.

KASTENBAUM, R. (1975) "Is death a life crisis? on the confrontation with death in theory and practice," pp. 19-50 in N. Datan and L. H. Ginsburg (eds.) Life-Span Developmental Psychology: Normative Life Crises. New York: Academic Press.

KATZ, E. (1979) "The uses of Becker, Blumler, and Swanson." Communication Research 6: 74-83.

——— J. G. BLUMLER, and M. GUREVITCH (1974) "Utilization of mass communication by the individual," pp. 19-34 in J. G. Blumler and E. Katz (eds.) The Uses of Mass Communications. Beverly Hills: Sage.

KATZ, E., M. GUREVITCH, and H. HAAS (1973) "On the use of the mass media for important things." Amer. Soc. Rev. 38 (April): 164-181.

KIMMEL, D. C. (1974) Adulthood and Aging. New York: John Wiley.

KLINE, F. G. (1977) "Time in communication research," pp. 187-204 in P. M. Hirsch, P. V. Miller, and F. G. Kline (eds.) Strategies for Communication Research. Beverly Hills: Sage.

——— P. V. MILLER, and A. J. MORRISON (1974) "Adolescents and family planning information: an exploration of audience needs and media effects," pp. 113-136 in J. Blumler and E. Katz (eds.) The Uses of Mass Communications. Beverly Hills: Sage.

KUHLEN, R. G. (1964) "Developmental changes in motivation during the adult years," in J. E. Birren (ed.) Relations of Development and Aging. Springfield, IL: Charles C. Thomas.

LYLE, J. and H. HOFFMAN (1971) "Children's use of television and other media," pp. 129-256 in E. Rubenstein et al. (eds.) Television and Social Behavior. Washington, DC: Government Printing Office.

McGUIRE, W. J. (1974) "Psychological motives and communication gratification," pp. 167-196 in J. G. Blumler and E. Katz (ed.) The Uses of Mass Communications. Beverly Hills: Sage.

McLEOD, J. M. and G. J. O'KEEFE (1972) "The socialization perspective and communication behavior," in F. G. Kline and P. J. Tichenor (eds.) Current Perspectives in Mass Communication Research. Beverly Hills: Sage.

MARCH, J. G. and H. A. SIMON (1958) Organizations. New York: John Wiley.

MEINE, F. J. (1941) "Radio and the press among young people," pp. 189-222 in P. F. Lazarsfeld and F. M. Stanton (eds.) Radio Research 1941. New York: Duell, Sloan, and Pearce.

NESSELROADE, J. F. and H. W. REESE [eds.] (1973) Life-Span Developmental Psychology. New York: Academic Press.

NUNNALLY, J. C. (1973) "Research strategies and measurement methods for investigating human development," pp. 87-106 in J. R. Nesselroade and H. W. Reese (eds.) Life-Span Developmental Psychology. New York: Academic Press.

OVERTON, W. F. and H. W. REESE (1973) "Models of development: methodological implications," pp. 65-86 in J. R. Nesselroade and H. W. Reese (eds.) Life-Span Developmental Psychology. New York: Academic Press.

RARICK, F. [ed.] (1971) News Research for Better Newspapers, Vol. 6. Washington, DC: American Newspaper Publishers Assn. Foundation.

RIEGEL, K. F. (1975) "Adult life crises: a dialectic interpretation of development," pp. 99-128 in N. Datan and I. H. Ginsburg (eds.) Life-Span Developmental Psychology: Normative Life Crises. New York: Academic Press.

RUBIN, A. M. (1979) "Television use by children and adolescents." Human Communication Research 5: 109-120.

——— (1977) "Television usage, attitudes and viewing behaviors of children and adolescents." J. of Broadcasting 21: 353-369.

SWANK, C. (1977) "Media and non-media sources of gratification." Ph.D. dissertation, University of Iowa.

SWANSON, D. L. (1979) "Political communication research and the uses and gratifications model: a critique." Communication Research 6: 37-53.

TERMAN, L. M. and M. H. ODEN (1959) Genetic Studies of Genius. V. 1. 5: The Gifted Group at Mid-Life. Palo Alto: Stanford Univ. Press.

TUROW, J. (1974) "Talk show radio as interpersonal communication." J. of Broadcasting 18: 171-179.

VEROFF, J. and J. VEROFF (1971) "Theoretical notes on power motivation," Merrill-Palmer Q. 17: 59-69.

WARTELLA, E. (1979) "The developmental perspective," in E. Wartella (ed.) Children Communicating. Beverly Hills: Sage.

WENNER, L. (1976) "Functional analyses of TV viewing for older adults." J. of Broadcasting 20: 79-88.

WOHLWILL, J. F. (1970) "Methodology and research strategy in the study of developmental change," pp. 50-190 in L. R. Goulet and P. B. Baltes (eds.) Life-Span Developmental Psychology: Research and Theory. New York: Academic Press.

Cogent discussions of the validity of content analysis are rare, so this article is unusual. Digby C. Anderson and W. W. Sharrock are unmerciful in their attack on studies of news bias of some prominent British media scholars, but the piece raises critical questions. First, the authors legitimately question application of the notion of bias to media studies. They question the idea that the mass media should be expected to be impartial. Clearly, they say, neither audiences nor journalists are neutral, so the idea of news impartiality is, at best, relative. But the major problem of content analysis is that it rarely makes simple distinctions between form and content, rendering the analysis insensitive to problems of story construction and audience behavior in reading texts. Dr. Anderson is an Education Fellow at the University of Nottingham. Dr. Sharrock is a senior lecturer in sociology at the University of Manchester.

17

BIASING THE NEWS
Technical Issues in "Media Studies"

Digby C. Anderson and W. W. Sharrock

Introduction

WE became interested in 'media studies'[1] when our interest in the analysis of texts (including newspaper stories) was responded to as though it were an intrusion into the field of media analysis, and was accordingly criticized for failing to take into account other developments in this currently burgeoning field. On inspection of some recent and supposedly leading examples of media studies we found that they were unacceptable to us, deficient in their methodology, insensitive in the treatment of their materials and dubious in their conclusions.[2] Insofar as such studies do concern themselves with texts[3] they treat the analysis of them only as a necessary, but auxiliary, part of their argument about the media. They do not really have any continuing or integrated concern with the investigation of texts of the sort which we would claim but, in order that we may set aside the argument that we should attend to the corpus of media studies we shall in this paper first outline some of the general deficiencies which we find in these studies; difficulties which greatly restrict our willingness to treat such studies as analytical or methodological models. We shall then deal in detail with the way in which one prominent student of the media handles his materials.

In order to facilitate understanding, let us try to say what our argumentative strategy is. We are not trying to argue that one *cannot* arrive at the kinds of conclusions that media scholars reach. We argue only that these conclusions are not *necessarily* to be drawn from those materials, *and* that those conclusions are not the only ones which can legitimately be drawn from those same materials. That the materials are amenable to other readings does pose some sharp difficulties for media scholars because their arguments require that 'members of the society' give certain kinds of interpretations to media output, but their 'theories'[4] do not ensure that

From Digby C. Anderson and W. W. Sharrock, "Biasing the News: Technical Issues in 'Media Studies,'" *Sociology,* the journal of the British Sociological Association, 13, 3 (September 1979) 367-385. Reprinted by permission.

members of the society *will* elect those readings. We do not then dispute that the media can be read in the way that media scholars read them, we ask only if the fact that they can be read in that fashion has any especial significance over the fact that they can be read in quite other ways.

I

Producing Significance

Within the brief scope of this paper we cannot argue all the topics that, in media studies, seem to us debatable. We have only sufficient room to concentrate on one topic, that of bias. We want to argue against the recurring theme that the media are biased.[5] We shall argue that they are not significantly biased in the way that they are often claimed to be; that whether or not they are biased is a trivial matter; and that there are more interesting, important, even fundamental, aspects of the media than bias. We shall argue that the significance and extent of bias are produced by media scholars, rather than by the media themselves. In this section we shall show that claims of bias are inflated and in the next we shall argue that the methods by which claimants find bias are superficial. We refer to these two aspects as 'producing significance' and 'locating bias'.

One basic method for the production of significant bias is through contrived surprise. The theorist assigns to the member of the society, in the form of a 'popular belief', the conviction that the media are neutral, and then proceeds to prove that far from being neutral, the media are cultural phenomena which are 'biased' by the assumptions, prejudices, etc., of the culture in which they are embedded.[6] This 'finding' should not, of course, come as any surprise to anyone who has completed a first year course in sociology, not do we think that it will particularly astonish those whose belief in the neutrality of the media this 'finding' supposedly contradicts.

Harold Garfinkel has pointed out[7] that assignments of attitude must work under the auspices of the *et cetera* principle. We cannot therefore suppose that a faith in someone's neutrality is equivalent to the belief that they are neutral between all possible, or even all actual, points of view: 'neutral between whom?', 'neutral over what', seem to us inevitable questions that must be answered before any characterization of neutrality is made. Insofar as the neutrality of television news is concerned, it seems to us likely that the public faith in its neutrality is one that has to do with the major parliamentary parties, for it is surely in this respect in which there is argument and controversy about bias. The media scholars do not, however, seem concerned with this kind of bias (presumably because many would subscribe to the view that there is so little material difference between the parties that the media would be hard put to take the side of one against the other). These scholars seem rather more concerned to reveal that the news is biased in regard to the class struggle, against extra-parliamentary left-wingers, trade unionists, and so forth. It is far from clear to us, however, that *anyone* has ever claimed impartiality for the media in such cases. It is very clear that all kinds of people – bombers, scroungers, paedophiles, child pornographers, sociologists, Provos, etc., etc., for the list is a long one – are quite openly disapproved by broadcasters and reporters.[8] There is no suggestion that atheists should be given equal time to match the output of religious broadcasting, the National Front the Labour Party, or perverts Mrs. Whitehouse. The television companies have open policies which relate television time to electoral popularity. Who in the world supposes otherwise? Who in the world supposes that where there are detectable minority positions against which 'we' are united in disapproval, that the broadcaster is neutral? Assuredly he is not. The presumption of neutrality which is assigned to those simple minded readers and viewers who figure in many media studies should in our view be seen as rather more sophisticated than it is usually allowed to be, a neutrality specified by relevances, not a notional universal impartiality.

Significant bias is not, then, to be found by identifying some under-represented viewpoint. Nor can it be established by reference to the validity and accuracy of what is reported since these are practical matters which are governed by, and are recognized to be governed by, limitations. Further, the claim that the media are biased is one which it seems to us can only be assessed relative to the claims which the media themselves actually make concerning impartiality but it does not seem to us that media scholars have been particularly assiduous in detailing the actual policies and programme of the media. Only if we know what we have been promised shall we know if we have been deceived.[9]

Whatever they do promise, media men are treated as if they have signed up to be professional sociologists and have fallen down on the job. They are alleged to distort events (if not 'Reality' itself) in their reports, where the measure of distortion is precisely the extent of discrepancy between their account and that given by the favoured sociological theories of the media scholars. For example, media theorists are often inclined to see deviance as the product of 'structured social strain'[10] and to feel that the actions of deviants are 'rational' relative to the circumstances in which they take place. The media are seen as 'distorting' the realities of deviance by presenting them as the products of individual psychological characteristics, e.g., psychological inadequacies, mental illness, etc. The media are, therefore, to be accused of misrepresentation and distortion, as though they were to be understood as propagating some generalized *psychological* theory and were then to be derogated because they subscribe to a psychological theory rather than a sociological one.[11] In effect, then, charges of distortion could equally well be reformulated as statements that the media men disagree with their sociologically minded critics. This reformulation is desirable because claims that the media 'distort' reality surely allow far too much credit to sociological theories which are, even within their own discipline, matters of controversy and which are remote from acceptance as definitive theories of, say, the nature and causes of deviance. In any case, we are far from confident that the accusations made against the media in this connection are correct. We could say that one has to distort the things that the press and television say in order to commit the media to the kinds of 'theories' that sociologists sometimes claim are expressed by them. That part of the press which favours the return of capital punishment, for example, seems to credit 'the deviant' with a high degree of rationality, to such an extent that they think that the commission of a deviant act is an outcome of calculation and that such actions can be prevented if the costs of commission are made so great as to be inhibiting.[12] Of course, it is possible to complain that we are, here, using a rather restricted notion of rationality, somewhat different to that which is often employed by those who emphasize the rationality of deviant acts. However, it is precisely our point that judgments of rationality are complex ones (no less circumstantial than are judgments of impartiality) and that charges that the media deny the rationality of deviants can easily be rebutted: they may deny the rationality of some aspects of some deviant acts but they are prone to recognize the rational aspects of some others. Chibnall's complaint[13] that Fleet Street denies a rational ideology to political deviants compares oddly with his own quotation from *The Sun* that 'The Trots and the Reds know all there is to be known about making the tail wag the dog';[14] if anything the Trots and Reds are a little bit too rational for the liking of *The Sun*.[15]

It is far from clear to us that the media are as systematic and consistent as their critics/analysts would have us believe (or, more accurately, that they are consistent and systematic *in the ways* these commentators suggest). We are not sure that the positions which these scholars ascribe to the media can be properly attributed as their consistent and exclusive standpoint. However, when it comes to the reading of the media as an expression of systematic theories, we are not so much doubtful about the accuracy with which the theories are identified as we are about the tendency to treat the media as though they should be expressing candidate sociological theories. There is a substantial amount of theorizing done in the press but it is typically of the practical and instant kind, done in the course of gathering materials for telling and writing stories: the theorizing is not offered as having the status 'theoretical system for further analysis and empirical research'. However, the continued focus upon the news as a source of candidate sociological theories ensures that little attention is paid to the prominent fact that we are dealing with *news*, and that in the news the media are less involved with general, systematic accounts of things than they are with *stories* about *these* people, *this* event, *this* place, *our* troubles and so on.[16] Further, such stories are presumably of interest to media men not only because they are (or might be) true but because they have attention grabbing, eyebrow raising, indignation arousing, titillating, tension generating, interest holding, and amusing characteristics (amongst others). We might even go so far as to suggest that except for those publications which imagine themselves as 'newspapers of record' and for those television outlets imbued with a Reithian desire for authoritative status, such considerations as we have just enumerated are vastly more important than are those of correctness, objectivity and the like.

Suppose we were to concede in its crudest form the thesis of many media scholars, *viz.* that the media indoctrinate the masses with capitalist ideology or, (as the fashionable phrase now has it) sustain the capitalist hegemony, we should still have to observe that they do so only by getting and holding a reader's attention,[17] mobilizing his emotions, directing his attention, manipulating his reasoning and so forth. The corpus of media studies does not provide any analytical account of the ways in which, through the construction of attention grabbing, interest holding, indignation arousing stories the media do accomplish the task they have been assigned. If the media are transmitting the generalized message they must do so through the particularized materials they employ and any adequate account of their operation must show how they do so. However, media theorists seem utterly indifferent to the 'particulars' of their materials and hence to the kinds of problems that *we* would like to see examined.

It might seem that if we wanted, say, to show that the press were biased or distorted the truth, that we could do so by examining stories as told in the news and by then investigating those same events by way of other sources on them (such as might be available in memoirs, records, etc.) in much the way that assassination freaks have interrogated the report of the Warren Commission or that Philip Knightley questions the objectivity and accuracy of the press in war reportage.[18] We would, that is, be aiming to show that the discrepancy between the media accounts and 'what really happened' on the number of separate occasions was such as to lead to the expectation of a recurrent bias, an expectation which might be confirmed by further studies. This is not, however, how media scholars typically undertake to prove bias; they do not usually[19] make independent investigations of the events the media report but rely on the media for materials on the events and then seek to controvert the media's way of accounting for those events. They typically wish to call into question *the entire way of accounting* employed by the media and can therefore only proceed at the level of type, contrasting one type of explanation with another. Their strategy most basically involves showing that events which are accounted for by the media in one way *could* equally well be accounted for in another, different way.

As we have noted, one of the favoured cases for media scholars is that of the deviant. We would suggest that the treatment that they give to the reporting of deviance in the press is similar to that which Szasz described Freud as assigning to the 'malingerer' in his creation of pyschoanalysis, namely a conceptual reconstruction of motivation rather than any empirical or investigative study.[20]

The strategy of the media scholars is to show that the media portray deviants in negative terms as irrational creatures, moved by psychological failings or personal maleficence and to argue that the doing of those deviants could equally well be seen as 'socially expressive', as an expression of the deviant's alienation from the official structures of the society, as an expression of the weaknesses and failings of the social system itself. If such a reconstruction were of an empirical kind it would, then, be a question for investigation as to whether or not different acts of deviance were motivated by malice or were socially expressive but, of course, this kind of question does not arise at all for the simple reason that the media scholars taking this kind of line simply do not contemplate malice or psychological deficiency as genuine motives, any more than Freud would allow genuineness to the idea of malingering. Most scholars of this persuasion then are satisfied to show that the events reported in the press can be explained otherwise than the press chooses to explain them, but, in our view, that is a very long way from showing that the press account is inadequate or that the socially expressive account must be accepted. The mere availability of an imaginable alternative account does not invalidate that to which it is an alternative.

In any case, the choice between two rival accounts of this sort may not be between one which is right and one which is wrong, but (for example) between different ways of construing motives which are more or less humane.

In much of the literature, then, it is not the details of media reportage which are in question, but the perceptual set which is adopted toward them. If anything, the media scholars are inclined to assign the media a good deal of actual reliability, impartiality, objectivity and the like for they are dependent upon the media as a source of information as to 'what happened' in many cases they examine. In one classic instance the authors of *Bad News* seek to reveal the bias of T.V. news by comparing its reports with those which are found in *Management Today* and *The Financial Times*. These last are taken as reporting objectively 'what happened' in order that the television report may be shown to have been 'selective'. It appears then that despite their more attention grabbing, interest holding, indignation arousing assertions about the media, media scholars are *in practice* apt to adopt the same piecemeal approach to the media as it is likely most readers and viewers do, treating them often as the sources of accredited facts and, equally often, complaining of their biased and erroneous character. Regular consumers of newspaper and television output are well aware of the prospects for bias, error, falsification, selectivity, misrepresentation, deception, concealment, equivocality, and the like because the media collectively feature a substantial amount of coverage of just such things (after all the letters columns of most newspapers provide an ample supply of charges and evidence of bias, etc.). The media scholars *appear* to be offering revelations of less familiar and much more systematic biases but, so far as we can judge, they really do not fulfil those promises. On the whole, these studies merely show that the media do not accept the same theories that are presently (and probably temporarily) fashionable within sociology: to that extent the media are just as biased as they are against alchemy, for they do not accept or expound that either.

Locating Bias

If the ubiquity of bias were proven (which we do not think it has been) we would face the question of the *source* of bias. We can think of four places in which a researcher could look for the origins of bias: (1) in the practices of news producers; (2) in the background to news production; (3) in the produced text; (4) in the reading of the text.

1. The practices of news producers

Here the mechanisms of selection and 'shaping' are inspected, patterns, collusions, and conspiracies found, and assertions made that producers wittingly or unwittingly, primarily or as agents, collaboratively or individually, directly or indirectly, bias the news. In terms of research strategy this involves very impressionistic ethnographic work at production points,[21] extremely crude content analysis where the categories to be counted are either implicitly organizational[22] or argumentatively oriented.[23] One tool is to erect an input-output model relating what went into the agency and what came out of it, to find that the agency has selected/biased the choice of outputs.[24] The accessibility of the input to the researchers is not systematically explained, i.e., we do not know how they are able to decide *what might have been news* but was not in fact broadcast/published as such. Unless we can know this we cannot assess the ways in which they do their counting nor place any credibility in their numbers. One other feature of this area is the willingness of the theorist to leave the work of analysis to the reader, to leave the reader to decide who did what. This means, in practical terms, an extensive use of passive constructions and impersonal subjects (reminiscent of vulgar functionalism): consider in Murdock[25] 'two things stand out . . . they (stories) focus . . . they counterpose two stereotypes . . . the basic contrast is between . . . if it is explained at all . . . is seen . . . what is missing'. Any reader collecting these deeds referred to in the Murdock studies and looking for one perpetrator to blame is going to be disappointed for much of this biasing is, it turns out, done by disembodied subjects.

2. The background to news production

This is the Rachel's pitcher of removed causes. The technique is to look 'behind' the news into the bottomless pit of the world and its entire history, wandering across space and time until one falls upon an ideologically allowable cause. If, as is usual, that cause is far removed from its effect then it does not need careful exposition beyond such amorphous characterization as 'the cultural air we breathe',[26] 'society' or 'capitalism'. A more sophisticated device is the use of knowledge-of-the-world-as-it-really-is in pejorative contrast with the-world-as-presented.[27] We have already noted that 'the world as it really is' is all too often only the world as the theorists says it is, and we can only say that the evidence for the influence of 'objective reality' upon media content remains still at the level of indicating structural correspondences between features of the social setting and features of media output. This kind of technique has been the stock in trade of cultural studies for an extremely long time and, before that, under the name 'the spirit of the age' it did sterling service for historians. However, if we are *now* required to credit such proposed correspondences we are entitled to demand much more effective and detailed specification of the causal chains which we are to believe, connect the related features. The appearance of Mannheim's work long ago invited a chorus of objections to the 'It is no accident that . . .' style of 'explanation' but it seems to us that those objections are now more pressing than ever before: such inadequate forms of proof and explanation become less acceptable with the passage of time as they are recurrently employed in place of better evidence or fuller explanation.

3. The produced text

This is subject to little in the way of careful and detailed examination, being mainly used in illustrative service of preconceived themes. There is, thus, primarily a 'content analysis' kind of approach to those materials which examines them for themes without any apparent concern for the form which the medium of their expression will assign them. We would have thought that the extensive work which is done in many fields on the expressive forms of the media – in literary criticism, linguistics, film criticism, information theory, to mention only a few – would give any analyst pause for thought before entering upon crude thematic characterizations but we seem to be wrong. Some reflection on the all-too-familiar difficulties encountered in such fields of study with regard to the determination of the sense of a single text should discourage hasty conclusions about the presence of cultural themes and ideological elements.

One simple test which has sometimes been suggested for the adequacy of social science theories is the 'replication procedure'; the specifications of the theory should be such as to enable someone to produce further instances of the conduct which the theory purports to cover. We do not realistically think that such a demand can be made (at the present moment) of any sociological theory but the imaginative use of such a test can highlight the inadequacies of a theory. If we required someone to reconstruct news articles and programmes from the theory provided by the media scholars they would be in no position to reconstruct the material as news: there is no reason why the reconstruction should resemble news more than, say, an overtly didactic text, a lecture, sermon or any other vehicle for the expression of ideas. The theories in question provide us with no information on how to deal with the problems of story construction, beginnings, titles, narrative structure, prefaces, character distribution, motive ascription, moral making, narrative flow, all of which are, amongst many other things, practical and inescapable features of the production of news stories. The fact that such matters are unattended suggests that the technique of 'content analysis' is still used in ways which presupposed that one can make simple distinctions between form and content but which realistically mean only that materials are handled coarsely.

4. The reading of the text

Before analysis can be done on a text it must be read. Analysis, is therefore, analysis of a reading. Texts can be read, and TV sets viewed, in different ways. An obvious question then is, does anyone else read them and view them in the same way as media scholars do? Unfortunately the media scholars seem uninterested in this question and hence in the related problem of the connection between their way of reading and that of others. 'The reader' does not make many appearances in the media literature as anything other than a passive dope:[28] in what we estimate as some eleven thousand sentences making up *Bad News* we cannot find any that make the viewer their subject. It does not seem to occur to these theorists that the viewer may be no less capable than they, 'the experts', of exercising judgment, wit, scepticism, a sense of proportion, a different conceptual scheme, an appreciation that it's only a newspaper story, or a television item, or even a quasi-Marxist suspicion of capitalist institutions and organization. If such capacities are extended to the otherwise witless and uncritical viewer, the media simply cannot fulfil their hegemonic task. Of course, it may just be that media scholars are rather like those participants in pornography trials who are not going to be corrupted by reading/viewing the relevant porn in the course of their duties in court but who are confident that other people are not so incorruptible, who know that the work in question will debilitate servants and the lower orders in general.[29]

II

The Dark Side of the Leicester Mercury

We began by saying that the second part of our paper would examine in detail the way one media theorist handles his materials. We use an article by Murdock.[30] In choosing this piece for analysis we do not accord it any special position or implicate a specified field of application. Ours is simply a study in depth of a piece by a prominent media scholar. It is generalizable insofar as it is formal and if the reader feels it treats too little data then that is due to the exigencies of the space to which depth and breadth must be sacrificed. In summary our argument is that the headlines analysed by Murdock do not attribute the qualities to Youth which Murdock says they do for they are not 'about' youth at all.

Harvey Sacks, in an elaborate discussion of the difference between talking of 'everyone lying' and e.g., 'protestants lying', suggests that there may, contrary to popular belief, be greater difficulty in establishing the second than the first.[31] The aspect of this which is pertinent to our concern is that sentences with subjects such as 'Protestants' or 'the boys' or 'the working class' or 'the youth' are read differently according to circumstances and context. One difference is the extent to which the identification of the subject is trivializable. A prototypical case involves 'confusion' over whether an actor doing something did it because of his categorization as protestant, young or whatever. We put 'confusion' in inverted commas because we do not wish to suggest that members actually are confused over such issues. They 'solve' such problems by reference outside the sentence to other sentences and to commonsense.

This 'problem' points to the uneasy relationship between 'scientific' argument and natural language. It also points again to the possible uses of that relationship for persuasive purposes. The work of Sacks and his colleagues on the Membership Categorization Device[32] stresses the inter-dependence of identifications of activities and actors, of terms and relationships, of recognition and normative expectation.[33] To invoke commonsense understanding and recognition of ordinary words is to invoke commonsense schemes of 'logical' and normative relationship. It is most difficult if not impossible, to hold down statements in natural language to a simple complementary reference of two denotata. One simple persuasive device then is to use an apparently trivialized identification to do significant work. This device can almost be elevated to a principle. He who wishes to persuade through recognition, should reproduce faithfully a reported activity while changing its argumentative product. Make the same utterance do different work.

This device may involve cutting out and working up.[34] Just as citation, in moving a 'fact' from one page and context to another, deprives it of the original literary context and surrounds it with a new one, so what is acceptable commonsense may be faithfully reproduced, its original context cut out and a new one worked up, so that it is recognizable as what anyone knows but does the persuasive work of its new master.

We shall focus on the section which commences at line twenty eight of the original:

'One of the quickest ways to gain a general impression of prevailing ideas about young people is to look at the kinds of images which are pumped out day after day in the news media. Here for example, is a random selection of stories taken from my local paper, the *Leicester Mercury*. There is nothing unique or special about them. They are not particularly exciting or sensational. None of them made the front page. They are however, typical of the routine news coverage of young people.

    1.   YOUTH FINED FOR INDECENT EXPOSURE

    2.   BOY, 16, SWIMS THE CHANNEL

Both from p. 5 for 4th September 1975. Two more from a week later, 11th September.

    3.   YOUTH THREATENED WITH KNIFE AS GANG GO ON RAMPAGE (p. 13).

    4.   MEDAL BOYS THROW PARTY. Eight boys who, over the last four years have worked for their Duke of Edinburgh Awards, last night threw a party for the people who had helped them (p. 7).

And finally two adjacent stories from p. 21 for 12th November.

    5.   SHOP FIGHT RINGLEADER TO FACE CROWN COURT. Carlton Gregory (17) pleaded guilty to causing Mr. Malcolm Harding actual bodily harm and having an offensive weapon – a hat stand – in Lewis's.

    6.   LOUISE GOES INTO EUROPE. Louise Riddlington, the 15-year-old winner of a 'Leicester in Europe' competition is having the time of her life. Wyggeston Girls' School pupil Louise won a two-day trip to Brussels for two – and went off with her mum to enjoy it.

Taking these stories together, two things stand out. Firstly, they all focus on ways of spending spare time, and more particularly on the contrast between the wholesome recreations sponsored and organized by adults, and the deviant and dangerous things that teenagers are likely to get up to if left to wander about the streets unsupervised. Secondly, and more generally, they counterpose two stereotypes of contemporary youth. On the one hand stand the model adolescents who have knuckled down and achieved something worthwhile – the prizewinners, award winners and channel swimmers; and on the other stand the anti-social elements – the delinquents, hooligans and sexually precocious. The basic contrast is between adolescents who have been successfully socialized into adult society and those who have failed and can't or won't conform. Further, this difference, if it is explained at all, is seen as the outcome of differences in individual ability and motivation, so that deviance is mainly a matter of instability or bloody-mindedness. What is missing from these accounts is any real consideration of the ways in which success and failure, conformity and deviance, are rooted in social situations, and in that complex web of advantage and deprivation which makes up the British class system.'

Convenient Combination

In his essay 'On the Analysability of Stories by Children'[35] Sacks provides a machinery to account for how we hear certain items together. The Membership Categorization Device with its collection and rules of application can be used to tie two categories, an activity and a category incumbent, and (as a variant of activity and actors), knowledge and an owner.[36] Two aspects of the machinery are of particular note in the present context: the economy rule and the (modified) consistency rule: 'A single category from any membership device can be referentially adequate.'[37] 'If a hearer has a second category which can be heard as consistent with one locus of the first, then the first is to be heard as *at least* consistent with the second.'[38]

We know that various categories are ambiguous, the same term occurring in different devices with different references. The economy rule and consistency rule explain our recognition and combination of referents given that ambiguity. The description is recognizable through combinations of its surrounding categories. The device that permits recognition of possible description works negatively as well. It involves the elimination of ambiguity and the de-combination of category from other 'possible' contexts.

Simplistically put: a device that suggests certain orientations does so, at least partly, by suggesting that we do *not* orient to certain other possibilities. Yet the description can still be adequate by the economy rule. It is by virtue of this that the apparatus for recognition may also be an apparatus for persuasion.

Murdock asks us to find several things in these passages from a newspaper and provides us with the machinery for the search. We are to find that the excerpts are *about* youth, at least initially;

'They are . . . typical of the routine news coverage of young people'.

Later we shall 'find' that they are not only, perhaps not at all, about youth but are rooted in an unequal class structure. The prime resource for our seeing the actors as young people is that youth is one categorization that *can* embrace them all. We are to see a categorization that will embrace them all because the six excerpts are collected together. We might summarize the procedure at least up to the good/bad contrast as follows:

(1) Take these stories together, do not look at them individually. Do not see their categories of actor (Youth, Youth, Boy 16, Medal Boys, Ringleader, Louise) as members of other possible collections. Collect them as in the same group 'youth'.

(2) Within that 'one' group make the following divisions. Put the examples into two groups of three; group A consisting of examples 1, 3 and 5; group B consisting of examples 2, 4 and 6. Do not collect these items in any other permutations. You will find that the items have been spaced and divided by context references so as to help this collection and there are two collection titles available under which you can selectively list the two groups: 'Model adolescents who have knuckled down and achieved something worthwhile – the prizewinners, award winners and channel swimmers; and on the other hand the anti-social elements – delinquents, hooligans and sexually precocious.' The characteristics of each group can be seen together not as separate. See e.g. prizewinning and channel swimming together and in contrast to delinquents and hooligans and find one device that will explain both the collection and the contrast and that is successful socialization/non-conformity.

(3) *Do* contrast the two groups. Do *not*, for example put them on a continuum either together or separately. The titles will provide you with ways to see them as opposites and no ways to scale them on a continuum.

(4) You now have one type of actor (youth) and two sorts of actions. Find those two sorts of actions in the excerpts ignoring 'irrelevancies'.

(5) Having characterized the actions in one way only, you are able to postulate the sort of actor in one way. The act adequately defines the actor. The contrast is no longer between different types of action but two different groups of actor.

(6) We can now see the inappropriateness of explaining group traits as idiosyncratic action especially if we are sociologists.

(7) If you scan the reports you will find little (no) author announced explanation of the behaviour. But if you use my (Murdock's) translations of the behaviour you will find that you can read in motivations according to the contrast. By using language more recognizable as that of the newswriter than the sociological researcher (the two 'possible' authors) I can make my motives appear to be theirs, e.g.,

'knuckled under . . . hooligan . . . won't conform' which contrast with the rest of Murdock's language but are collatable with such newspaper language as 'Mum' or 'rampage'.

Through the use of such language and the categorization of the two groups as stereotypes, I can indicate my exception to the views expressed therein but trade off the two groups produced thereby to introduce (a two) class analysis.

This summary does no justice to the elegance of Murdock's argument. It is obviously not an adequate analysis of his presentational work. But it does show the working up operation that the reader is asked to do. That working up is itself achieved relative to a cutting out. The two are interdependent operations. The sort of 'other' readings that the reader 'could' do is massively restricted in 'following' the argument. Those readings are largely a matter of speculation and depend on the context and concerns of the reader. Yet one set that appears more than likely derives from the fact, almost totally obscured by Murdock that these excerpts appeared in a local newspaper.

Convenient Abstraction: The Annihilation of Technical Context

Murdock contends, amongst other things, that these excerpts are 'about' youth and that they present stereotypes. He organizes them into two stereotype groups, 1, 3, 5 and 2, 4, 6. Another way to divide them would be into excerpts that were only headings (1, 2 and 3) and excerpts in which some of the story was included (4, 5 and 6). The justification for this is that the reader usually does different things with the two groups. Such a division is part of the technical context of the excerpts. Other parts include the fact that the newspaper was 'local' and that these are all 'stories', not for example 'comment' or 'serials'. In order to read intelligibly, reader searches for such directions as these. We do not say that everybody reads in this way but that many readers do use such features to facilitate their reading and that failure to do so may be held to invalidate readings of the piece in a subsequent lay discussion. We shall look specially at the 'headline only' group.

We, then, and we think many others, use headlines to find what may follow. We know that local papers include comment, serials, features, letters, advertisements, etc., and we use the headline to find what the subsequent text may be out of that range. Possibly we look at the length and make a decision to start reading or not. Journalists, at any rate think so, and spend time designing headlines with this, amongst other things, in view. None of this prevents someone scanning a newspaper to find headlines to bolster their stereotypes of youth. Whilst such a strategic reading is *possible*, as indeed are a legion of other things, it is highly *likely* that the technical reading of the headline is made. The technical and substantive parts of the piece are not independent. Our assessment of the technical context of the piece will effect any subsequent substantive reading. Fairly obviously, attributions of quality made in something we read as an advertisement are read differently to similar attributions in a review of competing products. The knowledge of what the piece is doing (trying to sell us something/informing us) instructs us to do quite different things to two sentences of the same words. That knowledge is frequently to be found in the headline.

'Youth fined for indecent exposure' is a headline for a story. The reader will expect a story relating to some of the events that 'led up to' the event of fining. The fact that the story occurs in a local weekly newspaper is one thing that suggests we see the fining, that is the event reported, as recent.[39] Lots of concerns could be tied to the fining. One of them is to treat fining as the end of a process started by indecent exposure. Such a reading is at least grounded in the observation of the co-presence[40] of fining and indecent exposure in the heading. That co-presence and the consequent possible orientation to process provides for a reading of the heading as a story preface. As a story it will involve particular events of particular individuals. We then read the heading as instructing us to find below a story that ends in a fine. That instruction is useful since we know that newspapers contain other things as well as stories, e.g., comment, situation analyses, etc. We further recognize that they contain serialized stories and stories which are presented as trends, e.g., 'another case of'. There are also headings which indicate stories with a moral. Whatever might have followed this heading there is little indication *in the heading* of anything like a serial, comment, moral, etc. Such serials, comment and morals are ways in which particular events can be generalized. In consequence unlike Murdock we find no instructions in the heading to read youth as implicative of a social group 'youth'. We find no instructions to attribute the blame for the indecent exposure to anyone beyond the person fined. We find nothing *in the text* to lead us to invoke a charge of stereotyping.

Of course, the term youth permits the reader who wishes, to tie the behaviour to youth as a group. But he would have to do some additional work. If we look to possible reactions to the heading as confirmations of the sort of story it is, then while 'Disgusting' or 'Interesting' would be immediately intelligible, 'Typical' would produce something to the effect of 'What of?' The term youth is not, however, gratuitous. It can help us to see the act of exposure in certain ways and to read certain motivations in and rule others out. Acknowledging and bypassing such considerations, we return to the possibility of using 'youth' to generalize as Murdock does. There are two further problems with this.

Some headings such as the elegant 'Girl Guide aged 14 raped at Hell's Angels' Convention' analysed by Lee,[41] provide for the reading of a fairly specific connection between act and actor and indeed contrast with other (in this case victim). Our heading does not. While 'Mother of six fined for shoplifting' provides for a reason for the act in the categorization of the actor, 'youth' does not. If we use youth to contrast with adult then we find that some, not remarkably less, adults also expose themselves and the contrast fails. If we try to generalize exposure to a substantial section of youth we run up against the unnatural/unusual nature of exposure. We cannot see exposure as *typical* behaviour for a section of youth, nor can we contrast such a section with a non-offending adult. We could list exposure with hooliganism and other undesirable things. We could do lots of tying operations. But the instructions to do them are not discoverable in the heading. Such operations are reader elections. It is Murdock that stereotypes youth not the local newspaper.

Newsworthiness

'Boy 16, swims the Channel'.

We have already seen that it is useful to consider what a headline may do technically to discern what it may do substantively. It can, by announcing which of a variety of newspaper activities is to follow, encourage us to read in one of several ways. In this argument it can particularly instruct us to generalize or read as an individual interest story. A headline in a newspaper also seeks to interest, to be newsworthy and this is known by most readers. Headlines then may be read to make news. They may attain newsworthiness by announcing that something we need to know is contained in the subsequent text; by announcing a continuation or conclusion to something we are already interested in or by announcing that something extraordinary has happened. There is a sense in which 'Boy 16, swims the Channel' is not about youth at all but about the unlikely achievement of a difficult task. At least one possible response to it would be the same as to:

Man who only learned to swim last year swims channel.
Handicapped woman swims Channel.
Eighty year old swims Channel.
Boy 16, climbs Everest.
Eighty year old climbs Everest.

Formally the newsworthy elements that provoke the response of amazement are the unlikely nature of the actor for the act. These formal elements establish the force of the response. According to the views of the reader that force may show itself in 'How very splendid' or 'How very stupid'. The essence of this particular newsworthiness resides in its outstanding mentionability. If we say 'How very stupid', the headline remains a good headline. What this amounts to is that 'boy' is not a mentionable in its own right. This headline is not about youth but about juxtaposition. Once again the reader is free to generalize about the virtues of some section of youth or to generalize in countless other ways but there are no instructions so to do in the headline. The term 'boy' is a means to an end in the headline. It is assimilable not into the category youth in the stage of life device but into the category of agents unlikely to swim the Channel; a category which includes other age groups (eighty year old) and non-age groups (handicapped woman).

The headline should not, of course, satisfy but arouse the reader's curiosity. It announces newsworthy events to be described below. Most readers know the formal elements of a routinely recounted news story. It is as if the headline precises which blanks will be filled in below. Thus: 'Youth threatened with knife as gang go on rampage' does not only tell reader by virtue of it being a headline that there is more to come, but the reader knows what sort of blanks might be filled in because of his knowledge of the normal formats of local newspapers and because the terms of the headline narrow such expectations. A rampage is a series of actions; a threatening is one action. An effort to relate the two juxtaposed items may result in the threatening being seen as one of a series of actions. There may then be others to be disclosed and the seriality provides for the possibility of them being of a similar order of gravity to threatening with a knife. The paper is local, the reader probably local: the headlines announce that a series of serious unruly offences have taken place in the reader's locality. For details see below. Such details include when, where, the names and addresses of participants, the gravity of individual events, etc. Readers may peruse to find out such details or to find that they occurred some distance away and reassure themselves.

Rampages are accountable actions which involve people whose duty it is to stop them. They need to have their origins explained ('The trouble started when a group of . . .'); their continuance, development and possible escalation accounted for ('Things got worse when' . . .); their response accounted for ('The police . . .'). A little lay knowledge of the form of newspapers and a brief reading of the heading as a heading promises the answers to such things. Once again the heading contains no stereotypical picture of youth. The gang is not even identified as young.

When we say that these headlines contain no stereotypes of youth, what we mean is that they do not produce them in the way that Murdock claims as products. We have already said that the headlines use highly generalized concepts as a means. If we wish to visualize the indecent exposure scene, then the age of the actor provides one of the resources for so doing. If we wish to visualize the swimming of the Channel scene and to see why the feat is unlikely then the age of the actors can help us. We orient to the description of most actors to see the act and vice versa. But, as we have shown, there is no attempt to typify the act to the generalized actor, or monopolize the act to the generalized actor. It would seem that Murdock is confusing the practical everyday need for generalized attributions as tools, with the practice of holding transsituational stereotypes. That an actor who is young and who is announced as being youth commits an act is little resource for suggesting the announcer to have a stereotype. It does, however, highlight the generalized and transsituational way that some sociologists treat variables such as age compared to the practical and particular way that lay members use such generalizations.

Conclusion

By examining one instance of media analysis in detail we have tried to show that we can equally plausibly, economically, and with no remainder, but with an extended appreciation of detail, read the text employed in that analysis and can show that the texts in question do not constrain the reader's inferences in such a way as to lead the reader to the conclusions that the media analyst wants to claim are implicit in them. It is the simple fact that these conclusions are not implicit in the text that, we suggest, throws heavy doubt upon the media theorists' interpretations of the nature and function of such texts. We do not claim to have used other than very elementary techniques on the relevant texts but we think that even such elementary procedures reveal the heavy handed and crude character of the methodology employed in much media analysis. Bourgeois sociology may be decadent, but it seems that some of its old, even outdated methods such as cultural thematization and content analysis are adequate to the needs of those who are supposedly exposing that decadence.[42]

Notes

1. The literature from British sociology on the media is expanding rapidly and a guide to it would be extensive. The expansion of the literature is in part attributable to the existence of some prolific 'centres' for 'cultural studies' such as the Birmingham centre for contemporary cultural studies, the Leicester centre for mass communications research, the Glasgow media group and, in the future no doubt, Goldsmith's college to which some luminaries in this field have now migrated. The work of Stuart Hall, James Halloran, Richard Hoggart, Graham Murdock, Philip Elliot, the collection *The manufacture of news*, edited by S. Cohen and J. Young, Constable, 1973, and the Working and Occasional Papers of the Birmingham centre should provide a wide sample of the things now regarded as media or (alternatively) cultural studies.

   The extensiveness of the research into newspapers and television leads us to speculate about the amount of time British sociologists are contributing to the consumption of media output and the apparent willingness of these same sociologists to contribute to that output leads us to wonder if Freud would not have something to say about the possibility of a deep and unhealthy ambivalence.

2. Insofar as these *are* conclusions, and not opinions formed and held prior to the research which would be insisted upon in any case.

3. By texts we intend here not only written documents but tape recordings, films and the like.

4. Of course, by any stringent criteria these discursive speculations are not theories, any more than are most of the supposed theories of sociology.

5. The Glasgow Media Group's *Bad News*, Routledge, 1977, and Steve Chibnall's, *Law-and-Order News*, Tavistock, 1977, will serve as prime examples for much of what we have to say. A paper by Graham Murdock will be the object of our detailed attention, see below p. 375-80 and fn. 30.

6. The treatment of 'the problem' of the mass media as a primarily *cognitive* one is most peculiar from our point of view and one which throughout leads these researchers to look upon news gathering as a surrogate form of scientific enquiry. Naturally, we must only expect that since news gathering is *not* scientific enquiry, it won't do as well at scientific enquiry as scientific enquiry will do. Of course, we need to ask whether newspapers are meant, or are usefully meant, to be treated as though they were producing scientifically verifiable findings.

7. Cf. Harold Garfinkel, *Studies in Ethnomethodology*, Prentice Hall, 1967, p. 73.

8. Much of what is treated as a matter of bias by the media scholars seems to us much more simply, elegantly, and accurately treated as having to do with opposition, disapproval and the like.

9. Alfred Schutz' description of the stock of knowledge in the possession of the 'well-informed-citizen' see ('The Well Informed Citizen', *Selected Papers*, vol. 2, Nijhoff 1964) would seem to us much more like the kind of characterization of the 'outlook' of any section of the press or media than does the emphasis upon a 'world view'. Of course the wonderful thing about the idea of 'world view' is that it can be used to attribute a homogeneous attitude to a collection of persons who quite obviously do not have such an homogeneous attitude. Chibnall (with the italics added by us) says 'any elucidation of "the ideology of the press" must be a candidate for charges of overgeneralization. I agree that the press is far from being a homogeneous collection of papers and I have no desire to portray it as an ideological monolith, *but there are sufficient similarities among the various newspapers to justify discussion of core elements of a general world view (even though the ideology of a particular newspaper may not possess all those elements in the same combination)*. The popular press probably conforms more closely to the ideal type outlined here than do the 'heavies' which *tend to surround their ideological themes with a more complex network of qualification.*' (Chibnall, p. 269, fn. 2 to chap. 2).

The notion of world-view and ideology, it seems to us, can be looked on (as it is by its proponents) as a means of revealing the 'hidden' behind the 'appearances' but it can equally well be looked upon as we prefer to see it, as a licence to ignore difference, qualification, and nuance, and to resolutely refuse to deal with the empirical complexity of the phenomena homogenized under such notions.

10. That we use Parsonian terminology to identify their theories will perhaps lead them to think we are accusing them of having a Parsonian theory. They are not, we think, so far from Parsons as they would like to believe but we are not attributing to them a Parsonian theory of deviance, merely notion that their theory is of the type identified by Parsons as theories of 'structured social strain'.

11. We should say, of course, that the trouble with the media is that they do not use *the* sociological theory, i.e. one (usually of a quasi-Marxist kind) favoured by their sociological critics.

12. Since even heavy qualification does not prevent one being attributed a given ideology, we should say very explicitly that *we* do not favour capital punishment, and while doing so, add that we have no great respect for the press and television news. Indeed, it is our

lack of awe for these magical institutions which leads us to think that such inefficient and ineffective organizations are incapable of serving as real instruments of a serious hegemonic struggle.

13. Chibnall, p. 108.

14. Ibid., p. 20.

15. Much of the complaint about the media is, it seems to us, of the very familiar sort, that the media call people 'terrorists' who look upon themselves as 'freedom fighters' and call people 'freedom fighters' who could equally well be seen as 'terrorists' (in the case of trade unionists, of course, it's 'socialists' who are called 'militants' or 'extremists'). Of course, as everyone knows, it's a matter of whether they are on our side or the other one that is the decider in the selection of such terms. We will suggest that the press do not, wholesale, ascribe or deny rationality to political deviants but, often ascribe or withhold rationality from those of whom they disapprove depending whether or not rationality would be an attractive or unattractive thing to attribute in such a context. It seems to us, say, that the British press would very often put something quite 'irrational' – such as loyalty to one's country – above the rational calculation of advantage. As for the claimed emphasis of the media upon 'impartiality' over 'bias' we can only suggest that Chibnall turn his attention to the football pages, where partisanship is an unquestioned virtue.

16. The massively particularized, localized, personalized character of news should make it apparent that it is incommensurable with the abstract, generalized, depersonalized concern with types that is the leading character of social science. Comparison of the media and social science is comparison of incomparables.

17. We often use 'reader' to mean 'viewer and reader' and are similarly loose in our use of expressions like 'media', 'press', 'TV', 'news' and so on.

18. 'The First Casualty', Quartet, 1978.

19. A rare exception, J. Halloran, P. Elliot, and G. Murdock, Demonstration and Communication, Penguin, 1970.

20. Cf. The Myth of Mental Illness, Hoeber/Harper, New York, 1961, The 'socially expressive' view just does not allow the idea of 'action for no good reason', and this results in its utter incomprehension of the kinds of explanations that other people might give for 'deviant' activities. Thus 'Unless one believes that a particular minority of football supporters are gripped or possessed by the Devil every Saturday from lunchtime onwards, there must be reasons for their behaviour' (Stuart Hall, cited on the cover of Football Hooliganism, by Roger Ingham, et al., Inter-action Inprint, 1978). Unpalatable as the idea of 'action for no good reason' is to those of sociologistic bent, it is not the equivalent of attributions of demonic possession, but to treat it as though it were enables one to avoid having to think seriously about the kind of alternative it might present, or to understand how it works. One might well reply to the 'socially expressive view' by saying that unless one accepts the view that a minority of football supporters are gripped by the Devil etc. one must take the contrary view that football supporters' clubs are communities of saints, people incapable of a malicious, spiteful, whimsical, destructive or pointless action.

21. Cf. Bad News, chap. 3, Chibnall, passim.

22. That is, derived from the organization and transferred to the research without explication of their role, in either context (see note 21).

23. Derived from the end of the argument they are meant to justify and 'retrospectively' constructed.

24. See especially the case studies in Bad News.

25. Murdock is discussed in detail below, pp. 375-80.

26. Richard Hoggart, in Bad News, pp. x.

27. As, for example in that very different study of 'culture' which is done by 'cognitive anthropologists', cf. Stephen Tyler, Cognitive Anthropology. Holt, Rinehart, Winston, 1971.

28. Garfinkel uses the phrase judgmental dope to characterize the social actor featured in most sociological theories, including those of the media theorists, see *Studies in Ethnomethodology, op. cit.*, pp. 68-70.

29. We are apt to wonder if those who argue so strongly for the mind shaping power of the media would be, inconsistently, amongst those who at such trials are apt to argue that the works in question do not have the effects, cannot have the effects, the prosecution are inclined to claim for them.

30. G. Murdock, 'Youth in Contemporary Britain: Misleading Imagery and Misapplied Action', in D. Marsland and M. Day (eds.), *Youth Service; Youth Work and the Future,* N.Y.B. occasional paper, 12 March, 1976, pp. 15-17.

31. H. Sacks, 'Everyone has to Lie', in M. Sanches and B. G. Blount (eds.), *Sociocultural Dimensions of Language Use,* Academic Press, 1975.

32. H. Sacks, 'On the Analysability of Stories by Children', in R. Turner (ed.), *Ethnomethodology,* Harmondsworth, Penguin, 1974.

33. *Ibid.,* pp. 225-6.

34. Terms borrowed from D. Smith as in ' "K Is Mentally Ill": the Anatomy of a Factual Account', *Sociology,* vol: 12 no. 1, 1978.

35. H. Sacks, 'On the analysability . . .', *op. cit.*

36. W. W. Sharrock, 'On Owning Knowledge', in R. Turner, *op. cit.*

37. H. Sacks, 'On the analysability . . .', *op. cit.*, p. 219.

38. H. Sacks, *ibid.,* p. 220

39. That is presented as 'recent' as news.

40. As suggested in J. R. E. Lee, 'Innocent Victims of Evil Doers', unpublished manuscript, University of Manchester.

41. *Idem.*

42. Accepted 10.5.78.

Biographical Note: DIGBY C. ANDERSON, PhD, is Education Fellow, Leverhulme Health Education Project, University of Nottingham.

WESLEY W. SHARROCK, PhD, is Senior Lecturer in Sociology at the University of Manchester.

Some of the most significant questions in mass communication are historical, leading to a growing body of exciting work by journalism historians. In this piece, Carolyn Stewart Dyer, assistant professor of journalism at the University of Iowa, describes some of her work in using quantitative methods. Dr. Dyer summarizes and explains a number of quantitative studies that pose propositions and questions about the press raised by traditional historians. For example, using dates of post office and newspaper establishment in Wisconsin and Iowa frontier communities, Dyer finds questionable Daniel Boorstin's argument that frontier newspapers were among the first institutions in pioneer communities. Plowing through 1.2 million names in census data, she compiles a list of a thousand newspapermen in the 1850s to find them younger and slightly more propertied than older adult males in other jobs. The article includes some cautions, particularly in arguing that the historian's use of quantitative approaches is often distinctly different from other behavioral applications, primarily because of the problem of missing data. This article first appeared in Clio, *the newsletter of the history division of the Association for Education in Journalism.*

18

QUANTITATIVE ANALYSIS IN JOURNALISM HISTORY

Some Examples and Advice

Carolyn Stewart Dyer

There has been much discussion of what I call the "What *you* should do, *I* think" school of journalism historiography.[1] The questions raised by this discussion are based on the assumption that a division of labor is possible in historical research between those who frame questions and the others who attempt to find answers. David Hackett Fischer calls this assumption the "fallacy of 'potentially verifiable' questions" (1970: 36-37). Rather than deal in hypothetical uses of quantitative methods in journalism history, I would like to concentrate on examples from my own work in order to stimulate others to ask related questions in areas of their interest and to try to understand the utility of quantitative methods. A second reason for discussing my own work is that I cannot say with conviction that the solutions to all or even most problems in journalism history are to be found in the use of

From Carolyn Stewart Dyer, "Quantitative Analysis in Journalism History: Some Examples and Advice," original manuscript.

quantitative methods any more than I would agree that the cultural approach is the answer, that intellectual history is where we should be directing our attention, or that one more study of new material in an old framework is to be rejected. In a field so little studied in any manner, I think every approach that raises significant questions and leads to credible answers is to be encouraged.

My use of quantitative methods, though quite diverse, is supplemented with traditional methods of historical analysis, and the requirements for evaluating the accuracy and reliability of sources common to other historical research are necessary components of quantitative methodology. In some instances, elaborate, but not particularly sophisticated, quantitative methods have been the primary means of answering my major questions about the business history of antebellum Wisconsin newspapers (Dyer, 1978). In others, a few simple calculations were made to answer simple questions and replace assumptions based on bits of anecdotal evidence. An example of the latter is the question whether newspapers were, as Boorstin has said, usually among the first establishments in a frontier community (1965). Probably because of my inclination to use quantitative data to answer questions of sequence of events, amount, duration, and the like, I tested Boorstin's proposition on Wisconsin's frontier newspapers. The test simply involved comparing the dates of the opening of the first post office in a community—which was almost a prerequisite to permanent settlement—with the establishment of the first newspaper there and getting an average difference in years. I found there was an average of seven years' lag between the time the post office was established and the time the first newspaper began publication in antebellum Wisconsin communities. Roy Atwood (1980) found an average lag of more than six years between the time a community was established as a county seat in Iowa and the time the first newspaper was established in that community. Atwood and I both found considerable variation in our data, making the averages less than perfect summaries, but clearly contradicting Boorstin. Generalizing from imperfect, though accurate, averages based on the experience of every relevant community seems sounder than the alternative of using a few dramatic examples as the basis for a general statement, as Boorstin has on this subject.

This bit of information was used in a study on the growth and spread of newspapers in Wisconsin between 1833 and 1860. Summary statistics, primarily totals, averages, and ranges, made it possible to characterize the demographic qualities of nearly 400 newspapers operating at some time in that period. The raw data used were starting and ending dates of all newspapers, derived from newspaper bibliographies, county histories, and other incidental sources; location, political position, language, frequency of issue, number of editions, and circulation of all newspapers enumerated in the 1850 and 1860 U.S. censuses of Wisconsin drawn from the manuscript census reports; and county population and statewide population divided into ethnic groups from the same two federal censuses and intermediate state censuses. A list will indicate the kind of information I was able to derive from these data, information that had not previously been available at all:

- growth in the number of newspapers starting and operating each year and the decline in failures, all of which were strongly related to population growth;
- the average longevity of all newspapers and the gradual increase in longevity;
- growth in total newspaper circulation between 1850 and 1860 and relative growth of total circulation to population and total circulation to the number of households and lack of significant growth in average circulation of individual newspapers;
- growth in circulation penetration and different rates of penetration of daily and weekly editions and different penetration rates in rural and urban areas;
- change in party affiliation from primarily Democratic to primarily Republican over a short period after the founding of the Republican Party in 1854; and
- growth of the foreign-language press relative to the foreign-born population, with a rough estimate of the penetration of the foreign-language press among the foreign-born.

This list is merely representative of the data base used to describe the press of early Wisconsin in terms other than the biography of individual newspapers and their operators. In combination with traditional methods of historical analysis and other data, many more substantial, conceptual questions could be answered (and some were), or clear alternative answers could be identified for further study. For example, it was found that weekly circulation penetration was particularly high in the counties with the smallest population and in counties with the largest population. Other evidence provided several explanations. Weekly editions of large city dailies generally were circulated statewide, thereby increasing penetration when circulation was compared to population in the county in which newspapers were published. In sparsely settled counties two factors explained the high penetration rates: One was circulation of these newspapers to outsiders to attract settlers and the infusion of government funds for "internal improvements" such as canals and harbors; the other was the fact that many of the smallest communities had two newspapers, one serving each of the two dominant political parties.

A related study resulted in a collective biography of 1000 newspapermen enumerated in the 1850 and/or 1860 population censuses. Some of the techniques of that study and the preliminary findings were reported in other papers (Dyer, 1974, 1977). The manuscript census entries for individuals include, among other things, name, age, birthplace, occupation title, wealth, whether the individual attended school in the previous year, and the same information about everyone with whom the individual lived. The objective of my use of these data was to determine what sort of person, generically, was involved in the newspaper business in the frontier period of Wisconsin press history. My interest was not just the elite class about whom individual biographies have been written, but also the mass of apprentices, journeymen printers, editors, and publishers, in an attempt to reconcile two conflicting characterizations of the frontier newspaperman—an influential member of the community who helped build the state and its institutions or a tramp printer who sold his soul and press to the highest bidder. The result of the collective biography is a catalog of characteristics that provides a background against which to measure the elite and attempt to determine whether they were elite because they were unique or because they were perhaps the most successful and visible of the mass of ordinary newspapermen. Among other things, I found that newspapermen were younger than other adult men, had a bit more property than other men in their age groups, and continued in the newspaper business for a rather brief period in their lives, particularly if they were in their teens and twenties when they were identified as newspapermen.

Another set of census data permitted an examination of the economics of the newspaper business in Wisconsin in 1860. Again, the findings are discussed elsewhere (Dyer, 1979). The Products of Industry schedule of the census included data on capital investment, cost and amount of raw materials, number and pay of employees, and value of newspaper and job printing produced. From these I calculated the return, a rough estimate of profits. The methods of analysis included the calculation of averages and the use of simple regression to determine, for example, the cost of producing an additional copy of a newspaper or an additional dollar's worth of job printing. (I found that newspaper publishing was more expensive and less profitable than job printing.) By combining the figures from the industrial census data analysis with data from the collective biography of newspapermen and the statistical analysis of the growth and spread of newspapers throughout the state, it was possible to learn even more about the newspaper business, often refuting common assumptions or clarifying murky issues in the process.

Consider these findings on capital investment and annual cost of operations in the average weekly newspaper shop. The average investment was about $1500 and cost of operation about $1700 in 1860. The investment figure is comparable to what I found several specific newspaper operators spent to buy all new equipment for their operations. Thus the average, together with anecdotal evidence, suggests that the average weekly newspaper was started with new equipment rather than secondhand materials, as we are told in much narrative history. Other evidence supports this conclusion as being logical. Since more newspapers were born in Wisconsin each year than died, there would not have been enough used equipment available within the state for many newspapers to use. Although some papers were started with used equipment, it was more common in Wisconsin to buy whole newspaper offices, including subscription lists and accounts receivable, and the cost was usually more than starting from scratch rather than less. Another implication of the capital investment and cost figures comes from their comparison with the average personal wealth of all newspaper operators in 1860, including those operating combination daily-weekly-semiweekly papers as well as those operating only weeklies. The average personal wealth was $1500. Thus the average newspaper operator did not have enough individual wealth to capitalize his paper, purchase supplies, and pay labor on his own. He would have required the assistance of a partner, an outside investor, or a loan or mortgage. All of these alternatives indicate that the frontier Wisconsin weekly could not have been as economically independent as the impression of the tramp printer starting papers at will.

A final example of my quantitative research in journalism history is an attempt to determine whether business relationships among newspapers—chains, joint operating agreements, etc.—resulted in a similarity of newspaper content. In the political press, which most antebellum newspapers in Wisconsin were, editorial opinion on political issues seemed an appropriate subject to use for the analysis. I also studied the exchange of copy among newspapers. The hypotheses were that related newspapers would share more political opinions and copy than unrelated newspapers. The content study itself was simple, but the analysis was complex. I studied editorial opinion on the first Wisconsin Constitution in 1846 and 1847, determining simply whether newspapers supported, opposed, or failed to state opinions on various provisions of the constitution. The statistical technique I used, cluster-bloc analysis, is usually used to analyze legislative voting records to identify groups of legislators that agree often and form voting blocs. By this method, I determined the relative amount of agreement among all newspapers and found that two pairs of related newspapers shared the highest level of agreement, even though one pair had one Democratic and one Whig newspaper. A pair of related Democratic newspapers also shared copy more frequently than all other newspapers.

Unlike the situation in survey or simple experimental research, in which all data can be collected and made ready for analysis within a few weeks, quantitative historical analysis is often more time-consuming than traditional historical analysis. One must find data that exist in comparable form, such as census manuscripts or newspaper ledgers, or develop comparable data from disparate sources. To find the 1000 newspapermen in the censuses, for example, I went through 1.2 million names, looking for persons with newspaper occupations. To get newspaper start and end dates, I had to analyze the accuracy of several bibliographies and determine for each the definition of a newspaper start and stop. (Were mergers of two papers considered the death of one and continuation of the other, and if so, which was which? Or were they considered the death of two and birth of one new newspaper?) Finally, I had to develop my own definition and then apply it to all the sources; thus, it took several months just getting together a list of newspapers with their start and stop dates. In preparing to gather data for quantitative analysis, one must also anticipate nearly every use that will be made of the data in order that one will collect all the relevant information and not have to return to the original for one more item. For example, the population censuses listed whether an individual had attended school in the year prior to the census. When I began collecting data, I could not imagine a use for that bit of information, so I ignored it. But later I found that many apprentices were school-age German immigrants. I speculated that these boys may have been in apprenticeships on German-language newspapers rather than in schools conducted in English. It would have been helpful to have had the data to know whether that supposition was correct. But however helpful or interesting, the answer to that question was not worth the time of wading through 1.2 million names again.

Gathering data for quantitative historical analysis is not inherently interesting, particularly gathering data from the census manuscripts. It is certainly not as engaging as reading old newspapers or personal papers. Stephan Thernstrom (1968) has described his research for the pioneering social history of occupational mobility in Newburyport, Massachusetts as being "as much drudgery as the ordinary historian can stand." There are rewards for the effort. They include the ability to answer questions that cannot be answered in any other way and the ability to make sound generalizations based on all of the relevant data rather than information about a few, probably unusual, individuals. A by-product of learning quantitative methods for history is the ability to read, criticize, and use the work of the "new" social, political, economic, and other historians.

What one needs to do quantitative history is an understanding of the statistical tools for historians and a basic knowledge of some simple, packaged computer programs. I use SPSS (Statistical Package for the Social Sciences; Nie, 1975) which is available in many university computer centers and can be self-taught if necessary. I emphasize quantitative methods *for historians,* specifically. While training in social science statistics—in sociology or educational psychology departments, for example—or mathematical statistics and familiarity with the work of our colleagues in behavioral and experimental communication research are of some help, their applicability is limited. Reliance on these methods and acceptance of the inappropriate conventions of their use may lead historians astray and be unnecessarily discouraging. Even asking advice of quantitative researchers in journalism schools on problems with analysis of historical data can cause rather than solve problems. (The advice is often, "You can't do that.") The reason is that many of the statistical tests and the standards of statistical significance appropriate for survey research, for example, are either inappropriate or not usable for historical data that are often plagued with missing information. Survey and experimental researchers generally regard data with missing items as useless and often delete a subject's responses altogether if they are not complete. If that approach were taken to analysis of historical data, quantitative analysis could rarely be done. There are, however, special statistical methods for dealing with missing data that are particularly useful for historians. If one has some background in social science statistics and needs retraining for statistical analysis of historical data, I recommend Dollar and Jensen (1971) or another text on statistics for historians.[2]

There is one more point to be made about learning and doing quantitative history: It lends itself to collective effort and a division of labor in some of the routine aspects of data-gathering and analysis. Thus, a journalism history research seminar could include instructor and students in the execution of a substantial research project that involves learning by doing. It could be a project that involves much drudgery for the ordinary, individual historian. From a pedagogical standpoint, that is a significant quality of quantitative research, a quality our colleagues in survey research have been able to use well.

NOTES

1. I used to use the title of Larry Woiwode's novel, *What I'm Going To Do, I Think,* but I revised the characterization to more accurately reflect the message of some recent critiques of journalism history research.

2. For formal instruction, quantitative methods courses in history departments are best. Probably next best, with some reservations, are courses in political science and beginning courses in economics that focus on quantitative analysis. For working journalism historians and advanced graduate students, an efficient way of learning almost all one needs to know to become facile in the use of quantitative methods is to attend the Newberry Library Summer Institute in Quantitative History. The Summer Institute is sponsored by the Family and Community History Center (Newberry Library, 60 West Walton Street, Chicago, IL 60610). The program is funded by a grant from the National Endowment for the Humanities. It is an intensive one-month program open to absolute neophytes and those with experience in statistics, computer usage, and quantitative methods. When I attended in 1979, a couple of middle-aged historians had learned relatively advanced statistical methods by the end of the program though neither had ever studied algebra or taken math since high school. Those in advanced classes had already done quantitative research and/or studied in history departments where quantitative methods are routinely taught or required. As encouragement, I might add that older participants were generally in the beginning classes and most of those in the advanced sections were younger graduate students.

REFERENCES

Atwood, R. (1980) "Handwritten newspapers on the Iowa frontier, 1844-1854." Warren C. Price paper presented to the History Division, Association for Education in Journalism, Boston, Mass.

Boorstin, D. (1965) "The booster press," Ch. 17 in The Americans: The Democratic Experience. New York: Random House.

Dollar, C. and Jensen, R. (1971) Historian's Guide to Statistics. New York: Holt, Rinehart and Winston.

Dyer, C. (1979) "The financial affairs of 1860 Wisconsin newspapers: an analysis of the manuscript products of industry returns from the U.S. Census of 1860." Presented to the History Division, Association for Education in Journalism, Houston, Texas.

———(1978) "The business history of the antebellum Wisconsin newspaper, 1833-1860: a study of concentration of ownership and diversity of views." Ph.D. dissertation, University of Wisconsin.

———(1977) "The antebellum Wisconsin newspaperman: a group portrait." Presented to the History Division, Association for Education in Journalism, Madison, Wisconsin.

———(1974) "Counting newsmen's noses: a key to the economic history of the nineteenth century newspaper." The AEJ History Division Newsletter, Summer.

Fischer, D. (1970) Historians' Fallacies. New York: Harper & Row.

Nie, N., et al. (1975) Statistical Package for the Social Sciences. New York: McGraw-Hill.

Thernstrom, S. (1968) "Quantitative methods in history: some notes," in S. Lipset and R. Hofstadter (eds.), Sociology and History: Methods. New York: Basic Books.

———(1964) Poverty and Progress. Cambridge: Harvard University Press.

Woiwode, L. (1969) What I'm Going To Do, I Think. New York: Farrar, Straus and Giroux.

PART III

NATURE OF NEWS AND REPORTING

Research on journalists and their institutional setting is gaining increasing attention, particularly among schools of journalism researchers and in departments of sociology and speech communication. The emerging subfield of inquiry, particularly in the United States, is what many call communicator studies.

This section, newly added in this volume, leads off with a classic example of secondary analysis of a massive data set to explore the predictors of professional and organizational commitment of journalists. Not only does this work tell us that the antecedents of the two kinds of commitment may not be the same, it points the way to other necessary studies on the social-intellectual climate of journalists.

The remaining articles use observational approaches to describe journalists at work. A journalistic group crucial to the public understanding of science is found to be structured in ways that facilitate *and* retard science reporting. An "inner club" of science writers provides expertise and accuracy checks for each other but may hamper the variety of science news coverage.

Two local television news staffs are probed in the two final studies. The first looks at the coverage of a gubernatorial race in a major Midwestern industrial state; the other is an analysis of general news processing in a TV station in the West. The study of local television political coverage uncovers surprising independence of news definition by the TV journalists, who seemed determined to avoid being duped by pseudo-events and campaign rhetoric. The second piece finds that specialization hampers initiative and autonomy of TV newsmen, hence the questionable analogy of the factory assembly line. This work is typical of the recent sociological analysis of news that rediscovers that journalists often work within the context of an organization.

Despite limited comparability and narrow focus, such investigations of journalists and news organizations provide rich data. And, they supplement inquiry focusing on audiences to produce more complete understanding of what is called (in a later article) the "agenda-building" process.

Predictors of organizational and professional commitment of U.S. journalists are studied here in a major secondary analysis of data collected by John W. C. Johnstone and his associates at the University of Illinois, Chicago Circle. Lee B. Becker, Idowu A. Sobowale, and Robin E. Cobbey have taken the massive data set and asked highly significant questions of it. Discriminant analysis showed that job satisfaction was a significant predictor of both organizational and professional commitment, but training and background were significant only for professional allegiance, which was also associated with married journalists having families, larger number of professional involvements, a less critical stance on the media in general, and nonguild status.

19

REPORTERS AND THEIR PROFESSIONAL
AND ORGANIZATIONAL COMMITMENT

Lee B. Becker, Idowu A. Sobowale, and
Robin E. Cobbey

Secondary analysis of data of
Johnstone et al finds
same variables do not predict
both professional and
organizational commitment.

▶ One of the less obvious, though perhaps ultimately more significant, ways in which journalists differ from members of other professions stems from the journalists' relationship to the mass media organizations. While members of

[1] While definitions of commitment have varied, most researchers seem to agree that commitment involves some form of psychological bond between the individual and the organization or the profession. See, particularly, Howard S. Becker, "Notes on the Concept of Commitment," *American Journal of Sociology*, 66:32-40 (July 1960). Bruce Buchanan, "Building Organizational Commitment: The Socialization of Managers in Work Organizations," *Administrative Science Quarterly*, 19:533-46 (December 1974) holds that commitment has three components. These are a) identification, or adopting as one's own the goals and values of the organization, b) involvement, or psychological immersion or absorption in the activities of one's work role, and c) loyalty, 'a feeling of affection for and attachment to the organization or profession.

[2] This distinction also has been made by, among others, Sang M. Lee, "An Empirical Analysis of Organizational Identification," *Academy of Management Journal*, 14:213-26 (June 1971); Mary E. Sheldon, "Investments and Involvements as Mechanisms Producing Commitment to the Organization," *Administrative Science Quarterly*, 16:143-50 (June 1971); Lawrence R. Jauch, William F. Glueck, and Richard N. Osborn, "Organizational Loyalty, Professional Commitment, and Academic Research Productivity," *Academy of Management Journal*, 21:84-92 (March 1978). Rodney W. Star, made a somewhat similar distinction in "Policy and the Pros: An Organizational Analysis of a Metropolitan Newspaper, *Berkeley Journal of Sociology*, 7:11-31 (Spring 1962) Howard S. Becker and James Carper, "The Elements of Identification with an Occupation," *American Sociological Review*, 21:341-48 (June 1956) and Thomas Rotondi, "Organizational Identification and Group Involvement," *Academy of Management Journal*, 18:892-97 (December 1975) also have distinguished between these two types of commitment and task commitment. See Idowu A. Sobowale, "Characteristics and Professional Attitudes of Nigerian Journalists," unpublished Ph.D. dissertation, Syracuse University, 1978, for a discussion of task commitment among journalists.

[3] C. Edward Wilson, "Why Canadian Newsmen Leave Their Papers," JOURNALISM QUARTERLY, 43:769-72 (Winter 1966).

the legal and medical professions are free and able to practice without organizational support, journalists are almost totally dependent on organizations for dissemination of their products. Without those organizations, journalists can gather and write the news, but they cannot distribute it.

It is therefore meaningful to speak of a journalist's level of organizational commitment as quite distinct from his or her level of professional commitment.[1] Any given journalist can feel loyalty to the profession without necessarily feeling loyalty to the specific organization for which he or she is presently working. And the reverse is true as well.[2]

The levels of commitment that journalists have to both their profession and their organizations are of considerable significance. Organizations respond to low levels of loyalty by creating incentives to hold old members and devising hiring strategies to find new ones. The profession must have similar strategies.

The literature suggests some specific reasons why journalists decide to leave the media. Wilson found in his study of Canadian journalists who had left the media that pay was a primary reason for departure.[3] Samuelson similarly found that newspeople were much more likely

▶ Lee B. Becker is an associate professor in the School of Journalism at the Ohio State University. Idowu A. Sobowale is an assistant lecturer in the Department of Mass Communication at the University of Lagos. Robin E. Cobbey is research manager for Knight-Ridder Newspapers. Inc. The authors thank John W.C. Johnstone, professor of sociology at the University of Illinois at Chicago Circle, for making his data available for secondary analysis.

From Lee B. Becker, Idowu A. Sobowale, and Robin E. Cobbey, "Reporters and Their Professional and Organizational Commitment," *Journalism Quarterly* (Winter 1979) 753-763, 770. Reprinted by permission.

than former newspeople to feel they were underpaid for their services.[4] But pay does not seem to be the only factor. Wilson found that many of the former journalists said the working conditions of the media—long hours and demanding schedules—and lack of satisfaction with the kind of work they were required to do led them to other jobs.

Johnstone, Slawski and Bowman, in their national study of working journalists, found that younger journalists were more likely to be uncommitted to either their news organizations or the news profession than older journalists.[5] And among those younger journalists, males were more likely than females to leave their organizations and the profession. Those young persons planning to leave the organizations also tended to be highly educated. The college educated holding journalism degrees, however, tended to be committed to the profession, though not necessarily to the organization. Among the younger journalists, those in the broadcast sector tended to be less loyal to the organization than those in print. The unloyal also were more likely to believe the media should play an active, dynamic role in the news dissemination process than those loyal to the profession and the organization.

For those uncommitted to a specific organization, another job within the news industry may seem to hold considerable promise. For those uncommitted to the profession, the opportunity to practice communication skills in another profession, such as public relations, often presents itself.

Model of Commitment: Even in the absence of a large body of research on the commitment of journalists it is possible to develop a set of expectations regarding factors which should be related to commitment to the profession and to the organization.

First, the training and the social background of the journalists ought to be a factor in determining commitment. The educational experiences as well as those acquired in other ways should influence

the commitment the individual has to the work setting.[6]

In addition to these background characteristics, individuals entering the job setting have some specific orientations to the profession. Journalists vary in the way they see the task before them. Some are high in values associated with the professions; others are less professional in outlook. Sentiments such as these also ought to have influence on the feelings of commitment the individual has.[7]

The media organization also should have considerable influence on commitment of the working journalists. Some organizations have work settings which would seem to thwart journalists. Others are more supportive.[8]

In addition to these organizational variables, a myriad of influences on the individual arise not from the work setting but from the non-work environments in which the individual finds himself or herself. These non-work factors also ought to have influence on commitment to the field and to the organization.[9]

Not only should the objective characteristics of the organizations and the other social units which impinge on the individual influence commitment, but also the sentiments the individual has for the

[4] Merrill Samuelson, "A Standardized Test to Measure Job Satisfaction," JOURNALISM QUARTERLY, 39:285-91 (Summer 1962).

[5] John W. C. Johnstone, Edward J. Slawski and William W. Bowman, *The News People* (Urbana, Ill.: University of Illinois Press, 1976).

[6] Empirical support for this position can be found in: Howard S. Becker and James W. Carper, "The Development of Identification With an Occupation," *American Journal of Sociology*, 61:289-98 (January 1956); Oscar Grusky, "Career Mobility and Organizational Commitment," *Administrative Science Quarterly* 10:488-503 (March 1966); Lee, *op. cit.*, Sheldon, *op. cit.*; and Lawrence G. Hrebiniak and Joseph A. Alutto, "Personal and Role-Related Factors in the Development of Organizational Commitment," *Administrative Science Quarterly*, 17:555-72 (December 1972).

[7] Lee, *op. cit.*, has found evidence supporting this link.

[8] See: David I. Sheppard, "Relationship of Job Satisfaction to Situational and Personal Characteristics of Terminating Employees," *Personnel Journal*, 46:567-71 (October 1967); Martin Patchen, *Participation, Achievement, and Involvement on the Job* (Englewood Cliffs, N.J.: Prentice Hall, 1970); Lee, *op. cit.*; Sheldon, *op. cit.*; Hrebiniak and Alutto, *op. cit.*; and Buchanan, *op. cit.*

[9] Empirical support for this position can be found in: Becker and Carper, "The Development of Identification with an Occupation," *op. cit.*; Lee, *op. cit.*; Sheldon, *op. cit.*; Hrebiniak and Alutto, *op. cit.*; and Buchanan, *op. cit.*

organization and key people in the work organization should influence commitment. Specifically, such sentiments as respect for superiors and professional evaluations of the organization itself should influence commitment.[10]

Finally, general feelings of job satisfaction should be related to commitment to the field. How an individual feels about a given job should have influence on general feelings about the occupation itself as well as commitment to the profession.[11]

These factors or types of influences are not independent of each other. It is possible to order them temporally so that background and training influences precede occupational sentiments, which may be a consequence, particularly, of the training. Occupational sentiments precede job selection. As a consequence, they are temporally prior to the influences of organizational and extra-organizational variables. These variables, in turn, precede specific job sentiments, which are followed by job satisfaction.[12]

Figure 1 lists the major types of variables expected to impact commitment and indicates the general nature of the relationships expected between the clusters. General types rather than specific

variables are used to indicate the general nature of the model rather than the relationships expected for specific variables. Also note that no distinction is made in the model between organizational and professional commitment. Rather, the model is expected to look much the same for these types of commitment.

Data Base: An examination of the data gathered by Johnstone, Slawski and Bowman in their national study of U.S. journalists indicated that a preliminary test of key aspects of the model was possible with existing data.[13] Sufficient measures of each of the variable types shown in Figure 1 were available in the data set. And the 1971 national study, which included lengthy telephone interviews with over 1,300 editorial personnel in daily and weekly newspapers, news magazines, wire services and the news departments of radio and television stations and networks, is clearly the most comprehensive to date on U.S. journalists.

While Johnstone and his colleagues had performed some analyses using job commitment as a focal variable, most of those reported were only for journalists between the ages of 25 and 34. And these analyses, while helpful and sufficient given the scope of the book, spoke only indirectly to many of the questions raised by the model discussed here. In addition, one key limitation of the reported analyses, from the point of view discussed here, is that they were somewhat insensitive to differences in the work situations of persons in the news media. Because the study was designed to represent all personnel in the media, relatively little effort was made to differentiate between the problems and tasks of media managers and of those actually doing the reporting and editing of the news.

The decision was made in re-examining the Johnstone data to restrict the analyses to those persons who actually did news reporting at least once a week. Approximately half the sample members could

[10] See: Patchen, *op. cit.*; Lee, *op. cit.*; Hrebiniak and Alutto, *op. cit.*; and Joseph Schneider, "The 'Greener Grass' Phenomenon: Differential Effects of a Work Context Alternative on Organizational Participation and Withdrawal Intentions," *Organizational Behavior and Human Performance,* 16:308-33 (1976).

[11] See: Frederick Herzberg, Bernard Mausner, Richard Peterson and Dora F. Capwell, *Job Attitudes: Review of Research and Opinion* (Pittsburgh: Psychological Service of Pittsburgh, 1957); Lee, *op. cit.*; William H. Mobley, "Intermediate Linkages in the Relationship Between Job Satisfaction and Employee Turnover," *Journal of Applied Psychology,* 62:237-40 (No. 2 1977); and Yoash Wiener and Arthur S. Gechman, "Commitment: A Behavioral Approach to Job Involvement," *Journal of Vocational Behavior,* 10:47-52 (No. 1 1977). The literature on job satisfaction in the newsroom is reviewed in Harold C. Shaver, "Job Satisfaction and Dissatisfaction Among Journalism Graduates," *Journalism Quarterly,* 55:54-61 (Spring 1978).

[12] This model is generally consistent with that of Robert Dubin, R. Alan Hedley and Thomas C. Taveggia, "Attachment to Work," in Robert Dubin, ed., *Handbook of Work, Organization and Society* (Chicago: Rand McNally, 1976), pp. 281-341 as well as the model of Bill McKelvey and Uma Sekaran, "Toward a Career-Based Theory of Job Involvement: A Study of Scientists and Engineers," *Administrative Science Quarterly,* 22:281-305 (June 1977).

[13] Johnstone, Slawski and Bowman, *op. cit.*

FIGURE 1

Model of Commitment

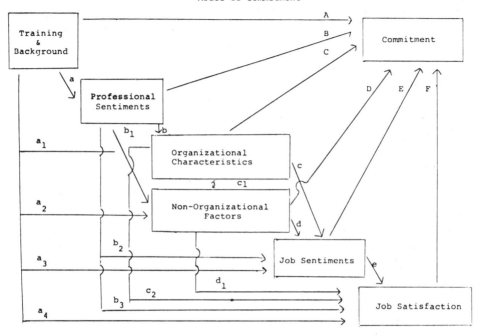

be so classified.[14] The decision to restrict the analyses to reporters is generally sensitive to the realities of the news profession. Most—though certainly not all—persons coming into the profession enter as reporters. So the problems and frustrations of reporting are very much the problems of the field.

The measure of commitment used by Johnstone, Slawski and Bowman was based on two questions. The first simply asked respondents: "Do you hope to be working for the same organization five years from now, or would you prefer to be working somewhere else by then?" This was followed, for those who hoped to be working somewhere else, with: "Where would you most like to be working in five years—in the news media, or somewhere else?" Almost 60% of the reporters in the sample said they hoped to stay with the same news organization.[15] Another 25% said they hoped to stay in journalism, but wanted to move to another organization. The 60% hoping to stay with the same organization were con-

sidered to be committed to that organization. The 85% hoping to remain in the field were considered to be committed to the profession.[16]

Measures of the various independent variables are listed in Table 1.[17] The training and background measures are straightforward. Several items designed to measure professional and non-professional orientations were included on the questionnaire.[18] These items were

[14] Editors were eliminated because of the small number of persons in this role who do not also serve in a managerial role and because different questions were asked regarding problems on the job from those asked reporters.

[15] Those intending to retire in five years were eliminated from these and subsequent analysis since the measure is not sensitive to their level of commitment.

[16] Consistent with the view that public relations is a separate profession, those hoping to move to public relations were labeled as uncommitted.

[17] In effect, the questionnaire was content analyzed to classify questions according to the conceptual scheme developed here. See Lee B. Becker, "Secondary Analysis," in Guido Stempel and Bruce H. Westley, eds., Research Methods in Mass Communication (Englewood Cliffs, N.J.: Prentice-Hall, forthcoming) for a discussion of this strategy.

[18] Items were similar to those used in the literature on professionalization of newsmen. See particularly Jack M. Mc-

(Continued)

summed to form two separate indices. Items also were included to measure the respondent's assessment of the proper role of the media in society. These items also were summed to form two indices, one for participant orientation and the other for a neutral orientation.[19] The organizational measures were derived either from information obtained in the interviews or from records available to Johnstone and his colleagues.[20] The non-organizational and job sentiment measures were obtained from items on the interview schedule, as were the two job satisfaction measures.[21] The first job satisfaction measure is based on a weighting of satisfaction for those aspects of the job which the respondent indicated was important. The second measure is more global.[22]

Results

Because the measures of the two types of commitment are nominal, while most of the measures of the independent variables at least approach interval-level, discriminant analysis was chosen as the method for testing the model. The results of the univariate analysis for each of the independent variables are shown in Table 1. To perform this analysis, respondents were classified according to their professional and organizational commitment. Commitment groups were then examined

Leod and Searle F. Hawley, "Professionalization Among Newsmen," JOURNALISM QUARTERLY, 41:529-39 (Autumn 1964). The professional and non-professional indices, which were created after item analyses, were found to be empirically unrelated (r = .01). This is consistent with the findings of Swedish journalists reported by Swen Windahl and Karl Erik Rosengren, "Newsmen's Professionalization: Some Methodological Problems," JOURNALISM QUARTERLY, 55:466-73 (1978).

[19] Johnstone and his colleagues used these same labels for similarly constructed indices. Several of the items used by Johnstone were not included here, however, after item analyses indicated problems resulting in part from missing data. The indices used were not highly correlated (r = .06).

[20] On the public access data tape, the identities of the media organizations were deleted. Prestige rankings for the various media organizations, used by Johnstone and his colleagues, consequently were not available for these analyses.

[21] Several of the job sentiment measures were specific to the reporting situation, as noted above, making comparisons across task difficult.

[22] The correlation between the two measures is high (r = .53).

[23] Respondents with missing data on any of the variables were eliminated, as were those expecting to retire from the profession in five years.

for differences on the independent variables. The results of these simple analysis of variance tests are summarized in Table 1. The responses of 570 reporters were used.[23]

These univariate findings, of course, easily can be misinterpreted since many of the relationships may be spurious. The more important questions have to do with the predictive power of the variable clusters and the controls implied in Figure 1. The zero-order relationships were used only to eliminate variables not making even a weak contribution to the distinction between the committment types. Those variables not showing an F significant at the .10 level in a two-tailed test were eliminated.

In Table 2 are shown the relative contributions of the variable clusters in discriminating between the commitment groups. The variable clusters were considered in the reverse order from what is shown in Figure 1. In other words, the discriminatory power of job sentiments was examined only after the contribution of job satisfaction was examined. In such a way it is possible to get a rough indication as to the strength of direct links between the clusters and commitment (A-F in Figure 1).

It is clear that job satisfaction is a significant factor in explaining both types of commitment. Job sentiments, on the other hand, are of significance only for organizational commitment and even here the relationship is not overly strong. Non-organizational factors are of some significance for both types of commitment, as are organizational characteristics. Professional sentiments are of some importance in distinguishing between commitment groups for both types of commitment. Training and background, however, seem only to be significant for occupational commitment. In general, the variable types chosen seem to be much better predictors of organizational commitment than occupational commitment. There is no evidence that the relationships represented by A and E in Figure 1 hold for professional commitment.

TABLE 1

Zero-Order Relationships with Commitment [a]

Measure	Summary
Training and Background	
Education: Highest year of school completed	c
Major: Journalism instruction or not	-
Father's Education: Highest year completed	c
Age	c
Sex	-
Ideology: Self-description of political learnings	bc
Professional Sentiments	
Professional Values: Finds freedom from supervision, helping people, editorial policies, autonomy important in a job	-
Non-Professional Values: Finds pay, fringe benefits, security and chance to get ahead important in a job	bc
Participant Orientation: Think it important for the media to provide analysis and interpretation	-
Neutral Orientation: Think it important for the media to get information to public quickly, provide entertainment, avoid controversial materials, concentrate on news of widest interest	bc
Evaluation of Media: How good of a job are the media doing	b
Organizational Characteristics	
Media Type: Print or broadcast	c
Size of Controlling Company: Number of units owned	c
Size of Organization: Number of editorial employees	bc
Labor Organization: Guild or not	b
Communication with Boss: Frequency of meetings with superior to discuss stories	b
Vertical Feedback: Frequency of reactions on work from superiors	-
Horizontal Feedback: Frequency of reactions on work from people on same level	c
Social Network: Percentage of people seen socially working for same organization	-
Income: Current salary from organization	c
Non-Organizational Factors	
Marital Status: Married or not	bc
Family Size: Number of children under 18	bc
Community Feedback: Frequency of reactions on work from readers	c
Community Involvement: Number of general organizational memberships	c
Professional Involvement: Number of professional memberships	bc

Professional Network: Percentage of people seen socially
connected to journalism or communications ... c

Professional Feedback: Frequency of reactions on work from
professional colleagues not at organization ... -

Contacts with Other Organizations: Feelers or job offers ... c

Job Sentiments

Evaluation of Organization: How good of a job is your own
news organization doing ... bc

Respect for Boss: How much respect do you have for him or
her professionally ... c

Agreement with Organization: How often do you agree with editorial
stands ... bc

Value of work: How often do you work on stories of news value;
how often work on stories of public controversy ... c

Time Restraints: How often do you feel you have enough time to
prepare story adequately ... c

Autonomy in Decision-Making: How much freedom do you have
in selecting stories; how much freedom in deciding which
aspects of story to emphasize ... bc

Job Satisfaction

Satisfaction with Salient Characteristics of Job: Is present job
providing for selected professional and non-professional needs ... bc

Satisfaction in General: All things considered, how satisfied are
you with present job ... bc

[a] F tests were performed by sorting respondents first according to their professional commitment type and then according to their organizational commitment type and then comparing these types in terms of the levels of the independent variables. The number of persons classified as committed to the profession was 485. The number of uncommitted was 85. The number of persons committed to the organization was 333. The number of uncommitted was 152. The 85 persons uncommitted to the profession were not used for the analyses of organizational commitment.

[b] The professionally committed differ significantly (.10 level, two-tailed test) from the professionally uncommitted on this variable.

[c] The organizationally committed differ significantly (.10 level, two-tailed test) from the organizationally uncommitted on this variable.

In Table 3, discriminant coefficients are shown to give indicants of the specific measures contributing to the differentiation between the committed and the uncommitted. A positive coefficient indicates the measure, after controlling for other measures in the equation, is positively related to commitment.

Controlling for other variables, we find the professionally committed are higher in non-professional values, more neutral and less critical of the media. They also are less likely to be Guild members and less likely to work for large organizations. They are more likely to be married with families and be high in professional involvement. And they are satisfied with their jobs.

The profile of the organizationally committed is somewhat different. As the coefficients in Table 3 indicate, these persons are less educated, older and more

TABLE 2

Discriminatory Power of Variable Types: Commitment as Dependent Variables

	Professional Commitment (N = 570)	
Independent Variables	Rao's V [a]	Changes in Rao's V
Job Satisfaction	41.02	41.02
Job Sentiments	-	-
Non-Organizational Factors	58.21	17.19
Organizational Characteristics	64.53	6.32
Professional Sentiments	72.61	8.08
Training & Background	-	-
	Organizational Commitment (N = 485)	
Job Satisfaction	128.07	128.07
Job Sentiments	144.04	15.97
Non-Organizational Factors	204.62	60.58
Organizational Factors	246.12	41.50
Professional Sentiments	259.79	13.67
Training & Background	310.33	50.54

[a] This statistic indicates discriminatory power of the independent variable types in differentiating between dependent variable groups, in this case, the committed and the uncommitted. Independent variables were introduced in the order shown, and a variables actually entered the equation only if its partial multivariate F ratio was larger than 1.0. Partial F reflects the discriminatory power of a variable after taking into account the other variables already used. The V statistics shown are sums for all variables of the indicated type which actually were used in the equation.

conservative than the uncommitted. They are somewhat high in non-professional values and likely to feel the media should be neutral. They are somewhat better paid, do not get a lot of feedback from colleagues, and work for large, print organizations. They are married and have families. They get feedback from the community and are involved in the formal aspects of their profession to some degree. They do not have a network of professional friends and do not have contacts with other media organizations. They are supportive of their organizations, agree with the editorial stands taken by these organizations and respect their bosses. In general, they are satisfied with their jobs.

The data in Table 1 through 3 speak only to the relationships between the variable clusters and commitment. In Table 4 data are shown relevant to the interrelationships of these clusters. The data result from cannonical correlation analyses of these variable clusters. All variables shown in Table 1, even those not having a direct effect on commitment, were examined since the variables may still have an indirect effect through other variables shown in the model.

As was expected, the general pattern of relationships shown in Table 4 is for a given cluster to be more highly correlated with a nearby cluster than with a more distant one. The training and background cluster shows this most clearly (a is greater than a_4)..

To a considerable degree the relationship between training and background and professional sentiments is explained by

TABLE 3

Discriminant Function Coefficients: Commitment as Dependent Variables

	Coefficient [a]	
Independent Variables	Professional Commitment	Organizational Commitment
Training & Background		
Education	-	-.06
Father's Education	-	-
Age	-	.25
Ideology (high = conservative)	-	.22
Professional Sentiments		
Non-Professional Values	.18	03
Neutral Orientation	.11	.09
Evaluation of Media	.21	-
Organizational Characteristics		
Media Type (high = print)	-	.09
Size of Controlling Company	-	-
Size of Organization	-.16	.23
Labor Organization (high = Guild)	-.15	-
Horizontal Feedback	-	-.11
Income	-	.07
Non-Organizational Factors		
Marital Status (high = married)	.33	.13
Family Size	.16	.17
Community Feedback	-	.07
Professional Involvement	.18	06
Professional Network	-	-.04
Contacts with Other Organizations	-	-.09
Job Sentiments		
Evaluation of Organization	-	.05
Respect for Boss	-	.11
Agreement with Organization	-	.11
Value of work	-	-
Time restraints	-	-
Autonomy in Decision-Making	-	-
Job Satisfaction		
Satisfaction with Salient Characteristics of Job	.36	.13
Satisfaction in General	.34	.45

[a] Coefficients are analogous to beta weights in regression analysis. A positive coefficient means a high value of the independent variable is associated with a high commitment. Where a dash appears, the variable did not enter into the equation because it added virtually no discriminant power. See the note for Table 2.

TABLE 4

Eigenvalues for Relationships in Figure 1

Relationship in Figure 1	Eigenvalue [a]
a	.296
a_1	.296
a_2	.237
a_3	.169
a_4	.030
b	.239
b_1	.070
b_2	.415
b_3	.552
c	.384
c_1	.894
c_2	.124
d	.070
d_1	.050
e	.359

[a] The eigenvalues indicating the percentage of variance shared by the two variable clusters connected by the arrow indicated at left were derived from cannonical correlation analysis. The figures reported are the total shared variance for significant cannonical variates.

the link between ideology and the active and neutral sentiments (liberals are more active and less neutral). But there also are some sex differences here of note. Women reporters are more professionally oriented than male reporters and less non-professionally oriented and neutralist. Sex, as Table 1 indicates, was not a factor in determining commitment.[24]

The link between training and background and organizational characteristics is explained by the positive relationship of both age and education with organizational size and reporter income. Male reporters also are better paid than female reporters. Older reporters are more likely to be print reporters.

The training and background link with non-organizational characteristics results from the fact that a larger percentage of the friends of younger reporters are in the profession, women get more feedback from the community than men, and the better educated are more likely to have both professional and community involvement.

The training and background link to job sentiments results from the links between ideology, education and age with the evaluations of the organization and job. The liberals are more likely to disagree with the editorial stands of the organization but feel they work on valuable stories and evaluate their own organizations highly. Education and age show similar relationships.

Professional sentiments are linked to organizational characteristics in several ways. Having an active orientation is positively associated with size of the organization and income. The neutral orientation shows parallel negative relationships.

Professional sentiments are linked to job sentiments through the relationship of evaluation of the media in general (a professional sentiment) and evaluation of one's own organization (a job sentiment). Since these very similarly worded questions were used one after the other in the survey instrument, b_2 may be overestimated.

The relationship between professional sentiments and job satisfaction (b_3) also may be overestimated in Table 4. This relationship seems to result in part from the use of the professional measures in building one of the indicants of satisfaction. When the more general indicant of job satisfaction is used, little link between professional sentiments and job satisfaction appears.

There is no basis for arguing that c in Table 4 should exceed c_1. Indeed, both are large. And both are larger than c_2. The link between organizational characteristics and job sentiments (c) results from the positive relationship between communication with the boss and agreement with the organization's editorials, the positive relationships of ver-

[24] This represents one of the several differences between the conclusions reached here and those of Johnstone, Slawski and Bowman. Johnstone and his colleagues, as noted earlier, found males to be less committed than females. Johnstone also found that a journalism education served to hold journalists to the profession, though the analyses reported here suggest major is of little overall importance. An active orientation also was associated with low commitment in the Johnstone analysis, though not in those presented here. The Johnstone inferences, however, were only for the young journalists—those between 25 and 34—and did not differentiate between reporters and others in the profession.

tical feedback and size of the organization with value of the reporter's work, and the negative relationship of size of the organization and autonomy.[25]

The organizational and non-organizational linkage is quite strong, Table 4 indicates. These variables are not always distinct, of course, and the classifications used for these analyses are somewhat arbitrary. Social network and professional network are highly related. And belonging to the Guild is associated, perhaps somewhat artifactually, with professional involvement. Vertical feedback is associated with contacts with other organizations. Size of organization is negatively associated with community feedback.

Organizational characteristics are linked with job satisfaction because of the positive relationship of income and satisfaction, the negative relationship of size of controlling company and satisfaction, and the positive link between communication with boss and satisfaction.

Job sentiments are linked to job satisfaction as follows. Evaluation of organization, respect for boss, agreement with organization, value of work, and autonomy are positively linked to satisfaction. Time restraints are negatively related to satisfaction.

In summary, the data support the following paths in Figure 1: a, a₁, a₂, a₃, b, c, c₁, c₂, and e.

In summary, the data support the following paths in Figure 1: a, a_1, a_2, a_3, b, c, c_1, c_2, and e.

[25] Johnstone has made much of this link between size of the organization and autonomy. See John W. C. Johnstone, "Organizational Constraints on Newswork," JOURNALISM QUARTERLY, 53:5-13 (Spring 1976). A re-examination of the data, however, suggested media type is the more important variable. For example, the differences between weekly newspapers and daily newspapers were greater than differences among daily newspapers of differing sizes. See Lee B. Becker, "Organizational Variables and the Study of Newsroom Behavior: A Review and Discussion of U.S. Research," paper presented at a Round Table Discussion on Communicator Research at the 11th Conference of the International Association for Mass Communication Research, Warsaw, Poland, 1978.

[26] For examples of additional questions see: Hrebiniak and Alutto, op. cit., Buchanan, op. cit., and Wiener and Gechman, op. cit.

[27] Warren Breed, "Social Control in the Newsroom: A Functional Analysis," Social Forces, 33:326-35 (May 1955). For a more recent example and a review of this research see D. Charles Whitney, "'Information Overload' in the Newsroom: Two Case Studies," unpublished Ph.D. dissertation, University of Minnesota, 1978.

Conclusions

Several limitations of the secondary analyses performed here are worthy of note. First, the conclusions must be considered somewhat tentative for the simple reason that not all relevant variables were included in the study. For example, the list of training and background variables used here is small given the breadth of that area. More detailed questions about the educational experiences of the reporters might well have boosted the impact of this type of variable.

Second, the dependent variables are measured here in a rather limiting way. Commitment is operationalized by only two questions, where a battery clearly would have been more suitable.[26] Finally, commitment is examined at only one point in time and only for those persons in the profession at that time. Persons who left the profession represent the extreme in terms of commitment. An analysis of their experiences would be most helpful in understanding the nature of this variable.

Despite these limitations, however, some important conclusions regarding commitment can be reached. The data seem to argue that the model offered to explain commitment is sound, at least where organizational commitment is concerned. Professional commitment does seem to be less well explained by the factors selected for analysis here. Two of the factors, background and training and job sentiments, seem particularly unimportant for professional commitment. But other factors, such as occupational sentiments and organizational characteristics, do predict to professional commitment. Perhaps what is needed is a modification of the model for this type of commitment. A total rejection does not seem in order.

The news reporter is under considerable organizational control, the classic analysis of Breed as well as more recent research has underscored.[27] He or she is not free to practice the profession independent of the forces of the newsroom. It is in terms of such matters as commitment, however, that the reporter has impact on the organization and the profession. The reporter always retains the right to walk away from the job, thereby forcing the organization and ultimately the profession to process a replacement.

Given this perspective, it is important to understand the determinants of commitment. Such factors as the background and training of the reporter, the professional orientation he or she brings to the job situation, the characteristics of the organization as well as related and unrelated aspects of the reporter's life, the sentiments the reporter has regarding the job, and overall job satisfaction help to determine commitment. Such factors discriminate between those committed to an organization and those who are not. And to a lesser extent, they also differentiate those committed to the profession from the uncommitted.

A great deal has been written about science journalists, but few studies have looked at them at work. Sharon Dunwoody, assistant professor of journalism at Ohio State University, used content analysis, observation, and interviews to research news coverage of the 1977 Convention of the American Association for the Advancement of Science (AAAS). Some 300-600 journalists, many of whom are full-time science reporters, attend the annual meetings, making them one of the largest scientific gatherings in the United States. Dr. Dunwoody found that a group of 28 reporters—deemed an "inner club" by many of their colleagues—greatly affected news coverage of the meeting. This group appears to maximize cooperative rather than competitive behavior among themselves, enhancing story accuracy and validating for each other what is newsworthy. A possible negative effect of the cooperation is to reduce the variety of coverage of the scientific event. Dunwoody finds the reporters ranked space and astronomy most frequently as topics of interest, with social science ranked last.

20

THE SCIENCE WRITING INNER CLUB
A Communication Link Between Science and the Lay Public

Sharon Dunwoody

Since the mid-1960's, a relatively small group of specialty reporters has played a large part in determining what the U.S. public has learned about significant scientific happenings. Nonscientists depend primarily on print media for news about science;[1] therefore, science writers employed by major newspapers and wire services have played crucial roles within the last fifteen years as translators of scientific information for a wide range of publics. However, although the names of these journalists may be familiar to many of us, we know very little about how they do their jobs.

In an effort to find out, I studied the news-gathering behaviors of a sample of the top U.S. mass media science writers at the annual meeting of the American Association for the Advancement of Science.[2] The study, conducted during 1976–78, consisted of three parts: (1) face-to-face interviews with the journalists, with questions primarily directed to reporters' perceptions of how they select news and gather information; (2) observation of the journalists as they covered the AAAS annual meeting; and (3) content analysis of the nearly 800 stories about the meeting that were published in U.S. daily newspapers.[3]

The study found that the U.S. mass media science writing community is dominated by a relatively small group of newspaper, magazine and wire service reporters who, since the mid-1960's, have largely determined what the public has read about significant scientific events. These individuals, who at any one time total no more than 25 or 30 journalists, form a closely knit, informal social network that I call an "inner club."[4] Many of its members have been a part of this club for more than 10 years; in fact, its stability over time may be unique among informal networks. And the club is worth studying precisely because it

affects the news selection and news-gathering behaviors of its members.

It does so mainly by emphasizing *cooperative* behaviors among reporters in situations that should be highly *competitive*. Cooperation provides a number of benefits for members, but it also exacts certain costs when the larger notion of "responsible science coverage" is taken into account. For example, inner club membership enhances story accuracy by making a wider pool of resources available to a journalist. But cooperative story selection also has the negative effect of reducing variety in science news coverage by fostering a homogeneous notion of "what's news" at a given event.

The Genesis of the Inner Club

Members of this informal science-writing network readily acknowledge the bond that exists among them. Said one, for example:

> There is a group of very experienced science writers in this country, and we do form—gee, I hate to use the term—something of a clique. We keep each other apprised of what's going on. . . . A bond of trust has grown up between us.

Another similarly viewed the relationships among his colleagues as something akin to a "fraternity," characterizing the club as "kind of an in-group . . . we're all friends. We've worked together for a long time and, obviously, . . . it evolves over time."

Most of the members agree that the group coalesced in the 1960's when some of them were suddenly dubbed science writers and sent by their newspapers or wire services to cover the great science story of the decade: the manned landings on the moon. Many of the journalists who journeyed to Cape Canaveral or to Houston possessed little scientific expertise. They had been pulled from general reporting backgrounds, and their educations had been primarily journalistic. Their editors knew even less about science, however; so, despite their lack of experience, these new science journalists were expected to know what they were doing. This meant they were responsible for front-page stories that were both substantive and accurate, yet they could not expect much help from home.

Consequently, they turned to one another. Away from their city rooms for weeks, they became socialized to *each other* rather than to their peers in the home newsroom.[5] As one science writer noted:

> At the height of it [the space program], they were making a major launch every three months, and you would be down there at the Cape for two-and-a-half weeks at a time. The result was that it [the group of science writers] became your family. There were love affairs, there were hates and fights. . . . It became a traveling road show with the same people showing up time and time again, going to the same places and doing the same things. There was great cohesiveness.

Another agreed that covering events away from the city room played a large part in the evolution of the group:

> We see more of each other because of going to these meetings, covering these stories. You're with each other for several days at a time, most of the day and most of the evening; you tend to go out and eat dinner together. So you get to be very good friends. You've got a common interest, like I have more in common with science writers from other papers than I do with reporters here on the ————————————, because we're covering the same stories, we interview the same people, and we see each other not just casually. So we all get to be pretty good friends.

The major emphasis of the club as it evolved was on cooperation. Cooperation seemed a good strategy because by sharing expertise, the group could evaluate scientific information better than could an individual with limited knowledge. Also, when the normal reporter/source problems arose, the journalists could close ranks and collectively negotiate a solution, a procedure that promised more success than did individual efforts. The science writers had also become close friends, so cooperative behavior seemed a better strategy for preserving those relationships than did competitive behavior. Finally, the quality of a reporter's work was judged by his editor in relation to what the other reporters were producing. The reporter, therefore, could satisfy his editor not by "scooping" his fellow science writers but by producing the *same story* each day. Cooperative behavior helped to ensure that.

The Inner Club Today

Inner club members today (Table 1) share several characteristics. They generally are affiliated with the prestige print media, media that can afford to make science a national or even international beat. Unlike most reporters, they travel regularly, spending days at a time away from the city room. They see each other regularly at large scientific meetings, at events such as the 1976 Viking landings on Mars (covered at the Jet Propulsion Center in California), or the Legionnaire's Disease crisis in Pennsylvania. They have been working as science writers for a number of years, long enough for close personal relationships to develop. And they share an intense concern for professional aspects of science writing, for the quality and accuracy of what they do.

The majority of inner club members in this study are male; most hold bachelor's degrees in journalism or some other non-science field, but have taken graduate courses in science or science writing. As students, they had no interest in becoming science writers, and most worked as general reporters for some years before concentrating on science reporting.

As of 1979, the average inner club member in this study had been a full-time science writer for 15 years. They are most likely to work for a morning metropolitan newspaper with a circulation of 300,000 or more. The majority prefer space, astronomy and the hard sciences in general to other areas of science and perceive themselves to be very autonomous of the newsroom, with the option of selecting their own story topics at least 80 percent of the time.[6] In fact, they are likely to act as science editors on their newspapers whether they actually have the title or not. Editors may defer to their judgment when evaluating the quality of science stories written by others. The majority of respondents in this study travel at least five times a year, usually to scientific meetings. And the news criteria they perceive themselves to be using are quite similar to those utilized by other journalists in other coverage areas: reader interest, potential significance of information to reader, newness of information, information that interests either the journalist or his editor, prominence of source, uniqueness of information, proximity, and the intrinsic importance of the information to science.

The Inner Club's Effects on News Gathering

The inner club network has an effect on news-making primarily when science journalists converge on one event or meeting. Although this is not a daily (or even weekly) occurrence, it does increase the likelihood that coverage of any scientific event significant enough to attract groups of journalists will be affected by the network. Understanding the workings of the inner club may not help us to interpret the how's and why's of daily newspaper science coverage; but, when a major scientific "happening" takes place, knowledge of inner club effects can provide some insight to mass media coverage of that event.

TABLE 1

Names of Science Journalists Suggested by Colleagues for Inner Club Status,
with Titles and Media Affiliations
at Time of Study

*George Alexander	Science writer	Los Angeles Times
Stuart Auerbach	Medical/Science writer	The Washington Post
*Jerry Bishop	Staff reporter	The Wall Street Journal
Al Blakeslee	Science writer	Associated Press (retired)
Jane Brody	Medical writer	The New York Times
Victor Cohn	Science writer	The Washington Post
*Bob Cooke	Science editor	Boston Globe
Lewis Cope	Science writer	The Minneapolis Tribune
Donald Drake	Science/Medicine writer	Philadelphia Inquirer
*Ed Edelson	Science editor	The New York News
*Peter Gwynne	General editor	Newsweek
Bill Hines	Science writer	Chicago Sun-Times
*Don Kirkman	Science writer	Scripps-Howard Newspapers
*Ron Kotulak	Science editor	Chicago Tribune
*John Langone	Medical/Science editor	Boston Herald-American
Harry Nelson	Medical writer	Los Angeles Times
*Tom O'Toole	Science editor	The Washington Post
*David Perlman	Science editor	San Francisco Chronicle
David Prowitt	Science correspondent	Public Broadcasting System
*Judy Randal	Science correspondent	The New York News
*Joann Rodgers	Medical writer	Baltimore News-American
*Al Rossiter	Science editor	United Press International
*Joel Shurkin	Science writer	Philadelphia Inquirer
Art Snider	Science editor	Chicago Sun-Times
*Brian Sullivan	Science writer	Associated Press
*Walter Sullivan	Science editor	The New York Times
John Noble Wilford	Science writer	The New York Times
*Patrick Young	Science writer	The National Observer (now free lance)

n=28
* Participants in study (n=17)

The effects are substantial. Inner club journalists may constitute only a small proportion of science writers who converge on any scientific event, but they significantly affect news coverage primarily because they work for either the major wire services (Associated Press and United Press International) or the elite print media, who also participate in wire service operations (such as *The New York Times* wire service, Scripps-Howard, Knight-Ridder and the *Los Angeles Times/ Washington Post* service). Wire copy accounts for a substantial portion of the editorial diet of most newspapers in this country. Thus, although only a few science journalists belong to the inner club, they can greatly influence what the public eventually will read about an event.[7]

To study the inner club in action, I chose as a "laboratory" the annual meeting of the American Association for the Advancement of Science. The meeting is one of the largest scientific gatherings in the country and annually draws more journalists than almost any other scientific occurrence; average newsroom attendance ranges from 300 to 600. The event is so popular among science writers, in fact, that the National Association of Science Writers, Inc., conducts its business meeting each year at AAAS.[8] Since most inner club reporters consider it a "required" annual trip, the meeting provided an ideal setting for observation of inner club interactions.[9]

Various cooperative behaviors among inner club members affected two points in the newsmaking process at the meeting: topic selection and information gathering.

Topic selection. The most frequently mentioned type of cooperation was helping one another select stories. At a meeting like that of AAAS, much of the practice seems to be a matter of discussing story possibilities informally and listening to colleagues weigh the potential of particular press conferences or evaluate the "quotability" of particular scientists. The end result is a consensus among club members about what or who is news at a given moment. Such a consensus seems to provide three major benefits for participants:

1) It allows them to "neutralize" the competitive aspects of the coverage situation. Journalism is traditionally a competitive business, with one newspaper pitted against another, one journalist trying to scoop his or her colleagues. But at events such as the AAAS meeting, the inner club member is faced with a paradox. Since the club is made up of journalists from the prestige media, members are not only close friends but also each other's main competition. The inner club member handles this contradiction by nullifying the competitive aspects. Each journalist knows that his editor is watching the competing newspapers and wire services and is evaluating what he produces *in relation to* what the competition publishes. If he produces something different, he may be in trouble; at the very least he will have to defend his choice. But if all competitors produce the same story for the day, then each editor assumes his reporter has done a good job. As one inner club member noted:

> A science writer will come back and say 'Hey, I've found a good one,' and ears will prick up. I'll sometimes do the same. You share with friends and they share with their friends and it gets around. Everybody's in the same boat, trying to please editors and get a good story done.

2) Collective story selection provides each reporter with the personal reassurance that he has found a "newsworthy" story. Just as editors gauge the quality of their reporters' story selections against the competition, the reporters come to depend on each other to validate what is news on a given day. It is difficult to select one story and then watch one's colleagues choose another. One journalist who is not an inner club member remarked that "everybody tends to agree on what is the important story" at a meeting and she finds that "a little bit unsettling. When you go to those meetings . . . there's a little bit more of that pack mentality in terms of everybody pressuring everybody else" to agree jointly on a major story for the day.

3) Selecting stories collectively allows the inner club also to pool its expertise. One reporter may be able to warn another away from a risky story; a third writer may be able to suggest a different story possibility altogether. As one inner club member noted: "I'm likely to change my mind (about a story topic) if it's an area that I don't know much about and if I know some other reporter knows a lot about it."

One example from the 1978 AAAS meeting sheds some light on this process. A number of inner club members attended a press conference at which a scientist presented findings of a study of Seventh Day Adventists that indicated consumption of red meat is linked to increased rates of heart attacks, increased cancer rates and decreased life expectancy. After the press conference, one inner club member warned her colleagues to obtain a copy of the research findings before writing anything; she felt the study may not have controlled for other confounding factors in the respondents' lifestyles and suggested the journalists make sure the study was a valid one before going ahead with a story. Several club members took her advice.

Information gathering. Although science writers are not eager to talk about cooperative information-gathering behaviors, I observed at least four types of information sharing during the 1977 AAAS meeting.

1) Providing scientific information. Perhaps most common among information-gathering behaviors was the tendency of the inner club to act as a pool of resources for its members. Journalists with science questions would corral one another, searching for definitions, clarifications, examples and analogues. At times, the rooms where reporters typed their stories would be alive with questions and answers, as one reporter depended on another's expertise. Information was always freely given.

2) Sharing notes and interviews. Inner club members respect one another's journalistic abilities, and cooperative information gathering would sometimes extend to the actual sharing of interview notes or of the interview sessions themselves. In one instance, the science writer for a large eastern newspaper set up an interview with an astronomer and then invited a colleague—who happened to work for a competing eastern newspaper—to sit in with him. Another journalist recounted an instance, at an earlier AAAS meeting, when he and a fellow science writer wanted to attend four different symposia at the same time and managed to do so by each attending one and leaving tape recorders at the other two. "We wound up—the two of us—covering four separate meetings simultaneously," he said. "And we swapped notes . . . covered ourselves that way."

3) Supportive questioning at press conferences. Journalists generally find press conferences frustrating because they have so little control over the "event"; reporters rarely work together, so questions are disparate with little or no followup. This is not the case among the inner club. The cooperative nature of the group encourages reporters to take their leads from each other, to ask followup questions, to work together. By doing so,

reporters can gain some control over the interview situation and can focus lines of questioning as necessary. At the 1977 AAAS meeting, for example, three inner club members attended a press conference at which a scientist discussed his attempts to identify infant behaviors that might be useful predictors of Sudden Infant Death Syndrome (SIDS). The three inner club members had written frequently about SIDS in other contexts, and when one began questioning the scientist closely about the predictive nature of his work, the other two joined what became a rather heated exchange. The journalists argued that they did not want to write stories that might provide false hope to readers, and the scientist in turn argued that he could not generalize any further from his data than he had already done. In the end, none of the three journalists wrote stories about the SIDS research. Both scientist and journalists were angry, but one science writer on the sideline felt that such intense, cooperative questioning was justified in cases such as this. He explained that a number of writers have been "burned" by scientists claiming to have found the explanation for SIDS. He felt that when a journalist is writing a SIDS story, he is justified in pushing the scientist to the limit, and the technique of following up on one another's questions at a press conference is a good way of doing that.

4) Acting as warning systems for one another. Just as inner club members warn each other away from potentially risky topics or scientists, so do they also flag information that must be interpreted cautiously. And if they feel a colleague is "going beyond the data" in drawing conclusions, they will take the time to warn him or her about it. An incident that took place at the 1977 AAAS meeting illustrates this point. One of the most popular press conferences at that meeting was on new Viking data about Mars and its moon, Phobos. During the press conference, astronomer Carl Sagan noted that new measurements of Phobos indicated it was made up to some extent of carbonaceous chondrites and constituted "a big lump of organic matter orbiting Mars." The main point of the discussion was that the data lent credence to the hypothesis that Phobos may be a captured asteroid. But one science writer came away from the press conference with the news that "there's oil on Phobos. Phobos is a little Saudi Arabia!" He apparently had made the conceptual leap from long-chain hydrocarbons to oil. Several inner club members were visibly dis-

turbed by the oil comment and talked further with Sagan. One reporter then corralled the colleague who had come up with the Saudi Arabia statement and warned him, "Sagan just called [another reporter] down on that [mentioning oil]. You can have long-chain hydrocarbons without it being anything like oil." Ultimately, the idea of oil on Phobos was either played down in or even eliminated from inner club stories.

Advantages and Disadvantages of Inner Club Membership

The main function of the inner club, then, seems to be to turn what should be a highly competitive media situation into a cooperative one for its members.[10] Resulting cooperative strategies seem to help inner club members to produce news more efficiently and more accurately.

Most inner club members come to science meetings saddled with deadline demands. They do not have the luxury of taking two or three days to gather information for a story; in many cases they may be expected to produce two stories a day, and time is of the essence. Sharing information is one way to cut down on the gathering time. Being able to look at a colleague's interview notes means you do not need to interview the scientist yourself. Collaborative questioning in a press conference may provide sufficient information to eliminate the need for further discussion with the scientists after the conference. Sharing information is, thus, an efficient strategy for news production.

Sharing also may increase accuracy. Because the information they cover is so technical, science writers worry about the accuracy of their products. Accuracy is enhanced when a journalist avails him- or herself of a pool of resources—such as the inner club. A number of science writers have accumulated expertise in specific areas of science and are able to provide detailed information to their colleagues. By emphasizing sharing, the club encourages interaction and the type of behavior monitoring illustrated by the Phobos incident.

However, while these behaviors probably increase the accuracy of the scientific information presented to the public, I think they also have had two negative effects on inner club coverage of science. One is standardization in story selection, and the other is the emphasis on some areas of science to the neglect of others. When the inner club attends a meeting such as that of AAAS, most factors encourage a homogeneous output. Cooperative newsgathering favors duplication; a large number of talented writers concentrate on a relatively small number of topics. The concentration of time and effort is not intrinsically bad—any one reporter could not possibly produce stories about more than a miniscule part of the meeting. However, if reporters ignore topics at a science meeting, they should do so according to some relevant criteria. What readers see or read about the event should in some way be more important, more relevant to them perhaps, than what they don't.

It is not clear that cooperative story selections by the inner club are based on such criteria. Members may define news less by judgments of the intrinsic importance of information than by the notion that if others have done this story, then it must in fact be important. In other words, duplication may be a strategy for satisfying *internal* (organizational) pressures but may have little meaning outside the reporting selection process. Inner club standardization of story choices at a scientific event thus means that lay readers will be exposed to only a small portion of the event itself and, in addition, will be given no help in understanding the criteria used to select that small pool of stories.

My data indicate that these journalists also tend to cover areas of science with which they are familiar. Such a situation is not a problem if backgrounds are diverse, but homogeneous science interests among reporters lay the groundwork for neglect of certain areas of science by the club's majority. As Table 2 attests, there is a certain amount of homogeneity in reporter interests within the club. Since many members spent most of their early science-writing years with the space program, the physical sciences and astronomy rank high. Others have developed interests in specific fields such as climatology or geology,[11] but areas of little interest to most club members are likely to be neglected. And the fields generating the *least* amount of interest among these respondents are the social sciences.

Science writers—of all journalists—should be equipped to report on the social sciences; in fact, they are not. Few feel they know enough about social science research techniques to evaluate studies and make news decisions. The typical response is to avoid social science or at least to view lack of evaluative skills as no great barrier to writing. "I'm not very well equipped to evaluate sociology," said one inner club member, "but it can't hurt anybody so I figure it's not going to do too much damage if I get it a little screwed up." So what's news to the inner club is *not* likely to be social science. And even when a social science story is picked up, inner club membership may not be of much help in ensuring accuracy. None of the inner club members studied in this project professed to have any social science expertise. A social sciences "pool of resources" simply may not exist among these elite science writers.

The Future of the Inner Club

The inner club will continue to influence science news coverage in the United States for some time; members are relatively young and show no intention of stepping aside. Nevertheless, I believe that the club's influence *is* likely to diminish over time.

Science writers appear to be shifting emphasis and resources away from coverage of discrete *events* to coverage of complex *issues*, such as the nationwide use of solar technologies or the industrial potential of recombinant DNA techniques. This shift may be partly adaptive; few scientific events today can rival the manned space shots for excitement and front-page potential. The shift also may signal a recognition that science's important effects on society do not lend themselves to an event orientation in news stories. Such a switch from event to non-event coverage of science does, however, reduce the frequency with which the inner club is coming together. An informal network that depends on personal interactions will be likely to suffer.

A second major reason for the club's diminishing influence is that a number of "new" journalists moving up in the mass media ranks have not become socialized to the inner club.[12] Most simply have not been around long enough—less than 10 years in most cases—but they also bring very different backgrounds to the profession.

TABLE 2

Scientific Interests of the Inner Club Ranked by Frequency of Mention

Topic	Number of mentions
Space	14
Astronomy	13
Other physical sciences, particularly geology	12
Medicine/biology	10
Environment/energy	9
Anthropology/archaeology	8
Technology	7
Political/social aspects of science	6
Social science/behavior	4

Total number of respondents in study: 17

Many of them majored in science in college, knew as students that they wanted to become science reporters, and began their mass media careers not as general reporters but as science writers. Few of them were around when the manned space program was in full swing, and they seem to be very interested in covering political, economic, sociological and technological aspects of science. Although inner club members do not avoid such areas, the younger journalists seem to place higher priority on the integration of "pure" science with its social ramifications.

The inner club will, of course, not disappear. However, as young science journalists are hired and opportunities to become socialized to one another at scientific events decline, the incidence of intense cooperation among journalists that so characterizes the inner club today should decrease. Such an evolution may give individual science writers sufficient independence to allow development of personal newsmaking strategies while at the same time enabling the science writing *community* to retain enough cooperative behaviors to give members access to some of the distinct advantages of peer monitoring and assistance.

NOTES

1. See, for example, Hillier Krieghbaum, *Science, the News, and the Public* (New York: New York University Press, 1958), pp. 12–16; James W. Swinehart and Jack M. McLeod, "News About Science: Channels, Audiences and Effects," 24 *Public Opinion Quarterly* (Winter 1960): 583–589; and Orest Dubas and Lisa Martel, *Science, Mass Media and the Public*, vol. 2 of *Media Impact* (Ottawa: Information Canada, 1975), pp. 34–36.

2. Study findings discussed in this article constitute a part of the author's doctoral dissertation, "Science Journalists: A Study of Factors Affecting the Selection of News at a Scientific Meeting," Indiana University, 1978. Data were collected with the aid of a grant from the Gannett Newspaper Foundation via the Indiana University Center for New Communications. Other components of the larger study *not* discussed here include comparisons of the news selection patterns of the top mass media science writers with those of journalists with much less expertise in science. Also included in the dissertation are analyses of the stories produced about the meeting, including comparisons between newspaper and broadcast coverage, between local (Denver) and nonlocal coverage, between media that sent reporters to the meeting and media that did not, and between wire service organizations and newspapers.

3. Details of the study methodology are available from the author. I suspected that I would find a small but cohesive network of experienced science writers in the United States, so I set out to construct a sample of those very individuals through a self-selection method. Three prominent science writers and four public information persons who work for national scientific institutions were asked to provide names of journalists whom they *regularly* encounter in major science news situations. Those providing names were David Perlman, then science editor of the *San Francisco Chronicle*; Ron Kotulak, science editor for the *Chicago Tribune*; Ed Edelson, science editor for *The New York News*; Don Phillips, senior project specialist for the American Hospital Association; Audrey Likely, director of public relations for the American Institute

of Physics; Dorothy P. Smith, manager of the news service for the American Chemical Society; and Carol Rogers, public information officer for the American Association for the Advancement of Science. The resulting lists were then merged and the names ranked according to the number of mentions they received. Those science journalists named by three or more of the seven persons were considered likely candidates for this experienced "inner circle" of science writers that the author wished to study. Table 1 provides names of all persons on that final list. The author then included in the sample *all* persons on the list who indicated they intended to cover the 1977 AAAS annual meeting, the event around which the study was designed. Of the 28 names on the list, 17 ultimately were included in the study.

4. This term originally was used by Timothy Crouse to describe the social network established among national political reporters who were covering presidential candidates during the 1972 U.S. election. His book, *The Boys on the Bus* (New York: Ballantine Books, 1973), provides a number of accounts of behaviors that closely parallel what I observed among the science writing inner club.

5. Socialization across media organizations, the situation described here, is not common in journalism. Studies such as the classical one by Warren Breed ["Social Control in the Newsroom," 33 *Social Forces* (May 1955): 326–335] have consistently found that journalists become socialized to peers *within* their own newsrooms. The exceptions to the rule seem to be specialty reporters, who establish relationships with similar reporters from other news organizations. Descriptions of this specialist phenomenon are provided by Jeremy Tunstall, *Journalists at Work* (London: Constable, 1971) and by Steve Chibnall, *Law-and-Order News* (London: Tavistock Publications Limited, 1977).

6. This percentage represents a high level of autonomy when compared to editorial personnel in general. A national study of American journalists by Johnstone, Slawski and Bowman titled *The News People* (Urbana: University of Illinois Press, 1976) found that only 46.2% of the respondents were able to make any of their own story assignments independently of their editors. In large media

organizations with more than 100 editorial employees, where science writers are likely to be employed, the percentage drops to 36.2.

7. Additional data gathered for this study corroborated this argument. A total of 88 mass media print journalists covered the 1977 AAAS meeting. Of that group, 14 were inner club members. Although the inner club constituted only 16% of all reporters, the group accounted for 56% of the 772 newspaper and news magazine stories published throughout the country in ensuing weeks. When coverage by the two local (Denver) newspapers was eliminated from the analysis, the percentage of stories attributable to inner club members increased to 64% (n = 583).

8. It should be emphasized that the AAAS meeting was selected primarily because it is a setting that *predictably* attracts the inner club each year. The meeting is sufficiently different from other scientific meetings to make one cautious about generalizing the study results to them, but the number of science stories generated by the AAAS meeting alone is sufficient to warrant examination of the event. And subsequent discussions of the study findings with science writers involved in this research have elicited numerous acknowledgments that behaviors observed at the AAAS meeting parallel those that take place when the inner club gathers to cover other events as well. I would like to thank the AAAS and particularly Arthur Herschman, head of the meetings and publications division, and Carol Rogers, public information officer, for their cooperation with the study.

9. Data were gathered at the 1977 AAAS meeting in Denver through the use of four trained observers who were stationed at points throughout the press area of the meeting. Additionally, the author has subsequently gathered further observational data at both the 1978 Washington and 1979 Houston meetings.

10. Observation of the inner club at several AAAS meetings indicates that the kinds of information sharing discussed here take place primarily among members. The informal network is based on close personal ties that have developed over time and, like anyone, an inner club member will interact most with his or her friends. Members will certainly provide information to non-members when asked, but they will rarely initiate communication with journalists outside the network. This means that reporters who are new to science writing, who perhaps need more help with information than anyone, are often the most isolated at these meetings.

11. Don Kirkman of Scripps-Howard, for example, developed an interest in weather from several years as a weather observer for both the U.S. Navy and the U.S. Weather Bureau. Al Rossiter of UPI majored in geology as an undergraduate and even spent a year in graduate school taking geology courses before turning to journalism.

12. Among these journalists are Ira Flatow, science reporter for National Public Radio in Washington, D.C.; Cristine Russell, science-medicine reporter for *The Washington Star*; Jon Franklin, science writer for the *Baltimore Evening Sun*; Bob Gillette, science writer for the *Los Angeles Times*; and David Salisbury, science writer for the *Christian Science Monitor*.

National broadcast coverage has received considerable research attention in recent years, but very little published work looks at TV reporting of state and local politics. David H. Ostroff studied television coverage of the 1978 gubernatorial race in Ohio, an important Midwestern industrial state. Based in the capitol city of Columbus, Ostroff used participant observation, interviews, and case study materials to analyze the contest between incumbent James Rhoades and challenger Richard C. Celeste. Ostroff concludes that the three Columbus TV stations were highly selective in their coverage, consciously resisted being "used" by pseudoevents, and were skeptical of the incumbent's attempts to use official activities as campaign events. The stations gave the challenger more coverage than the incumbent, primarily because Mr. Celeste waged a more personal, Columbus-oriented campaign. The stations used their own productions more frequently than wire service coverage, largely because of the need for visuals. However, Ostroff sees much less reliance on visuals than in TV coverage of national politics.

21

A PARTICIPANT-OBSERVER STUDY OF
TV CAMPAIGN COVERAGE

David H. Ostroff

Coverage of gubernatorial campaign relatively light partly because TV news persons were skeptical of news value of many campaign events.

▶ The viewer of television network news generally receives a continuous report about presidential election campaigns. Each night's newscasts include descriptions, and usually film or videotape, of the candidates' activities of the day, no matter how trivial or similar to previous activities. As two observers have noted, the networks:

devote most of their election coverage to the trivia of political campaigning that make for flashy pictures. Hecklers, crowds, motorcades, balloons, rallies, and gossip—these are the regular subjects of network campaign stories.[1]

As important and pervasive as network television coverage of presidential campaigns may be, there is no evidence that local television news coverage of non-presidential campaigns is comparable. This study represents an effort to explore systematically the question of how local television news organizations go about the task of covering local campaigns, particularly a gubernatorial campaign. It seeks to determine what information viewers in one area, Columbus, Ohio, received about the campaign from television, and why the news organizations behaved as they did.

There is considerable evidence television news is an important factor in political campaigns:

In modern politics, rallies are merely a device to get the candidate good television coverage. At virtually all political rallies today, the candidate is not talking to the people in front of him, but to the people he hopes will see him on television.[2]

One observer reports that in the 1976 presidential campaign "getting the candidate on the network evening news was the *sine qua non* of each day's plan; everything else revolved around that objective."[3]

There have been numerous analyses of different aspects of television news coverage of political campaigns.[4] As noted, however, the focus of scholarly research has been upon network television and presidential campaigns. Literature about other types of television news organizations and

[1] Thomas E. Patterson and Robert D. McClure, *The Unseeing Eye: The Myth of Television Power in National Elections* (New York: G.P. Putnam's Sons, 1976), p. 22.

[2] David Lee Rosenbloom, *The Election Men: Professional Campaign Managers and American Democracy* (New York: Quadrangle Books, 1973), p. 14.

[3] Jules Witcover, *Marathon: The Pursuit of the Presidency 1972-1976* (New York: The Viking Press, 1977), p. 15.

[4] An extensive summary of these studies can be found in Sidney Kraus and Dennis Davis, *The Effects of Mass Communication on Political Behavior* (University Park: The Pennsylvania State University Press, 1976). More recent studies include F. Christopher Arterton, "Campaign Organizations Confront the Media-Political Environment," in *Race for the Presidency: The Media and the Nominating Process*, ed. James David Barber (Englewood Cliffs, N.J.: Prentice-Hall, Inc., 1978), pp. 3-25; William E. Bicker, "Network Television News and the 1976 Presidential Primaries: A Look from the Networks' Side of the Camera," in Barber, *Race for the Presidency*, pp. 79-110; C. Richard Hofstetter and Cliff Zukin, "TV Network News and Advertising in the Nixon and McGovern Campaigns," JOURNALISM QUARTERLY, 56:106-115, 152 (Spring 1979); and Wenmouth Williams, Jr., and William D. Semlak, "Structural Effects of TV Coverage on Political Agendas," *Journal of Communication*, 28:114-19 (Autumn 1978).

▶ The author is on the speech communication faculty at Bowling Green State University. This article is based on his dissertation at Ohio University under the direction of Dr. Charles Clift III.

From David H. Ostroff, "A Participant-Observer Study of TV Campaign Coverage," *Journalism Quarterly* (Autumn 1980) 415-419. Reprinted by permission.

coverage of non-presidential campaigns is limited.[5]

Methodology

This study focuses upon the news coverage of the 1978 Ohio election campaigns by the three commercial television stations in Columbus. Particular attention was devoted to the campaign activities of the Democratic gubernatorial candidate, Lt. Gov. Richard C. Celeste. Celeste was defeated by the incumbent governor, Republican James A. Rhodes.[6]

The primary method of data collection was participant-observation, "a manner of conducting a scientific investigation wherein the observer maintains a face-to-face involvement with the members of a particular social setting for purposes of scientific inquiry."[7] The researcher attended campaign activities independently, and with Columbus television news crews; closely observed the activities and practices within the newsroom of one of the stations prior to, during, and after the campaign period; and conducted interviews with members of the campaign staffs of the two major gubernatorial candidates, and with the news directors, producers, reporters and photographers of the three stations.

Case studies were made of news organization behavior surrounding particular gubernatorial campaign events. The researcher attended the events and conducted interviews with important participants from the news organizations and campaign organizations. Videotapes and/or scripts of the news stories presented on the respective news programs enabled the researcher to compare the news stories with his own impressions of the event and the treatments of the event by the different television news organizations, and to seek the reactions and comments of participants. In cases where one or more stations decided not to cover an event, reasons for such decisions were probed.

Finally, to provide a context for the observations, the researcher briefly enumerated and classified all of the campaign news stories presented by the three stations in the early evening and 11 p.m. weeknight newscasts during the period from Oct. 2 to

election day.[8] The bases for these data were the scripts of the newscasts kept on file by the stations.

Results

Amount of Coverage. Judged by the amount of air time and the number of stories devoted to all candidates and issues during the 1978 campaign by the Columbus stations, television did not provide a large quantity of information (see Table 1). The amount of time devoted to election activities by the television stations is further qualified by the fact many of the stories presented in the 11 p.m. newscasts were repeats—often abridged—from the newscasts of the early evening.[9]

Many local races or issues were of interest only to portions of the audience. However, as Table 2 indicates, even stories about the governor's race received relatively little air time. In the case of WTVN and WBNS, a large proportion of the time can be attributed to a single story. Each station produced on "campaign report" about the governor's race, which summarized the personalities and major issues of the campaign. WTVN's story lasted two minutes and 55 seconds, and was shown in both the 5:30 p.m. and 11 p.m. newscasts; WBNS presented its three minute and 20

[5] Virtually the only studies touching upon the subject have been Gene Wyckoff, *The Image Candidates* (New York: The MacMillan Company, 1968); Leonard Tipton, Roger D. Haney, and John R. Basehart, "Media Agenda-Setting in City and State Elections," JOURNALISM QUARTERLY, 52:15-22 (Spring 1975); and Robert George Finney, "Television News Messages and their Perceived Effects in a Congressional Election Campaign," (Ph.D. dissertation, Ohio State University, 1971).

[6] Although the Democrats maintained control of both houses of the legislature, and swept the other statewide offices, Rhodes received 1,393,627 votes to 1,345,151 votes for Celeste; three minor party candidates polled a total of 90,390 votes. Rhodes campaigned on his ability to bring new industry and jobs to the state; and on Celeste's supposed lack of administrative experience. Celeste's campaign was built around three issues: the need for more jobs in Ohio; the need for lower utility rates; and the need to shift educational financing from local property taxes to state sources such as income and sales taxes. This last issue dominated the campaign.

[7] J.M. Johnson, *Doing Field Research* (New York: Free Press, 1975), pp. ix-x.

[8] WTVN presented 30-minute programs at 5:30 p.m. and 11 p.m.; WCMH at 6 p.m. and 11 p.m.; and WBNS at 6 p.m., 7 p.m., and 11 p.m.

[9] Repeating stories is not necessarily a negative practice. It allows viewers who might have missed the earlier newscast to be exposed to the information; further, the viewer seeing a story a second time might be more likely to learn the information because of the repeated exposure.

TABLE 1

Total Stories and Time Devoted
to Campaign Activities

Station	Number of Stories	Minutes
WTVN		
5:30	26	30:00
11	26	36:10
WCMH		
6	39	33:02
11	26	18:37
WBNS		
6	34	45:35
7	23	42:55
11	18	12:45

TABLE 2

Time and Stories Devoted
to the Governor's Campaign

Station	Number of Stories	Minutes
WTVN		
5:30	Rhodes 3	1:45
	Celeste 5	3:05
	Others 1	:20
11	Rhodes 2	2:28
	Celeste 3	4:27
WCMH		
6	Rhodes 10	4:00
	Celeste 8	3:52
11	Rhodes 6	1:50
	Celeste 8	4:12
WBNS		
6	Rhodes 5	4:15
	Celeste 6	6:00
7	Rhodes 1	1:30
	Celeste 5	6:05
11	Rhodes 5	4:00
	Celeste 6	3:05

The Rhodes and Celeste totals include that candidate's proportion of the time devoted to him in the "campaign report" stories presented by WTVN and WBNS.

[10] Not all of the "official duty" stories were necessarily favorable to Rhodes's campaign. For example, on the Friday before the election state employees received a letter with their paychecks describing likely pay increases under a new Rhodes administration. All three Columbus stations telecast stories about complaints from the employees' union that the letters represented an illegal campaign activity on the part of the governor.

TABLE 3

Time and Stories Devoted to
Rhodes' Official Duties

Station	Number of Stories	Minutes
WTVN		
5:30	5	2:35
11	1	:15
WCMH		
6	2	:30
11	4	:58
WBNS		
6	1	:50
7	0	
11	1	:45

second "campaign report" in only one newscast.

Celeste conducted a more active personal campaign than did Rhodes, especially in the Columbus area; this probably explains why the Democrat received greater air time than did his opponent. Rhode's campaign staff felt confident he would carry the Columbus area, so the governor concentrated his personal efforts in other sections of the state.

Of course, as an incumbent Rhodes might have been expected to use his office to "make news." However, the Colmbus television news personnel indicated they tried to exercise care to avoid covering the Governor's "official activities" which seemed to have been undertaken primarily to score campaign points. As Table 3 indicates, the total time devoted to stories about Rhodes's official duties was just over five minutes.[10]

Campaign News Gathering and Reporting. Counting and classifying news stories does not provide a complete picture of how the television news organizations reported the campaigns. Observation and interviews provided further information.

The data point to some differences between the behavior of the local television news organizations and that which has been reported about the networks' coverage of presidential campaigns. The most striking was the selectivity of coverage provided by the Columbus stations, a behavior the news persons attributed to a sensitivity to being "used" by political candidates.

The news persons believed that while they had a responsibility to inform their viewers about the campaigns, most of the candidates' activities were designed to achieve campaign goals, rather than to enlighten the public. One reporter who regularly covered the gubernatorial campaign sometimes expressed distaste at being assigned to some events; she said if the candidates wanted to "advertise" themselves, "let them buy the time."

Interviews with news and campaign personnel provided an impression of a highly competitive "struggle" for the advantage in determining the content of political campaign news stories. The executive producer of one television news organization commented about publications describing manipulation of the news media by candidates: "I don't believe the candidates are as successful as they once were. After all, we've read those books, too."

Illustrating the efforts by the news organizations to maintain, or regain, control over the campaign news content, one station's coverage of the campaign consisted primarily of two to three minute summaries, or "campaign reports." Only one "campaign report" was presented about each of the major state and local races, and about the two statewide ballot issues.

The "campaign reports" were presented in WTVN's 5:30 p.m. newscast, and repeated at 11 p.m. Only the reporter's voice was used in the audio portion; according to the news director the candidates did not explain their own issue positions because such interviews "take up too much air time, but provide little useful information." Thus, the television news organization felt it was better able to use the medium to explain matters to the audience than would the candidates.[11]

In some instances the news organizations made concerted efforts to avoid being "manipulated." An illustration is provided by news organization behavior in response

to a "Get Out the Vote" rally sponsored by a Columbus black political organization. The television reporters concentrated their attention, and their stories, on the "guest of honor," U.N. Ambassador Andrew Young; the television reporters ignored gubernatorial candidate Richard Celeste, who spoke to the rally, and other candidates who attended. As one television reporter explained, even before the start of the rally, "We're just here to cover Andrew Young. We won't mention the candidates; we're not going to play into their hands."

In another instance, a local candidate scheduled a news conference at which he would be endorsed by a national political figure visiting Columbus. In assigning a reporter to cover the news conference, a news executive at one station told him to concentrate his questions on the political aspirations of the national newsmaker. The story which was eventually prepared about the news conference did not mention the local candidate, who was, indeed, endorsed by the visiting politician.

Contributing to the selectivity exercised by the news organizations was the fact their personnel gathered most of the stories used in the newscasts; with a limited number of crews available assignment editors and producers were careful in choosing the stories to which reporters would be assigned.[12] Unlike the networks, the Columbus television news organizations could not, or would not, afford the luxury of permanently assigning reporters to election coverage in general, or to individual races or candidates. Thus, most of the stories telecast about the campaign took place in the Columbus area.

The primary reason the Columbus news organizations gave for using stories gathered by their own personnel, rather than by the wire services, was a desire to include film or videotape accompaniment

---

[11] The reports, in fact, seemed to be an effective use of television for "instructional" purposes. In addition to the narration and normal videotaped visual accompaniment, visual reinforcement for the reporter's comments was provided in the form of information about the particular race printed on the screen; the information was inserted electronically with a device called a "vidifont."

[12] The smallest news organization had five crews available during weekdays, the largest about a dozen. Fewer crews were available at nights and on weekends.

to the stories.[13] However, contrary to the literature, "exciting" visual media events did not guarantee coverage of campaign activities; similarly, the absence of visual material did not preclude the presentation of campaign stories on the Columbus television news programs.

Of course, the news crews attempted to find visual material to illustrate their stories. However, editors and producers gave greater weight to the importance of the information contained in a story when determining whether or not to use it in a newscast. An example is provided by the news organizations' behavior in covering a news conference conducted jointly by Richard Celeste and the Democratic candidate for secretary of state.

The theme of the news conference was the need for "new" blood in Ohio's statewide offices. The Democratic candidates pointed out their opponents had first sought statewide office in the 1950's, and noted the many changes in the world since that time. As a visual backdrop to the news conference the campaign organizations constructed a large billboard using electronically reproduced newspaper headlines from the 1950s to the present. Although the reproductions were not dark enough to provide usable television pictures, two of the Columbus stations telecast stories about the news conference. The third station sent a reporter, but she decided not to prepare a story: in her judgment neither candidate "said anything newsworthy."

One type of "media event" was almost guaranteed to attract the Columbus television news crews: the appearance by a bona fide national newsmaker at a campaign activity. Both major political parties made use of such people to attract television coverage to campaigns. For example, a Democratic rally featuring Rosalyn Carter received extensive air time on all three stations; an appearance by Gerald Ford at a Republican fundraiser received similar attention by the television news organizations. However, while some local candi-

dates received television news exposure because of these appearances, the news organizations often ignored the local candidates entirely.

Discussion

This study provides evidence of differences between the news coverage of nonpresidential campaigns by local television stations, and network coverage of presidential campaigns. The most striking differences were the selectivity of coverage by the stations, and the cautious, almost cynical, attitude of the television news personnel towards the "news value" of most campaign activities.

These attitudes are probably a reaction to the reputed success of "media events" conducted in recent years. A successful media event implies that the news organizations are being manipulated, and have lost their control over the content of written and broadcast news stories. During the 1978 campaign the Columbus television news organizations were apparently acting in ways designed to regain control.

For the electorate and the candidates, however, the selective, relatively sparse coverage provided by local television news organizations has potentially negative consequences. The local candidates may be unable to gain access to the electorate, much of which, we are told, looks to television as its most important source of news. Therefore, the candidate may be increasingly forced to purchase access to the voter via advertising, direct mail, and similar means.

On a more positive note, the evidence presented here suggests television news organizations may be seeking to cover campaign activities which contain elements of substance, rather than simply containing "balloons and parades." The unanswered question about this behavior is whether campaign organizations will accede to this "requirement," and provide more useful information to the public, or whether they will increase their access to the television news audience through more imaginative "packaging" of their campaign activities.

[13] The executive producer of one news organization said he *always* tried to have film or videotape. "After all," he explained, "we call our program 'Action News.'"

Team observation and interviews are used in this research on a Western local television station newsroom in 1977. The authors admit their use of the analogy of the factory is strained, but conclude that television newswork at the Western station lacked flexibility and personal investment in the news product, and fostered an evaluation of news in productivity terms and a mismatch between expectations of news workers and supervisors. The authors studied the station at a time of considerable organizational tension, which makes their results especially tenuous. However, their observations are consistent with the news routinization hypothesis of many sociologists who have looked at isolated newsrooms. Charles R. Bantz is assistant professor of speech-communication at the University of Minnesota. Suzanne McCorkle is assistant professor of communication at Boise State University. Roberta C. Baade is an assistant professor at Pepperdine College.

22

THE NEWS FACTORY

Charles R. Bantz, Suzanne McCorkle, and Robert C. Baade

In the winter and spring of 1977, a research team of three members with diverse backgrounds spent 14 weeks observing a western metropolis television newsroom.[1] After utilizing methods of participant-observation research,[2] we were able to synthesize the team's various experience and observations into several characterizations of a television news organization's communicative environment. This essay includes a historic overview of factors that constrain the typical *local* television news organization and a descrip-

---

AUTHORS' NOTE: An earlier version of this article was presented at the meeting of the Western Speech Communication Association, Los Angeles, February 1979. Steven Chaffee's comments on that occasion and those of anonymous Communication Research *reviewer were essential to our revision of this article.*

tive characterization of the organizational nature of WEST-TV news.[3]

THE ROUTINIZATION OF NEWSWORK: AN OVERVIEW

While the popular conceptions of television news usually encompass some image of the glamorous on-the-air news personality, television has an underlying structure little different from any other organization that markets a product (see Hirsch, 1977). Like other organizations, television news is affected by a myriad of historic, technological, and "chance" factors that constrain the realm of possibilities within the organization.

We believe, as do others, the world of television news contains organizational and environmental pressures that have fostered a trend toward the "routinization" of newswork (see Altheide and Rasmussen, 1976; Tuchman, 1973a, 1977; see also Perrow, 1967). At WEST and other news organizations, five factors appear to have encouraged newswork routinization: (1) the nature of news staffs, (2) technological developments, (3) the impact of news consultants, (4) considerations of profit, and (5) constraints on the organization's product. Each of these factors has received considerable comment from observers of local television news. Here we demonstrate how these interdependent factors have combined to circumscribe the independent activity of reporters and photographers.

THE NEWS STAFF

A principal characteristic of television news staffs is their mobility. Broadcast journalists change jobs throughout their careers, holding more jobs and receiving more job offers than print journalists (Johnstone et al. 1976). When these changes involve on-the-air talent, the moves are as visible as they are frequent.[4] A pattern of continuous personnel turnover compounds the need for news organizations to develop uniform structures and routine methods of work to facilitate the assimilation of new staff persons into working "team" members.

In recent years, news departments have experienced an increase in size (Barrett, 1978) and supervisory and managerial positions. The emergence of the producer on most television news staffs is the most visible example of a new supervisory position. As the title suggests, the "producer's" speciality is the presentation or appearance of the news show. In the early days of television news, the news director or anchorperson was responsible for overseeing the newscast. Gradually, the position of producer was adopted in many local operations. As supervision of the newscast was assigned to a producer, other organizational members also shifted into more specialized roles. For example, in some news organizations, the anchorperson now has little responsibility in preparing or coordinating the news show, often becoming a "talent" specialist whose job is to read copy. Similarly, the news director often became more of an administrator—hiring personnel, setting policy, and managing budgets. In Boulding's (1953) terms, local television news organizations have undergone not only simple growth (more personnel) but also structural growth (with more supervisory personnel and more specialized tasks for other personnel). The structural growth produces more specialized responsibility for the newscast, personnel, budgets, presentation, and so forth, producing greater control and routinization of the news organization.

TECHNOLOGY

As in all organizations, the development of technology altered the nature of news departments (Thompson, 1967; Tuchman, 1972, 1973b). In television news, the most important recent technological developments are portable video equipment and the subsequent introduction of microwave relays.

Traditionally, news programs used film in their productions. Film, however, takes time to photograph, process, and edit; and the cost of film constitutes a substantial expense for the organization.

The emergent video technology—portable video cameras and videotape machines—offered news departments faster production (instant playback capabilities) and lower expense (reusability of tape). One can, in theory, quickly edit the tape and be ready to broadcast. However, tape has limitations that encourage the organization to restrict its use. The equipment is more complex than film and requires constant maintenance. On an even more basic level, the effective use of video equipment in the field may require the presence of an additional person to carry the videotape recorder. In the absence of the extra person, the reporter and photographer must cope with the problems involved in physical manipulation of too much equipment. Unless the reporter helps carry the equipment, the team does not have the physical mobility to attain the desired visuals; if the reporter helps, he/she is inhibited in covering the story. Finally, the editing of videotape is time-consuming and requires an expensive editing machine. Hence, there are few machines and a great demand for them. Technology has increased the need for role specialists and coordinative activities in the newsroom. If this need is not met, long delays can result as equipment breaks down, tape does not get edited, and ultimately the news show is affected adversely.

The most recent technological development in television news, microwave transmission, has brought live, on-the-spot reporting into reality. However, new technology introduces new constraints. The skill and planning required for effective, quality broadcast are immense. The technical limitations of microwave's line-of-sight transmission means the crew, including a new specialist in microwave technology, must locate the equipment to avoid buildings and mountains. Further, many stations have only one microwave unit, so its use is planned carefully to maximize its value to the news department.[5] The microwave technology represents a financial investment that necessitates scheduling and planning to maximize the everyday use of the equipment. Unfortunately, rigid scheduling minimizes the equipment's availability for "instant coverage." Thus, economic and scheduling factors may constrain the organization's ability to meet its goals.

CONSULTANTS

One of the most debated trends in local television news programs is the use of news consultants (see Powers, 1977; Whitehead, 1978). The pervasive impact of consultants, such as Frank Magid Associates or McHugh Hoffman, was reflected in the claim (made by a WEST-TV staff member) that one could identify a station's consulting firm simply by watching the newscast. For example, KSTP in Minneapolis-St. Paul and KOA in Denver have shared a visual style promoted by Magid, while KMGH in Denver and WCCO in Minneapolis-St. Paul have shared a style promoted by McHugh Hoffman. Overlooked in comments about visual style, however, are the organizational consequences of consultant recommendations, e.g., encouraging stories of certain lengths or certain numbers of stories per newscast, stressing highly visual newscasts and/or promoting reporter "involvement" in stories (Diamond, 1975; Eden, 1977). We observed an operative rule that news stories ran from 75 to 105 seconds. Not surprisingly, the activities or reporters and photographers produced only enough film and copy to fill that time. The system offered little reason to invest time and film in developing a longer story, as it would have a minimal chance of being aired. The only exceptions we observed were commissioned stories that would be split into several segments broadcast on different days, lead stories, and some feature stories. Whether the time limits had been set by consultant suggestion or were the by-products of other constraints (time and money), the effect at WEST was a functional law limiting the length of most stories.

Consultants almost uniformly have urged the use of more visuals in news (Diamond, 1975; Eden, 1977; Powers,

1977). Newsworkers are expected to provide usable film/ tape for virtually every story. At WEST, a lack of "appropriate" visuals often meant an assigned story was no longer desirable and was dropped from the show. Hence, newsworkers avoided any story without good visuals and/or invested a substantial amount of time pondering how to "visualize" a story (see Altheide, 1976; Crouse, 1974).

Finally, consultants also have played a role in the high mobility of news personnel by facilitating movement of newsworkers among stations. Carmody's (1977) and our observations indicate consultants will provide their clients with videotapes of newsworkers, enabling the client to view a wide range of potential employees quickly and easily.

PROFIT

In the not-too-distant past, local television stations treated their news operations as a necessary evil—necessary to demonstrate the station was serving the public as required by law, evil because news cost money and returned little profit. Today, local news programs are an integral part of the profit making of stations (Altheide, 1976; Diamond, 1975). As a result, upper management in most stations takes a strong interest in the news programs' ratings, sales, format, and talent.[6] At WEST, the level of management involvement was indicated by the fact the news consultants reported to the station's manager.

PRODUCT

The demands of profit, consultants, producers, and technology combine to constrain the type of product a news organization produces. The emphasis is on technically uniform, visually sophisticated, easy to understand, fast-paced, people-oriented stories that are produced in a minimum amount of time (see Rosenfield et al., 1976). These requirements mean the organization depends on a well-defined task structure, role specialization, speed, interchangeability of personnel, and commonly held conceptions of what the product should be.[7]

The manner in which news staffs, technology, consultants, and profit combine within an organization to yield a uniform product suggests functionalism's principle of equifinality may be in operation (see Stinchcombe, 1968). These factors and the description developed below reflect an organization structuring itself to yield a uniform product in the face of variable events, resources, and time. The attempt to routinize newswork is an attempt to regulate organizational activity so the organization not only meets the deadline but also produces a news show that the organization defines (with the help of consultants and ratings) as *good*.

WEST AS A TELEVISION NEWS FACTORY

The constraints described above are common to most local television news organizations, but are significant in their synergistic operation—as they build to increase routinization. In this section we present a characterization of how organizational constraints manifested themselves at WEST. We argue that, descriptively, a *factory model*[8] is a heuristic metaphor for how work was accomplished within WEST's television news department. Before that description, however, several cautions are necessary.

First, the generalizability of our observations may be limited. While WEST typified the national trends discussed above, a high level of organizational and interpersonal conflict may make it atypical of local news departments and our case study approach lacks the comparative data necessary to judge impact of the conflict on our observations. Second, the present study is not a long-term longitudinal study, thus precluding us from reporting historical developments. The reader should note, therefore, any claims presented below about historical developments reflect the *perceptions of the newsworkers*, not the researcher's long-term observations. Third, our use of the factory model in the discussion below is analogical, rather than literal. As an analogy, we feel the factory model provides insight into television news organizations that is obscured from other viewpoints.

THE NEWS FACTORY MODEL

The factory metaphor for the newsroom is not a precise duplication of the traditional factory.[9] It follows the form of an assembly line factory—breaking tasks into smaller "chunks" but it has the chunks being performed by newsworkers with varying degrees of skill who employ complex technology. The news factory divides tasks into larger pieces (hence "chunks") and for different reasons than a typical assembly line does. The size of the piece is related directly to the skill of the worker, rather than the amount of time necessary to perform the task (an auto assembly line may break tasks into one-minute pieces so the line can produce 60 autos per hour). A reporter, who is experienced and/or educated, has a larger chunk of the process than does a film editor.[10] Therefore, the news factory is a mixed assembly line, with varying amounts of responsibilities among employees.

WEST's news department is modeled as an assembly line in Figure 1. The elements of a newscast segment[11] flow through the factory, being processed step by step, with the amount of processing related to the complexity of each segment. The systematic flow of the elements through the assembly line leading to a newscast consists of five steps: story ideation, task assignment, gathering and structuring materials, assembling materials, and presenting the newscast. The operation of the news factory model is best explained by detailing each step in the assembly line.[12]

Step One: Story Ideation

Enacting story ideas, the first step in the assembly line at WEST, involved two related activities.[13] First, individual newsworkers assessed the information flowing into the

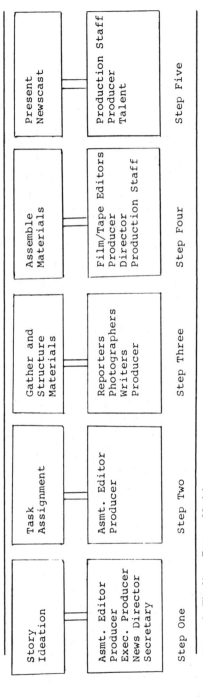

Figure 1: The News Factory Model

newsroom from various sources: press releases, general mail, newspapers, magazines, reporter ideas, police-fire-FBI radios, wire services, phone calls, and so on. The principal person performing this assesment was the assignment editor who received the bulk of information (see Kasindorf, 1972). At WEST, however, the producer took major responsibility for the wire service stories and on some occasions other newsworkers (e.g., news director, executive producer, or secretary) evaluated the information. The assessment involved rapid processing of information and enactment of those items deemed potential stories. Such items were either filed for future reference or prepared for immediate news factory processing.

Second, story ideas were enacted collectively in the daily story meeting, which functioned in conjunction with the individual assessment of information described above. At this daily meeting, the assignment person, news director, early evening producer, and executive producer discussed a variety of topics, but directed most of their attention to that day's early evening newscast. The assignment editor usually had a list of assignments sketched out by the meeting time; the list formed the basis of the discussions. The story meeting functioned to modify, expand, and approve the tentative plan of assignments for the day. It is notable that the story meeting, while open to reporters and photographers, functioned as a meeting of management and supervisors to approve the day's work schedule.[14] The meeting narrowed the range of news inputs by committing the bulk of reporters' time, thus limiting their ability to generate additional items, and by emphasizing the ideation of a few individuals who enacted story concepts from a limited range of sources (see Tuchman, 1978).

Step Two: Task Assignment

Immediately after the story meeting, the assignment editor began his or her supervisory function, assigning tasks to the newsworkers as they arrived in the newsroom. The tasks often were assigned directly, with the assignment person informing (sometimes by two-way radio) the personnel involved of their duties. In addition, the assignment editor usually wrote the schedule of assignments on a large wallboard listing the story by title, reporter, photographer, completion time, type of equipment, and type of segment required. Like the "big board" in manufacturing plants, the story board functioned to inform personnel of their tasks for that day. As reporters and photographers moved in and out of the newsroom, they checked the board to monitor their duties and to evaluate the newsday. In a smoothly functioning television news factory, reporters and photographers would flow into the newsroom, receive a story assignment, move quickly to complete the task, and be ready for reassignment.

Some task assignments were made by the producers who would either ask a writer to rewrite wire copy for broadcast or assign the task to themselves. Similarly, the producers would often assign themselves the task of selecting items from the network's morning or afternoon news feeds and write any copy necessary for the items.

Step Three: Gather and Structure Materials

Once a story was assigned, the newsworkers set out to gather and almost simultaneously structure the materials into a story. We observed, as have others, an interdependence of the gathering and structuring processes (gathering and structuring may occur simultaneously or either process may precede the other), which is why we join them here (see Altheide, 1976; Epstein, 1973; Roshco, 1975; Tuchman, 1972, 1973b).

In its most simplistic form, this involved nothing more than taking a wire story, writing it for the newscast, and requesting appropriate available visuals. More often, however, this process involved five related tasks: (1) obtaining any information the assigner had (news release, newspaper clippings), (2) talking to someone on the phone or in person,

(3) going somewhere to gather material, (4) shooting film/ tape, and (5) writing copy.

Although the reporters and photographers often worked together during this process, each person also performed specialized tasks. Reporters sought information, wrote material to read, and coordinated the field work. Photographers had a creative technical task requiring specific skills —an ability to handle equipment and a good visual sense— combined with frugality. Reporter and photographer worked together but the different skills and differing levels of power and authority meant their rolls were clearly differentiated.[15] The division of labor was most pronounced when a photographer was sent into the field to shoot film/tape on order— "get 30 seconds of air pollution"—while the reporter or writer remained in the newsroom to write the story.

The structuring of materials was formalized in the "shot sheet," which informed the film/tape editor what parts of the film/tape should be selected, what sound elements should be used, and in what order they should be assembled. The vast majority of times this sheet was made out before the reporter even saw the processed film or the videotape. Questions about the length of a segment were sometimes raised as the shot sheet was prepared; however, the manner in which the materials were gathered would have prohibited structuring a long (e.g., five-minute) segment, even if the producer desired one.

Step Four: Assemble Materials

The assembly of materials involved two activities: constructing individual segments and assembling the segments into the newscast. While the two activities are to some extent sequential, a segment's assembly is affected by and affects the show's assembly.

The assembly of a segment was performed by a film/tape editor who edited the film/tape according to the instructions on the shot sheet. If the editor saw alternative modes for editing the film/tape, he or she could have altered the sequences, sometimes with or sometimes without the reporters knowledge. The assembly of a segment was a technical operation, which could be time-consuming—particularly when editing tape.

The assembly process brought together the various elements of a newscast (except the newscasters) and prepared them for use during the program. The producer and director oversaw the assembly process, spending the last hour before airtime going over the script, adjusting times, and planning while the other newsworkers completed their own work.

Step Five: Present Newscast

Shortly before airtime, the parts of the newscast—script, film, tape—were turned over to the production staff, who were responsible for the broadcast itself. The production staff performed the technical coordination of the visual and oral elements during the newscast.

The producer remained involved with the news product throughout the telecast. He or she oversaw the progress of the program—watching the time, dropping stories if necessary, informing the newscasters of any new information. News personnel were involved in the production by reading copy and presenting the weather and sports.

THE ASSEMBLY LINE

While there are links between these five steps and some personnel are involved in several stages, a newscast is nonetheless a product of a series of activities that are performed separately. The idea for a segment seldom came from a reporter or photographer (except in the rare case when a reporter or photographer was assigned a permanent beat). Idea selection at WEST occurred at higher levels in the organization: news director, executive producer, producer and assignment editors.

The assignment editor had the most direct influence on story ideation and was the supervisor of the newsroom, with the assignment desk being the focal spot in the flow of information to the reporters and photographers. The assignment editor's work was circumscribed, however, once an assignment was made.

Reporter responsibilities were to gather and structure materials, with occasional responsibility for assembly and presentation. The regular on-the-air talent for the weekday evening newscast were not active reporters. The photographers' principal responsibilities were gathering materials, but they also often functioned as film/tape editors. The film/tape editors assembled stories, with little or no feedback to the reporter, and had no role in any other processes. The news writers wrote copy and often filled other roles in the organization where they performed additional tasks (e.g., noon producer, assistant producer, editorial writer).

Of all the members of the organization, the producer was most likely to be found performing tasks in each step. The producer was an active supervisor, who coordinated the flow of segments and structured the entire show. The producer worked within the constraints of time, visuals available, segments prepared, show format, newsworkers availability, and technical limitations to prepare a show that met product requirements. The division of labor was pronounced and likely would have been even more pronounced if WEST was a union shop, with contracts limiting movement across job descriptions.

The only persons immediately responsible for the entire product—the newscast—were the producer and director—the former for the content and the latter for the coordination of the technical elements. Thus the reporter, who from the outside is often seen as the central figure in news organizations, was responsible—at best—for a segment or two in the telecast and those segments could be altered or dropped completely without the reporter's knowledge. While the reporter had freedom to leave the place of work (unlike a typical factory worker) and some ability to identify his or her contribution to the company's product, the broadcast reporter had no lasting control over his or her own work and no control whatsoever over the remainder of the newscast

(Argyris, 1974, discusses the former problem in print organizations). Despite arguments for newsworkers' professionalism, the task distribution of the television news organization we observed shared more characteristics of a factory
than it did the characteristics of a professional organization
(see Tuchman 1978; Tunstall, 1971; Ritzer, 1977).

ORGANIZATIONAL CONSEQUENCES OF FACTORY NEWS

The development of a factory news model, with its assembly line approach, in conjunction with the trends toward
routinization appear to have at least four organizational
consequences: (1) the news factory lacks flexibility, (2) there
is a lack of personal investment in the news product, (3)
newswork becomes evaluated in productivity terms, and (4)
goal incongruence emerges between newsworkers' job expectations and job reality. Significantly, throughout our
observations, newsworkers negatively characterized specific instances of these consequences.

Lack of Flexibility

Scene 1. It is 2:30 in the afternoon. One of the two videotape editing machines is not working. There are 15 videotape segments to be edited before the evening telecast. One
segment has been waiting to be edited since 12:30. An argument ensues about the impossibility of editing all 15 segments by newstime. Several stories are dropped. Several
tape segments are modified and partially edited. During the
newscast the director improvises as some tapes are incomplete. After the show the producer sarcastically comments:
"Isn't television exciting?" A meeting about the problem
produces a suggestion that editing time be scheduled.
Scene 2. A mild snowstorm turns into a major blizzard.
Both the assignment editor and news secretary leave early
to beat the blizzard home, creating a gap in the normal flow
of information through the newsroom. The news director,
producer, and executive producer decide a live remote is
necessary to cover the storm. The only reporter in the news-

room is told to do the remote on overtime. The microwave van operator is told about the live remote and angrily responds: "It wasn't planned!"

These two scenes are illustrative of the lack of flexibility in a factory production system. As Figure 1 shows, it is necessary for each story idea to pass sequentially through three steps before it is ready to be a segment on the newscast. A breakdown at any point requires adjustments to continue production. The lack of flexibility means the factory finds itself increasingly incapable of coping with such breakdowns and yet meeting self-imposed standards of production.

The technology involved in steps three, four, and five is critical. If, as in Scene 1, the assembling technology breaks down or even slows down, the progress of the story through the assembly line is impaired and the product must be modified. Organizational evaluation of system breakdowns produced plans to prevent the need for such last-minute improvisation in the future—i.e., to make the task accomplishment more routine (see Altheide and Rasmussen, 1976).

The newsworkers do exhibit, at times, a clock-punching syndrome. Scene 2 illustrates this with the remote operator being angered by a change in plans. Further, there are examples of newsworkers "working to contract," with a reluctance or even resistance to being assigned tasks not designated as their own. (Remember, WEST was *non*union). For example, on several occasions the reporter who did investigative reports was angered when taken from his semi-autonomous work to do general reporting. The emergence of work rules, both institutionalized (several work rule memos appeared during our observations) and self-imposed, is indicative of routinization.

The combination of increasing technology, task specialization, and adherence to work rules encourages more rigidity in the news factory. When rigidity merges with the demands of consultants and the requirements of a sophisticated product, the time required to assemble the product is increased, while the tolerance for error is decreased. This encourages the system to take a more carefully pre-scribed approach to gathering, structuring, and assembling the news. At WEST, these requirements were spelled out in detailed memos, instructing the staff on exactly how seg-ments were to be prepared. The goal is not to simply meet the deadline, but to do so with a sophisticated, visual pro-duct (which is defined as necessary for a good show).

The television news factory, given the trends in tele-vision news and the operation we observed, appears to lose flexibility as it attempts to cope with technology and other requirements. The frustration this produces was bitterly summed up by the executive producer after the news the night of Scene 2: "This place doesn't respond to anything but a real disaster."

Personal Investment

The factory system reduces a newsworker's personal investment both in the segment he or she helps produce and in the entire newscast. This is a consequence of the interchangeability of newsworkers [16] and the newsworkers' lack of control over the final product. While a number of re-porters have specialities, the assumption was any WEST re-porter could be assigned to any topic and expected to pro-duce a story (see Epstein, 1973; Tuchman, 1978). Similarly, photographers are expected to handle any assignment even though some are credited with being better with certain types of photography—such as sports or features.

Interchangeability means not only that any reporter could be assigned any story but also that any pairing of reporter and photographer is possible. The news factory assumption is that any type A part (reporter) can be paired with any type B part (photographer) to make a product C (story). While the wise assignment editor may avoid certain pairings because of past conflicts, personal strengths, or differences in work style, if necessary any pairing of personnel will be, and is, used.

The newsworkers' lack of control over the final product is apparent in the model. Neither the photographer nor the reporter can claim complete responsibility for a segment—each contributes to the material gathering and structuring. The assembly of the segment may be performed by a third person with constraints introduced by a fourth (the producer). Finally, the appearance of the segment is under the control of the producer and director, rather than the photographers or reporters.

The consequence of this system, with its interchangeability of personnel and lack of control, was demonstrated lack of personal involvement. Several newsworkers admitted they simply wanted to get a story done on time and be done with work. We rarely observed a reporter or photographer ripping a breaking story off the newswire. Several reporters admitted they seldom watched the newscast. These patterns indicate a lack of involvement with the news product and the station. Further, the public job hunting of several persons demonstrated this lack of involvement with others in the newsroom.

This consequence of the general factory operation was highlighted by the contrast provided by a reporter and photographer who were treated as a team, assigned a regular feature slot, and granted much autonomy and control over their work. These two followed through the first four steps of the process: they generated ideas, gathered material, structured it, assembled most material, and sometimes even participated in presenting it. Not surprisingly, their work was distinctly different than their colleagues', and the team treated it differently, often promoting it for network syndication.

Productivity

The emergence of a factory model of news—combined with the demands for a high story count, for profit, and for cost-efficient use of sophisticated equipment—has directed the news organization toward evaluating newswork in productivity terms. Specifically, productivity is defined as doing one's assignment and doing it on time.

Under this measure of newswork, good workers are ones who get their work done on time; bad workers do not (with the consequences that the producer has to alter the show's rundown and perhaps the script, which in turn requires the director to change his or her plans for the telecast). The importance of this measure of productivity appeared in the supervisor's hostile response to the announcement that a story would be late and in the sharp criticism slow reporters and photographers received from faster newsworkers (who would have to produce more work to make up for the slower workers).

The productivity measure is significant for what it does not consider—any evaluation of quality, whether in the eyes of management, the reporters, or the outside journalistic establishment. With the exception of one series, we observed little discussion among newsworkers of "good" or "bad" newswork.

The popular guideline for WEST newsroom could read (1) only do the assignments given, (2) only attempt to complete them, and (3) meet the time deadline. The effect of the productivity measure is epitomized in the "quick and dirty": a story which would be treated simply, gathered and structured quickly, and evoke little personal investment from the newsworkers because they did not understand the purpose of the assignment.[17]

Expectations and the Factory

A fundamental problem of the mechanization of newswork is that newsworkers were not told newswork is factory work (see Johnstone et al., 1976). It may seem overdrawn, but we suspect (and Johnstone et al.'s 1976 data indicate) newspeople—like much of the public—have images of newswork similar to the popularized values portrayed in Bernstein and Woodward's (1974) *All the President's Men* and the personalized glamour of the network superstars or local anchorpersons.

In addition to these expectations, newsworkers are affected by the recognition television provides. On-the-air reporters are recognized on the street and invited to charity affairs and other public activities. In the era of eyewitness news, reporters are aware they are often hired not simply for reporting skills but also because they *look* good. Without the aid of comparative data on self-evaluation, we cannot support a claim that newsworkers have higher levels of self-value than other workers. We would note, however, several reporters commented that the television news business is full of people with large egos. Based on our observations, we would hazard the claim that newsworkers' self-valuation exceeds that of most workers in factory settings.

These circumstances produce a straightforward problem for the news factory. The factory newsworker values public service, autonomy, and freedom from supervision (Johnstone et al., 1976) and appears to have a strong sense of self-value. These same workers are in an organization that mechanizes their work, emphasizes worker interchangeability, encourages rapidity in production, has high employee turnover, and seldom offers qualitative evaluation of work. Thus, newsworkers concerned about being professional (Johnstone et al., 1976) find themselves in a climate in which work must be completed quickly within only minimum standards—no matter what complications develop—and then must relinquish the work to a factory assembly line (see Waters, 1978).

CONCLUSION

It is clear a newsroom is not an assembly line as most persons conceive of one. However, newswork is accomplished within steps of organizing that are designed to use nearly identical reporters and photographers to produce a uniform product within a limited period of time. The trends in television news—the turnover of newsworkers, the influence of consultants, the producer supervision, the increased technical sophistication, increasing organizational size, and the emergence of the news as a profit center— have contributed to local television news' development of a highly constrained, routinized approach to news.

The consequences of mechanizing newswork in television are a lack of flexibility, lack of personal investment in the product, an evaluation of newswork in productivity terms, and a mismatch between newsworkers' expectations and the factory in which they work. Throughout our observations, specific instances of these consequences were labeled negatively by newsworkers. Both supervisors and reporters would criticize the lack of flexibility for causing disagreements and as being "stupid." Instances of lack of personal involvement would appear as supervisors criticized newsworkers for "not following through" and some newsworkers criticized others for being "lazy." Some newsworkers complained that management's emphasis on productivity prevented them from doing a complete job. There were confrontations between newsworkers who sought autonomy and supervisors who demanded adherence to work routines. In their words and through their behavior many newsworkers defined these four consequences as negative. The implications of the consequences for the viewing public remain to be evaluated.

NOTES

1. Members of the team varied in age, credentials, media knowledge, and personal style, providing for a wider range of possible experiences and observations within the organization.

2. The organization's members were aware of the team's identity and purpose. Techniques varied from unobtrusive observation to near participation in work activities. Because of the team's composition and the wealth of different experiences afforded to each researcher, factors that similarly emerged from our individual field notes were considered significant and comprised the basis for the development of this report.

3. WEST-TV is a pseudonym. Please note we are restricting our comments to local news organizations. There is reason to believe the operation of network news differs from the argument we present below.

4. Barbara Walters and Harry Reasoner are two highly visible network examples; David Schoumacher and Connie Chung exemplify the moves from net-

work to local operations; we suspect most readers can provide examples of station switching within one's own local market.

5. As we observed, maximation of value can have different meanings for different members of the organization. For some it is to save film expense, for some to show off the station's new toy, for some it is to get the news fast, and for others merely being sure the microwave unit is used at least once a day.

6. This interest can produce serious conflict between management and the news department, as illustrated in the highly publicized conflict at WCCO-TV, Minneapolis-St. Paul (Demick, 1978).

7. Role specialization and interchangeability are complimentary processes. Even as role specialization develops, workers are expected to be able to do the work of any person within their work class. Thus a legislative reporter can be assigned a nonlegislative story. Reporters are assumed capable of reporting any story (see Tuchman, 1978). Photographers are assumed capable of filming any story. As technical specialization increases, the work class narrows and the interchangeability is limited. Thus, not all photographers are assumed capable of running microwave equipment even though it is a subspeciality of photography. Thus, role specialization and technology interact making the functioning of the news organization more fragile.

8. The traditional factory model was born in the Industrial Revolution and is epitomized by the assembly line, where tasks are broken into tiny bits, with each worker adding his or her piece to the ever-growing product (see Kranzberg and Gies, 1975).

9. See Tunstall (1971) who argues journalists are part of a nonroutine bureaucracy; while we would not dispute television workers must deal with exceptional cases, comparing our observations and others' (Altheide, 1976; Altheide and Rasmussen, 1976) with studies examining print news (Tuchman, 1978, emphasizes print) suggests television news is more routine than print news and seeks to increase its routinization for the reasons discussed above.

10. This relationship was illustrated when an experienced film editor was dealing with an inexperienced reporter. In those cases, the editor assumed greater control over the assembly of the segment, while the reporter lost some of his or her control.

11. A segment would be: wire copy written for reading with or without visuals, film or videotape to be shown with the copy being read (a voice-over), a film or tape package (incorporating all the visual and oral elements of a story, except the introduction), a live remote, and in-studio material (e.g., the weather).

12. In explicating the model we will focus on the news component of a telecast (as opposed to sports and weather). The sports and weather segments are produced by the sports and weather persons, who operate semi-independently of the assembly line process; however, if they choose to use the resources of the factory (e.g., a photographer), the sports or weather segment becomes part of the assembly line process.

13. The terms *enacting* and *enactment* are used to suggest the active, meaning-creating nature of story ideation (Weick, 1969)—in contrast with the "story sorting" concept that dominates gatekeeper studies (e.g., White, 1950).

14. Wire stories were rewritten for broadcast as they came in and were not a regular feature on the story meeting agenda.

15. There were examples of open reporter-photographer conflict at WEST. In some cases this appeared to be the result of one exerting dominance over the other.

16. "Ford established the final proposition of the theory of industrial manu-facture—not only that the parts of the finished product be interchangeable, but that the men who build the products be themselves interchangeable parts" (Doc-torow, 1975: 113).

17. There were newsworkers who sought to do more than meet a deadline; however, the system made productivity its primary measure of work.

REFERENCES

ALTHEIDE, D. L. (1976) Creating Reality: How TV News Distorts Events. Beverly Hills, CA: Sage.

——— and P. K. RASMUSSEN (1976) "Becoming news: a study of two news-rooms." Sociology of Work and Occupations 3: 223-246.

ARGYRIS, C. (1974) Behind the Front Page: Organizational Self-Renewal in a Metropolitan Newspaper. San Francisco: Jossey-Bass.

BARRETT, M. (1978) Rich News, Poor News. New York: Crowell.

BERNSTEIN, C. and B. WOODWARD (1974) All the President's Men. New York: Simon and Schuster.

BOULDING, K. E. (1953) "Toward a general theory of growth." Canadian J. of Eco-nomics and Pol. Sci. 19: 326-340.

CARMODY, J. (1977) "'Cosmetic' or 'overrated,' consultants do influence TV." Denver Post (April 10): 27-28.

CROUSE, T. (1974) The Boys on the Bus. New York: Ballantine.

DEMICK, B. (1978) "News victory: WCCO boss resigns; wanted happy talk." [More] 8 (January): 10-11.

DIAMOND, E. (1975) The Tin Kazoo: Television, Politics, and the News. Cambridge, MA: MIT Press.

DOCTOROW, E. L. (1975) Ragtime. New York: Random House.

EDEN, D. (1977) "'News doctor' orders 'happy talk.'" Minneapolis Star (December 30): 1C; 12C.

EPSTEIN, E. J. (1973) News from Nowhere: Television and the News. New York: Random House.

HIRSCH, P. M. (1977) "Occupational, organizational, and institutional models in mass media research: toward an integrated framework" pp. 13-42 in P. M. Hirsch et al. (eds.), Strategies for Communication Research. Beverly Hills, CA: Sage.

JOHNSTONE, J.W.C., E. J. SLAWSKI, and W. W. BOWMAN (1976) The News People: A Sociological Portrait of American Journalists and Their Work. Ur-bana: Univ. of Illinois Press.

KASINDORF, .I (1972) "Spending a day on the hot seat." TV Guide 20 (July 1): 6-8.

KRANZBERG, M and J. GIES (1975) By the Sweat of Thy Brow: Work in the West-ern World. New York: Putnam.

PERROW, C. (1967) "A framework for the comparative analysis of organizations." Amer. Soc. Rev. 32: 194-208.

POWERS, R. (1977) The Newscasters. New York: St. Martin's.

RITZER, G. (1977) Working: Conflict and Change. Englewood Cliffs, NJ: Prentice Hall.

ROSENFIELD. W. W., L. S. HAYES, and T. S. FRENTZ (1976) The Communicative Experience. Boston: Allyn and Bacon.

ROSHCO, B. (1975) Newsmaking. Chicago: Univ. of Chicago Press.

STINCHCOMBE, A. L. (1968) Constructing Social Theories. New York: Harcourt Brace Janovich.

THOMPSON, J. D. (1967) Organizations in Action: Social Science Basis of Administrative Theory. New York: McGraw-Hill.

TUCHMAN G. (1978) Making News: A Study in the Construction of Reality. New York: Macmillan.

——— (1977) "The exception proves the rule: the study of routine news practices" pp. 43-62 in P. M. Hirsch et al. (eds.), Strategies for Communication Research. Beverly Hills, CA: Sage.

——— (1973a) "Making news by doing work: routinizing the unexpected." Amer. J. of Sociology 79: 110-131.

——— (1973b) "The technology of objectivity: doing 'objective' tv news film." Urban Life and Culture 2 (April): 3-26.

——— (1972) "Objectivity as strategic ritual: an examination of newsmen's notions of objectivity." Amer. J. of Sociology 77: 660-679.

TUNSTALL, J. (1971) Journalists at Work: Specialist Correspondents, Their News Organizations, News Sources, and Competitor-Colleagues. Beverly Hills, CA: Sage.

WATERS, H. F. (1978) "The local-news blues." Newsweek (January 16): 82-83.

WEICK, K. E. (1969) The Social Psychology of Organizing. Reading, MA: Addison-Wesley.

WHITE, D. M. (1950) "The 'gatekeeper': a case study in the selection of news." Journalism Q. 27: 383-390.

WHITEHEAD, R., Jr. (1978) "Show news." Columbia Journalism Rev. (March/April): 58-59.

Charles R. Bantz is Assistant Professor of Speech-Communication at the University of Minnesota. He received his Ph.D. from Ohio State University and his major research interests are organizational communication, television news, and comparative communication research.

Suzanne McCorkle is Assistant Professor of Communication at Boise State University. She received her Ph.D. from the University of Colorado and her major research interests are rhetorical criticism and computerized textual analysis.

Roberta C. Baade is an Instructor at Pepperdine College. She is completing her Ph.D. at the University of Colorado. Her major interest is organizational communication.

PART IV

INFORMATION PROCESSING AND THE MASS MEDIA

Research in this section is exemplary of expanding work on information processing, the critical link between message dissemination and media impact. The lead article describes a program on news comprehension conducted at Swedish Radio in Stockholm. An example of increasingly significant studies done by audience research departments of European broadcasting corporations, the work finds that the "causal" context of events in television news stories is related to overall comprehension of news by viewers. Unfortunately, the authors find that TV news rarely includes the causal element.

Following the Swedish study is a report of television news learning among Wisconsin school children. This unusual research suggests that children who saw the news as informational in function had greater comprehension than those who viewed it as entertainment.

The next article describes a highly theoretical research project that attempts to test and extend Richard Carter's stopping theory of message processing on TV news. The innovative experiment finds support for Carter's theory.

Concluding Part IV is work that connects the notion of televised "scripts" to the everyday life scripts of interpersonal communication. The research propositions posed in this provocative piece—about whether life scripts are affected by vignettes in television news and drama—may lead to an intriguing theoretical bridge in the search for media effects.

An extensive program of news comprehension research is reported in this article by Olle Findahl and Birgitta Höijer, both research scientists in the audience research department of Swedish Radio, Stockholm. Findahl and Höijer combine field experimentation and content analysis to look at the relationship of knowledge levels, news production methods, and dimensions of news comprehension on four major issues in Sweden. Their work suggests that broadcast news in Sweden often ignores causal, interpretive perspectives, which Findahl and Höijer's field experiments indicate are important elements in news comprehension. They argue that broadcast news in Sweden is designed basically for the "initiated," those persons already highly knowledgeable about events. Findahl and Höijer's report is an excellent example of the kind of programmatic research conducted by the larger audience research services of European television systems.

23

STUDIES OF NEWS FROM THE PERSPECTIVE OF HUMAN COMPREHENSION

Olle Findahl and Birgitta Höijer

"It's odd, sitting there watching news on TV. It's as though I somehow wasn't listening, though I'm sitting there listening, all the same."

So sighed a middle-aged woman with little formal schooling who participated in one of our studies. This woman was not exceptional. For many there is a sort of invisible barrier between what happens on the TV-screen and the people watching that screen. The words refer to things beyond the realm of the listener's knowledge and experience, and thus the basic preconditions for communication are lacking. The news programs take for granted that members of the audience possess the same body of "silent" knowledge and have the same frameworks as the highly educated, middle-aged individuals who produce them. But a majority of the audience have other frames of references and are not acquainted with the background and conditions of the news stories.

One consequence of this is that a lot of people in the public catch only fragments or loose details of the news programs. Fragmentation is characteristic of the perception of news items. People most easily catch

From Olle Findahl and Birgitta Höijer, "Studies of News from the Perspective of Human Comprehension," original manuscript.

geographical place names, where an event has occurred, and names of a person or thing involved, such as "Something happened in Paris" or "Carter said something."

In all news reporting there is a major risk that what is communicated amounts to no more than fragments of news events, fragments isolated from their contexts. The reasons for this are many. Some of them are discussed in this paper with a point of departure taken from a long-term project dealing with the comprehension of news. The project includes both experimental research with fictitious but realistic news programs and thorough analysis of daily news broadcasts.

On the following pages we will discuss some of the conclusions we have drawn from this project. We will try to characterize the comprehension of news by the general audience and consider the obstacles, and we will also point out the problems that news research must deal with and the complexity of its task.

News can, of course, be studied with different approaches and from different perspectives. As cognitive psychologists we have a special interest in the process of knowledge: How do people get to know the world outside their own experiences? What is made known to the audience through the news? This interest has strongly influenced our research and the formulation of our research problem: What are the basic preconditions that must be fulfilled if the audience demand for comprehensible information is to be met? What aspects in the content and presentation of broadcast news influence the audience's perception and understanding? What kind of audience do the news programs address?

We have conducted experiments with fictitious but realistic news programs in which we tested different ways of presenting and structuring the news. We have also, during the last years, analyzed closely the daily news broadcasts to find out how they are composed and how the content is structured and presented.

Three main factors are at play here: the human comprehension process, the program content, and the manner in which the content is presented. The manner of presentation and the content structure are the object of our research; the human comprehension process is the starting point.

HUMAN COMPREHENSION PROCESS

While there is no complete theory as to the specific mental functions involved in comprehension, certain basic principles have been established.[1] The comprehension process occurs on different levels *(Luria, 1976)*. Processes on the lower levels usually occur automatically and unconsciously. If we confine our discussion for the moment to the spoken word, the impulses reaching us consist of words, intonations, and pauses. The next step in the process is one of grouping these impulses. The most important bits are sorted out and ordered hierarchically. Toward the end of this process, when grammatical and prosodic characteristics come into the picture, we are ready for the next phase of the process, which involves the reduction and condensation of the organized bits into a form of "inner language." It is on the basis of this condensed, inner register that we attempt to synthesize and grasp the gist of the message: What does it all mean? What is it about? In this process of interpretation we use our own previous experiences and our conceptions of reality as a framework or scheme for processing the information.

Here we may regard our comprehension of a message as the result of a recollection in connection with the implicit subconscious question: "Is there any interpretation of this message that will make it meaningful in terms of what I already know?" A positive answer to this question constitutes one of the basic preconditions for communication. If a speaker wishes to be understood, he must adapt his manner of speaking to the persons he addresses. This is a silent agreement, and as long as it is observed the listener will make an effort to understand what the speaker says. The communication between them rests all the while on a basis of their shared knowledge.

In the world of broadcast news the agreement has been broken if the newscaster should start talking about something entirely foreign to his viewers and does so without giving them an orientation or background information. It is no longer a question of communication. The viewer/listener no longer feels like a viewer/listener, and many will shrug their shoulders, saying "This is nothing for me," or "Words, words, words!"

COMPREHENSION AND PREVIOUS KNOWLEDGE

Let us now look at some of the findings from our studies to see if these preconditions are satisfied. Let us start by looking more closely at audience recall after viewing a news broadcast.

The most striking characteristic of information recall is its variety. At first glance, there would seem to be no common pattern whatsoever. Some people recall information here and there throughout the program, some recall only a few items, while others recall entirely different ones. The viewer who has had to leave his home in the north of Sweden to look for work in Stockholm has no trouble recalling an item about the expanding firm in the northern community, Piteå. Another, whose brother seriously injured his finger while working at a lathe, will readily recall an item about on-the-job accidents, while the viewer who handles the family's Christmas and New Year correspondence will know how much letter postage will increase.

Studying the responses of individual viewers, we thus find an enormous variation in what they recall as a result of their specific experience and respective walks of life. But the more responses we compile, the more clearly a pattern emerges. Some items are easy to remember—nearly everyone recalls them—while only very few viewers recall others. The most easily recalled items are those closely related to everyday life and of direct concern to many people. They are "close," but not necessarily in any geographical sense, measurable in meters or miles or by a distinction between domestic and foreign news. Rather, they represent psychological closeness in that they are related to people's knowledge and personal experiences.

In one of our studies (Findahl and Höijer, 1974) the participants were taking a knowledge test,[2] a question-and-answer test of general knowledge on current topics of the sort which is common in mass media. They were also shown a fictitious but completely realistic news program and then asked a series of questions on the program content. The results revealed that people with high general knowledge were able to recall considerably more of the program content compared to people with little general knowledge, despite equal attention to the program. (See Figure 23.1.) We obtained these groups through a Q-segmentation analysis.[3] Let us first consider the patterns of general knowledge. We can see that one group knew much about all topics. The two groups had similar knowledge about Swedish social policy, some disparity of knowledge when the questions are about labor unions and labor conditions, and great differences on foreign topics.

We also find great differences in patterns of recall for the two groups— especially for news items about Swedish industry and the labor market, and for news about Latin America, Eastern Europe, and a summit conference. But we can also find a reverse difference on everyday-life subjects.

Possession of good knowledge reserves is apparently no guarantee that one absorbs all information in the news. *But poor knowledge reserves always implies that one fails to absorb very much of the program content.* As a concrete example we can look at a news item about a state emergency in Peru. Those who knew nothing about Latin America (that Peru is a country in Latin America, etc.) did not recall anything of the news item about Peru. Only those with knowledge about Latin America did recall the news item.

What kind of persons characterize these groups? In one group we find many middle-aged men with college educations. In the other group we find many women, both young and elderly, with elementary-school educations, none with college educations. The last group, whose members were poorly informed, particularly with respect to world affairs and Swedish industrial conditions, recalled few of the news items except those items closely related to everyday life and particularly to women's life situations: rising prices, maternity benefits, children's risk of hereditary defects. Nearly all of them recalled these items, and they recalled them better than other groups in the audience.

Another characteristic of information people recall is the many misconceptions and distortions of the original content (Findahl and Hoijer, 1973). Such misconceptions are seldom random. The listener "fills in" the gaps in his recollection or reconstructs "new" events by mixing together

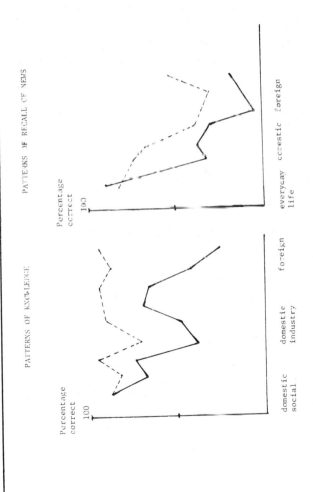

PATTERNS OF KNOWLEDGE   PATTERNS OF RECALL OF NEWS

Percentage correct 100

domestic social   domestic industry   foreign

Percentage correct 100

everyday life   domestic   foreign

NOTE: – – – – –   This group largely consists of middle-aged men with college education.
————————   This group largely consists of young and elderly women with elementary-school education.

Figure 23.1: Knowledge of domestic and foreign matters and recall of news with different content for two separate groups in the audience. 617 persons, randomly selected, participated in the study

portions of various items and by adding details from his previous knowledge and experience. As an example, we mention the confusion of two different news items about demonstrations. One concerned clashes between police and demonstrators in Paris and the other reported a bicycle demonstration in a Swedish city sponsored by the urban environment group. In contrast to the demonstration in Paris, the Swedish demonstration was entirely without violence and no police were involved. Nevertheless, many listeners confused the two items, thinking that the bicycle demonstration had resulted in a clash with the police and that some of the Swedish demonstrators were seriously injured.

There are many factors that can contribute to misconceptions and distortions, but we shall not discuss those factors here. Let us just point out that there is no simple relationship between the difficulty of a news item and the misunderstanding of its content that can arise. It is a far more complex question.

REPETITIONS AND REFORMULATIONS IN THE NEWSTEXT

Repetition is a tried and true pedagogic technique. The technique is often associated with more or less mechanical learning. But repetition need not imply "inundation," nor literal iteration for that matter. When naturally woven into the text of a news item, and when used to emphasize vital elements of the message, repetition can give the listener a better opportunity to examine and assess the information presented. In such cases, repetition can counteract fragmentation—that is, the tendency for listeners to recall no more than scattered details of what they have heard.

In an experiment with a radio news broadcast, we started with quite condensed and concise messages within the program and studied what happened with listener recall when different parts of the news messages were repeated (Findahl and Höijer, 1975). As mentioned earlier, listeners/viewers most readily recall concrete details, such as where an event occurred and who or what was involved. Causes and consequences of events are recalled with considerably greater difficulty. This applies not only to news content, but is a well-known recall phenomenon. Repetition of precisely these two elements—usually a placename or the name of a more or less well-known figure—is far from uncommon in news broadcasts, however. The simple, concrete elements in the item thereby assume even greater prominence in listeners' recollection. Tendencies toward fragmentation are not counteracted; on the contrary, they are accentuated.

Repetition of the cause or consequences (effect) of an event, on the other hand, brings about a more general improvement. These aspects, in themselves difficult to remember, are recalled much better. In addition, an improvement in recall of the rest of the content is also achieved despite its not being particularly stressed. When stress is placed on the causal relation, it serves to "tie together" the elements of the message and so provide a framework for the listeners' cognitive organization of the content.

The amount of repetition is not the important thing. While it does have some effect, retention does not at all increase in proportion to the amount of repetitions included in the message. The crucial point is what the repetition emphasizes. It is a question of making the causes and consequences of an event explicit and giving them a prominent place in the news item. Then the listeners are able to form a complete mental image of what it is all about.

VISUAL ILLUSTRATIONS IN THE NEWS

In an enlarged follow-up study (Findahl and Höijer, 1976) we used television news broadcasts and studied the role of the TV picture. When is it an aid? When does it distract viewers' attention from the essential message? How do visuals interact with the spoken word?[4] (See Figure 23.2.)

Let us start with the audience recall of a news item presented in brief with no other visual illustration than the on-camera newscaster. The more concrete content of the news is often central in people's recollection, as we can see, while other, more abstracted or complex relations do not register nearly as well.

What happens now when we are utilizing pictures and illustrations in presenting the news? Using a map with captions indicating the locations of the event, many more viewers did recall where the event occurred. Maps and pictures of places and more or less well-known persons often result in viewers being able to recall these things only, while few can recall the causal relations that make the news understandable. However, when the persons and things involved are placed in a proper milieu or at the scene of the event, viewer recall is more complete. Such illustrations provide cues to several other elements of the content, and they may also serve as a background to the verbal message, placing the event in a "here and now."

When a still photo of the consequence of the event is used, viewer recall is improved with respect not only to what the photo illustrates but to the whole item. Viewers' mental images of the news item no longer consist of isolated details, although an imbalance is still apparent. But we can complement the consequence-photo by amplifying the newstext with verbal repetition of the cause and the consequence of the event. (The repetition is woven naturally into the text.) The audience now has a complete memory picture of the news item, and fragmentation has been overcome.

The results of the experiments suggest that the key to audience apprehension and understanding lies in emphasizing the causal relations and explanations that explicitly outline the background of the news events.

This brings us to the third point—the content and the content structure. How can we find out what is important in a program? What is essential for understanding?

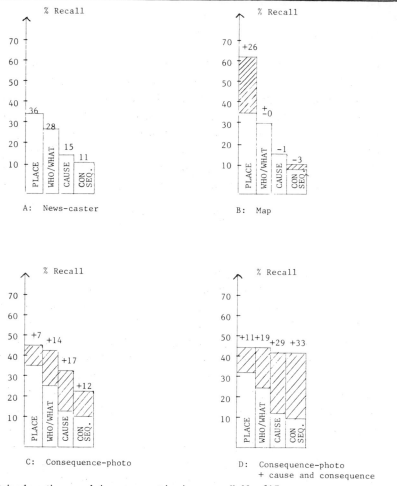

NOTE: Striped portion equals improvement in viewer recall. N = 617.

Figure 23.2: Audience recall of news items presented in brief with no other visual illustration than the on-camera news-caster, compared with different kinds of presentation

CONTENT STRUCTURE OF THE NEWS

News texts are produced within a certain historical tradition and follow strict standard patterns. News is mostly about events, especially events that have recently occurred. The event involves actors and other principals who are fixed in time and place. There is a background of causes and motives, and the event has, or will have, consequences.

Though this schema is very simple it has—as far as we can see—a psychological relevance, and most news can be analyzed according to it.

However, the actual content structures of the news subjects are much more complicated. Usually more than one event is involved; the causal factors and the consequences may be many and complex. Thus, different combinations of the basic elements are possible, and there are also temporal and geographic relations that give news items a far more complex structure than the model suggests.

As a part of a series analyses for Swedish Radio, we analyzed 30 TV news stories in three important areas: atomic energy, central labor contract negotiations, and employee-controlled investment funds. We tried to answer two questions: What do people learn about these matters? Are the news stories presented in a way that the audience's demand for comprehensible information is fulfilled?

Assessed from the point of view of the human comprehension process, the news items presented many difficulties that denied listeners and viewers the opportunity to be informed. The major points at issue often were kept in the background while more spectacular aspects were magnified and given a dominant place in news stories. The more fundamental questions of comprehensibility and what it was all about were made into side issues; ambiguous and irrelevant statements were made into main points.

Some stories contained information about several different events, but failed to tell how they were related. Others went off on tangents that had little to do with the main story. Such faults cause confusion; viewers mix up the details of the respective elements and, for lack of a unifying structure, fail to grasp the whole of the message.

Many items were not ended logically but simply ended, whereupon the next item was presented. This causes problems in that viewers are not given enough time to sort out the information in their minds and must either cast it aside unprocessed or miss the succeeding content.

Several of the items contained apparently contradictory information. Such inconsistencies naturally cause confusion among viewers, who are neither able to reconcile different parts of the message nor given enough time to figure out why. Another frequent source of trouble was the omission of defining key concepts and terminology.

NEWS FOR THE INITIATED

Our findings may be summarized in one phrase: Broadcast news is written for the initiated. The failure to describe background factors in many items meant that they were only understood by people who already knew something about the news event and could thus place the information offered in context on their own. The common failure to define key terms and concepts must have caused many items to float in midair for viewers unacquainted with the jargon of technology and bureaucracy. Other factors had the same effect. Time and again, our analysis found implicit references in the items that only the initiated would be able to understand.

Results from the experimental research reveal the impact of the visual and verbal formulations of news items. The crucial point is not the technique of presentation, however, but what parts of the news content the visual or verbal formulation stresses. It is a question of making the causal relations and background explanations explicit to the audience. It is necessary to provide listeners and viewers with a framework upon which they can form a conception of the way various circumstances and events are interrelated.

Our analysis amply shows that the tacit agreement observed by radio and TV journalists is one between them and a well-informed minority of Swedes. Any such agreement with the rest of the audience is often broken.

Communication rests on the basis of shared knowledge between listeners and speaker. If the speaker wishes to be understood, he must adapt his manner of speaking to the knowledge of his audience. This is a fundamental precondition of making something known to others. The close analysis of comprehensibility in Swedish news broadcasts reveals many inherent difficulties in the news items. Frequently the preconditions of communication are not fulfilled. The findings might be summed up in one phrase: News for the initiated.

NOTES

1. Kintsch and vanDijk (1974) have attempted to specify what such a global theory would entail. It would require theories of structure and comprehension concerning both the micro- (proposition) and macro- (discourse) levels. Further, a theory is needed that relates these structures and offers principles for the reduction of complex semantic information. A synoptical theory that relates history-specific structures to the logic and discourse of the document is needed. Finally, the body of theory concerning the relation of verbal and narrative structures to cognitive processes must be significantly augmented.

2. A total of 617 persons, randomly selected, participated in the study. There were roughly as many men as women, aged 16-65 years, with varying levels of formal education.

3. This is a method of data analysis developed at the Audience and Programme Research Department of the Swedish Broadcasting Corporation. Briefly, the method involves grouping together individuals who resemble one another in any particular respect. Examining the patterns of response, the computer was able to distinguish five groups, whose members resembled one another with respect to pattern of knowledge and retention but differed from the members of other groups in this respect. Here we have discussed two of these groups.

4. Twenty-seven versions of the experimental news program were recorded. These were exactly identical, save for the manner in which five of the items were presented. Various versions, with respect to visual and verbal composition, of these five items were tested. A total of 617 persons participated in the study. See note 2.

REFERENCES

FINDAHL. OLLE (1971) "The Effect of Visual Illustrations on Perception and Retention of News Programmes." Sveriges Radio/PUB, Stockholm.

———— and BIRGITTA HÖIJER (1973) "An Analysis of Errors in the Recollection of a News Program." Sveriges Radio/PUB, Stockholm.

————(1974) "On Knowledge, Social Privilege and the News." Sveriges Radio/PUB, Stockholm.

————(1975) "Effect of Additional Verbal Information on Retention of a Radio News Program." Journalism Quarterly (Summer, 1975) Vol. 52, No. 3, pp. 493-498.

————(1976) "Fragments of Reality. An Experiment with News and TV-Visuals." Sveriges Radio/PUB, Stockholm.

————(1977) "How Important is Presentation?" Sveriges Radio/PUB, Stockholm.

————(1977) "Recall or Recognition. Some Studies of Methodology Around Multiple Choice and Open Questions." Sveriges Radio/PUB, Stockholm.

————(1979) "What Does the News Tell Us? Part 1. Crisis in Swedish Industry." Sveriges Radio/PUB, Stockholm.

————(1980) "What Does the News Tell Us? Part 2. Wage Negotiations, Atomic Energy, Employee-controlled Funds." Sveriges Radio/PUB, Stockholm.

KINTSCH, WALTER, and TEUN A. VANDIJK (1975) "Comment On Se Rappelle et On Résume des Histoires." Langages, Vol. 40, pp. 98-116, Paris.

LURIA, A.R. (1976) "Basic Problems of Neurolinguistics." Mouton, The Hague.

Too little is known about the way children respond to television news, especially news segments designed especially for them. This experiment uses a large group of third- through seventh-grade students in Wisconsin to test the learning process in response to a Saturday morning segment of CBS "In the News." The research suggests that believability, liking the story, and understanding story function are all significant predictors of news learning. The most critical finding is that children's perceptions may be just as important as production variables in news learning, lending support to those who urge that children should be taught to consume news intelligently. Dan Drew is associate professor and Bvron Reeves is assistant professor at the School of Journalism and Mass Communication at the University of Wisconsin—Madison.

24

LEARNING FROM A TELEVISION NEWS STORY

Dan Drew and Byron Reeves

Several studies show that substantial numbers of children watch television news. Atkin and Gantz (1975) reported that one-quarter of the six-year-olds they surveyed watch one of the national evening newscasts "every day." In a later study, Atkin (1978) found that nearly one-third of kindergarten through fifth-grade students said they watched one of these programs "almost every day." McLeod et al. (1972) reported that 30% of sixth-grade students "often" watch national newscasts. Of a sample of third

AUTHORS' NOTE: *This project was supported by a University of Wisconsin Graduate School Grant. Research Assistant Warren Bechtolt helped with the data analysis.*

through sixth graders, 11% claimed to watch a national news program "almost every day."

There also is evidence that children learn from this exposure to news and public affairs programming. Chaffee et al. (1970) found that public affairs media exposure during the 1968 presidential campaign was moderately related to adolescents' political knowledge, although it did not affect overt behavior such as political activity. Atkin and Gantz (1975) found that amount of national news exposure was associated with childrens' ability to identify leaders, issues, cities, and countries in the news. Similarly, Conway et al. (1975) showed that exposure to television news increased preadolescents' ability to differentiate the policies of political parties, their awareness of the law-making process in government, and knowledge of governmental roles. Another study (Dominick, 1972) has even shown that adolescents themselves report that television is their dominant source for information about the president, vice president, and Congress.

However, these studies do not attempt to deal with the underlying process through which learning occurs. For this reason, the present study focuses on the process by which children learn from a television news story. This project assumes that learning from the news is dependent on a mediating process of interpretation, and perception (McLeod and Reeves, 1977) and therefore examines several variables, including the context in which the news story appears, perceived function of the content, liking the content, and believing the content. The study tests the assumption that a child's perceptions of the program affect learning, and the child's perceptions are in turn affected by age and the program context.

These variables were chosen because they appear to be logically related to the dependent variable and some have been useful predictors in research dealing with entertainment programs. Because related research does not deal directly with the questions asked in this study, there is little empirical and theoretical support for predictions about the direction of effects. For this reason, the present study is exploratory and deals primarily with a series of research questions rather than hypotheses. The rationale for using the variables follows.

Perceived function. Several authors say that children make distinctions about the functions of various media. Among the earlier studies, Schramm et al. (1961) found that teenagers did not like educational television because they considered television to be an entertainment medium and thought educational television was an "unnatural" use of the medium. Wilson and Shaffer (1965) also found perception of function to be important. Children said they preferred to use textbooks rather than comic books to learn material about how fish swim—the youngsters explained that textbooks were for information and comics were for entertainment. Among more recent studies, Greenberg (1974) and Lometti et al. (1977) also found that children tend to ascribe different functions to different mass communication channels.

Although these studies did not deal with the relationship of perceived function to learning, they raise interesting questions about television news. Because news possibly could serve both entertainment and information functions, the individual's perception of the communicator's motivation may help determine the amount of learning that takes place. Perhaps those who think a story was presented to serve an information function learn more from it than those who believe it was included as entertainment because the former is consistent with the learning process. This question is different than those asked in uses and gratifications research. Typically, children have been asked what they get from content, while this study deals with why the content was presented. The question becomes: Does a child's perception of the communicator's purpose for showing a television news story affect learning from that story?

Believability. In a journalistic setting believability might be defined as the receiver's perception of the accuracy of a media representation of a real-world event. Although numerous studies have dealt with credibility, they used adults as subjects and some measure of attitude change as a dependent variable (McGuire, 1968). It is possible that children's perceptions of believability change as they learn about the media in school and have greater contact with news and public affairs programming. The perception of believability may affect acceptance of factual content of the news. The research question posed here is whether children's perceptions of believability of a news story affect learning from that story.

Liking the program and story. It is possible to develop conflicting hypotheses about the effect of liking a news story on learning. One could argue that liking the message increases attention, which in turn enhances learning. On the other hand, it is possible that liking distracts children from the informational content and reduces learning. This study separates the content of the news story from the content of the program in which it appears, because it is possible a child will like one and not the other. This poses two research questions: What is the effect of liking the program on learning from a news story, and what is the effect of liking the story and learning from the story?

Age. Research dealing with entertainment films has looked at the relationship between age and learning. Collins (1970) and Hawkins (1973) found positive relationships between age and learning content relevant to the central plot of a film. They also found curvilinear relationships between peripheral learning and age. This study deals with information that is a central part of a news story, so we also would expect to find a linear relationship with older children learning more than younger ones.

In addition to this direct effect of age on learning one might also expect indirect effects through perceptual variables. Because of the opportunity for greater exposure to news and public affairs content and classroom discussion of the news media, it is possible that children's perceptions of the media change and that these changes may then affect learning for the reasons outlined above. This study predicts a positive relationship between age and learning and asks the question: Does age affect learning through the perceptual variables?

Story context. Children see news stories that are placed in different contexts. Some, designed especially for children, are shown in the context of Saturday morning cartoons and fantasy drama, while similar stories, designed for adults, are presented in the context of more serious public affairs formats. It is possible that the differing contexts alter perceptions, which in turn affect learning. For example, youngsters who see a story in a cartoon context may like it more and learn more from it than those who see it embedded in an adult newscast. On the other hand, children who see the story in an adult newscast might think it serves an information function and, therefore, learn more from it than those who see it in the cartoon context. This could result in greater learning in the newscast condition. Because of these conflicting possibilities, the question is asked: Does news story context affect a child's perception of a news story and learning from it?

Age/context interaction. No prediction is made about the age-by-context interaction. The possibilities, however, are interesting: older children may be bored by the cartoons and learn more from the newscast, while younger children do the opposite. In addition, younger children may be less able to distinguish between the fantasy content of the cartoons and the reality content of the news story, and this could affect learning. The final research question asks: Is there an interaction effect of age and context on children's learning from a television news story?

METHOD

The study was conducted with 435 third- through seventh-grade students in Janesville, Wisconsin, in the spring of 1977. Each student was asked to answer questions about television and news viewing. The children were then asked to watch a 10-minute videotape containing the manipulation of viewing context. Four classes in each grade were randomly assigned to the two viewing conditions. After watching the videotape, all children answered the same multiple-choice questions about factual material in the story and their perceptions of the story.

The news story context was manipulated by showing children in the two viewing conditions the same one and one-half minute-long news story about a new fine arts museum in Paris, France, that was taken from a Saturday morning "In the News" program. In the first condition the story was surrounded by typical Saturday morning programming—two cartoon segments and five 30-second commercials along with the original "In the News" open and close. In the second condition, the same story appeared with an introduction by Hughes Rudd as the fourth item in a "CBS Morning News" segment. The newscast also contained commercials, and the story appeared at the same time in each viewing condition.

The news story used in the experiment explained the controversy that had developed in France about construction of a new national fine arts museum. The dispute centered on the design of the modern glass and steel structure in which pipes, supports, and escalators were located outside the building to preserve large areas of open space inside. Critics said the building looked like a giant erector set. The film and script were well coordinated with the video-reinforced points made by the script.

Two questions were used to measure perceived function of the story. The first question asked: "Why did they show the story about the new building in Paris? Put a number 1 next to the most important reason." Children could choose from two entertainment responses—"because it's fun to watch" or "because it's fun to look at pictures of the new building" or two information functions—"so we would know what people in other countries are doing" or "because some people didn't like the new building." The second question used the same responses, but asked: "Put a number 2 next to the second most important reason they showed the story about the new building."

Children were then categorized on a scale from low information function to high information function: low information if they chose two entertainment responses, slightly higher if they chose an entertainment function as first choice and information as second. The next highest group reversed those choices with information first, while the highest group chose two information responses.

The believability measure asked: "Did you believe what they said about the new building in Paris?" Responses were: "yes," "I'm not sure," and "no."

Liking the program was measured with a 4-point scale. Children were asked, "How much did you like watching the program we showed you?" Responses were "very much," "a little," "not very much," and "not at all."

The same scale was used to measure liking the story; this question read: "How much did you like watching the story about the new building in Paris?"

Dependent variable. The dependent measure was a 10-item, multiple choice quiz that asked factual questions about the stimulus news story. Children were asked what the building was for, what most people thought of the new building, where the building was located, what people said the new building looked like, what was located on the outside of the new building, why people who lived next to the new building did not like it, what else they showed in the news story that was in the same city, and why pipes and supports were located outside the building.

Children were given a score of one for each correct answer, and the items were summed for a measure of learning. The measure of test reliability using Chronbach's alpha was .77.

RESULTS

The data were analyzed in two stages, each using hierarchical regression.[1] The first set of regression equations predicted learning from the television news story using all of the independent and perceptual variables in the study. The second predicted the perceptual variables using the two antecedent variables: grade and context. The analysis procedure was designed to indicate whether the antecedent variables affect learning directly and/or indirectly through the perceptual variables.

The first regression analysis, predicting learning, is shown in Table 1. The five perceptual variables were entered as a block because they were expected to have main effects on learning, and there was no theoretical reason for ordering. Grade and context were entered in the equation next to see if they predicted any additional variance not accounted for by the perceptual variables. The interaction between grade and context was added last.

The first equation in Table 1 shows that the four perceptual variables—like program, believability, story function, and like story—had significant main effects on learning. Story function was the best predictor of learning, while believability accounted for the least amount of variance.

The second equation in Table 1 indicates that the manipulation of the context in which the story appeared had no independent effect on learning beyond that accounted for by the perceptual variables. Grade, however, produced a very strong direct effect on learning. The addition of grade substantially decreased the regression coefficient for liking the program by making it statistically insignificant.

TABLE 1

Heirarchical Regression Analysis of Seven Predictors of Children's
Learning from a Television News Story (N = 435)

Predictor Variables	Regression 1	Regression 2	Regression[a] 3
Like Program	.15 **	.04	
Believability	.10 *	.11	
Story Function[b]	.39 ***	.29 ***	
Like Story	.25 ***	.21 ***	
Context[c]		-.04	
Grade		.30 ***	
Context/Grade Interaction			
Multiple R	.546 ***	.609 ***	.615 ***
Increment in R		.073 ***	.006 *

$*p < .05$
$**p < .01$
$***p < .001$

a. Beta weights are not shown for the equation in which the interaction term is included because they are not empirically meaningful. The best measurement of importance of the interaction term is the increment added to R^2 by the inclusion of the product term (Assison, 1977).
b. Story function was measured on a 4-point scale ranging from no information function (1) to high information function (4).
c. Viewing context was coded: news context = (-1); cartoon context = $(+1)$.

It also decreased somewhat the beta weight for function of the story, indicating that age did affect learning through these two intervening variables.

The data in Table 1 also show a statistically significant grade-by-context interaction. A closer look at the means shows that children in the third, fourth, and fifth grades learn more from the news story imbedded in the newscast than they did from the story in the cartoon context. On the other hand, the sixth and seventh graders learned more from the story in the cartoon context (see Figure 1).

The regression equations for the second stage of the analysis are shown in Table 2. Grade and context were regressed against the four perceptual variables to see

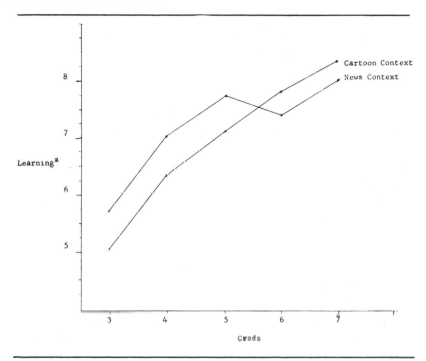

Figure 1: Plot of the Experimental Condition by Grade Interaction in Relation to Children's Learning from a Television News Story

a. An index representing learning from the news story was created by summing the number of questions out of nine each child answered correctly about the story.

if either accounted for any of the variances of the perceptual variables.

Although the context was expected to affect a number of the perceptual variables, it accounted for a significant portion of the variance in only one—liking the program. As might be expected, children liked the stimulus tape with the cartoon more than they liked the one with the newscast. It is interesting to note, however, that context did not affect how much they liked the news story itself.

Grade predicted two of the perceptual variables—liking the program and story function: older children liked the entire stimulus package less than the younger children, and older children were more likely to perceive the story function as being one of information rather than entertainment.

TABLE 2

Heirarchical Regression Analysis of Grade and Story Context
as Predictors of Children's Perceptions of a Television
News Story (N = 435)

	Regression 1	Regression[a] 2
Dependent Variable: Believability		
Story Context	.05	
Grade	-.02	
Story Context/Grade Interaction		
R	.05	.07
Increment in R		.02
Dependent Variable: Story Function		
Story Context	.00	
Grade	.35 ***	
Story Context/Grade Interaction		
R	.35 ***	.35 ***
Increment in R		.00
Dependent Variable: Like Story		
Story Context	.04	
Grade	.01	
Story Context/Grade Interaction		
R	.04	.09
Increment in R		.05
Dependent Variable: Like Program		
Story Context	.35 ***	
Grade	-.29 ***	
Story Context/Grade Interaction		
R	.45 ***	.45 ***
Increment in R		.00

a. See footnote a in Table 1.

Because context did not have a main effect on learning
and it predicted only one perceptual variable—liking the
program—which did not affect learning, it appears that
context had neither a direct nor indirect effect on learning
from a news story. Grade also predicted liking the program,

which did not affect learning, and story function, which had a positive relationship with learning. Thus, it appears that grade acted on learning directly and indirectly through story function.

The grade-by-context interaction did not predict any of the perceptual variables.

DISCUSSION

The variables in this study account for a significant portion (37%) of the variance in children's learning from a television news story. This prediction seems especially accurate considering that no intelligence measures were used. Believability, liking the story, and understanding the function of the story all were significant predictors of learning. The strongest and most interesting predictor was story function, indicating that those who understood the information function of the story learned the most from it.

Manipulation of the context in which the news story appeared did not directly affect learning from the story, nor did it affect learning indirectly by altering the children's perception of story function or the extent to which they liked the story or believed the story. This seems to indicate that placing reality content in a fantasy setting has little impact —in terms of the variables listed above—on children in third through seventh grades.

Even though context did not affect learning or perceptions in this study, it may have an important effect in a real-world setting. Children liked the cartoon program context much more than they did the news context, as one would expect. Children in this field experiment setting had no alternative to watching the program the researchers presented, but given a choice in their own living rooms, they may watch the "In the News" programs and ignore the regular news formats.

The data do not explain the weak age-by-context interaction on learning shown in Figure 1. However, a possibility may be that children in the six and seventh grades make more sophisticated judgments about the importance of content than those in the younger grades. Younger children may see news as generally more important than cartoons and may therefore learn more from news. By the time they reach sixth and seventh grades, children may begin to make distinctions about the importance of content within program context, perhaps basing judgments on individual stories rather than types of programs.

For example, older children may learn more from the news story in the cartoon context because they perceive it as being more important than the cartoons and give it greater attention. In the news context, however, they may see a story about a museum in Paris as being less important than the hard news stories that surrounded it and therefore give it less attention.

This may be related to the curvilinear relationship Collins (1970) found for peripheral learning in entertainment programs. The interaction found in this study occurs between fifth and sixth grade, whereas Collins found a change between seventh and eighth grade. It is possible that the distinction between content that is central or peripheral to the plot of a story is even more sophisticated than the judgment mentioned above and occurs a bit later.

The data are interesting in terms of uses and gratifications research also. The tendency of children who thought the story was presented for information to learn more than those who thought it was aired for entertainment raises an interesting question about the relationship between perceived intent of the communicator and the uses of television content. Perceived intent may help determine use. For example, children who perceive that a source's intent is to entertain may then use the program primarily for entertainment, and those who judge the intent to be informational may use the content to learn. On the other hand, it is possible that the gratifications children receive from a program set the expectation for later contacts with that type of program. A child who watches a news program and is entertained by it may approach similar programs in the future expecting to be entertained. Consistency between perceived intent and use also may be related to other dependent variables, such as satisfaction with content. Those who expect to be entertained by content and are entertained may be more satisfied with the content than those who expect to be informed and are entertained.

In summary, the data here indicate that children's *perceptions* should not be overlooked in efforts to increase learning from news and public affairs programs. Although there is often a tendency to concentrate on production variables to enhance learning, it also may be worthwhile to try to change or develop perceptions. It appears that the more children understand the information function of news, like the news, and believe the news story, the more information they will take away from it. This also should support educators in their efforts to teach children to become knowledgeable consumers of the news media.

One final observation is that the multiple R reported in this study (.61), produced by regressing perceptual variables on the learning scores, is much larger than that reported in a number of television entertainment effects studies using the same variables singly. This may indicate that there is value in using actual programming in the classroom to establish a specific referent for measuring children's reactions to television. For example, children's perceptions of course motivation was a particularly strong predictor of learning. It may have been much easier for the children to react to a specific message rather than answer a question about a category of messages.

NOTE

1. Path analysis was not used for two reasons: there is multicollinearity among the variables and the general model is underidentified.

REFERENCES

ATKIN, C. K. (1978) "Broadcast news programming and the child audience.'
J. of Broadcasting 22: 47-61.
——— and W. GANTZ (1975) "The role of television news in the political sociali-
zation of children." Presented at the annual convention of the International
Communication Association, Chicago.
CHAFFEE, S. H., S. WARD, and L. TIPTON (1970) "Mass communication and
political socialization." Journalism Q. 47: 647-659.
COLLINS, W. A. (1970) "Learning of media content: a developmental study."
Child Development 41: 1133-1142.
CONWAY, M. M., A. J. STEVENS, and R. G. SMITH (1975) "The relation between
media use and children's civic awareness." Journalism Q. 52: 531-538.
DOMINICK, J. (1972) "Television and political socialization." Educ. Broadcasting
Rev. 6: 48-52.
GREENBERG, B. S. (1974) "Gratifications of television viewing and their cor-
relates for British children," in J. G. Blumler and E. Katz (eds.) The Uses of
Mass Communications: Current Perspectives on Gratification Research.
Beverly Hills, CA: Sage.
HAWKINS, R. P. (1973) "Learning of peripheral content in films: a developmental
study." Child Development 44: 2134-217.
LOMETTI, G. E., B. REEVES, and C. R. BYBEE (1977) "Investigating the Assump-
tions of uses and gratifications research." Communication Research 4: 321-
338.
McGUIRE, W. J. (1968) "The nature of attitudes and attitude change," in G.
Lindzey and E. Aronson (eds.) The Handbook of Social Psychology, Vol. III.
Reading, MA: Addison-Wesley.
McCLEOD, J. M., C. K. ATKIN, and S. H. CHAFFEE (1972) "Adolescents, parents
and television use: self-report and other-report measures from the Wisconsin
sample," in G. A. Comstock and E. A. Rubinstein (eds.) Television and Social
Behavior, Vol. 3. Washington, DC: U.S. Government Printing Office.
McLEOD, J. M. and B. REEVES (1977) "The nature of mass media effects." (un-
published)
SCHRAMM, W., J. LYLE, and E. B. PARKER (1961) Television in the Lives of Our
Children. Stanford: Stanford Univ. Press.
WILSON, R. C. and E. J. SCHAFFER (1965) "Reading comics to learn." Elementary
School 66: 81-82.

*Dan Drew is Assistant Professor in the School of Journalism and Mass
Communication at the University of Wisconsin—Madison. Drew received
his Ph.D. in the Mass Communication Program at Indiana University. He is
interested in research dealing with socialization of children to the news
media and by the news media.*

*Byron Reeves is Assistant Professor in the School of Journalism and Mass
Communication at the University of Wisconsin—Madison. Reeves received
his Ph.D. in communication from Michigan State University in 1976 and has
since been interested in research on media and child socialization.*

An innovative experiment designed to validate and extend the ideas of Richard Carter on information processing is described here. Thomas McCain and Mark G. Ross used computerized monitoring and content analysis of an open-ended questionnaire to measure Ohio State University students' cognitive switching while watching television news. The experiment suggests that the respondents "unitize" the TV news in the four modes suggested by Carter— agree, disagree, think, and question—regardless of the varying news content. Dr. McCain is an associate professor of communication at Ohio State University. Mr. Ross is an assistant professor at Purdue University.

25

COGNITIVE SWITCHING
A Behavioral Trace of Human Information Processing for Television Newscasts

Thomas A. McCain and Mark G. Ross

Television news has for many years been identified as the primary source of information about what is going on in the world (Roper, 1977). Further, television's credibility has consistently been demonstrated to be relatively higher than those of other media. Roper, for example, reports that television is believed over other media accounts of news events, even for many people who indicate they do not receive most of their information from television. Even though television is such an ubiquitous medium, whose effects and uses have been widely studied, we know precious little about how people process televised information during the actual viewing situation. Such is the concern of this investigation.

Human beings monitor and process information constantly. Even while sleeping, people process information from their environment and rearrange their experiences (Travers, 1970). Although humans are not always in active information-seeking modes, they continue to monitor their environment. Background noise, while not actively sought, is constantly monitored for potentially important information (Moray, 1959). The critical point is that humans cannot not process information.

The purpose of the present study was to develop a descriptive picture of how people organize and process television newscasts. The assumptions concerning information-processing and the theoretical rationale which guided our investigation are presented below.

Assumption I: Human Information-processing is Limited by Time and Space Factors

The capability of the human information-processing system is not infinite. Posner and Keele (1970) identified two kinds of limitations on the processing system which are related to human performance. These are limitations of time and space. The time limitations are related to both the length of time that stored information persists (Keele, 1973) as well as the amount of time required for transformation of information from persistent and abstract

Thomas A. McCain (Ph.D., University of Wisconsin, 1972) is an associate professor of communication at Ohio State University, Columbus, Ohio, 43210. *Mark G. Ross* (M.A., Ohio State University, 1975) is a teaching associate and Ph.D. candidate at Ohio State University, Columbus, Ohio, 43210. This study accepted for publication August 8, 1978.

representations (Keele, 1973, p. 3). Spatial limitations are related to the finite capacity of the processing systems (Keele, 1973, p. 4).

Posner and Keele (1970) noted that some information is stored for only a few seconds before it is lost from memory, since varying amounts of time are required for retrieval of differing kinds of information. Certain information-processing tasks require more memory space than others. Television-viewing, for example, seems to require more memory space than other activities. Posner and Keele (1970) found that when subjects tried to do two tasks (television-viewing and conversing) at the same time, performance on both tasks suffered. This finding suggested that somewhere in a person's information-processing system there is a limitation or bottleneck which allocates limited memory space for processing information. Both spatial and temporal limitations of the information-processing system contribute to this bottleneck.

Proposition I: People Process Information Discretely

The basic thrust of the single-channel theory of information-processing is that people process information serially, or discretely (Broadbent, 1958; Welford, 1960; Posner, 1964; Attneave, 1966; Travers, 1970; Keele, 1973). Memorial systems are of a limited capacity and cannot process information in a bulk or parallel fashion (Haber, 1969). Broadbent's (1958) experiments indicated that a person's central information processor or "P-system" operates in a serial fashion. Travers indicated that our information utilization channel is a "limited capacity system that can handle only a given amount of information in a given time. The system handles one thing at a time and thus is referred to as a single channel system" (1970, p. 101). Welford (1960) found that reaction times to two closely occurring stimuli were different, with the reaction time to the second stimulus always longer than the first. The time needed to process the first stimulus apparently causes the reaction time for the second stimulus to be delayed. This phenomenon is termed central intermittency. Bertelson's (1966) review of central intermittency research strongly supports the single-channel theory of information-processing.

Because the memorial system functions as a single channel, the central processing of information appears to operate in a discrete fashion.

Assumption II: Cognitive Switching is the Process by Which People Organize Incoming Information

Researchers in information-processing have examined human performance in relation to various stimuli. There appears to be general consensus among human performance scholars that while human receptors can *attend* to a multitude of stimuli in a parallel fashion, the cognitive processing of this input is prioritized and handled in a unitary fashion (Keele, 1973). Sperling (1960), for example, suggests that there is a "rehearsal buffer" which aids in the processing of complex stimuli. Broadbent's (1958) p-system is further support for this filtering phenomenon.

We call the mechanism people use to establish hierarchies of input and to handle the plethora of information bombarding their information-processing systems cognitive switching. It is in part an analogue of the single-channel theory of information-processing, for if people process input in a unitary fashion, then they must organize this information and switch between various information or sensory sources.

A second rationale for cognitive switching is found in the work of Richard Carter (1971; Carter et al., 1973) and his signaled stopping technique (SST). Carter argues that a stop defines a boundary for a unit of information appropriate to the information processor. People stop, according to Carter, because of "nonsingularity of cognition" (Carter et al., 1973, p. 19). This nonsingularity of cognition, in essence, represents a parallel processing situation for the information processor. When such an incidence occurs, people must cognitively switch from one cognitive state to another. Carter labels this unitization of the information stream stopping.

Carter suggested that humans employ differing modes of information-processing. He called these modes of information-processing "content states" (1973, p. 16). According to Carter, as people process information, they switch from one content state to another. For example, a person may be viewing a newscaster giving an editorial comment and generally agreeing, when suddenly something is said that results in questioning the issue—the viewer has switched modes. Carter argues that in order to switch from the agreeing mode to the questioning mode suggested above, the switch must be indexed with a stop.

Switching behavior is not usually observed. If, however, subjects are equipped with an instrument (SST) to signal a stop, then the switch is observable. With this information, the researcher can distinguish the boundaries of content states which are unique for individuals.

Carter's notions suggest that humans process information in a discrete fashion. Although information itself is obviously available in a continuous flow, people can only process it in one content state at a time. Humans cannot both agree and disagree with incoming information simultaneously; they must cognitively switch from one content state to another.

Carter's concerns with communication messages are clearly more complex than those of the human performance researchers. Most of the human performance studies used reaction times to simple stimuli for their measure of information-processing. Signaled stopping research has employed newspaper articles as the independent variable and concerned itself not with simple reaction times to the varying stimuli, but to the type and frequency of stops signaled by the subjects. Our assumption here is that Carter's notion of signaled stopping is analogous to the single-channel phenomenon observed in human performance research. People unitize information macroscopically as well as microscopically. This macroscopic chunking is the process by which people organize incoming information in a unitary fashion. We label this phenomenon cognitive switching.

Proposition II: Cognitive Switching is the Process of Unitizing Information

Three elements of cognitive switching as an information-processing activity have been extrapolated from past research. We have labeled them: state location, state interval, and state function.

State location is the point in time that a switch occurs for a subject. Posner (1964), Haber (1969),

Broadbent (1958), Travers (1970), and others have been primarily interested in identifying the point in time that a subject responds to a stimulus. In a broader context, Carter et al.'s (1973) research in signaled stopping has focused on the location of cognitive switches in printed copy.

State interval is the length of time a subject is in any given cognitive switching state. Welford (1960) and Broadbent's (1958) research is illustrative of the state *interval* notion. This research focused on the relationships between interstimulus interval and reaction time.

State function is the cognitive switching mode a subject is in at any one state interval—it is the reason why a person switches. Carter et al.'s research (1973) suggested that there were four relevant types of stops analogous to state function. People stop to: agree, disagree, think, and question. Carter's support for these four categories was derived from subjects' written comments and personal interviews.

Cognitive switching may be examined according to the relationships of the location, interval, and function of the switches as they persistently occur.

Proposition III: People Exhibit Similar Cognitive Switching Behaviors in Similar Information-processing Situations

Heffner (1972), in a study of stopping behavior, concluded that groups of subjects that were given the same instructions on a task were much closer in their stopping, than were groups with differing instructions. Carter and Simpson (Carter et al., 1973) used subjects' attitudes as an independent condition. They discovered that subjects with similar preconceptions tended to stop similarly in response to a given stimulus. Grunig (1974) studied the effects of differing writing styles of scientific material on stopping behavior. He concluded that groups of people presented with the same content but differing message styles showed significant differences in their stopping behavior.

We would expect, therefore, that subjects in similar information-processing situations should exhibit similar cognitive switching patterns over time. That is, individuals should leave similar behavioral traces of their cognitive switching activity.

HYPOTHESES

Before the general hypotheses are presented, several points about the state of research in cognitive switching are important. First, the relationship between state location and state function has never been examined in a dynamic mass media setting such as a television-viewing situation. This is most likely due to the lack of instruments with sufficient sophistication to record switches as they occur. Second, signaled stopping research, which has examined some aspects of cognitive switching, has treated switches as the sum of stops across varying conditions (Heffner, 1970; Carter, 1971; Heffner, 1972; Jacoubovitch, 1972; Carter, et al., 1983; Grunig, 1974). Finally, in the majority of SST research, the temporal sequencing of switches has not been preserved; stops have been lumped together (Carter, 1971; Carter, et al., 1973; Grunig, 1974).

The theory developed above suggests that people process information discretely and that there must, by necessity, be a way individuals can unitize input into their systems. The cognitive switching model developed in proposition II tacitly assumes the existence of the four state functions (agreeing, disagreeing, thinking, and questioning) as the thought processes people use in order to unitize input. The validity of these functions has not, however, been systematically examined.

The specific purpose of this research was primarily descriptive. Its focus was to validate the utility and viability of state location and state function for a continuous, time-bound communication transaction—viewing television newscasts. Since this research is in its infancy, the need to describe phenomena and validate the basic constructs of the budding theory were viewed as the primary concern.

The following hypotheses were specifically tested:

H₁: Subjects who cognitively switch for specified state functions (agree, disagree, think, question) will exhibit similar distributions of switching behavior as subjects with nonspecified state functions, while viewing television newscasts.

H₂: Subject-generated reasons for cognitively switching will be positively related to the four state functions of agreeing, disagreeing, thinking, and questioning.

H₃: Subjects' cognitive switching distributions will be similar over time from newscast₁ to newscast₅.

The hypotheses were directed toward validation of the concept of cognitive switching and assessing the explanatory power of the four state functions. The presumption was that subjects who had been trained in the use of the four state functions to trace their cognitive switching behavior would be similar to those who were unaware of the specific nature of these functional switches. The validity problem was to attempt to assess the similarities or nondifferences between these two groups. This, in conjunction with the conceptual nature of the data, represents a nonordinary validity problem, due to the time series nature of subjects' cognitive switching behaviors.

PROCEDURES FOR DATA COLLECTION

Hypotheses 1 and 3 were assessed, using a specially designed audience response machine (ARM). Each subject was supplied with a hand-held sender unit whereby he/she could trace his/her switching behavior. An interface was constructed which linked the ARM with a computer terminal. The interface could scan the subjects' responses at any predetermined rate. Each interface scan was then automatically recorded on the output of the computer terminal.

The ARM allowed for a quasi-continuous over time record of subject responses. Subjects responded by depressing an appropriate button on their hand-held sender units. Subject responses were scanned and recorded every 1.33 seconds.

Thirty subjects participated in the experiment over five trials. All subjects responded to five different videotaped recordings of the "CBS Evening News with Walter Cronkite."

One-half of the subjects were assigned to a four state function treatment group. Subjects in this group were instructed to specify their switches by depressing one of four buttons (A through D) on their sender units. The four buttons corresponded to Carter's four types of signaled stops: agree, disagree, think, and question—respectively.

The other half of the subjects were randomly placed in a nonspecified state function treatment group. Subjects in this group were instructed to trace their switching behavior whenever it occurred by depressing button A on their sender unit. They were not informed of the four state functions.

The data were collected in the Audience Response Laboratory at Ohio State University. The laboratory offers a quasi-livingroom atmosphere with couches, comfortable chairs, and indirect lighting. The furniture was clustered around two different black and white television monitors, so that subjects viewed in small groups no larger than five. All subjects received two weeks of prior training in the use of the ARM.

PROCEDURES FOR DATA ANALYSIS

Two major problems were encountered. First, how can the stream of subject responses be categorized in such a way as to preserve its processual nature? Each newscast was approximately 26 minutes long. The data were coded into 24 one-minute intervals, representing common intervals for all trials and groups. In this fashion, 24 frequency location scores were calculated for each subject, representing the total number of switches within each one-minute segment of the newscast. Although arbitrary, this conceptualization of the data still preserves some of the sequential nature of the cognitive switching process.

The second, and perhaps more critical, validity problem dealt with demonstrating similarities between the treatment groups. The use of various statistical and analytical tools was employed in an attempt to offer multimethod evidence of similarity. Obviously, inferential statistics are designed to evaluate differences between populations, not similarities. The statistical tests should not be viewed as sufficient evidence of similarity in and of themselves, since some of the assumptions of the statistics were violated. No single definitive tests of the hypotheses are available; therefore, the analyses are presented as a triangulation of proofs. The specific procedures for assessing each hypothesis are presented below.

Hypothesis 1 was investigated by assessing the degree of relationship between the two treatment groups. To the extent that these two treatment groups left similar behavioral traces, the validity of Carter's four state functions was enhanced. Data were analyzed by correlating the response distributions of the two groups at each of the five newscasts and by a graphic procedure whereby the number of stops were graphed over time for each treatment group across the five newscasts.

At first inspection it might appear that a more sensitive way to intercorrelate the two treatment groups would be to calculate correlations based on subjects' raw scores at each of the one-minute intervals and then to derive an overall average correlation. This avenue was considered, but the amount of data generated in a one-minute time interval was small and considered to be inadequate for analysis due to lack of error randomization inherent in such a short time frame.

Hypothesis 2 was investigated by a content analysis of an open-ended questionnaire that was administered on the last trial of the experiment. Subjects were instructed to list any reasons they could think of for switching.

Three judges were each given a copy of the instructions that were administered to the four-category group at each session. Judges were then asked to code any statement that dealt with the cognitive process of thinking in the *think* category, any statement that dealt with *questioning*, *agreeing*, or *disagreeing* into the appropriate category. Any statement that could not be coded into one of these categories was coded into a category called *other*. Judges were assessed for intercoder (unitizing) reliability by intercorrelating the frequencies of units in the five categories across the three judges.

To the extent that the four-category scheme exhausted the universe of state functions created through the questionnaire and to the extent that separate content analyses of statements generated by each of the treatment groups reflected similar findings, the validity of Hypothesis 2 was enhanced.

TABLE 1
Correlation Between Treatments
Across Five Newscasts

News-cast 1	News-cast 2	News-cast 3	News-cast 4	News-cast 5
.58*	.59*	.52*	.51*	.54*

N = 24
* p < .01

Hypothesis 3 was assessed by treating all subjects as if they were using the nonspecified state function instrument. Only state location over time was considered in this analysis. A one-way ANOVA repeated measures design was performed across the five newscasts. To the extent that the between columns F ratio showed no significant differences and to the extent that the Beta level was low, Hypothesis 3 was supported.

A test-retest reliability assessment procedure was also conducted. On what would have been the sixth trial of the experiment, subjects viewed and responded to the same newscast they had seen the week before. Subject responses were coded and their response distributions (24 one-minute segments) correlated from $time_1$ to $time_2$.

RESULTS

Hypothesis 1

The reliability assessment procedure was completed first. This analysis yielded a test-retest reliability coefficient of .90 (Spearman Rho).

Subject switching behaviors were then coded across all newscasts into the one-minute intervals and the two treatment group distributions correlated for each newscast. The results of this Pearson r analysis are reported in Table 1. The correlations ranged from .5 to .6.

The moderate relationships illustrated by the correlations are viewed as strikingly high when other factors are taken into account. The first factor in need of consideration is the negatively biasing effect of calculating correlation coefficients based on two different groups of subjects. The second factor involves the intercorrelating of *functionally* differ-

TABLE 2
Mean and Standard Deviation Comparisons
Between Two Treatments
Across Five Newscasts

News-cast		Non-Specified	Four Category
1	$\bar{x}$	2.19	2.28
	sd	.03	.28
2	$\bar{x}$	2.21	2.35
	sd	.21	.21
3	$\bar{x}$	1.73	2.00
	sd	.27	.29
4	$\bar{x}$	1.00	1.51
	sd	.27	.27
5	$\bar{x}$	1.06	1.43
	sd	.34	.34

ent instruments (four-category vs. nonspecified). Although it was predicted that both instruments would be highly related, the functional differences in the instruments would lead one to believe the four-category group would generate more switches by virtue of the fact that the four-category instrument provided subjects with more sensitivity. They would switch more frequently, thus negatively biasing the degree of relationship between the two groups. Table 2 bears this notion out. It compares the means and standard deviations of the two groups across the five newscasts.

The means of the four-category group are consistently higher than those of the nonspecified group, while the standard deviations of the groups show only slight differences.

Furthermore, a mean proportional analysis yielded inconsequential differences in means across the groups. Mean proportions were calculated by dividing the mean switching score for any single one-minute time interval by the total number of switches the particular treatment group signaled and calculating a grand average. The grand means for the nonspecified and four-category groups respectively were: newscast 1: 5.6, 5.6; newscast 2: 4.2, 4.1; newscast 3: 4.2, 4.2; newscast 4: 4.1, 4.1; newscast 5: 4.2, 4.1. Taking into account the inherent sensitivity of the four-category instrument, by calculating proportions, reveals that the two groups are essentially identical.

The degree of similarity between the two groups'

TABLE 3
Comparison of the Frequency of Occurrence of Five Types of Subject Generated Statements Across Two Treatments

Type of Switch	Non-Specified Function Treatment		Four Function Treatment	
Think	31	(32.2%)	29	(29.5%)
Agree	16	(16.6%)	21	(23.8%)
Disagree	20	(20.8%)	19	(21.5%)
Question	14	(14.5%)	12	(13.6%)
Other	15	(15.6%)	10	(11.3%)

Spearman Rho = .80.

switching behaviors was also illustrated graphically. The average number of switches (for each one-minute time interval) was plotted across all subjects in each treatment group for each of the five newscasts.[1]

The mean number of switches per minute for each subject ranged from 2.41 to 1.5, and did not significantly vary across the five newscasts. The specified four-function group switched more often than the nonspecified group, but the distributions of both groups switching over time show a remarkable similarity, given the limitations outlined above. The moderate correlations further indicate a reasonably consistent relationship between the two groups.

Hypothesis 2

Hypothesis 2 suggested that the two treatment groups would be similar in their reasons for cognitive switching. A content analysis procedure of the five types of possible subject generated reasons for switching was employed, and the results are presented in Table 3.

There appear to be few differences in frequency of responses of the subjects across the two groups as to the reasons why they cognitively switched. A Spearman Rho correlation of .80 revealed further support of the similarities of the two groups. It is important to note that even for the subjects without knowledge of the four state function categories, 84 percent of their reasons for switching were accounted for by thinking, agreeing, disagreeing, and questioning.

The consistency of the three judges was computed for intercoder unitizing reliability. The aver-

age intercoder reliability coefficient was .92. The results of the judges coding for both groups were further assessed, utilizing chi-square goodness-of-fit tests on the data presented in Table 3. The two resulting significant chi-squares ($X^2 = 10.08$, df=4, p<.05; $X^2 - 9.81$, df=4, p<.05) indicate that the judges were not coding the responses in a random fashion. These analyses further support the reliability of the judges.

Hypothesis 3

This hypothesis was assessed through the use of a one-way analysis of variance repeated measures design. The result of this analysis yielded a significant between rows F ratio (7.38, df=29, 116; p<.01). This finding indicates significant variance due to individual differences between the television viewers. The nonsignificant between columns F ratio (.59, df=4, 116) indicates that differences between the newscasts were not significant.

DISCUSSION

Hypotheses 1 and 2, which were directed toward assessing the validity of the four state functions, were supported. The correlations, means, and graphing procedures indicate a strong relationship between groups of subjects who were supplied the four state functions in order to indicate their switching behavior and those who were unaware of the four specific state functions. Further, the content analysis of subject-generated reasons for switching tended to fall along the four state functions originally specified by Carter. People appear to unitize information with at least four functional filters: agreeing, disagreeing, questioning, and thinking.

Hypothesis 3, which argued that switching behavior (i.e., number of switching units) would persist in a similar fashion over time, was supported through a somewhat circuitous procedure.

Predicting the null hypothesis (no differences) is certainly not a definitive way to test a hypothesis; however, an analysis of the between columns F ratio suggests that a fairly large alpha level would have been required to interpret the F ratio as significant. An F ratio of 5.74 or greater was required to interpret the differences between the groups as being significant at the p=.05 level of confidence. The alpha level required to interpret the derived F ratio of .59 as indicating significant differences across the five newscasts was higher than p=.5 (Owen, 1962, p. 80). Since alpha levels are inversely related to beta levels, this inflated alpha level would necessarily decrease the beta level involved in the test. This decreased beta level would therefore decrease the chances of making a Type II error, which is the main interest when predicting no differences between groups (Blalock, 1972, pp. 160-162).

The distributions of state locations appear to persist for subjects over five different newscasts. That is, people tended to switch about the same number of times at all 24 locations from one newscast to another. It is critical to emphasize that the analyses presented here should not be viewed in isolation, but rather as supportive and complementary. Since no definitive tests of the hypothesis were available, the results are displayed as a triangulation of proofs concerning the validity of the cognitive switching model.

Companion research has investigated the factors which account for the individual differences between the subjects as their switching persisted over time. There is some indication that people develop an information-processing style which varies along state function configurations (Ross, 1975; McCain & Ross, 1977).

LIMITATIONS

The sample was drawn entirely from the student population at the Ohio State University; inferences drawn from this study are probably only generalizable to that population. The sample size for the study was small (n=30). The large amounts of data generated and the tedious data-coding process required a small sample (over 450 feet of raw data were handcoded centimeter by centimeter, into one-minute time intervals). In this small a sample, error is difficult to randomize.

Another potential limitation of the study is that the judges employed for the content analysis knew the five categories into which they could code the data. A less biased way to perform this analysis would have been to allow the judges to generate their own categories and then to test to determine the

extent that these categories correspond with the four Carter categories.

The one-minute time intervals in which the data were coded were arbitrarily chosen. The one-minute interval was the easiest to work with in terms of analytical and coding procedures. Another interval might be more applicable.

Another problem may have resulted, in that by the time the last newscast was viewed, it was five weeks old. The first newscast subjects viewed was only one day old. This may have had a confounding effect on subjects' responses.

There are also some limitations specific to the audience response machine, which should be noted. Subjects were required to press buttons on their sender units. The buttons were not always as quiet as would be desired. This could have added obtrusiveness to the experimental setting. Secondly, the machine was set up to take readings every 1.33 seconds. Some subjects' switches could have been lost simply because the machine was not fast enough.

IMPLICATIONS FOR FUTURE RESEARCH

The four categories that were employed here are certainly very broad. Further refinement of these categories is needed especially for the thinking function. Thinking covers a multitude of sins—it includes pondering the information in order to put new input in perspective and also daydreaming, or tuning out. Future research should try to differentiate these two broad functional switches.

The content analysis showed that some variance was accounted for by the "other" category. The type of reasons that filled this category should also be investigated.

Another dimension in need of further study is the state interval of the switch. Some subjects left traces lasting one second, others for 20 seconds. Possibly, the longer the interval of the switch, the greater the effect the message is having. If subjects think for long durations, the message may be more complex. There are numerous hypotheses which should be dealt with in this area.

There is some evidence that there might be "critical" time intervals that have strong effects on cognitive switching behavior. In the graphs of subject switching distributions, there seemed to be points in every newscast where switching frequency was at a minimum.

Companion research investigated the relationship between the state function/location of switching patterns and the verbal and nonverbal content of one of the newscasts. Specific methods of presentation, news topics, and news sources were found to differentially effect degrees of cognitive switching (McCain, Ross et al., 1977). Perceived saliency of the issues may also have an effect on subject switching behavior. In any event, there is a need for further research into the nature of the stimulus message and its effects on the distribution of subject switches.

We were particularly encouraged that the functions of cognitive switching: agree, disagree, think, and question have some validity for explaining how people unitize continuous television news messages. Further, the finding that people tend to unitize similar information (i.e., newscasts) in a similar fashion, regardless of the varying content of the stories in the newscast, has significant implications for unraveling the differential uses that television news serves for people. The observed differences in viewing the five different newscasts were differences within groups, rather than differences due to the content of the newscasts themselves. This suggests to us that people bring to the news-viewing situation a cognitive switching style which they employ in a systematic manner in order to make sense of the news content and to cope with the spatial and temporal limitations of their information-processing systems.

NOTE

1. Copies of these graphs are available from the authors upon request.

REFERENCES

ATTNEAVE, F. Spatial coding of tactual stimulation. *Journal of Experimental Psychology*, 1969, 81, 216-222.

BERTELSON, P. Central intermittency twenty years later. *Quarterly Journal of Experimental Psychology*, 1966, 18, 153-163.

BLALOCK, H.M. *Social Statistics*. 2nd Ed. New York: McGraw-Hill, 1972.

BROADBENT, D. *Perception and communication*. New York: Pergamon Press, 1958.

CARTER, R.F., & RUGGELS, W.L. Research on stopping: A new approach to research on communication effects. Research proposal, 1970.

CARTER, R.F. Theoretical development in the use of signaled stopping. Paper prepared for the Division of Theory and Methodology, Association for Education in Journalism, 1971.

CARTER, R.F. et al. Application of signaled stopping technique to communication research. In Peter Clark (Ed.), *New Models for mass communication research*. Beverly Hills: Sage Publication Co., 1973.

GRUNIG, J. Three stopping experiments on the communication of science. *Journalism Quarterly*, Autumn 1974.

HABER, R.N. Perception and thought: An information processing analysis. In J F Voss (Ed.), *Approaches to thought*. Columbus, Ohio: Merrill Publishing Co., 1969.

HEFFNER, M.B. Innoculation and stopping behavior. Paper read at Association for Education in Journalism convention, 1972.

HEFFNER, M.B. The possibility of communicative accuracy. Ph.D. dissertation. Seattle: University of Washington, 1972.

JACKSON, K.M. Monitoring communication activity, new techniques of observation. *Journalism Quarterly*, 1974, 51, 47-56.

JACOUBOVITCH, M.D. Communication consequences of signification. Masters thesis. Seattle: University of Washington, 1972.

KEELE, S.W. *Attention and human performance*. Pacific Palisades, California: Goodyear Publishing Co., Inc., 1973.

KERLINGER, F.N. *Foundations of behavioral research*. New York: Holt, Rinehart and Winston, Inc., 1973.

McCAIN, T.A., & ROSS, M.G. with LEFFINGWELL, R., SCHIEBER, D., SIEGERDT, G. Cognitive switching. An information processing measure of television news viewing. Paper presented at International Communication Association Convention, Berlin, 1977.

MORAY, N. Attention in dichotic listening: Affective cues and the influence of instructions. *Quarterly Journal of Experimental Psychology*, 1959, 11, 56-60.

OWEN, D.B. *Handbook of Statistical Tables*. London: Pergamon Press, 1962.

POSNER, M.I. Information reduction in the analysis of sequential tasks. *Psychological Review*, 1964, 71, 491-504.

POSNER, M.I., & KEELE, S.W. Time and space as measures of mental operations. Paper read at the 78th Annual Convention of the American Psychological Association, September, 1970.

ROPER ORGANIZATION. Changing public attitudes toward television and other mass media, 1959-1976. New York: Television Information Office, 1977.

ROSS, M.G. Signaled stopping: Development of a measure of human information processing. Unpublished masters thesis, Ohio State University, 1975.

SPERLING, G.A. The information available in brief visual presentation. *Psychological Monographs*, 1960, 74.

TRAVERS, R.M. *Man's information system*. Scranton, Pa.: Chandler Publishing Co., 1970.

WELFORD, A.T. The measurement of sensory-motor performance: Survey and reappraisal of twelve years progress. *Ergonomics*, 1960, 3, 189-230.

ZEISEL, H. *Say it with figures*. New York: Harper & Row, Publishers, 1968.

Research on the possible linkages between mass media content and interpersonal behavior has assumed new directions. Michael E. Roloff presents an unusual perspective in which he uses the notion of scripts—coherent projections of actual or perceived vignettes of human actions in response to a situation or problem—to link media content to interpersonal relations. Dr. Roloff, who is in the department of communication studies at Northwestern University, reviews research that describes interpersonal behavior in terms of scripts and other work which links probabilities of realizing certain scripts to media exposure. He develops five propositions that may lead to a theory of media-script utilization. This article is based on a paper presented at the Speech Communication Association meeting in San Antonio, Texas, in November 1979.

26

INTERPERSONAL AND MASS COMMUNICATION SCRIPTS

An Interdisciplinary Link

Michael E. Roloff

Scholars have noted that cultural portrayals of interpersonal life in the theater often provide important insights into our actual interpersonal relationships. Goffman (1959) has suggested that the same skills that are used by actors on a stage are employed by interpersonal communicators, and Harré (1974) has gone so far as to suggest that theorists and researchers can learn more about interpersonal communication from playwrights than from theorists in the natural sciences. Despite this recognition by some interpersonal theorists that mass communication portrayals of interpersonal communication bear a great deal of resemblance to actual interactions, little social scientific research has been generated investigating this correspondence. The position taken here argues that this neglected area represents a potentially rich well of research in the interpersonal communication area, particularly conflict situations.[1] This paper presents an analysis of an area of overlap between mass media portrayals of interpersonal communication and actual interpersonal communication.

From Michael E. Roloff, "Interpersonal and Mass Communication Scripts: An Interdisciplinary Link," original manuscript.

INTERPERSONAL CONFLICT:
IT IS EVERYWHERE

The tendency to attempt to project and maintain one's own self-image has been noted by several theorists (for example, Shaver, 1975; McCall and Simmons, 1978). However, despite this "positivity bias," interpersonal conflict is pervasive. Indeed, a number of studies suggest that this tendency to reinforce each other's self-concept may actually be an attempt to resolve a conflict through conflict avoidance or denial (Rausch et al., 1974; Fitzpatrick, 1977; Sillars, 1979). Frost and Wilmot (1978:9) define interpersonal conflict as "an expressed struggle between at least two interdependent parties, who perceive incompatible goals, scarce rewards, and interference from the other party in achieving their goals." In their view, conflict in interpersonal relationships is inevitable and serves the positive function of relational growth. While conflict is not inherently destructive, the methods which people employ to resolve their conflicts are not always constructive (Roloff, 1976; Deutsch, 1977). Several studies have found that the use of violence between family members to resolve conflicts is quite common (Levinger, 1966; O'Brien, 1971; Gelles, 1972). In addition, some people engage in avoidance behaviors that decrease their understanding of one another (Knudson et al., 1980).

While a variety of issues are cited as causing conflict, a plausible underlying cause of interpersonal conflict stems from the very nature of relationships. Several interpersonal theorists have noted the importance of exchanging rewards in relationships. For example, Scanzoni writes (1972:53), "what is lifelong is the notion of an ongoing quest or seeking for rewards, or the best bargain possible. Therefore, persons today bargain during courtship, during the decision to marry, and furthermore, they continue this bargaining on through the length of their marriage." Because of inequities in the exchange of relational rewards, Scanzoni argues that interpersonal conflict is inevitable and unavoidable.

If interpersonal conflict is as pervasive as suggested by this analysis, it should be reflected in the mass media. Indeed, some analyses of media content suggest that interpersonal conflict is frequently portrayed and can be found in at least two types of media content. First, interpersonal conflict is an important part of fictional presentations. Greenberg (1969) reviewed several content analyses concerning the prevalence of violent conflict in a variety of media. Conflict was broadly defined as the establishment of problem situations, the interaction of antagonistic forces. His review suggested that conflict was often portrayed in a variety of media but particularly in dramatic content. The most frequent resolution of dramatic media portrayals of conflict involved violence. Greenberg suggests that the structure of media presentations is inherently limited in how much background material can be presented about a conflict. Therefore, the media tend to present violent resolutions of conflict since minimal explanation about the character is necessitated.

Felsenthal (1976:34) also has noted the prevalence of conflict in dramatic presentations in the media: "Conflict has always been a dominant theme in any dramatic presentation, be it a Greek tragedy, a play by Shakespeare, a motion picture, or a television series." Although both Felsenthal and Greenberg use conflict to include situations not normally thought to be interpersonal (for example, war) the necessity of including conflict in dramatic portrayals underscores the potential relevance of media presentations to actual interpersonal conflicts.

A second type of media content involves presenting conflict in informational contexts. The current popularity of "self-help" books suggests that authors have a medium for describing the conflicts that are emerging in family interactions or in work situations (for example, Dyer, 1976, 1978; Ringer, 1978). In addition to books, conflict is often described in the news. In an analysis of six major daily newspapers, Cony (1953) found 53 percent of news stories dealt with some type of conflict. Of that, more than one-fourth dealt with crime reports involving individuals. Bagdikian (1974:127) pointed out the importance of conflict to television news: "The high value placed on action footage intensifies the traditional tendency to put a high priority on conflict even more for television than for radio or print."

In an examination of long-term trends in media portrayals of violence, Clark and Blankenburg (1971) found that the frequency of violence in the movies and on newspaper front pages has increased. Violence in mass circulation magazine fiction has been on a downward trend since the mid-1950s but still remains relatively high.

Comstock et al. (1978) noted that the relative frequency of violence in drama and news is about the same. The proportion of violent items in newscasts and violent programs in prime time is similar. In addition, the proportion of reports of violence in television news and on newspaper front pages is similar, although television tends to provide illustrations of the violence more than do newspapers.

While violence is but one means of conflict resolution and might be used to resolve a variety of conflicts other than interpersonal ones, the high incidence of violence in the media suggests that interpersonal conflict is prevalent in media portrayals. Thus, we have a situation in which interpersonal conflict is pervasive in real life and is so reflected in media presentations. The correspondence between the two represents an important area of research. The question becomes, How do we go about looking at this correspondence?

SCRIPTS AS A BASIS OF BEHAVIOR

In contrast to traditional explanations of human behavior in terms of attitudes, Schank and Abelson (1977) have argued that human behavior can be best understood in terms of cognitive scripts. Abelson (1976:33) recently defined a script as a "coherent sequence of events expected by the individual involving him or her either as a participant or as an observer." He suggests that scripts are composed of linked vignettes; a single vignette consists of an image of a perceived event and conceptual representation of the event. Vignettes may be stored by the individual as single episodes or experiences, categories defined by their use in a given situation, or hypothetical groupings based upon features abstracted from a variety of vignettes. Since scripts are composed of vignettes, Abelson argues that scripts may also be stored in the same manner.

Although Schank and Abelson recognize the difficulty of developing a taxonomy of scripts, they tentatively identify three types: situational, personal and instrumental. Situational scripts are those in which a given situation is specified, the participants within the situation have interlocking roles, and the individuals in the situation share an understanding of what will happen in the situation. Personal scripts are those which exist in the mind of the main participant in the situation. They may occur when two individuals do not have a situational script, such as in novel situations. However, personal scripts may also be used in conjunction with situational scripts. Instrumental scripts prescribe a sequence of actions that one individual will engage in to achieve a given goal. Usually the sequence is quite rigid and is associated with a task. Finally, Abelson (1976:42) suggests that scripts are related to behavior in the following manner: "Cognitively mediated social behavior depends on the joint occurrence of two processes: (a) the selection of a particular script to represent the given situation and (b) the taking of a participant role within that script."

This approach is not altogether unique. Stebbins (1972) presents a similar analysis of the definition of the situation. He argues that people categorize situations on the basis of their self-perceptions and perceptions of others. These definitions may be cultural, habitual, or personal. Cultural definitions are collective representations embedded in the culture as a whole or some subpart of it that are learned through socialization. They are standardized and recognized by members of a social system. Habitual definitions are those circumstances in which the definition of the situation holds the same meaning for a particular class of people participating in it but in which each participant is more or less unaware that people like him or her who have the same kind of experiences define them similarly. Personal definitions are the regular meanings employed by categories of actors in specific kinds of situations that are not shared.

Abelson makes a similar point when he notes that some people develop different scripts through socialization but that some scripts are so over-learned they become universal within a given group of people. However, an important difference emerges in the recent thinking on scripts. The definition of the situation assumes a great deal of cognitive activity and self-awareness in the selection of a definition.

While Stebbins recognizes that people may not be aware of the degree of consensus about a given definition, the process by which the definition affects behavior assumes a *conscious* selection of the definition. Initially, Schank and Abelson (1977:67-68) recognized that the use of scripts in behavior may involve little cognitive activity: "A human understander comes equipped with thousands of scripts. He uses these scripts almost without thinking."

Langer (1978) has expanded this point by arguing that most human behavior follows well-learned scripts and therefore requires so little cognitive activity that much human behavior might be characterized as "mindless." Langer (1978:39) writes, "The more often we have engaged in the activity the more likely it is that we will rely on scripts for the completion of the activity and the less likely it is that there will be any correspondence between our actions and those thoughts of ours that occur simultaneously." She argues that there may not be a relationship between our cognitions and concomitant behavior, and that there may be few cognitions occurring at all. Langer suggests that our reliance on scripts allows our minds to be virtually at rest. Langer suggests that "mindful" behavior occurs only in certain situations.

Social scientific research utilizing the notion of scripts has focused on two issues: (1) identifying factors that influence recall of scripts and (2) exploring the conditions which prompt "mindful" as opposed to "mindless" behavior. In general, research looking at the recall of scripts has employed a methodology in which subjects are presented with written scripts and asked to recall actions within the script after some experimental manipulation.[2]

The adoption of a theoretical framework such as that suggested by Schank and Abelson and revised by Langer offers a fruitful approach to looking at the correspondence between mass media portrayals of interpersonal conflict and actual interpersonal conflict. The position that will be presented in the remaining portion of this paper will focus on similarities between media conflict scripts and the scripts that are recognized in interpersonal conflicts. At this juncture, however, it is important to note that some differences are likely to be found between media scripts and the sequences of conflict behaviors that people actually perform in interpersonal relationships. *First,* it is likely that most media scripts are more structured than their interpersonal counterparts. Watzlawick et al. (1967) have noted that people often see interpersonal communication as an uninterrupted sequence of interactions and are forced to punctuate these sequences in order to determine some meaning for them. Similarly, Newtson (1976) has noted a variety of factors that affect the way in which people organize continuous behavior into discrete actions. Because of the processual nature of interpersonal communication, we might expect a great deal of variation in how people organize it.

Mass media scripts are more likely presented in a discrete fashion to begin with. The author has created a sequence of behavior with a beginning and end in mind. In essence, the author has punctuated the sequence for the recipient of a mass media script (Withey, 1980:15).

Second, characters acting within media scripts are better known to observers than characters within interpersonal situations. Berger and Calabrese (1975) have noted the importance of uncertainty about another in interpersonal communication. Individuals participating in interpersonal communication are often forced to make inferences about others. In mass media scripts, information about the characters is communicated at some point in time. For example, Rose (1979) has pointed out that soap operas make their plots and character analyses explicit. Some uncertainty exists in media scripts (for example, in mystery novels), but at some point resolution about character motivations generally occurs.

Third, mass media scripts are more recoverable than interpersonal scripts. After an interpersonal sequence is observed, the possibility of viewing it again or even experiencing it in a similar manner is very low. While people may differ in their reaction to a media script even when it is viewed again, the opportunity to view it as originally presented is greater than in interpersonal communication.

Fourth, interpersonal scripts may be viewed as being more reality based than mass media scripts. Certainly, the media provides an author with the opportunity to create interactions in contexts which are beyond the reach of current interpersonal communication (for example, science fiction). Other differences may exist, and their impact on the correspondence between interpersonal conflict scripts and media portrayals of interpersonal conflict should be studied.

INTERPERSONAL CONFLICT SCRIPTS: INDIRECT EVIDENCE

While no studies have directly investigated the use of conflict scripts as they are described here, several theorists and researchers have noted patterns of behavior that resemble scripts. Frost and Wilmot (1978) refer to ritualistic styles of conflict. The notion of ritual is similar to that of a script. The two participants are bound into a set of interlocking roles in which initially both seem to be aware of the behaviors in which each will engage. Importantly, Frost and Wilmot note that these conflict rituals allow individuals in ongoing relationships to add a sense of order to their interactions. Because the two individuals seemingly became comfortable with the rituals, one might also expect that after a period of time they can engage in them without being "mindful" *(a la* Langer) of their scripted behavior.

Interestingly, Scanzoni (1972:66) suggests that bargaining for relational rewards which are often the basis of interpersonal conflict takes place without a great deal of "mindful" behavior: "The bargaining need not be conscious, not rationally or explicitly calculated. Indeed, it may be quite unconscious and often husbands and wives may not in the least be aware that they are engaged in bargaining, or in efforts to make the exchange between them more equitable." Thus, it is possible that the ritualistic conflicts between men and women over rewards may reach the point where the participants are not aware of what they are doing.

Empirical research on interpersonal conflict has looked for regularities by investigating conflict behavior or by constructing conflict scenarios and assessing the likelihood that the subjects report they would use a variety of modes of conflict resolution. Both types of methodologies have discovered potential scripts.[3] Much research suggests that people tend to behave in a regular manner within conflict situations; they also report intentions that vary with the situation. These typical behaviors appear to be similar to scripts. However, an important question remains: "What are the interpersonal conflict scripts presented via the media?"

INTERPERSONAL CONFLICT SCRIPTS
IN THE MASS MEDIA

The incidence of interpersonal conflict in the media has been established. However, it is important to examine the form in which conflict is presented. The presentations made in the media may be similar to Abelson's notion of a script.

Greenberg (1969:44) points out that the typical plot of mass media fiction involves "(1) a sympathetic hero (2) struggling (3) against great odds or problems (4) to obtain (5) some worthwhile goal." Within this outline a variety of behaviors are carried out for many reasons, and considerable regularity occurs. Gerbner and Gross (1976:182) note: "Values and forces come into play through characterizations; good is a certain type of attractiveness, evil is a personality defect, and right is the might that wins. Plots weave a thread of causality into the fabric of dramatic ritual, as stock characters act out familiar parts and confirm preferred notions of what's what, who's who, and who counts for what."

Several analyses of television scripts have been done. Gerbner and Gross report a thorough analysis of the use of violence in television; they indicate that types of television programs differ in the use of violence, with action adventure programs contributing the most violence. In addition, their analysis examined the relationship between the victim and killer. Typically, the victim and killer are strangers. Certain categories such as old, married, lower-class, foreign, and nonwhite men were most likely to get killed rather than kill. Women were typically more likely to be victims than killers, particularly old, poor, and black women.

While Gerbner and Gross focused primarily on violence, Greenberg et al. (1977) examined a variety of pro- and antisocial actions on prime-time television. Antisocial actions consisted of physical aggression, verbal aggression, and deceit. Pro-social actions consisted of altruism, affection, expressing one's own feelings, and expressing the feelings of others. Their analysis suggests that approximately the same number of pro- and antisocial acts occurred during the average television hour. The most frequent antisocial act was verbal aggression, followed by physical aggression, and then by deceit. Of the pro-social acts, altruism and expressing one's own feelings were most frequent, followed by affection and expressing other's feelings. Again, differences were observed between television program type in the use of pro- and antisocial behavior. Cartoons were the most antisocial, family dramas, the least. Situation comedies were the most pro-social. Most antisocial actions were accompanied by some motive, usually material gain. In comparison, pro-social actions were infrequently accompanied by motives.

Recently, Dominick et al. (1979) content-analyzed prime-time and Saturday television programs for how characters resolved five types of problems: physical, property, authority, self-esteem, and affect/sentiment/ romance. Their analysis indicated that heroes in prime time tended to resolve problems through assertiveness or helping behaviors rather than aggression. Prime-time villains tended to resort to aggression rather than other modes of resolution. Saturday television heroes and villains both used aggression as their most likely resolution technique. Interestingly, assertive attempts to resolve a conflict were successful 70 percent of the time and aggression 60 percent of the time. On both prime-time and Saturday programming, aggressive resolutions were used when the conflict threatened life, while assertive solutions were paramount in the other conflict categories.

Barbatsis et al. (1979) content-analyzed the interaction between television characters within prime-time television, daytime soap operas, and Saturday morning cartoons. Their findings indicated that much of the interpersonal communication of both males and females involved attempts to establish dominance over another. This was true regardless of program type. In general, both males and females tended to send a great deal of dominance messages. However, females tended to receive a greater number of powerful dominance messages than did males. However, males received a greater proportion of nonsupportive messages. In essence, the study indicated a great deal of conflict between men and women in a variety of television scripts.

While these analyses focus exclusively on television, they do suggest regular observable behaviors in television scripts of conflict. In addition, the antisocial behaviors within the conflict are associated with given motives for the behavior.

INTERPERSONAL AND MEDIA CONFLICT
SCRIPTS: THE CRUCIAL COMPARISON

A critical question concerning the conflict scripts in real life and in the media focuses on whether consumers of the media perceive any correspondence between the two. Although no direct research has been conducted to test this issue, two studies provide some indirect evidence. Roloff and Greenberg (1979a) were concerned with the relationship between the perceived use of modes of conflict resolution by an adolescent's favorite TV character and the adolescent's intention to use a given mode of conflict resolution. Subjects were given a conflict scenario which they indicated their likelihood of resolving with a variety of behaviors. They also indicated how likely their favorite TV character would engage in the same behaviors in a similar scenario. The following results were obtained.

First, similar modes of conflict resolution were likely to be used by the favorite TV character and adolescent. Separate factor analyses of the responses indicated that five modes emerged: verbal aggression, physical aggression, revenge, regression, and pro-social. Second, an unreported canonical correlation was computed between the adolescent's intentions to use each conflict behavior and perception of favorite TV character's intentions. Eight significant canonical varieties ranging from .895 to .798 were observed, indicating a strong relationship between perceptions and behavioral intentions.

Third, differences were observed in the perceptions of how types of TV characters would handle the conflict. Action/adventure characters were perceived as more likely to engage in physical aggression than situation comedy/family drama characters. However, situation comedy/family drama characters were perceived as more likely to engage in revenge, verbal aggression, and regression. No differences were perceived in the use of pro-social.

In another study, Meyer (1973) asked children how they would respond to a variety of conflict situations. The children also described how their favorite television character, best friend, and parents would react to the situations. The results indicated that the children believed their favorite television character would respond in a pro-social manner, although some males believed their favorites would engage in violence to resolve the conflicts, similar to the child's own behavior.

While these two studies focused only on television, they suggest that people see some similarities in the scripts presented via one medium and their lives. Other research needs to be conducted with other media.

PROPOSITIONS FOR ANALYZING
SCRIPTED CONFLICT BEHAVIOR

While the research discussed here is only partially relevant to scripts, speculative propositions can be presented which might be used to generate research in the correspondence between media and interpersonal conflict scripts.

(1) Interpersonal conflict scripts are derived from a variety of social observations. The position suggested in this proposition is similar to the analysis presented by Schank and Abelson. From childhood, individuals observe their environment and construct scripts about what they observe. Sources of conflict scripts likely include family interactions, peer behavior as well as media scripts (Lefkowitz et al., 1977; Roloff and Greenberg, in press). To argue that one source is dominant for every individual all of his or her life would be an unrealistic position. Instead, research should attempt to focus on a variety of potential sources of scripts.

(2) Media portrayals of interpersonal conflict scripts may increase the awareness of certain conflict scripts or parts of these scripts. Within this analysis of scripts, it has been suggested that people are not always aware of the scripts of which they are part. This suggests that individuals may not be aware of their own scripted behavior and that large numbers of people may not be aware that they share similar scripts. In the case of self-awareness, it is possible that media users may become "mindful" of their own scripted behavior as a result of seeing it in the media. Seeing the portrayal of an interpersonal conflict as an outside observer, they may come to recognize similarities with their own conflict behavior.

In addition, media users may come to recognize habitual scripts and recognize that others feel the same way. This second form of awareness may be similar to the awareness that men and women as interest groups are in conflict with each other for institutional rewards. As the media portray or report conflicts between men and women over equal employment, ERA, or rape within marriage, women may become aware of their relative reward deprivation and focus their attention on conflict within their interpersonal relationships with men. Coser (1964) notes that awareness is necessary for conflicts to emerge. Scanzoni (1972) and Deutsch (1977) have made similar judgments about the women's movement.

As the awareness of the conflict increases, it is possible that the script will no longer be habitual but may move to a cultural or institutional level where people become universally aware of it. Certainly, such movement may take a long time, but represents an important area of research.

Another area of increased awareness may not stem from the entire script but from certain aspects of it. Gerbner and Gross have pointed out that subjects who are high viewers of violent television tend to generalize the incidence of televised violence into their perception of real violence. In other words, certain behaviors within scripts may be given added prominence because of media portrayals. In addition to behaviors, some scripts include statements about the cause of conflict. For example, Vogelmann-Sine et al. (1979) found that men and women differ in terms of the attributions of intent in written episodes of sexual contact between men and women. Gelles (1972) observed that battered wives often attributed personal responsibilities to themselves for their role of victim. A variety of studies have found that divorced people spend a great deal of time seeking explanations for their marital conflicts (Harvey et al., 1978; Newman and Langer, 1977). Because the media provide information about why people engage in conflict behaviors, media scripts may provide insight into our perception of why other people as well as ourselves engage in a given conflict behavior.

It should be noted that this proposition does not imply that awareness will necessarily affect behavior. It is possible that awareness may create certain types of behavior changes. Tversky and Kahneman (1974) have noted that vivid mental images may bias decision-making, and Janis (1980) has suggested that such images may be provided by the mass media in the form of scripts. However, as I shall note later, awareness of a script does not necessarily lead to particular behaviors.

(3) Media portrayals of interpersonal conflict will likely reflect different scripts. The justification for this proposition comes from several sources. First, some media presentation may be more relevant to interpersonal conflict than others. For example, soap operas have been found to contain a great deal of information about interpersonal relationships and their resultant problems (Katzman, 1972; Downing, 1974). Other media events may have little interpersonal conflict.

Second, media presentations may differ in their views of conflict scripts. Feminist literature and plays may focus on different causes of a male and female conflict within a script than what is presented in "men's magazines."

Since people differ in the media they consume, it will be important for researchers to be specific in terms of the media content to be studied and media mix of the sample. A reanalysis of data reported by Roloff and Greenberg (in press) found that the type of television watched by subjects may influence their view of conflict behaviors within scripts. Subjects who reported being high viewers of police/adventure programs but infrequent viewers of nonpolice action programs and situation comedies were more likely to say they would engage in physical aggression with a stranger ($t = 2.5$, $p < .017$) and a friend ($t = 1.8$, $p < .086$) than subjects who were high viewers of nonpolice action programs and situation comedies but infrequent viewers of police/adventure programs. In other words, the frequency with which a person is exposed to a variety of scripts may be an important factor in awareness of the scripts.

(4) People differ in their ability to acquire interpersonal conflict scripts from mass media portrayals of interpersonal conflict. While a variety of factors may influence the ability to recognize and learn scripts from the media, an important one deals with development of cognitive processes during maturation. Collins (1979) has pointed out that the ability to recall information from television differs with age. He argues that adult processing of information from the media is a sophisticated process involving the selection of stimuli from the portrayal, the organization of that stimuli, and making inferences about implicit processes in the portrayal. A variety of studies support his notion that recall of essential behaviors within a television script increases between childhood to adulthood (Collins, 1970, 1973; Collins et al., 1978). In addition, the ability to recall nonessential information also increases during early childhood, although it declines after junior high school. When examining the ability to make inferences about implied events in a television script, the same pattern of increasing ability with maturation has been found. In other words, the ability to understand and acquire scripts may be dependent upon factors such as maturation.

(5) The likelihood that a person will use a given interpersonal conflict script depends upon his or her prior use of the script in a given situation and the opportunity to use that script in a current situation. An important problem stemming from this analysis concerns the likelihood that a script acquired or recognized as a result of media exposure will actually be used. In general, Abelson (1976) predicts that after the initial participation in a script, the likelihood increases that it will be used in a similar situation in the future. However, what prompts initial use of a script is still unclear. Thus, after initial use, cues in a stimulus situation become the causal agents prompting the engagement of a script.

In addition, Abelson has noted that a person acquires some scripts that one may never have the opportunity to use. Indeed, one might argue that some mass media scripts are so unrealistic that the likelihood a person will encounter a situation that prompts the use of the script is very low.

The importance of Abelson's approach is seen when one considers the difficulty in predicting behavioral effects from media exposure. In the case of the relationship between viewing televised violence and viewer aggression, the correlations have been positive but of low magnitude. From Abelson's view, these weak correlations may be the result of two factors. First, it is possible that some subjects may have rarely engaged in aggressive behaviors to begin with. As a result, the subject is put into the position of engaging in a violence script for the first time. Since, we have limited understanding of the initial use of scripts, it is not surprising that we have trouble producing them. Some support for this position may stem from studies indicating that televised violence has greater impact on children who are initially aggressive than those children who are not (Surgeon General, 1972).

Second, the lack of a great behavioral impact may be due to the situation following the media exposure. Unless proper stimuli existed in the post-exposure situation, there is no reason to expect that the script would be used.

Too often, we have assumed that exposure to a behavior is sufficient to prompt that behavior. We need to examine the situational cues that prompt a given script to be used and then create those cues in our experimental situation.

Research conducted by Leifer and Roberts (1972) may provide a useful model for examining the acquisition of scripts. They created conflict scenarios typical among children of various age groups. After viewing a television segment, the children were asked how likely it was that they would deal with the situations through pro-social coping, leaving the situation, verbal aggression, or physical aggression. Children observing the aggressive sequences were more likely to say they would deal with conflict through physical aggression. Leifer and Roberts may well have created awareness of a new aspect of a script. Whether that new aspect would be used in an actual conflict is a different question and depends upon the prior use of aggression or the stimulus situation the child encounters. In any case, two critical effects are involved: awareness of the script or aspects of a script and the use of the script in a real situation.

The approach taken here assumes that people understand their environment through scripts. These scripts are acquired through observation of interpersonal or media models. An attempt has been made to specify propositions which might guide our investigations into the correspondence between media and interpersonal scripts.

NOTES

1. See these studies: Altman and Taylor (1973), Peters (1974), Miller and Steinberg (1975), McCall and Simmons (1978), Cushman and Craig (1976), Rogers (1973), Bittner (1977), DeFleur and Ball-Rokeach (1975), and Felsenthal (1976).

2. See these studies: Chiesi et al. (1979), Spilich et al. (1979), Black and Bower (1979), Graesser et al. (1979), Langer et al. (1978), Langer and Newman (1979).

3. See these studies: Gelles (1972), Rausch et al. (1974), Foa and Foa (1974), Foa et al. (1972), Donnenwerth and Foa (1974), Marwell and Schmitt (1967), Miller et al. (1977), Lorr et al. (1969), Roloff and Barnicott (1978, 1979), Sillars (1979), Baxter and Shepherd (1978), Kelley et al. (1978), Roloff (1978), Roloff and Greenberg (1979b).

REFERENCES

ABELSON, R. (1976) "Script processing in attitude formation and decision-making," pp. 33-45 in J. Carroll and J. Payne (eds.), Cognition and social behavior. Hillsdale, NJ: Lawrence Erlbaum.

ALTMAN, I and TAYLOR, D. (1973) Social penetration: The development of interpersonal relationships. New York: Holt, Rinehart & Winston.

BAGDIKIAN, B. (1974) "Professional personnel and organizational structure in mass media," pp. 122-142 in W. Davison and F.T.C. Yu (eds.), Mass communication research: Major issues and future directions. New York: Praeger.

BARBATSIS, G., WONG, M., and HEREK, G. (1979) "A struggle for dominance: Relational communication messages in television programming." Paper presented at the annual convention of the Speech Communication Association, November, 10-14. San Antonio, Texas.

BAXTER, L. and SHEPHERD, T. (1978) "Sex role identity, sex of other, and affective relationship as determinants of interpersonal conflict management styles." Sex Roles: A Journal of Research 4: 813-826.

BERGER, C. and CALABRESE, R. (1975) "Some explorations in initial interaction and beyond: Toward a developmental theory of interpersonal communication." Human Communication Research 1: 99-112.

BITTNER, J. (1977) Mass communication: An introduction. Englewood Cliffs, NJ. Prentice Hall.

BLACK, J. and BOWER, G. (1979) "Episodes as chunks in narrative memory." Journal of Verbal Learning and Verbal Behavior 18: 309-318.

CHIESI, H., SPILICH, G., and VOSS, J. (1979) "Acquisition of domain-related information in relation to high and low domain knowledge." Journal of Verbal Learning and Verbal Behavior 18: 257-273.

CLARK, D. and BLANKENBURG, W. (1971) "Trends in violent content in selected mass media," pp. 188-243 in G. Comstock and E. Rubinstein (eds.), Television and social behavior, Volume 1: Media content and control. Washington, DC: Government Printing Office.

COLLINS, W. (1970) "Learning of media content: A developmental study." Child Development 41: 1133-1142.

―――― (1973) "Effect of temporal separation between motivation, aggression, and consequences: A developmental study." Developmental Psychology 8: 215-221.

―――― (1979) "Children's comprehension of television content," pp. 21-52 in E. Wartella (ed.), Children communicating: Media and development of thought, speech, understanding. Beverly Hills, CA: Sage.

―――― WELLMAN, H., KENISTON, A., and WESTBY, S. (1978) "Age-related aspects of comprehension and inferences from a televised narrative." Child Development 49: 389-399.

COMSTOCK, G., CHAFFEE, S., KATZMAN, N., McCOMBS, M., and ROBERTS, D. (1978) Television and human behavior. New York: Columbia University Press.

CONY, E. (1953) "Conflict-cooperation content of five American dailies." Journalism Quarterly 30: 15-22.

COSER, L. (1964) The functions of social conflict. New York: Free Press.

CUSHMAN, D. and CRAIG, R. (1976) "Communication systems: Interpersonal implications," pp. 37-58 in G. Miller (ed.), Explorations in interpersonal communication. Beverly Hills, CA: Sage.

DeFLEUR, M. and BALL-ROKEACH, S. (1975) Theories of mass communication. New York: David McKay.

DEUTSCH, M. (1977) The resolution of conflict: Constructive and destructive processes. New Haven, CT: Yale University Press.

DOMINICK, J., RICHMAN, S., and WURTZEL, A. (1979) "Problem-solving in TV shows popular with children: Assertion vs. aggression." Journalism Quarterly 56: 455-463.

DONNENWERTH, G. and FOA, U. (1974) "Effect of resource class on retaliation to injustice in interpersonal exchange." Journal of Personality and Social Psychology 29: 785-793.

DOWNING, M. (1974) "Heroine of the daytime serial." Journal of Communication 24: 130-137.

DYER, W. (1976) Your erroneous zone. New York: Funk and Wagnalls.
———(1978) Pulling your own string. New York: Funk and Wagnalls.
FELSENTHAL, N. (1976) Orientations to mass communication. Chicago: Science Research Associates.
FITZPATRICK, M. (1977) "A typological approach to communication in relationships," pp. 263-275 in B. Ruben (ed.), Communication yearbook I. New Brunswick, NJ: Transaction Books.
FOA, U. and FOA, E. (1974) Social structures of the mind. Springfield, IL: Charles C. Thomas.
FOA, E., TURNER, J., and FOA, U. (1972) "Response generalization in aggression." Human Relations 25: 337-350.
FROST, J. and WILMOT, W. (1978) Interpersonal conflict. Dubuque, IA: William C. Brown.
GELLES, R. (1972) The violent home: A study of physical aggression between husbands and wives. Beverly Hills, CA: Sage.
GERBNER, G. and GROSS, L. (1976) "Living with television: The violence profile." Journal of Communication 26: 173-199.
GOFFMAN, E. (1959) The presentation of self in everyday life. New York: Doubleday.
GRAESSER, A., GORDON, S., and SAWYER, J. (1979) "Recognition memory for typical and atypical action in scripted activities: Tests of a script pointer + tag hypothesis." Journal of Verbal Learning and Verbal Behavior 18: 319-332.
GREENBERG, B. (1969) "The content and context of violence in the mass media," pp. 423-452 in R. Baker and S. Ball (eds.), Mass media and violence: A staff report to the National Commission on the Causes and Prevention of Violence. Washington, DC: Government Printing Office.
——— ATKIN, C., EDISON, N., and KORZENNY, F. (1977) Pro-social and anti-social behaviors on commercial television in 1975-76. Washington, DC: Office of Child Development.
HARRÉ, R. (1974) "Some remarks on 'rule' as a scientific concept," pp. 143-184 in T. Mischel (ed.), Understanding other persons. Oxford, England: Basil Blackwell.
HARVEY, J., WELLS, G., and ALVAREZ, M. (1978) "Attribution in the context of conflict and separation in close relationships," pp. 235-260 in J. Harvey, W. Ickes, and R. Kidd (eds.), New Directions in attribution research, volume 2. Hillsdale, NJ: Lawrence Erlbaum.
JANIS, I. (1980) "The influence of television on personal decision-making," pp. 161-190 in S. Withey and R. Abeles (eds.), Television and social behavior: Beyond violence and children. Hillsdale, NJ: Lawrence Erlbaum.
KATZMAN, N. (1972) "Television soap operas: What's been going on anyway?" Public Opinion Quarterly 36: 200-212.
KELLEY, H., CUNNINGHAM, J., GRISHAM, J., LEBEBVRE, L., SINK, C., and YABLON, G. (1978) "Sex differences in comments made during conflict within close heterosexual pairs." Sex Role: A Journal of Research 4: 473-492.
KNUDSON, R., SOMMERS, A., and GOLDING, S. (1980) "Interpersonal perception and mode of resolution in marital conflict." Journal of Personality and Social Psychology 38: 751-763.
LANGER, E. (1978) "Rethinking the role of thought in social interaction," pp. 35-58 in J. Harvey, W. Ickes, and R. Kidd (eds.), New directions in attribution research, volume 2. Hillsdale, NJ: Lawrence Erlbaum.
——— and NEWMAN, H. (1979) "The role of mindlessness in a typical social psychological experiment." Personality and Social Psychology Bulletin 5: 295-298.
LANGER, E., BLANK, A., and CHANOWITZ, B. (1978) "The mindlessness of ostensibly thoughtful action: The role of 'placebic' information in interpersonal interaction." Journal of Personality and Social Psychology 36: 635-642.
LEFKOWITZ, M., ERON, L., WALDER, L., and HUESMANN, L. (1977) Growing up to be violent: A longitudinal study of the development of aggression. New York: Pergamon.

LEIFER, A. and ROBERTS, D. (1972) "Children's responses to television violence," pp. 43-180 in J. Murray, E. Rubinstein, and G. Comstock (eds.), Television and social behavior, volume 2. Washington, DC: Department of Health, Education and Welfare.

LEVINGER, G. (1966) "Sources of marital dissatisfaction among applicants for divorce." American Journal of Orthopsychiatry 26: 126-132.

LORR, M., SUZIDELIS, A., and KINNANE, J. (1969) "Characteristic response modes of interpersonal situations." Multivariate Behavioral Research 4: 445-458.

McCALL, G. and SIMMONS, J. (1978) Identities and interactions: An examination of human associations in everyday life. New York: Free Press.

MARWELL, G. and SCHMITT, D. (1967) "Dimensions of compliance-gaining behavior: An empirical analysis." Sociometry 30: 350-364.

MEYER, T. (1973) "Children's perceptions of favorite television characters as behavioral models." Educational Broadcasting Review 7: 25-33.

MILLER, G. and STEINBERG, M. (1975) Between people: A new analysis of interpersonal communication. Chicago: Science Research Associates.

MILLER, G., BOSTER, F., ROLOFF, M., and SEIBOLD, D. (1977) "Compliance-gaining message strategies: A typology and some findings concerning effects of situational differences." Communication Monographs 44: 37-51.

NEWMAN, H. and LANGER, E. (1977) "Post-divorce adaptation as a function of the attribution of responsibility for the divorce." (unpublished)

NEWTSON, D. (1976) "Foundations of attribution: The perception of ongoing behavior," pp. 223-247 in J. Harvey, W. Ickes, and R. Kidd (eds.), New Directions in attribution research, volume 1. Hillsdale, NJ: Lawrence Erlbaum.

O'BRIEN, J. (1971) "Violence in divorce prone families." Journal of Marriage and the Family 33: 692-698.

PETERS, R. (1974) "Personal understanding and relationships," pp. 37-65 in T. Mischel (ed.), Understanding other persons. Oxford, England: Basil Blackwell.

RAUSCH, H., BARRY, W., HERTEL, R., and SWAIN, M. (1974) Communication, conflict and marriage. San Francisco: Jossey-Bass.

RINGER, R. (1978) Looking out for number one. Greenwich, CT: Fawcett.

ROGERS, E. (1973) "Mass media and interpersonal communication," pp. 290-310 in I. de Sola Pool, F. Frey, W. Schramm, N. Maccoby, and E. Parker (eds.), Handbook of communication. Chicago: Rand McNally.

ROLOFF, M. (1976) "Communication strategies, relationships, and relational changes," pp. 173-196 in G. Miller (ed.), Explorations in interpersonal communication. Beverly Hills, CA: Sage.

———(1978) "The influence of sex, nature of relationship, and modes of conflict resolution on conflict resolution communication." Presented at the annual convention of the Speech Communication Association, Minneapolis, Minnesota, November 2-5.

——— and BARNICOTT, E. (1978) "The situational use of pro- and anti-social compliance-gaining strategies by high and low Machiavellians," pp. 193-208 in B. Ruben (ed.), Communication yearbook 2. New Brunswick, NJ: Transaction.

———(1979) "The influence of dogmatism on the situational use of pro- and anti-social compliance-gaining strategies." Southern Speech Communication Journal 45: 37-54.

ROLOFF, M. and GREENBERG, B. (1979a) "Resolving conflict: Methods used by TV characters and teenage viewers." Journal of Broadcasting 23: 285-295.

———(1979b) "Sex differences in choice of modes of conflict resolution in real-life and television." Communication Quarterly 27: 3-12.

———(in press) "TV, peer, and parent models for pro- and anti-social conflict behaviors." Human Communication Research.

ROSE, B. (1979) "Thickening the plot." Journal of Communication 29: 81-84.

SCANZONI, J. (1972) Sexual bargaining: Power politics in the American marriage. Englewood Cliffs, NJ: Prentice-Hall.

SCHANK, R. and ABELSON, R. (1977) Scripts plans goals and understanding: An inquiry into human knowledge structures. Hillsdale, NJ: Lawrence Erlbaum.

SHAVER, K. (1975) An introduction to attribution processes. Cambridge, MA: Winthrop.

SILLARS, A. (1979) "Attributions and communication in roommate conflicts." Presented at the annual meeting of the Speech Communication Association, San Antonio, Texas, November 10-14.

SPILICH, G., VESONDER, G., CHIESI, H., and VOSS, J. (1979) "Text processing of domain-related information for individuals with high and low domain knowledge." Journal of Verbal Learning and Verbal Behavior 18: 275-290.

STEBBINS, R. (1972) "Studying the definition of the situation: Theory and field research strategies," pp. 337-354 in J. Manis and B. Metzler (eds.), Symbolic interaction: A reader in social psychology. Boston: Allyn and Bacon.

Surgeon General's Scientific Advisory Committee on Television and Social Behavior (1972) Television and growing up: The impact of televised violence. Washington, DC: Department of Health, Education and Welfare.

TVERSKY, A. and KAHNEMAN, D. (1974) "Judgment under uncertainty." Science 185: 1124-1131.

VOGELMANN-SINE, S., ERVINE, E., CHRISTENSEN, R., WARMSUN, C., and ULLMANN, L. (1979) "Sex differences in feelings attributed to a woman in situations involving coercion and sexual advances." Journal of Personality 47: 420-431.

WITHEY, S. (1980) "An ecological, cultural, and scripting view of television and social behavior," pp. 9-16 in S. Withey and R. Abeles (eds.), Television and social behavior: Beyond violence and children. Hillsdale, NJ: Lawrence Erlbaum.

WATZLAWICK, P., BEAVIN, J., and JACKSON, D. (1967) Pragmatics of human communication: A study of interactional patterns, pathologies, and paradoxes. New York: Norton.

PART V

POLITICAL COMMUNICATION

Linking research on mass communication to the political system and the public opinion process has always been one of the most exciting, yet difficult, challenges in the field. With the eclipse of the multistep flow theories and limited effects traditions by new perspectives of agenda-setting and information-processing, new conceptual work is needed. A landmark effort toward a coherent framework of political communication is represented in the lead article in this section. The Langs' study of Watergate, published here for the first time, leads toward reconceptualizing agenda-setting as the *agenda-building* process. Issue attributes are linked to media coverage and public opinion to frame a comprehensive model of the political opinion process.

Two studies follow that add new dimensions to knowledge gap theory. A look at the 1976 presidential debates and their function for various types of voters points toward a crucial, necessary broadening in knowledge gap studies. This work finds evidence of *equivalence* of informed political participation as a result of the debates, even though the debates themselves were more likely to be viewed by the "information rich" than the "information poor."

A similar expansion of our understanding of the conditions whereby the knowledge gap may be bridged is represented in the final study, which suggests that news interest may not always follow traditional socioeconomic status. Social interest in news topics, which may cut across educational and socioeconomic lines, appears to be related to both news consumption and information gain.

Agenda-setting research findings are seen by most thinkers as fitting into an overall framework of the public opinion process, but few have carefully conceptualized them as such. Two leading scholars in the field attempt to do that in this paper. Gladys Engel Lang and Kurt Lang use secondary analysis of opinion data and news coverage of the Watergate scandal to develop an argument for transforming the agenda-setting function into a larger framework of the agenda-building process. They argue that issues have special attributes and are not just topics or concerns covered by media. Categorizing topics according to threshold—economic matters being low threshold (readily identified with by everyone), and certain discrete problems such as the plight of Vietnam refugees as high threshold topics—the Langs argue that the media potentially have their greatest impact on high threshold topics. But to have that impact, the media must establish linkages from high threshold problems to other symbols and concepts, such as the general credibility of a president. Mere frequency of coverage is not enough. In the case of Watergate, a high threshold problem, the events of Watergate did not become a highly salient issue until the news of the unfolding scandal overcame incredulity by both the media and the larger, mass audience. The suspension of disbelief that a president could condone such illegal acts coincided with saturation coverage of Watergate events as they unfolded. Thus, media attention clearly was necessary for Watergate to emerge as an issue, but the content of that coverage had to combine with a reciprocal political and social psychological process for Watergate to become salient enough to topple a president. The Langs see the traditional interpretation of the agenda-setting function as both too much and too little, and argue for an agenda-building model that incorporates a collective process. This piece, written especially for Mass Communication Review Yearbook, is a preview of their book, which is in press. The Langs are sociologists at the State University of New York at Stony Brook.

27

WATERGATE

An Exploration of the Agenda-Building Process

Gladys Engel Lang
Kurt Lang

The conviction that mass communications are a powerful political force has survived the frustration of researchers trying to tease out direct effects from the fabric of surrounding social influences. During the past decade the conviction has gained new strength from studies documenting the correspondence between the amount of media attention a problem receives and the

From Gladys Engel Lang and Kurt Lang, "Watergate: An Exploration of the Agenda-Building Process," original manuscript.

amount of public concern, findings that have been cast into the language of "agenda setting." The theorem that the mass media set the public agenda boils down to the proposition that, during a political campaign and on other occasions, "people learn from the media what the important issues are." As a result, the search for political effects has changed direction. The focus of inquiry has turned away from persuasion and toward changes in the salience of certain objects on the political landscape; away from the content of public opinion (what people think) and toward the things about which the public has opinions (what people think about).

The apparent simplicity of this reformulation helps explain much of its attractiveness. Almost any observed correlation between aggregate measure of content on one hand and the cognitions of the audience on the other is consistent with the agenda-setting hypothesis. This is certainly how McCombs and Shaw,[1] in introducing the neologism into communication research, interpreted the match they found between what voters said were key issues in the 1968 election and the emphasis given these issues in the media coverage of the campaign.

The hypothesis also rests firmly on a simple and highly plausible premise: The perceptions people have of the larger universe, of the things they cannot see for themselves, which includes most of the political environment, are rarely the result of direct observation and experience. They are, as Lippmann[2] was among the first to point out, known only secondhand, derived mostly from mass media reports. In the political realm, other organized and interpersonal channels, important and effective as they may be, play only a supplementary role, operating within a larger symbolic context provided by media messages. Public recognition by media can also add a new dimension to people's experience, even where the objects or events in the news are familiar or already directly known to them.[3]

Since the publication of McCombs and Shaw's trend-setting article, there has been a host of "quick, almost casual, empirical forays" into agenda-setting.[4] The value of many of these studies, which we have no intention of reviewing here, is diminished both by certain methodological inadequacies and the lack of a clear theoretical framework. There is no question that such a framework is needed, and it is toward this objective that the present paper, drawing on material about Watergate, makes a modest step. We start from the observation that the agenda-setting hypothesis—the bland and unqualified statement that the mass media set the agenda for political campaigns—attributes to the media at one and the same time too little and too much influence. The whole question of how issues originate is sidestepped, nor is there any recognition of the process through which agendas are built or through which an object that has caught public attention, by being big news, gives rise to a political issue. In other words, while agenda-setting research, like most research, suffers from methodological shortcomings, the more basic problems are conceptual.

SOME CONCEPTUAL PROBLEMS

What follows is a brief annotated catalogue of some of these problems. First, there is the distinction between content and salience. What people think may not be as easily separable from what they think about, as the various formulations of agenda-setting have implied.[5] On the contrary, many differences of opinion originate from the different weights people attach to elements in a complex situation.[6] Therefore, the clever campaigner will seek to persuade by focusing on those issues that work in his or her favor while deliberately playing down those that might work for the opponent. Salience is related to content insofar as a problem with only minimal recognition by the media may be perceived as welcome news and judged important because it is the preferred talking point of one's candidate or party. Watergate—to cite the issue that serves as a vehicle for illuminating agenda-setting—was perceived as a McGovern issue throughout the 1972 campaign and therefore considered important by many of his more dedicated supporters.[7] What they thought about the break-in and its implications made them think it important. Most people did not think about it because they did not think it a serious matter.

Second, some of the observed correlations between salience and media content may be nothing more than an artifact of the subject categories under which specific news items are classified. In other words, that they may be produced by the research method and not by the media can best be illustrated by a comparison of the original study by McCombs and Shaw and another by Robert Frank,[8] who used questions from the Gallup Poll to see if news emphasis matched public concerns. The first of these studies found an impressive correlation of +.979, concluding that the composite of the media coverage was reflected in the judgment of voters on five major issue categories: foreign policy, law and order, fiscal policy, public welfare, and civil rights. Foreign policy ranked far above the other four both in media coverage and as the object of voter concern in 1968. Frank's 1972 data showed "international problems" to be the most overrepresented network news category, in the sense that the public "could not care less" about this part of the news; contrariwise, the Vietnam war was of "even greater interest to the American people than the relatively large amount of airtime devoted to the subject."[9] These discrepancies showed up only because Frank had put all Vietnam items into a separate category instead of subsuming them under foreign policy, as had McCombs and Shaw. Granted, the two studies were conducted four years apart, but would the 1968 study have found as great a correlation had Vietnam been introduced as a sixth category distinct from other international problems faced by the United States?

The third question relates to the matter of causal influence. Instantaneous effects are improbable except under conditions of crisis, where the reported event signals a danger threatening most everyone, so that a media buildup is generally expected to precede any rise in public concern. According to one study, the strongest relationship between media emphasis and issue salience was obtained when correlations were lagged by four months.[10] However, the time element may vary, and the number of other factors that operate during the buildup period with potentially reinforcing effects on the issue's salience should make us cautious about the direction of any media effect. Salience can dictate media coverage. Some events, moreover, operate as sleepers; concern rises as media attention diminishes. For example, a school strike usually receives maximum coverage during its early days but becomes a cause of increasing concern, even with sporadic news treatment, as children who miss their classes fall further and further behind in their school work. Coverage usually picks up again, briefly, until a settlement reduces parental concern.

A fourth question turns on the unit of analysis: Is it the individual who is made aware of a problem and comes to recognize its importance after having learned of it from the mass media, or is agenda-setting a process through which an issue develops? Although we clearly opt for the latter alternative, it remains indisputable that individuals have different thresholds of sensitivity and that not everyone is apt to respond to the same coverage in the same way. How much an individual's awareness and perceptions of salience are affected by the amount of coverage depends on certain dispositional factors. In particular, it is the potential utility of news items—that is, the belief that they depict developments with some bearing on their own situation—that makes some people pay attention. Others with no perceived stake in the outcome of events may follow the same developments, mainly to satisfy a more diffuse interest in political news of all kinds. Different dispositions can make a problem reported by the press salient for both groups, even where the coverage is less than phenomenal. To the extent that this happens, stepping up the amount of news cannot do much to raise the salience the problem has for this group—a ceiling has already been approached. This ceiling effect may, at a stage in the development of the issue, yield empirical observations that at first glance seem to refute the agenda-setting function of the mass media. After an issue has made headlines for some time, the largest increases in salience are recorded not among the most interested but among the least interested and therefore the least exposed to the mass media. It does not follow from this finding that media exposure has a negative effect. Such findings only demonstrate, first, how much it can take for an issue to break through to public consciousness and, second, that patterns of individual responses need always to be analyzed within the framework of a larger collective process—in the case of Watergate, the framework of the transformation of the problem from campaign infighting readily dismissed to a matter of national importance.

This raises the fifth and probably most basic question: What is an issue? Without a clear definition, the concept of agenda-setting becomes so all-embracing as to be rendered practically meaningless. Thus, when Becker et al., in their review article,[11] have it cover *any* causal relationship "between the media coverage and the salience of topics in the minds of individuals in the audience," they obliterate any distinction between the personal and the political, between the many things that may enter discussion among intimates and the systemic agenda that stands for the range of the controversies that fall within the legitimate concern of the polity.[12] In fact, issues have been variously conceptualized as (1) *concerns,* the things about which people are personally worried; (2) *perceptions of key problems* facing the country, about which the government should do something; (3) the existence of *policy alternatives* between which people must choose (whether or not to support SALT II, an antiabortion amendment, and so on); (4) a *public controversy,* such as the one over Watergate; and (5) the "reasons" or underlying *determinants of political cleavage* (the "issue" most closely related to an electoral outcome or certain objective interests, such as class/occupation or race, even though these symbols may not enter the debate).

There is naturally some overlap in what would be included within each of the five definitions. A personal concern can also be identified as one of the most important problems facing the country, as an object of considerable public controversy or as the basis for an electoral decision. When there is much anxiety about its passage, even a policy alternative can become a matter of grave personal concern. To illustrate the point by a concrete example: McCombs and Shaw[13] asked respondents to name the "key" issues in the campaign—namely, the things the "government should concentrate on doing something about." The wording allows for a good deal of leeway but basically invites respondents to state their uppermost concerns (such as rising prices or crime in the streets), their perceptions of the most important "problem" (the economy or energy shortages), and the main "controversies" connected with a campaign (peace in Vietnam). The examples, though hypothetical, should make clear that the "issues" elicited as responses are not necessarily those critics have in mind when they blame the press for not paying more attention to the policy differences between the candidates. Nor are the "issues" apt to be named those on which electoral decisions are normally based.[14]

Most voters, whatever their specific concerns, still vote for the man or the party they believe has their own best interest at heart or simply for the one they believe would do the "better job."[15] This holds even for members of single-issue constituencies, who are guided by endorsements rather than by what the candidates say or avoid saying. Yet most people, when asked what they see as the "issues," are not at all hesitant to name one or the other, and the ones most often mentioned are those the candidates have stressed and the media have singled out for attention. They name issues even when they do not perceive differences in the candidates' positions on the issues named or even incorrectly associate their own policy preference with the candidate of their choice. Thus, in 1972, McGovern failed to hold enough of the natural "dovish" constituency that he needed to win, mainly because they had come to doubt his ability to make good, even on peace in Vietnam. While for them peace was the big issue facing the country, it was not at issue in their vote.

What is an issue? In the last analysis, it is whatever is in contention among a relevant public. The objects of potential controversy are diverse. A policy, a party and its platform or past performance, a personality, a particular act, or even a theory about such things as the state of the economy or the causes of a disease can stir public debate. Of course, many controversies—even political ones—remain invisible. Discussion may be confined to the political bodies legally charged with responsibility for making decisions. They may seek expert advice or be responsive to special interests. But it is not with politics on the more esoteric level that agenda-setting research is concerned. The public agenda, as opposed to the various institutional agendas, consists of only those issues on which "the people" form opinions and are inclined to take sides. This degree of participation can develop only through some medium of communication that links the polity and the public at large. In assessing the role of the media, one is compelled to take account of the different thresholds of attention, not only among individuals but also among issues.

ISSUE THRESHOLDS

Some issues arise out of conditions that *directly affect nearly everybody* in the same way, such as inflation, high taxes, and gasoline shortages, and therefore exhibit a strong propensity to show up as personal concerns. A different type is related to a situation whose effects are *selectively experienced,* such as urban congestion or draft calls. Last, there are conditions and developments whose effects are *generally remote* from just about everyone, such as the plight of refugees from Vietnam or wrongdoing high up in the government. The three categories, we argue, have vastly different thresholds of sensitivity, and the nature of the influence exerted by the media varies accordingly.

Economic conditions that affect nearly everyone tend to have low thresholds. The problem would be of general concern even without attention from the news media. However, concern is apt to be boosted in two ways: through media recognition that puts the problem into the public domain and through statements by political figures trying to mobilize certain constituencies with promises, by fixing blame, or courting support for some kind of political action. The "economic" issue moves onto the political agenda quite naturally. As it does, the political relevance of the voters' own economic position compared with that of the previous year recedes while the relevance of their perception of the state of economic affairs increases.[16] These perceptions are basically media generated, though as the number feeling personally worse off continues to increase, it becomes more difficult to believe prosperity is just around the corner, whatever is reported.

On other matters that are more selectively experienced, such as urban crime, the problem itself is made more visible and concern increased by media recognition. Reports of a crime wave can make even those not personally victimized cautious about walking the streets, even when there is little potential danger. Sensational media coverage can exaggerate the dimensions of a problem; it can also create a problem where none exists. For instance, speculations about an impending oil shortage helped spawn a run on existing supplies that led to a real shortage.[17] While continuing attention by the media helps keep a problem alive, lagging media recognition can slow the rise of concern, particularly when those most directly affected are few and/or powerless. The majority either remains unaware of the problem or down-grades its importance, as in the case of ghetto conditions that suddenly erupt into riots.[18]

The potential influence of the media is greatest when the public has no direct contact with the problem. Whether or not a major event, like the launching of the first Soviet sputnik or an American moon landing, becomes an issue depends on whether it is reported in a context of crisis and partisanship or as a unifying achievement. The style of coverage reflects, in turn, the existing political situation and the ability of political figures to seize on the event as an issue.

Problems compete for attention.[19] Therefore, the salience an issue has for elites or for the mass public is not just an absolute but to some extent a relative matter. A potentially explosive issue surfacing at the wrong time, when other controversies are dominating the polity and the news media, is apt to be ignored until the time is ripe for it. Here, too, thresholds are relevant. High-threshold issues encounter greater difficulties in gaining the attention of the news media, and even when they do (as through some sensational expose or foreign policy crisis) much depends on the ability of an administration, party, or candidate to identify with the cause or to steer clear of the negative implications. The controversy may affect political support without entering the list of most important problems. By contrast, low-threshold issues, because of their link to personal concerns, almost compel attention from political elites as well as the news media. This increases the likelihood that they will either displace or become assimilated into issues already on public agendas.

In analyzing the role of the mass media in structuring the issues of a campaign or the controversies of an era, one must go beyond a search for simple correspondences between the treatment of certain topics in the press and the extent to which the mass public is aware, informed, and concerned about these matters.

Watergate provides a prima facie case through which to consider the role of the mass media in agenda-setting. It allows us to examine, first, the failure of Watergate to become a significant factor in the outcome of the 1972 election and, second, the way Watergate erupted into a major controversy just five months later. As to the election, the press has been criticized for not giving sufficient coverage to Watergate and thereby burying the issue. On the other hand, the media have been lavishly praised for their key role in mobilizing the public; without their dogged pursuit of the facts, the scandal would have expired and the Nixon administration would not have been held accountable. Neither version quite accords with the evidence.

CAMPAIGN 1972:
WHY WATERGATE WAS NOT AN ISSUE

James Perry of the *National Observer* commented after Nixon had resigned: "Watergate should have been an issue in the election and it really wasn't. If we had worked harder and dug deeper, could we have made Watergate the issue it should have been?"[20] In saying this, Perry implies a direct causal relationship between press inattention and the lack of public concern in line with the agenda-setting hypothesis.

It is true that most of the press failed to follow the Washington *Post* in its effort to get at the full facts behind the break-in at the Democratic National Headquarters. But it is also true that much of the basic story that goes under the code name "Watergate" was in the public domain by the time the 1972 campaign reached its climax. That story included not only the details of the bungled break-in on June 17, 1972 to the headquarters of the National Democratic Committee but such related issues as the deliberate circumvention of campaign finance laws, "dirty tricks" perpetrated by persons in the employ of the Committee to Re-elect the President, and the illegal use of federal agencies by the White House against its political "enemies." During the campaign some of these stories had surfaced only as unverified press exposés or as allegations by persons with axes to grind, but they had been aired before election day.

Coverage of Watergate during the campaign was far from negligible, yet it was highly uneven. The regional and local papers gave it much less space than the more "cosmopolitan" papers with their own reporters in Washington, such as the New York *Times* and the Los Angeles *Times*. In addition, the treatment of Watergate was apt to vary in accordance with a paper's editorial endorsement of one or the other of the two presidential candidates. Bagdikian[21] showed that papers which had endorsed Nixon more often delayed or deemphasized three Watergate stories than did those that had endorsed McGovern. Also, Watergate received considerable emphasis on national television. Whatever the deficiencies of television news, the proportion of air time devoted to Watergate was greater than that of space in newspapers. Throughout the campaign, Watergate and corruption were second only to Vietnam.[22] It would be wrong to infer from criticisms of the news coverage that the media had covered Watergate with a curtain of silence.

Indeed, there was sufficient coverage of Watergate during the campaign for clear majorities of the public to have become aware of Watergate. When Gallup asked in September 1972, "Have you read or heard about Watergate?" 52 percent of a national sample said they had. While this level of awareness may not stagger the imagination, it is impressive when put into context. It accords roughly with the proportion of Americans who, in 1970, could correctly name their congressmen or who, in 1971, had "read or heard about the articles first published in the New York *Times* about how we got involved in the Vietnam War" (that is, the Pentagon Papers). On the other hand, by this same measure, the public at this time was less aware of

Watergate than it had been of Nixon's new welfare proposals (1969) and his new economic program to fight inflation (1971), both of which achieved awareness scores in the 70 percentile range a week after their unveiling on television.[23]

The Gallup reading, taken in mid-September, may actually underestimate the extent of awareness, inasmuch as "Watergate," as a code name for the break-in and its ramifications, may not yet have caught on among people aware of the incident. Thus, when a Harris Poll, conducted at about the same time, asked more specifically, "Have you heard, or not, about the men who were caught trying to install wire-taps in the Democratic National Head-quarters in Washington?" even with no mention of Watergate, 76 percent indicated their awareness.[24] And by October, 87 percent of the voters in Summit County, Ohio, said they were aware of the "Watergate break-in."[25]

Awareness is only a precondition for taking a stand in a controversy. Polls taken during the campaign provide no evidence that, for the most part, citizens were outraged and prepared to charge the Nixon administration the political price for its various trespasses. Rather, most people looked on this kind of wiretapping, whether or not they believed it to be an invasion of individual rights,[26] as a commonplace occurrence, the usual kind of skull-duggery to be expected, especially during a campaign.[27] Moreover, the various Watergate stories led very few voters (17 percent) to link the break-in even to the Committee to Re-elect the President, not to mention the White House; most (73 percent) were content to reserve judgment about who was to blame for the incident.[28] McGovern's attempt in the latter phase of the campaign to use Watergate as evidence of widespread corruption in the Nixon admin-istration made very limited headway.[29] This is not to say that there were no doubts about the Republican disclaimers; only that hardly anyone—a mere one percent—connected the break-in with Nixon. Surveys show that Nixon lost some ground between September and October as a "man of high integrity,"[30] but the news did not tarnish his image as President. Nixon's performance ratings remained just about where they had been—about three-fifths approving.[31]

Nor did Watergate play any perceptible role in the electoral outcome. Fewer than one percent of the comments by respondents in the 1972 election survey by the University of Michigan's Center for Political Studies about what they liked or disliked about the presidential candidates mentioned the subject.[32] Equally revealing of the general attitude is the response to a question by ORC in its October 13-15 survey. "If it were proven that the charges against the President's re-election committee are true, will this [make you] less likely to vote for President Nixon, or wouldn't it have any effect on your vote?" Only 21 percent said it would, and 68 percent said it would make no difference. Watergate remained first and foremost an argument for confirmed Democrats. Though potentially explosive, it caused very few Republican defections, and very few voters found the Watergate break-in "personally important" in making up their minds how to vote.[33]

Watergate obviously belongs in the category of high threshold "issues." The problem it signified was outside the range of most people's immediate concerns. The details of the incident seemed outlandish and their import difficult to fathom. Surfacing during a campaign, the whole story could more easily be dismissed, since denunciations of the opposition for unfair electioneering methods and low-level campaign tactics are endemic to American politics. Still, it is not unheard of for such charges as those leveled by McGovern to stick and for "corruption" and "dirty politics" to become a concern and provoke controversy in the heat of a campaign. Whether this happens is more contingent on recognition of the problem by the media than in the case of problems that directly impinge on everyone. For the "high threshold" issue mere recognition is not enough. It requires a buildup, which is a function of more than the amount of space and/or time the media devote to the story. The latter may push it past the threshold of inattention, but one must also look at the kind of coverage to explain how a remote incident like Watergate becomes an issue.

The apparent lack of impact of the Watergate news coverage can only be understood if one takes account of the political context: the fact that the story broke during an electoral contest and that it had to compete for attention against other political controversies.

To belittle the significance of Watergate was an obvious and essential part of the Nixon strategy to counter its potential effect. The media, sometimes unintentionally, played into his hands. Both the metaphors adopted in the coverage and the way editors seemed to lean over backward to be fair and balanced by presenting "two sides" to every question, even when there may have been only one, made it easier to dismiss the incident and the charges growing out of it as just the usual campaign politics. A week after the break-in (June 24), the New York *Times* reported that the break-in was popularly known in the capital as the "Watergate caper." Ziegler had made headlines when he called it a "third-rate burglary," and Nixon, in his first televised press conference dealing with Watergate (August 29), referred to it as "this very bizarre incident," the kind of act with which no responsible person, not the President's advisors and certainly not the President himself, could have anything to do. "Caper" as a descriptor did not, however, so far as we have been able to ascertain, originate with Republicans. Its first appearance was in the headline of a Washington *Post* story, though not in the story itself, on June 19, two days after the break-in.[34] By June 21, a *Post* editorial, entitled "Mission Incredible," likening it to the CBS show, *Mission Impossible,* cited the "Watergate caper now unfolding in weird and scarcely believable detail" as an example of life imitating art. The editorial raised a number of serious questions, but the Watergate label stuck and was used all through the summer and into the fall. On September 13, David Brinkley (NBC) discussed the "caper," noting how it fell flat as an issue, influenced few votes, and was without effect on the important issues of the campaign. It was to discredit this epithet that Walter Cronkite opened an extended discussion of Watergate, as part of the October 27 CBS evening news, "At first it was called the Watergate caper." The rest of this 16-minute report and its shorter sequel four days later, which alarmed the White House,[35] pulled together bits and pieces of information to show there was more to the break-in than just a bungled effort to place some telephone tape. But the campaign was over except for the voting.

More generally, the press, under fire from the administration for its allegedly antiadministration bias, retreated to some kind of mathematical balance, whereby Republican and Democratic stories were given equal play and space each day. What Bagdikian calls "twinning" was widely employed during the 1972 campaign.[36] All too often this meant holding back on a Watergate story damaging to Nixon until it could be coupled with a denial that generally neutralized its impact. If no denial was forthcoming, reporters would seek it. One instance cited by Bagdikian concerns the handling of a Washington *Post* story about a $25,000 campaign contribution that was "laundered" and wound up in the bank account of one Watergate burglar. ABC held back on the story for a day until it could be coupled with news that Nixon had given instructions for a GAO probe into the matter. The Chicago *Tribune's* report (August 2) was captioned "GAO to Audit Finances of Nixon's Campaign Committee."

This concern over giving equal play fitted the Republican strategy in yet another way. Throughout the campaign, Nixon tried to make news only in his capacity as President, keeping as much distance as possible between himself and reporters and forcing them to settle for surrogates in reporting the Republican side. Charles Guggenheim, McGovern's media advisor, tried to persuade Democratic National Chairman Laurence O'Brien to write the networks and say the Democrats would not accept responses from surrogates as constituting equal time, since that put them at a disadvantage.[37] The media made little effort to expose this strategy. Mainly, they reported the campaign as it was actually run—McGovern against the Nixon surrogates—without making an issue of Nixon's nonappearances. Their responsibility as journalists, as they saw it, was to reflect the "reality" of the campaign, but this reality, as later became clear, was greatly influenced by a strategy of which Watergate was an integral part. The efforts during the campaign to deceive the press and public, to intimidate the press with threats, and to head off investigations that could have made headlines, thereby increasing the salience of Watergate for the electoral preferences of voters, obviously paid off. Whether the strategy would have succeeded to the extent it did, had the news media focused on it, remains a moot question.

Next to consider is the concrete political situation in which Watergate was injected into the electoral campaign. Much of Nixon's first term had been dominated by controversy over Vietnam, a problem that continued to be perceived as important and politically relevant by a large number of people. It remained prominent in the news. Yet, even had more of the press acted so as to make Watergate the big issue it ought to have been, this might not have been enough. The overriding "issue" of the 1972 campaign, the perception most salient for voters' choices, was the relative credibility of the two candidates, their ability to achieve peace in Vietnam, to cope with rising economic difficulties, and to deal effectively with the crime and drug problems that were uppermost in the minds of most people.[38] To become a major factor in the election, Watergate had to be perceived as relevant to Nixon's credibility. It was not so identified, and the question is, why not?

The answer lies, first, in the loss of credibility suffered by McGovern during the course of his fight to win the nomination and during the campaign, which made his charges against the Nixon administration appear as a desperate attempt to divert attention from the problems plaguing his own candidacy. The campaign had begun with McGovern the clear underdog. Every poll showed Nixon with a big lead. Still, Nixon's lead was no greater than it had been at the same point four years earlier when he won by the smallest conceivable margin. But unlike Humphrey in 1968, McGovern seemed unable to close the gap. His harping on the signs of possible complicity in the break-in, making an issue of the secret campaign fund, even of Donald Segretti's "dirty tricks," fell mainly on deaf ears. Earlier mistakes had cost the Democratic nominee dearly in credibility and damaged his reputation for decisiveness. In the end, many people even lost confidence that McGovern, who had gained prominence as a peace candidate, could do the better job in ending the Vietnam war.[39]

McGovern had been especially hurt by his handling of the Eagleton affair less than two weeks after his nomination. When the press revealed that Senator Eagleton, McGovern's vice-presidential running mate, had previously been hospitalized for psychiatric treatment, McGovern's inept handling of the problem—the way he first said he was "1000 percent" behind Eagleton and then, a few days later, asked Eagleton to take himself off the ticket—did not improve his image. Most people, including many Democrats, reacted negatively.[40] The issue dominated the news for some days, into early August, and Republicans had little to do but exploit it for all it was worth. In his July 27 press conference, Nixon was asked four questions about Eagleton but none about the investigation of Watergate.

But if one reason Watergate did not "take off" was McGovern's lack of credibility, we have also to explain why Watergate did not "rub off" and tarnish Nixon's image. First, we have noted the success of the media strategy whereby Nixon remained in the White House, appearing only on those occasions when he could be shown addressing audiences chosen so as to ensure him an enthusiastic reception. The distance he kept, as President, between himself and the press in order to escape the close scrutiny given McGovern's every move and statement also enabled him to stonewall on Watergate. By letting others carry the burden of responding to Watergate charges, he managed not only to stave off suspicions concerning his personal involvement but to stay personally above the whole affair.

A still more basic explanation for the reluctance to point a finger at the President is to be found in the phenomenon of incredulity.[41] There is no greater fallacy than the belief that facts speak for themselves. The charge that a president should have involved his own staff in a "third-rate burglary" or in "laundering of campaign funds" or would report to the people about a "most thorough investigation ever" that would later prove pure fiction appeared outlandish to most people. This alone gave a certain weight to official denials. In 1972 the American people might have been ready to believe that a mayor or a governor might so sully the office but not a president who had taken a sacred oath of office, at the beginning of his term, "with the whole world watching."

The awe of the office of President, which rubs off on the incumbent, was shared by a large part of the press and inhibited them from pursuing the case as hard as they might have. The same was true of politicians. The McGovern camp long remained hesitant about exploiting Watergate, afraid that a negative strategy might backfire. According to an ORC poll in early October, 51 percent agreed that this was "simply a political charge by a desperate politician who is behind"; only 29 percent thought that Nixon needed to "answer and explain these charges," with the other 20 percent having no opinion. When the question was repeated three weeks later, after news stories had linked Haldeman to the break-in, the gain for McGovern was slight.

In sum, then, the news coverage had created awareness of Watergate, but this did not translate directly into a politically relevant response. In the 1972 campaign, with evaluation of the candidates' suitability for office clearly the decisive factor, Watergate never became a concern linked in most people's minds with Nixon's fitness to be President. Unlike high prices or a gasoline shortage, Watergate did not impinge on people's lives; and while few persons might consider illegal election eavesdropping and political sabotage acceptable campaign practices, the crime was perceived as that of politicians against other politicians and thereby sufficiently remote from everyday concerns not to agitate the ordinary voter.

HOW THE ISSUE MADE THE AGENDA

A half-year after Nixon's landslide victory, Watergate had become the center of a full-blown political controversy. Not only was nearly everybody aware of it,[42] but far more people than during the election expressed concern. Even before the televised hearings of the Senate Watergate Committee were to begin in May, Watergate had made its way, for the first time, onto the Gallup list of "most important problems facing the country today." Though clearly still lagging behind such low-threshold issues as "the high cost of living," mentioned by three out of five people, "Watergate and/or corruption in government" with 16 percent was in close competition with "crime and lawlessness" (17 percent) and "drugs" (16 percent) for second place.[43]

Meanwhile, the number of people willing to play ostrich and simply write the whole matter off as "just more politics," though still a plurality, had been steadily dwindling, and the number for whom the "bugging attempt" was "really something serious" had been going up correspondingly. ORC found that just three percent of their respondents believed in February that Nixon had ordered the break-in. Gallup and Harris, which did not resume polling on Watergate until April, registered similar increases in seriousness.

By April a new element had entered the controversy. At issue now was how to proceed with the investigation so that the full truth could be flushed out. Near two-thirds (63 percent) of the citizenry, in mid-April, believed Nixon had "withheld important information" about Watergate; only nine percent thought he had been "frank and honest."[44] More people had come to suspect that the President had either ordered the wiretapping of the Democratic headquarters or, more likely, that he had prior knowledge of the operation, which they now were associating with the White House in a way they had not done during the campaign. And, accordingly, Nixon was earning a strongly negative rating on his "handling of the Watergate case." His past acts were seen as a coverup attempt.[45]

Since few pollsters asked any questions about Watergate between October 1972 and April 1973, the only real trend data available are the month-by-month ratings of the presidency.[46] These must be read with some caution, because the peak ratings Nixon had enjoyed in the aftermath of the February peace agreement and the return of the POWs were bound to have slipped even without the albatross of Watergate around his neck. It appears that Watergate did not rub off on Nixon until early in April, when it began to take its toll. In that month, his *net* approval rating (that is, the percentage of "positive" minus the percentage of "negative" responses) in the Gallup poll fell abruptly below the average of the previous four years. By early May—within little more than a month—it had fallen from a 2-to-1 favorable ratio to just about an even split. The same trend is evidenced by other measures.[47]

That Nixon on his relatively rare public appearances was now apt to be greeted with "Watergate" rather than "Vietnam" signs should not be misread: There was no public clamor for Nixon's head; most still regarded the President as a man of high integrity whom they held in high repute.[48] Reporters visiting college campuses found national issues, including Watergate, being all but ignored by students.[49] Congressmen were not subject to the spontaneous outpouring of letters, phone calls, and telegrams, such as was to occur after the controversy heated up. But many found their constituents, when asked about their opinions, wondering just where it all would end.[50]

This cautious assessment of the public mood seems to have been shared by Nixon, when he told H.R. Haldeman, White House Chief of Staff, that "despite all the polls . . . I think there's still a hell of a lot of people out there, and from what I've seen . . . they want to believe. That's the point, isn't it?"[51]

That was, indeed, the point. Although fewer people now thought Watergate merely another routine political squabble, and there was some erosion of presidential credibility, the majority, unable to understand what was going on, still wanted to believe in the President. Getting at the truth was becoming an issue.

EVENTS AND SATURATION COVERAGE

Does the postelection coverage of Watergate, the great "sleeper" issue of the 1972 campaign, account for its emergence as an issue?

First, Watergate never altogether dropped out of sight. The death in December of the wife of Watergate defendant H.L. Hunt in the crash of an airliner at Chicago made national news when she was found to have had in her possession an unusually large sum of money in bills of $100 denomination. Other news centered on Judge Sirica, whose court had jurisdiction over the Watergate trial. In December, Sirica had been involved in a dispute with the Los Angeles *Times* over the publication of an interview with former FBI agent Baldwin, a possible key witness in the upcoming trial. Throughout January, it was the trial itself that drew attention as the defendants entered their guilty pleas and Sirica charged at the end that the full facts still had to be unearthed. Then, in early February, the Senate began to move ahead with its own investigation. Although these and other items often made headlines as well as the network news on television, they were overshadowed by other events. Not only was there the ending of the war in Vietnam and the return of the POWs to compel attention, but also the devaluation of the dollar by 10 percent, in February, and a continuing dollar crisis, which worsened in March and temporarily closed foreign exchange markets in Europe and Japan. Of less personal concern to most of the public but more sensational and "good copy" was a 37-day armed confrontation between militant Indian leaders and federal troops around the Ogalala Sioux hamlet of Wounded Knee, South Dakota. Only in March did the Watergate coverage once again approach the level reached the previous fall. Beginning in late March newspaper space and broadcast time given Watergate rose rapidly. A peak was reached in May when the New York *Times* carried an average of 14 items a day, nearly eight times the average of the previous October.[52] Coverage in other papers rose correspondingly,[53] and the increase for television is even more dramatic, considering the time strictures of the network newscast. In May, before the televised Watergate hearings, between 20 and 25 percent of the roughly 20 minutes available for hard news on the typical network newscast was devoted to Watergate items.[54]

Second, the increase amounted to a change in kind: the onset of a *saturation coverage* such as had been experienced only for brief intervals in 1972. Saturation is judged by two criteria: (1) prominent placement—on the front page of a newspaper to ensure visibility or as an item lasting 60 seconds or longer on television—and (2) continuity—by having such items appear on four out of five successive days—to fix the basic elements in people's minds while developing the story.[55] For a high-threshold event such as Watergate, to break through the barrier of inattention and to become a dominant concern that overshadows others requires dramatic presentation and continuous reinforcement. How much of both depends on the political context.

Third, after the campaign, it was events that kept Watergate in the news and, by early April, culminated in a saturation of the news media with Watergate that lasted, with little interruption, until after Nixon resigned. This stood in clear contrast to the coverage during the campaign when most news was the product of press initiative in digging up information the Nixon camp had been eager to hide. Then the only Watergate-related event to draw simultaneous saturation coverage from at least two networks and the New York *Times* occurred in late August during the controversy over the release of the GAO report on illegal campaign contributions. No other event or set of events during the campaign received quite the same uniform and simultaneous play from several media. The networks, too, varied in their emphasis. In October, while all three focused essentially on the same events, CBS was "Watergate-saturated" from October 13 through November 1, ABC from October 3 through 12, and NBC from October 13 through 25.

By contrast, the periods of saturation coverage after the election were in response to events and developments in which the media were not in any sense prime movers. What first breathed new life into a story that had almost expired was the start of the trial of the Watergate defendants. It was scheduled and held in Washington with its unique concentration of news staffs. For much of January, the trial provided a continuous flow of news for the networks. But the real breakthrough did not come until much later. On March 23, the day his sentence was to be set, McCord's letter was read in open court. A bombshell, it spoke of "political pressure" on all the defendants to remain silent, of perjury during the trial, of higher-ups (not named) who were implicated in the Watergate operation. From this point on the disclosures began to fit together. They had too much plausibility not to call for answers. The possibility of a scandal could no longer be ignored, even by the regional press still favorable to Nixon. After a brief break in Watergate headlines in early April, every one of five papers examined gave Watergate continuous and prominent coverage through the entire month before the Senate hearings. During this same month, 56 percent of the evening newscasts over the 23 weekdays led off with a Watergate story. No longer was it the "bugging incident." Enough evidence was out to persuade even the more hesitant editors that a major scandal was shaping up.

THE MEDIA CONTEXT

Does saturation coverage suffice to explain the increased concern and changes in the perception of Watergate? The two trends indeed coincide, lending credence to the agenda-setting hypothesis that the media set the public agenda by informing the public of the important issues. The simple parallelism fails, however, to clarify the process by which this occurs. More than simple learning is involved.

We know of only two empirical studies that directly address the influence of the mass media on attitudes toward Watergate during this period. In May 1973, Weaver, McCombs, and Spellman contacted people by phone in a North Carolina community whom they had interviewed in an election survey the previous October.[56] The amount of *change* in the perceived importance of Watergate during the interim was negatively correlated with heavy use of the media for political information during the campaign, as gauged from responses by three questions about newspaper reading, television viewing, and subscribing to news magazines. Change in Watergate salience also correlated negatively with the frequency of political discussion during the campaign period. While both these correlations were weak, there was no correspondence, positive or negative, between increased salience and recent media use and/or discussion.

What is one to make of these findings? Other evidence from the study suggests that change among the heavy users was subject to a ceiling effect. Among those who had followed the campaign closely—whatever their party identification or presidential preference, whatever the medium used— Watergate had already broken through the threshold, limiting the room for influence from the spate of Watergate stories in the spring. The perception of importance was more likely to increase among those who had not been paying attention earlier on. Now the saturation coverage compelled them to pay attention, to recognize that there was a problem and that the problem was serious. Although the explanation by Weaver et al. pursues a different path, the "need for orientation" variable they introduce does not preclude the concomitant operation of the hypothesized ceiling effect.

Correlations between media use and Watergate salience during the campaign would be weakened by political factors. Voters are apt to ignore discrepant campaign material, and Nixon supporters had every motive to accept the White House belittling of Watergate. Once the election was over, the issue resurfaced in a different context. It was up to the courts and Congress to deal with charges that could no longer be dismissed as campaign rhetoric. Especially after the McCord letter, the issue became to some extent bipartisan; some prominent Republicans joined the demand that Nixon clear up the matter.

Still another factor to be considered is the nature of the information which people were being asked to accept. Where the situation that gives rise to an issue can be known only through the media—where the news is about events that are communicated and totally outside the range of most people's experience—the believability of the accounts or, in this case, of the charges is an important determinant of what people will believe. This distinction between credibility, which is an attribute of a source, and credulity, the tendency to believe or disbelieve, made by Edelstein and Tefft in their discussion of Watergate helps to understand Watergate as a high-threshold issue. Not only did the break-in and the related events seem at first to have no relation to people's lives, except perhaps as one of those more salacious campaign stories, but there was something about the things that were supposed to have happened or to be happening that many people found hard to believe. Any tendency toward disbelief would have been reinforced by skepticism about sources of information, since many of the charges were emanating from politicians whose credibility could be discounted and from journalists suspected of bias against Nixon.

The accounts by people in Longview, Washington, who were interviewed by Edelstein and Tefft in May and June 1973[57] of their reaction upon first hearing or reading about Watergate indicate that their disbelief centered more on the facts of the case—that is, on the events and actions described as having taken place within the President's own circle—than on the credibility or trustworthiness of the media or of any specific medium as sources of information. There were so many things they found hard to believe that, even before they could consider the importance of the issue, they first had to be convinced that a number of facts were indeed believable, or at least beyond disbelief.

What changed by late March and April was that many more people were willing to believe the "facts" or to grant them enough credence to want to have them clarified. Suspending disbelief, for many, did not mean they were ready to believe either in White House involvement or that Nixon was not telling the "truth," only that they believed he was not revealing all he knew.

That "getting the facts out" had become both a concern and an issue is also apparent from responses to Nixon's April 30 speech, announcing the resignations of Haldeman, Ehrlichman, and Dean, a move that the President hoped would turn attention to other political matters. Political leaders of both parties, while expressing relief that Nixon had broken his long silence on Watergate, were nevertheless insistent that investigation be turned over to a special prosecutor. Public response echoed this sentiment. Politically, the reactions of the seven out of ten adult Americans who had watched or listened to the speech were split. But more than three-fourths (78 percent) agreed that: "There are still so many unanswered questions left about Watergate that only a completely independent investigation of the affair by people not controlled by the President will get at the truth."[58] What the largest number found difficult to believe was that President Nixon should not have known about the planning and the later coverup of the break-in and that it had taken him a full nine months to find out about this. This issue was not whether there should be an investigation but what kind of an investigation there should be. People may have wanted to believe the Nixon version, but parts of it strained their credulity.

To create a Watergate issue, the media had to do more than just give the problem publicity. They had to stir up enough controversy to make it politically relevant, not only on the elite level but also to give the bystander public a reason for taking sides. By spring 1973, the public, for the most part, was still not outraged, but it was making its presence felt. The intense press coverage made it evident to political actors that, as more and more people were taking Watergate seriously, they would probably react negatively to anything that gave the appearance of a continuing attempt at coverup. Those in Congress insistent on a full investigation were able to exploit the widespread feeling that the whole truth about Watergate had not yet come out and maneuver the opposition into a corner. The many things from the closed hearings that found their way into the press stirred up enough controversy for the Watergate issue to mushroom into a full-blown scandal. As yet it did not appear as a personal threat, personally touching people's lives, as it would later, when the extent to which the administration had engaged in illegal electronic eavesdropping and other retribution against political enemies became public knowledge. But the public could not be called "apathetic," as it had been as late as March.[59]

AGENDA-BUILDING

To say that they set the agenda is to claim both too much and too little for the media of mass communication. There are, after all, concerns that do not originate from the media, in that they fall within most people's direct experience. Media recognition helps put these concerns into the public domain. What was a widespread concern is thereby "politicized." With regard to high-threshold issues, the media assume a still more important role. Except for the news reports about Watergate, most people would not have even known there was a problem. Media attention was a necessary condition for the emergence of the Watergate issue. Without it there would not have been the same amount of controversy. But the media do not operate in total autonomy from the political system, and their gradual saturation with Watergate news must be viewed in relation to political developments in which the press itself was one of the movers. Agenda building is a collective process with some degree of reciprocity.

The Watergate issue had broken into public consciousness only after the media, by covering developments and by the way it covered them, had created a sense of real crisis. It was not something they had created out of whole cloth. The coverage, which stirred interest, was dictated by events, but the media were themselves part of the field of action. Political figures made use of whatever publicity they could attract to advance their own goals and interests, increasing the number of Watergate events there to be covered until the coverage escalated to reach saturation level, with Watergate on the front page and on the evening news day after day. The headlines alone would not have been enough to transform a problem so removed from most people's daily concerns into an issue, but there was enough continuity to rivet attention to the developing story. The process was circular with media exposure, political interest, and events on the elite level feeding one another.

Let us summarize the part played by the news media. First, the news media highlight some events, activities, groups, personalities, and so forth to make them stand out. Different kinds of issues require different amounts and kinds of coverage to gain attention. This common focus affects what people will think or talk about.

Second, the object that is the focus of attention still needs to be framed. It must come to stand for something—some problem or concern. The media can play up or down the more serious aspects of a situation.

The third step in the buildup links the object or event to secondary symbols, so that it becomes a part of the recognized political landscape. Something like interest aggregation is involved, since the line of division on the particular issue does not always coincide with the cleavage between the organized political parties or between other sharply defined groups. The media tend to weave discrete events into a continuing story, often a political one.

Finally, spokesmen who can articulate demands must make their appearance. Their effectiveness stems in good part from their ability to command media attention.

The process is a continuous one, involving a number of feedback loops, most important among which are the way political figures see their own image mirrored in the media, the pooling of information within the press corps, and the various indicators of the public response. We argue that a topic, problem, or key concern to which political leaders are or should be paying attention is not yet an *issue*. Important as the media may be in focusing attention, neither awareness nor perceived importance makes an issue. However, once the above-mentioned links are established, a topic may continue to be an issue even if other topics receive greater emphasis from the media.

NOTES

1. M.E. McCombs and D.L. Shaw (1972) "The Agenda-Setting Function of Mass Media." *Public Opinion Quarterly*, 36, pp. 176-187.

2. Walter Lippmann (1922) *Public Opinion*. New York. Lippmann developed his ideas during service with the Inter-Allied Propaganda Commission, and his bitterness at the "peace" settlement to World War II makes for fascinating reading in Ronald Steel, *Walter Lippmann and the American Century*. Boston, 1980.

3. See W.P. Davison (1960) "Political Significance of Recognition via Mass Media—an Illustration from the Berlin Blockade. *Public Opinion Quarterly*, 20, pp. 327-333.

4. M.E. McCombs (1979) *Setting the Agenda for Agenda-Setting Research*. Communication Research Center, Newhouse School of Public Communication, Syracuse University, June 1979 (mimeo), p. 3 states that fifty papers were produced in six years.

5. This formulation comes from Bernard Cohen, *The Press and Foreign Policy*. Princeton, N.J.: Princeton University Press, 1963, p. 120. Our own words, likewise cited by McCombs and Shaw in the above article, were "the mass media force attention to certain issues by suggesting what individuals in the mass should think about, know about, have feelings about." See also Kurt Lang & Gladys E. Lang, "The Mass Media and Voting," in E. Burdick and A.J. Brodbeck (eds.) *American Voting Behavior*. New York: Free Press, 1959, p. 232.

6. A. Lawrence Lowell (1913) *Public Opinion and Popular Government*. New York: Longman's, Green.

7. T.E. Patterson and R.D. McClure (1976) *The Unseeing Eye; the Myth of Television Power in National Politics*. New York: Putnam, p. 27.

8. R.S. Frank, *Message Dimensions of Television News*. Lexington, Mass.: Lexington Books, 1973.

9. Ibid, p. 61.

10. J.P. Winter, "An Agenda-Setting Time Frame for the Civil Rights Issue 1954-1976." Presented at the annual meeting of the American Association for Public Opinion Research, May 1979.

11. L.B. Becker, M.E. McCombs and J.M. McLeod (1975) "The Development of Political Cognitions," in S.H. Chaffee (ed.) *Political Communication*. Beverly Hills, Cal.: Sage, p. 38.

12. R. W. Cobb and C. D. Elder (1971) "The Politics of Agenda-Building: An Alternative Perspective for Modern Democratic Theory." *Journal of Politics*, 33, pp. 892-915.

13. McCombs and Shaw, op. cit

14. A. Campbell et al. (1960) *The American Voter*. New York: John Wiley.

15. S. L. Popkin et al. (1976) "Toward an Investment Theory of Voting." *American Political Science Review*, 70, pp. 779-805.

16. D. R. Kinder and D. R. Kiewiet (1979) "Economic Discontent and Political Behavior: The Role of Personal Grievances and Collective Economic Judgments in Congressional Voting." *American Journal of Political Science*, 23, pp. 495-523.

17. H. M. Kepplinger and H. Roth (1979) "Creating a Crisis: German Mass Media and the Oil Supply in 1973-1974." *Public Opinion Quarterly*, 43, pp. 285-296.

18. National Advisory Commission on Civil Disorder (1968) *Report*. Washington: GPO.

19. T. W. Smith (1980) "America's Most Important Problem—A Trend Analysis." *Public Opinion Quarterly*, 44, pp. 164-180.

20. J. Perry (1973) *Us and Them; How the Press Covered the 1972 Election*. New York: Clarkson N. Potter.

21. B. Bagdikian (1973) "The Fruits of 'Agnewism.' " *Columbia Journalism Review*, Jan./Feb., p. 12.

22. The most complete study of the television coverage of the 1972 by Hofstetter does not have a category for Watergate but subsumes this subject under either "Republican party affairs" or "government functioning." C. Richard Hofstetter (1976) *Bias in the News*. Columbus: Ohio State University Press. Our conclusion is based on (1) an unpublished paper by Lawrence W. Lichty, "Network News Reporting of Watergate During the 1972 Election," Madison, Wisconsin, 1974; (2) Diamond, op. cit.; and (3) Patterson and McClure, op. cit. for television; and on J. R. Holz (1976) "Watergate and Mass Communication: A Case Study in Public Agenda-Setting." Unpublished Master's thesis, University of Pennsylvania for the New York *Times* coverage. This has been supplemented by an analysis of the four papers indexed in the Bell & Howell Newspaper Index. For a comparison between television and newspapers, see D. A. Graber (1976) "The Press and TV as Opinion Resources in Presidential Campaigns." *Public Opinion Quarterly*, 40, pp. 285-303.

23. Gallup Opinion Index, 1935-1937.

24. ORC data were made available through the courtesy of Harry O'Neill and is gratefully acknowledged.

25. H. Mendelsohn and G. J. O'Keefe (1976) *The People Chose a President*. New York: Praeger, p. 200.

26. According to a Harris poll in mid-September 1972, 84 percent considered the attempt to wiretap another party's headquarters "a basic violation of individual freedom."

27. The same Harris poll showed 57 percent believing it a commonplace occurrence with another 15 percent uncertain.

28. ORC, August 28-30, 1973.

29. Ibid.

30. Both the Harris and the Time/Yankelovich polls give evidence of slippage.

31. The Harris Survey.

32. A. H. Miller and W. E. Miller (1975) "Issues, Candidates and Partisan Divisions in the 1972 American Presidential Election." *Journal of Political Science*, 5, pp. 393-434.

33. D. H. Weaver et al. (1975) "Watergate and the Media: A Case Study of Agenda-Setting." *American Politics Quarterly*, 3, pp. 452-472.

34. A byline story by Ronald Kessler.

35. We have omitted here any discussion of the controversy over the delay and the alleged reduction in the length of the second part of this enterprise.

36. Bagdikian, op. cit.

37. E. R. May and J. Fraser, eds. (1973) *Campaign '72: The Managers Speak*. Cambridge: Harvard, p. 207.

38. Popkin et al., op. cit.

39. *The Harris Yearbook 1972*, p. 70, 72. In October, a majority believed that McGovern would get peace on the wrong terms and nearly as many thought his election would slow down the return of American prisoners as thought would speed it up.

40. Miller and Miller, op. cit.

41. A. S. Edelstein and D. P. Tefft (1976) "Media Credibility and Respondent Credulity with Respect to Watergate." *Communication Research*, 4, pp. 426-439.

42. Gallup showed public awareness of "Watergate" at 52 percent in September 1972, at 83 percent in early April, 91 percent in mid-May. ORC showed it at near-saturation (85 percent) as early as mid-February.

43. *Gallup Opinion Index* # 100, October 1973, p. 11.

44. *The Harris Yearbook 1973.*

45. Ibid.

46. The exact Gallup question was "Do you approve or disapprove of the way Nixon is handling his job as President?"

47. The exact Harris questions were "How would you rate the job President Nixon is doing as President? . . . on inspiring confidence in the White House personally? . . . on handling corruption in the government?"

48. The net rating (i.e., the percentage of positive minus the percentage of negative responses) in the Harris poll was + 35 in May—down from +48 in February.

49. New York *Times,* April 20, 1973.

50. New York *Times,* April 26, 1973.

51. From transcript of telephone conversation, April 25, 1973, as published in the New York *Times,* November 22, 1974, p. 20.

52. Holz, op. cit.

53. Based on an examination of the Bell & Howell Index for four newspapers—the Chicago *Tribune,* the Los Angeles *Times,* the New Orleans *Times-Picayune,* and the Washington *Post.*

54. Based on the *Television News Index and Abstracts,* Vanderbilt University. This index is not suited for a full content analysis but enables us to trace increases in time devoted to Watergate.

55. The criterion for saturation is four successive days, five out of seven, six out of nine and no break for longer than three days. This was done largely to allow for Sunday and Monday doldrums in the coverage. For television, the criterion was four out of five successive weekdays.

56. Weaver et al., op. cit.

57. Edelstein and Tefft, op. cit.

58. The Harris Survey, May 8, 1973—Special Bonus Column.

59. On March 25, 1973, the New York *Times* editorially despaired of the "monumental apathy" of Americans in the face of this serious trend in corruption.

Knowledge-gap studies have argued that the mass media may increase the discrepancies in knowledge between the less and more advantaged segments of society. This research uses the 1976 presidential debates to look closely at the question: Did the debates contribute to the quality and quantity of political participation among all segments of society? Using a panel design with samples of eligible voters in Madison, Wisconsin, the study suggests that less politically interested persons spent less time watching the debates than others, but that the effects of the debates were roughly equivalent for all segments of the electorate. Debate-watching increased involvement and participation in the campaign, and was a marginal help in candidate choice. Knowledge appeared unaffected by the debates. Thus, the implication for knowledge-gap research is that the findings need to be interpreted in a larger, systemic framework of possible media effects. Jack M. McLeod is professor of journalism and mass communication at the University of Wisconsin. Carl R. Bybee is assistant professor of communication at Purdue University. Jean A. Durall is assistant professor of communication at Northwestern University.

28

EQUIVALENCE OF INFORMED POLITICAL PARTICIPATION
The 1976 Presidential Debates as a Source of Influence

Jack M. McLeod, Carl R. Bybee, and Jean A. Durall

There is an understandable temptation to treat the 1976 presidential debates as historic media events. For the first

AUTHORS' NOTE: *Earlier versions of this article were presented to the annual conventions of the Association for Education in Journalism, Madison, Wisconsin, in 1977 and the International Communication Association, Chicago, in 1978. The research was supported in part by grants from the Markle Foundation and the Graduate School of the University of Wisconsin.*

time in 166 years and for only the second time in history, a confrontation of the two major presidential candidates was brought directly to the American people by the media. In the excitement of finding out "who won" the contests and how they may have affected the vote, we should not lose sight of our responsibility to systematically evaluate the debates as forms of political communication having potential impact on the political system beyond any immediate effect on the particular election outcome.

Two major problems combine to frustrate attempts at systematic evaluation of the debates. First, there is an almost limitless number of audience reactions that might have implications for the social system. This abundance of potential effects thus requires a careful specification of a limited number of criteria to serve as standards for evaluation. The second problem arises from the complexity of the debates as sources of effects. Their highly salient format set off various behaviors, reactions, and communication processes whose influence should be investigated along with the effects of debate-watching. In addition, the debates were only one among many sources of campaign information and their impact in comparison with these sources must be considered.

CRITERIA FOR EVALUATION

The evaluation research task was to identify functional requirements for the social system and to develop appropriate ways of measuring these requirements: What did we hope the debates would accomplish? for whom? and how would we know if they did so? Normative democratic political theory suggests that societal institutions can be judged on the basis of how well they facilitate broadly based and well-informed participation in the political decision-making process (Lasswell, 1948; Berelson et al., 1954; Verba and Nie, 1972; Wright, 1975). If we are willing to further assume that the present state of American political life can be characterized as having wide disparities in the level of participation among various sets of status categories, we can say that sources of political communication can be judged by their contribution to the participation of less active sectors of society. The research question then becomes: Did the debates contribute to the quantity and quality of political participation among all sectors of society? While this is not likely to be universally accepted as an adequate criterion—particularly not by elite democratic political theorists (Lipset, 1963)—it is at least clear enough to illustrate our approach to the problem. We call this criterion the *equivalence of informed political participation.*

Informed political participation. Measurement of informed political participation can be approached through consideration of various functions that political communication might serve for individuals. Five such functions can be seen as leading directly or indirectly to informed political participation: (1) to stimulate involvement (gain attention, motivate); (2) to inform (increase knowledge); (3) to facilitate decision-making (clarify issues and images, establish vote preferences); (4) to stimulate participation (campaigning, likelihood of voting); and (5) to strengthen attachment to the more abstract political system (values of efficacy and trust).

Equivalence. To the extent that the debates fostered informed political participation, it is necessary to estimate the equivalence or evenness of such effects across status groups. Equivalence is complicated by the fact that it is a distributional property of the political system and, hence, cannot be inferred from individual behavior alone. In this respect the investigation of equivalence resembles research testing the knowledge gap hypothesis, which asserts that the mass media often act to increase the discrepancies in knowledge between the more and the less advantaged sectors of society (Tichenor et al., 1970; Robinson, 1972; Donohue et al., 1975).

Our examination of equivalence does, however, differ from the knowledge gap literature in several ways. The primary difference lies in the scope of the criterion variables for which equalization effects are considered. Whereas the knowledge gap literature has been restricted to an examination of the equalization of information holding, this criterion represents only one of five variables in the present study. These additional variables will enable us to examine equivalence at several stages of a complex behavioral sequence.

A second difference derives from our inclusion of several media sources, in addition to the debates, to be used for comparative purposes. While it is important to determine whether or not the debates had equalizing effects, it is just as important from a policy standpoint to determine whether or not these equalizing effects were any greater or less than those of conventional political communication sources.

The present study also differs from the knowledge gap research in going beyond the division of the sample by education to examine the gap between the young and the old and between the politically interested and the politically uninterested. The use of contingent subgroups may help to avoid the confounds that are inherent in a single division, such as the instrumentality of the information, its availability, and the ability of groups to decode the information.

A final difference from the knowledge gap research lies in our use of a longitudinal research design. The majority of knowledge gap studies are cross-sectional in design and therefore yield, at best, correlational evidence; seldom is a control for the prior level of knowledge included. Our panel data provide for comparative tests of knowledge *gain* (along with increments in other participation measures) in relation to exposure to communication sources within educational, age, and interest levels. This allows for more direct tests of communication effects gap hypotheses.

We can assert equivalence in the present study if we can show that the debates contributed as much or more to the participation of groups usually less active in politics as they did to those with higher participation rates. We have used age, education, and political interest as contingent variables for equivalence analyses, since each consistently has been found to be a strong predictor of political participation (Milbrath and Goel, 1977; Verba and Nie, 1972). They are termed contingent variables in that they potentially delimit or mediate the effects of the communication variables and can be used to analyze two distinctive forms of equivalence. The first, equivalence of *exposure*, refers to the consistent use of a given media or interpersonal source across levels of the contingent variable. For example, to the extent that a source is used more often by the highly educated than by the lesser educated, we can say that there is evidence of *non*equivalence of exposure. The second form, equivalence of *predictive strength*, deals with the relative potency of the source's impact across contingency levels *per unit* of exposure. If a given source produces stronger associations with participation gains among the more educated than among the lesser educated, for example, we can assert *non*equivalence of predictive strength. A simple medical analogy may be helpful. The comparative effectiveness of a drug in helping cure a disease in various populations is a function of two factors: how widespread its application is (level of exposure) and its relative effectiveness in curing the disease once the drug is applied (likelihood of producing the cure).

Together, the two forms of equivalence comprise the more general criterion of *equivalence of effect*. If debate-viewing and its impact are less among the less interested, the lesser educated, and the young, then we can infer support for extending the knowledge gap hypothesis to the debates. On the other hand, if we find greater or equal usage and effects among the less participatory groups, then we might infer that the debates had consequences of equalizing social status differences and socializing the low-participation groups into the political system.

DEBATES AS FORMS OF POLITICAL COMMUNICATION

Treating the debates as unique "media events" is likely to divert attention from the fact that they were by no means the only source of campaign information. Long before the first debate in September, the standard print and electronic news sources were providing information about the candidates and the campaign. Complete coverage had been devoted to the political campaigns earlier in the summer and the full onslaught of political advertising was about to be felt. This implies that we should examine the more complicated questions of comparative evaluation in order to assess the role of each information source in the political process.

Certain aspects of the debate format seem to be uniquely relevant to the question of equivalence. First, the fact that the debates occupied several hours of prime-time television under virtual monopoly conditions (except for cable television) implies the likelihood of much higher viewing levels than is common to other formats. Only the coverage of the political conventions approached these ideal conditions. Prime-time coverage meant that avid television viewers who customarily do not pay much attention to public affiars may have been induced to watch. The excitement of the debates as spectator contests may have added to audience size. These factors should make equivalence or compensatory equivalence more likely because the less participatory groups would be drawn into the audience.

Another attribute of the debates that may have had consequences for equivalence is their high level of visibility. The advance publicity and postevent analyses associated with the debates were likely to set off public discussion and scrutiny not common to other information sources whose impact is more dispersed over time. This makes the debates an extremely complex set of events and implies that we look beyond the level of exposure to other social processes connected with the debates to determine their impact. This attribute also should mean greater impact on the less participatory categories, at least relative to the less focused standard sources of information.

STUDY DESIGN

Hour-long personal interviews were conducted with 353 eligible voters in Madison, Wisconsin, during late October of 1976. Since the main purpose of our larger research program was to analyze the political communication of young voters, persons under 27 years old were overrepresented in all samples. A month earlier and one week before the first debate, 97 of the respondents were interviewed by telephone. Another portion of the main sample included 133 respondents who had been interviewed during the off-year Congressional election in October 1974. Finally, 323 of the main sample were contacted by telephone in the weeks following the November 1976 election. The two panels constitute the data sets examined here.

Our research strategy examined potential debate effects in five areas, each represented by a sum of two or more standardized items or indices taken from the post-debate interviews and contrasted to their predebate levels.

(1) *Stimulating involvement:* changes in levels of campaign interest and campaign discussion (alpha = .75 predebate and .63 postdebate).

(2) *Conveying knowledge:* changes in accuracy of the two candidates' positions on three issues: federal jobs programs, building the B-1 bomber, and reorganizing the federal government (alpha = .48 predebate and .56 postdebate).

(3) *Facilitating vote decisions:* changes in discrimination between candidates (regardless of which chosen) on four criteria: vote preference; proximity of each candidate to respondent's position on issues; difference between the candidates' ratings on a "feeling thermometer"; and discrepancy between the candidates' images (alpha = .38 predebate and .64 postdebate).

(4) *Increasing participation:* changes in levels of likelihood of voting on election day and five specific types of campaigning (wearing buttons, giving money; alpha = .73 in 1974 and .65 postdebate).

(5) *Strengthening of system values:* changes in levels of political efficacy, political trust, and strength of party affiliation (alpha = .64 in 1974 and .19 in postdebate). The marked downward shift in reliability was due to party affiliation becoming almost unrelated to the other two system indices in 1976.

Since the intent was to study changes in these five criteria that took place during the debate period, the predebate measures of each criterion were used as a prior control. Identical measures were available for all items except for campaign interest, where predebate surrogates (paying attention to the campaign on television and in the print media) were substituted. Prior measures for involvement, knowledge, and vote decision were taken from the immediate predebate telephone interviews (n = 97), while those for participation and system values were obtained from the 1974 wave of the 1974-1976 panel (n = 133).

Debate-watching was measured by summing viewing levels across the first three debates as reported on a four-point scale. Five other debate variables were also included: level of attention, discussion with other people, following debate analyses in various media, evaluation of debate helpfulness, and the perception of who won (seeing Carter winning was scored as high). Four standard media sources were used for comparison: television news, entertainment television, television advertising, and newspaper public affairs content. All media measures were based on self-reports of exposure except for television advertising, which was indexed by the number of political ads recalled. We did not expect watching of entertainment shows to increase informed participation, but we included it for comparative purposes.

The three contingent variables—political interest, education, and age—were treated as continuous variables in their relationship to the various debate and media sources. The strength of the positive correlation of each with a given source variable constituted a measure of exposure *non*-equivalence; a zero or negligible association would indicate equivalence, while a substantial negative correlation could be called *compensatory* equivalence in overcoming status differences in exposure. Equivalence of predictive strength was analyzed in a more complex fashion. The postdebate dependent variables were regressed using their predebate levels as the first predictor block so that subsequent blocks were in effect analyzing increments of the participation indices. Separate analyses were conducted for each contingent variable using the individual contingency as the second block. The individual source variable was entered as the third block, with the multiplicative interaction between the contingent and source variable being brought in as the fourth and final block. Incremental R^2 tests were used to test for statistical significance.

RESULTS

EQUIVALENCE OF EXPOSURE

Our conceptualization of the debates as highly publicized, prime-time televised "events" suggested that the less participatory citizens who usually ignore public affairs media content might be lured into viewing the presidential confrontations. It is apparent from the first row in Table 1 that the debates rather clearly failed to achieve this democratic ideal of equivalent exposure. Although a very broad audience viewed at least part of the debates (McLeod et al., forthcoming), the significant positive correlations of debate-watching with all three contingency variables indicate

TABLE 1

Correlation of Contingent Variables with Debate
and Other Media Variables

Source Variable	Political Interest		Education		Age	
	Pre-post Panel	1974-76 Panel	Pre-post Panel	1974-76 Panel	Pre-post Panel	1974-76 Panel
Debate watching	.38[a]	.42[a]	.37[a]	.18[b]	.26[b]	.09
Other debate variables						
Attention	.40[a]	.36[a]	.19[c]	.03	.21[b]	.01
Discussion	.34[a]	.40[a]	.31[a]	.12	.04	-.05
Followed analyses	.30[a]	.33[a]	.21[b]	-.13	.01	.10
Evaluated favorably	.12	.22[b]	-.23[b]	.06	.06	-.02
Saw Carter as winner	.32[a]	.34[a]	.24[b]	-.06	-.07	.01
Other media sources						
Television news	.17	.21[b]	-.03	-.05	.39[a]	.32[a]
Television entertainment	-.12	-.10	-.50[a]	-.21[b]	.06	.23[b]
Television advertising	.17	.18[b]	.13	.18[b]	-.22[b]	-.22[b]
Newspaper news	.46[a]	.59[a]	.40[a]	-.35[a]	.26[b]	.46[a]

NOTE: N = 94 for Pre-post panel, 133 for 1974-76 panel. Significance is indicated:
a = $<.01$; b = $<.05$; c = $<.10$, two-tailed test.

that the more interested, better-educated, and older voters were much more likely to have spent time watching them in depth.

The processes resulting from debate-watching also tended to show nonequivalence of exposure. Particularly the more politically interested respondents were also more likely to pay close attention to the debates, to discuss them with other people, to follow their analyses in the media, to evaluate them favorably, and to see Carter as winning them (Table 1). The nonequivalence for education is less clear, since differences occur only in the pre-post debate panel. Age was much less of a contingency for debate processes. The only difference was in the pre-post panel, where the older respondents tended to pay closer attention.

The exposure equivalence correlations for the debate variables are perhaps best interpreted by comparison with the standard media sources. With respect to political interest, all debate variables except for favorable evaluation are more nonequivalent than any of the three television source measures (Table 1). The reading of political content in the newspaper is a different matter, in that it correlates more highly with political interest than does any debate variable. In the education comparisons there is equivalence in the use of television. In addition, there was an unexpected reversal between panels for newspaper news. Age correlations reveal a rather different pattern, with older respondents considerably more likely than the young to both view television news and read political content in the newspaper. Age, then, shows the only evidence among the three contingent variables that the debates and the processes they stimulated were more equivalent in the audiences they reached than were the standard news sources. The recall of advertising that shows negative associations with age in Table 1 is the only instance of compensatory equivalence in exposure other than the heavy use of entertainment viewing by the lesser educated

EQUIVALENCE OF PREDICTIVE STRENGTH

The ability of a given media source to induce political change among the more and the less participatory citizens was considered independently of the ability of that source's equivalence of exposure. To the extent that our three contingent variables altered the effects of the source variables on the informed participation criteria, they provided evidence for nonequivalence or, alternatively, for compensatory equivalence. Operationally, the alteration of source effects is indexed by the variance accounted for by the source exposure by contingent variable interaction. If a given source has a main effect on a participation criterion but no interaction effect with the contingent variable indicated, we have evidence for the equivalence of effect.

Results for the debate source variables and the first three participation criteria are shown in Table 2. While

TABLE 2

Percentage of Incremental Variance in Involvement, Knowledge,
and Decisions Accounted for by Contingent and Debate
Variables and their Interactions (pre-post study)

		Post-debate Dependent Variables					
		Involvement		Knowledge		Decision	
Predictor	Block	%	Dir.	%	Dir.	%	Dir.
Pre-debate measure	(1)	29.4[a]	+	37.0[a]	+	30.9[a]	+
Contingent variables							
Political interest	(2)	34.1[a]	+	8.3[a]	+	3.0[c]	+
Education	(2)	4.7[b]	+	4.7[b]	+	-	
Age	(2)	-		-		5.9[b]	+
Debate variables							
Debate watching	(3)	5.3[b]	+	-		2.5[c]	+
Watching x interest	(4)	1.1	+	-		-	
Watching x education	(4)	-		1.7	-	1.6	-
Watching x age	(4)	-		-		-	
Debate attention	(3)	11.3[a]	+	2.0	+	4.1[b]	+
Attention x interest	(4)	-		-		1.3	-
Attention x education	(4)	-		1.1	-	-	
Attention x age	(4)	-		-		1.2	+
Debate discussion	(3)	15.4[a]	+	1.1	+	5.6[b]	+
Discussion x interest	(4)	-		-		-	
Discussion x education	(4)	1.9	+	-		-	
Discussion x age	(4)	2.2	+	2.3	+	-	
Debate analyses	(3)	4.1[b]	+	4.1[b]	+	3.0[c]	+
Analyses x interest	(4)	-		-		4.8[b]	+
Analyses x education	(4)	-		-		-	
Analyses x age	(4)	5.6[b]	+	-		4.2[b]	+
Debate evaluation	(3)	2.6[c]	+	-		-	
Evaluation x interest	(4)	-		-		-	
Evaluation x education	(4)	-		2.2	+	3.0[c]	+
Evaluation x age	(4)	-		-		-	
Debate winner	(3)	5.8[a]	+	6.5[a]	+	-	
Winner x interest	(4)	1.7	-	1.1	-	-	
Winner x education	(4)	1.5	+	-		-	
Winner x age	(4)	1.5	-	1.4	-	-	

NOTE: N = 94. Entries are percentages of incremental variance accounted for by a given predictor relative to the amount of variance not accounted for by previous predictor blocks. Percentages less than 1.0 are eliminated from the table. A plus (+) for direction of an interaction indicates that the effect was greater in the more participatory contingent group; a minus (—) shows a tendency to lessen the "effects gap." Significance is indicated: a = $<.01$; b = $<.05$; c = $<.10$.

accounting for more than 3% of the incremental variance is
required for statistical significance, predictive strength
of 1% or more is shown in the table in order to avoid type II

error. As expected, the predebate measures of each dependent variable criterion account for a considerable proportion of the postdebate variance when entered as the first block in the regression analyses (first row of Table 2). The three contingent variables, entered singly as main effects in the second predictor block, account for widely differing proportions of incremental variance. Political interest, for example, is strongly related to involvement, indicating that those most interested in politics generally were also those that were the most likely to increase their involvement in the campaign during the debate period. They were also more likely than others to gain knowledge, and showed some tendency to come to a more firm decision during the same period. Less strong educational differences are shown, but again it is the more participatory the more educated respondents—who become more involved and more informed. Education was unrelated to decision-making. Age was unrelated to gains in involvement and knowledge, but the older respondents were more likely to become more decisive in their presidential choices. Overall, the main effects found for the contingent variables showed gains for those already most participatory. Thus, any effect of the media sources toward equivalence must overcome an overall trend toward an increasing participation gap during the late campaign period.

The direct effects of debate-watching for the first three criteria were not overwhelming except for its stimulation of involvement and, marginally, its aid in decision-making (row five of Table 2). But our previous research has shown that the greatest impact of debate-viewing was *indirect*, through the stimulation of discussion and other postdebate processes and cognitions (McLeod et al., forthcoming). Those watching the debates more often paid closer attention to them, discussed them more often, were more likely to follow their analyses in the media, and evaluated them more highly than did those watching less frequently. These processes and cognitions subsequently tended to have stronger effects on participation, beliefs, and attitudes.

More important to equivalence, however, are the relationships shown for the interaction of watching with the three contingent variables (rows 6 through 8). None of the nine possible interactions with debate-watching is significant, and only three account for more than 1% of the incremental variance (one positive or nonequivalence and two negative or compensatory equivalence). The overall finding is, then, that the modest effects of debate-watching tended to be equivalent in their effect.

The effects of the first subprocess stimulated by debate-watching were similar. Those paying closest attention to the debates were more likely than others to become more involved and to make more firm decisions (Table 2). As with debate-viewing, the effects tended to be equivalent, with only three of nine possible interactions accounting for as much as 1% of the incremental variance. The amount of debate discussion also aided involvement and decision-making. Again, none of the interactions was significant.

Following debate analyses in the media produced positive effects on all three criteria, perhaps most importantly for increased knowledge of the candidates' positions on issues (Table 2). The relationship of following analyses to *knowledge* produced no significant interactions with the contingent variables, but a significant interaction was found in predicting *involvement* such that older respondents were much more likely than the young to increase their campaign interest and discussion as a result of attending to debate analyses. The use of debate analyses to make more firm decisions was also restricted to the older voters. A nonequivalent interaction was also shown for analyses and interest in which the more interested were more likely to use these interpretations to make decisions. The debate analyses, then, produced the only clear evidence for nonequivalence among the debate variables.

Favorable evaluation of the debates had little impact on the first three dependent variable criteria, revealing only a marginally equivalent relationship with an increase in involvement (Table 2). Perceiving Carter as winning, however, was clearly and somewhat surprisingly related to both increased involvement and knowledge. None of the interactions is significant, but the direction is toward compensatory equivalence for the interactions between Carter winning and both interest and age, with a hint of nonequivalence for Carter winning and education. The decision-making criterion was unaffected by seeing Carter as winning the debates, but our previous research (McLeod et al., forthcoming) indicates that perception of winning did lead to voting for the judged victor. The effects were thus cancelled out in the decision index used here.

The results for the two criteria using the 1974-1976 panel data are shown in Table 3. The 1974 measures do account for considerable variance in the postdebate criteria, but the strength is considerably less for participation than for any other criterion. Among the main effects of the contingent variables both political interest and education predicted positively to increased participation, but not to strengthened system values. Age is unrelated to either criterion.

Debate-watching is related to heightened levels of participation, but not to changes in system values (Table 3). The lack of any trace of interaction indicates that the stimulation of participation is equivalent across the contingent variable levels. Among the other debate variables, the level of attention and the amount of discussion were unrelated to either 1974 or 1976 criterion. Following debate analyses was related to more frequent campaigning activity, an effect largely confined to the more highly educated respondents. On the other hand, the more educated tended to show *weakened* system values among those following the debate analyses most closely. The other high participation subgroups—the more interested and older citizens—showed positive nonequivalent associations in their interactions with following analyses with respect to system values.

TABLE 3

Percentage of Incremental Variance in Participation and System
Values Accounted for by Contingent and Debate Variables
and their Interactions (1974-76 study)

| Predictor | Block | 1976 Post-debate Dependent Variables | | | |
| | | Participation | | System Values | |
		%	Dir.	%	Dir.
1974 measure	(1)	10.1[a]	+	22.5[a]	+
Contingent variables					
Political interest	(2)	8.2[a]	+	-	
Education	(2)	5.2[a]	-	1.6	+
Age	(2)	-		-	
Debate variables					
Debate watching	(3)	3.2[b]	+	-	
Watching x interest	(4)	-		2.0	+
Watching x education	(4)	-		-	
Watching x age	(4)	-		-	
Debate attention	(3)	1.2	+	-	
Attention x interest	(4)	1.2	-	-	
Attention x education	(4)	-		-	
Attention x age	(4)	-		-	
Debate discussion	(3)	2.3	+	-	
Discussion x interest	(4)	1.5	+	2.7[c]	+
Discussion x education	(4)	1.8	+	-	
Discussion x age	(4)	-		-	
Debate analyses	(3)	4.7[a]	+	1.0	-
Analyses x interest	(4)	-		3.9[b]	+
Analyses x education	(4)	6.0[a]	+	2.6[c]	-
Analyses x age	(4)	2.3	-	2.9[c]	+
Debate evaluation	(3)	-		7.9[a]	+
Evaluation x interest	(4)	-		2.9[c]	+
Evaluation x education	(4)	-		-	
Evaluation x age	(4)	-		-	
Debate winner	(3)	4.5[a]	+	-	
Winner x interest	(4)	1.1	-	6.1[a]	+
Winner x education	(4)	1.4	+	-	
Winner x age	(4)	-		1.9	+

NOTE: N = 94. Entries are percentages of incremental variance accounted for by a given predictor relative to the amount of variance not accounted for by previous predictor blocks. Percentage less than 1.0 are eliminated from the table. A plus (+) for direction of an interaction indicates that the effect was greater in the more participatory contingent group; a minus (—) shows a tendency to lessen the "effects gap." Significance is indicated: a = $<.01$; b = $<.05$; c = $<.10$.

Favorable evaluation of the debates, which was unrelated to all other criteria, did reveal a clear positive relationship to strengthened system values (Table 3). In a nonequivalent interaction, the more interested were more likely than others to show a link between evaluating the debates and system values. Seeing Carter as winning the debates was related to increased participation in the presidential campaign. This produced no interactions, but in direction the effect appears to have been somewhat stronger among the less interested but more educated respondents. Although no main effect was shown, those most interested in politics who saw Carter as winning tended to reveal stronger system values. Conversely, it is also true that the less interested who saw Ford as winning tended to show weaker trust, efficacy, and party identification than they had expressed two years earlier.

In general, the results for the 1974-1976 panel analyses of participation parallel those for the pre-post debate panel on first three criteria. Of the six debate variables, three predict increases in participation and these effects tend to be equivalent with one exception (nonequivalence for analyses by education). System values, on the other hand, revealed only one main effect, but substantial interactions generally in the direction of increasing the discrepancy between the active and inactive in their regard for the political system appeared.

The four other media sources and their impact on the first three participation criteria are shown in Table 4. Television news appears to have little impact on involvement, knowledge gain, or decision-making (row 5). There is some evidence for interaction in increasing involvement of less educated (compensatory equivalence) but older (nonequivalence) news viewers.

Television entertainment viewing has only marginal effects on involvement and knowledge and these are in the direction of the *low* watchers becoming more interested and learning more (Table 4). This supressant effect was not unexpected, but positive effects might have been expected for the more heralded television advertising (Patterson and McClure, 1976). The recall of television campaign

TABLE 4

Percentage of Incremental Variance in Involvement, Knowledge, and Decisions Accounted for by Contingent and Media Variables and their Interactions (pre-post study)

Predictor	Block	Post-debate Dependent Variables					
		Involvement		Knowledge		Decision	
		%	Dir.	%	Dir.	%	Dir.
Pre-debate measure	(1)	29.4[a]	+	37.0[a]	+	30.9[a]	+
Contingent variables							
Political interest	(2)	34.1[a]	+	8.3[a]	+	3.0[c]	+
Education	(2)	4.7[b]		4.7[b]	+	-	
Age	(2)	-		-		5.9[b]	+
Media variables							
Television news	(3)	1.4	+	-		2.2	+
TV news x interest	(4)	-		-		-	
TV news x education	(4)	4.9[b]	-	-		-	
TV news x age	(4)	3.2[c]	+	1.1	+	-	
Television entertainment	(3)	2.4[c]	-	3.4[c]	-	1.1	-
TV entertmt. x interest	(4)	-		-		-	
TV entertmt. x education	(4)	-		-		2.1	-
TV entertmt. x age	(4)	2.8[c]	+	-		-	
Television advertising	(3)	2.3	+	-		-	
TV advertising x interest	(4)	-		-		-	
TV advertising x education	(4)	-		-		-	
TV advertising x age	(4)	-		-		-	
Newspaper news	(3)	11.3[a]	+	2.8[c]	+	1.3	+
Newspaper news x interest	(4)	-		-		-	
Newspaper news x education	(4)	-		3.3[c]	-	-	
Newspaper news x age	(4)	-		2.2	+	-	

NOTE: N = 133. Entries are percentages of incremental variance accounted for by a given predictor relative to the amount of variance not accounted for by previous predictor blocks. Percentages less than 1.0 are eliminated from the table. A plus (+) for direction of an interaction indicates that the effect was greater in the more participatory contingent group; a minus (−) shows a tendency to lessen the "effects gap." Significance is indicated: a = $<.01$; b = $<.05$; c = $<.10$.

advertising predicted to none of the three criteria, and no interaction is shown. Reading political content in the newspaper offers a marked contrast to the television variables; avid readers were much more likely than others to become more involved during the campaign period and showed a tendency to increase their knowledge of the candidates' positions. Knowledge also shows an interesting although marginal interaction in the form of increased issue accuracy among the lesser-educated avid readers.

The relationship of the other media variables to the final set of criteria from the 1974-1976 panel are shown in Table 5. Television news again plays only a minor role in being marginally associated with an increase in campaign participation. The compensatory equivalence potential of television news is shown, however, in the significant negative interaction with age. It is the younger, more frequent news viewers who are the most likely to increase their participation in the campaign. News viewing is unrelated to changes in system values, but there is a marginal interaction: the older frequent news watchers are the most likely to maintain or enhance their commitment to the political system.

Results for television entertainment-viewing are more difficult to interpret. Although there is no main effect on participation, there is a significant interaction with age and a marginally significant positive one with interest. Since there is no main effect for either entertainment viewing or age, the former interaction becomes very difficult to interpret. No relationship for entertainment and system values is indicated.

Recall of television political advertising is tied to gains in campaign participation (Table 5). The effect is equivalent for interest and age, but shows compensatory equivalence in being concentrated among the less educated respondents. It shows no impact on system values, but there is a marginal interaction indicating the possibility of effects among the more highly educated.

The reading of political content in the press has a marked impact on more active campaign participation (Table 5). All three interactions are significant: news reading is tied to increased campaigning among the better-educated citizens, but also among the less interested and the young. Its interactive effects reverse for system values, with reading leading to equal or strengthened commitment among the older but less educated respondents. Newspaper news-reading clearly varies between nonequivalence and compensatory equivalence depending upon the contingent variable and the criterion considered.

TABLE 5

Percentage of Incremental Variance in Participation and System Values Accounted for by Contingent and Media Variables and their Interactions (1974-76 study)

		1976 Post-debate Dependent Variables	
		Participation	System Values
Predictor	Block	% Dir.	% Dir.
1974 measure	(1)	10.1[a] +	28.5[a] +
Contingent variables			
Political interest	(2)	8.2[a] +	-
Education	(2)	5.2[a] -	1.6 +
Age	(2)	-	-
Media variables			
Television news	(3)	2.5[c] +	-
TV news x interest	(4)	-	-
TV news x education	(4)	-	-
TV news x age	(4)	3.2[b] -	2.8[c] +
Television entertainment	(3)	-	-
TV entertmt. x interest	(4)	2.2[c] +	-
TV entertmt. x education	(4)	2.0 +	-
TV entertmt. x age	(4)	6.2[a] -	1.5 +
Television ads	(3)	3.9[b] +	-
TV ads x interest	(4)	-	-
TV ads x education	(4)	4.2[b] -	2.5[c] +
TV ads x age	(4)	-	-
Newspaper news	(3)	4.3[b] +	1.0 -
Newsp. news x interest	(4)	4.1[b] -	-
Newsp. news x education	(4)	6.0[a] +	3.6[b] -
Newsp. news x age	(4)	3.8[b] -	3.8[b] +

NOTE: N = 133. Entries are percentages of incremental variance accounted for by a given predictor relative to the amount of variance not accounted for by previous predictor blocks. Percentages less than 1.0 are eliminated from the table. A plus (+) for direction of an interaction indicates that the effect was greater in the more participatory contingent group; a minus (—) shows a tendency to lessen the "effects gap." Significance is indicated: a = $<.01$; b = $<.05$; c = $<.10$.

CONCLUSIONS

The 1976 presidential debates were evaluated as an innovation in political communication formats that might overcome existing gaps in electoral participation between the more and the less active sectors of society. Since existing media sources of information (television news, newspaper news) are alleged to produce "effects gaps" that widen differentials in participation, it was reasonable to test whether the debates as highly publicized prime-time media events might be more equivalent than standard news sources in activating the less participatory citizens in the election campaign.

Effects gaps or nonequivalence of a political communication source can result if either of two conditions are present: first, the less participatory sectors may use the source less frequently than other people and, hence, will be less exposed to activating information. Second, the less involved groups may benefit less per unit of exposure to such information. To distinguish the two types we have labeled the former condition nonequivalence of exposure and the latter nonequivalence of predictive strength.

With respect to the criterion of exposure equivalence, it was apparent that the debates failed to sustain the depth of viewing among the less active respondents. The less politically interested were particularly likely to spend less time watching the debates, and this nonequivalence is greater than for any television measure (news, entertainment, and advertising recall) and not significantly less than for reading political content in the newspaper. This leads to the pessimistic conclusion that increased opportunity for exposure will not automatically lead to actual use among the less interested citizens. Monopoly conditions and heavy advance publicity may initially enlarge the audience, but sustaining attention across a series a debates may depend on creating formats that appeal to disparate groups of viewers.

Analysis of the second criterion, predictive strength equivalence, obviously requires that debate-watching must have had an impact on at least some segment of the public. Debate-watching was found to have significant direct effects on increasing involvement and participation in the campaign and a marginal effect in helping people to make voting decisions. It had no direct impact on the final two areas measured, increasing knowledge and strengthening system values. The major outcome of debate-watching was indirect, however, in such processes as discussion of the debates and following them in subsequent media analyses. These variables, in turn, had substantial effects on all five types of dependent variables.

As measured by the lack of interaction with the three contingent variables (interest, education, and age), the effects of debate-watching were consistently equivalent. They were as likely to have stimulated the less interested, educated, and the young as they were to have activated the more participatory groups. Among the other five debate variables, only following debate analyses revealed a substantial proportion of nonequivalent effects. None of the debate variables showed clear indications of compensatory equivalence in reaching the less participatory groups more effectively.

In summary, the debates and the processes they stimulated tended to be nonequivalent in exposure, but equivalent in effect. That is, they unfortunately reached more effectively those already best served by the standard media sources, but to the extent that less active citizens did view the debates, they benefited equally with their more involved counterparts. Some 43% of the main effects of the six debate variables were statistically significant, as compared with less than 8% (6 of 80 comparisons) for their interactions with the three contingent variables.

The predictive strength equivalence of the debate variables stands in sharp contrast to the results for the standard media sources. Exclusive of television entertainment (which was not expected to influence participation), the three standard sources produced significant main effects in only 20% of the comparisons, but 60% of their interactions with the contingent variables were found to be significant. The reasons why the standard media sources produced interactive effects so much more frequently than did the debate variables is not entirely clear. Perhaps the more habitual sources of information have more structured processing patterns than do the debates, and thereby produce less across-the-board effects.

The interactions of the standard media sources more often showed compensatory equivalence (closing the effects gap) than nonequivalence (widening the gap). The dominance of compensatory equivalence in effect held even for newspaper news that was so clearly nonequivalent in exposure. A variety of explanations for the compensatory equivalence might be offered. Among these is the possibility that a ceiling effect (Ettema and Kline, 1977) might have restricted the participation gain of the more interested and educated older respondents. However, a separate analysis of the means and variances of the pre- and postmeasure of the dependent variables within dichotomized contingent subgroups tends to cast doubt on this methodological explanation.

Another possible explanation for the compensatory equivalent effects of the traditional sources is that election campaigns are highly salient events that generate conflict and levels of interpersonal processes and information-seeking that have as their consequence the leveling out of effects gaps that characterize the between-election situation. This would be consonant with the findings of Donohue et al. (1975) that knowledge gaps tend to narrow when conflict is raised about community issues. If this reasoning holds, then election campaigns and the media that cover them do act to make the level of informed participation more equivalent. Our data indicate the debates added involvement and a focus to the campaign that may have contributed to this objective.

Our results have considerable relevance for the "knowledge gap" literature at an even more general level. First, it appears essential to distinguish between the *equivalence of exposure* and the *equivalence of predictive strength* for any given source. Both debate-watching and newspaper news-reading, for example, were nonequivalent in *exposure* by being more heavily used among the more active sectors of the public, but tended to show equivalence in *effect*, as evidenced by the lack of significant interactions between exposure to debates and newspapers and the three contingent variables. That is, the more interested, better-educated, older respondents gained an additional advantage in informed participation during the campaign by their media exposure patterns, but they did *not* receive further increments by being able to use these sources more effectively than did the less active groups. The less interested, less educated, and younger people gained just as much as others per amount of debate-viewing and newspaper-reading. The net consequence for the political system is a combination of these two equivalence types. Nonequivalence of either variety may be sufficient to foster inequality of participation.

Second, the degree of equivalence very much depends upon which contingent variable we are describing. A given source sometimes showed a positive interaction with one contingent variable and a negative interaction with another. It is ironic that across 50 comparisons (ten sources and five dependent variables) education—the variable most often used for analysis in the knowledge gap literature—showed the *most even* ratio of positive and negative interactions; for both political interest and age, nonequivalence (positive interactions) was much more likely than was compensatory equivalence (negative interactions).

A final implication for the knowledge gap literature is also ironic in that knowledge gain among our five dependent variables showed the *lowest* levels of nonequivalence. That is, the concentration of research efforts on gaps in knowledge may have obscured even larger differentials in other areas of effects. In the present study, for example, strengthening of system values reveals much greater levels of nonequivalence. It appears that generalizations about media effects gaps must be cautiously restricted to the particular combination of effects criterion, media source, and contingent variable being considered. The questions of differential source effects seem increasingly complicated.

REFERENCES

BERELSON, B. R., P. F. LAZARSFELD, and W. N. McPHEE (1954) Voting. Chicago: Univ. of Chicago Press.

DONOHUE, G. A., P. J. TICHENOR, and C. N. OLIEN (1975) "Mass media and the knowledge gap: a hypothesis reconsidered." Communication Research 2: 3-23.

ETTEMA, J. S. and F. G. KLINE (1977) "Deficits, differences, and ceilings: contingent conditions for understanding the knowledge gap." Communication Research 4: 179-202.

LASSWELL, H. D. (1948) "The structure and function of communication in society," in L. Bryson (ed.) The Communication of Ideas. New York: Harper & Row.

LIPSET, S. M. (1963) Political Man. Garden City, NY. Anchor.

McLEOD, J. M., J. A. DURALL, D. A. ZIEMKE, and C. R. BYBEE (forthcoming) "Expanding the context of debate effects," in S. Kraus (ed.) Great Debates: 1976—Ford vs. Carter. Bloomington: Indiana Univ. Press.

MILBRATH, L. W. and M. L. GOEL (1977) Political Participation: How and Why Do People Get Involved in Politics? Chicago: Rand McNally.

PATTERSON, T. E. and R. D. McCLURE (1976) The Unseeing Eye: The Myth of Television Power in National Elections. New York: Putnam.

ROBINSON, J. (1972) "Mass communication and information diffusion," in F. G. Kline and P. J. Tichenor (eds.) Current Perspectives in Mass Communication Research. Beverly Hills, CA: Sage.

TICHENOR, P. J., G. A. DONOHUE, and C. N. OLIEN (1970) "Mass media flow and differential growth of knowledge." Public Opinion Q. 34: 159-170.

WRIGHT, D. R. (1975) Mass Communication: A Sociological Perspective. New York: Random House.

VERBA, S. and N. H. NIE (1972) Participation in America: Political Democracy and Social Equality. New York: Harper & Row.

Jack M. McLeod is Professor in the School of Journalism and Mass Communication at the University of Wisconsin, Madison and Chairman of the Mass Communications Research Center at that university.

Carl R. Bybee is Assistant Professor in the Department of Communication at Purdue University.

Jean A. Durall is Assistant Professor in the Department of Communication Studies at Northwestern University.

As did the preceding article by McLeod and others, this piece tackles interest as a crucial variable in the test of the knowledge-gap hypothesis. A panel design using a large sample of mid-Michigan respondents tests the comparative role of educational level (traditionally a main predictor in knowledge-gap studies) with self-interest and social interest in two news topics, the Nixon impeachment controversy and a National Football League strike. In addition, two levels of knowledge are assessed: factual and structural. Social interest was a stronger predictor of structural knowledge than education, and it was equal to education as a predictor of factual knowledge. Self-interest was not a factor. These findings are consistent with the McLeod study in pointing to alternative routes to understanding and narrowing the information gap. B.K.L. Genova is an assistant professor at Syracuse University's School of Information Studies. Bradley S. Greenberg is professor of communication and telecommunication at Michigan State University.

29

INTERESTS IN NEWS AND
THE KNOWLEDGE GAP

B. K. L. Genova and Bradley S. Greenberg

THE knowledge gap hypothesis proposes that socioeconomic factors are the crucial determinant in identifying citizens who are more likely to be knowledgeable about public affairs news events. In their seminal work on this issue, Tichenor et al. chose education to index SES in assessing public knowledge about current print-media news events. Their secondary analysis of several U.S. studies led to this proposition: "As the infusion of mass media information into a social system increases, segments of the population with higher socioeconomic status tend to acquire this information at a faster rate than lower status segments, so that the gap in knowledge between them tends to increase rather than decrease" (Tichenor et al., 1970:159–60).

This statement conveys the pessimism that the information-rich will become richer, and it bears supporting evidence. The same explanation has been applied to the impact of the television series "Sesame Street." Advantaged children who infrequently watched that series gained more in cognitive skills than disadvantaged children with the same viewing pattern (Ball and Bogatz, 1970). News events have been demonstrated to diffuse somewhat more rapidly to high SES adults than to lower SES citizens (Budd et al., 1966).

There is no quarrel with the proposition that certain background characteristics such as education contribute to the capacities of audience members to respond to and assimilate incoming media information (Wade and Schramm, 1969). Hyman et al. (1975) have written that the process of education creates an "enduring" receptivity to knowledge. There is, however, a body of research evidence which posits that the choice of media information to consume and the consequent learning of media information stem more immediately and directly from motivational interests of the public (Ettema and Kline, 1977). For example, one study of audience attention to television commercials for two gubernatorial campaigns showed strong ties with campaign interest and little support for demographic locators, such as education or occupation (Atkin et al., 1973). Another found interest strongly related to knowledge about an ongoing sports event (Greenberg et al., 1965). One domestic and one foreign study sought to isolate factors playing a role in political knowledge acquisition. Both concurred on the role played by interest predictors, suggesting that the process moves from interest through media use to political knowledge (Johnson, 1973; Bishop and McMartin, 1973). The correlation of political interest with political knowledge was as strong as that of media use with political knowledge in each study.

These representative studies suggest that the interests of the public may be a central factor in what public affairs knowledge is gained. Implicit is the notion that interests may have something to do with education or socioeconomic status, but nowhere is that issue directly assessed, nor are the demographic locators separated from interest predispositions, within the knowledge gap scheme. Although education is likely to widen an individual's overall scope of interest, it is not necessary and perhaps not reasonable to assume that there are homogenous interests among similarly educated citizens, whether high or low in education.

This study focuses on interest as a key component in assessing public affairs news information learning within the framework of the knowledge gap phenomenon. Here it is proposed that an interest-based model will permit a more sensitive examination of news information gain processes and will help trace the patterns of knowledge differences among mass media audiences. Figure 1 displays the model used. News information items are portrayed as having different distributions in their perceived interest for receivers, and information gain is presented as a function of those interests. Knowledge gains grow more rapidly among more interested public segments, during early

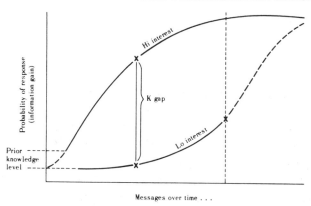

Figure 1. Information Gain Response Functions

and more intermediate stages of dissemination of information about continuing news events. If any message were publicized indefinitely or at least for relatively long periods, expectations are that the knowledge gap regarding basic information about the event would eventually narrow and close. Given media news patterns and the fragility of news coverage on any given topic, that would rarely occur. The magnitude of the gap would seem to depend on how long the media publicity continues.

Interest itself is not an unambiguous concept and has been variously explicated in the literature. Adams et al. (1965) based a distinction on potential social utility, while Greenberg et al. (1965) found news interest based more on perceived personal utility for the information. Hanneman and Greenberg (1973) used composite measures of relevance (importance) and salience (interest) to predict differential news information processing. McCombs (1972) studied relevance as both discussion of the event and interest in the event interchangeably.

From these approaches, two components of interest emerge for specific examination in this study. One is the perceived usefulness of news information for one's self. Self-interest is pertinent to information areas which are scanned because they are judged by the individual to have some functional utility in daily coping behaviors (Atkin, 1973). Self-interests are likely to be determined by personal exigencies, e.g., "What is happening to me?" They may be of primacy in orienting what a person chooses to learn. An individual with relatively constant spheres of activity and stable social networks should persist in using certain criteria to select information areas.

The second component of interest is the perceived utility of the information to the individual's social milieu, to the kinds of interpersonal networks important to the individual. In terms of information seeking, but not information gain, Chaffee and McLeod (1973) have reported that social contacts account better for that behavior than do individual differences. Social interests are more likely to be influenced by the agenda-setting role of the mass media's choices of news events to report. Thus, changes in the individual's spheres of activity and/or social milieu should result in changing perceptions of informational utility, and perhaps the formation of new interest areas.

Within this framework, the study model proceeded to test certain specific propositions. First, the relative predictive power of interest versus education in assessing news knowledge gain was examined, as well as the distinction between self-interest and social interest. Second, it was anticipated that citizens with stronger interests would have more knowledge than those with weaker interests in specific events, and that the former would acquire additional information more rapidly as new mass media information was made available to the social system, thus widening the knowledge gap between them. Finally, for news events with longer durations of media coverage, the knowledge gap was expected to begin to narrow between the more and less interested public segments.

Method

A structured interview was used to measure separate components of interest and knowledge about two well-publicized news events in August 1974, from a panel survey of adults at two points in time, 10 days apart.

SAMPLE

The survey site was a mid-Michigan area of 15 communities with an estimated population of 115,000 excluding an urban center. A systematic probability sample of 400 telephone numbers was drawn from the area telephone directory. Respondent selection within each household among adults eighteen years of age and over followed the procedure recommended by Troldahl and Carter (1964). In all, 63 percent usable interviews ($N = 253$) were completed during the first wave, with 28 percent refusals, disconnects, and no answers, 2 percent ineligible, and 7 percent who said they would not be reinterviewed. Comparisons between the obtained sample and 1970 census characteristics yielded comparable distributions for sex and age, with some discrepancy for education and occupation. The sample was 48 percent male, compared to 46 percent in the census. Both the sample and the census contained 59 percent aged eighteen to thirty, and 14 percent in their forties. The sample included 32 percent in labor and service jobs, with 36 percent in the census; the sample had a higher proportion of professionals (31 percent versus 14 percent) and a lower proportion of students (7 percent versus 23 percent) than did the census, in large part because the data collection occurred during the summer, when far fewer students reside in the area.

NEWS EVENTS

The questionnaire assessed respondent interest and knowledge about two different news events, the ongoing National Football League strike and the Nixon impeachment developments, at two points in time. These two events met several necessary criteria. First, they met the need for two news topics contrasting in the likely interest they would hold for different audience segments. Second, they were likely to have different durations of display in the mass media, with the football strike a relatively short-lived event and the impeachment events developing a longer history. Third, both events had to remain in the news throughout the 10-day study period.

VARIABLES

The key independent variables were self-interest and social interest. To tap *self-interest,* respondents were asked four questions about the event's influence on their own life, their job or that of someone close to them, the cost of living, and their general satisfaction with things around them. To tap *social interest,* respondents were asked if they had discussed the event with friends, relatives, people at work, or anyone else. Questionnaire items were evaluated for inclusion on their posited self- or social interest indices on the basis of results from a principal axis factor analysis with a quartimax rotation. For example, at time one, the four items tapping social interest in the NFL event had factor loadings ranging from .57 to .88 with no loading on these items exceeding .15 on the self-interest factor. In parallel, the items comprising self-interest had factor loadings ranging from .51 to .81 with no loading exceeding .16 on the social interest factor. The standard deviation of the constructed interest indices were .89 and .94. The proportion of variance accounted for by items posited to establish these two factors of interest were 95 percent and 91 percent. Factor scores for all the extracted factor items were summed to form the indices of interest.[1] Composite interest was an index obtained by summing the single index scores of self-interest and social interest.

[1] Independent variable indexing entailed the following steps: First, factor analyses were obtained with a quartimax of each group of component variables, in order to arrive at a factor score coefficient for each component. Next, factor scores were created for each respondent on the chosen factor, i.e., multiplying a respondent's

The events examined differed by interest levels, as anticipated. There was little interest in the NFL strike, either in terms of self-interest or social interest measures at time one; about 80 percent of the sample chose low interest responses on both measures. In contrast, 60 percent of the sample selected high interest responses for the impeachment event during the first interview.

The use of a panel design carries with it some potential contamination problem. Here, the contamination argument would be that the first wave of questioning could have stimulated interest in the two news events. However, between the two waves, more respondents decreased in interest for each event than increased. For the NFL event, 78 reported less interest and 4 percent reported more interest; for the impeachment, 44 percent decreased and 40 percent increased in interest. If there was any contamination problem, it did not have the expected outcome.

The dependent variables were measures of *factual* and *structural* knowledge about each news event (Akin and Greenberg, 1974). Factual knowledge tapped the respondent's knowledge of specific items, names, dates, places, facts, and figures, related to specific news occurrences. Factual knowledge items asked for the names of quarterbacks crossing picketlines, the amount of presidential pension, etc. Structural knowledge indexed the respondent's understanding of the relationships manifested in an event, how or why it took place, and the event's place in the broader framework of related phenomena. Structural knowledge items asked about Ed Garvey's role in the NFL strike, the implications of presidential censure, etc. From a pretest, three items were selected for each knowledge component, and scored as correct or not. Two of the six knowledge items remained constant across both interviews, while four more current questions during wave two replaced prior items from wave one. A single index for each knowledge variable was created by summing standardized response scores across knowledge items at each time period.

Six standard categories assessed the respondents' highest education level: Less than sixth grade completion, seventh grade through some high school, high school diploma, some college, college degree, and graduate work.

After all indices had been constructed and before analyses to test the study hypotheses, the relationship between interest and education was examined. If these were strongly interrelated, much of the proposed analysis would be unwarranted. At time one, the composite

---

standardized score on the component variables by the factor score coefficient for that variable. The final index score was obtained by summing a respondent's standardized scores on N component measures, each multiplied by the appropriate factor score coefficient. Items, distributions, and related information are available from the authors.

measure of interest in the NFL strike was correlated .14 with education, and interest in the impeachment developments was correlated .23 with education. At time two, the same measures of interest were correlated .08 and .18, respectively, with education. The relatively low magnitude of these correlations permits direct comparisons of the roles of education and interest in explaining potential knowledge gap differences.

Findings

First, the independent and combined impacts of interest and education on public affairs knowledge were examined. For both events at both time periods, the correlation of interest with knowledge exceeded that of education with knowledge (Table 1a). At time one, the differences between the correlations were not significant, but in the predicted direction; at time two, each difference was significant ($p <$ .01). The interest-knowledge correlations ranged from .32 to .39, and the education-knowledge correlations ranged from .23 to .29, demonstrating no overlap in the ranges. Further, as anticipated, the multiple correlations of education and interest, ranging from .40 to .44, exceeded the individual correlations.

This basic analysis was repeated with the conceptually and operationally distinct components of factual and structural knowledge, in Table 1b and 1c. The interest-knowledge and education-knowledge relationships have distinctive and contrasting patterns. For factual knowledge, there are small and inconsistent differences in the correlations between education and interest with knowledge. Twice education yields a higher correlation, and twice interest does, but they vary little. Thus, for discrete bits of information about such news events as these, education and interest are functionally equivalent as predictors.

Table 1. Public Affairs Knowledge by Interest and Education

| | 1a. Composite Knowledge | | | | 1b. Factual Knowledge | | | | 1c. Structural Knowledge | | | |
| | NFL | | IMP | | NFL | | IMP | | NFL | | IMP | |
	T_1	T_2	T_1	T_2	T_1	T_2	T_1	T_2	T_1	T_2	T_1	T_2
Interest	.32	.36	.35	.39	.24	.24	.23	.28	.34	.40	.36	.40
Education	.29	.23	.29	.26	.32	.18	.26	.21	.19	.24	.24	.24
Multiple correlation[a]	.40	.41	.41	.44	.38	.29	.31	.33	.37	.45	.39	.44

[a] The Betas for Interest and Education with Composite Knowledge for T1 (NFL) were .28 and .25; for T2 (NFL), .34 and .21; for T1 (IMP), .29 and .23; for T2 (IMP), .36 and .20. All Betas were statistically significant at $p < .001$.

Table 1c shows that the learning of structural knowledge is far more susceptible to interest differences than to education differences. The range of education-knowledge correlations is .19 to .24, while the range of interest-knowledge correlations is .34 to .40, all statistically significant differences ($p < .001$). Furthermore, the multiple correlations add trivially, from .03 to .05, to the correlations obtained with the variable of interest alone. For learning information about a news event which requires an understanding of processual elements, interest is a better predictor than education, and education adds virtually nothing to the prediction obtained from interest alone.

It also was anticipated that self-interest would be a better predictor of knowledge than social interest. The results in Table 2 are surprising, but clarify Table 1. First, self-interest is not a better predictor of knowledge, but a worse predictor. In all comparisons, it yields lower correlations with both factual and structural knowledge than does social interest in the news events. Further, it yields generally lower correlations with both knowledge components than does education, more so for the NFL event than for the impeachment events.

Whereas a tentative conclusion from Table 1 suggested that factual knowledge was equally predictable from the composite interest index and education, Table 2 shows that social interest, i.e., talking with people about the event, consistently is a stronger predictor about both factual and structural knowledge, for the NFL strike event. Social interest is also a stronger predictor of both kinds of knowledges for the impeachment event at time two, and for structural knowledge at time one. As judged by these respondents, the impact of these events on their personal well-being was not a determinant of how much they learned. Their ability to use the news in social situations was.

Further, it was posited that at any point in time, more interested citizens would have a higher level of knowledge than those less interested in a news event, i.e., that differing levels of interest would generate a knowledge gap. Figure 2 examines this proposition for each event at two points in time. The knowledge differences between those with high and low interests are significantly different for each

Table 2. Self-Interest and Social Interest by Factual and Structural Knowledge

| | Time One | | | | | Time Two | | | | |
| | Interest | | | | | Interest | | | | |
	Self		Social		Education	Self		Social		Education
NFL										
Factual	.06	<	.43	>	.32	.06	<	.31	>	.18
Structural	.14	<	.43	>	.19	.16	<	.46	>	.24
IMP										
Factual	.13	<	.20	<	.26	.17	<	.30	>	.21
Structural	.21	<	.29	>	.24	.29	<	.37	>	.24

Table 3a. New Knowledge Gap by Interest in Two News Events at Time Two

	N	Mean	t	df	p
NFL					
High interest	76	1.96	7.51	176	<.001
Low interest	102	0.67			
IMP					
High interest	78	2.32	3.32	154	<.001
Low interest	78	1.63			

event at each point in time, for all four possible independent comparisons (t-values range from 3.81 to 7.34, all at $p < .001$). Those with more interest knew more than those with less interest. This established the existence of a significant knowledge gap. Given such a gap, it was possible to investigate the notion that those with a higher level of interest would acquire new information faster than those less interested, thereby widening the knowledge gap between them.

At time two, a series of four new information questions, two structural and two factual, was asked for each event. These new information items reflected event developments after the first interview. The analysis in Table 3a included those respondents who retained the same interest level as they had at time one, which was two-thirds of each news event group. For each event, those with continuing high interest in the event learned significantly more of the newly available information than those who remained disinterested.

Also examined were the data for old knowledge, or the items which remained constant during both waves. The analysis in Table 3b includes respondents who retained the same interest level throughout the study. The means on the repeated information items are presented for each subgroup. The same general pattern emerges; for both events, more interested respondents displayed a consistently higher level of knowledge. A similar finding emerged from subanalyses of the switchers, regarding interest in the impeachment event. Interest gainers between the two time waves knew significantly more at the second testing than interest losers ($p < .05$). For NFL, the numbers who switched were too small for analysis.

Table 3b. Old Knowledge Gap by Interest in Two News Events

	Time One Mean	Time Two Mean
NFL		
High interest	.92[a]	1.14[a]
Low interest	.27	.32
IMP		
High interest	1.09	1.68[a]
Low interest	.88	1.40

[a] High interest–Low interest differences are significant at $p < 01$.

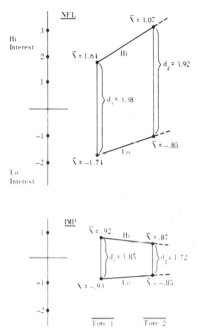

Figure 2. Mean Knowledge Comparisons over Time

The study model made one further tentative proposition: As information dissemination on a topic continues over an extended time period, the knowledge gap between those more and less interested would begin to decrease. Ideally, this would have been tested among several events of equivalent interest but differing in duration of media coverage. The impeachment proceedings had been newsworthy for a much longer period than the NFL strike, but they were much higher in self-interest and social interest at both time periods. Therefore, only a partial test of this idea is possible from the study data. Figure 2 presents relevant evidence. At the second testing for the impeachment news event, the difference between the more and less interested was negligibly smaller than at time one. The parallel difference for the NFL news event was substantially larger than it had been at the first testing. The directional differences between the two events support the model's assertion. However, additional time segments and more varied news events are necessary to adequately examine this idea.

Discussion

The news interest knowledge gain model examined has yielded strong preliminary findings. This evidence suggests that specialized interests in ongoing news events can yield more sensitive expectations about public information gain than such socioeconomic factors as education. Interests can be identified which cut across educationally developed preferences. This is a more optimistic proposition than the original knowledge gap hypothesis; it offers an alternative route by which public knowledge could be expanded. At the same time that national efforts are directed at improving citizen educational opportunities, independent efforts might well be centered on (a) conducting an interests assessment study of information-needy segments of the population, (b) tying major interests identified in such a study to news informational packages targeted for population subgroups, and (c) conducting appropriate studies to determine if the distribution of knowledge achieves greater parity from this approach. Before such a grand design is implemented, however, some more specific issues may be culled from the present study. For one, self-interest was negligible as a contributor to explaining knowledge gain. Either the news events studied did not activate self-interest, or self-interest was inadequately conceived and/or operationalized here. Before deleting it from the model, a test needs to be carried out to detect its presence among other topic areas which may be more susceptible to the influence of self-interest. For example, news events encompassing certain religious, economic, ethical, or legal topics may be more responsive to personal perceptions of well-being. It remains reasonable that the information contained in some kinds of news events would be assessed as of high personal import and strongly attended to for that reason. As yet, we have not demonstrated that.

Since social interest was dominant, it is worthy of continued examination. The least complicated interpretation of that variable is that it represents communicative facilitation between an individual and his/her social groupings. However, social communication is likely to vary among different groups within one's social milieu. Some news issues may more likely be discussed with close friends than with co-workers; others with family members more so than with nonfamily friends. Considered this way, social interest should be examined subsequently in terms of who are the co-communicants in relation to which topics of social exchange.

These findings also point to an important distinction in the definition of knowledge. The present subdivision into factual and structural knowledge is relatively crude, but prior studies which made no differentiation as to the type of information gained ignored a useful discriminant. When one wishes to consider the transference of knowledge among different population segments, it may be increasingly important to move beyond superficial knowledge increments to the audience's understanding of processes and structural components associated with developing public events.

The proposed interest-knowledge gain model receives additional support through some post hoc analyses conducted. For one, the argument remains that the model should proceed from education through interest into knowledge gain, to the extent that education contributes to an individual's entire configuration of news interests. To examine this possibility, education was partialed out of the interest-knowledge relationships to determine to what extent those relationships would be altered. They changed very little. For NFL, at time one, the correlation changed from .326 to .307; at time two, from .355 to .346; for impeachment at time one, from .341 to .301; for time two, from .391 to .362. These results provide little support for that alternative explanation.

Further, the underlying causal flow from interest to knowledge at two time points was examined by means of the cross-lagged correlational technique. The Rozelle-Campbell (1969) baseline criterion was applied to assess causal relationships between the two variables. In the resulting analyses, it was apparent that both diagonals exceeded the baseline criterion for both events, so that each association (that of time one interest with time two knowledge and time one knowledge with time two interest) was functional and each variable appeared to affect the other in a mutual interaction. For the NFL event, of relatively brief duration, the association between knowledge at time one with interest at time two (.374) exceeded the reverse association (.302). For impeachment, the longer-lasting event, the correlation between interest at time one and knowledge at time two (.277) was greater than the reverse (.212). This suggests that the causal flow from interest to knowledge may be the slower process, and may not have manifested itself yet with the NFL event. Future work should compare news events of equivalent as well as different durations in the mass media to better ascertain the soundness of these tentative observations.

Finally, some consideration should be given to what it is that may be generating self-interest and/or social interest in news events on the part of audience subgroups, given that education is not a particularly strong explanation. Interest is contributing to knowledge gaps, and the resulting unequal distribution of knowledge is then adding to further specialization in public affairs expertise. The social argument to be examined is that it may be feasible to tap into existing interests and to augment those interests with usable information. But the origins of those interests remain to be identified.

References

Adams, J. B., J. J. Mullen, and H. M. Wilson
    1969   "Diffusion of a minor foreign affairs news event." Journalism Quarterly 46:545–51.
Atkin, C.
    1973   "Instrumental utilities and information seeking," in P. Clarke (ed.),

New Models for Mass Communication Research, Vol. 2, Sage Annual Reviews of Communication Research.

Atkin, C., L. Bowen, O. Nayman, and K. Sheinkopf
 1973 "Quality versus quantity in televised political ads." Public Opinion Quarterly 37:209–24.

Atkin, C., and B. Greenberg
 1974 Public Television and Political Socialization. Michigan State University Report to the Corporation for Public Broadcasting.

Ball, S., and G. A. Bogatz
 1970 The First Year of Sesame Street: An Evaluation. Princeton, N.J.: Educational Testing Services.

Bishop, M., and P. McMartin
 1973 "Toward a socio-psychological definition of transitional persons." Journal of Broadcasting 17:333–44.

Budd, R., M. S. MacLean, Jr., and A. Barnes
 1966 "Regularities in the diffusion of two major news events." Journalism Quarterly 43:221–30.

Chaffee, S., and J. McLeod
 1973 "Individual versus social predictors of information seeking." Journalism Quarterly 50:237–45.

Ettema, J., and F. G. Kline
 1977 "Deficits, differences and ceiling: contingent conditions for understanding the knowledge gap." Communication Research April: 179–202.

Greenberg, B., J. Brinton, and R. S. Farr
 1965 "Diffusion of news about an anticipated news event." Journal of Broadcasting 9:129–42.

Hanneman, G., and B. Greenberg
 1973 "Relevance and the diffusion of minor and major foreign affairs events." Journalism Quarterly 50:443–447.

Hyman, H. H., C. R. Wright, and J. S. Reed
 1975 The Enduring Effects of Education. Chicago: University of Chicago Press.

Johnson, N.
 1973 "Television and politicization: A test of competing models." Journalism Quarterly 50:447–55.

McCombs, M.
 1972 "Mass communication in political campaigns: information gratification, and persuasion," in G. Kline and P. Tichenor (eds.), Current Perspectives in Mass Communication Research, Vol. 1, Sage Annual Reviews of Communication Research.

Rozelle, R., and D. Campbell
 1969 "More plausible rival hypotheses in the cross-lagged panel correlation technique." Psychological Bulletin 71:74–80.

Tichenor, P. J., G. A. Donohue, and C. N. Olien
 1970 "Mass media flow and differential growth of knowledge." Public Opinion Quarterly 34:159–70.

Troldahl, V., and R. Carter, Jr.
 1964 "Random selection of respondents within households in phone surveys." Journal of Marketing Research May, 71–76.

Wade, S., and W. Schramm
 1969 "The mass media as sources of public affairs, science and health knowledge." Public Opinion Quarterly 33:197–209.

PART VI

IMPACT OF MASS COMMUNICATION

In Volume 1 of the *Yearbook,* an entire section was devoted to crime and violence in mass communication. That section concentrated on the findings of, and the resulting debate about, the annual violence profiles and cultivation analyses of the Annenberg Cultural Indicators research group.

In this book, the Annenberg work, and response to it, lead the section on impact of mass communication. Clearly, the work speaks directly to media impact, even though its authors see the research program as underpinning a much broader social theory than is generally subsumed under a media effects purview. It is the "effects" link of the cultivation analysis that attracts the most scrutiny and controversy at present.

The most recent violence profile, reprinted here, found a slight decline in televised violence and what the research team sees as even more solid evidence of a cultivation effect of television. Challenges to the cultivation link, however, are gaining momentum, as the second piece demonstrates. Reanalysis of the same data set used by the Annenberg group casts fresh skepticism by arguing that the nonviewer appears to have the scariest perceived world of all. The debate is a hot one, and it bodes well for the field. For the first time, there are enough researchers at work to enable the kind of replication that is needed to strengthen our research.

Building on the solid base of the ambitious syntheses of empirical work on the social effects of television, published in Volume 1, this section contains a rare synthesis of more than a thousand studies from around the world on TV effects on children and adults. The work is unusual and significant not only in its international exhaustiveness but also in its attempt to organize the research into pertinent theoretical perspectives.

Closing this section are research projects that are examples of major mass media information campaigns that worked—one in California and another in Holland—and another campaign in Austria that had minimal effects.

The Dutch study of the impact of *Holocaust* (a five-part NBC series televised in 1979) and a national information campaign organized around the program is a classic. Based on a rigorous longitudinal design, the findings suggest that Dutch young people were influenced significantly and positively in the long term by the *Holocaust* campaign.

The Austrian research, dealing with the entire adult population, has a less happy conclusion but one consistent with prior research that attitudes based in deep, long-term experiences are highly resistant to change. The California study, however, offers excellent evidence that selective exposure was not a major factor in a cardiovascular health campaign in the mass media of that state.

Media violence profiles and cultivation analysis from the Annenberg School continue to be among the most widely discussed work in the field. In this piece, the Annenberg team reports decline in mass media violence and victimization from 1978 to 1979, accounted for largely by reduction in violence on the ABC network. More importantly, the authors report further support for the cultivation effects of television in the United States. They rebut challenges to their findings (reported in Volume 1 of Mass Communication Review Yearbook *by Anthony Doob and Glenn E. MacDonald) by other researchers. Comparing low income, urban dwellers (presumably those likeliest to live in high-crime areas) with high-income, urban dwellers, the authors still find a positive, slight correlation between high television watching and high scores on perceptions of danger by the low-income persons. They interpret these findings as supporting cultivation theory. George Gerbner is dean of the Annenberg School of Communications of the University of Pennsylvania. Larry Gross is associate professor of communication at Annenberg. Michael Morgan and Nancy Signorielli are assistant professors of communication at Annenberg. All are members of the cultural indicators research team at the Annenberg School.*

30

THE 'MAINSTREAMING' OF AMERICA
Violence Profile No. 11

George Gerbner, Larry Gross,
Michael Morgan, and Nancy Signorielli

New findings of the Cultural Indicators research
project support earlier results and lead to elaboration
of the concepts of "mainstreaming" and "resonance."

Television makes specific and measurable contributions to viewers' conceptions of reality. These contributions relate both to the synthetic world television presents and to viewers' real life circumstances. These are the basic findings of our long-range research project called Cultural Indicators, and they have been supported, extended, and refined in a series of studies. Here we shall report new findings and introduce theoretical developments dealing with the dynamics of the cultivation of general concepts of social reality (which we shall call "mainstreaming") and of the amplification of issues particularly salient to certain groups of viewers (which we shall call "resonance").

The design of our research consists of two interrelated parts: message system analysis and cultivation analysis. Message system analysis is the annual monitoring of samples of prime-time and weekend daytime network dramatic programming (including series, other plays, comedies, movies, and cartoons). Cultivation analysis is the investigation of viewer conceptions of social reality associated with the most recurrent features of the world of television. Our studies since 1967-68 have traced some conceptual and behavioral correlates of growing up and living with a television world in which men outnumber women three to one, young people comprise one-third and old people one-fifth of their real numbers, professionals and law-enforcers dominate the occupations, and an

AUTHORS' NOTE: George Gerbner, Larry Gross, Michael Morgan, and Nancy Signorielli are members of the Cultural Indicators research team at The Annenberg School of Communications, University of Pennsylvania. This research is conducted under grants from the National Institute of Mental Health, the American Medical Association, and the Administration on Aging. A Technical Report with details of methodology and results (25) and "Highlights" containing the most important tabulations are available.

average of five acts of violence per prime time hour (and four times that number per weekend daytime hour) involve more than half of all leading characters.

These results have been published in a series of Violence Profiles (11, 12, 17, 19, 22, 26) and in studies dealing with aging (27, 63, 65), sex roles and minorities (28, 30, 49, 62), children (16), occupational conceptions (39, 41, 64), educational achievements and aspirations (48, 50, 51, 52), family images and impact (24, 40, 53), sexual depictions and lessons (15), and death and dying (14).

The basic theories and recurrent findings of our research have been replicated and reanalyzed in many areas by independent investigators. Some, replicating our design or employing different methodologies, have confirmed, extended, or refined our work.[1] Others have presented critiques of our published reports on both methodological and theoretical grounds.[2] Our own reports have reflected these and other developments, and this report is no exception. In addition to bringing the Violence Profile up to date, we present a new formulation of our methodological and theoretical position based on new findings and relating to the work of these investigators.

The Violence Index is based on the analysis of week-long samples of prime-time and weekend-daytime network dramatic programming broadcast from 1967 through 1979.

For purposes of this analysis,[3] we define violence as the overt expression of physical force (with or without a weapon, against self or others) compelling action against one's will on pain of being hurt and/or killed or threatened to be so victimized as part of the plot. Idle threats, verbal abuse, or gestures without credible violent consequences are not coded as violence. However, "accidental"

---

[1] See, for example, findings by Volgy and Schwarz on doctor shows (69), Neville on mistrust (56), Gonzalez on aging (29), Pingree et al. on interpersonal mistrust (58), Zill on fear (71), Harr-Mazer on children's role (33), Rothschild on sexism and occupations (61), Doob and Macdonald on conceptions of violence in high crime urban areas (but not elsewhere, a point we discuss in this report) (7), Pingree and Hawkins on mistrust and perception of violence in Australia (34, 35, 59), and laboratory studies by Tan on role expectations (68) and Bryant et al. on anxiety (4). See also a comprehensive evaluative review of this and related research by Murray and Kippax (54), and the survey of studies prepared for the ten-year update of the report of the Surgeon General's Scientific Advisory Committee on Television and Social Behavior by Hawkins and Pingree (36).

[2] In this article we shall report on the statistical and empirical characteristics of the Violence Index and other methodological points contested by Owen (57; see also 13), Coffin and Tuchman (5, 6; see also 8, 9), and Blank (2, 3; see also 20, 21). We shall touch upon some points raised by Wober (70; see also 23) and Newcomb (55; see also 18). We shall also deal with the attempted replications and objections by Doob and Macdonald (7), Hughes (38), and Hirsch (37). One lengthy critique by law professors Krattenmaker and Powe (45) came to our attention two years after its publication and is too much of an idiosyncratic mixture of perceptive and puzzling statements to be dealt with seriously in this article.

[3] Many aspects of program content are coded for analysis; this report is limited to those aspects which relate to violence.

and "natural" violence (always purposeful dramatic actions that do victimize certain characters) are, of course, included.

A violent act that fits the definition is recorded, whatever the context. This definition includes violence that occurs in a fantasy or "humorous" context as well as violence presented in a realistic or "serious" context. There is substantial evidence that fantasy and comedy are effective forms in which to convey serious lessons (1, 10, 47). Thus eliminating fantasy or comic violence, as well as violence of an "accidental" nature, would be a major analytical error.

All items are coded by pairs of trained coders (see 22 and 25) and are subjected to an extensive reliability analysis (see 46). Only those items meeting acceptable standards of reliability (.6 or above) are included in the analysis.

The Violence Index combines three sets of observations in order to provide a single indicator sensitive to a range of program characteristics. These observations measure the extent to which violence occurs at all in the programs sampled, the frequency and rate of violent episodes, and the number of roles calling for characterization as violents, victims, or both.[4] These three measures have achieved high inter-coder reliability over the years we have been collecting these data. Although here we report only the Index, the component measures are always reported in our full technical reports (e.g., 25).

We have also established that the Index meets the critical statistical and empirical requirements of an index: unidimensionality and internal homogeneity (see 25, 32). For prime-time programs, factor analysis of our thirteen-year data base reveals only one factor underlying the components of the Index, which accounts for 70 percent of the variance. The internal homogeneity, as measured by Cronbach's alpha, is very high (alpha = .89). In weekend-daytime programs, the internal homogeneity is somewhat lower, but still acceptable (alpha = .66).[5]

The frequency of violence and the patterns of victimization in the world of dramatic television are remarkably stable from year to year. Overall, the Fall

---

[4] These data sets are called prevalence, rate, and role, respectively. Prevalence (%P) is the percent of programs in a particular sample containing any violence. Rate expresses the frequency of violent actions in units of programming and in units of time. The number of violent acts divided by the total number of programs gives the rate per program (R/P) while the rate per hour (R/H) is the number of violent actions divided by the number of program hours in the sample. The latter measures the saturation of violence in time, and compensates for the difference in rates between a long program unit, such as a movie, and a short one, such as a cartoon.

Role is defined as the portrayal of characters as violents (committing violence) or victims (subjected to violence) or both, and yields two measures. They are the percent violents or victims or both (%V) and the percent involved in killing, either as killers, as killed, or both (%K). The Index is the sum of these five measures with the rates weighted by a factor of two. It is represented as: VI = %P + 2 R/H + 2 R/P + %V + %K.

[5] In weekend-daytime programs the internal homogeneity and degree of unidimensionality of the Index is reduced by one item—the percent of characters involved in killing. These programs generally have the highest rates of violent acts and the greatest number of programs containing violence. But they also have the smallest proportion of characters involved in killing. In fact, within these programs killing and other measures of violence are negatively related. Moreover, the weights included in the Index enhance its internal homogeneity. In each time period (and overall) weighting the rate per hour and rate per program (by a factor of 2) adds about .05 to the alpha.

1979 Violence Index shows some decline over the 1978 Index, much of which
can be accounted for by a reduction of violence on ABC. Violence also declined
after 9 p.m. but rose in the 1979 "family viewing" time (8:00 to 9:00 p.m. EST)
(see Figure 1). Although still way above the level in prime time, violence in
weekend-daytime (children's) programs also declined. The largest increase in violence in the 1979 sample was in new prime-time programs, especially in the
former "family hour" and particularly on NBC. The largest reductions in violence were in the late evening by ABC and NBC and on weekend-daytime programs by all networks, but especially NBC.

In prime time, 70 percent of all programs still contained violence. The rate
of violent episodes was 5.7 per hour, up from 4.5 in 1978. Nearly 54 percent of
all leading characters were involved in some violence, about the same as in
1978. In weekend-daytime (children's) programs, 92 percent of all programs
contained some violence, down from 98 percent in 1978. The rate of violent episodes was 17 per hour, down from 25 the year before. Nearly 75 percent of all
leading characters were involved in violence, down from 86 percent in 1978.

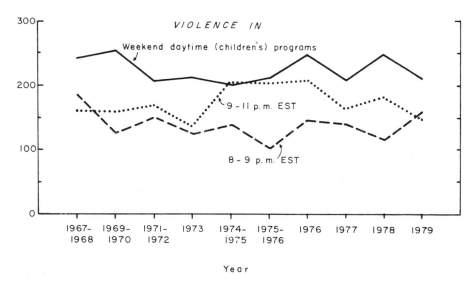

Figure 1: Violence Index in children's and prime-time programming, 1967-1979

Overall, the percent of characters involved in violence has remained fairly
steady since 1969. About two-thirds of the males and nearly half of the females
are involved. When involved, female characters are more likely than male characters to be the victims rather than the perpetrators of violence. Only one group
of male characters—young boys—are among the ten groups who are most likely
to be victimized. Women cast in minority roles (old women, upper-class
women, non-white women, young women, and lower-class women) are especially more likely to suffer rather than to inflict violence. Only two groups of

characters—old men and "bad" women—are more likely to hurt others than to be hurt themselves (for details of these and other message analysis findings, see 25).

We now turn to the theory of cultivation and to findings relating to conceptions of a mean world and its dangers.

Television is the central and most pervasive mass medium in American culture and it plays a distinctive and historically unprecedented role. Other media are accessible to the individual (usually at the point of literacy and mobility) only after the socializing functions of home and family life have begun. In the case of television, however, the individual is introduced virtually at birth into its powerful flow of messages and images. The television set has become a key member of the family, the one who tells most of the stories most of the time. Its massive flow of stories showing what things are, how things work, and what to do about them has become the common socializer of our times. These stories form a coherent if mythical "world" in every home. Television dominates the symbolic environment of modern life.

Cultivation analysis is the investigation of the consequences of this ongoing and pervasive system of cultural messages. Given our premise that television's images cultivate the dominant tendencies of our culture's beliefs, ideologies, and world views, the observable independent contributions of television can only be relatively small. But just as an average temperature shift of a few degrees can lead to an ice age or the outcomes of elections can be determined by slight margins, so too can a relatively small but pervasive influence make a crucial difference. The "size" of an "effect" is far less critical than the direction of its steady contribution.

We have found that amount of exposure to television is an important indicator of the strength of its contributions to ways of thinking and acting. For heavy viewers, television virtually monopolizes and subsumes other sources of information, ideas, and consciousness. Thus, we have suggested that the more time one spends "living" in the world of television, the more likely one is to report perceptions of social reality which can be traced to (or are congruent with) television's most persistent representations of life and society. Accordingly, we have examined the difference that amount of viewing makes in people's images, expectations, assumptions, and behaviors.[6]

In previous reports, we have stressed across-the-board consequences of television viewing. Thus, we expected heavier viewers to be more likely to give the "television answers" to a series of informational and opinion questions than lighter viewers. This theoretical perspective still holds and provides some of the

---

[6] We refer to this difference as the "cultivation differential" (CD) which is the spread between the percentages of light and heavy viewers who give a "television answer" to questions about social reality. The classification of respondents as relatively light, medium, and heavy viewers is determined by the distribution of amount of viewing in a given sample. Consequently, the actual proportions of lighter and heavier viewers will vary from one sample to another.

most compelling evidence for the existence of television's contributions to conceptions of social reality. But further examination of previously analyzed and new data reveals there are substantially different patterns of associations for different social groups between amount of viewing and certain conceptions of social reality.

Television's cultivation of conceptions and behaviors is a consistent process but is integrated in different ways and with different results into different patterns of life. Therefore, a fuller understanding of television's contribution may be achieved by paying particular attention to differences across different subgroups.

Many differences between groups of viewers can be explained in terms of one of two systematic processes which we call "mainstreaming" and "resonance."

The "mainstream" can be thought of as a relative commonality of outlooks that television tends to cultivate. By "mainstreaming" we mean the sharing of that commonality among heavy viewers in those demographic groups whose light viewers hold divergent views. In other words, differences deriving from other factors and social forces may be diminished or even absent among heavy viewers. Thus, in some cases we should only find evidence for cultivation within those groups who are "out" of the mainstream. In other cases, we may find that viewing "moderates" attitudes in groups whose light viewers tend to hold extreme views. But in all cases, more viewing appears to signal a convergence of outlooks rather than absolute, across-the-board increments in all groups.

For example, it is well documented that more educated, higher income groups have the most diversified patterns of cultural opportunities and activities; therefore, they tend to be lighter viewers. We found that, when they are light viewers, they also tend to be the least imbued with the television view of the world. But the heavy viewers in the higher education/high income groups respond differently. Their responses to our questions are more like those of other heavy viewers, most of whom have less education and income. It is the college-educated, higher income light viewers who diverge from the "mainstream" cultivated by television; heavy viewers of all groups tend to share a relatively homogeneous outlook.

But the relationship of real life experience to television's cultivation of conceptions of reality entails not only this generalized notion of "mainstreaming" but also special cases of particular salience to specific issues. This is what we call "resonance." When what people see on television is most congruent with everyday reality (or even *perceived* reality), the combination may result in a coherent and powerful "double dose" of the television message and significantly boost cultivation. Thus, the congruence of the television world and real-life circumstances may "resonate" and lead to markedly amplified cultivation patterns.

These processes are not the only possible mechanisms which might explain variations in susceptibility to cultivation. For example, related analyses of children and adolescents suggest that cultivation may be most pronounced when

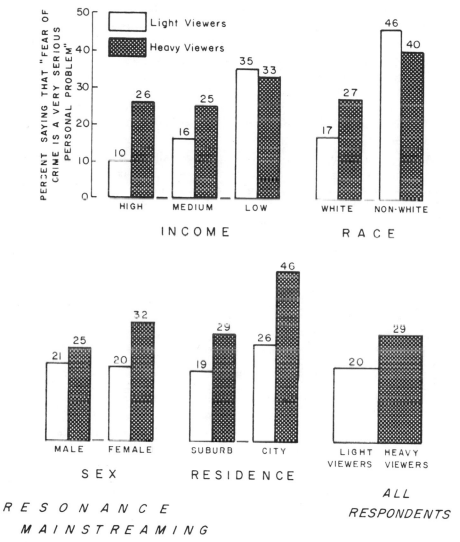

Data source: Opinion Research Corporation, March 1979

Figure 2: Examples of mainstreaming and resonance in terms of respondents saying that "fear of crime the relationship between amount of viewing and percent of is a very serious personal problem"

parents are not involved in their children's viewing (31) or when children are less integrated into cohesive peer groups (61). Furthermore, the constructs of "mainstreaming" and "resonance" are still being developed and investigated. Although the number of empirical instances of each is rapidly growing, too few have been accumulated to allow for predictions of when one or the other—or neither—will occur. Nonetheless, we believe that the results we will report here suggest that these concepts merit serious consideration.

Before we present findings further illuminating the two phenomena, it may help to illustrate them graphically. The data for this illustration come from our most recent sample of adults, collected in March 1979 by the Opinion Research Corporation (ORC).[7] In this sample we found instances of "mainstreaming" and "resonance" in the differential patterns of responses to a single question which may tap some conceptions cultivated by the violent and dangerous world of television. Figure 2 presents two examples of each in terms of the relationship between amount of viewing and responding that "fear of crime is a very serious personal problem."

As shown in Figure 2 this relationship holds only for respondents with medium or high incomes; low-income respondents are more likely to agree, regardless of viewing. The proportion of light viewers giving the "television answer" is much lower in the higher income groups; yet the middle- and high-income heavy viewers are in the "mainstream." When we look at the responses by race we see a consistent but different pattern. The relationship between viewing and fear is positive for whites but slightly negative for non-whites. Non-white light viewers are especially likely to express the notion that fear of crime is a "very serious personal problem." Heavy viewing among non-whites may moderate this outlook; thus, they are closer to the "mainstream."

The right-hand section of Figure 2 also shows that the association is strongest among females and among those who live in cities. To a large extent, this fear may be most salient to such respondents. Accordingly, real-life circumstances and environmental factors may "resonate" with television's messages and augment them.

> *We shall now examine both mainstreaming and*
> *resonance in light of new data and in response*
> *to critiques of our earlier analyses.*

Examples of "mainstreaming" can be found in analyses of questions relating to what we have called the "mean world syndrome." We combined three items from the 1975 and 1978 National Opinion Research Center (NORC) General Social Surveys to form an index of interpersonal mistrust (alpha = .68) similar to Rosenberg's "faith in people" scale (60). The three items—which form the Mean World Index—measure the degree to which respondents agree that most people are just looking out for themselves, that you can't be too careful in dealing with people, and that most people would take advantage of you if they got a chance. As shown in Table 1, which presents within-group partial correlations between amount of viewing and this Index, television viewing overall is significantly associated with the tendency to express mistrust (r = .12, p < .001). This relation-

---

[7] These data were collected as part of an Administration on Aging research grant (No. 90-A-1299) on "Aging with Television." George Gerbner, Larry Gross, and Nancy Signorielli were co-principal investigators (see 27).

Table 1: Within-group partial correlations between amount of television viewing and the Mean World Index

	Overall	Education		Income			Race	
		No college	Some college	Low	Med.	High	White	Non-white
Simple r	.12***	.06**	.14***	.03	.16***	.08	.12***	−.08
Controlling for:								
Sex	.12***	.06**	.15***	.03	.17***	.09*	.12***	−.07
Age	.12***	.06**	.14***	.02	.16***	.08	.12***	−.08
Newspaper reading	.11***	.06**	.14***	.03	.16***	.08	.12***	−.08
Subjective social class	.10***	.05**	.13***	.02	.15***	.07	.10***	.07
Education	.07***	.06**	.12***	.01	.12***	.04	.07***	−.08
Income	.09***	.04*	.12**	—	—	—	.09***	−.11*
Race	.09***	.04	.10**	−.01	.15***	.08	—	—
Occupational prestige	.08***	.04*	.13***	.01	.13***	.04	.08***	−.08
All controls	.04*	.02	.08**	.02	.11***	.04	.06**	−.10*
Final d.f. (8th order)	(2727)	(1853)	(861)	(1091)	(1290)	(317)	(2431)	(288)

Data source: NORC General Social Surveys, 1975 and 1978

* p ≤ .05
** p ≤ .01
*** p ≤ .001

ship is not fully accounted for by any individual control. Simultaneous controls greatly reduce its strength, but the relationship remains statistically significant.

Even more revealing than this small overall correlation is the relationship between television viewing and mistrust for specific groups of the population. The relationship is strongest for respondents who have had some college education—those who are also least likely to express interpersonal mistrust. (The correlation between education and the Mean World Index is −.28, p < .001.) The most striking specifications emerge for whites and non-whites. As a group, non-whites score higher on the Mean World Index (r = .23, p < .001). Yet, there is a significant *negative* association among non-whites between television and this index (r = −.10, p < .05). The relationship for whites, however, remains positive. Thus, those groups who in general are *least* likely to hold a television-related attitude are *most* likely to be influenced toward the "mainstream" television view; and those who are most likely to hold a view *more* extreme than the TV view may be "coaxed back" to the "mainstream" position.

Similar patterns can be found by examining the relationship between amount of viewing and feelings of alienation. In the 1977 NORC survey, alienation was measured by three of Srole's (66) anomie items—the lot of the average man is getting worse, it is hardly fair to bring a child into the world, and most public officials are not interested in the lot of the average man. We had previously reported (22) that the relationship between amount of viewing and the tendency to agree with these statements holds up in most groups. When these items were reanalyzed by Stevens (67), Hughes (38), and Hirsch (37), they all found that the overall association disappears when several demographic variables are controlled all at once.

> *But the lack of an overall relationship*
> *does not mean that the relationship does not*
> *hold for any specific group of respondents.*

We combined these items into an index (alpha = .61) and found that the best predictor of anomie appeared to be education (r = −.31, p < .001). When the relationship between television viewing and endorsing statements of alienation is examined within educational subgroups, the relationship persists for those respondents who, as a group, are far less likely to express alienation—again, those with some college education. This relationship withstands the implementation of a large number of controls, either singly or simultaneously (r = .14, p < .01; see Table 2). For respondents with less education, who are relatively alienated to begin with, television viewing has no apparent relationship with anomie. Again, we see that television may influence a convergence of outlooks toward its "mainstream" rather than cultivating absolute across-the-board changes.

New data from a national probability sample of adults (ORC) provide numerous examples of this "mainstreaming" phenomenon with regard to people's conceptions about crime and violence. Using a question that replicates some of our earlier work, we asked respondents whether chances of being involved in violence in any given week are one in ten or one in a hundred. Our basic expectation is that relatively more heavy than light viewers will answer that their chances of encountering violence are higher.

As Table 3 reveals, heavy viewers are indeed significantly more likely to give this response, overall and within most subgroups. Yet, there are important specifications. A large majority (84 percent) of both light and heavy viewers *with low incomes* give the higher risk response, and thus show no evidence of a relationship between amount of viewing and responses to this question. When we examine the middle- and upper-income groups, however, we find that the proportion of light viewers giving the "television answer" drops; "only" 62 percent of light viewers with higher incomes overestimate their chances of being involved in violence. Yet, the *difference* between light and heavy viewers rises sharply. Light viewers with middle and upper incomes are considerably less likely to express a high expectation of encountering violence, while heavy viewers with middle or high incomes exhibit almost the same level of perceived risk as the low-income group.

Such differences could be explained in terms of a ceiling effect. However, we think that the results we have found are a strong indication that television

Table 2: Partial correlations between amount of viewing and anomie by educational level

	Less than high school	High school	Some college
Simple r	.01	.06*	.14**
Controlling for:			
Sex	−.00	.06*	.15**
Age	.01	.06*	.14*
Newspaper reading	.01	.06*	.15**
Urban proximity	.01	.06*	.14*
Subjective social class	.01	.05	14*
Education	.01	.06	.14*
Income	−.01	.03	.15**
Race	.01	.05	.13*
All controls	−.03	.01	.14*
Final d.f. (8th order)	(455)	(686)	(729)

Data source: NORC General Social Survey, 1977

* p ≤ .05
** p ≤ .01

does contribute to the cultivation of common perspectives. In particular, heavy viewing may serve to cultivate beliefs of otherwise disparate and divergent groups toward a more homogeneous "mainstream" view.

The other important refinement of our theory suggests that cultivation will be most pronounced when other aspects of one's social environment are most congruent and thereby "resonate" with television's message.

Among Canadians, Doob and Macdonald (7) found the strongest positive associations between amount of television viewing and fear of crime among those who live in high crime centers. Although they interpreted this finding as evidence of spuriousness of the relationship between television viewing and fear of crime, clearly the concept of neighborhood does not "explain" the observed relationship. Rather, it points to an important specification. For those urban dwellers who live in high crime centers, television's violent imagery may be most congruent with their real-life perceptions. These people receive a "double dose" of messages that the world is violent, and consequently show the strongest associations between viewing and fear.

We have found parallel results in an analysis of data from our most recent national survey of adults (ORC). We asked people about how safe they felt walking around alone, at night, in their own neighborhoods, and assumed that those who lived in urban areas would also be most likely to express fear. We found, as would be expected (see Table 3), that those who live in large cities are much more likely to be afraid in their own neighborhoods at night, regardless of amount of viewing. But city dwellers also "resonate" most—they show the strongest association between amount of viewing and expressing this fear.

Table 3: Summary of analyses of questions relating to fear and violence in the 1979 ORC survey

	Percent overestimating chances of involvement in violence			Percent agreeing that women are more likely to be victims of crime			Percent saying their neighborhoods are only somewhat safe or not safe at all			Percent saying that fear of crime is a very serious problem			Percent agreeing that crime is rising		
	%L	CD	g	%L	CD	g	%L	CD	g	%L	CD	g	%L	CD	g
Overall	71	+10	.14***	72	+10	.18***	55	+11	.10***	20	+9	.12***	94	+4	.30***
Controlling for:															
Age															
18–29	76	+14	.28***	73	+6	.11**	49	+11	.09**	16	+11	.21***	93	+4	.27***
30–54	68	+9	.11**	70	+10	.18***	53	+12	.09***	17	+11	.12***	96	+3	.27**
Over 55	71	+4	.07*	77	+10	.22***	65	+9	.06*	31	+1	−.01	94	+4	.38***
Education															
No college	76	+7	.13***	70	+12	.20***	58	+10	.07***	24	+8	.11***	96	+3	.28***
Some college	63	+9	.10*	76	+7	.06	49	+9	.07*	13	+5	.09*	91	+5	.22**
Newspaper reading															
Sometimes	75	+14	.25***	70	+15	.26***	58	+17	.10***	23	+11	.14***	94	+4	.27***
Everyday	69	+7	.10***	74	+17	.13***	53	+8	.09***	18	+8	.11***	95	+4	.36***
Race															
White	69	+10	.13***	73	+9	.17***	53	+10	.09***	17	+10	.14***	94	+4	.29***
Non-white	86	+7	.25**	70	+12	.21**	72	+16	.09*	46	−6	−.07	95	+4	.37**
Urban proximity															
City over 250,000	69	+10	.13**	77	0	−.00	71	+14	.19***	26	+20	.19***	88	+10	.52***
City under 250,000	74	+3	.05	64	+24	.42***	59	+8	.04	22	+5	.09*	89	+11	.57***
Suburban	67	+13	.18***	75	+10	.19***	50	+13	.13***	19	+10	.12***	96	+2	.13
Non-metropolitan	77	+8	.13**	70	+9	.17***	51	+7	.01	18	+2	.08**	98	0	.10
Income															
Under $10,000	84	0	.04	67	+18	.32***	61	+14	.10***	35	−2	−.00	96	+4	.51***
$10–$25,000	68	+8	.12***	74	+6	.12***	55	+6	.04	16	+9	.16***	93	+5	.35***
Over $25,000	62	+18	.13**	76	0	−.03	49	+1	−.01	10	+16	.11**	96	−1	−.13
Sex															
Male	68	+8	.09**	68	+10	.20***	38	+16	.16***	21	+4	.07**	95	+2	.07
Female	76	+8	.15***	78	+6	.14***	73	+1	−.01	20	+12	.14***	94	+5	.55***

Data source: Opinion Research Corporation, March 1979

  * p ≤ .05 (tau)
 ** p ≤ .01 (tau)
*** p ≤ .001 (tau)

Note: Viewing was measured by the following question: "On the average weekday, about how many hours do you personally watch television?" Light: under 2 hours; Medium: 2–4 hours; or Heavy: over 4 hours. % L (percent light viewers) refers to the percent of light viewers giving the "television answer." CD or Cultivation Differential refers to the percent of heavy viewers minus the percent of light viewers giving the "television answer"; g refers to gamma.

To provide further evidence we tried to approximate Doob and Macdonald's high crime/low crime distinction for respondents who live in cities. We assumed that respondents who live in larger cities *and* have lower incomes are likely to live in areas with relatively high crime rates, while high-income urban residents arguably live in less dangerous areas. We used the five questions from the 1979 ORC survey shown in Table 3 to form a Perceptions of Danger Index-I.[8] When amount of television viewing was correlated with the Perceptions of Danger Index-I scores, the relationship was much stronger for residents in low-income (presumably high crime) urban areas (r = .26, p < .001) than for those in high-income (presumably low crime) urban areas (r = .05; see Table 4.)

Table 4: Within-group partial correlations for residence and income between amount of viewing and the Perceptions of Danger Index-I

	City		Suburban, non-metropolitan	
	Low income	High income	Low income	High income
Simple r	26***	.05	.10***	.20***
Controlling for:				
Sex	.27***	.05	.01***	.16***
Age	.24***	.05	.09***	.20***
Income	.26***	.02	.10***	.18***
Newspaper reading	.26***	.04	.10***	.20***
Education	.14***	.02	.11***	.15***
Race	.21***	.03	.11***	.20***
All controls	.13***	.00	.10***	.12***
Final d.f. (7th order)	(969)	(656)	(2017)	(1886)

Data source: Opinion Research Corporation, March 1979

* p ≤ .05
** p ≤ .01
*** p ≤ .001

This relationship remains positive and significant (r = .13, p < .001) for urban dwellers with low incomes and falls to zero for high-income urban residents when within-group controls for demographic factors are implemented simultaneously. While the correspondence between income and neighborhood crime is ambiguous in suburban and non-metropolitan areas, it is worth noting that the association between amount of viewing and these images of danger, crime, and violence remains significant despite controls. Thus, the role of television in the

[8] These items essentially tap discrete dimensions; their conceptual link, however, is that they examine various aspects of television's portrayal of violence. Thus, it is not surprising that while these questions are all positively and significantly related to each other, their additive index has relatively low internal homogeneity (alpha = .34). At the same time, there is only one factor underlying the five items, indicating a high degree of unidimensionality. This index is called the Images of Violence Index in Violence Profile No. 11 (25).

cultivation of attitudes and fears may be most pronounced when an issue has direct relevance to the respondent's life.

A further example of "resonance" from the same survey focuses upon the assumption that older people are more likely than younger people to be victims of crime (an assumption contrary to the facts). Young and middle-aged respondents show no overall relationship between amount of viewing and the tendency to think that the elderly are most likely to be victimized. But, among older respondents, there is a significant positive association between television viewing and expressing this belief (gamma = .27, p < .001). In particular, this holds for older respondents in those demographic groups in which light viewers are less likely to respond this way.

We must stress that these specifications do not exhaust cultivation results. Amount of viewing remains significantly related to scores on the Perceptions of Danger Index-I, over and above the effects of education, income, sex, race, age, urban proximity, and newspaper reading (seventh order partial r = .11, p < .001). Although the amount of the variance in these scores explained by television viewing is small, with other things being held constant its predictive power is equal to or greater than that of age, race, urban proximity, income, or newspaper reading. But even where a relationship disappears for an entire sample, as Hirsch (37), Hughes (38), and Stevens (64) have found, it may quite clearly hold up in certain groups.

Thus, we have seen two distinct processes which help explain differential susceptibility to cultivation. "Resonance" may occur when a feature of the television world has special salience for a group, e.g., greater fear among city dwellers, or perceived over-victimization by the elderly. In these cases, the correlates of heavy viewing are most apparent among those for whom the topic holds considerable personal relevance. "Mainstreaming," on the other hand, may be related more to general and widespread images and norms of social reality.

> *Data from our three-year longitudinal study*
> *of adolescents also provide strong evidence*
> *for both an overall effect of viewing*
> *and important specification/interaction effects.*

In the second and third years of this study we included two dependent measures—the Mean World Index (see above) and an index of Perceptions of Danger-II. The Perceptions of Danger Index-II was composed of four questions relating to estimates of the chances of encountering violence, aspects of murders and killings, and the importance of knowing self-defense. Agreement with these beliefs was interpreted as reflecting a strong image of the world as a dangerous place.[9]

---

[9] The exact wording of the questions asked of our adolescent respondents and used in the Perceptions of Danger Index-II are presented in Violence Profile No. 11 (25). Both Perceptions of Danger Indices were called the Images of Violence Indices. The names of both indices have been changed to distinguish them from the Violence Index used in the message system analysis. The two Perceptions of Danger Indices tap similar concepts but are made up of different questions.

These data were analyzed in the form of structural equation models, using Jöreskog's LISREL program (see 42, 43, 44). This technique, a sophisticated form of path analysis, performs a maximum likelihood estimation of parameters in causal models. It also takes measurement error into account and reveals how well the hypothesized model fits the observed data. This procedure can simultaneously evaluate a "measurement model" (how well the observed indicators relate to the "true," underlying concepts) and a "causal model" (patterns of association among "true" observed constructs). All of the observed indicators show reasonably strong links with the "true" variables.[10]

Figure 3 presents the maximum likelihood solution of this model. The third year scores on the Mean World and Perceptions of Danger-II Indices are controlled for their second year scores, SES, and IQ, and thus represent "new information" or "change" in attitudes that is not attributable to previous levels or demographics. We see that those who were heavy viewers in the second year reveal greater fear and mistrust in the third year, even controlling for demographics and second year index scores.[11] Thus, amount of viewing has a positive impact on subsequent scores on the Mean World and Perceptions of Danger-II Indices for these adolescents.

Most importantly, the model provides a good fit to the observed data. Using the chi-square test (see Figure 3), the likelihood ratio is 1.86 (the lower the ratio, the better the fit). When measurement error is removed and even when IQ and SES are held constant, adolescents' perceptions of fear, danger, and mistrust vary over time as a function of earlier viewing.

Finally, the longitudinal data provide evidence of yet another specification. Among boys, there is an interaction between second year viewing and second year scores on the Perceptions of Danger Index-II upon the third Perceptions of Danger Index-II scores. With IQ, SES, grade, early viewing, and early scores on the Perceptions of Danger Index-II already in a regression equation, there is still a negative and significant interaction (partial $r = -.30$, $F = 6.26$, d.f. = 1, 64, $p < .05$). This means that for those boys who had low Perceptions of Danger Index-II scores and watched more television in the second year, third year scores increased. But among those who were initially *more* afraid, heavy viewing led to less fear.

This is a dramatic and significant demonstration of the power of television to cultivate mainstream outlooks. There are, to be sure, significant "main effects,"

[10] For SES, the coefficients linking concepts to indicators range from .66 for mother's education to .90 for father's occupational prestige. For IQ, they are .77 for verbal aptitude and .76 for nonverbal aptitude. Television viewing coefficients range from .56 to .85. The items measuring interpersonal mistrust produce links between .44 and .59. As for the adults, the Perceptions of Danger-II items are essentially discrete concepts, so the links are slightly weaker (.30 to .60).

[11] The conclusion is not challenged by the finding that it seems also to run the other way. In this case the "effects" of different variables cannot be "compared" because they are measured in different units. The finding that television viewing exerts a longitudinal causal influence on attitudes of fear and mistrust is not negated by the finding that these variables also affect viewing. The two causal processes are by no means mutually exclusive. The important thing, from our perspective, is that television demonstrably affects attitudes towards violence and mistrust among adolescents.

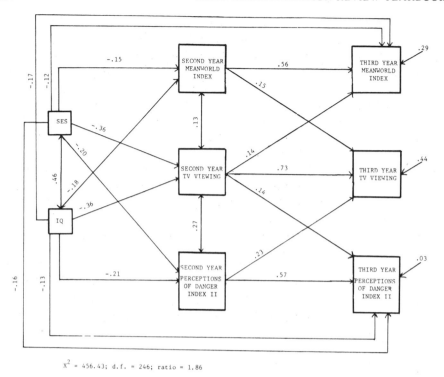

$$x^2 = 456.43; \quad d.f. = 246; \quad ratio = 1.86$$

Figure 3: Structural equation model of the longitudinal relationship between viewing, fear, and mistrust

in a generally positive direction. But perhaps the more fundamental underlying process is that of convergence into a "mainstream" television view of the world, regardless of starting points. The ultimate homogenization of initially different perspectives may be the critical consequence of living with television.

The results reported here confirm, amplify, extend, and specify previous findings. The basic stability of the Violence Index and the apparent convergence of different programming parts (with the disappearance of the former "family hour" as a relatively low-violence zone) are the most noteworthy findings of message analysis. The cultivation analysis provides further strong support for the theory of pervasive cultivation of mistrust, apprehension, danger, and exaggerated "mean world" perceptions. Important specifications suggest that television viewing is associated with a cultural "mainstream" that tends to absorb or assimilate groups that otherwise diverge from it, and that the salience of certain real-life circumstances is likely to boost television's cultivating potential.

REFERENCES

1. Bandura, Albert, Dorothea Ross, and Sheila Ross. "Transmission of Aggression through Imitation of Aggressive Models." *Journal of Abnormal and Social Psychology* 63, 1967, pp. 575-582.
2. Blank, David. "The Gerbner Violence Profile." *Journal of Broadcasting* 21(3), 1977, pp. 273-279.

3. Blank, David. "Final Comments on the Violence Profile." *Journal of Broadcasting* 21(3), 1977, pp. 287-296.

4. Bryant, Jennings, Rodney A. Carveth, and Dan Brown. "Does Heavy Television Viewing Produce Anxiety? Or does Anxiety Promote Heavy Television Viewing?: An Experimental Examination of Alternative Hypotheses." Paper presented in a "top twelve" session, Mass Communication Division, Annual Meeting of the International Communication Association, Acapulco, Mexico, 1980.

5. Coffin, Thomas E. and Sam Tuchman. "Rating Television Programs for Violence: A Comparison of Five Surveys." *Journal of Broadcasting* 17(1), 1972-73, pp. 3-20.

6. Coffin, Thomas and Sam Tuchman. "A Question of Validity: Some Comments on 'Apples, Oranges, and the Kitchen Sink.'" *Journal of Broadcasting* 17(1), 1972-73, pp. 31-33.

7. Doob, Anthony N. and Glenn E. Macdonald. "Television Viewing and Fear of Victimization: Is the Relationship Causal?" *Journal of Personality and Social Psychology* 37(2), 1979, pp. 170-179.

8. Eleey, Michael, George Gerbner, and Nancy (Tedesco) Signorielli. "Apples, Oranges, and the Kitchen Sink: An Analysis and Guide to the Comparison of 'Violence Ratings.'" *Journal of Broadcasting* 17(1), 1972-73, pp. 21-30.

9. Eleey, Michael, George Gerbner, and Nancy (Tedesco) Signorielli. "Validity Indeed!" *Journal of Broadcasting* 17(1), 1972-73, pp. 34-35.

10. Ellis, Glenn T. and Francis Sekura III. "The Effect of Aggressive Cartoons on the Behavior of First Grade Children." *Journal of Psychology* 81, 1972, pp. 7-43.

11. Gerbner, George. "Dimensions of Violence in Television Drama." In Robert K. Baker and Sandra J. Ball (Eds.) *Violence in the Media*. Staff report to the National Commission on the Causes and Prevention of Violence. Washington, D.C.: U.S. Govt. Printing Office, 1969.

12. Gerbner, George. "Violence and Television Drama: Trends and Symbolic Functions." In G. A. Comstock and E. A. Rubinstein (Eds.) *Television and Social Behavior*, Vol. 1: *Content and Control*. Washington, D.C.: U.S. Government Printing Office, 1972.

13. Gerbner, George. "Comments on 'Measuring Violence on Television: The Gerbner Index.'" Unpublished manuscript, The Annenberg School of Communications, University of Pennsylvania, July 1972.

14. Gerbner, George. "Death in Prime-Time: Notes on the Symbolic Functions of Dying in the Mass Media." *Annals of the American Academy of Political and Social Science* 447, January 1980, pp. 64-70.

15. Gerbner, George. "Sex on Television and What Viewers Learn From It." Paper presented to the National Association of Television Program Executives Annual Conference, San Francisco, February 1980.

16. Gerbner, George. "Children and Power on Television: The Other Side of the Picture." In George Gerbner, Catherine J. Ross, and Edward Ziegler (Eds.) *Child Abuse: An Analysis and Agenda for Action*. New York: Oxford University Press, 1980.

17. Gerbner, George and Larry Gross. "Living with Television: The Violence Profile." *Journal of Communication* 26(2), Spring 1976, pp. 173-199.

18. Gerbner, George and Larry Gross. "Editorial Response: A Reply to Newcomb's 'Humanistic Critique.'" *Communication Research* 6, 1979, pp. 223-230.

19. Gerbner, George, Larry Gross, Michael F. Eleey, Marilyn Jackson-Beeck, Suzanne Jeffries-Fox, and Nancy Signorielli. "TV Violence Profile No. 8: The Highlights." *Journal of Communication* 27(2), Spring 1977, pp. 171-180.

20. Gerbner, George, Larry Gross, Michael Eleey, Marilyn Jackson-Beeck, Suzanne Jeffries-Fox, and Nancy Signorielli. "'The Gerbner Violence Profile'—An Analysis of the CBS Report." *Journal of Broadcasting* 21(3), 1977, pp. 280-286.

21. Gerbner, George, Larry Gross, Michael Eleey, Marilyn Jackson-Beeck, Suzanne Jeffries-Fox, and Nancy Signorielli. "One More Time: An Analysis of the CBS 'Final Comments on the Violence Profile.'" *Journal of Broadcasting* 21(3), 1977, pp. 297-303.

22. Gerbner, George, Larry Gross, Marilyn Jackson-Beeck, Suzanne Jeffries-Fox, and Nancy Signorielli. "Cultural Indicators: Violence Profile No. 9." *Journal of Communication* 28(3), Summer 1978, pp. 176-207.

23. Gerbner, George, Larry Gross, Michael Morgan, and Nancy Signorielli. "On Wober's 'Televised Violence and Paranoid Perception: The View from Great Britain.'" *Public Opinion Quarterly* 43, Spring 1979, pp. 123-124.

24. Gerbner, George, Larry Gross, Michael Morgan, and Nancy Signorielli. "Media and the Family: Images and Impact." Paper for the National Research Forum on Family Issues, White House Conference on Families, April 1980.

25. Gerbner, George, Larry Gross, Michael Morgan, and Nancy Signorielli. "Violence Profile No. 11: Trends in Network Television Drama and Viewer Conceptions of Social Reality, 1967-1979." Technical Report, The Annenberg School of Communications, University of Pennsylvania, May 1980.

26. Gerbner, George, Larry Gross, Nancy Signorielli, Michael Morgan, and Marilyn Jackson-Beeck. "The Demonstration of Power: Violence Profile No. 10." *Journal of Communication* 29(3), Summer 1979, pp. 177-196.

27. Gerbner, George, Larry Gross, Nancy Signorielli, and Michael Morgan. "Aging with Television: Images on Television Drama and Conceptions of Social Reality." *Journal of Communication* 30(1), Winter 1980, pp. 37-47.

28. Gerbner, George and Nancy Signorielli. "Women and Minorities in Television Drama 1969-1978." The Annenberg School of Communications, University of Pennsylvania, 1979.

29. Gonzalez, Mark. "Television and People's Images of Old Age." Unpublished master's thesis, The Annenberg School of Communications, University of Pennsylvania, 1979.

30. Gross, Larry and Suzanne Jeffries-Fox. "What Do You Want To Be When You Grow Up, Little Girl?" In Gaye Tuchman *et al.* (Eds.) *Hearth and Home: Images of Women in the Mass Media.* New York: Oxford University Press, 1977.

31. Gross, Larry and Michael Morgan. "Television and Enculturation." In J. R. Dominick and J. Fletcher (Eds.) *Broadcasting Research Methods: A Reader.* Boston: Allyn and Bacon, in press.

32. Gross, Larry, Michael Morgan, and Nancy Signorielli. "Violence in Television Programs: Ten Years Later." In National Institute of Mental Health, *Television and Behavior: Ten Years of Scientific Progress and Implications for the 80's,* in press.

33. Harr-Mazer, Heather. "Television's Victimized Children." Unpublished master's thesis, The Annenberg School of Communications, University of Pennsylvania, 1980.

34. Hawkins, Robert P. and Suzanne Pingree. "Some Processes in the Cultivation Effect." *Communication Research,* April 1980.

35. Hawkins, Robert P. and Suzanne Pingree. "Television Viewing and Cultural Indicators: Some Notes on Theory and Measurement." Paper presented in a "top twelve" session, Mass Communication Division, Annual Meeting of the International Communication Association, Acapulco, Mexico, 1980.

36. Hawkins, Robert P. and Suzanne Pingree. "TV Influence on Social Reality and Conceptions of the World." In National Institute of Mental Health, *Television and Behavior: Ten Years of Scientific Progress and Implications for the 80's,* in press.

37. Hirsch, Paul. "The 'Scary World' of the Nonviewer and Other Anomalies: A Reanalysis of Findings on the Cultivation Hypothesis, Part I." Paper presented at the 35th Annual Conference of the American Association for Public Opinion Research, Cincinnati, May 1980. Also, *Communication Research,* in press.

38. Hughes, Michael. "The Fruits of Cultivation Analysis: A Re-examination of the Effects of Television Watching on Fear of Victimization, Alienation, and the Approval of Violence." *Public Opinion Quarterly,* in press.

39. Jeffries-Fox, Suzanne. "Television's Contribution to Children's Ideas about Occupations." Unpublished Ph.D. dissertation, University of Pennsylvania, 1978.

40. Jeffries-Fox, Suzanne and George Gerbner. "Television and the Family." *Fernsehen und Bildung* 11(3), 1977.

41. Jeffries-Fox, Suzanne and Nancy Signorielli. "Television and Children's Conceptions about Occupations." In Herb S. Dordick (Ed.) *Proceedings of the Sixth Annual Telecommunications Policy Research Conference.* Lexington, Mass.: Lexington Books, 1979.

42. Jöreskog, K. G. "A General Method for Estimating a Linear Structural Equation System." In A. S. Goldberger and O. D. Duncan (Eds.) *Structural Equation Models in the Social Sciences.* New York: Seminar Press, 1973, pp. 85-112.

43. Jöreskog, K. G. "Structural Equation Models in the Social Sciences: Specification, Estimation, and Testing." In P. R. Krishnaiah (Ed.) *Applications of Statistics.* Amsterdam: North Holland Publishing Co., 1977.

44. Jöreskog, K. G. "Structural Analysis of Covariance and Correlation Matrices." *Psychometrika* 43, 1978, pp. 443-477.

45. Krattenmaker, Thomas G. and L. A. Powe, Jr. "Televised Violence: First Amendment Principles and Social Science Theory." *Virginia Law Review* 64(8), December 1978, pp. 1123-1297.

46. Krippendorff, Klaus. "Bivariate Agreement Coefficients for the Reliability of Data." In E. F. Borgatta and G. W. Bohrnstedt (Eds.) *Sociological Methodology 1970.* San Francisco: Jossey-Bass, 1970.

47. Lovas, O. I. "Effects of Exposure to Symbolic Aggression on Aggressive Behavior." *Child Development* 32, 1061, pp. 37-44.

48. Morgan, Michael. "Television and Reading: Does More Equal Better?" *Journal of Communication* 30(1), Winter 1980, pp. 159-165.

49. Morgan, Michael. "Longitudinal Patterns of Television Viewing and Adolescent Role Socialization." Unpublished Ph.D. dissertation, University of Pennsylvania, 1980.

50. Morgan, Michael and Larry Gross. "Television, IQ, and School Achievement." In S. Scheuyer (Ed.) *The TV Annual 1978-1979.* New York: Macmillan, 1979.

51. Morgan, Michael and Larry Gross. "Reading, Writing and Watching: Television Viewing, IQ, and Academic Achievement." *Journal of Broadcasting,* in press.

52. Morgan, Michael and Larry Gross. "Television and Educational Achievement and Aspirations." In National Institute of Mental Health, *Television and Behavior: Ten Years of Scientific Progress and Implications for the 80's,* in press.

53. Morgan, Michael and Heather Harr-Mazer. "Television and Adolescents' Family Life Expectations." Unpublished manuscript, The Annenberg School of Communications, University of Pennsylvania, 1980.

54. Murray, John P. and Susan Kippax. "From the Early Window to the Late Night Show: International Trends in the Study of Television's Impact on Children and Adults." *Advances in Experimental Social Psychology* 12, 1979, pp. 253-320.

55. Newcomb, Horace. "Assessing the Violence Profile of Gerbner and Gross: A Humanistic Critique and Suggestions." *Communication Research* 5, 1978, pp. 264-282.

56. Neville, T. "Television Viewing and the Expression of Interpersonal Mistrust." Unpublished Ph.D. dissertation, Princeton University, 1980.

57. Owen, Bruce M. "Measuring Violence on Television: The Gerbner Index." Staff Research Paper, Office of Telecommunications Policy, OTP-SP-7, Washington, D.C., June 1972.

58. Pingree, S., S. Starrett, and R. Hawkins. "Soap Opera Viewers and Social Reality." Unpublished manuscript, Women's Studies Program, University of Wisconsin-Madison, 1979.

59. Pingree, Suzanne and Robert P. Hawkins. "American Programs on Australian Television: The Cultivation Effect in Australia." *Journal of Communication,* 1980 (in press).

60. Rosenberg, Morris. *Occupations and Values.* Glencoe, Ill.: Free Press, 1957.

61. Rothschild, Nancy F. "Group as a Mediating Factor in the Cultivation Process Among Young Children." Unpublished master's thesis, The Annenberg School of Communications, University of Pennsylvania, 1979.

62. Signorielli, Nancy. "Television's Contribution to Sex Role Socialization." Paper presented at the Seventh Annual Telecommunications Policy Research Conference, Skytop, Pennsylvania, April 1979.

63. Signorielli, Nancy. "Aging and Television: Portrayals in Prime-Time Drama and Conceptions of Social Reality." Paper presented at the 34th Annual Conference of the American Association for Public Opinion Research, Buck Hill Falls, Pennsylvania, June 1979.

64. Signorielli, Nancy. "The Valuation of Occupations on Television." Paper presented at Conference on Public Views of Doctors and Lawyers, The Annenberg School of Communications, University of Pennsylvania, October 1979.

65. Signorielli, Nancy and George Gerbner. "The Image of the Elderly in Prime-Time Television Drama." *Generations*, Fall 1978.

66. Srole, Leo. "Social Integration and Certain Correlaries: An Exploratory Study." *American Sociological Review* 21, 1956, pp. 709-712.

67. Stevens, Geoffrey. "TV and Attitudes of Fear and Alienation." Unpublished master's thesis, The Annenberg School of Communications, University of Pennsylvania, 1980.

68. Tan, Alexis. "TV Beauty Ads and Role Expectations of Adolescent Female Viewers." *Journalism Quarterly* 56, 1979, pp. 283-288.

69. Volgy, T. and J. Schwarz. "Television Entertainment Programming and Sociopolitical Attitudes." *Journalism Quarterly*, in press.

70. Wober, J. M. "Televised Violence and Paranoid Perception: The View from Great Britain." *Public Opinion Quarterly* 42, 1978, pp. 315-321.

71. Zill, Nicholas. "Television and Children's Intellectual Development: Results from a National Sample of Youth." Presented at the 35th Annual Conference of the American Association for Public Opinion Research, Cincinnati, May 1980.

Using the same NORC data set analyzed by the Gerbner-Annenberg team, Paul M. Hirsch replicates their study on the cultivation effects of television. Isolating nonviewers and extreme viewers, Hirsch turns up disturbing findings. On a majority of 18 relevant questionnaire items, the nonviewers *are more frequently fearful, alienated, and favorable to suicide than the* light viewers. Extreme viewers *appear to perceive a less scary world than* heavy viewers, *as defined by Gerbner. Using multiple controls simultaneously on age, sex, and education greatly reduces support for the cultivation hypothesis in Hirsch's replication. Dr. Hirsch concludes that the cultivation hypothesis remains an interesting but unsupported speculation. Hirsch is associate professor of sociology at the University of Chicago's School of Business.*

31

THE "SCARY WORLD" OF
THE NONVIEWER AND OTHER ANOMALIES
A Reanalysis of Gerbner et al.'s Findings on
Cultivation Analysis

Paul M. Hirsch

SUMMATIVE INTRODUCTION

This article reports a reanalysis of the NORC data set which Gerbner et al. claim provides much of the empirical support for their "cultivation hypothesis"—that television-viewing inculcates fear, anomia, and a perception by heavy viewers of the world as a "mean" place to live. Although the NORC General Social Survey is publicly available, no one

AUTHOR'S NOTE: *This research was generously supported by a grant from the John and Mary R. Markle Foundation to facilitate dialogue between the social sciences and humanities in the field of mass communication. The research was initiated at the suggestion of Horace Newcomb (1978), an English professor who insisted that findings presented in support of the cultivation hypothesis by the Annenberg group were logically suspect and*

From Paul M. Hirsch, "The 'Scary World' of the Nonviewer and Other Anomalies: A Reanalysis of Gerbner et al.'s Findings on Cultivation Analysis," *Communication Research* 7, 4 (October 1980) 403-456. Copyright 1980 by Sage Publications, Inc.

independent of the Annenberg School has previously reanalyzed its contents concerning television-viewing and its
correlates. The reanalysis finds remarkably little support for
the hypothesis. It is especially weakest when nonviewers
and extreme viewers are included in the analysis. Over 18
relevant items, *nonviewers* are consistently more fearful,
alienated, and favorable to suicide than "light" viewers;
extreme viewers are *less* perturbed than heavy viewers.
These findings severely undermine the contention that any
relationship between TV-viewing and the provision of "television answers" to attitude items is linear or monotonic.
Additional findings include: (1) what few bivariate relationships appeared in the analysis by Gerbner et al. are virtually
wiped out by the addition of (any two) multiple controls; and
(2) at least one previously unreported item from the NORC
data set goes directly counter (despite controls) to the
cultivation hypothesis. Furthermore—as will be detailed in
Part II of this article—(3) the attitudes of people in such
victimized categories as blacks, females, and the elderly are
independent of their amount of television-viewing; (4) non-
demographic variables, such as amount of radio-listening
and reported health, are as statistically significant as TV-
viewing in their (albeit weak) ability to predict attitudes
about the world across the population; and (5) respondents'
astrological sign (as a proxy for a random number table)
significantly predicts whether persons are heavy viewers.

We therefore conclude that acceptance of the cultivation
hypothesis as anything more than an interesting but unsupported speculation is premature and unwarranted at this

*warranted reanalysis by the social science community. I am grateful to
Delores Conway, Elihu Katz, Peter Miller, Horace Newcomb, and John
Robinson for their contributions to and critical readings of this article. While
they did not always concur with how each point was weighted or with every
conclusion, all agreed that the issues raised, given the prominence of the
Annenberg projects, need to be formalized for discussion. I am also greatly
indebted to Sally Kilgore, Tom Panelas, and Stephen Struhl for their original
contributions and first-rate research assistance.*

time. In Part II, alternative explanations for heavy television-viewing, and alternative interpretations and conceptualizations of television's effects will be proposed and outlined.

INTRODUCTION

Two approaches are available for interpreting [these results]. One is that what may be true in America is not true in Britain, for which difference it will be useful to explore the reasons. The second is that the Gerbner thesis has still not been demonstrated convincingly enough in America, and the effect exists neither there nor in Britain [Wober, 1978: 320].

Most researchers interested in mass media and communication research are keenly aware of the violence profiles and cultivation analyses published annually by Dr. George Gerbner and his colleagues at the University of Pennsylvania's Annenberg School of Communication. The violence profiles present frame-by-frame content analyses of television programs, taken over a week's period of prime-time viewing hours; the cumulative profiles provide one set of valuable indicators about what is shown and available to viewers of American network television productions. Focusing primarily on dominance relations, they follow in a long tradition of reporting the frequencies and proportions of characters from specific ethnic and social groups found to portray villains or heroes, aggressors or victims, manipulators or manipulated. The second body of reports, entitled "Cultivation Analysis," seeks to demonstrate that the "television reality" shown in the violence and content profiles is meaningful to and understood by the viewing population. Further, it is proposed that viewers interpret television content in a manner which supports the argument that watching television engenders perceptions in heavy viewers significantly different from what they might otherwise feel or think if they viewed television less. The argument has been that the more television a survey respondent reports viewing, the more his or her perception of the "real world" approaches the "mean" and "scary" world of television (as yielded by the content categories set forth in the profiles).

The Annenberg projects on television content and effects have strongly influenced the research agendas and theoretical bases of current research on mass communications. Graduate students across disciplines and professional researchers seldom launch a project about television without first seeking to relate it to the Annenberg results and/or adopting that school's paradigm(s). This rapid acceptance is unusual in the sociology of science, where assertions of strong results or important effects are more typically reanalyzed, debated among scholars, replicated, and then supported, rejected, or left to await further research. Recent controversies over sociobiology (Wilson, 1975; Sahlins, 1977; Caplan, 1978), Maslow's theory of job satisfaction (Salancik and Pfeffer, 1977; Alderfer, 1977), Coleman's findings on busing (Moynihan and Mosteller, 1972), and Shockley's assertions on IQ and heredity (Kamin, 1974) provide examples of social science research bearing on public policy being tested and retested within the academic community.

Mass communication research, in contrast, has been remarkably free of such active efforts at reanalysis and replication. Efforts to replicate the reported results of the Annenberg group's cultivation analysis have met with mixed success. Wober (1978) found no evidence of a paranoic effect of television viewing on British audiences. Doob and MacDonald (1979: 170), controlling for the crime rate in respondents' neighborhoods, found "no overall relationship between television and fear of being a victim of crime." Hawkins and Pingree (1980) found partial support in Australia for the cultivation hypothesis. To date, however, there have been no reanalyses by anyone independent of having been trained at or otherwise associated with the Annenberg school.[1] This is especially surprising, insofar as a major and critical source of the data on which the project has relied is the General Social Survey of the National Opinion Research Center, an omnibus survey conducted annually and available to any interested user for $25.00. Of all the surveys reported by the Annenberg group, NORC's General Social Survey, along with the University of Michigan (Survey Research Center's) Center for Political Studies 1976 election survey, are the only two nationally representative probability samples they have drawn from and therefore are the most important for reanalysis. If either survey's results fail to hold up, the cultivation hypothesis must be called into serious question.

Conceptually, this article begins at that point where Gerbner et al. seek to impose their categories for purposes of content analysis onto the interpretive mind of the viewer.[2] There is, of course, some question about whether examining a single survey item and its correlates is adequate to this task (Newcomb, 1970; Himmelwoit et al., 1980). However, accepting this presumption for the sake of argument, this article presents a reanalysis of a significant body of data on which much in the cultivation analysis reports are based. The reanalysis is based on the data in the National Opinion Research Center's General Social Surveys of 1975, 1977, and 1978.

We will see that both the items and the codings chosen across surveys by Gerbner et al. are unusually selective and arbitrary: There are unreported items which do not support the model they present, as well as ambiguities in what they have reported, that cast grave doubts on its validity. In almost every case, especially with the addition of multiple controls (practically any two) on the relationship between hours of television watched and its correlates, there is neither statistical significance nor a plausible argument that the results, though insignificant, move in the expected direction. In fact, I will provide instances showing that where patterns do emerge, they are as likely to move in the *opposite* direction. Based on the *cumulative number* of questionable statistical procedures and interpretations on which the Annenberg group's assertions about cultivation analysis are based—rather than the single instances over which researchers might normally disagree—I will propose that (1) because the NORC data set fails to support most of the inferences and conclusions which have been drawn and is one of the best of the many samples to have been reported to support them, (2) the assertion of cultivation analysis should be transformed from the status of scientific finding to an (albeit interesting) armchair hypothesis. *Note that there is no claim made here about "disproving" its possible validity.* Rather, the attempt is more simply to show that the NORC data, properly analyzed, contain precious little which can be found to support cultivation analysis.

The following sections will take up, in sequence, (1) The General Social Survey data set, comparing it with the others and examining what items and question wordings are available in each; (2) reported and unreported discrepancies across samples; (3) the substantially different results obtained once variables are added or recoded. Over 18 relevant items, *nonviewers* are consistently more fearful, alienated, and favorable to suicide than light viewers. *Extreme* viewers are less perturbed than heavy viewers. These findings severely undermine the contention that any relationship between TV-viewing and the provision of "television answers" to attitude items is linear or even monotonic. Finally, (4) when *multiple controls* are placed on the (already weak) bivariate relationships, the added effect of television hours viewed—over and above such standard controls as education, race, sex, and employment status—is shown to be negligible at best.

In Part II, the major findings reported will include (5) a near-total absence of association between the attitudes of population subgroups (women, elderly, blacks) and the amount of television viewed by each. Indeed, the former is shown to be independent of the latter, and subgroups' attitudes often move in directions *counter* to the "mean world" hypothesis' expectations about their relation to number of hours viewed. Part II will also discuss (6) anomalous results from items available but not reported by the Annenberg group. Here we find, for example, heavy viewers are *less* favorable than light viewers regarding the use of actual physical violence. Respondents' reported number of television hours viewed also vary significantly with zodiac signs, taken as proxy for a random number table. (I will *not* argue that certain zodiac signs therefore "cultivate" or cause heavy television-viewing.)

THE GENERAL SOCIAL SURVEY
AS DATA
SET AND RESOURCE

The General Social Survey has been conducted by the National Opinion Research Center annually since 1972 to generate a data base for social science researchers and to make available "fresh, interesting, and high quality data" to a wide population of interested users (Davis et al., 1978: v). Each survey is administered and coded at NORC, but the data analysis is left entirely to the interest and discretion of the user community. Over 600 items have been asked since the survey's inception; many are asked every year, while others rotate and a small number appear only one time. Interviews average one hour in length. Each sample of approximately 1500 respondents is independently drawn from English-speaking persons 18 years of age or older living in noninstitutionalized arrangements within the continental United States. The national samples are designed to be representative of the general population.

Three items on media use have been included for particular years:

(1) How often do you read the newspaper—every day, a few times a week, once a week, less than once a week, or never? (1972, 1975, 1977, 1978)

(2) Do you ever listen to the radio? (If yes): On the average, about how many hours a day do you usually listen to the radio? (1978 only)

(3) On the average day, about how many hours do you personally watch television? (1975, 1977, 1978)

All of the Annenberg group's reports on cultivation analysis focus on the third item, hours of reported television-viewing per day. Responses of "light," "medium," and "heavy" viewers to other items and scales, on a wide variety of surveys, constitute the data base employed:

> Our approach reflects the hypothesis that heavier viewers of television, those more exposed than lighter viewers to its messages, are more likely to understand social reality in terms of the "facts of life" they see on television. To investigate this hypothesis, we partition the population and our samples according to television exposure. By contrasting light and heavy viewers, some of the difference television makes in people's conception of social reality can be examined [Gerbner et al., 1978: 194].

The distribution of respondents in the NORC data file on each of these items is presented in Table 1. For both radio and television, over half the samples listen to or watch two hours or less per day. The means (3.2 and 2.9, respectively) are higher, reflecting the skewness of the distribution. Interestingly, about 85% of the respondents fall within one standard deviation of the mean, leaving only 15% as outliers in the distribution. These are nonviewers and those exposed to television or radio for approximately five or more hours. These media use variables are better fitted by a gamma distribution than a normal distribution, suggesting that respondents watching from one to five hours of television daily are less deviant, statistically, than those who watch none at all or more than five hours. In Table 1, we also see that well over half the respondents are "heavy readers" of the daily newspaper, with 80% reporting they read one daily or several times a week.

TABLE 1
Frequency Distributions and Summary Statistics for Media Use Items on NORC General Social Survey (cumulative for 1975, 1977, 1978)

Hours/Day Watching TV				Hours/Day Listening to Radio				Times/Week Reading Newspaper			
Years Available: 1975/77/78				Year Available: 1978				Years Available: 1975/77/78			
No. Hrs.	%	Cum	N	No. Hrs.	%	Cum	N	Times/Wk	%	Cum%	N
0	5	5	209	0	9	9	137	Never	5	5	217
1	20	24	892	1	36	45	547				
2	26	51	1198	2	19	64	293				
3	20	70	889	3	8	72	124				
4	14	84	616	4	7	80	112	Less than			
5	7	91	313	5	4	83	54	once	6	11	294
6	4	95	203	6	4	87	62	a week			
7	1	96	43	7	1	88	13				
8	2	98	78	8	6	94	84				
9	0	98	10	9	1	95	12	Once a wk	9	20	428
10	1	99	34	10	2	97	36				
11	0	99	2	11	0	97	1				
12	1	100	28	12	2	99	26				
13	0	100	3	13	0	99	1	A few times	6	38	793
14	0	100	2	14	0	99	2	a week			
15	0	100	7	15	0	99	5				
16	0	100	4	16	0	99	1				
17	0	100	1	17	*	99	-	Every day	62	100	2807
18	0	100	1	18	0	99	2				
20	0	100	2	20	0	99	1				
24	0	100	1	24	0	100	7				

Mean: 2.9
Median: 2.4
Standard Deviation: 2.1
Skewness: 2.1

Mean: 3.0
Median: 1.8
Standard Deviation: 3.3
Skewness: 2.5

In Gerbner et al.'s treatment of the NORC TV-viewing data, the sample is divided into three categories, defined as follows:

Survey	No. hours viewed	Viewer Category	% Cumulative Sample (3 available years)
NORC	0-2	Light	51
	3	Medium	19
	4-24	Heavy	30

This categorization is used consistently through all of the Annenberg group's reporting of NORC data (Gerbner et al., 1976, 1977, 1978). It is *very roughly* comparable to the coding employed in their secondary analysis of data from the 1976 Michigan Center for Political Studies Election Survey. There, in answer to the item, "How often do you watch evening entertainment programs about crime and police?" the analogue to NORC's total hours viewed (out of 24 and across all programs, not evening-only crime and police shows) becomes:

Survey	Frequency of Viewing	Viewer Category	% of Sample
Michigan	"Rarely" or "Never"	Light	37
CPS	"Sometimes"	Medium	37
	"Frequently"	Heavy	26

Since daytime viewing and all news and "nonviolent" entertainment programs are excluded from the Michigan item, it is easier for a respondent to show up as a "light" viewer in the Michigan election (CPS) survey than in the NORC data, and possible for the same persons coded as "light" in the CPS file to fall into the "medium" or "heavy" viewing categories derived from the more inclusive NORC item.[3] Nevertheless—perhaps because respondents did not see "rarely" or "never" as converging with zero through two hours—it is unexpectedly from the NORC data set that Gerbner et al. obtain 13% more "light" viewers; the percentage coded as "medium" is 17% lower, while the proportion of "heavy" viewers remains about the same.[4]

While Michigan and NORC surveys share the advantage of being large, national, representative samples, both the sample base and coding of data into viewing categories become much more problematic when Gerbner et al. present convenience samples of children under 18 years of age. Table 2 collects in one place the widely discrepant definitions of viewing categories employed in the Annenberg group's Profiles 9 (1978) and 10 (1979a, 1979b). Although the text of each "Violence Profile" reads as though there is consistency across samples by use of the descriptive terms "heavy" and "light" viewers, we now have seen six different definitions of these concepts employed across samples and used interchangeably. In Violence Profile 10, for example, *if a child reported viewing three hours of tele-*

TABLE 2

Categorization of Viewing Employed in Gerbner et al.'s Reporting on Children Under 18 Years of Age

"Light"	"Medium"	"Heavy"	Sample Description	In Violence Profile #
Less than 4 hours	Dropped	More than 4 hours	"Suburban/rural" 7-8 grades in New Jersey School (N = 477)	10
2 hours or less *	2-6 hours *	6 hours or more *	"Suburban/rural" children in New Jersey School (N = 625)	9
Less than 2 hours	Dropped	2 hours or more	"New York School children," aged 10-17 at private school in New York	10
Less than 2 hours	2 hours or more	Dropped	Bank Street School, a [well-known] private school in New York City (N = 116)	9

*These category intervals overlap, providing insufficient information on how responses were actually coded for this survey.

vision in the New Jersey school, he or she would be coded as a "light" viewer. The same child, if transported to the New York school, is coded as a "heavy" viewer. As we shall see in the next section, the extent to which simple bivariate relationships appear linear and monotonic can be substantially influenced by (1) the number of reported hours selected to define each viewing category and (2) the distribution of respondents falling in each of the hours collapsed to form each viewing category. Writ large, this issue raises obvious questions concerning the computation and comparability of "cultivation differentials" both within and among samples. If, as Gerbner et al. suggest in Profile 10 (1979b), each "latest" statistical treatment is to supersede all previous reported results, the most recent is also the *most* susceptible to distortion when comparisons are made across surveys; for where each sample is broken at the median of its TV-hours distribution, as in the latest profile (1979a: 189), the definitions of "light" and "heavy" become entirely determined by the idiosyncracies of each sample (for example, the TV-hours distribution of 116 middle-class children in one school is treated as comparable or equatable with the viewing hours distribution of the NORC or SRC national probability samples of the adult U.S. population).[5]

REPORTED AND UNREPORTED DISCREPANCIES IN RESULTS ACROSS SAMPLES

Given the wide variations in the size and representativeness of the samples employed and discrepancies in the coding of variables, the question arises whether important issues covered by one or more of the samples are reported at all and, if so, reported accurately. Tables 3 and 4 present the responses of three samples to two comparable items on respondents' approval of the commission of actual physical violence. In Table 3, as reported by Gerbner et al. (1978: 197), more heavy than light viewers among two convenience samples of children (N = 116 and N = 625)—for whom the definitions of "heavy" and "light" are themselves

TABLE 3

Percentage of Children Agreeing: "It's Almost Always All Right To Hit Someone If You Are Mad At Them"*** (by Level of Television Viewing)[1]

	New Jersey School					Bank Street School				
	Television Viewing[2]			CD Difference %Heavy-%Light	gamma		Television Viewing[2]		CD Difference %Medium-%Light	gamma
	Light (N=141)	Medium (N=339)	Heavy (N=161)				Light (N=65)	Medium (N=61)		
Overall (N=625)	31	35	41	+10	.13**	Overall (N=116)	10	24	+14	.49**
Controlling for:										
Grade in School						**Age**				
sixth (N=68)	20	37	44	+24	.28*	9 – 11 (N=43)	18	35	+17	.42*
seventh (N=266)	35	32	41	+ 6	-.09	12-14 (N=30)	5	19	+14	.63**
eighth (N=230)	35	39	40	+ 5	.06					
ninth (N=68)	17	28	33	+16	.28					
Sex						**Sex**				
Male (N=304)	37	44	39	+ 2	-.04	Male (N=56)	14	42	+28	.62**
Female (N=328)	24	26	42	+18	.27**	Female (N=67)	6	10	+ 4	.28
Parents' Education						**Father's Education**				
Neither went to college (N=228)	29	40	47	+18	.20**	No college (N=11)	20	53	+33	.33
Father or both went to college (N=349)	33	29	36	+ 3	.05	Some college (N=103)	9	24	+15	.53*

1. Question for New Jersey School: "How often is it all right to hit someone if you are mad at the person for a good reason?"
Question for Bank Street School: "How often is it all right to hit someone if you are mad at them?"
2. "Altogether, about how many hours a day do you usually spend watching TV, including morning, afternoon and evening?"
New Jersey School: light—2 hours or less; medium—2 to 6 hours; heavy—6 hours or more.
Bank Street School: light—less than 2 hours; medium—2 hours or more.

*p ≤ .05 (tau); **p ≤ .01 (tau); ***Reprinted from Gerbner et al. (1978: 197).

TABLE 4

Percentage Approving of Ever Punching a Male by TV-Viewing Hours, Controlling for Age, Sex, Education

	LIGHT VIEWERS	MEDIUM VIEWERS	HEAVY VIEWERS	GAMMA
Overall	71	72	62	.14
Controlling for:				
EDUCATION:				
11 years or less (N=946)	56	60	53	.06
12 years (N=997)	72	78	71	.00
13 years or more (N=924)	81	79	66	.23**
SEX:				
Male (N=1253)	71	73	63	.12*
Female (N=1622)	71	71	62	.15**
AGE:				
Under 30 (N=793)	75	76	68	.13*
30-55 (N=1238)	75	78	69	.07
55+ (N=844)	62	59	50	.17*

SOURCE: NORC General Social Surveys, 1975 and 1978.

*P ≤ .05 (tau); **P ≤ .001 (tau)

not comparable and the distributions within each category not provided—responded affirmatively to the following item, worded in one case as: "How often is it alright to hit someone if you are mad at them? Is it almost always alright or almost never right?"

For the larger sample, the item's wording added "for a good reason" at the end of the first sentence. In their coding of this item to distinguish respondents giving the "television answers" from those better reflecting the "real world," the Annenberg group define a child's positive response to the idea of hitting someone as the former and a negative response as the latter.

In Table 4, we present the cumulated responses (N = 2875) from NORC's large probability sample of people 18 and older to the following item, available for 1975 and 1978 but never discussed or referred to by Gerbner et al.

Are there any situations you can imagine in which you would approve a man punching an adult male stranger?

Using the same criteria for significance and the same bivariate controls (plus age) employed by Gerbner et al. in Table 3, the *opposite results shown* for the NORC probability sample are especially striking. *Here, there is not a single row in which "heavy" viewers are more favorable toward actual physical violence than are "medium" or "light" viewers*— quite the contrary: in five of the eight rows, the difference in the percentage of heavy viewers expressing a positive distaste for violence is statistically significant at either the .05 or .01 level. Table 4 is especially damaging to the cultivation hypothesis and will be discussed at greater length in other sections of this article. It is one of the few tables in the NORC data set whose statistical significance remains after the imposition of multiple controls, whereas most of the findings reported by Gerbner et al. as their strongest virtually evaporate on exposure to multiple classification analysis. Theoretically, it is critical because respondents' orientation to actual physical violence ties up directly to the content analysis portions and are found here to run directly counter to expectations generated in the content analysis parts of the Violence Profiles.[7]

Table 4 provides no support for the repeated contention that scientific findings support the assertions that heavy viewers are "more likely than light viewers to choose answers that reflect television perspectives" and that " 'living' in the world of television cultivates conceptions of its own conventionalized reality" (Gerbner et al., 1978: 175; 1976: 194, respectively). Rather, it raises the possibility that in failing to ensure crosssample comparability, introduce multiple controls, and report items where the data do not support the argument for television's "cultivation" of beliefs and attitudes, the Annenberg group has itself contributed to distorting scientific reality. To eschew the importance of statistical significance when it is not found, while simultaneously presenting it whenever it appears, further contributes to the existing confusion over how to interpret results they have reported.

RECODING TV HOURS IN THE GENERAL SOCIAL SURVEY TO ANALYZE NONVIEWERS AND EXTREME VIEWERS

Because Gerbner et al. present no theoretical or statistical rationale for defining the NORC sample into the viewing hour categories (0-2, Light; 3, Medium; 4 or more, Heavy), several alternative formulations were developed for reasons of logic or experimentation. Taking the log of TV hours, for example, reduces the skewness of the distribution, enabling it to more closely approximate normalcy. Similarly, recoding the categories so that the number of viewers called light (0-1), medium (2-3), and heavy (4 or more) is more equal enables the median to fall into the medium viewer category (rather than the light) and the distribution to appear more normal. Finally, breaking out nonviewers (0 hours) and extreme viewers (8 or more hours) by expanding the number of viewing categories facilitates the isolation of interesting cultural and statistical "deviates" whose viewing patterns fall beyond one standard deviation from the mean of the distribution and differ from 90% of the population (which views between one and five hours per day; see the earlier discussion).

With the exception of this last redefinition of viewing categories, none of these reformulations yields associations with other variables in the data set which depart from results obtained employing the categories used by the Annenberg group. *One reason is that amount of television-viewing independently predicts or explains so little variation in virtually any of the dependent variables that there is little difference for the recoding of viewing categories to make.*[8] In expanding the number of categories to allow for analysis of the extremes of the distribution, however, a number of surprises emerge. In terms of Gerbner et al.'s assertion that heavy viewers learn lessons in life from television content and that this "cultivates" high scores on items tapping fear, anomia, and alienation, the most important finding is that *on many of these items, the scores of nonviewers are higher than those of television's light, medium, heavy, and/or extreme viewers.*

In other words, what small relationships there are between viewing and other variables are *nonlinear* wherever people who watch *no* television turn out to be more fearful, alienated, or anomic than those classified as light, medium or heavy viewers. This finding is clearly counter to the cultivation hypothesis, in which it is the responses of those least exposed to the "messages" about life transmitted by "television reality" which should be closest to the "real world" in terms of a more positive view of their personal affairs, life chances, and fellow man.

As we shall see, the consistent and important patterns throughout the data set are:

(1) *The only viewing category where respondents least often provide the "TV answer" and most consistently give the "non-television response" is that of light viewers (1-2*

*hours per day). However, there is no clear-cut pattern be-
yond that for respondents coded as nonviewers, medium,
heavy, or extreme. For example, persons providing "television answers" do not cluster in any of these categories. In
terms of the attitude items, only the light viewers' mean
scores are (statistically) "normal," and all other categories,
including nonviewers, exhibit no stable pattern. Since 50%
of the sample are light viewers, we think this suggests
more about Americans' lifestyles and demographics (Bogart,
1973) than about the experience of television-watching or
its effects.*

*(2) Where viewing categories form any pattern at all, it tends to
be curvilinear. In a number of interesting cases, across
attitude items, the scores of nonviewers and extreme viewers are closer to each other than to the scores of light
viewers.*

THE "SCARY WORLD" OF THE NONVIEWER

It is surprising to find that the scores of nonviewers on all
of the items analyzed for television viewers have been
neither reported nor discussed in the Annenberg group's
articles on the cultivation hypothesis. This is not because
nonviewers' responses are excluded in their analyses of the
NORC and CPS data. Rather, *in both cases nonviewers have
been defined as light viewers and their scores coded into
that category.* Simultaneously, the importance of nonviewers for assessing the impact of television has been noted in
the same articles; for example: "Without control groups of
nonviewers it is difficult to isolate television's impact"
(Gerbner et al., 1978: 193-194).

One possible argument for excluding them might be that
in any one survey, the frequency of nonviewers may be too
small to provide sufficient numbers (for example, for cells in
contingency tables) once one or more controls are introduced. In this case, one would expect them to be excluded
from the statistical analyses rather than retained and collapsed into the category of light viewers. Indeed, since

nonviewers comprise the bottom 4% of the viewing hours distribution, it would then also make sense to exclude (or separately examine) viewers of eight hours or more, who comprise the top 4%. The small numbers problem for both groups is potentially alleviated by combining samples of several years of the GSS. Depending on the other items asked in a given year, it is possible to obtain up to 209 nonviewers from the NORC surveys for 1975, 1977, and 1978, the three years in which respondents were asked their number of viewing hours on an average day. This number will increase as the annual administration of the survey continues and whenever television-viewing and other items of interest are included in the questionnaire.

A second possible reason for excluding nonviewers from the data analysis might conceivably follow from Violence Profile co-author Jackson-Beeck's (1977: 71-72) contention that the data from NORC's 1975 survey

> do not support continued reference to nonviewers as if they were a meaningful population subgroup. . . . The most appropriate characterization of the television nonviewer . . . appears to be none at all. Certainly, there are considerable differences between viewers and nonviewers on a number of specific variables. But . . . from the macro perspective, they seem socially insignificant.

Jackson-Beeck found that the nonviewers' profile includes less unemployment, higher education, but also lower incomes than the profile for all viewers. She interpreted this as providing inconsistent signals for constructing a demographic profile that "hangs together." Quite possibly, of course, the nonviewer category could include several demographic segments. But even if it did not, its cultural and theoretical importance is too great to warrant its manifest omission from the Violence Profiles. (Her article does not report nonviewers' responses to any of the attitude items put forth by the profile's authors as relevant to the cultivation hypothesis.)

While the analysis of cumulated nonviewers' demographic characteristics replicates many of Jackson-Beeck's
comparisons with *all* television viewers, it also raises serious questions of comparability between nonviewers and
those reporting an average of one to two hours of viewing
daily. By collapsing both into the category of light viewers,
Gerbner et al. ignore (by averaging together) significant
differences in these groups' composition. Light viewers (1-2
hours) report much higher family incomes (47% above
$15,000 and 12% below $5000) than nonviewers (32% and
27%, respectively); are far more likely to be currently
married (65%) than nonviewers (42%); and are less likely to
have obtained schooling beyond high school (39%) than
nonviewers (48%). Substantial differences appear in the
responses of these groups to many items in the GSS, but
these are masked and obscured by the procedure of combining them into a single category. The disproportionately
larger number of cases in the 1-2-hour category always
ensures that the average scores, across 0-2 hours, remains
close to the mean of the 1-2-hour group, regardless of how
far away the mean response of the nonviewer group may be
for the same item.

Tables 5 and 6 present items for which the Annenberg
group has constructed "television answers" and show that
*nonviewers consistently provide the "TV answer" more
frequently than do viewers of one or two hours daily.* The
questions are:

> Would you say that most of the time people try to be helpful,
> or that they are mostly just looking out for themselves?
> [Table 6]
>
> In spite of what some people say, the lot of the average man
> is getting worse, not better. [Table 5]

Using the same single controls reported in their presentation of Table 5 (Gerbner et al., 1978: 203), we find seven of
the nine comparisons between nonviewers and light view-

TABLE 5

Percentage Agreeing with "Television Answer" to Anomia Statement that "The Lot of The Average Man is Getting Worse, Not Better"

	Television Viewing		CULTIVATION DIFFERENTIAL BETWEEN NONVIEWERS AND LIGHT VIEWERS*
	NONVIEWERS (N=57)	LIGHT (N=679)	
Overall (N=1461)	61	50	-11
Controlling for:			
AGE			
Under 30 (N=155)	54	59	5
30-54 (N=385)	65	46	-19
55 and over (N=196)	59	51	-8
SEX			
Male (N=381)	59	50	-9
Female (N=355)	63	50	-13
Years in School			
11 or less (N=212)	84	65	-19
12 (HSG) (N=239)	75	52	-23
13 or more (N=284)	38	38	0

*Computed by subtracting the percentage of nonviewers agreeing with the "television answer" from the percentage of light viewers. A positive sign supports the cultivation hypothesis, for agreement with the "television answer" would be associated with more viewing. A negative sign suggests there is no relationship between them.

TABLE 6

Percentage Giving "Television Answer" to "Mean World" Question of Whether People Try to be Helpful or Mostly Look Out for Themselves

	Television Viewing		CULTIVATION DIFFERENTIAL BETWEEN NONVIEWERS AND LIGHT VIEWERS*
	NONVIEWERS (N=134)	LIGHT (N=1293)	
Overall (N=2819)	37	35	-2
Controlling for:			
AGE			
Under 30 (N=346)	42	38	-4
30-54 (N=687)	26	33	7
55 and older	48	35	-3
SEX			
Male (N=679)	45	41	-4
Female (N=748)	30	29	-1
Years of Education			
Less than 11 years (N=392)	56	51	-5
12 (HSG) (N=462)	30	32	2
13 or more (N=569)	30	25	-5

*See note to Table 5.

ers moving in the opposite direction from what the cultivation hypothesis would predict. For Table 6, where the number of nonviewers is greater because the item is available for two years, seven of the nine comparisons (though smaller in magnitude) again run in the "wrong" direction. Comparing the "cultivation differentials"[9] here (column 3) to those reported by the Annenberg group for the same items (but with different viewing categories), we see that the sign of the percentage differences in most rows reverses dramatically: *The interpretation by Gerbner et al. that heavy viewers are more likely to give the "television answer" than light viewers because they see more television is confounded by the (column 3) figures showing that nonviewers are more likely to give the "television answer" as well.*

This finding is not restricted to these illustrative examples; it is replicated within categories of each of these single controls across other relevant items in the NORC General Social Survey. Included here are six of the nine rows for both of the remaining two Anomia items reported by Gerbner et al. (1978: 203)[11] and for the item, "Do you think that most people would try to take advantage of you if they got a chance or would they try to be fair?" (reported in Gerbner et al., 1977, and available for two years of the NORC surveys).

In addition, for two unreported sets of items, one on the 1977 NORC survey and the other on 1977 and 1978, nonviewers remain far more disposed than light viewers to what we estimate Gerbner et al. would say is the answer to be expected from respondents most exposed to television.

The first set of items taps attitudes toward suicide. Respondents were asked if "a person has a right to end his or her own life if this person (a) has an incurable disease; (b) has gone bankrupt; (c) has dishonored his or her family, or (d) is tired of living and ready to die." Whereas a fair inference from the Violence Profiles is that television viewing "cultivates" doubts about life's sanctity and raises fear levels about the likelihood of being a victim, we find that both television nonviewers and extreme viewers are the *least likely* to see any of these circumstances as justifying the taking of one's own life. Comparing the percentages of nonviewers approving any form of suicide with those of light viewers, overall and by age, sex, and education, nonviewers are persistently and consistently more negative in their evaluation.[12] The second set of items consists of six questions seeking to measure if the respondent is "alienated" and one similar to the Anomia items discussed earlier. Nonviewers and light viewers divide equally here, with the majority of rows for three of the "Alienation" tables showing the percentage of "alienated" nonviewers to be greater than the corresponding percentage for light viewers.[13] For the remaining three items, the direction reverses such that in a majority of the nine rows, the percentage of light viewers providing the "television answer" is higher than the corresponding percentage of nonviewers.[14]

In sum, we have reviewed 18 items in the NORC data set to see if viewers of one to two hours of television daily provide the "television response" more frequently than nonviewers, and find they do not across 13 (72%) of the 18 items. Each was examined, following Gerbner et al.'s example, with controls placed on age, sex, and education, singly. For six of the seven items reported by Gerbner et al. as providing support for the "cultivation hypothesis," nonviewers more often gave a "mean world" response than did the light viewers, with whom their responses were averaged by the Annenberg group.[15] For seven of the 10 remaining items reported here for the first time, the percentage of nonviewers providing the "television answer" also was greater.[16] All of the attitude items we have examined in the NORC General Social Survey are reported here, whether or not responses to them undermine or lend support to the cultivation hypothesis. If there are more and they are not reported here, their theoretical relevance to the television item has not occurred to us.

TELEVISION'S EXTREME VIEWERS

At the opposite end of the viewing hours distribution for television's heaviest viewers, the "cultivation hypothesis" requires that the percentages providing the "television" or "mean world" answers for these items be higher than for "light," "medium," and nonviewers. Gerbner et al. define "heavy" viewers as all persons reporting they watch four to 24 hours daily. In this section, we examine how well NORC data support this hypothesis by subdividing their "heavy" viewing category into two groups—"heavy," now recoded as four to seven hours, and "extreme," recorded as eight or more. Extreme viewers, as defined here, comprise four percent of the entire sample (about the same proportion as nonviewers), and attain an N of 173 wherever the three years of General Social Surveys asking the TV use item can be combined. Just as nonviewers are one standard deviation below the mean of 2.9 hours for the entire sample, these extreme viewers fall beyond one standard deviation above the mean. The questions we will pose are (1) How consistently are extreme viewers more likely to provide "television answers" than heavy viewers? and (2) How consistently do heavy and extreme viewers provide responses different from light, medium and nonviewers and in the expected (that is, "mean world") direction?

Table 7 shows that the demographic character of television's heavy and extreme viewers is clear cut and unambiguous. Seventy-two percent of the extreme and 62% of heavy viewers are women. Two thirds (67%) of the extreme and half of the heavy viewers are housewives or retired workers. Forty-one percent of the extreme and 36% of heavy viewers report their health as "fair" or "poor." Not only are people in these categories undestandably more "available" for television-viewing than most; they are also likely to be included disproportionately among the 40% of Americans engaged in viewing as a secondary activity (Robinson, 1969). For example, doing housework or other things while the set is on defines viewing as a secondary activity rather than as the primary focus of the viewer's attention. Secondary viewing also is widely reported to be found disproportionately among those income and status groups which also constitute television's heavy and extreme viewers.

Television's heavy and extreme viewers also are disproportionately black (15% and 24%, respectively), uneducated (43% and 58%, respectively, without a high school degree), and report relatively high self-identification as lower class (8% and 13%, respectively). While heavy viewers do not differ noticeably from all others on family income or self-

TABLE 7
Background Characteristics of Respondents by Amount of Television-Viewing Percentages (numbers in parentheses)

Amount of Television Viewing

	Overall (Sample Mean)	Extreme (8 hrs & over)	Heavy (4-7 hrs)	Medium (3 hrs)	Light (1-2 hrs)	Nonviewer (0 hrs)
AGE						
Under 30	26 (1177)	42 (72)	30 (551)	25 (226)	23 (473)	26 (55)
30-54	43 (1974)	30 (51)	34 (400)	44 (393)	49 (1032)	47 (98)
55 and over	31 (1385)	29 (50)	36 (424)	30 (270)	42 (585)	26 (56)
	100	100	100	100	100	100
SEX						
Male	44 (2001)	27 (47)	38 (448)	43 (386)	49 (1025)	45 (95)
Female	56 (2535)	72 (126)	62 (727)	57 (503)	51 (1065)	55 (114)
RACE						
White	89 (4007)	76 (131)	85 (995)	90 (798)	92 (1900)	88 (183)
Black	11 (494)	24 (41)	15 (175)	10 (85)	8 (169)	12 (24)
EDUCATION						
11 years or less	35 (1576)	58 (100)	43 (505)	35 (311)	29 (599)	29 (61)
12 years	34 (1543)	31 (53)	38 (443)	36 (317)	33 (683)	23 (47)
13 years or more	31 (1401)	11 (19)	19 (223)	29 (257)	39 (802)	48 (100)

TABLE 7 (Continued)

	Overall (Sample Mean)	Extreme (8 hrs & over)	Heavy (4-7 hrs)	Medium (3 hrs)	Light (1-2 hrs)	Nonviewer (0 hrs)
FAMILY INCOME						
Under $5,000	17 (714)	40 (62)	22 (237)	15 (119)	12 (242)	27 (54)
$5,000-$9,999	22 (940)	26 (41)	28 (301)	23 (189)	19 (366)	22 (43)
$10,000-$14,999	22 (912)	21 (32)	22 (238)	22 (180)	22 (423)	20 (39)
$15,000-$24,999	27 (1131)	10 (16)	22 (262)	29 (235)	29 (575)	22 (43)
$25,000 and over	13 (548)	3 (5)	6 (70)	12 (97)	18 (357)	10 (19)
WORK STATUS						
Working full time	47 (2102)	9 (16)	51 (362)	47 (414)	58 (1202)	52 (108)
Working part time	9 (392)	7 (12)	7 (85)	9 (78)	9 (195)	9 (19)
Keeping house	25 (1132)	54 (92)	36 (428)	25 (220)	17 (331)	20 (41)
Retired	11 (473)	13 (22)	14 (163)	11 (94)	8 (177)	8 (17)
School	3 (122)	1 (5)	3 (36)	3 (21)	3 (52)	3 (8)
Unemployed, temporarily out of work	5 (241)	10 (18)	6 (73)	6 (49)	5 (94)	4 (7)
HEALTH						
Excellent	32 (963)	17 (19)	25 (266)	29 (177)	38 (518)	36 (43)
Good	40 (1212)	42 (48)	40 (325)	43 (259)	40 (536)	37 (44)
Fair	21 (630)	30 (34)	26 (209)	21 (127)	18 (241)	16 (19)
Poor	7 (201)	11 (12)	10 (79)	6 (39)	4 (59)	10 (12)
Self Reported HAPPINESS						
Very happy	34 (1536)	28 (48)	33 (382)	32 (283)	35 (742)	39 (81)
Pretty happy	55 (2459)	53 (92)	54 (637)	56 (499)	54 (1129)	49 (102)
Not too happy	12 (521)	19 (33)	13 (151)	12 (103)	10 (209)	12 (25)
Self Reported Class Identification						
Lower class	5 (222)	13 (22)	8 (91)	4 (34)	3 (64)	5 (11)
Working class	48 (2164)	47 (81)	50 (582)	54 (482)	45 (928)	44 (91)
Middle class	44 (1992)	37 (64)	41 (475)	39 (348)	49 (1007)	48 (98)
Upper class	3 (135)	3 (5)	2 (25)	3 (23)	4 (77)	2 (5)

SOURCE: NORC General Social Survey, cumulative for 1975, 1977 and 1978.
*Percentages for each category and within each column add to 100%, or deviate slightly due to rounding to the nearest integer.

reported general unhappiness, television's extreme viewers are noticeably different, with 40% reporting family incomes of $5000 or less and 19% reporting that they are unhappy. Also of interest here is the NORC interviewers' collective judgment that among the minority of respondents who least understood the questions asked them, people reporting four or more hours of daily television viewing were 40% less likely than light viewers to comprehend the questions.

The cultivation hypothesis proposes that persons exposed to the largest amount of television will provide "television answers" to survey items more often than persons exposed to TV fewer hours per day. By subdividing the Annenberg group's heavy viewer category, which collapsed 4-24 hours of viewing per day into heavy (4-7) and extreme (8 or more), it becomes possible to examine these groups separately to see if the responses of the extreme viewers go in the expected (television answer) direction. As with the comparisons between nonviewers and light viewers, we are inquiring into the logic of collapsing both into a single category (heavy) and expect that the mean scores of each group on the same items may vary substantially.

The responses of heavy and extreme viewers on the same 18 items reported in the nonviewer-light viewer comparisons are analyzed in this section. Following Gerbner et al.'s format in the Violence Profiles, we compared the percentage of heavy and extreme viewers providing the television answer with each question—for both groups (overall) and also when the controls of age, sex, and educaton are applied singly. If the percentage of extreme viewers providing the television answer is greater than that of heavy viewers (4-7 hours), its direction supports the expectations of the cultivation hypothesis. Where the percentage of viewers exposed to eight or more hours of television and providing the television response is *lower* than that for viewers of four to seven hours daily, its direction runs opposite to the expectations of the hypothesis. Each of the tables generated by this procedure has nine rows: If the absolute percentage for extreme viewers is higher in five or more rows of each table, we interpret the item as supporting the hypothesis.[17]

On the 18 NORC items described earlier, extreme viewers provide the television answer *less often* than heavy viewers for a majority of the rows in 11 (61%) of the 18 tables. These are: two of the three "mean world" items employed by Gerbner et al. (on whether people are helpful, and on if they can be trusted); the item "fear of walking within one mile from home" employed by Gerbner et al.; the item on whether there are circumstances justifying a man's punching an adult male (this item and those immediately following are not reported by Gerbner et al.); three of the four items tapping attitude toward suicide (types 1, 2 and 3); and four of the items tapping alienation (numbers 2, 3, 5, and 6). On six other items (33%), extreme viewers provided the television response more often than heavy viewers. These were the three Anomia items (on the "lot of the average man," "bringing children into the world," and public officials being indifferent) employed by Gerbner et al.; one of the three "mean world" items ("people try to be fair"), also employed by Gerbner et al.; and one each of the suicide (type 4) and alienation (number 1) items.[18]

By breaking out the nonviewers and extreme viewers from the categories into which they were collapsed by the Annenberg group, we have shown that the cultivation hypothesis receives strikingly little support from the two groups of viewers by whom television's "lessons" and "messages" should be most strongly reflected. *Nonviewers gave the television answer more often than those viewing one to two hours daily, and the extreme viewers gave the television answer less often than those viewing four to seven hours per day.* The fundamental weakness of the Annenberg group's coding of viewing categories and its interpretation is perhaps best illustrated in Table 8. Here we see not only that the percentage of respondents endorsing the use of physical violence generally *decreases* as we move from the light to heavy viewing categories; but also

TABLE 8

Percentage Giving "Television Answer" (Answering "Yes") to Question of Whether There are Any Circumstances in which They Would Approve of Someone Hitting an Adult Male

	NONVIEWERS	LIGHT	MEDIUM	HEAVY	EXTREME	GAMMA
Overall (N=2875)	72	71	72	63	60	.13 **
Controlling for:						
AGE						
Under 30 (N=793)	76	75	76	70	60	.13 *
30-54 (N=1238)	79	74	78	68	74	.07 **
55 and older (N=844)	56	62	58	51	44	.15 **
SEX						
Male (N=1253)	71	72	73	65	46	.11 *
Female (N=1622)	73	71	71	61	63	.14 **
EDUCATION						
11 years or less (N=946)	46	58	60	54	47	.05
12 years (N=997)	74	72	78	70	77	.00
13 years or more (N=924)	84	80	79	66	67	.21 **

*p ≤ .05 (tau); **p ≤ .01 (tau)

that it is the *extreme* viewers who disapprove most of the idea, and the *nonviewers* who are most likely to embrace such "aggression." These outcomes clearly provide no support for the assertion that television cultivates a higher tolerance for violent acts—which Gerbner et al. argued earlier in their coding as the television answer, the response by children that "it's almost always alright to hit someone if you are mad at them."

Up to this point we have reanalyzed items from the NORC data set reported by the Annenberg group and presented others asked on one or more of these surveys, all in the same statistical framework set up by Gerbner et al. in the Violence Profiles. In none of these instances have two (or more) statistical controls been placed on any item in the surveys, nor have a number of relevant and available variables appeared consistently (or at all) as single controls. We now expand the reanalysis of the NORC data to include multiple controls.

MULTIVARIATE ANALYSIS AND THE ISSUE OF CAUSALITY

Throughout the corpus of Violence Profiles, the Annenberg researchers have sought to distinguish and separate the concept of causality from cultivation while simultaneously employing the language of causal analysis and its assumptions. The following excerpts, from three different years' Profiles, illustrate this ambiguity by moving from an argument eschewing causality straight into the framework and rhetoric of statistical language associated with the search for causal relations.

> Cultivation analysis is the study of what is usually called effects or impact. . . . We consider the latter terms inappropriate to the study of broad cultural influences. The "effects" of a pervasive medium upon the composition and structure of the symbolic environment are subtle, complex, and

intermingled with other influences. Also, the concept of causation, borrowed from simpler experimental studies in the physical and biological sciences, is not fully applicable to the steady flow of images and messages that comprise much contemporary popular culture [Gerbner et al., 1978: 193].

Heavy viewing is part and parcel of a complex syndrome which also includes lower education, lower mobility, lower aspirations, higher anxieties, and other class, age, and sex related characteristics. We assume, indeed, that viewing helps to hold together and cultivate elements of that syndrome. But it does more than that. *Television viewing also makes a separate and independent contribution to the "biasing" of conceptions of social reality within most age, sex, educational, and other groupings, including those presumably most "immune" to its effects* [Gerbner and Gross, 1976: 191; italics added].

These findings provide considerable support for the conclusion that heavy television viewers perceive social reality differently from light television viewers, even when other factors are held constant. There is considerable variation between groups in the scope and magnitude of these patterns: the extent of television's contribution is mediated, enhanced, or diminished by powerful personal, social and cultural variables, as well as by other information sources. Yet the relationships remain positive in almost every case. The amount of viewing makes a consistent difference in the responses [Gerbner et al., 1979: 193].

The first statement reflects a misunderstanding of causal reasoning, as conventionally employed in social science. Both "causal" and "cultivation" analysts should find no difficulty agreeing that observed differences can be subtle and that, while differences among groups may not be statistically significant, data may yield patterns that are real and consequential. While television's effects may indeed be complex and subtle, the use of survey data presupposes a minimal level of shared assumptions about the nature of evidence in empirical research. If only to counter the suggestion that an observed relationship is spurious, the areas of shared agreement already include the use of control variables (compare statements two and three) and the ideas that certain events are prior to others and that their occurrence is patterned. In short, by seeming to reject the relevance of "causal" analysis, the Annenberg group understates the conceptual common ground between causal and cultivation analysis and obscures the degree to which both are bound by the same rules of evidence before either can claim empirical support.

To garner such support, cultivation analysis has consistently employed the logic of introducing the single controls of age, sex, and education on the relationship between television-viewing and selected dependent variables. Since all agree that relationships of this sort are indeed complex, this is clearly an instance for which multiple controls are needed for reliable tests of hypotheses. In this section, we extend the analysis to include multiple controls such as age, sex, and education taken simultaneously, and by examining the evidence for arguing (in statement two) that television-viewing exerts a "separate and independent contribution to" (or influence or effect on) "conceptions of social reality within most age, sex, educational, and other groupings." To so assert, one must go on to show that viewing actually adds to the amount of variance explained, that this continues to hold up (as in statements two and three) after the introduction of multiple controls, and that the adjusted percentages by viewing category are different and in the direction predicted by the cultivation hypothesis. Beyond that, in order to substantiate causal or cultivation inferences about any discovered relationship, it is important to carefully examine the beta coefficients yielded in regression analyses.

Multivariate analyses of the statistical relation between television-viewing and items tapping fear, anomia, alienation, and attitudes toward suicide, strangers, and actual physical violence are shown in Tables 10-16. The basic findings are summarized in Table 9. Following Gerbner et al.'s (1978) example of combining "mean world" items into an index, we have clustered these and the multiple questions on anomia, alienation, and suicide, respectively, into four indexes. The 16 items comprising them and reported individually earlier are now included in one of these four indexes.[19] The remaining two questions—on fear of walking alone within one mile from home and attitude toward physical violence—are still shown separately.

In Tables 10-16, the grand mean for the entire sample on the dependent variables is displayed at the top. Each table's "unadjusted" column shows the deviation from the grand mean for each category of respondents providing the "television answer" for the dependent variable, by hours of viewing, years of school, sex, and age.[20] The first adjusted column shows how much this deviation is narrowed for each of these predictor variables when controlling for the other three simultaneously. For each table these controls are television-viewing, education, sex, and age, selected to coincide with the Annenberg group's presentation of these (as single controls) in most of the tables they present. In the second adjusted column we add race as an additional variable of conceptual interest to see if its introduction further narrows the percentage differences obtained when the others are simultaneously controlled.[21] For added clarity, Table 11 reformats the same findings on anomia by amount of TV-viewing contained in Table 10. The unadjusted row presents the grand mean, followed by the percentage of viewers providing "television answers" to the anomia items on the General Social Survey. The adjusted row shows how the apparent effect of television-viewing disappears after controlling for age, sex, education, and race simultaneously. The percentages in each row are easily derived by adding the grand mean and the deviations from it for each viewing category presented in the unadjusted and second adjusted columns for TV-viewing in Table 10.

The R^2 statistics at the bottom of the adjusted columns in Tables 10-16 tell how much variation in the attitude items is explained by all of the control variables taken together. For each of these "predictors" separately, two indicators of its relative effect are the Eta (N) and Beta (B) statistics displayed at the bottom row of each control variable. An indicator of each predictor's relative contribution to explained variance is the percentage spread between each variable's component categories compared with the same differential in the other three. The "High-Low Differential" column shows the percentage spread for each variable, and notes the one (or two, if tied) with the largest differential. (If this does not exceed two percentage points, nothing is circled). This statistic is based on (and includes) the "cultivation differential" developed by Gerbner et al. to report the absolute differences between the percentage of heavy and light viewers giving the "television answer" to "scary" or "mean world" items.

In Table 9's summary of these analyses, we see that (1) *the total amount of variance explained (column one) by all four controls, taken together, is consistently minimal, ranging from .08 to .18 and exceeding 10 percent in only three of six instances.* In the context of such low R^2 findings television viewing's minimal relative effect—across all of the dependent variables—is especially significant: It clearly refutes the Annenberg group's assertion of a "separate and independent" effect and severely undermines their conceptual argument. Table 9 shows television-viewing to be a lesser among equals, whose total combination is itself strikingly unimpressive. (2) Television viewing's standardized dummy regression coefficients (Beta) range from .03 to .08 across all of the dependent variables. That variable and sex are consistently the weakest contributors to the amount of variance explained by the control variables. (3) Of all the potential effects, only education shows any consistent independent strength as a predictor. This is evidenced by its relatively large Betas and the percentage spreads between its "high" and "low" categories after adjusting for the other predictor variables. It is instructive to compare them with the cultivation differentials for television-viewing (column

TABLE 9

**Summary Statistics on Television Viewing's "Separate and Independent Contribution"
to the Variance Explained Below**

Variable	Multiple R^2 for Television Viewing, Education, Sex, and Race	High-Low Differential for Television Viewing and Linearity (Y=Yes)	High-Low Differential for Largest Contributor to R^2	Beta for Education	Adjusted Beta of Television Viewing
Alienation	0.08	-2.42 (No)	-20.64 (Education)	.26	0.06
Anomia	0.13	-2.36 (No)	-28.50 (Education)	.32	0.08
Fear	0.18	-6.13 (No)	39.68 (Sex)	.01	0.03
Actual Violence	0.07	-3.33 (No)	16.67 (Education)	.15	0.05
Mean World	0.12	3.81 (No)	-25.03 (Education) 22.19 (Race)	.25	0.06
Suicide	0.07	-6.91 (Y)	10.91 (Education	.19	0.06

2), which they dwarf. Education's high-low differentials and Betas are the highest, with those of race and age in the middle and television and sex (except for fear of walking alone) typically the lowest. (4) The "high-low" or "cultivation" differential for television viewers runs in the opposite direction, after adjustment, to what Gerbner et al. assert; that is, the negative sign in five of the six cases means that television's heaviest viewers provide the "television answer" in smaller percentages than nonviewers.

Furthermore, the (No) following the differentials in five of the six instances shows that there is no pattern of evidence where the mean percentage of respondents providing "television answers" increases monotonically with hours viewed. Most frequently, it is light viewers who least often yield "mean" or "scary" world responses. Both nonviewers and medium viewers generally provide higher percentages of "television answers." After adjusting for the other variables, the percentage of heavy and extreme viewers giving these responses follows no pattern at all. Were the cultivation differential computed by subtracting the percentage of light from heavy viewers, as Gerbner et al. have done, the resulting improvement in size and sign for the hypothesis would be due largely to the marked deviation in the response of light viewers from all other viewing categories in the direction away from the "television answer." This is reflected in the general finding of nonlinearity in the responses of all categories of television-watching, including those of nonviewers. In the one instance where the cultivation differential is linear, it moves in the direction *opposite* to that proposed by the cultivation hypothesis: Here, the percentage of heavy and extreme viewers opposed to actual physical violence remains higher than that of light and nonviewers, even after the multiple controls are introduced. For only one scale, the "mean world" index, is the sign of the high-low differential positive, in the direction proposed by the cultivation hypothesis.

Tables 10-16 also yield additional information on the relation of television and these "controls" to the dependent variables. Most importantly, we can see that the final, adjusted breakdowns on television-viewing give no support to the Annenberg group's claims on five of the six dependent variables. Only one, the "mean world" index, shows some results which are linear in the hypothesized direction. To list only the most salient anomalies to the cultivation hypothesis: (1) The Heaviest viewers give the television answer *less* frequently than nonviewers. The "cultivation differential," which we adopt from Gerbner et al.'s practice of subtracting the mean score of the highest viewing category from that of the lowest, is *negative* for five of the six dependent variables. (2) Even if we drop these two extreme viewing categories and compute the cultivation differential as Gerbner et al. do, by subtracting the scores of light viewers from those of heavy viewers, we still get negative differentials for three of six dependent variables (fear of walking alone at night, attitude toward actual violence, and attitude toward suicide). (3) For three of the six dependent variables, alienation, fear, and attitude toward suicide, it is the heaviest viewers who give the television answer the *least* often. (4) For two of the six dependent variables, anomia and attitude toward suicide, it is nonviewers who give the television answer more often than any other group. (5) For two of the dependent variables, attitude toward actual violence and attitude toward suicide, we find nearly perfect monotonic *reductions* in the percentage of television answers across viewing categories when adjustments are made; that is, there is a linear relationship between television-viewing and so-called "television answers" which runs *directly contrary* to the cultivation. hypothesis.

Although the percentage of blacks in the sample is small, thus mitigating the possible effect of race as a suppressor variable, differences between blacks and whites on all

(text continues on page 574)

TABLE 10
MCA of Anomia by TV-Viewing (TV), Education (E), Sex (S), Age (A), and Race (R)

Grand Mean = 53.12

Variable	N	Unadjusted Deviation	Adjusted for TV, E, S, A	Adjusted for TV, E, S, A, R	Hi-Lo Differential
TV Viewing					
NV	54	2.45	4.94	5.37	
L	655	-5.80	-5.25	-5.10	
M	284	3.80	2.90	3.09	
H	353	5.42	2.39	2.01	
EX	52	12.90	5.72	5.01	-2.36
		Eta=.16	Beta=.08	Beta=.03	
Education					
11 years or less	494	14.69	14.79	14.29	
12 years	478	-2.22	-2.69	-2.30	
13 years or more	426	-14.55	-14.09	-14.21	28.50
		Eta=.33	Beta=.32	Beta=.32	
Sex					
M	649	-1.97	-1.30	-1.09	
F	749	1.70	1.13	.94	
		Eta=.05	Beta=.03	Beta=.03	
Age					
Under 30	343	1.50	4.58	2.71	
30-54	637	-2.94	-1.37	4.38	
55 and over	418	3.26	-1.68	-8.99	11.70
		Eta=.08	Beta=.07	Beta=.07	
			$R^2 = 0.122$	$R^2 = .13$	

TABLE 11

Alternative Format for MCA of Anomia by Television Viewing, Education, Sex, and Race

BY VIEWING CATEGORY

	Overall Grand Mean	Nonviewers	Light	Medium	Heavy	Extreme
UNADJUSTED:*	53	56	47	57	58	66
ADJUSTED FOR:**	53	58	50	56	55	56

Age
Race
Sex
Education

together

*Unadjusted roughly supports cultivation hypothesis.
**Adjusted wipes out the "television effect."

TABLE 12
MCA of Alienation by TV-Viewing (TV), Education (E), Sex (S), Age (A), and Race (R)

Grand Mean = 55.77

Variable	N	Unadjusted Deviation	Adjusted for TV E, S, A	Adjusted for TV, E, S, A, R	Hi-Lo Differential
NV	74	-1.48	-0.41	-0.25	
L	579	-2.8?	-.34	-1.28	
M	230	0.09	-.43	-0.15	
H	291	5.23	2.44	3.16	
EX	47	3.80	-.99	-2.67	-2.42
		Eta=.11	Beta=.06	Beta=.06	
Education					
≤11	360	0.06	10.51	10.50	
12	440	1.50	1.05	1.11	
≥13	421	-10.17	-10.10	-10.14	20.64
		Eta=.26	Beta=.26	Beta=.26	
Sex					
M	526	0.09	1.27	1.07	
F	695	-0.07	-0.97	-0.81	1.88
		Eta=.03	Beta=.04	Beta=.03	
Age					
<30	338	3.79	4.76	4.67	
30-54	535	-2.44	-0.97	-1.14	
≥55	348	0.07	-3.11	-2.79	7.46
		Eta=.08	Beta=.10	Beta=.09	
Race					
W	1095	-0.81		-0.46	
B	126	7.06		4.01	4.47
		Eta=.08 R^2=0.04		Beta=.04 R^2=0.082	

569

TABLE 13
MCA of Fear by TV-Viewing (TV), Education (E), Sex (S), Age (A), and Race (R)

Grand Mean = 45.03

Variable	N	Unadjusted Deviation	Adjusted for TV, E, S, A	Adjusted for TV, E, S, A, R	Hi-Lo Differential
TV Viewing					
NV	60	-.03	1.17	.84	
L	698	-2.19	.85	1.10	
M	307	-1.05	-1.90	-1.64	
H	386	4.46	.39	.02	
EX	57	2.34	-4.02	-5.29	-6.13
		Eta=.06	Beta=.03	Beta=.03	
Education					
< 11	551	2.89	1.33	.56	
12	505	.12	-1.35	-.82	
≥ 13	452	-3.65	-.12	.24	.32
		Eta=.05	Beta=.02	Beta=.01	
Sex					
M	684	-21.93	-21.91	-21.75	
F	824	18.20	18.19	17.93	39.68
		Eta=.40	Beta=.40	Beta=.40	
Age					
< 30		-4.42	-3.10	-3.69	
30-54		-3.70	-3.47	-3.46	
≥ 55		8.84	7.47	7.85	10.95
		Eta=.05	Beta=.02	Beta=.11	
Race					
W	1323	-2.24		-2.01	
B	171	17.33	Beta=.02	15.56	
		Eta=.13		Beta=-.11	R^2=.18

TABLE 14
MCA of Attitude Toward Actual Violence by TV-Viewing (TV), Education (E), Sex (S), Age (A), and Race (R)

Grand Mean = 68.78

Variable	N	Unadjusted Deviation	Adjusted for TV, E, S, F	Adjusted for TV, E, S, A, R	Hi-Lo Differential
TV Viewing					
NV	138	2.96	0.75	.39	
L	1320	2.51	1.10	.78	
M	560	3.36	3.32	2.93	
H	740	-6.22	-3.82	-3.24	
EX	109	-9.15	-5.37	-2.94	-3.33
		Eta=.09	Beta=.06	Beta=.05	
Education					
≤ 11	946	-12.97	-10.51	-9.55	
12	997	3.73	3.08	2.48	
≥ 13	924	9.25	7.43	7.12	16.67
		Eta=.20	Beta=.16	Beta=.15	
Sex					
M	1250	0.82	-0.09	-.13	
F	1617	-0.63	0.07	.10	
		Eta=.02	Beta=.00	Beta=.00	0.23
Age					
< 30	793	4.9	2.38	2.71	
30-54	1236	4.8	3.89	4.38	
≥ 55	838	-11.4	-7.99	-8.99	11.70
		Eta=.16	Beta=.11	Beta=.13	
Race					
W	2550	1.91		1.62	
B	298	-16.31		-13.87	11.70
		Eta=.12		Beta=.10	

$R^2 = .068$

TABLE 15

MCA of Mean World by TV-Viewing (TV), Education (E), Sex (S), Age (A), and Race (R)

Grand Mean = 48.24

Variable	N	Unadjusted Deviation	Adjusted for TV, E, S, A	Adjusted for TV, E, S, A, R	Hi-Lo Differential
TV Viewing					
NV	129	-6.38	-3.64	-3.23	
L	1233	-4.68	-2.59	-2.12	
M	527	2.43	2.05	2.53	
H	697	6.14	3.19	2.35	
EX	106	9.78	3.48	0.58	3.81
		Eta=.13	Beta=.07	Beta=.06	
Education					
≤ 11	897	13.19	14.01	12.96	
12	955	-1.48	-2.18	-1.55	
≥ 13	840	-12.40	-12.45	-12.07	-25.03
		Eta=.26	Beta=.27	Beta=.25	
Sex					
M	1182	0.66	1.92	1.75	
F	1510	-0.52	-1.50	-1.37	-3.12
		Eta=.01	Beta=.04	Beta=.04	
Age					
< 30	738	6.17	8.41	8.08	
30-54	1155	-4.43	-2.79	-3.29	
≥ 55	799	0.70	-3.73	-2.72	-10.8
		Eta=.11	Beta=.13	Beta=.12	
Race					
W	2418	-2.76		-2.26	
B	274	24.39		19.93	22.19
		Eta=.20		Beta=.17	
			$R^2=0.087$	$R^2=0.116$	

TABLE 16
MCA of Attitude Toward Suicide by TV-Viewing (TV), Education (E), Sex (S), Age (A), and Race (R)

Grand Mean = 16.26

Variable	N	Unadjusted Deviation	Adjusted for TV, E, S, A	Adjusted for TV, E, S, A, R	Hi-Lo Differential
TV Viewing					
NV	145	6.84	4.78	4.74	
L	1365	1.59	0.74	.62	
M	570	-0.43	-0.03	-.08	
H	711	-3.43	-1.99	-1.75	
EX	111	-4.33	-2.47	-2.17	
		Eta=.10	Beta=.06	Beta=.06	-6.91
Education					
≤11	983	-4.69	-3.71	-3.44	
12	1006	-3.12	-3.16	-3.36	
≥13	913	8.49	7.47	7.51	
		Eta .22	Beta .19	Beta=.19	10.91
Sex					
M	1270	2.57	1.83	1.72	
F	1632	-2.00	-1.43	-1.33	
		Eta=.09	Beta=.0	Beta=.06	3.05
Age					
< 30	747	4.22	3.58	3.87	
30-54	1282	-0.02	-0.68	-.66	
≥55	873	-3.58	-2.06	-2.34	
		Eta=.11	Beta=.0	Beta=.09	6.21
Race					
W	2557	.70		.63	
B	318	-5.63		-5.06	
		Eta=.08		Beta=.07	

$R^2=.065$ $R^2=.063$

dependent variables are sharp. Interestingly, the black/ white percentage difference does not run in the same direction with respect to the "television answers" in each case. While racial differences are striking for all dependent variables, in the case of attitude toward actual violence (Table 14) and attitude toward suicide (Table 16), blacks give the television answer with considerably less frequency than whites. This suggests that the sentiments tapped by the various attitude questions are quite distinct and that the relationship of attitudes to socioeconomic status, as well as to television-viewing, is more complex than in the Annenberg group's formulation. The impact of race on the "mean world" index, the only one of the dependent variables which gives any support to the cultivation hypothesis, is also of interest. This can be seen by comparing the first and second columns of adjusted deviations with respect to television-viewing in Table 15. In the first column of adjustments, before race had been added, there is a monotonic increase in mean world attitudes across viewing levels. Once race is controlled, the percentages of mean world answers by those in the heavy and extreme categories drop below those of medium viewers, with the percentages of extreme viewers being lower than those respondents in the heavy viewing category. If we take race as a rough proxy for neighorhood crime rate, this finding underscores and supports Doob and MacDonald's (1979) discovery that controlling for local crime rates undercuts the presumed effect of television on fear of victimization.

While sex has a negligible effect on most dependent variables, it is not surprising to find that its effect swamps that of all other independent variables on fear of walking alone at night. Once controls are added, the already weak relationship between television-viewing and fear collapses, and it is evidently sex which is most responsible for this. Considerable disparities exist across age groupings on several dependent variables, but these are not consistently in the same direction, nor are they linear. The oldest respondents (55 and over) give the lowest number of television answers for four of the six dependent variables but are also by far the highest on fear of walking alone at night, again suggesting that objective vulnerability is the only operative factor in this fear.

CONCLUSION

This article has systematically analyzed responses to the National Opinion Research Center's General Social Survey claimed by George Gerbner et al. to support the assertion that television-viewing "cultivates" misconceptions of the "real world." In Part I of this report, I have shown how the assertion is found severely wanting when standard statistical techniques employed in social science research are applied to these data. Across most of the attitude items reported by the Annenberg group, as well as for others they chose not to report, the effect of television-viewing is clearly minimal when the responses of nonviewers and extreme viewers are analyzed separately. When two or more controls were applied simultaneously, we found the "separate and independent" effect of television viewing to be nonexistent.

A more serious issue raised by the results of the multivariate analysis is that the total amount of variance explained by all of the predictor variables—that is, their combined ability to explain respondents' attitudes—is usually less than .10 and never above 15%. Since most social scientists find such low R^2 statistics evidence of nonfindings and clearly not reportable as positive results, one cannot help being impressed at the minimal contribution of television-viewing to even this low amount of explained variance. (In relative terms, education explained the most.) Indeed, if all of them combined explain so little, and we found television-viewing to add virtually nothing to the others before it, to then argue that these data *support* the cultivation hypothesis is itself an ironic distortion of the "real world" of data analysis.

Another serious problem addressed in this report was the lack of comparability between the items and samples treated by Gerbner et al. as cumulative empirical evidence in their efforts to build a case for cultivation effects. The lack of consistent results within and between samples suggests more a pattern of randomness than evidence for a linear, or even a monotonic, relationship between television-viewing and perceptions of a "mean" or "scary" world.

Two larger purposes of this reanalysis have been to open a scholarly dialogue on the virtues and defects of the Annenberg group's cultural indicators project, and to point up a need for more and expanded research frameworks to study the role and impact of television in society. Dr. Gerbner's violence profiles have articulated and set the stage for such expanded discussions. His efforts to empirically link content analysis to audience perceptions are rightly regarded as important and systematic contributions to communication research. Nevertheless, the demographic profile of extreme viewers reported here (mainly housewives, the elderly, and those in poor health) suggest viewer availability as a key prior determinant of viewing behavior and as indicative of associated attitude clusters. Combined with the relative absence of cultivation effects found for this viewing category, it is clear that the theory specified by Gerbner et al. is incomplete and needs further development.

The methodology of taking single survey items and their attitudinal correlates needs to be expanded by other investigations focusing on the relation of specific genres and programs to viewer interpretations and perceptions—as Gans did in both *The Urban Villagers* (1962) and in more recent work (1980). The complexity of viewers' perceptions also requires more careful treatment—as provided, for example, in Dorr's (1980) integration of the literature on children and television. Most important, researchers and graduate students must be encouraged to work with and develop alternative frameworks and paradigms since most of the work in the Violence Profiles, as shown here, still awaits replication and support and is best represented as only one among many possible research strategies and designs for studying communications content and effects.

Part II of this report will take up these theoretical issues in more detail and outline one such alternative strategy. In addition, I will complete the analysis of responses in NORC's data set and show that the attitudes of population sub-groups (women, elderly, blacks) are independent of television hours viewed and often move in directions counter to expectations of the "mean world" hypothesis. Also included will be a series of other anomalies, such as findings relating radio-listening to items Gerbner et al. assert tap the "mean" or "scary" world portrayed on television.

NOTES

1. The National Opinion Research Center keeps records of papers and publications making use of its data. NORC has nothing on this in its files, and we are aware of no published or unpublished attempts to reanalyze the Annenberg group's findings with the same data sources they used.

2. There is, of course, a long history of findings and discussion over the documented absence of linkage between the conveyance of specific messages and an awareness by or impact on the intended recipient. The "hypodermic needle" or "magic bullet" model has long been viewed by communication researchers as problematic, due to the intervening filtering mechanisms exerted by selective perception, differential salience, viewer predispositions, and personal influence. For a review of the relevant literature, see DeFleur and Ball-Rokeach (1975).

3. For example, if I watched two hours of morning and evening news, plus two hours of daytime serials and three situation comedies at night, I would appear as a heavy viewer if surveyed by NORC but as light in the CPS data file.

4. When it is employed as a control on TV-viewing, the coding for education varies *within* the analysis of the NORC data. In Gerbner et al. (1978), where NORC and CPS surveys are presented side by side, the breaks for education in the NORC samples appear as either (1) No high school, High School grad, and Some college (pp. 198, 201, 203), or (2) No college and Some college (p. 204). Here, the first two

entries in version 1 are collapsed in version 2. This lack of consistency in coding categories becomes more problematic as we move on to different samples.

5. This problem also arises when Gerbner et al. present correlation coefficients for these very different samples without noting how their differences in composition and size also cast doubt on the significance and comparability of the results. In Profile 8 (1978: 177), for example, a series of partial correlations is presented between amount of television viewed and answers on the attitude items concerning violence and law enforcement. Not surprisingly, the size of the coefficients is highest for the least representative samples (the New York City private school children, the suburban/rural children, and a "quota sample" of adults). They are smallest for the national probability sample (apparently CPS), ranging from .05 to .09, but reported nevertheless as attaining statistical significance—a likely artifact of sample size, for N here is 1627, in contrast to the New York children's N of 133. Results for these very different samples are presented side by side.

6. Within the children's samples reprinted in Table 3, note that the presumed effects are themselves inconsistent and conceivably random. Statistical significance is attained only for girls in the New Jersey school and for boys only in the New York school; for children of *non*-college-educated parents only, in New Jersey, but for children of (at least) some college-educated parents only in New York. The "effects" by age group are similarly contradictory. These inconsistencies actually raise more questions than they purport to answer.

7. The presumption here that a favorable attitude toward actual physical violence constitutes the "television answer" is based on Gerbner et al.'s own coding of the similar items discussed above and inferred from the text accompanying the violence profiles. I do not interpret Table 4 to mean that heavy viewers are therefore more peace-loving than anyone else. The point is more simply that even in terms of the analysis framework set up by Gerbner et al., there are unreported items like this one that severely undermine the case he asserts so vigorously. Since comparisons between samples of children and adults are presented elsewhere in their articles (for example, 1977: 177-178), it is not the age differential which would account for Gerbner et al.'s omission of the NORC items from their reports.

8. For a dramatic illustration of this point, see Gerbner et al.'s (1978: Table 9, p. 198) interpretation of "Percent of Adults Who Would Be Afraid to Walk Alone at Night." Here they separately provide responses to this item by respondents in both the NORC and CPS surveys. In the former, of eight gamma coefficients of association reported where a single control is introduced, all are statistically *insignificant.* The ninth, a zero-order coefficient of .08 for the entire sample (N=1516) is "significant" but must be discounted due to the large N. In the CPS survey, the zero-order coefficient is insignificant as well, as are six out of the eight partial gammas reported. (One colleague has noted that if this table were reported but the text changed, it could persuasively support a case for "no effects.") Our finding, given the pervasive insignificance of the table, is that the same insignificance remains after alternative codings of viewing categories are introduced. When the same single controls are introduced, the frequency of consistent upward movements of the percentage from "light" through "heavy" viewing falls from

three rows out of nine to only one in the nine. The two alternative coding categories employed here were (1) 0 hours = nonviewers, 1 = light, 2-3 = medium, 4-7 = heavy, 8 or more = extreme; and (2) 0 hours = nonviewers, 1-2 hours = light, 3-4 = medium, 5-7 = heavy, 8 or more = extreme.

9. The "cultivation differential" is a measure employed by Gerbner et al. to show the percentage difference obtained by subtracting the percentage of light viewers giving the "television answer" from the percentage of heavy viewers. In column 3 of Tables 5 and 6, we compute the same statistic by subtracting the percentage of nonviewers giving the "television answer" from the percentage of light viewers giving the same response to a particular question. A negative sign means the direction is counter to the expectations of the cultivation hypothesis.

10. Another way to interpret these differences is that if there is *any* pattern of discrepancies between the percentages of nonviewers and light viewers responding to survey items, the two categories should not be combined. By this criterion, if the percentages are different enough, the direction of the response is immaterial. In Table 6, for example, if 48% of nonviewers 55 and older compared with 35% of light viewers in that category had *disagreed* that people look out mostly for themselves, the 13% differential would be seen as arguing against combining them, even though in this instance it would have been the nonviewers whose response was furthest from the "television answer." Similarly, one would then discount instances where their percentages differed only by small magnitudes.

11. "It's hardly fair to bring a child into the world with the way things look for the future." "Most public officials are not really interested in the problems of the average man."

12. The format of these tables (not shown here) is the same as in Tables 5 and 6. For the nine rows in each of four tables for suicide, nonviewers are less favorable than light viewers in (a) eight out of nine rows of three tables and in (b) five out of nine where an incurable disease is listed as the motive. The procedure employed in this part of the reanalysis is further described in the section comparing television's heavy and extreme viewers. See, for example, footnote 1.

13. These three items are:

(1) "The rich get richer and the poor get poorer."
(2) "You're left out of things going on around you."
(3) "The people running the country don't really care what happens to you."

The single controls, applied after showing the "overall" percentages, continue to be age, sex, and education.

14. These three items are:

(1) "What you think doesn't count very much any more."
(2) "Most of the people with power try to take advantage of people like yourself."
(3) "The people in Washington, D.C. are out of touch with the rest of the country."

15. The one item for which nonviewers did not conform to this pattern is: "Generally speaking, would you say that most people can be trusted or that you can't be too careful in dealing with people?"

16. The three (alienation) items for which this did not occur are described in note 15. We have not examined two items from the NORC Survey discussed by Gerbner et al. in Violence Profile 8 (1977). These pertain to the respondent's views on the likelihood of a war within the next ten years and on isolationism. Our main reason for excluding them is that Gerbner et al.'s basis for deriving a "television answer" for them is too obscure for us to feel comfortable in adopting it.

17. The resulting "pattern" of support or nonsupport is thus based on the frequencies of the upward or downwards movement of percentages across 153

rows of 17 tables. The aggregated result is of theoretical significance, given Gerbner et al.'s strong inferences from similar tables in which both extremes of the distribution are distorted. Significant gamma statistics occur in some rows but not others (as in the tables reported by Gerbner et al.). These are omitted here, as they are essentially irrelevant to the search for "patterns" which they claim to have found and which is so central to their argument. While cell sizes, as noted earlier, are far from ideal in some instances, the sheer number and magnitude of the patterns running counter to the cultivation hypothesis, and the conceptual damage they create for the assertion of cultivation effects, outweigh any argument for their exclusion.

18. The actual wording of each question was provided earlier in this article. The item which tied was the fourth alienation question.

19. For four of these items—anomia, alienation, attitudes toward suicide, and attitudes toward strangers—we constructed indexes from groups of questions designed by NORC to measure different dimensions of each attitude. To determine the undimensionality of each set of questions, intercorrelations of index items were inspected using gamma measures. All were sufficient and high. For the three questions comprising our anomia index, the average gamma was .65; for the six questions in the alienation scale, the mean gamma was .61; for the four items in the attitude toward suicide scale, .98; and for the three questions in the index of attitudes toward strangers—or what we will henceforth be calling our "mean world" index following Gerbner et al.'s term for these questions in Violence Profile No. 8 (1977)—the average gamma was .76.

20. If the grand mean is 50 and the mean percentage of nonviewers is 53, the number in the "Unadjusted" column will appear as + 3. In this case, 50% of the total sample would have given the "television answer," while the percentage of nonviewers giving the same response is 53. See Table 11 for an additional illustration of this procedure.

21. We introduce only one additional control here due to restrictions inherent in both cell sizes and the SPSS package's MCA program. Multiple Classification Analysis is a dummy variable regression program designed to correct the predictive power of a given independent variable for each of the other predictors in the model. The technique and its application to survey data are described in Andrews et al. (1972).

REFERENCES

ALDERFER, C. P. (1977) "A critique of Salancik and Pfeffer's examination of need satisfaction theories." Admin. Science Q. 22: 658-669.

ANDREWS, F., J. MORGAN, and J. SONQUIST (1972) Multiple Classification Analysis. Ann Arbor: University of Michigan Survey Research Center.

BOGART, L. (1973) The Age of Television. New York: Unger.

CAPLAN, A. [ed.] (1978) Sociobiology Debate. New York: Harper & Row.

DAVIS, J. A., T. A. SMITH, and C. B. STEPHENSON (1978) General Social Surveys, 1972-1978: Cumulative Codebook. Chicago: National Opinion Research Center.

DeFLEUR, M. L. and S. BALL-ROKEACH (1975) Theories of Mass Communication. New York: Longman.

DOOB, A. and G. E. MacDONALD (1979) "Television viewing and fear of victimization: is the relationship causal?" J. of Social Psychology and Personality 37: 170-179.

DORR, A. (1980) "When I was a child I thought as a child," in S. Withey and R. Abeles (eds.) Television and Social Behavior: Beyond Violence and Children. Hillsdale, NJ: Lawrence Erlbaum.

GANS, H. (1980) "The audience for television and in television research," in S. Withey and R. Abeles (eds.) Television and Social Behavior: Beyond Violence and Children. Hillsdale, NJ: Lawrence Erlbaum.

——— (1962) The Urban Villagers. New York: Free Press.

GERBNER, G. and L. GROSS (1976) "Living with television: the violence profile." J. of Communication 26: 173-199.

——— N. SIGNORIELLI, M. MORGAN, and M. JACKSON-BEECK (1979a) "The demonstration of power: Violence Profile No. 10." J. of Communication 29: 177-196.

——— (1979b) Violence Profile No. 10. Philadelphia: Annenberg School of Communication.

GERBNER, G., L. GROSS, M. JACKSON-BEECK, S. JEFFERIES-FOX, and N. SIGNORIELLI (1978) "Cultural indicators: Violence Profile No. 9." J. of Communication 28: 176-206.

GERBNER, G., L. GROSS, M. F. ELEEY, M. JACKSON-BEECK, S. JEFFRIES-FOX, and N. SIGNORIELLI (1977) "TV Violence Profile No. 8: highlights." J. of Communication 27: 171-180.

HAWKINS, R. and S. PINGREE (1980) "Some processes in the cultivation effect." Communication Research 7: 193-226.

HIMMELWEIT, H., B. SWIFT, and M. E. JAEGER (1980) "The audience as critic: an approach to the study of entertainment," in P. Tannenbaum (ed.) Television Entertainment. Hillsdale, NJ: Lawrence Erlbaum.

JACKSON-BEECK, M. (1977) "The nonviewers: who are they?" J. of Communication 27: 65-72.

KAMIN, L. (1974) The Science and Politics of I.Q. New York: Halsted Press.

MOYNIHAN, D. P. and F. MOSTELLER [ed.] (1972) On Equality of Educational Opportunity. New York: Random House.

NEWCOMB, H. (1978) "Assessing the violence profiles of Gerbner and Gross: a humanistic critique and suggestion." Communication Research 5: 264-282.

ROBINSON, J. (1969) "Television and leisure times: yesterday, today and (maybe) tomorrow." Public Opinion Q. 33: 210-222.

SAHLINS, M. (1977) The Use and Abuse of Biology. Ann Arbor: Univ. of Michigan Press.

SALANCIK, G. R. and J. PFEFFER (1977) "An examination of need satisfaction models of job attitudes." Admin. Science Q. 22: 427-455.

WILSON, E. O. (1975) Sociobiology. Cambridge, MA: Belknap Press.

WOBER, J. M. (1978) "Televised violence and paranoid perception: the view from Great Britain." Public Opinion Q. 42: 315-321.

In an ambitious attempt to synthesize work conducted around the world on the role and effects of television, John P. Murray and Susan Kippax place more than 1000 studies in a comparative-cultural framework. Beginning with a description of world television systems, the article summarizes and analyzes the implications of research for television's impact on daily life and the effects of televised violence. The authors argue that the cultivation analysis perspective associated with George Gerbner may be a promising way to synthesize uses-gratifications and effects approaches for a fuller perspective on future research. Dr. Murray is a scientist and science writer at the Boys Town Center for the Study of Youth Development, Boys Town, Nebraska. Dr. Kippax is Associate Professor of Psychology in the School of Behavioural Sciences at Macquarie University, Sydney, Australia.

32

TELEVISION'S IMPACT ON CHILDREN AND ADULTS
International Perspectives on Theory and Research

John P. Murray and Susan Kippax

I. Introduction

This paper is designed to evaluate television's influence within the social context in which the medium is used. The inclusion of contextual variables is important because it emphasizes the notion that television does not affect the individual in isolation, but that its influence must be seen in terms of the audience member's "construal" of the televised message. How the audience will interpret what it views will depend not only upon the content of the programs but also on the nature of the viewer and the context in which the viewing occurs. The mass media are only one source of meanings in the communication of ideas and these meanings coexist with the ideas and meanings inherent in the individual's social situation—both in the narrow sense of the individual's immediate setting and in the broad sense of the individual's cultural context.

Research on the mass media has occupied the talents and time of a large number of researchers in very many countries around the world. However, there have been very few reviews of the literature which compare the results of the efforts of one country with those of another. This paper is an attempt to overcome this deficiency. We not only review the results of studies conducted in a variety of countries, but we attempt to place those results within the cultural contexts of the countries in which the research has been conducted. The nature of television varies from country to country in terms of such factors as the number of broadcast hours available, whether the medium is publicly or commercially owned, and the characteristics of the program content. So, also, there is variation in the characteristics of the audience and the perspectives and orientation of the researchers. It is our aim to reflect this cultural diversity.

The 16 countries from which we have gathered information are Australia, Austria, Canada, Denmark, Finland, France, Germany, Israel, Italy, Japan, Norway, Poland, Sweden, Switzerland, the United Kingdom, and the United States. Each of these countries has a particular view of the nature of television's influence on the lives of its citizens and yet, to some extent, the research results on which this view is based are relatively similar.

From John P. Murray and Susan Kippax, "From the Early Window to the Late Show: International Trends in the Study of Television's Impact on Children and Adults," L. Berkowitz, ed., *Advances in Experimental Social Psychology, Volume 12,* pp. 253-320. Copyright 1979 by Academic Press, Inc. Reprinted by permission.

The variation in research strategies and theoretical assumptions is quite evident in even the most casual perusal of the cross-national literature. For example, much of the early American research was strongly influenced by learning theory, and particularly social-learning theory. In some of this research there was an overemphasis on the view of the individual as passive rather than active or purposive and the media were seen to affect the individual in a unidirectional rather than in an interactive manner. Later research incorporated societal variables into the framework but often these were reduced to the status of individual variables, such as educational level or socioeconomic status. Similarly, in England and Israel the tendency to emphasize individualistic rather than social perspectives is evident in some aspects of the "uses and gratifications" approach to media research. A basic postulate of this research is that audience members use the media in accordance with the needs that they believe will be satisfied by the media or media content. There is an acceptance of the purposiveness of the individual but the essentially social nature of the media experience is by-passed in as much as these researchers seem to forget that these needs or predispositions of the audience members are socially derived. More recently, in America (Gerbner, 1972; Gerbner & Gross, 1976a, 1976b) and England (McCron, 1976) there has been a move away from the individualistic bias to a social or sociological approach. The mass media are seen to permeate everyday life as major elements in leisure activities. They are also seen as providing information about the wider society as well as establishing a framework of explanations about social and political processes. This framework is not simply a reflection of reality but is, itself, a function of the social, economic, and political contexts within which the media operate. Gerbner and Gross (1976a) nicely summarize this viewpoint: "We begin with the assertion that television is the central arm of American society . . . its function is, in a word, enculturation" (p. 175).

The above view of the media as a definer of social reality, together with the view of the audience as active, is evident in the work of Murdock and McCron (1976) in England and in that of Nordenstreng (1970; 1974) in Finland. Nordenstreng argues that we need both a theory of knowledge and a theory of society in order to understand the role of the media. In other words, first, we need a theory about how an individual's subjective consciousness is formed and how this is related to objective reality (the media constituting part of the input into the formation of this consciousness). Second, we need a theory of society and social relations between members of the society in order to understand how the individual acts on and incorporates the "reality" provided for him or her in part by the media.

With these orientations and perspectives in mind, and with the view that the material conditions and ideologies of the researchers influence the type of research that they do, we turn to the main task of assembling a review of the cross-national evidence concerning television's impact on children and adults. We first look at the manner in which the characteristics of television vary from country to country. Second, we review the ways in which the introduction of television affects the daily lives of children and adults and examine which activities are displaced by television. Third, we examine the effects of televised violence on the viewer's aggressive behavior. Then we summarize other aspects of television's impact, such as the influence of prosocial messages and advertising. Next, we review the area of "uses and gratifications" research and examine the notion that the audience is selective in its use of television. Finally, we shall describe recent research on television as a definer of "reality" and the role that television plays as an agenda setter and purveyor of attitudes and values. In a concluding section, we summarize the main streams of research evidence on television's influence and the likely implications for both further research and the development and implementation of social policy.

II. Television's Culture Context

A. BROADCASTING STRUCTURES

In order to understand the context of the research and research issues, it is necessary to appreciate the extent and nature of the variation in television's characteristics in the countries from which we have drawn the core literature for this review. This description of the nature of television in each country can be summarized in terms of the extent and type of available programming, the mode of ownership and control, and the regulations or proscriptions concerning particular content, such as violence. More detailed descriptions of the structures of television in these countries can be found in the report of the Canadian violence inquiry (Royal Commission on Violence in the Communications Industry, 1976) and a report of an international comparison of children's television which was commissioned by Action for Children's Television (1978). The major aspects of television's structure in 16 countries are outlined in Table I. The emerging picture of the nature of television can be described in terms of geographical and historical similarities.

In the Scandinavian countries, Denmark, Norway, and Sweden, television is controlled by a government monopoly. There is no advertising and television viewing time is generally restricted to about 50 hr/week. There is a strong emphasis on educational and informational programs and a consistently high standard of quality entertainment programs. In Finland a similar picture emerges, although there is a mixed media ownership, both private and government, and limited advertising is allowed.

In the western European countries, Austria, France, Italy, Switzerland, and West Germany, there is a monopolistic control of television by either government-licensed private companies, as in Switzerland, or by government-funded independent broadcast authorities. Viewing time is generally restricted to about 70 hr/week and morning broadcasts are devoted to educational and school programs. In some cases there is very limited advertising, while in other cases more time is devoted to advertising, but none of these broadcasting systems is very dependent on revenue from commercial sources. The programming appears to be slightly "lighter" than that in the Scandinavian countries, but in each country there is special attention given to minority audiences and information and educational programs.

In the only eastern European country examined, Poland, the picture is similar to that of the Scandinavian countries. In Poland, there is a government monopoly and there is very limited advertising. Viewing time is restricted to approximately 50 hr/week on one channel and the second channel, which is devoted to minority interests and cultural and educational programs, is restricted to 22 hr/week.

Israel, the only middle eastern country examined, has a broadcast structure which is modeled on the BBC but is similar to the Scandinavian countries in that there is limited broadcast time (about 30 hr/week) and there is no advertising on television.

In all of the broadcast systems in the countries described above, there are only one or two channels available (there are three exceptions, with three channels) and broadcast time is somewhat restricted. However, when we turn to the Anglo-Saxon countries there is a marked change in the nature of television.

In England, there is no monopolistic ownership of television broadcasting. Of the three channels, two are publicly owned and the third is commercially owned. The average viewing time available is longer in England than in the other countries previously reviewed (broadcasting time is about 90 hr/week). In addition, while the BBC carries educational, information, and quality entertainment programs, the IBA network generally broadcasts "lighter" fare.

In three other Anglo-Saxon countries, Australia, Canada, and the United States, again there is no monopoly ownership of television. Also, in these countries there is a much heavier emphasis on commercial control rather than public broadcasting than is the case in the United Kingdom. All three countries broadcast more hours per week on more channels than any other countries reviewed so far. Furthermore, the commercial networks in these countries carry, or are allowed to carry, much more advertising than any of the other countries above. As both Australia and Canada import many of their programs from the United States (and Canada can receive direct transmissions across the border), there is great similarity in the programming available in all three countries. In general, it would be fair to say that although all three countries have a public television service, the nature of television is dominated by commercial interests which dictate homogeneous programming of a less "heavy" kind than any of the other countries that we have discussed above. There is less attention paid to education,

TABLE I

The Structure of Television Broadcasting in Sixteen Countries

Country	Date of onset	Number of channels or networks and ownership	Broadcast hours	Advertising[a]	Control of violence		Imported content (allowed/ actual, %)
					Formal	Informal	
Australia	1956	1 public	100 hr/week	None	X		50
		3 commercial	140 hr/week	11 min/hr, P			
				13 min/hr, O			
Austria	1957	1 public	12 hr/day	None		X	
		1 public	4 hr/day	20 min/day			
Canada	1952	1 public	18 hr/day	12 min/hr		X	40
		1 commercial	18 hr/day				
Denmark	1954	1 public	4 hr/day	None		X	52
Finland	1957	2 govt./private	16 hr/day	15%	X		35
France	1945	2 public		Minimal		X	60
		1 public		None			
Germany	1945	1 public	3 hr/day			X	40
		2 public	8 hr/day	20 min/day		X	

Country	Year	Stations	Hours	Advertising			
Israel	1968	1 public	4 hr/day	None		X	50
Italy	1948	1 public	7 hr/day	5%		X	Minimal
		1 public	4 hr/day	5%			
Japan	1953	1 public	18 hr/day	None	X	X	10
		1 commercial	18 hr/day	18%		X	
Norway	1960	1 public	50 hr/week	None		X	50
Poland	1954	1 public	9 hr/day	Minimal	X		18
		1 public	22 hr/week				
Sweden	1956	1 public	100 hr/week	None		X	40
		1 public	100 hr/week				
Switzerland		3 govt./private	20 min/day		X		
United Kingdom	1936	1 public	82 hr/week	6 min/hr		X	14
		1 public	42 hr/week				
		1 commercial	105 hr/week				
United States	1939	1 public	16 hr/day	None		X	Minimal
		3 commercial	24 hr/day	5 min/hr, P			
				13 min/hr, O			

ᵃP, prime time, usually 5 to 9 pm; O, other times.

science, and the arts. It is also of interest to note that both Australia and Canada are concerned about the amount of local content shown on their television and are somewhat anxious about the dominance of American programming.

Finally, the last country in our geographical–historical comparison is Japan. It is here that one finds a unique mixture of the European and American broadcast systems. Japan has a very strong and well-regarded public television structure (NHK) as well as an extensive commercial system (NTV). The public system is modeled on the BBC and the commercial system conforms to the American network model. This is not surprising when one considers the history of Japanese broadcasting: an initially British public system which was Americanized following the Second World War.

B. STRUCTURE AND CONTENT

One might ask, at this point, what is the relationship between these broadcasting structures and program policy and content. It would seem that where there is monopoly control and there is little or no advertising (and these two characteristics of the broadcast structure tend to go together), television policy and programming differ from those instances in which there is private ownership supported by commercial interests. In the former instance, the broadcast day is of a shorter duration, more time is spent on pursuing educational and cultural interests, and the programs, in general, are of a higher quality. Where the broadcasting is primarily supported by commercial interests, as in the United States, Canada, Australia, and Japan, not only are there more hours of television, but less of the programming is devoted to educational and cultural pursuits and more of it is given over to televised violence. There appears to be a relationship between the presence of advertising and the relative predominance of violence on these nation's television screens. This relationship is discussed in more detail in Section IV.

With this summary of the historical and cultural contexts of television in the various countries from which we have drawn the core of the cross-national research, we can now turn to a review of the research findings which are products of these varying milieus.

III.   Television's Impact on Daily Life

A. TELEVISION USE

1. Children's Viewing

In the United Kingdom, Greenberg (1976) reports that children spend about 2¾ hr/day watching television. For older children (12–15 years), the average viewing time increases to 3 or 3½ hr/day. These findings for British children accord with the recent results of a survey of the viewing patterns of children and youth (5–18 years) in Australia (Tindall & Reid, 1975; Tindall, Reid, & Goodwin, 1977): (a) children viewed an average of 3 hr/day, with heavier viewing on weekends versus weekdays; and (b) there was a constant rise in the amount of viewing by older children (7–9 years) and preteens (10–12 years). In the United States, various studies (Lyle & Hoffman, 1972; Murray, 1972; Schramm, Lyle, & Parker, 1961) have indicated that children view between 2 and 3 hr/day, and that the amount of viewing increases to a peak in preteen–early teen years and then declines. In Canada, a similar pattern occurs (Canadian Broadcasting Corporation, 1973; 1975) in which young children (2–6 years) watch about 20 hr/week, while older children (7–11 years) watch about 22 hr/week.

In West Germany and Austria, Saxer (in Prix Jeunesse, 1976) reports that the average viewing time for 3- to 13-year-olds is 79 min/day in West Germany and 58 min/day in Austria. An Italian study of the viewing patterns of children aged 0–3 years (Radiotelevisione Italiana, 1974; 1975a) reports considerable contact with television beginning at 4 months. However, these precocious infant viewers were observed to scan the television screen for only brief intervals lasting, at most, only 6 min.

In Switzerland, the picture is very similar to that in Austria and West Germany. A survey of children's viewing, conducted by Schweizerisch Radio- und Fernsehgesellschaft (1974a) indicated that the average amount of viewing was 78 min/day in German Switzerland, 108 min/day in French Switzerland, and almost 2 hr/day in Italian Switzerland. As in other countries, viewing reaches a peak at around 13 years and then declines.

In Sweden, von Feilitzen (1975, 1976) and Filipson (1976) report that the majority of Swedish children start paying serious attention to television at about 3 years. Once they have acquired concentration, preschool children view for about 1½ hr/day. The amount of viewing increases to about 2 hr/day for 10- to 14-year-olds and then, as in other countries, declines rapidly. In Norway, Werner (1971) reports a pattern similar to Sweden, with the average viewing time holding at about 1½ hr/day. In Finland, the average viewing time, according to Haapasalo (1974), is about 2 hr/day.

In Japan, Furu (1971) reports that the average fourth-grade child watches about 2 hr/day, while the tenth-grade child watches about 3 hr/day.

In Israel, where there are only 4 hr of programming per evening, with 3 hr in Hebrew and 1 hr in Arabic, the average amount of viewing is between 2 and 3 hr [despite the fact that there is only a half-hour of children's programming and a half-hour of family programs, such as *Bewitched* (Katz & Gurevitch, 1976; Shinar, Parnes, & Caspi, 1972].

The general pattern that emerges is that countries where there is a large amount of television available (i.e., Australia, Canada, Japan, the United Kingdom, and the United States) are associated with greater viewing on the part of young children, about 2–3 hr/day. In the Scandinavian and European countries for which information was available, the viewing time tended to be lower (i.e., 1–2 hr vs. 2–3 hr). However, in all countries, the age-related pattern of viewing is identical: a gradual rise in viewing time to a peak in early adolescence and then a sharp decline. The differential amount of viewing in these two groups of countries is obviously related to the amount of programming available, both the sheer numbers of hours and the timing of broadcasts (e.g., the first group of countries frequently has programming available in the early morning hours as well as evening–afternoon periods). However, simple magnitude of available television is not the entire explanation because that does not account for the Israeli variation nor the variation in viewing by children living in German, French, and Italian Switzerland.

One further caveat: The figures that we have quoted above are averages and there is a number of variables which are associated with changes in viewing for particular types of children, such as (1) age and intelligence: Among very young children, the bright child tends to spend more time watching than his or her less bright peer, but this pattern reverses in early school years (Lyle & Hoffman, 1972); (2) socioeconomic status: the higher the status the fewer hours spent watching (Dominick & Greenberg, 1970; Bogart, 1972); (3) self-esteem: the higher the self-esteem, the fewer hours spent watching (Edgar, 1977a); (4) sex (Greenberg, 1976); (5) whether the child is a "high media user" or a "high print user" (Furu, 1971); and (6) parental and family viewing patterns (Brown & Linné, 1976). In addition, it is important to note that the amount of time spent viewing television is not normally distributed but is very heavily negatively skewed. For example, Australian data (Murray & Kippax, 1978; Tindall, Reid, & Goodwin, 1977) demonstrate that the majority of children watch, on the average, about 15 hr/week but the overall averages from most studies are inflated because there is a minority (perhaps a substantial minority, e.g., 25%) who view 30–80 hr/week.

2. Adult's Viewing

When we turn to the viewing behavior of adults, a relatively similar general pattern emerges across various countries. In Australia, the mean viewing time for adults is around 17 hr/week, although the majority of adults watch between 9 and 14 hr/week. The heaviest viewers are females, the old, and those from lower socioeconomic groups (Kippax & Murray, 1976, 1977; Murray & Kippax, 1977). Chaffee and Wilson (1975) present a similar picture for the United States. This pattern is echoed by von Feilitzen (1976) for Swedish adult viewers, except it is the men and not the women who are the heaviest viewers—probably because viewing time is limited to the evenings when women are busy with housework. In general, adults, except those over 50 years, spend less time viewing than do children. In Anglo-Saxon countries adults view about 2 hr/day and slightly fewer in the other countries examined, with the exception of Israel, where adults view between 2 and 3 hr/day.

One may ask what changes take place when television is introduced into a community; are some activities displaced and/or does television stimulate other activities? The major studies of the impact of television on children and adults include: Belson (1967), Himmelweit, Oppenheim, and Vince (1958) and Himmelweit and Swift (1976) in England; Coffin (1955) and Schramm, Lyle, and Parker (1961) in North America; and Furu (1962, 1971) in Japan. In addition, smaller scale studies have been conducted in Australia (Murray & Kippax, 1977, 1978), Canada (Williams, 1977), Finland (Nordenstreng, 1969), Italy (Radiotelevisione Italiana, 1975b), Jamaica (Lasker, 1975), Norway (Werner, 1971), Scotland (Brown, Cramond, & Wilde, 1974), Switzerland (Schweizerisch Radio-und Fernsehgesellschaft, 1974a, 1974b), and the United States-Alaska (Corporation for Public Broadcasting, 1975). In general, the results of these studies suggest that there are decreases in radio listening and cinema attendance as well as changes in patterns of daily living, such as sleeping and modifications of social activities, such as visiting friends. However, precise specification of the nature of television's influence is hampered by the difficulty of obtaining sufficiently large, naturally occurring samples of people who do not view television but live in social contexts that are directly comparable to those of the television viewers.

Some of the more recent studies have attempted to gauge television's impact on social life by comparing the daily time budgets of persons living in homes with or without television (e.g., Katz & Gurevitch, 1976; Robinson, 1972a; Edgar, 1977) or in countries with markedly different states of television diffusion (e.g., Szalai, 1972). However, Coffin (1955) and Robinson (1972a) have provided extensive discussion of the methodological problems involved in comparing television owners and nonowners drawn from geographical areas where television is available to both groups as in the case of Edgar's (1977b) study in Australia. Moreover, Belson (1967) has noted that these problems are not resolved by sampling from areas with or without television if the towns are markedly different or are sampled at different historical periods in the diffusion of television. However, with these warnings in mind, we have found that the findings of the various studies, using different approaches in different countries, are remarkably consistent, especially with reference to radio listening, cinema attendance, and reading.

1.   Effects on Children

a.   *Radio listening.*   Schramm, Lyle, and Parker (1961) reported that children from the sixth and tenth grades in Radiotown, a Canadian town without access to television, spent about 3 hr/day listening to radio, while their peers in

Teletown listened to the radio for only 1.3 hr/day. A similar displacement of radio was found in Australia by Murray and Kippax (1978) when they compared the radio listening of 8- to 12-year-old children living in a town without television with the radio listening of their peers who lived in a low-TV town (one channel, for only 1 year) or a high-TV town (two channels, 5-years experience). The children in the no-TV town listened to the radio for more than 4 hr/day, while those in the high-TV and low-TV towns listened for 3 and 2 hr/day, respectively. Himmelweit, Oppenheim, and Vince (1958) reported that their English school children who were the nonviewing controls listened to the radio five times longer than the children who had television. However, they also point out that future viewers were keener radio listeners than the controls before television arrived. In Scotland, Brown, Cramond and Wilde (1974) also noted a marked decrease in radio listening when television was introduced into a small Scottish town. Also, Werner (1971), in Norway, reports decreases in listening to "speech-only" radio programs among younger children while, for adolescents, there was no decline in listening to popular music on radio.

b. Cinema. A similar pattern of decline in cinema attendance is reported in most countries examined, and many cinemas have been closed. Schramm, Lyle and Parker (1961) in Canada and the United States; Himmelweit, Oppenheim and Vince (1958) in England; Werner (1971) in Norway; and Murray and Kippax 1978) in Australia all report major reductions in cinema attendance. Also, as with radio, the Australian study found a novelty effect in which the largest reductions in cinema attendance occurred among children in the low-TV town, for whom television was newest. In addition, Himmelweit *et al.* (1958) reported that the reduction in cinema was most marked among the 10- to 11-year-olds and the effect was not evident among the 13- to 14-year-olds. The authors suggested that television served the same functions as cinema for the preadolescent, namely, free audiovisual entertainment. However, the function of cinema for the adolescent had little to do with the content that was being shown, serving rather as a reason to leave home and a meeting place for social engagements. Further support for this notion comes from the Australian finding that 1 year after the closure of the only cinema in the high-TV town, parents and youth groups combined to establish an informal weekend cinema in a church hall. We shall return to this topic in the discussion of uses and gratifications research (Section VI).

c. Reading. The results of various studies of television's impact on reading are somewhat inconsistent. However, it appears that some of this inconsistency can be explained by differentiating between reading comics and reading books. Murray and Kippax (1978) found that reading in general declined when television was available. However, other measures confirmed that the decline was operative only for comics, while book reading actually increased with increasing experience with television. Similarly, Schramm *et al.* (1961), Himmelweit *et al.* (1958), and Brown *et al.* (1974) all report declines in comic reading. With regard to book reading, Schramm reports no difference between viewers and nonviewers, Himmelweit *et al.* report a decrease in book reading followed by a return to pretelevision patterns, and Werner (1971) in Norway reports a drop in the number of books read when television arrived, and this is supported by Furu (1962, 1971) among Japanese children. However, another approach to the question of television's impact on reading is Corteen's (1977) analysis of children's reading skills in three Canadian towns with and without television (Notel, Unitel, and Multitel) as well as before and after the introduction of television in Notel. Corteen found that at time 1 (i.e., before television came to Notel) children in grades 2 and 3 in Notel were superior to their peers in Unitel, and these in turn were superior to the children in Multitel. At time 2 (2 years after television came to Notel) the previous sample was retested and an age-cohort sample was added. The results indicated that the level of reading skills in the Notel children had significantly deteriorated. However, it should be noted that for children in grade 8, there were no differences either across the towns or from time 1 to time 2.

  d. Social life and leisure. It is more difficult to unravel the effects of television on the social life of the child. This is due, partly, to the different categories used by the various researchers. In general, it is the unstructured outdoor activities that appear to suffer most. Himmelweit *et al.* found a greater decline in walking and being out with friends than in playing or watching sport. Similarly, Murray and Kippax (1978) found linear decreases across the three towns (with increasing television) in general unstructured outdoor activities, but watching sport was also affected. However, the initially large decrement that occurred in the town in which television had just been introduced (low-TV) recovered in the high-TV town.

  Organized social activities, such as dances and clubs, are only very slightly affected by television. Werner (1971), Murray and Kippax (1978), and Himmelweit, Oppenheim and Vince (1958) all report similar results. Once again, moreover, in the Australian study, there was a decline in such activities as clubs, indoor games, and parties with the introduction of television, but the effect was ameliorated with increasing television experience.

  Unlike Himmelweit's *et al.*, the Australian study did not find any decrement in "sitting around doing nothing" nor was there a decrement in playing with friends. This difference between the English and Australian studies may relate to cultural differences in the manner in which these different groups of children conceptualize the dimensions of their daily time budgets. For example, we cannot be sure the "doing nothing" in these two cultures would include the same range of "nonactivities."

e. Overall effects. The patterns of television's influence on the life styles of children living in America, Australia, Canada, England, and Norway is one of an initial marked decrement in a wide range of activities following the introduction of television, followed by a modest return of interest in these displaced activities. Alternative media (i.e., cinema, radio, and comics) and some unstructured outdoor activities are much more profoundly and persistently affected. However, in the studies in which the design allowed for the measurement of recovery effects, cinema and radio listening manifested some slight return toward the pretelevision levels, although Corteen's (1977) finding of a deterioration in reading skills with increasing experience with television in three Canadian towns raises concern about the qualitative (as opposed to the quantitative) changes in reading that are associated with television viewing. Related to these findings is the continued decrement in reading of comic books which may underscore the functional equivalence of television and comics but not television and books (for comics, the function may be time filling). The decrements in outdoor activities are difficult to explain, but with increasing availability of television, there may be a gain in indoor activity at the expense of outdoor interests. Nevertheless, the overall result is one of a return to pretelevision levels. It is possible that this reemergence of displaced activities is actually stimulated by television viewing. This hypothesis is supported by the increase found for playing with friends (Murray & Kippax, 1978) and the increases in time spent on hobbies (Murray & Kippax, 1978; Werner, 1971). Thus, television, although an initial displacer of social activities, may ultimately foster increased interpersonal contact by serving as a focal point for shared activities, particularly inside the viewer's home.

2. Effects on Adults

When one turns to studies of television's impact on the life styles of adults, one finds that the results are similar to those described for children but the number of studies is smaller. Murray and Kippax (1977) have studied the patterns of leisure and social activities of adults living in three towns with differing television experiences; Himmelweit (1977) and Himmelweit and Swift (1976) have followed up their sample of children (Himmelweit, Oppenheim, & Vince, 1958) studied during the period of the introduction of television in England; Robinson (1972a) in a UNESCO study (Szalai, 1972), has examined the daily time budgets of television owners and nonowners in 12 countries; Coffin (1955), in the United States, and Belson (1967), in England, have examined alternative media use in competition with the newly arrived television set; Haapsalo (1974), in Finland, has examined the effect of the introduction of television on adult radio listening; and the impact of television on cinema attendance in several countries has been examined by the Royal Commission on Violence in the Communications Industry (1976).

All the above studies found, where examined, decreases in radio listening, cinema attendance, and book reading. However, with the exception of cinema, Murray and Kippax (1977) report a slight recovery effect with increasing experience with television. Thus, as with children, the initial decrements are in part a function of the novelty of television, and with increasing experience with television there is a tendency to return to the abandoned alternative media. The Canadian violence inquiry (Royal Commission on Violence in the Communications Industry, 1976) reported a drop in cinema attendance of about two-thirds of the initial audience during the 10 years following the advent of television in Austria, Denmark, Finland, Germany, and Sweden. In Switzerland there was a 25% drop, while in Norway there was a 50% decrease, but it now seems to be stabilizing and perhaps even increasing. A similar stabilizing effect is now seen in Canada, England, and the United States, where decreases were initially in the range of 50–60%. The younger adults (17–24 years) are the ones who appear to be returning to the cinema. Similarly, in Poland, although 300 cinemas were originally closed down, new cinemas are now being constructed. These results suggest that, although television may serve a function that is similar to cinema, the cinema serves additional functions, particularly for the young

Robinson's (1972a) analysis of the daily time budgets of television owners and nonowners who were participants in a UNESCO study of life patterns in 12 countries found some interesting increases as well as decreases associated with television ownership. There appear to be decreases in such activities as household care, personal grooming, and some social engagement activities but there are also increases in the time devoted to child care and at-home social contacts. This result mirrors, to some extent, the impact of television on children's activities and, again, there is an increase in home-centered activities. The findings of a recent survey in England (I.P.C., 1975) suggest that television does not eat into leisure time, although it is a large part of it. In general increases were found in some outdoor activities, such as sport, and in the more active pursuits in the home, such as crafts, hobbies, pets, and games. Moreover, Murray and Kippax (1977) found no differences among adults living in the three towns in terms of organized social and club activities and there was an increase in the time devoted to hobbies. However, Williams and Handford (1977), in Canada, have reported that there tends to be a decrease in involvement in community activities in the 2 years following the inception of television, particularly for older adults.

C.   CONCLUSIONS

In general, it seems clear that the introduction of television does result in the displacement of some activities for both children and adults. However, it appears that with increasing experience with television, some of this displacement effect dissipates. This rather robust finding can best be illustrated by looking at clusters of activities, such as the use of alternative media or social contacts. In this regard, the data presented in Fig. 1 are drawn from the analysis of the leisure activities and life styles of children and parents living in three Australian towns which have differing levels of experience with television. As described previously, the television experience ranges from none (no-TV) to 1 year and one channel (low-TV) to 5 years and two channels (high-TV). The four clusters of activities that were examined were: alternative media (radio, reading, records, cinema, theater–concerts, and public talks); social engagement (visiting friends, dances–clubs, indoor activities, group activities, outdoor activities, playing sport, and watching live sporting events); individual interests (hobbies and animal care); and time filling (driving around and sitting around doing nothing). It can be seen, in Fig. 1, that as one moves from the no-TV town to the low-TV town, there are marked decrements in all four clusters for children and in three of

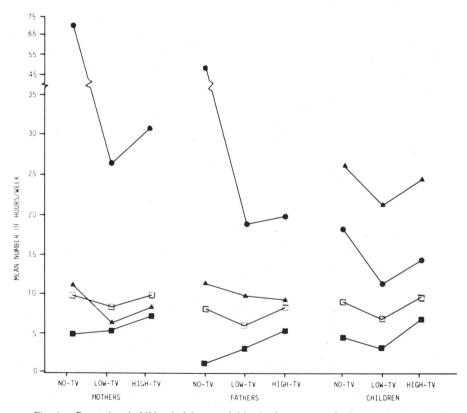

Fig. 1.   Parents' and children's leisure activities in three towns. ▲, Social engagement; ■, individual interests; ●, alternative media; □, time filling.

the four clusters for mothers and fathers. Also, the most dramatic decrements were those for mothers' and fathers' involvement in alternative media. However, the other important feature that is evident in Fig. 1 is the fact that many of the activities which were severely depressed in the low-TV town begin to manifest some recovery in the patterns of adults and children's behavior in the high-TV town. Although the recovery effect is most marked for children, there are some modest recovery trends for parents as well. In general, it appears that television does not have a long-lasting displacing effect on adults' and children's life styles. Most of the changes reported in the various studies discussed above were observed when television was establishing itself as a major element in our lives but, as Himmelweit (1977) suggests, when television becomes extensively used, it becomes part of the background of leisure. The foreground, she suggests, is occupied by other things, such as people, music, sport, and hobbies. Those who watch television most are the preadolescent child and the older adult, those from lower socioeconomic background, and the less well educated. Television may be serving a time-filling function for these people; it may fill in time and kill time for those who do not have the education, money, or ability for other outlets. Television is cheap and convenient; it is on tap to be turned to when there is nothing else available.

Another important pattern that emerges from the studies reviewed above is the suggestion that television is, in some ways, functionally similar to radio and cinema. As Himmelweit (1977) points out: "The principle of functional equivalence predicts that an entertainment or activity will be displaced by the newer one provided it serves the same needs as the established activity but does so more cheaply or conveniently" (p. 6). However, it is important to remember that this process of functional equivalence and displacement will vary from individual to individual, or for the same individual at different periods in his or her life. For example, it appears that for adolescents television does not provide the venue for dating that the cinema does, nor does it serve the same function as radio in purveying popular music knowledge which is a coin of exchange for adolescent social contacts (see Chaffee & Tims, 1976).

The notion that television is, at least for adults and younger children, somewhat functionally equivalent to radio and cinema and that the functions served by these media are, to some extent, time filling, is supported by a recent study of families without television in Australia (Edgar, 1977b). These 298 families who answered an advertisement in a Melbourne newspaper had never owned a television set or had got rid of it. Those who participated in this study were middle aged and of higher socioeconomic status and educational attainment than the general population. Ninety-two percent indicated that they belonged to at least one club, and 82% indicated that they had a religious affiliation. They read widely; they were more likely to go to the theater than to the cinema; the majority preferred classical music to other types of music; and over 40% played one or more musical instruments. The chief reason for not having a television set was the fear that it would destroy the quality of their lives. They felt that television "makes people more passive," "it is addictive," and it is a major threat to family relationships and to community life.

Another common feature of viewers' evaluation of television is the feeling that it is a waste of time and, indeed, heavy viewers frequently express feelings of guilt about spending so much time watching television (Bower, 1973; Furu, 1971; Steiner, 1963). Perhaps, television moves into the foreground of the lives of heavy viewers and becomes a habit for those with few other outlets. Thus, although viewing is perceived as a marginal activity, it is one on which a great deal of time is spent. This interpretation may account for the discrepancy in the Himmelweit, Oppenheim, and Vince (1958) result and the Murray and Kippax (1977, 1978) finding that there was no decrement in time-filling activities with the experienced viewers in the high-TV town (although there was an initial decrement in the low-TV town for parents—not children). It may be that, for the experienced heavy viewer, watching television becomes nothing more than fill-ing time by "sitting around doing nothing." We know that for the lighter viewer, television is often turned on for very specific reasons (Kippax & Murray, 1977). Moreover, the lighter viewers are more selective in the programs that they view (Kippax & Murray, 1977). We will return to the issue of the functions of tele-vision and the differential "reality" of light and heavy viewers in Section VI and VII.

IV. Impact of Televised Violence

There is probably no other question concerning television's impact that has generated as much public interest and professional study as the question about the influence of televised violence on the viewer's aggressive behavior. During the preceeding decade, there have been numerous reviews and commentaries de-voted to this issue (e.g., Bandura, 1973; Berkowitz, 1973; Comstock & Lindsey, 1975; Howitt & Cumberbatch, 1975; Kaplan & R. D. Singer, 1976; Klapper, 1968, 1976; Kniveton, 1976; Liebert, Neale, & Davidson, 1973; Liebert & Schwartzberg, 1977; Murray, 1973, 1976, 1977a; National Broadcasting Com-pany, 1977; Ontario Psychological Association, 1976; Pietila, 1977; J. L. Singer, 1971; Stein & Friedrich, 1975; Weiss, 1969), and not all reviewers are in agreement about the nature and extent of the effects of viewing televised vio-lence. For example, Howitt and Cumberbatch (1975), two British researchers, argued that "the mass media do not have any significant effect on the level of violence in society" (p. vii). However, in that same year, Comstock and Lindsey (1975), two American researchers who reviewed much of the same evidence as Howitt and Cumberbatch, stated: "The widespread belief that the Surgeon General's Scientific Advisory Committee's conclusion that the evidence suggests a causal link between violence viewing and aggression, is correct . . . '' (p. 8; see also Comstock, 1976). Furthermore, the Surgeon General, Dr. Jesse L. Steinfeld, in testimony before the United States Senate Committee which inaugurated the investigation, stated: ''While the committee report (Advisory Committee) is carefully phrased and qualified in language acceptable to social scientists, it is clear to me that the causal relationship between televised violence and anti-social behavior is sufficient to warrant appropriate and immediate remedial action. The data on social phenomena such as television and violence and/or aggressive behavior will never be clear enough for all social scientists to agree on the formulation of a succinct statement of causality. But there comes a time when the data are sufficient to justify action. That time has come'' (United States Senate, 1972). With this background of controversy we will plunge into the cross-national evidence on the impact of television violence.

The first, and most obvious, fact which emerges from a compilation of the international literature on televised violence is the observation that most of the research in this area has been conducted in the United States. For example, in Andison's (1977) review of 67 studies of television and violence, 54 were carried out in the United States and the remainder in England, Canada, Australia, Japan, and Germany. The only cross-cultural study (i.e., one in which the essential procedures of a study are replicated in another culture) that we have located is a recent study conducted in the United States and Belgium (Parke, Berkowitz, Leyens, West, & Sebastion, 1977). Of course, cross-national comparisons can be made to the extent that researchers have employed either basically similar methods or have based their research on similar theoretical orientations. Nevertheless, in the absence of cross-cultural studies, cross-national comparisons should be tempered by the possibility that the nature of aggression and the factors influencing its expression may vary from culture to culture. For example, Pictila (1976), in Finland, has demonstrated that the nature of violence portrayed on American versus that on Russian television programs differs markedly; in American programs, violence is used for personal gain, while in Russian programs violence is used to further the goals of the state.

A second important feature of the studies that we have assembled is the fact that certain methods are used more frequently with one particular age group rather than others. For example, experimental studies are more likely to be conducted with young children, while correlational studies are more frequent in the adolescent and adult literature on violence. This characteristic of the literature makes it rather difficult to provide direct comparisons across various age groups. However, there are a few studies which allow several points on the age continuum to be mapped. With these caveats in mind, we shall discuss the studies in three methodological clusters: experimental studies, correlational studies, and causal-correlational and field-experimental studies. In each grouping we consider the influence of developmental differences in terms of age and the influence of social and situational factors, where possible. In a fourth section we shall consider the evidence for and against the "catharsis" hypothesis.

A. EXPERIMENTAL STUDIES

The major initial studies of the impact of film and television violence were the experiments conducted in the United States by Bandura and his colleagues (Bandura, 1973; Bandura, Ross, & Ross, 1961, 1963; Bandura & Walters, 1963) with young children, and the studies by Berkowitz and his colleagues (Berkowitz, 1962, 1973; Berkowitz & Geen, 1966; Berkowitz & Rawlings, 1963) with older adolescents–young adults. In a typical study conducted by Bandura (e.g., Bandura, Ross, & Ross, 1963), young children were presented with a film, back-projected onto a television screen, in which an adult model displayed novel aggressive behavior toward an inflated plastic doll. After viewing this material, the child was placed in a playroom setting and the incidence of aggressive behavior was recorded (including, but not limited to, assaults on the plastic doll). The results of several of these studies indicated that the children who had viewed the aggressive film were more aggressive in this setting than those children who had not observed the aggressive model. Similarly, the results of Berkowitz's (e.g., Berkowitz & Rawlings, 1963) studies in which university students viewed violent film clips and then were allowed to express aggression in another setting (e.g., administering electric shocks to a recalcitrant "learner" peer) demonstrated increased aggression among those who had viewed the violent film material. These early studies were criticized because the film material consisted of either segments of a film or a specially produced film sequence and these stimuli were not directly comparable to typical television programs. Also, the studies were criticized because the measures of aggression were not considered to be representative of serious interpersonal aggression. Later studies have attempted to address these criticisms.

1. Children

A more recent example of experimental studies of the impact of televised violence on children's aggressive behavior is an American study conducted for the Surgeon General's research program by Liebert and Baron (1972). In this study, the authors addressed the criticisms of earlier research by studying young children's willingness to hurt another child after viewing videotaped sections of standard typical aggressive or neutral television programs. The aggressive program consisted of segments drawn from *The Untouchables,* while the neutral program featured a track race. Following viewing, the children were placed in a setting in which they could either help or hurt another child by pressing control buttons that would either facilitate or disrupt the game playing performance of the ostensible victim in an adjoining room. The main findings were that the children who viewed the aggressive program demonstrated a greater willingness to hurt another child. The youngest children who had viewed the aggressive program pressed the HURT button earlier and for a longer period of time than did their peers who had viewed an equally stimulating track race. Moreover, when the children were later observed during the free-play period, those who had viewed *The Untouchables* exhibited a greater preference for playing with weapons and aggressive toys than did the children who had watched the neutral programming.

There are, of course, other factors that might moderate the violence-viewing-to-aggressive-behavior equation, such as "selective attention" or "perceptual screening." In order to evaluate these possible contributors to the effects observed in the Liebert and Baron (1972) study, Ekman and his colleagues (Ekman, Liebert, Friesen, Harrison, Zlatchin, Malmstrom, & Baron, 1972), using the children from the study described above, assessed the relationship between children's emotional reactions while they were viewing televised violence and their subsequent aggressive behavior. Children's facial expressions were unobtrusively videotaped while they watched a segment of a violent television program. The researchers could then relate the child's aggressive behavior to facial expressions of emotion while viewing televised violence. They found that children whose facial expressions depicted the positive emotions of happiness, pleasure, interest, or involvement while viewing televised violence were more likely to hurt another child than were children whose facial expressions indicated disinterest or displeasure in such television content.

Further elaborations of more meaningful measures of aggressive behavior can be found in another American study by Drabman and Thomas (1974). These researchers assessed children's willingness to intervene in the ongoing disruptive and assaultive behavior of younger children, following the viewing of aggressive television content. In this instance, children who had viewed the aggressive program were slower to intervene and were more likely to wait until the disruptive behavior had escalated into presumed serious physical assault before they initiated intervention.

Several studies have demonstrated that one exposure to a violent cartoon leads to increased aggression (Ellis & Sekyra, 1972; Lovaas, 1961; Mussen & Rutherford, 1961; Ross, 1972). Hapkiewitz and Roden (1971) found no effects for violent cartoons on children's physical aggression but boys who saw the violent cartoons were less likely to share than their control group peers. In an Australian study (Murray, Hayes, & Smith, 1978a, 1978b), preschool children who had viewed aggressive cartoons, such as *Road Runner,* were more aggressive in a play group than those children who had viewed equally stimulating animated segments of *Sesame Street.* However, these results were mediated by the fact that live peer models of aggression provided by spontaneous play in the postviewing play group were better predictors of aggression than the television programs. The results suggested that viewing aggressive cartoons stimulated aggressive behaviors in some children who, by acting out their aggression, stimulated aggressive behavior in other members of the play group.

Several studies which evaluated children's willingness to use violence to resolve conflict situations following exposure to violent films or television programs (Collins, 1973; Leifer & Roberts, 1972) found somewhat mixed results. In one study conducted by Leifer and Roberts (1972), children who had viewed an aggressive program were clearly more likely to choose violent/aggressive solutions in these conflict situations. However, in another study in the Leifer and Roberts program which employed both violent and nonviolent programs there was no difference in postviewing selection of violent conflict resolution between experimental and control groups. A similar lack of differentiation on this type of measure of aggression was found for children exposed to aggressive or neutral films by Collins (1973).

In an experiment conducted with 5- and 6-year-old children in Sweden, Linné (1971) compared children who had seen 75% or more of the broadcasts of an aggressive American television program, *High Chaparral,* with those who had seen half or less of the series. She found that a higher proportion of the "high-exposure" children chose an aggressive mode of resolving conflict situations. However, she also found that the high-exposure children differed from the low-exposure children in a variety of important dimensions. For example, she found that the high-exposure children watched more television and that their mothers also watch more television. Furthermore, children who chose the aggressive conflict resolutions were more likely to go to bed immediately following viewing of *High Chaparral,* while those high-exposure children who chose nonaggressive solutions were more likely to stay up later and play before going to bed. This study points out a few of the background factors that must be taken into account when pursuing the relationship between television content and social behavior.

2. Preadolescents, Adolescents, and Adults

As mentioned previously, experimental studies of adolescents and adults are considerably less frequent than those conducted with children. However, of the available American studies, those conducted by Berkowitz and his colleagues (e.g., Berkowitz, 1973; Berkowitz, Corwin, & Heironimus, 1963; Berkowitz & Geen, 1966; Berkowitz & Rawlings, 1963), mostly with university students, suggest that exposure to violent films increases the likelihood and magnitude of subsequent aggressive behavior, particularly if the viewer has been previously angered or frustrated prior to viewing the filmed violence. Also, Leifer and Roberts (1972) found that adolescent males and females were more likely to choose aggressive modes of conflict resolution in direct relation to the amount of violence contained in the aggressive program that they had viewed in the experimental setting. Similarly, other studies (e.g., D. P. Hartmann, 1969; Walters & Thomas, 1963) found that male adolescents who had viewed aggressive films were more likely to deliver greater levels of electric shock to a peer in the experimental setting. However, another experimental study with adults conducted by Milgram and Shotland (1973) failed to find any effect on adults antisocial behavior (i.e., breaking into a plastic charity box) during the week following exposure to a television program which repeatedly depicted this act. However, Comstock (1974) provides a detailed review of the Milgram and Shotland study and suggests that the methodology employed was not appropriate to the question of the impact of televised antisocial behavior because the behavior in question (charity box smashing) has such a low environmental base rate that it would be impossible to obtain statistically significant differentials.

In a Swedish experimental study of the impact of televised violence, Linné (1974) examined the effect of both content and context of television/film violence on adult viewer's reactions. She presented adult women with one of three versions of a Swedish "thriller" produced by the professional production training department of Sveriges Radio (SR). Although the three versions contained the same amount of violence and the violent acts were identical in all three versions, the producers had edited the film to produce "low-excitement," "normal-excitement," and "high-excitement" versions. The subjects were told that their main task was to help SR select a new television newsreader but while they were waiting for the videotaped interviews with the five candidates to be arranged, they would be shown some recent films. During the screening of an initial irrelevant film, one of the potential newsreaders entered the room and caused a disruption, insulting the experimenter and the audience. Immediately following this disruption, the women viewed one of the three versions of the violent film. Next, they were asked to evaluate the interviews with the five candidates (including the protagonist). The results indicated that the women who had viewed the high-excitement film were more aggressive toward the newsreader (i.e., evaluated her more harshly) than those in the low-excitement group. In a related additional study, two different sets of films were produced: The first version contained a scene depicting the consequences of aggression in death; the second version did not contain the consequences. In both versions, there was a high-excitement and a low-excitement version. The subjects for this second study were obtained from a random sample of Stockholm adults. The results indicated that, again, those males and females who viewed the high-excitement films were more aggressive than those who viewed the low-excitement versions. However, the second hypothesis, namely, that those who view the full consequences of violence would be more aggressive was not confirmed. Rather, it appeared to be the excitement level which best predicted the extent of aggression following viewing. This arousal hypothesis is a concept that is supported by the results of several studies conducted by Tannenbaum and Zillmann (1975).

B. CORRELATIONAL STUDIES

Most of the studies which have attempted to relate television program preferences or viewing patterns to the viewer's aggressive behavior have tended to concentrate on older children and adolescents. However, a few experimental studies conducted with younger children have also investigated the relationship of home television viewing/preferences to aggressive attitudes and behavior in the experimental setting (e.g., Leifer & Roberts, 1972; Stein & Friedrich, 1972). As was the case with experimental studies of aggression, most of the correlational studies are American, with the exception of a study of television and juvenile delinquency in England (Halloran, Brown, & Chaney, 1970) and two studies in Australia in which an attempt was made to relate film and/or television violence to the viewer's perception/evaluation of violence and aggressive attitudes (Edgar, 1977a; Lovibond, 1967). In addition, the early surveys conducted when television was being introduced into England (Himmelweit, Oppenheim, & Vince, 1958), Australia (Campbell & Keogh, 1962), Japan (Furu, 1962, 1971), and North America (Schramm, Lyle, & Parker, 1961) investigated the relationship between program preferences and aggressive behavior/attitudes.

In general, the correlational studies are fairly consistent in demonstrating that viewing/preference for aggressive television content is related to aggressive behavior and attitudes. Although Himmelweit et al. (1958) failed to find a significant relationship between parent's or teachers' ratings of aggressiveness and the presence of a television set in the child's home, all of these early studies in which the researchers related the content viewed or preferred to measures of aggression found positive relationships. For example, Furu (1962, 1971) reported that Japanese children who were rated as high in conflict or high in aggressiveness were significantly more likely to espouse a preference for aggressive hero content. Similarly, Lovibond (1967) found that Australian children whose tastes in several media, such as comics, radio, and television, were aggressive were rated as more aggressive or antisocial. Similarly, Schramm, Lyle, and Parker (1961), reported that Canadian and American children who had high exposure to television and low exposure to print were more aggressive than those with the reverse pattern.

More recent correlational studies continue to support the conclusion that viewing televised violence is significantly related to aggressive behavior but question whether aggressive behavior is necessarily related to preference for violent television content. For example, McLeod, Atkin and Chaffee (1972a;

1972b) have found a strong positive correlation between viewing violence and ratings of aggressive behavior by self, peers, parents, and teachers, but Chaffee (Chaffee, 1972; Chaffee & McLeod, 1972) have reported that, although preference is related to viewing, preference for viewing violence is not strongly related to aggression. Thus, for example, McIntyre and Teevan (1972), who used preference rather than viewing indices, could only report a modest relationship between the violence level of favorite television programs and self-reports of antisocial behavior among older adolescents. However, clear relationships between content and behavior emerge when the studies obtain measures of television viewing. For example, Dominick and Greenberg (1972) found a relationship between extent of violence viewing and willingness to endorse the use of violence by 9- to 11-year-old boys. Also, Robinson and Bachman (1972) found a relationship between the number of hours of television viewing and adolescent self-reports of aggression. In a more extensive analysis of the nature of the content of children's viewing patterns and its relationship to aggressive behavior in 9- to 13-year-old boys and girls, Greenberg and Atkin (1977) found a strong relationship between the extent of violence viewed and aggressive behavior. They report that, on the average, aggressive responses were selected by 45% of the heavy violence viewers compared to 21% of the light violence viewers. Thus, it seems clear that viewing violence is related to aggressive behavior but the relationship between aggressive behavior and preference for televised violence is less clear.

Some of the problems associated with individual differences in children's perception of and reactions to televised violence are illustrated by an Australian study of children's responses to film violence (Edgar, 1977a). In this instance, Edgar found that self-esteem was an important variable in predicting children's reactions in that low-self-esteem children were less likely to understand the screen violence, less able to articulate their concern about disturbing realistic film violence, and less likely to be sufficiently interested in taking action to prevent the occurrence of such realistic violence. However, the picture is further complicated by the fact that these low-self-esteem children were also heavier television viewers, who preferred fantasy rather than realistic programs and tended to use the television set at an electronic companion because they had fewer friends and more disturbed interpersonal relationships.

In summary, it is clear that viewing violence is related to aggressive attitudes and actions. To some lesser extent, moreover, behaving aggressively is related to preference for televised violence. However, whether one is the cause of the other cannot be determined from correlational studies alone. Rather, causal relationships can only be demonstrated by experimental studies and, in some instances, inferred from time-series correlational studies which employ various combinations of partial-correlation or stable-correlate/automatic-interaction detection matching in conjunction with time-lagged correlations between violence preference/viewing and aggressive behavior. Two recent studies which employ some of these techniques are described in the next section.

C. CAUSAL-CORRELATIONAL AND FIELD-EXPERIMENTAL STUDIES

1. Causal-Correlational Analyses

One of the major problems with laboratory-based experimental studies such as those described in Section IV, A, is the fact that the aggressive behavior that can be evaluated in these settings is severely constrained by the obvious ethical concerns. However, this refracted aggression is, of course, criticized on the grounds that it is not identical to the types of aggression or violence that are at the root of the public concern about televised violence. Similarly, the typical correlational study, while dealing with real-life aggression, is usually powerless to elucidate the cause–effect relationship. Therefore, it is necessary to develop alternative strategies which may enhance the causal inference that may be drawn from correlational data. There are two recent studies which address this issue: Lefkowitz, Eron, Walder, and Huesmann (1972, 1977) and Belson (1978).

In the first study, Lefkowitz and his colleagues (Eron, Huesmann, Lefkowitz, & Walder, 1972; Huesmann, Eron, Lefkowitz, & Walder, 1973; Lefkowitz, Eron, Walder, & Huesmann, 1972) confront the issue of ecological validity in studies of televised violence by assessing the relationship between preferences for violent television programs during early childhood and socially significant aggressive behavior in childhood and adolescence. These investigators obtained peer-rated measures of aggressive behavior and preferences for various kinds of television, radio, and comic books when the children were 8 years old. Ten years later, when these young boys had become young men, the investigators again obtained measures of aggressive behavior and television program preferences. Eron (1963) had previously demonstrated a relationship between preference for violent media and aggressive behavior at age 8 but the questions now posed were: Would this relationship hold over a long segment of the child's life span; and, could adolescent aggressive behavior be predicted from knowledge of the person's television viewing habits in early childhood? Using a cross-lagged panel design, it was possible to describe potential causal agents in the televised violence-to-aggressive behavior equation. The simultaneous and time-lagged correlations between preference for violent television and aggressive behavior are presented in Fig. 2. It can be noted that preference for television violence at age 8 years was significantly related to aggression at age 8 years ($r = .21$) but preference for television violence at age 18 was not related to aggression at age 18 ($r = -.05$). When the cross-lagged correlations across the 10-year age span are considered, the important finding is a significant relationship between preference for violent television programs at age 8 years and aggression at

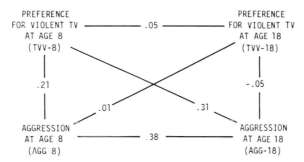

Fig. 2.   Correlations between preference for violent television and aggressive behavior for 8-
and 18-year-old boys. (Adapted from Lefkowitz, Eron, Walder & Huesmann, 1972.)

age 18 ($r = .31$). Equally important is the lack of a relationship in the reverse
direction (i.e., preference for television violence at age 18 and aggression at age
8 years ($r = .01$). The authors suggest that there is a number of possible interpretations of this pattern of correlations; especially when it is observed that the
strongest correlation in the matrix is that between aggression at age 8 years and
aggression at 18 ($r = .38$). Therefore, the ultimate interpretation rests upon
examining several alternative interpretations and selecting the most plausible.
After an examination of some of these alternatives, the authors conclude that:
"The single most plausible causal hypothesis is that a preference for watching
violent television in the third grade contributes to the development of aggressive
habits" (Eron et al., 1972, p. 258). One of the most likely rival candidates is the
suggestion that early aggression causes both early preference for violence and
later aggression. Figure 3 presents these two interpretations of the data. However, the authors point out that if a partial correlation is computed between
preference for violence at age eight and aggression at age 18 while controlling for
aggression at age eight, this partial correlation would have to be zero if the

Fig. 3.   Two possible causal hypotheses concerning the relation of preference for televised
violence and aggressive behavior. (Adapted from Eron, Huesmann, Lefkowitz & Walder, 1972.)

pattern diagrammed in Fig. 3b is correct. The partial correlation is .25, however, so 3b cannot be the whole explanation. Therefore, Eron and his colleagues favor the causal hypothesis diagrammed in Fig. 3a, namely that preference for televised violence at an early age causes later aggression.

It should be noted that this interpretation is not without controversy and some methodological issues have been raised (e.g., Becker, 1972; Howitt, 1972; Kaplan, 1972; Kay, 1972). Many of these issues have been settled by the reviews of other methodologists (i.e., Kenny, 1972, 1975; Neale, 1972) and the authors have refuted most of the remaining criticisms (Huesmann et al., 1972). However, one criticism that can never be refuted is the claim that both preference for televised violence and aggressive behavior are a product of some third variable. On this issue, however, the authors noted that the correlations between aggression and preference for televised violence were not significantly moderated when they controlled for the child's level of aggression at age eight, socioeconomic status, IQ, parental punishment, parental aggressiveness, parental aspirations for the child, and the number of hours of television watched by the child. However, the multiple regression analyses, for boys, show that preference for televised violence, parental mobility orientation, and identification with the opposite-sex parent are all equally good predictors of aggression at age 18. Also, parental mobility orientation and identification with the opposite-sex parent are good predictors of aggression in 18 year old girls, whereas a girl's preference for televised violence at age eight was negatively related to her aggressive behavior at age 18. It is possible that both preference for televised violence and aggressive behavior are partly related to these two variables, at least for boys.

Another causal–correlational approach to the impact of televised violence can be found in a study commissioned by the American television network, Columbia Broadcasting System, which was conducted in England by an Australian (how delightfully cross-national). Belson (1978) investigated the relationships between long-term exposure to televised violence and the violent behavior of adolescent boys. The results of this study are based upon interviews conducted with a representative sample of 12- to 17-year-old boys residing in London. The total number of persons interviewed in the main study was 1565. The interviews and test procedures conducted on several occasions were focused upon the extent of exposure to a sample of violent television programs broadcast during the period 1959-1971 and upon each boy's involvement in a range of violent acts during the 6 months preceding the interview. The level and types of violence in the television programs were rated by members of the British Broadcasting Corporation's viewing panel. Therefore, it was possible to obtain, for each boy, a measure of both the magnitude and the type of exposure to televised violence (e.g., realistic, fictional, cartoon, etc.). Each boy's level of violent behavior was determined by the frequency of his involvement in any of 53 categories of violent behavior. The degree of violence in the acts reported by the boys ranged from slightly violent aggravation to more serious and very violent behavior such as: ''I tried to force a girl to have sexual intercourse with me; I bashed a boy's head against a wall; I threatened to kill my father; I burned a boy on the chest with a cigarette while my mates held him down.''

The results of Belson's investigation indicated that approximately 50% of the 1565 boys were not involved in any violent acts during the 6-month period. However, of those who were involved in violence, 188 (12%) were involved in 10 or more acts during the 6-month period. When Belson compared the behavior of boys who had higher and those who had lower exposure to televised violence, and who had been matched on a wide variety of variables, he found that the high-violence viewers were more involved in serious violent behavior. Moreover, he found that serious interpersonal violence is increased by long-term exposure to: (a) plays or films in which close personal relationships are a major theme and which feature verbal or physical violence; (b) programs in which violence seems to be thrown in for its own sake or is not necessary to the plot; (c) programs featuring fictional violence of a realistic nature; (d) programs in which the violence is presented as being in a good cause; and (e) violent ''westerns.'' However, Belson also points out that even after a solid and searching matching procedure, it is still possible that the whole or part of this hypothesis is working in reverse. That is, the relationship between televised violence and aggression may be, at least in part, a reflection of the violent boys' tendency to watch the more violent programs just because these boys are violent.

Some additional aspects of Belson's study are, at first glance, rather puzzling, namely, the lack of any significant relationship between the boys' aggressive behavior and attitudes favorable toward the use of violence or callousness concerning aggression. It would seem that the attitudes of these boys were not affected by either viewing televised violence or actual involvement in violence. Certainly, this presents a problem in interpreting this aspect of the study because it is in conflict with the results of many of the correlational studies reviewed in Section IV, B. Belson suggests that this result may have been produced by subtle desensitization effects of viewing televised violence in which behavior change comes about in a gradual sequence in which the viewer adopts an aggressive style of interpersonal interaction but is ''unconscious'' of the reasons for his behavior and, hence, never consciously expresses violent attitudes. Although this rationale presents an intriguing theory, it would require substantially more evidence than is currently available.

2. Field Experiments

Another approach to preserving the ecological validity of both television viewing and response measures is demonstrated in several recent studies of the impact of television or film violence on the social behavior of children and adolescents residing in relatively natural environments, such as the kindergarten classrooms or playgrounds and in the living quarters and grounds of residential institutions.

In one American field experiment conducted with preschool children, Steuer, Applefield, and Smith (1971) attempted to assess the cumulative effects of viewing televised violence. In this small-scale study, 10 preschool children were assigned to five pairs matched on the basis of the amount of home television viewing. Each child was observed in free-play peer interaction for a baseline period of 10 days. Following the baseline period, one child in the matched pair viewed a series of aggressive cartoons and the other child viewed a series of nonaggressive programs. The daily viewing period extended for 11 days. During both the baseline and viewing periods, the frequency of aggressive interaction with peers was recorded for each child. The measures of aggressive behavior were focused on serious aggression, such as physical assaults in the form of hitting, kicking, squeezing, holding down, choking, and throwing an object at another child from a distance of more than 1 ft. The baseline observations indicated that the pairs of children were closely matched on initial level of aggressive behavior. However, by the end of 11 days of viewing, the children who had viewed the aggressive programs were displaying more aggressive behavior in their peer interaction than their matched controls who had viewed the nonaggressive programs. Thus, the significant feature of this study is the demonstrable cumulative effect of exposure to televised violence despite the relatively brief viewing period.

In another, longer term, American study, Stein and Friedrich (1972; Friedrich & Stein, 1973) presented 97 preschool children with a diet of either "antisocial, prosocial, or neutral" television programs. The antisocial diet consisted of 12 half-hour episodes of *Batman* and *Superman* cartoons. The prosocial diet was composed of 12 episodes of *Misteroger's Neighborhood* (a program that stresses such themes as sharing possessions and cooperative play). The neutral diet consisted of children's travelog films. The children were observed through a 9-week period which consisted of 3 weeks of previewing baseline, 4 weeks of television exposure, and 2 weeks of follow-up. All observations were conducted in a naturalistic setting while the children were engaged in daily activities. The observers recorded various forms of behavior that could be regarded as prosocial (i.e., helping, sharing, cooperative play) or antisocial (i.e., arguing, pushing, breaking toys). The overall results indicated that children who were adjudged to be initially somewhat more aggressive became significantly more aggressive as a result of viewing the *Batman* and *Superman* cartoons. Moreover, the children who viewed *Misteroger's Neighborhood* became more cooperative and willing to share toys and to delay gratification.

In a recent Canadian field experiment, the researchers (Joy, Kimball, & Zabrack, 1977) had an opportunity to observe the aggressive behavior of children living in three towns with or without television, Notel, Unitel, and Multitel, and to reassess the children 2 years after television was introduced into Notel. At time 1, the researchers selected a sample of five male and five female children from grades 1, 2, 4, and 5 and at time 2, from grades 1, 2, 3, and 4. In addition, the children who were observed at time 1 were observed again at time 2. Each child was observed for 21 1-min intervals during a 7- to 10-day period. In addition, teacher ratings and peer ratings of aggressive behavior were obtained on all children in the four grades included in the observational study. The results of the longitudinal study of 44 children observed at time 1 and time 2 indicated that there were no differences across the three towns at time 1 but, at time 2, the children in the former Notel were significantly more aggressive, both physically and verbally, than the children in the Unitel or Multitel towns. Moreover, only the children in Notel manifested any significant increase in physical and verbal aggression from time 1 to time 2. The cross-sectional study of 240 children in the three towns at two time periods indicated that children in Notel were significantly more aggressive than their peers in Unitel but not different from their age mates in Multitel. Males were more aggressive than females and children were more aggressive at time 2 than at time 1. For verbal aggression, children in Notel were significantly more aggressive at time 2 than at time 1, but the children in Unitel and Multitel did not increase from time 1 to time 2. The authors suggest that these dramatic increases in Notel at time 2, in contrast to a relatively stable level of aggression in the other towns, might be due to a "disinhibiting" effect rather than to the cumulative effect of viewing, a finding reminiscent of the pattern observed for other social behaviors in the three Australian towns (Murray & Kippax, 1978). The authors suggest that the vehicle by which this disinhibiting effect might operate is through an energizing, activation, or arousal effect, such as that demonstrated by Tannenbaum and Zillman (1975).

In another Canadian field experiment, McCabe and Moriarity (1977) assessed the influence of aggressive or prosocial televised sports programs on the behavior of children and adolescents who were involved in summer training programs in hockey, lacrosse, and baseball. In each of the three programs the children or adolescents were presented with two 30-min edited videotapes of teams playing the relevant sport. In the aggressive condition the tapes were edited to highlight the antisocial verbal or physical accompaniments not infrequently observed in the conduct of that particular sport. Conversely, the prosocial tapes emphasized the cooperative, supportive aspects of team play. The children and adolescents, ranging in age from 6 to 17 (hockey), 7 to 20 (lacrosse), and 6 to 12 (baseball), were observed for evidence of physical, verbal, and nonverbal symbolic aggression and prosocial behavior. The observations were conducted prior to viewing, on the viewing days, and on days following the viewing of the videotaped programs. The only trend in the results was a slight tendency toward an increase in prosocial behavior among the older team members who viewed the prosocial televised sport. It may be that the incidence of antisocial activities on the playing field, particularly for hockey and lacrosse, swamped the television effect, while conversely, the low incidence of naturally occurring prosocial behavior caused the prosocial programs to be something of a novelty for the older, more case-hardened players.

The next field experiment that we shall discuss is the only cross-cultural study of the impact of film or television violence that we have encountered. This series of studies, undertaken in the United States and Belgium, was designed to evaluate the influence of filmed violence on the aggressive behavior of adolescent delinquents (Parke, Berkowitz, Leyens, West, & Sebastian, 1977). All three field studies in this program included the presentation of either aggressive or nonaggressive, unedited, commercial films to groups of adolescent males who were living in small-group cottages in minimum security institutions. Furthermore, the measures of aggressive behavior were based upon naturalistic observations of the boys' behavior in their usual environment. The categories of aggressive behavior observed included physical threats (e.g., fist waving), verbal aggression (e.g., taunting, cursing), and physical attack (e.g., hitting, choking, kicking), as well as a variety of noninterpersonal physical and verbal aggression (e.g., destroying an object, cursing without a social target) and self-directed physical and verbal aggression.

In the first American study, boys in two separate cottages were exposed to a diet of five aggressive or neutral films. These boys had been observed for a 3-week baseline period, followed by a 1-week film-viewing period, followed by a 3-week postviewing observation period. The results of this study indicated that the boys who viewed the aggressive movies were significantly more aggressive in terms of interpersonal verbal and physical aggression ad well as of noninterpersonal verbal and physical aggression against objects and self. In addition, there was a tendency for the greatest increase in aggression to be associated with those boys who were initially somewhat more aggressive.

In the second American study, the duration of observation was increased in the baseline and postviewing periods and the extent of film viewing was varied so that two groups were exposed to five sessions of either aggressive or neutral films and two other groups were exposed to only one neutral or aggressive film. Therefore, the magnitude of effects in relation to the extent of exposure could be analyzed. In general, the results indicated that more dramatic effects of the aggressive movies were obtained in the five-movie diet than in the one-exposure condition. Also, there was an effect for initial level of aggression (those who were initially more aggressive increased most) in the one-film condition but the level of aggression effect was not found in the five-exposure group.

In the third study, the same basic design of the American studies was replicated in a minimum security institution for teenage boys in Belgium. The study included a 1-week baseline observation period, followed by 1 week of film viewing and a 1-week postviewing observation period. There were four cottages involved in which there were two cottages with high aggressive behavior and two with low levels of aggression. One of each pair of cottages was assigned to the aggressive film condition, while the other two viewed the neutral films. The results of this study indicated that only the two initially high-aggressive cottages were affected by the movies; those boys who saw the aggressive movies increased their level of aggression, while those who were exposed to the neutral films reduced their level of aggression. Thus, there is some evidence that predispositional factors related to aggressiveness may be catalysts in producing either increases or decreases in film-mediated behavior.

D. TELEVISION VIOLENCE AND CATHARSIS

Standing in opposition to these accumulated findings on the effects of media violence is a major study by Feshbach and R. D. Singer (1971) which suggests that viewing televised violence reduces the likelihood that the viewer will engage in aggressive behavior. The theory underlying this study stipulates that the child who views violence on television vicariously experiences the violence, identifies with the aggressive actor, and thereby discharges his pent-up anger, hostility, and frustration. In the Feshbach and Singer study, adolescent and preadolescent boys were presented with a "diet" of either aggressive or nonaggressive television programming over a 6-week period while the researchers concurrently measured the day-to-day aggressive behavior of these boys. The results indicated that, in some cases, the children who viewed the nonviolent television programs were more aggressive than the boys who viewed the aggressive programs. However, this research has been seriously questioned on methodological grounds (Liebert, Sobol, & Davidson, 1972; Liebert, Davidson, & Sobol, 1972); the authors have replied to some of these criticisms (Feshbach & Singer, 1972a, 1972b) but serious doubts remain. For example, the reliability of the main measure of aggressive behavior, daily ratings by institutional personnel (e.g., teachers, houseparents) was not clearly established during the study. Furthermore, the raters were untrained and, more serious, were knowledgeable about the treatment condition to which their ratees were assigned. In another instance, the boys who were supposedly restricted to nonaggressive programs were, in fact, allowed to routinely view their favorite program, *Batman* (one of the more violent programs in the aggressive diet).

There are however, more general problems with the catharsis notion when applied to the mass media. The concept of catharsis, as it is formulated in psychoanalytic or dynamic theories of personality development, requires the experiencing of a rather intense emotional involvement which, we know from both common observation and research, appears to be lacking in most television viewing contexts. The only media setting in which the intensity of involvement might possibly be sufficient to postulate the operation of catharsis is the reading of fairy tales to very young children (Bettelheim, 1976; Murray, 1977a). In this latter setting, it is possible that the parental mediation of the impact of the fairy tale by controlling intensity of emotion, sequencing of content, and pacing of development in response to the child's feedback, could bring about catharsis of aggressive fantasies; especially when there is an opportunity for a repeated "working through" of these feelings in subsequent repetition of a fairy tale selected by the child as one which deals most directly with emotional issues that are of immediate concern to that particular child.

More concretely, in terms of research findings, there is little evidence from other studies which would support the catharsis notion when applied to televised violence. For example, a replication of the Feshbach and Singer study by Wells (1973) failed to demonstrate the existence of a catharsis effect. Furthermore, the catharsis effect does not square with other, more general research findings to the extent that, if viewing televised violence leads to a decrease in aggressive behavior, then, in various other correlational studies, preference for and viewing of violent programs should be inversely related to aggressive behavior (i.e., by reducing aggressive behavior, aggressive children should ultimately cease viewing and preferring aggressive television programs). Of course, this is not the case. As Chaffee (1972) points out, children who are more aggressive are also more likely to view televised violence. For example, in summarizing a range of recent correlational studies, Chaffee suggests that some of the imprecise findings in the television violence and aggression literature are due to a failure to differentiate between the effects of preference for televised violence and actual viewing of violence. When the studies included actual measures of viewing rather than preference, there was a much stronger relationship of the type diagrammed in Fig. 4. Also, when one includes the findings from laboratory and field-experimental studies the causal process is clarified. Thus, the weight of the evidence on the televised violence issue warrants, at the very least, caution and concern as well as action. The type of action that has been or could be taken will

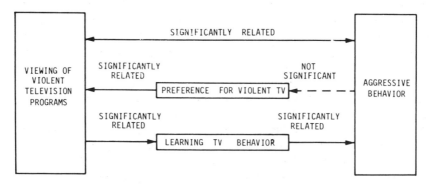

Fig. 4.   Relation of violence viewing to aggressive behavior. (Adapted from Chaffee, 1972.)

vary from culture to culture because we know that television is not the only cause of violence in society.

At this point in the state of the available research on catharsis, the most viable interpretation is the suggestion that, although for some children under some circumstances viewing televised violence may enable the child to discharge some of his or her aggressive feelings, for many children under many circumstances viewing aggression on television leads to an increase in aggressive feelings, attitudes, and behavior. Indeed, one of the principal proponents of the catharsis hypothesis, R. D. Singer, has recently acknowledged (Kaplan & Singer, 1976) that the original formulation of televised catharsis was likely to be erroneous (for a recent review of theory and research on catharsis, see Geen & Quanty, 1977).

E. CONCLUSIONS

Any attempt to provide a concise summary of the state of the research on televised violence and aggressive behavior is fraught with hazards. However, there is one broad conclusion which is quite clear, namely, that there is a relationship between violence on television and violence in society. The relationship is not straightforward and there are many aspects which, in the absence of firm, replicated findings, must be dealt with on the level of reasonable scientific guesstimates. For example, we know that there is a myriad of variables which must be entered into the violence-viewing-to-aggressive-behavior equation. We have outlined some of the major variables such as age, sex, socioeconomic status, preexisting aggressive tendencies, self-esteem, frustration, and other social-situational variables, such as family communication patterns, child-rearing practices, and family structure. Alas, moreover, all of these variables have a nasty tendency to interact, thereby making the task of presenting a succinct causal statement rather risky. However, despite these caveats, there is sufficient cumulative evidence to warrant the view that televised violence is one factor in the production and maintenance of violence in society. Other powerful candidates for the production of violence are such factors as the unequal distribution of income and resources as manifested in ethnic/racial/social class discrimination. Moreover, the questions raised in Section II concerning the intimate relationship between the existence of a commercial television structure and the prevalence of violence on a nation's television screens require further exploration. Thus, there is a need to examine the debate about televised violence within the broader social and cultural contexts in which television has developed in various countries. As Gerbner (1976) has noted, American television is concerned with, among other things, the making of consumers. Perhaps it is, as Halloran (1977) suggests, that the presentation of material goods through advertising "... may increase expectations unrealistically, aggravate existing problems, contribute to frustration, and consequently to the aggression and violence that may stem from this'' (p. 7).

*　　　　　　　*　　　　　　　*

V. Television and the "Real" World

A. CULTIVATION OF REALITY

All television programs, whether news, or documentary, drama, soap opera, or science fiction, present a reality—a televised reality. Television may be seen as a provider of definitions of reality. None of these definitions is necessarily true or false, correct or incorrect, and all of them may be more or less distorted. The viewer, however, is not a passive recipient of televised reality; he or she acts on, interprets, and matches the reality presented on the screen with his or her own view of the world.

Most viewers are prepared to believe that the events portrayed on a news program or in a news format are real (e.g., Feshbach, 1972, 1976). While most viewers have no difficulty in distinguishing entertainment from news programs, moreover, it is likely that entertainment programs also provide the viewer with versions of reality. Noble (1975) in England suggested that children's perceptions of occupational roles and ethnic stereotypes are related to the second-hand or vicarious experiences on television. Other studies conducted with English school children have confirmed the notion that the televised reality is most powerful when the child does not have any first-hand experience. For example, Faulkner (1975) found that Asian adolescent girls, living in Britain in a protected environment which prevented contact with English girls, tended to construe English girls and their families in a manner that resembled the media reality rather than veridical judgments. Similar distortions of reality, resulting from a media-based conception in instances in which the individual lacks first-hand experience, have been demonstrated for children's ethnic stereotypes (P. Hartmann & Husband, 1974).

In a recent study of American children, Greenberg and Reeves (1976) found that the amount of television viewed by 8- to 11-year-olds was related to perceived reality in that heavy viewers were much more likely to perceive television portrayals in entertainment programs as real. These results were strongest for the youngest and the least bright children. One of the surprising findings of this study was that the amount of personal experience with the type of person portrayed in the television programs increased rather than decreased the degree of perceived reality. However, it is difficult to estimate the children's personal experience, when Greenberg's children indicated that they knew policemen or blacks, it may have been a very superficial type of knowing, and such superficial experience would facilitate the acquisition of televised reality constructions.

Similar findings have been demonstrated for adults. In a series of studies in America, Gerbner (1974) and Gerbner and Gross (1976a, 1976b) contrasted the world views of heavy and light viewers of television. They found, in general, that heavy viewing was associated with cultural and social stereotypes, particularly, with regard to sex and occupational roles. They also found that heavy viewers and those adults under 30 (a group that was likely to have grown up with television in its homes) were more likely to exaggerate their estimates of the probability of a violent encounter than were the light viewers. An expanded study, conducted in 1976, confirmed the earlier findings for adults and extended the "cultivation analysis" to children. Thus, Gerbner and his associates (Gerbner, Gross, Eleey, Jackson-Beeck, Jeffries-Fox, & Signorielli, 1977) report: "Heavy viewers in all sex, age, education, income, reading and church attendance groups were more imbued with the television view of a mean world than were light viewers in the same groups" (p. 9). Furthermore, children tended to give more television-world view answers and to learn more of the televised reality.

Hartmann and Husband (1972), in England, demonstrated how the media define or help to define the audience member's view of race relations. Interviewing people both from areas with small and large immigrant populations, they found that those who lived in the more densely populated immigrant areas were more likely to rely on their own experience and less likely to rely on the media. In another study examining adults' conceptions of the role of union and management in industrial relations, Hartmann (1976) nicely captures the potential for media distortion—"who ever heard of a militant employer?"

B. AGENDA SETTING

Another way in which television can influence the viewer's conception of reality is through selective overemphasis on a restricted range of topics or issues. In this instance, the nature of the influence is not a direct imposition of particular content on the viewer in the sense that the viewer is told "what to think," but is told "what to think about." In other words, the media set the agenda and select particular issues that are deemed "important for public debate." It follows that to the extent that there is competition and variation across media, there may, at any one time, be a wide variety of agendas promulgated by newspapers, radio, television, and other media. However, when there is overlap among the various media, the agenda-setting function can be quite powerful. Most of the early research on agenda setting was concerned with political agenda setting during election periods and even very early studies of the impact of media on voting behavior (e.g., Berelson, Lazarsfeld, & McPhee, 1954) have noted that most elections are fought on the "salience" of issues rather than content. Thus, the basic concept of agenda setting has existed in the communications literature for many years, but it has been given new emphasis by the work of McCombs and Shaw (1972).

Following the recent reemergence of agenda setting, there has been considerable research activity in this area. There is a number of excellent reviews of this growing literature (e.g., Becker, McLeod, & McCombs, 1975; Comstock *et al.*, 1978; McLeod, Becker, & Byrnes, 1974) which demonstrate that there is a relationship between media agenda and public agenda in varying contexts. However, as Galloway (1977) points out, the relations between media and public agenda are rather gross and far more needs to be known about the conditions which maximize and minimize the relationship. One of these factors is, of course, the audience and, apart from the relationship of demographic variables, we know very little about which members of the audience are most receptive to the influence of agenda setting.

C. WHOSE REALITY?

In conclusion, it is clear, from the available evidence on agenda setting and cultivation analyses, that televised reality can influence and, in some cases, supplant the individual realities constructed by the viewer. It also has been suggested that the extent of media influence is maximized when the viewer has little personal experience which might provide a countervailing force against the televised reality. Those with relevant personal experience seem better able to negotiate a compromise between the televised and personal reality construction. Support for this explanation comes from a series of studies on the credibility that children and adults ascribe to television (Graves, 1976a, 1976b; Leifer, 1976). In a series of interviews with black and white adults, Graves (1976b) attempted to discover the ways in which viewers evaluated the reality of television portrayals of blacks and whites. Illustrative of some of the difficulties that viewers have in coming to grips with televised reality when they have only limited experience with the issues or characteristics portrayed is an excerpt from an interview with a white woman concerning the portrayal of blacks on American television: "I don't know much about it, but it seems that all the black shows are all the same. It seems that they're showing all the black people in *one way on almost all the shows, so maybe this is true* [emphasis added] . . . I think the white people are true-to-life and the black people must be true-to-life. I don't know much about them, but all the shows show them and have them act the same way" (p. 1).

It is clear that television can and does act as a socializing agent. However, whose reality or which version of reality is provided by television? There is a suggestion in the literature (e.g., Gerbner, 1976; Hartmann, 1976) that television is perceived to present a dominant or preferred view of society and the world. All of us may use television as an information source, as Noelle-Neumann (1974) points out. For all questions outside our immediate personal sphere, we are almost totally dependent upon the mass media for the facts and for our evaluation of the climate of opinion, i.e., opinion that can be voiced in public without fear of sanctions and upon which public action can be based. This leads to what Noelle-Neumann (1977) calls a "spiral of silence," whereby the only opinion that a person will voice is one which has come from the media, and the media in turn reiterates this opinion. This process may give rise to a homogene ous, dominant ideology which finds expression in the media and can thereby override or shape the individual's reality construction. Certainly each country presents its own view of the world, and most countries place restrictions on imported programming. However, the socializing process is an interactive one and the audience member will select from among the various definitions of reality provided and match them to his or her own experience.

*   *   *

VI. Conclusions, Implications, and Research Priorities

A. EFFECTS AND FUNCTIONS

It is not easy to summarize the role that television plays in the lives of children and adults. The use that is made of television and the impact of this use on the attitudes, values, and behavior of the viewer varies, to some extent, across cultures and, to a far greater extent, across age, sex, and social role status within a given culture. The research findings included in this review fall into two broad but differing approaches to media research; namely, effects and functions. Nevertheless, despite this continuing dichotomy in media research, which is reflected in our review, it is possible that the effects and functions approaches can find some common ground in the recent cultivation analysis and agenda-setting studies. Moreover, it would appear that research on the introduction of television, both the early studies (e.g., Furu, 1962; Himmelweit, Oppenheim, & Vince, 1958; Schramm, Lyle, & Parker, 1961) and the more recent additions (e.g., Brown, Cramond, & Wilde, 1974; Murray & Kippax, 1977, 1978;

Werner, 1971; Williams, 1977) have incorporated both effects and functions in their designs and analyses. Moreover, it should be apparent in this review that both effects and functions studies have important roles to play in explicating the puzzle that is television. Such an interpretation, in terms both of effects and of functions, allows for an understanding of the influences of television on its audiences in terms of the audience members' use of the medium, which, in turn, is a function of the particular audience member.

This is not to say that generalizations are not possible. With regard to television's impact on the daily life activities, the evidence suggests that there are extensive and enduring changes, such as a decrease in radio listening, as well as localized and limited changes, such as a change in children's reading habits. The introduction of television has a marked initial effect—a novelty effect. For a time, many activities, such as playing and watching sport, are displaced. However as television becomes more "normal" there is a recovery of many of these leisure activities. In general, the leisure activities that suffer most are those which appear most similar—functionally—to television. Cinema attendance declines, as does radio listening—and unlike nearly all other activities, these do not show a marked recovery. The reading of comic books by children and of some magazines by adults also declines and remains depressed, whereas overall reading by both adults and children, at least in Australia, England, and the United States, appears to be unaffected in the long term.

However, there are marked individual differences. There are some adolescents who do not stop going to the cinema; and there are some children who watch close to 70 hr of television per week and who, presumably, have little time for anything else. There are some families who rid themselves of their television sets, and others who use television to stifle family communication.

Again with regard to the impact of particular television content on the viewers' behavior, attitudes, and values, a general statement can be made. The pattern of results suggests that television content can and does influence the viewer at various levels from changing attitudes to modifying interpersonal behavior. Television does act as a socializing agent. Like the family, the school, and peer groups, television is a source of information and attitudes. It acts in this capacity for both adults and children, although perhaps it has a greater potential for influence on children. As von Feilitzen (1975) points out, it is obvious that children acquire a great deal of knowledge and information from television. "In the first place they learn—both in the short and long term—about what they have experience of and interest in, and which they perceive will be useful to them in their social environment.... But at the same time, television provides, both entertaining and informative programs, knowledge of the world outside, a second-hand information which is not based on personal experiences.... Television influences children's conceptions of reality—especially about people and places they haven't encountered first-hand" (pp. 72–73).

Similarly, Abruzzini (1974), in Italy, sees television as an instrument of information on extrafamily realities. He notes that its role will be more effective the more easily it is framed within a body of information and values of family derivation. He and De Domenico (1975) stress that the socialization effect of television must be seen within the setting of the family and the school. It is unlikely that television acts in isolation.

The evidence suggests that television is most influential when it is in accord with other sources of influence or when alternative sources are absent. In the latter case, television provides a definition of reality when the audience member has no or only second-hand experience of the phenomenon in question. When the reality provided by television overlaps with that provided by experience, the effect of the television will be mediated by that experience.

For some, especially those who view a great deal of violent television and/or have little knowledge of the crime statistics in our society, the world will be defined as a dangerous and mean place (Gerbner & Gross, 1976). For some, those who watch American and English detective and crime series, violence will be associated with crimes against property, while those who watch Russian programs will perceive violence as associated with crimes against the society or state (Pietila, 1976; Powell, 1975).

There is a plethora of experiments which clearly document that viewing televised violence causes increased aggressive behavior as well as anxiety and fear. Similarly, but to a lesser extent, viewing socially valued behavior results in modest increases in various aspects of altruism. However, controversy rages over the issue of the endurance of these effects and, in the case of violence, the representativeness of the measures of aggression employed in laboratory-based experiments. These latter questions recently have been explored with more panache and some success in field-experimental studies (e.g., Joy, Kimball, & Zabrack, 1977; Parke, Berkowitz, Leyens, West, & Sebastian, 1977; Stein & Friedrich, 1972) and time-series or causal-correlational studies over extended time periods (e.g., Belson, 1978; Lefkowitz, Eron, Walder, & Huesmann, 1972). However, it should be noted that many of these recent studies have also been criticized (e.g., Howitt & Cumberbatch, 1975; Kaplan & R. D. Singer, 1976; Klapper, 1976), although much of the criticism stems from differing philosophies rather than differing findings (Comstock, 1976).

Despite the controversies surrounding the interpretation of the results of specific studies, the pattern of results from this extensive body of literature is sufficiently robust to suggest that television content can and does influence the viewer at various levels from changing attitudes and values to modifying interpersonal behavior. Also, we know that the younger viewer is more likely to be more affected and, within this most susceptible group, there are probably some individuals who, because of previous social experiences, are more readily influenced by particular television content.

In examining the various influences of television, it becomes clear that the audience must be specified before the effects can be properly assessed. There is not an undifferentiated passive audience but a heterogeneous one. Some members of this audience will select from among the available programs, and all members of the audience act on and interpret the content in terms of their expectations concerning the medium and/or programs.

The selection among media, and within a single medium such as television, is complex and not clearly understood. However, we do know that television is seen to satisfy needs associated with information, social contact, entertainment or diversion, and personal identity (e.g., Katz, Gurevitch, & Haas, 1973; Kippax and Murray, 1976, 1977; McQuail, Blumler, & Brown, 1972; Robinson, 1972b). Similarly, cinema attendance and the use of popular music is also seen to fulfill certain needs for self-identity or self-definition as well as entertainment needs.

Evidence of active selection from among the media comes from the work of Cohen (1972), with "mods" and "rockers"; from Murdock and Phelps (1973), with school children; and from Troyna (1977), with adolescent male dropouts. In all three cases, the data suggest that these subgroups or subcultures actively select certain media (in these cases popular music and certain magazines and television programs) in order to identify with the subculture in question and to define themselves.

Other studies have characterized other groups in other ways. For example, Belson (1975) and Howitt and Dembo (1974) have identified delinquent subcultures with greater exposure to and use of the cinema, comic books, and popular music.

As Morley (1974) notes, the accumulated evidence points to a theory or an approach to the study of media which links differential use of the media back to the socioeconomic structure of the society. Such an approach shows how different members of different groups, and different classes, who share different cultural codes, use and interpret the messages provided by the media. This suggestion may be viewed in two ways: (a) that there is a heterogeneous audience reaching out to media which provide heterogeneous content; or (b) that the heterogeneous audience is reaching out to media which, for the most part, provide a preferred or dominant view of reality. Whatever the correct view (and this may vary from culture to culture), it is clear that the audience does select from the given messages. At the same time, it is equally clear that these given messages help us to form a picture of the world as well as help some of us to express ourselves through these messages. At the risk of stating the obvious, the media reflect a reality, or some limited number of realities, which in turn is/are used by the audience members to construct their own view of the world and to define a place for themselves in this constructed world.

The effects that the media may have on our attitudes, beliefs, knowledge, and behavior depends to a large extent on how we decode the given messages;

how we interpret the messages and fit them into our view of the world. In short, the effects may be mediated by the manner in which we use media.

With regard to television, there appear to be two main divisions which account for the bulk of the audience, namely, heavy and light viewers. Various studies in Australia, England, and the United States (e.g., Belson, 1967; Himmelweit & Swift, 1976; Kippax & Murray, 1977; Robinson, 1972b) have suggested that the heavy users of television tend to come from the lower socioeconomic groups in society, have lower educational attainments, and also tend to be those people who spend more time at home (i.e., housewives and elderly)—the "available" viewers. For these available viewers, television is on tap and little effort is needed to gain information, entertainment, or social contact. Himmelweit and Swift (1976) find a similar pattern in the use of the popular media. Heavy use of popular or "on-tap" media is characteristic of those with fewest resources, i.e., those with the poorest education, and those from a working-class background. Himmelweit and Swift (1976) found, as did Edgar (1977a) in Australia, that a good education and a middle-class environment led to a selective use of the popular media. They also found that, within similar ability, education, and socioeconomic groups, personality and outlook influenced both use and "taste." For example, gregariousness and a low need achievement were associated with heavy use of the popular media: "Together they form a dimension at the one end of which is success, adjustment, and a positive outlook, while at the other end is withdrawal, lack of success, and maladjusted passivity" (Himmelweit & Swift, 1976, p. 154).

Therefore, when one turns to a consideration of the effects of the amount of viewing or the content of programs viewed on the behavior of these viewers, it is important to be aware of the other social and situational factors that are associated with viewing. What effect does the content of a particular program have on the behavior of a person who espouses "escape" or diversion reasons for turning to television? Would the effects of televised violence be greater among persons who turn to television for social contact? Perhaps Gerbner's cultivation analyses will offer an opportunity to merge the effects and functions approaches. For example, he finds the greatest cultivation effect among the heavy viewers, and the results of some functional studies (e.g., Kippax & Murray, 1977) indicate the heavy viewers are the ones who are most likely to espouse "escapist" reasons for turning to television where they will watch anything that happens to be on the screen.

B. WHITHER RESEARCH?

In reviewing the history of communications research, Katz (1977) described three main periods in the relatively brief life span of this field of research endeavor. The first period, from 1935 to 1955, was described as the period of the "flowering and withering" of broadcasting research. During the period from 1955 to the early 1960s, the studies of the effects of the introduction of television began; and these studies reawakened the interest in the "uses and gratification" approach.

In the 1960s, several events which occurred outside the field of communications raised anew questions about the power of media. The first event was the upsurge of interest in media effects by a group of researchers who had had relatively little contact with traditional communications research. These new researchers were social or clinical/developmental psychologists whose interest in media effects was more directly related to their investigation of aggressive behavior or child development rather than media, per se. These researchers, unlike the earlier researchers, assumed that the media, particularly the new medium of television, were quite powerful and they set about to demonstrate the power of television.

The effect of these new "effects" studies was to polarize the research literature into effects and functions, and this dichotomy continues to be quite evident in the structure of the present review. It is also quite clear that the "effects" versus "functions" researchers tend to be drawn from differing theoretical/philosophical orientations. Many, but not all, effects studies tend to rely on learning theory, while functional studies employ phenomenological purposive concepts. Further, it should be apparent in this cross-national review that there is a modest geographical division, with most functional researchers residing in Britain/Europe, while effects researchers are to be found in North America, and Australia, which reflects Anglo-American influence, produces a mix of functional and effects studies.

Surveying the field, then, what are the important landmarks in the television research territory which are likely to be mapped in the near future? We feel that one area which has begun to expand, and which will continue to do so over the next few years, is research on cultivation analyses as initiated by Gerbner (Gerbner & Gross, 1976a, 1976b; Gerbner et al., 1977). The reason for predicting growth in this relatively new research topic is the fact that this is the one area in which "functions" and "effects" researchers can find some common ground. Also, cultivation research does not denigrate the power of the medium.

A second research topic, which is closely related to cultivation analyses, "agenda setting," is also a likely area for increased research activity and for largely the same reasons as those outlined for cultivation research (cf. McCombs & Shaw, 1972).

A third area, "formative" research, has evolved from effects studies, but in this instance the interest is in the formal, as opposed to the content, characteristics of television. Research in this area is most clearly demonstrated by the work of Salomon (1977) in Israel and by the work conducted either for or as a result of Sesame Street (e.g., Anderson, 1977; Flagg, 1977; Lesser, 1974).

Other areas which are well established but are also likely to expand are more refined content analyses and a growth in uses and gratification research—to the extent that these become allied to such areas as the cultivation analyses or, further afield, to studies of subcultural groups, in order to clarify functions and effects approaches.

One final area which has received increased attention in recent years is the impact of prosocial or socially valued television programming. Although much of this research is firmly rooted in an effects approach to the impact of television, by virtue of its close association with "formative" research on the production of television programs it is another strong candidate for bridging the gap between functions and effects studies.

One feature that many of these growth areas have in common is a somewhat more "applied" or pragmatic emphasis. It would appear that this change in emphasis has been brought about by the combined influence of the three major groups of "actors" involved in the television world: broadcasters, regulators, and citizen/consumer-action organizations. All three groups have started asking researchers to provide information relevant to their concerns. For example, Katz (1977), in his extensive interviews with BBC production staff, found that many persons, at all levels of creative and administrative responsibility, were concerned to discover whether their programs did in fact convey the message that the producer intended to the audience for which the program was designed. It seems reasonable to suggest that this is an appropriate question for researchers. Indeed, a good example of this type of research is a study conducted at Danmarks Radio (Linné & Marosi, 1976) which evaluated the impact of a British-produced documentary about Vietnam on viewer's attitudes and understanding of issues related to the war. In addition to this example of "evaluative" or "summative" research there are numerous examples of recent developments in "formative" research, which is designed to assist in the production process before the program is broadcast (e.g., Lesser, 1974; Palmer, 1973). In a similar manner, requests for more research directed toward informing social policy and planning are a result of the increased involvement of citizen-action groups in the formulation of the broadcasting policies of regulatory agencies.

The net result of increasing demands for relevant theoretical and research efforts may bring about a closer partnership of researcher and producer, which may also lead to a closer link between the functions and the effects of television.

REFERENCES

Abruzzini, P. *Television and the socialization of children.* Paper presented at the meeting of the International Association for Mass Communication Research, Leicester, August, 1976.

Action for children's television: An international survey of children's television. *Phaedrus,* 1978, **5** (1, whole issue).

Anderson, D. R. *Children's attention to television*. Paper presented at the biennial meeting of the Society for Research in Child Development, New Orleans, March, 1977.

Anderson, D. R., & Levin, S. R. Young children's attention to "Sesame Street." *Child Development*, 1976, **47**, 806-811.

Anderson, D. R., Alwitt, L. F., Pugzles-Lorch, S., & Levin, S. R. *Watching children watch television*. Manuscript, University of Massachusetts, 1978.

Anderson, D. R., Levin, S. R., & Sanders, J. A. *Attentional inertia in television viewing*. Manuscript, University of Massachusetts, 1977.

Andison, F. S. TV violence and viewer aggression: A cumulation of study results 1956-1976. *Public Opinion Quarterly*, 1977, **41**, 314-331.

Australian Broadcasting Tribunal. *Self-regulation for broadcasting?* Canberra: Australian Government Publishing Service, 1977.

Baker, R. K., & Ball, S. J. *Mass media and violence: A staff report to the National Commission on the Causes and Prevention of Violence*. Washington, D. C.: United States Government Printing Office, 1969.

Ball, S., & Bogatz, G. A. *The first year of Sesame Street: An evaluation*. Princeton: Educational Testing Service, 1970.

Bandura, A. *Aggression: A social learning analysis*. New York: Holt, Rinehart & Winston, 1973.

Bandura, A., & McDonald, F. J. The influence of social reinforcement on the behaviour of models in shaping children's moral judgment. *Journal of Personality & Social Psychology*, 1963, **67**, 274-281.

Bandura, A., Ross, D., & Ross, S. Transmission of aggression through imitation of aggressive models. *Journal of Abnormal and Social Psychology*, 1961, **63**, 575-582.

Bandura, A., Ross, D., & Ross, S. Imitation of film-mediated aggressive models. *Journal of Abnormal and Social Psychology*, 1963, **66**, 3-11.

Bandura, A., & Walters, R. H. Aggression. In H. Stevenson (Ed.), *Child psychology*. 62nd Yearbook of the National Society for the Study of Education (Part I). Chicago: University of Chicago Press, 1963.

Becker, G. Causal analysis in R-R studies: Television violence and aggression. *American Psychologist*, 1972, **27**, 967-968.

Becker, L. B., McLeod, J. M., & McCombs, M. E. The development of political cognition. In S. H. Chaffee (Ed.), *Political communication* (Vol. 4). Beverly Hills: Sage, 1975.

Belson, W. A. *The impact of television*. Melbourne: Cheshire, 1967.

Belson, W. A. *Juvenile theft: The causal factors*. London: Harper, 1975.

Belson, W. *Television violence and the adolescent boy*. Westmead, England: Saxon House, Teakfield Limited, 1978.

Berkowitz, L. *Aggression: A social psychological analysis*. New York: McGraw-Hill, 1962.

Berkowitz, L. The control of aggression. In B. Caldwell & H. Ricciuti (Eds.), *Review of child development research* (Vol. 3). Chicago: University of Chicago Press, 1973.

Berkowitz, L., & Geen, R. G. Film violence and the cue properties of available targets. *Journal of Personality and Social Psychology*, 1966, **3**, 525-530.

Berkowitz, L., Corwin, R., & Heironimus, M. Film violence and subsequent aggressive tendencies. *Public Opinion Quarterly*, 1963, **27**, 217-229.

Berkowitz, L, & Rawlings, E. Effects of film violence on inhibitions against subsequent aggression. *Journal of Abnormal and Social Psychology*, 1963, **66**, 405-412.

Berelson, B. R., Lazarsfeld, P. F., & McPhee, W. N. *Voting: A study of opinion formation in a presidential campaign*. Chicago: University of Chicago Press, 1954.

Bettelheim, B. *The uses of enchantment: The meaning and importance of fairy tales*. New York: Knopf, 1976.

Blumler, J. G., & McQuail, D. *Television in politics: Its uses and influences*. Chicago: University of Chicago Press, 1969.

Bogart, L. Warning, the Surgeon General has determined that TV violence is moderately dangerous to your child's mental health. *Public Opinion Quarterly*, 1972, **36**, 491-521.

Bower, R. T. *Television and the public*. New York: Holt, Rinehart & Winston, 1973.

Brown, J. R., & Linné, O. The family as a mediator of television's effects. In R. Brown (Ed.), *Children and television*. London: Collier Macmillan, 1976.

Brown, J. R., Cramond, J. K , & Wilde, R. J. Displacement effects of television and the child's functional orientation to media. In J. G. Blumler & E. Katz (Eds.), *The uses of mass communications*. Beverly Hills: Sage, 1974.

Campbell, W. J., & Keogh, R. *Television and the Australian adolescent*. Sydney. Angus & Robertson, 1962.

Canadian Broadcasting Corporation (CBC). *Patterns of television viewing in Canada*. Toronto: CBC, 1973.

Canadian Broadcasting Corporation (CBC). *Dimensions of audience response to television programs in Canada*. Toronto: CBC, 1975.

Chaffee, S. H. Television and adolescent aggressiveness (overview). In G. A. Comstock & E. A. Rubinstein (Eds.), *Television and social behavior* (Vol. 3); *Television and adolescent aggressiveness*. Washington, D. C.: United States Government Printing Office, 1972.

Chaffee, S. H., & McLeod, J. M. Adolescent television use in the family context. In G. A. Comstock & E. A. Rubinstein (Eds.), *Television and social behavior* (Vol. 3); *Television and adolescent aggressiveness*. Washington, D. C.: United States Government Printing Office, 1972.

Chaffee, S. H., & Tims, A. R. Interpersonal factors in adolescent television use. *Journal of Social Issues*, 1976, **32** (4), 98-115.

Chaffee, S. H., & Wilson, D *Adult life-cycle changes in mass media use*. Paper presented at the meeting of the Association for Education in Journalism, Ottawa, Canada, 1975.

Chaney, D. H. *The processes of mass communication*. New York: McGraw-Hill, 1972.

Coates, B., Pusser, H. E., & Goodman, I. The influence of "Sesame Street" and "Mister Rogers Neighborhood" on children's social behavior in the preschool. *Child Development*, 1976, **47**, 138 144.

Coffin, T. E. Television's impact on society. *American Psychologist*, 1955, **10**, 630-641.

Cohen, P. *Subcultural conflict and working-class community*. Working papers in cultural studies, University of Birmingham, 1972.

Collins, H. L. *The influence of prosocial television programs emphasizing the positive value of differences on children's attitudes toward differences and children's behavior in choice situations*. Unpublished doctoral dissertation, Pennsylvania State University, 1974.

Collins, W. A. Learning of media content: A developmental study. *Child Development*, 1970, **41**, 1133-1142

Collins, W. A. Effect of temporal separation between motivation, aggression, and consequences: A developmental study. *Developmental Psychology*, 1973, **3**, 215-221.

Collins, W. A. The developing child as viewer. *Journal of Communication*, 1975, **25** (4), 35-44.

Collins, W. A., Berndt, T. J., & Hess, V. L. Observational learning of motives and consequences for television aggression: A developmental study. *Child Development*, 1974, **45**, 799-802.

Collins, W. A., & Getz, S. K. Children's social responses following modeled reactions to provocation: Prosocial effects of a television drama. *Journal of Personality*, 1976, **44** (3), 488-500.

Collins, W. A., & Westby, S. *Children's processing of social information from televised dramatic programs*. Paper presented at the biennial meeting of the Society for Research in Child Development, Denver, April, 1975.

Columbia Broadcasting System (CBS). *A study of messages received by children who viewed an episode of Fat Albert and the Cosby Kids*. New York: CBS, 1974.

Columbia Broadcasting System (CBS). *Communicating with children through television*. New York: CBS, 1977.

Comstock, G. Milgram's scotch verdict on TV: A retrial. *Journal of Communication*, 1974, **24** (3), 155–158.

Comstock, G. An attack that misses the target. A review of *"Mass media violence and society"* by D. Howitt, & G. Cumberbatch. *Contemporary Psychology*, 1976, **21**, 269–270.

Comstock, G. A. *Television as a teacher: Television and social values*. Manuscript, Syracuse University, 1978.

Comstock, G., & Fisher, M. *Television and human behavior: A guide to the pertinent scientific literature*. Santa Monica, Calif.: The Rand Corporation, 1975.

Comstock, G., & Lindsey, G. *Television and human behaviour: The research horizon, future and present*. Santa Monica, Calif.: The Rand Corporation, 1975.

Comstock, G., Chaffee, S., Katzman, N., McCombs, M., & Roberts, D. *Television and human behavior*. New York: Columbia University Press, 1978.

Corporation for Public Broadcasting (CPB). *The impact of mini-TV stations in three remote communities in Alaska*. Manuscript, CPB, 1975.

Corteen, R. S. Television and reading skills. In T. M. Williams (Chair) *The impact of television: A natural experiment involving three communities*. A symposium presented at the annual meeting of the Canadian Psychological Association, Vancouver, June, 1977.

Cosgrove, M., & McIntyre, C. W. *The influence of "Mister Rogers' Neighborhood" on nursery school children's prosocial behavior*. Paper presented at the meeting of the Southeastern Regional Society for Research in Child Development, Chapel Hill, March, 1974.

Cowan, P. A., Langer, J., Heavenrich, J., & Nathanson, M. Social learning and Piaget's cognition theory of moral development. *Journal of Personality and Social Psychology*, 1969, **11**, 261–274.

Debus, R. L. Effects of brief observation of model behavior on conceptual tempo of impulsive children. *Developmental Psychology*, 1970, **2**, 22–32.

De Dominico, F. *Programs on television: Family and child socialization*. Rome: Servizio Opinioni, Italian Radio and Television Company (RAI), 1975.

Dominick, J. R., & Greenberg, B. S. Attitudes toward violence: The interaction of television exposure, family attitudes, and social class. In G. A. Comstock & E. A. Rubinstein (Eds.), *Television and social behavior* (Vol. 3); *Television and adolescent aggressiveness*. Washington, D. C.: United States Government Printing Office, 1972.

Drabman, R., & Thomas, M. H. Does media violence increase children's toleration of real-life aggression? *Developmental Psychology*, 1974, **10**, 418–421.

Edgar, P. *Children and screen violence*. St. Lucia: University of Queensland Press, 1977. (a)

Edgar, P. Families without television. *Journal of Communication*, 1977, **27**, 73–77. (b)

Ekman, P., Liebert, R. M., Friesen, W., Harrison, R., Zlatchin, C., Malmstrom, E. V., & Baron, R. A. Facial expressions of emotion as predictors of subsequent aggression. In G. A. Comstock, E. A. Rubinstein, & J. P. Murray (Eds.), *Television and social behavior* (Vol. 5); *Television's effects and further explorations*. Washington, D. C.: United States Government Printing Office, 1972.

Elliott, P. "Uses and gratification" research: A critique and a sociological alternative. In J. G. Blumler & E. Katz (Eds.), *The uses of mass communications*. Beverly Hills, Calif.: Sage Publications, 1974.

Ellis, G. T., & Sekyra, F. The effect of aggressive cartoons on the behavior of first grade children. *Journal of Psychology*, 1972, **81**, 37–43.

Eron, L. Relationship of TV viewing habits and aggressive behavior in children. *Journal of Abnormal and Social Psychology,* 1963, **67**, 193-196.

Eron, L. D., Huesmann, L. R., Lefkowitz, M. M., & Walder, L. O. Does television violence cause aggression? *American Psychologist,* 1972, **27**, 253-263.

Faith-Ell, P., von Feilitzen, C., Filipson, L., Rydin, I., & Schyller, I. Children's research Radio, *Barn och Kultur* [Children and culture], 1976, **4**, 88-91.

Faulkner, G. Media and identity: The Asian adolescent's dilemma. In C. Husband (Ed.), *White media and black Britain.* London: Arrow, 1975.

von Feilitzen, C. *Maternal observations of child behaviours in the course of home televiewing.* Stockholm: Sveriges Radio, 1972.

von Feilitzen, C. *Children and television in the socialization process.* Stockholm: Swedish Broadcasting Corporation (SR), 1975.

von Feilitzen, C. The functions served by the media. In R. Brown (Ed.), *Children and television.* London: Collier Macmillan, 1976.

Feshbach, S. Reality and fantasy in filmed violence. In J. P. Murray, E. A. Rubinstein, & G. A. Comstock (Eds.), *Television and social behavior* (Vol. 2); *Television and social learning.* Washington, D. C.: United States Government Printing Office, 1972.

Feshbach, S. The role of fantasy in the response to television. *Journal of Social Issues,* 1976, **32** (4), 71-85.

Feshbach, S., & Singer, R. D. *Television and aggression: An experimental field study.* San Francisco: Jossey-Bass, 1971.

Feshbach, S., & Singer, R. D. Television and aggression: A reply to Liebert, Sobol, and Davidson. In G. A. Comstock, E. A. Rubinstein, & J. P. Murray (Eds.), *Television and Social behavior* (Vol. 5); *Television's effects: Further explorations.* Washington, D. C.: United States Government Printing Office, 1972. (a)

Feshbach, S., & Singer, R. D. Television and aggression: Some reactions to the Liebert, Davidson, and Sobol review and response. In G. A. Comstock, E. A. Rubinstein, & J. P. Murray (Eds.), *Television and social behavior* (Vol. 5); *Television's effects: Further explorations.* Washington, D. C.: United States Government Printing Office, 1972. (b)

Filipson, L. *The role of radio and TV in the lives of pre-school children: Summary.* Stockholm: Swedish Broadcasting Corporation (SR), 1976.

Firsov, B. *Televideniye glazami sotsiologa.* [Television through the eyes of a sociologist.] Moscow: Progress Publishers, 1971.

Flagg, B. N. *Children and television: Effects of stimulus repetition on eye activity.* Manuscript, Harvard University, 1977.

Flagg, B. N., Allen, B. D., Geer, A. H., & Scinto, L. F. *Children's visual responses to "Sesame Street": A formative research report.* Manuscript, Harvard University, 1976.

Ford Foundation. *Television and children: Priorities for research.* New York: Ford Foundation, 1976.

Fox, S., Stein, A. H., Friedrich, L. C., & Kipnis, D. M. *Prosocial television and children's fantasy.* Paper presented at the biennial meeting of the Society for Research in Child Development, New Orleans, March, 1977.

Friedrich, L. K., & Stein, A. H. Aggressive and prosocial television programs and the natural behavior of preschool children. *Monographs of the Society for Research in Child Development,* 1973, **38** (4, Serial No. 151).

Friedrich, L. K., & Stein, A. H. Prosocial television and young children: The effects of verbal labeling and role playing on learning and behavior. *Child Development,* 1975, **46**, 27-38.

Furu, T. *Television and children's life: A before-after study.* Tokyo: Japan Broadcasting Corporation, (NHK) Corporation (NHK), 1962.

Furu, T. *The function of television for children and adolescents.* Tokyo: Sophia University Press, 1971.

Furu, T. *Cognitive style and television viewing patterns of children.* Research reports, Department of Audio-Visual Education, International Christian University, 1977.

Gadberry, S. *Television viewing and school grades: A cross-lagged longitudinal study.* Paper presented at the biennial meeting of the Society for Research in Child Development, New Orleans, March, 1977.

Galloway, J. The agenda setting function of mass media. In T. Mohen (Ed.), *Proceedings of a conference on interpersonal and mass communication.* Sydney: New South Wales Institute of Technology, 1977.

Geen, R. G., & Quanty, M. B. The catharsis of aggression: An evaluation of a hypothesis. In L. Berkowitz (Ed.), *Advances in experimental social psychology* (Vol. 10). New York: Academic Press, 1977.

Gerbner, G. Violence in television drama: Trends and symbolic functions. In G. A. Comstock & E. A. Rubinstein (Eds.), *Television and social behavior* (Vol. 1); *Media content and control.* Washington, D.C.: United States Government Printing Office, 1972.

Gerbner, G. *Where we are and where we should be going.* Paper presented at the meeting of the International Association for Mass Communication Research, Leicester, 1976.

Gerbner, G., & Gross, L. *Violence profile No. 6: Trends in network television drama and viewer conceptions of social reality 1967-1973.* Manuscript, University of Pennsylvania, 1974.

Gerbner, G., & Gross, L. Living with television: The violence profile. *Journal of Communication,* 1976, **26** (1), 173-199. (a)

Gerbner, G., & Gross, L. The scary world of TV's heavy viewer. *Psychology Today,* April, 1976, 41-45/89. (b)

Gerbner, G., Gross, L., Eleey, M. F., Jackson-Beeck, M., Jeffries-Fox, S., & Signorielli, N. TV violence profile No. 8: The highlights. *Journal of Communication,* 1977, **27** (2), 171-180.

Glushkova, Y. Effects of television viewing. Cited in: Radiotelevisione Italiana. *Televisione e bambini* (Vol. 8) *L'ascoloto della televisione de parte di bambini da 0 a 3 anni.* (Television and children: Television viewing of preschool children aged between 0-3 years) Rome: RAI Servizio Opinioni, 1975.

Graves, S. B. *Overview of the project Critical evaluation of television.* Paper presented at the annual meeting of the American Psychological Association, Washington, D. C., September, 1976. (a)

Graves, S. B. *Content attended to in evaluating television's credibility.* Paper presented at the annual meeting of the American Psychological Association, Washington, D. C., September, 1976. (b)

Greenberg, B. S. Viewing and listening parameters among British youngsters. In R. Brown (Ed.), *Children and television.* London: Collier Macmillan, 1976.

Greenberg, B. S., & Atkin, C. K. *Current trends in research on children and television: Social behavior content portrayals and effects in the family context.* Paper presented at the annual conference of the International Communication Association, Berlin, May, 1977.

Greenberg, B. S., & Gordon, T. F. Children's perceptions of television violence: A replication. In G. A. Comstock, E. A. Rubinstein, & J. P. Murray (Eds.), *Television and social behavior* (Vol. 5); *Television's effects: Further explorations.* Washington, D. C.: United States Government Printing Office, 1972.

Greenberg, B. S., & Reeves, B. Children and the perceived reality of television. *Journal of Social Issues,* 1976, **32** (4), 86-97.

Haapasalo, J. *The Finns as users of mass media.* Helsinki: *Oy Yleisradio Ab* Finnish Broadcasting Company, 1974.

Halloran, J. D. (Ed.). *Mass media and socialization.* Leeds: International Association for Mass Communication Research, 1976.

Halloran, J. D. *Violence and its causes: Mass communication—symptom or cause of violence.* Manuscript, University of Leicester, 1977.

Halloran, J. D., Brown, R. L., & Chaney, D. C. *Television and delinquency*. Leicester: Leicester University Press, 1970.

Hapkiewicz, W. G., & Roden, A. H. The effect of aggressive cartoons on children's interpersonal play. *Child Development*, 1971, **42**, 1583-1585.

Harrison, L. F., & Williams, T. M. *Television and cognitive development*. Paper presented at the annual meeting of the Canadian Psychological Association, Vancouver, June, 1977.

Hartmann, D. P. Influence of symbolically modeled instrumental aggression and pain cues on aggressive behavior. *Journal of Personality and Social Psychology*, 1969, **11**, 280-288.

Hartmann, P. *The media and industrial relations*. Manuscript, University of Leicester, 1976.

Hartmann, P., & Husband, C. The mass media and racial conflict. In D. McQuail (Ed.), *Sociology of mass communication*. Harmondsworth: Penguin, 1972.

Heller, M. S., & Polsky, S. *Studies in violence and television*. New York: American Broadcasting Company (ABC), 1976.

Herzog, H. What do we really know about daytime serial listening? In P. F. Lazarsfeld & F. N. Stanton (Eds.), *Radio research 1942-1943*. New York: Duell, Sloan, & Pearce, 1944.

Himmelweit, H. T. Yesterday's and tomorrow's television research on children. In D. Lerner & L. Nelson (Eds.), *Essays in honor of Wilber Schramm*. Honolulu: University of Hawaii Press, 1977.

Himmelweit, H. T., & Swift, B. Continuities and discontinuities in media us usage and taste: A longitudinal study. *Journal of Social Issues*, 1976, **32** (4), 133-156.

Himmelweit, H. T., Oppenheim, A. N., & Vince, P. *Television and the child: An empirical study of the effects of television on the young*. London: Oxford University Press, 1958.

Howitt, D. Television and aggression: A counterargument. *American Psychologist*, 1972, **27**, 969-970.

Howitt, D., & Cumberbatch, G. *Mass media, violence and society*. London: Paul Elek, 1975.

Howitt, D., & Dembo, R. A subcultural account of media effects. *Human Relations*, 1974, **27**, 25-42.

Huesmann, L. R., Eron, L. D., Lefkowitz, M. M., & Walder, L. O. Television violence and aggression: The causal effect remains. *American Psychologist*, 1973, **28**, 617-620.

Instituto Demoskopea. *Pubblicità televisiva e comportamento di consumo dei bambini* (Television advertising and the consumer behavior of young children). Rome: RAI, 1975.

International Publishing Corporation (I.P.C.). *Leisure*, Sociological Monographs, No. 12, 1975.

Joy, L. A., Kimball, M., & Zabrack, M. L. Television exposure and children's aggressive behaviour. In T. M. Williams (Chair) *The impact of television: A natural experiment involving three communities*. A symposium presented at the annual meeting of the Canadian Psychological Association, Vancouver, June, 1977.

Kaplan, R. M. On television as a cause of aggression. *American Psychologist*, 1972, **27**, 968-969.

Kaplan, R. M., & Singer, R. D. Television violence and viewer aggression: A reexamination of the evidence. *Journal of Social Issues*, 1976, **32** (4), 35-70.

Katz, D. The functional approach to the study of attitudes. *Public Opinion Quarterly*, 1960, **24**, 163-204.

Katz, E. *Social research on broadcasting: Proposals for further development*. London: British Broadcasting Corporation (BBC), 1977.

Katz, E., Blumler, J. G., & Gurevitch, M. Uses and gratifications research. *Public Opinion Quarterly*, 1974, **37**, 509-523.

Katz, E., & Foulkes, D. On the use of the mass media as "escape": Clarification of a concept. *Public Opinion Quarterly*, 1962, **26**, 377-388.

Katz, E., & Gurevitch, M. *The secularization of leisure: Culture and communication in Israel*. Cambridge, Mass.: Harvard University Press, 1976.

Katz, E., Gurevitch, M., & Haas, H. On the use of the mass media for important things. *American Sociological Review*, 1973, **38**, 164–181.

Kay, H. Weaknesses in the television-causes-aggression analysis by Eron *et al*. *American Psychologist*, 1972, **27**, 970–973.

Kenny, D. A. Threats to the internal validity of cross-lagged panel inference as related to television violence and child aggression: A followup study. In G. A. Comstock & E. A. Rubinstein (Eds.), *Television and social behavior* (Vol. 3); *Television and adolescent aggressiveness*. Washington, D. C.: United States Government Printing Office, 1972.

Kenny, D. A. Cross-lagged panel correlation: A test for spuriousness. *Psychological Bulletin*, 1975, **82** (6), 887–903.

Kippax, S., & Murray, J. P. *Using the mass media in Australia and Israel: Need gratification and perceived utility*. Manuscript, Macquarie University, 1976.

Kippax, S., & Murray, J. P. Using television: Programme content and need gratification. *Politics*, 1977, **12** (1), 56–69.

Kjellmor, S. *Basic subjective broadcasting media functions*. Paper presented at the Conference on Uses and Gratifications Studies, Stockholm, October, 1973.

Klapper, J. T. *The effects of mass communication*. New York: Free Press, 1960.

Klapper, J. T. The impact of viewing "aggression": Studies and problems of extrapolation. In O. N. Larsen (Ed.), *Violence in the mass media*. New York: Harper, 1968.

Klapper, J. T. Mass communication and social change. In I. Pilowsky (Ed.), *Cultures in collission: Proceedings of the 25th Congress of the World Federation for Mental Health*. Sydney: Australian National Association for Mental Health. Sydney: Australian National Association for Mental Health, 1976.

Kniveton, B. H. Social learning and imitation in relation to TV. In R. Brown (Ed.), *Children and television*. London: Collier Macmillan, 1976.

Kraus, S., & Davis, D. *The effects of mass communication on political behavior*. University Park: Pennsylvania State University, 1976.

Lasker, H. M. *The Jamaican project: Final report to the children's television workshop*. Manuscript, Center for Research in Children's Television, Harvard University, 1975.

Lefkowitz, H., Eron, L., Walder, L., & Huesmann, L. R. Television violence and child aggression: A follow-up study. In G. A. Comstock & E. A. Rubinstein (Eds.), *Television and social behavior* (Vol. 3); *Television and adolescent aggressiveness*. Washington, D. C.: United States Government Printing Office, 1972.

Lefkowitz, M., Eron, L., Walder, L., & Huesmann, L. R. *Growing up to be violent*. New York: Pergamon, 1977.

Leifer, A. D. *Factors which predict the credibility ascribed to television*. Paper presented at the annual meeting of the American Psychological Society, Washington, September, 1976.

Leifer, A. D., & Lesser, G. S. *The development of career awareness in young children*. Manuscript, Harvard University, 1976.

Leifer, A. D., & Roberts, D. F. Children's responses to television violence. In J. P. Murray, E. A. Rubinstein, & G. A. Comstock (Eds.), *Television and social behavior* (Vol. 2); *Television and social learning*. Washington, D. C.: United States Government Printing Office, 1972.

Lesser, G. *Children and television: Lessons from "Sesame Street."* New York: Vintage Books, 1974.

Levin, S. R., & Anderson, D. R. The development of attention. *Journal of Communication*, 1976, **26** (2), 126–135.

Liebert, R. M., & Baron, R. A. Short-term effects of televised aggression on children's aggressive behavior. In J. P. Murray, E. A. Rubinstein, & G. A. Comstock (Eds.), *Television and social behavior* (Vol. 2); *Television and social learning*. Washington, D. C.: United States Government Printing Office, 1972.

Liebert, R. M., & Schwartzberg, N. S. Effects of mass media. In *Annual Review of Psychology* (Vol. 28). Palo Alto: Annual Reviews, 1977.

Liebert, R. M., Davidson, E. S., & Sobol, M. P. Catharsis of aggression among institutionalized boys: Further discussion: In G. A. Comstock, E. A. Rubinstein, & J. P. Murray (Eds.), *Television and social behavior* (Vol. 5); *Television's effects: Further explorations.* Washington, D. C.: United States Government Printing Office, 1972.

Liebert, R. M., Neale, J. M., & Davidson, E. S. *The early window: Effects of television on children and youth.* New York: Pergamon, 1973.

Liebert, R. M., Sobol, M. D., & Davidson, E. S. Catharsis of aggression among institutionalized boys: Fact or artifact? In G. A. Comstock, E. A. Rubinstein, & J. P. Murray (Eds.), *Television and social behavior* (Vol. 5); *Television's effects: Further explorations.* Washington, D. C.: United States Government Printing Office, 1972.

Linné, O. *Reactions of children to violence on TV.* Stockholm: Swedish Broadcasting Corporation (SR), 1971.

Linné, O. *The viewer's aggression as a function of a variously edited TV-film: Two experiments.* Stockholm: Swedish Broadcasting Corporation (SR), 1974.

Linné, O., & Marosi, K. *Understanding television: A study of viewer reactions to a documentary film.* Copenhagen: Danish Radio (DR), 1976.

Lovaas, O. I. Effect of exposure to symbolic aggression on aggressive behavior. *Child Development,* 1961, **32**, 37–44.

Lovibond, S. H. The effect of media stressing crime and violence upon children's attitudes. *Social Problems,* 1967, **15**, 91–100.

Lyle, J., & Hoffman, H. R. Children's use of television and other media. In E. A. Rubinstein, G. A. Comstock & J. P. Murray (Eds.), *Television and social behavior* (Vol. 4): *Television in day-to-day life: Patterns of use.* Washington, D. C.: United States Government Printing Office, 1972.

Madigan, R. J., & Peterson, W. J. Television on the Bering Strait. *Journal of Communication,* 1977, **27** (4), 183–187.

McCabe, A. E., & Moriarity, R. J. *A laboratory/field study of television violence and aggression in children's sport.* Paper presented at the biennial meeting of the Society for Research in Child Development, New Orleans, March, 1977.

McCombs, M. E., & Shaw, D. L. The agenda-setting function of mass media. *Public Opinion Quarterly,* 1972, **36**, 176–187.

McCron, R. Changing perspectives in the study of mass media and socialization. In J. D. Halloran (Ed.), *Mass media and socialization.* Leeds: International Association for Mass Communication Research, 1976.

McIntyre, J. J., & Teevan, J. J. Television violence and deviant behavior. In G. A. Comstock & E. A. Rubinstein (Eds.), *Television and social behavior* (Vol. 3); *Television and adolescent aggressiveness.* Washington, D. C.: United States Government Printing Office, 1972.

McLeod, J. M., Atkin, C. K., & Chaffee, S. H. Adolescents, parents, and television use: Adolescent self-report measures from Maryland and Wisconsin samples. In G. A. Comstock & E. A. Rubinstein (Eds.), *Television and social behavior* (Vol. 3); *Television and adolescent aggressiveness.* Washington, D. C.: United States Government Printing Office, 1972, (a)

McLeod, J. M., Atkin, C. K., & Chaffee, S. H. Adolescents, parents and television use: Self-report and other report measures from the Wisconsin sample. In G. A. Comstock & E. A. Rubinstein (Eds.), *Television and social behavior* (Vol. 3); *Television and adolescent aggressiveness.* Washington, D. C.: United States Government Printing Office, 1972, (b).

McLeod, J. M., Becker, L. B., & Byrnes, J. E. Another look at the agenda-setting function of the press. *Communication Research,* 1974, **1** (2).

McLuhan, M. *Understanding media: The extension of man.* New York: McGraw-Hill, 1964.

McQuail, D. (Ed.). *Sociology of mass communications.* Harmondsworth: Penguin, 1972.

McQuail, D., Blumler, J. G., & Brown, J. R. The television audience: A revised perspective. In D. McQuail (Ed.), *Sociology of mass communications.* Harmondsworth: Penguin, 1972.

Mendelshon, H. A., & Crespi, I. *Polls, television and the new politics.* San Francisco: Chandler, 1970.

Milgram, S., & Shotland, R. L. *Television and antisocial behavior: Field experiments.* New York: Academic Press, 1973.

Morley, D. *Reconceptualizing the media audience: Towards an ethnography of audiences.* Manuscript, Birmingham University, 1974.

Murdock, G., & McCron, R. *Adolescent culture and the mass media.* Manuscript, University of Leicester, 1976.

Murdock, G., & Phelps, G. *Mass media and the secondary school.* London: Macmillan, 1973.

Murray, J. P. Television in inner-city homes: Viewing behavior of young boys. In E. A. Rubinstein, G. A. Comstock, & J. P. Murray (Eds.), *Television and social behavior* (Vol. 4); *Television in day-to-day life: Patterns of use.* Washington, D. C.: United States Government Printing Office, 1972.

Murray, J. P. Television and violence: Implications of the Surgeon-General's research program. *American Psychologist,* 1973, **28**, 472-478.

Murray, J. P. Social learning and cognitive development: Modelling effects on children's understanding of conservation. *British Journal of Psychology,* 1974, **65**, 151-160.

Murray, J. P. Beyond entertainment: Television's effects on children and youth. *Australian Psychologist,* 1976, **11**, (3), 291-302.

Murray, J. P. Of fairies and children. (A review of "The uses of enchantment: The meaning and importance of fairy tales," by B. Bettelheim) *Contemporary Psychology,* 1977, **22** (3), 195-196. (a)

Murray, J. P. Violence in children's television: Continuing research issues. *Media Information-Australia,* 1977, **3**, 1-18. (b)

Murray, J. P., & Ahammer, I. M. *Kindness in the kindergarten: A multidimensional program for facilitating altruism.* Paper presented to the biennial meeting of the Society for Research in Child Development, New Orleans, March, 1977.

Murray, J. P., & Kippax, S. Television diffusion and social behavior in three communities: A field experiment. *Australian Journal of Psychology,* 1977, **29**, (1), 31-43.

Murray, J. P., & Kippax, S. Children's social behavior in three towns with differing television experience. *Journal of Communication,* 1978, **28** (1), 19-29.

Murray, J. P., Hayes, A. J., & Smith, J. E. *When Bobo hits back: Impact of peer and televised models of aggression on behaviour in a preschool playgroup.* Manuscript, Macquarie University, 1978. (a)

Murray, J. P., Hayes, A. J., & Smith, J. E. Sequential analysis: Another Approach to describing the stream of behaviour in children's interactions. *Australian Journal of Psychology,* 1978, **30** (3), 207-215. (b)

Murray, J. P., Nayman, O. B., & Atkin, C. E. Television and the child: A research bibliography. *Journal of Broadcasting,* 1972, **26**, 21-35.

Mussen, P., & Rutherford, E. Effects of aggressive cartoons on children's aggressive play. *Journal of Abnormal and Social Psychology,* 1961, **62**, 461-464.

National Broadcasting Company (NBC). *Public television.* New York: NBC, Department of Social Research, 1976.

National Broadcasting Company (NBC). *Recent developments involving violence on television: A status report.* New York: NBC, Department of Social Research, 1977.

National Science Foundation. *Research on the effects of television advertising on children: A review of the literature and recommendations for future research.* Washington, D. C.: National Science Foundation, 1977.

Neale, J. M. Comment on television violence and child aggression: A follow-up study. In G. A. Comstock & E. A. Rubinstein (Eds.), *Television and social behavior* (Vol. 3); *Television and adolescent aggressiveness.* Washington, D. C.: United States Government Printing Office, 1972.

Noble, G. *Children in front of the small screen.* London: Constable, 1975.

Noelle-Neumann, E. Return to the concept of powerful mass media. *Studies in Broadcasting,* 1973, **9**, 66-112.

Noelle-Neuman, E. The spiral of silence: A theory of public opinion. *Journal of Communication,* 1974, **24** (2), 43-51.

Nordenstreng, K. Consumption of mass media in Finland. *Gazette,* 1969, **25** (4), 249-259.

Nordenstreng, K. Comments on 'gratifications research' in broadcasting. *Public Opinion Quarterly,* 1970, **34**, 130-132.

Nordenstreng, K. (Ed.). *Informational mass communication.* Helsinki: Tammi Publishers, 1974.

Ontario Psychological Association. Submission on violence in the media. In *Report of the Royal Commission on Violence in the Communications Industry* (Vol. 1); *Approaches, conclusions and recommendations.* Toronto: Queen's Printer for Ontario, 1976.

Palmer, E. L. Formative research in the production of television for children. In G. Gerbner, L. P. Gross, & W. H. Melody (Eds.), *Communications technology and social policy.* New York: Wiley, 1973.

Parke, R.D., Berkowitz, L., Leyens, J. P., West, S., & Sebastian, R. J. Some effects of violent and nonviolent movies on the behavior of juvenile delinquents. In L. Berkowitz (Ed.), *Advances in experimental social psychology* (Vol. 10). New York: Academic Press, 1977.

Pietila, V. *Gratifications and content choices in mass media use.* Manuscript, University of Tampere, 1974.

Pietila, V. Some notes about violence in our mass media—especially in fictitious TV programmes. *Instant Research on Peace and Violence,* 1976, **4**.

Pietila, V. On the effects of mass media: Some conceptual viewpoints. In M. Berg (Ed.), *Current theories in Scandinavian mass communication research.* Grenaa, Denmark: GMT, 1977.

Powell, D. E. Television in the USSR. *Public Opinion Quarterly,* 1975, **39** (3), 287-300.

Prix Jeunesse. *Television and socialization processes in the family: A documentation of the Prix Jeunesse Seminar 1975.* Munich: Verlag Dokumentation, 1976.

Radiotelevisione Italiana (RAI). *Televisione e bambini* (Vol. 5); *Televisione e sviluppo della creativita nei regazzi.* [Television and children: Television and the development of creative skills.] Rome: RAI Servizio Opinioni, 1973.

Radiotelevisione Italiana (RAI). *Televisione e bambini* (Vol. 6); *Risonanza di trasmissioni televisive in soggetti di eta scolare.* (Television and children: The impact of television broadcasts on primary school children.) Rome: RAI Servizio Opinioni, 1974.

Radiotelevisione Italiana (RAI). *Televisione e bambini* (Vol. 8); *L'ascolto della televisione da parte di bambini da 0 a 3 anni.* (Television and children: Television viewing of preschool children aged between 0-3 years). Rome: RAI Servizio Opinioni, 1975. (a)

Radiotelevisione Italiana (RAI). *Cambiamento sociale e sistemi di communicasione in un'area in via di sviluppo.* [Social change and mass media in developing areas.] Rome: RAI Servizio Opinioni, 1975. (b)

Reshetov, P., & Skurlatov, V. *Soviet youth: A socio-political outline.* Moscow: Progress Publishers, 1977.

Roberts, D. F., Herold, C., Hornby, M., King, S., Sterne, D., Whiteley, S., & Silverman, T. *Earth's a big blue marble: A report of the impact of a children's television series on children's opinions.* Manuscript, Stanford University, 1974.

Robinson, J. P. Television's impact on everyday life: Some crossnational evidence. In E. A. Rubin-
    stein, G. A. Comstock, & J. P. Murray (Eds.), *Television and social behavior* (Vol. 4); *Televi-
    sion in day-to-day life: Patterns of use*. Washington, D. C.: United States Government Printing
    Office. 1972. (a)

Robinson, J. P. Toward defining the functions of television. In E. A. Rubinstein, G. A. Comstock, &
    J. P. Murray (Eds.), *Television and social behavior* (Vol. 4); *Television in day-to-day life:
    Patterns of use*. Washington, D. C.: United States Government Printing Office, 1972. (b)

Robinson, J. P., & Bachman, J. G. Television viewing habits and aggression. In G. A. Comstock &
    E. A. Rubinstein (Eds.), *Television and social behavior* (Vol. 3); *Television and adolescent
    aggressiveness*. Washington, D. C.: United States Government Printing Office, 1972.

Ross, L. B. *The effect of aggressive cartoons on the group play of children*. Doctoral dissertation,
    Miami University, 1972.

Rota, J., Cojec, J. R., & Kozlowski, O. *Children and television in Mexico: The communication
    research center of Universidad Anahuac*. Paper presented at a meeting of the International
    Communication Association, Berlin, May, 1977.

Royal Commission on Violence in the Communications Industry. *Approaches, conclusions and
    recommendations* (Vol. 1). Toronto: Queen's Printer for Ontario, 1976.

Rubinstein, E. A. Warning: The Surgeon General's research program may be dangerous to precon-
    ceived notions. *Journal of Social Issues*, 1976, **32**, (4), 18-34.

Rubinstein, E. A., Liebert, R. M., Neale, J. M., & Poulos, R. W. *Assessing television's influence
    on childrens' prosocial behavior*. Stony Brook, N. Y.: Brookdale International Institute, 1974.

Rushton, J. P. Socialization and the altruistic behavior of children. *Psychological Bulletin*, 1976, **83**,
    (5), 898-913. (a)

Rushton, J. P. Television and prosocial behavior. In *Report of the Royal Commission on Violence in
    the Communications Industry*. Toronto: Queen's Printer for Ontario, 1976. (b)

Rushton, J. P. Effects of television and film material on the pro-social behavior of children. In L.
    Berkowitz (Ed.), *Advances in experimental social psychology*. New York: Academic Press,
    1979.

Rydin, I. *Information processes in pre-school children: I. How relevant and irrelevant verbal
    supplements affect retention of a factual radio programme*. Stockholm: Swedish Broadcasting
    Corporation (SR), 1972.

Rydin, I. *The tale of the seed: Facts and irrelevant details in a TV-programme for children*.
    Stockholm: Swedish Broadcasting Corporation (SR), 1972, 1976.

Rydin, I. *Children's understanding of television: Pre-school children's perception of an informative
    programme*. Stockholm: Swedish Broadcasting Corporation, (SR), 1976.

Rydin, I., & Hansson, G. *Information processes in preschool children: The Ability of children to
    comprehend television and radio programmes*. Stockholm: Swedish Broadcasting Corporation
    (SR), 1970.

Salomon, G. Can we affect cognitive skills through visual media: Explication of an hypothesis and
    initial findings. *AV Communication Review*, 1972, **20** (4), 401-423.

Salomon, G. Internalization of filmic schematic operations in interaction with learners' aptitudes.
    Journal of Educational Psychology, 1974, **66**, 499-511. (a)

Salomon, G. What is learned and how it is taught: The interaction between media, message, task and
    learner. In D. R. Olson (Ed.), *Media and symbols: The forms of expression, communications
    and education*. The Yearbook of the National Society for the Study of Education. Chicago:
    University of Chicago Press, 1974. (b)

Salomon, G. Cognitive skill learning across cultures. *Journal of Communication*, 1976, **26** (2),
    138-144.

Salomon, G. *The language of media and the cultivation of mental skills*. Manuscript, The Hebrew
    University of Jerusalem, 1977.

Schramm, W., Lyle, V., & Parker, E. B. *Television in the lives of our children.* Stanford: Stanford University Press, 1961.

Schweizerische Radio-und Fernsehgesellschaft. *Kind und Fernsehen: Eine Studie Über das Fernseh-und Freizeitverhalten der Kinder in der Schweiz* [A study of television and leisure-time behavior of Swiss children]. Basel: [Swiss Radio and Television Company]. (SRG), 1974. (a)

Schweizerische Radio- und Fernsehgesellschaft. *Die älteran Hörer und Zuschauer in der Schweiz.* [Older listeners and viewers in Switzerland]. Bern: [Swiss Radio and Television Company]. (SRG), 1974. (b)

Sherkovin, Y. A. Mass information processes and problems of personality socialization. In J. D. Halloran (Ed.), *Mass media and socialization.* Leeds: International Association for Mass Communication Research, 1976.

Shinar, D., Parnes, P., & Caspi, D. Structure and content of television broadcasting in Israel. In G. A. Comstock & E. A. Rubinstein (Eds.), *Television and social behavior* (Vol); *Media content and control.* Washington, D. C.: United States Government Printing Office, 1972.

Singer, J. L. The influence of violence portrayed in television or motion pictures upon overt aggressive behavior. In J. L. Singer (Ed.), *The control of aggression and violence: Cognitive and physiological factors.* New York: Academic Press, 1971.

Singer, J. L., & Singer, D. G. Can TV stimulate imaginative play? *Journal of Communication,* 1976, **26**, (3), 74–80.

Sprafkin, J., Liebert, R., & Poulos, R. Effects of a prosocial televised example on children's helping. *Journal of Experimental Child Psychology,* 1975, **20**, 119–126.

Stein, A. H., & Friedrich, L. K. Television content and young children's behavior. In J. P. Murray, E. A. Rubinstein, & G. A. Comstock (Eds.), *Television and social behavior* (Vol. 2); *Television and social learning.* Washington, D. C.: United States Government Printing Office, 1972.

Stein, A. H., & Friedrich, L. K. Impact of television on children and youth. In E. M. Hetherington (Ed.), *Review of child development research* (Vol. 5). Chicago: University of Chicago Press, 1975.

Stein, A. H., Friedrich, L. K., & Tahsler, S. *The effects of prosocial television and environmental cues on children's task persistence and conceptual tempo.* Manuscript, Pennsylvania State University, 1973.

Stein, A. H., & Wright, J. C. *Modeling the medium: Effects of formal properties of children's television programs.* Paper presented at the biennial meeting of the Society for Research in Child Development, New Orleans, March, 1977.

Steiner, G. A. *The people look at television.* New York: Knopf, 1963.

Sternglanz, S. H., & Serbin, L. Sex role stereotyping in children's television programs. *Developmental Psychology,* 1974, **10**, 710–715.

Steuer, F. B., Applefield, J. M., & Smith, R. Televised aggression and the interpersonal aggression of preschool children. *Journal of Experimental Child Psychology,* 1971, **11**, 442–447.

Sturm, H. The application of Piaget's criteria to television programmes. In P. Werner (Ed.), *Information programmes for children 7 to 12 years old: Fifth EBU [European Broadcast Union] workshop for producers and directors of television programmes for children.* Remscheid, April, 1976.

Surgeon General's Scientific Advisory Committee on Television and Social Behavior. *Television and growing up: The impact of televised violence.* Washington, D. C.: United States Government Printing Office, 1972.

Szalai, A. (Ed.). *The use of time: Daily activities of urban and suburban populations in twelve countries.* The Hague: Mouton, 1972.

Tannenbaum, P. H., & Zillmann, D. Emotional arousal in the facilitation of aggression through communication. In L. Berkowitz (Ed.), *Advances in experimental social psychology* (Vol. 8). New York: Academic Press, 1975.

Tindall, K., & Reid, D. *Television's children*. Sydney: Sydney Teachers College, 1975.

Tindall, K., Reid, D., & Goodwin, N. *Television: 20th century cyclops*. Sydney: Sydney Teachers College, 1977.

Tolley, H. *Children and war: Political socialization to international conflict*. New York: Columbia University Press, 1973.

Troyna, B. The reggae war. *New Society*, 10 March 1977, 481–482.

Tunstall, J. *The media are American: Anglo-American media in the world*. London: Constable, 1977.

United States Senate. *Hearings before the Subcommittee on Communications of the Committee on Interstate Commerce concerning the report of the Surgeon General's Scientific Advisory Committee on Television and Social Behavior, March, 1972*. Washington, D. C.: United States Government Printing Office, 1972.

Walters, R. H., & Thomas, E. L. Enhancement of punitiveness by visual and audio-visual displays. *Canadian Journal of Psychology*, 1963, **17**, 244–255.

Ward, S. Effects of television advertising on children and adolescents. In E. A. Rubinstein, G. A. Comstock, & J. P. Murray (Eds.), *Television and social behavior* (Vol. 4); *Television in day-to-day life: Patterns of use*. Washington, D. C.: United States Government Printing Office, 1972.

Ward, S., & Wackman, D. Television advertising and intrafamily influence: Children's purchase attempts and parental yielding. In E. A. Rubinstein, G. A. Comstock, & J. P. Murray (Eds.), *Television and social behavior* (Vol. 4); *Television in day-to-day life: Patterns of use*. Washington, D. C.: United States Government Printing Office, 1972.

Ward, S., Levinson, D., & Wackman, D. Children's attention to television advertising. In E. A. Rubinstein, G. A. Comstock, & J. P. Murray (Eds.) *Television and social behavior* (Vol. 4); *Television in day-to-day life: Patterns of use*. Washington, D. C.: United States Government Printing Office, 1972.

Ward, S., Wackman, D., & Wartella, E. *How children learn to buy: The development of consumer information-processing skills*. Beverly Hills, Calif.: Sage, 1977.

Weiss, W. Effects of the mass media of communication. In G. Lindzey & E. Aronson (Eds.), *Handbook of social psychology* (Vol. 5). Reading, Mass.: Addison-Wesley, 1969.

Wells, W. D. *Television and aggression: Replication of an experimental field study*. Manuscript, University of Chicago, 1973.

Werner, A. Children and television in Norway. *Gazette*, 1971, **16** (3), 133–151.

Williams, T. M. Introduction. In T. M. Williams (Chair) *The impact of television: A natural experiment involving three communities*. A symposium presented at the annual meeting of the Canadian Psychological Association, Vancouver, June, 1977.

Williams, T. M., & Handford, G. Television and community life. In T. M. Williams (Chair) *The impact of television: A natural experiment involving three communities*. A symposium presented at the annual meeting of the Canadian Psychological Association, Vancouver, June, 1977.

Zimmerman, B. J., & Rosenthal, T. L. Observational learning of rule-governed behavior by children. *Psychological Bulletin*, 1974, **81**, 29–42.

Worldwide broadcasting of the American five-part television series Holocaust *was the historic media event of 1979. Much research on the response to the series was conducted, primarily by audience research departments of the various European television systems. Two of the most extensive of those studies are reported here. In the first, Harold de Bock and Jan van Lil describe an elaborate field experimental-panel design carried out in the Netherlands. The research, which focuses on the impact of* Holocaust *and an imaginative interpersonal and mass media educational campaign on Dutch young people, is one of the most complete and rigorous assessments of a national information campaign in recent times. The study suggests that the total mass media and interpersonal "environment" created by* Holocaust *had significant long-term effects in increasing both knowledge of the history of World War II atrocities and disapproval of anti-Semitism. Dr. de Bock is director and Mr. van Lil is a senior researcher of the Audience Research Department of the Netherlands Broadcasting Corporation, Hilversum.*

33

HOLOCAUST IN THE NETHERLANDS[1]

Harold de Bock
Jan van Lil

On April 16-19, 1978, an estimated 120 million Americans watched some part of NBC's nine-hour docudrama *Holocaust,* portraying the Jewish persecution before and during World War II under National Socialist regimes.[2] During the year following the U.S. showing, *Holocaust* was shown in about 40 countries, provoking intense debates and occasional violence.[3] Many critics denounced the program as a trivial and romanticized version of the actual atrocities. Others praised *Holocaust,* saying it succeeded where historians failed: It confronted massive audiences with one of the darkest periods of modern history.

Dutch broadcasters saw *Holocaust* for the first time during the 1978 Cannes Television Festival. Three broadcasting organizations claimed the series for broadcasting in Holland.[4] The first claim, held by NCRV, the major Protestant broadcasting association, was dropped because NCRV feared the program would be too painful for those who had actually witnessed or suffered what *Holocaust* shows. Another broadcast association, TROS, the largest general company in Holland, held the second claim and decided to broadcast *Holocaust* in order to arouse interest in and add to the knowledge

From Harold de Bock and Jan van Lil,"*Holocaust* in the Netherlands," original manuscript.

of World War II and the Jewish persecution, especially among the younger, postwar generation. To make *Holocaust* as realistic as possible for the Dutch (who experienced five years of German occupation), TROS broadcast the German language version of *Holocaust.*

The five episodes of *Holocaust* were broadcast on four evenings: April 23, 28, 29, and May 4, 1979. The first two episodes were shown on one evening with a short intermission. The final episode was broadcast the evening on which the Netherlands traditionally commemorates its citizens who died during World War II, immediately preceding the national celebration of the liberation from German occupation, which is held on May 5.

To prepare the nation for the showing of *Holocaust,* TROS organized an extensive guidance and counseling operation. A special committee of seven Jewish and educational organizations advised on several projects. First, all secondary schools in the country received extensive written documentation with background information on *Holocaust* and on the Jewish persecution during World War II. It also contained suggestions for preparing students to watch the program. Five specials of the TROS regular public affairs television program *Aktua* were produced and broadcast to introduce the series and to conclude each episode. Special radio programs immediately following the *Holocaust* broadcasts provided an opportunity for the audience to react directly and in public to what it had seen on television. In addition, a national information conference was organized on March 2, prior to the first episode. Teachers and editors of student newspapers of all Dutch secondary schools were invited to see previews of the program and to discuss how students would be best prepared to watch it. So many applications for participation were received that a second conference was held on March 15. More than 2000 students and teachers attended the conference.

PURPOSE AND DESIGN OF PANEL STUDY

The Netherlands Broadcasting Corporation (NOS) Audience Research Department conducted an extensive study of the audience reaction to *Holocaust,* with a special emphasis on young viewers. Quantitative data on audience size and composition were derived from the regular NOS continuous audience measurement system.[5] Qualitative data were obtained from a longitudinal study including three waves of personal interviews with a national representation of secondary school students, with their mothers, and with their teachers (the latter using postal questionnaires) and including personal interviews with a control group of secondary school students at the time of the third wave to control possible panel effects. Student panel sizes were 794 in the first wave and 631 and 523 in the second and third waves. The first wave took place between March 19 and April 7; the second wave immediately following the *Holocaust* broadcasts between May 8 and June 11; and the third wave almost half a year later, between October 15 and

November 2. Mothers and teachers were surveyed at the time of the second wave.

The basic research question was this: "What, if any, are the effects of broadcasting *Holocaust* on secondary school students' attitudes towards and knowledge of Jewish persecution before and during World War II?"[6]

RESULTS

Audience size.   The five *Holocaust* episodes had an average audience rating of 34 percent among the Dutch population of 12 years and older. Audience size declined from 39 percent for the first episode to 30 percent for the last. Total cumulative rating was 54 percent. Thus, more than half the Dutch population (age 12 and over) watched at least one episode of *Holocaust:* These viewers averaged viewing *Holocaust* on 2.4 of the 4 broadcast evenings.[7]

For the first two episodes, audience ratings were higher in younger than in older age categories; the age categories differed little in viewing level for the other three episodes. Both data are exceptions to the Dutch regular evening viewing patterns of considerably higher audience ratings in older than in younger age categories.

The 12-14 and 15-19 age categories showed the highest average audience ratings (44 percent and 36 percent) as well as the highest cumulative ratings (61 percent and 67 percent). Thus, *Holocaust* had a remarkably strong appeal to young viewers of secondary school age.

Parental influence on students' viewing.   Secondary school students' viewing of *Holocaust* depended to some extent on parental attitudes or actions. The number of episodes students saw was larger if one or more of the following conditions were present:

1. If the mother considered it important for her children to know about what had happened during World War II.
2. If the mother had suffered herself considerably during World War II.
3. If the parents had discussed collaboration and resistance with their children.
4. If the parents had discussed World War II topics with their children after they had seen a World War II program.
5. If the mother considered broadcasting *Holocaust* a good idea.

Nevertheless, about two-thirds of the students whose mothers disapproved of broadcasting *Holocaust* had seen at least one episode.

General program evaluation.   The second survey wave—conducted within a few weeks after *Holocaust* had been broadcast—contained a number of questions mapping student viewers' general evaluation of the series. A large majority of student viewers (77 percent) considered broadcasting *Holocaust* a very (23 percent) or fairly (54 percent) good idea. They maintained primarily that *Holocaust* taught a lesson to all not to forget what had happened and to prevent history from ever repeating itself in this respect.

A minority of 18 percent did not think it a good idea to broadcast *Holocaust:* these student viewers argued that the war was so long ago that there was no reason to show all this misery. Student viewers who watched a majority of the episodes had a more positive opinion about broadcasting *Holocaust* than students who saw fewer episodes.

Almost half of the student viewers (46 percent) considered *Holocaust* a program "to really stay home for." Student viewers who saw a majority of the episodes thought so much more than did students who saw fewer episodes.

The message.   Most student viewers (66 percent) felt that *Holocaust* had a definite message. This opinion was independent of the number of episodes watched. First of all, *Holocaust* was seen to warn that what the program showed should never happen again. Second, *Holocaust* was seen as telling its audience to be on guard against phenomena such as discrimination of minorities in general—a projection to today.

Somewhat less than half of the student viewers (43 percent) reported they had been impressed by *Holocaust* "very much" (9 percent) or "quite a bit" (34 percent); most said (57 percent) they were not so much impressed. Student viewers who watched more episodes were more impressed with *Holocaust* than students who saw fewer episodes. A large majority of student viewers (77 percent) mentioned one or more parts of *Holocaust* that really made an impression. The Babi Yar mass execution and the gas chambers were mentioned most often. The number of episodes students had seen made no difference on this point.

Most student viewers (62 percent) supposed that reality had been worse than what *Holocaust* shows. Student viewers who saw more episodes thought so more than students who watched fewer episodes.

Student perceptions after six months.   Half a year later, during the third survey wave, about one-third of the student viewers (30 percent) reported they still think about *Holocaust* occasionally. On their minds was mainly how atrocious World War II had been in general and the execution and gas chambers scenes of *Holocaust* in particular.

None of the three evaluation points (checked for long-term effects) showed any change from the second survey wave. There was no change in the extent to which student viewers considered *Holocaust* a program "to really stay home for," to which they expected reality to have been worse, or to which they had felt it was a good idea to broadcast *Holocaust*. Data from the control sample indicated no panel effects had occurred.

Influence of Holocaust *on World War II attitudes and knowledge.*   To establish the influence of *Holocaust* on World War II attitudes and knowledge, first and second wave results were compared. The analysis included both student viewers and student nonviewers. This procedure was chosen because of the pervasiveness of the total *Holocaust* "environment."

Virtually everybody in Holland was exposed to it in some way even if they had not watched the program themselves: special radio and television programs, extensive newspaper and magazine articles, and debates about the merits of (broadcasting) *Holocaust.* Automatic interaction detection was used to analyze the separate influences of watching *Holocaust* itself and of exposure to the wider *Holocaust* environment.

More than half of all students (55 percent) reported they learned something from *Holocaust* or its environment. Students who watched more *Holocaust* episodes reported subjective learning more frequently than those who saw fewer episodes.

A large majority of the students (77 percent) said they obtained a reasonably good impression of what had happened during World War II. Again, students who had seen more *Holocaust* episodes more often reported learning than those who had watched fewer episodes.

Most students (57 percent) said they had become more aware of the background of the Jewish persecution. This subjective learning was slightly related to the number of *Holocaust* episodes seen, but was strongly related to exposure to the *Holocaust* environment. Half a year later, subjective learning was no different from these second wave data.

Knowledge of persecuted groups. Immediately after *Holocaust* had been broadcast, students showed an increase in knowledge of groups which had been persecuted during World War II in addition to the Jews. Before *Holocaust,* students mentioned an average of 0.7 of the following groups: resistance fighters, gypsies, mentally handicapped, homosexuals, Slavic people, and Jehovah Witnesses; afterwards this average was 1.4.

Half a year later, students showed no decline in knowledge. (A somewhat lower score in the control sample suggests a slight panel effect may have occurred.) The increase in knowledge was slightly related to the number of *Holocaust* episodes watched, but more strongly to exposure to the *Holocaust* environment, especially the Aktua (public affairs background) television programs and the discussions with parents, peers, and teachers.

Knowledge of concentration camps. Immediately after *Holocaust* had been broadcast, students were able to give more names of concentration camps (average 1.9) than before (1.0). The increase in knowledge was related to exposure to the *Holocaust* environment and had not declined half a year later.

Opinions about prosecution of war criminals. Immediately after the *Holocaust* broadcasts, students who said "Don't prosecute war criminals anymore" dropped from 35 percent to 23 percent. However, most changers had returned to their original position half a year later (35 percent "Don't prosecute"). The immediate *Holocaust* effect was related to the number of *Holocaust* episodes seen, to exposure to the Aktua television programs, and to discussions with parents and peers.

Opinions about Jewish resistance.   Immediately after *Holocaust* was broadcast, students were likelier than before to say that the Jews had put up too little resistance against their persecution: (25 percent before; 40 percent after). Half a year later, a tendency to return to the original position was found (32 percent thinking the Jews should have resisted more). The immediate attitudinal effect was not related to watching *Holocaust* itself, but to exposure to the Aktua television programs and other mass media content on *Holocaust.*

Pertinence to contemporary life.   Immediately after the *Holocaust* broadcasts, more students disagreed with the statement "Such things cannot happen anymore" (66 percent) than before (55 percent). Half a year later, there was a tendency toward the original position (59 percent). The immediate effect was not related to actually watching *Holocaust,* but was related to exposure to the Aktua television programs and other mass media content on *Holocaust.*

General interest, knowledge, and attitudes.   *Holocaust* appeared to have no measureable short-term or long-term effect on students' general interest in World War II. But, half a year after *Holocaust* had been broadcast, most students (63 percent) scored higher on a World War II knowledge scale than before.[8] This increase was related to the number of *Holocaust* episodes watched, to exposure to the Aktua television program, and to discussions with parents.

Half a year after *Holocaust* had been broadcast, almost half of the students (41 percent) scored higher on a Judaism knowledge scale than before the broadcasts.[9] This increase was slightly related to the number of *Holocaust* episodes watched, but more strongly to exposure to the total *Holocaust* environment.

In the interviews conducted half a year after *Holocaust* had been broadcast, no effects were measured on a number of students' more general attitudes which might determine their opinions and behavior on today's political issues.[10] No effects were found for these: confidence in people, intolerance toward others (especially minority groups), intolerance toward deviant behavior, liberalism (in its classic European sense), and acceptance of authority.

However, on two important dimensions, effects were obtained. Half a year after the *Holocaust* broadcasts, students *had increased* in their disapproval of anti-Semitism and in their approval of violent resistance to minority oppression. (See note 10 for the scale used.)

CONCLUSIONS

All three objectives of the *Holocaust* educational campaign appear to have been obtained. First, the target audience of 12-19-year-old school students showed the highest average and cumulative audience ratings. Even if their parents disapproved of (broadcasting) *Holocaust,* most students were exposed to at least one episode of the series. In addition to large-scale exposure, student viewers received the program quite favorably. Second, students' knowledge of World War II and the Jewish persecution increased after *Holocaust* was broadcast; this increase had not diminished half a year later. Exposure to the total *Holocaust* environment was especially helpful in creating this effect. Third, relevant students' attitudes were affected. The message came across: Events like the Jewish persecution should never happen again. Attitudinal changes about the desirability of war criminal prosecution, the conviction that the Jews put up too little resistance, and the possibility that similar events could take place today, were evidence of increased disapproval of what happened then and of a more skeptical (and alert) view of what present political conditions in the world may lead to. Again, exposure to the total *Holocaust* environment was particularly effective.

In evaluating *Holocaust* effects, the crucial question is whether the decline in attitudinal changes half a year after the broadcasts implies that these intended effects were short-term only. If so, *Holocaust* would be less likely to have influence on the target audience's future political attitudes and behaviors. *Holocaust* would not have succeeded to teach history's lesson to the postwar generation.

One remarkable finding contradicts this implication and suggests that the decline may be the result of students' increasingly historic perspective on what actually happened, as time passed after the broadcasts. In fact, a more profound effect appears to have occurred; students translated *Holocaust's* historic lesson to the political conditions of the world today. Half a year after *Holocaust* had been broadcast, students showed increased sympathy for violent resistance against minority oppression. Thus, *Holocaust* seems to have strengthened students' adolescent inclination to actively protest injustice. They became more convinced that violent resistance is justified in extreme circumstances. This, of course, is an effect of considerable political importance.

NOTES

1. This article is based on a more extensive research report by Dick Verzijden of the Veldkamp Market Research Bureau, which conducted the field work in the study. The Netherlands Broadcasting Corporation (NOS) is indebted to the National Foundation for Mental Health, to the Queen Juliana Foundation, and to the Television Radio Broadcasting Corporation (TROS) for grants that made this research possible.

2. New York *Times,* April 21, 1978, II, p. 4.

3. New York *Times,* April 28, 1978, III, p. 26; July 15, p. 16; Sept. 12, p. 84.

4. The "claim system" prevents competition between the eight major broadcasting organizations from forcing these organizations to pay excessively high prices for foreign programs. The first organization to claim a foreign program has the exclusive broadcasting rights; if this first claim is dropped, the organization holding the second claim is entitled to broadcast the program. For a description of the Dutch Broadcasting System, see Chr. De Brauw, "Broadcasting in the Netherlands," Journal of Broadcasting, vol. 18, no. 4 (fall 1974), pp.453-463.

5. The NOS Audience Research Department serves as central research facility for all Dutch broadcasting organizations. Its continuous audience measurement system operates a nationally representative television panel in which about 1800 persons (age 3 and over) of about 600 families use individual weekly television diaries to report which programs of the two Dutch television channels they have watched for at least 50 percent of their duration.

6. Data analysis used the following statistical techniques: Kendall correlation coefficient, automatic interaction detection for multivariate analysis, Mokken's version of the Guttman scaling technique for scale construction (or summation scales if items clustered in a factor analysis without forming a one-dimensional Mokken scale) and the Median test to trace changes between survey waves. Applying the Median test to dependent samples yields a slightly conservative estimate of the significance of obtained differences. For the Mokken scaling procedure, see R.J. Mokken, *A Theory and Procedure of Scaling Analysis*, The Hague, Mouton, 1970.

7. Average audience size per program (between 6:45 and 10:45 p.m.) during the second quarter of 1979 was 12 percent for the total Dutch population age 12 and over; it was 11 percent and 13 percent for the 12-14 and 15-19 age categories, respectively.

8. Seven items testing respondents' knowledge constituted a World War II knowledge scale: beginning and end of World War II, existence of concentration camps in the Netherlands, first country to be occupied by Germany, number of Jews killed in Europe, names of concentration camps, and gypsies and homosexuals named as persecuted groups. The seven items formed a moderately strong Mokken scale (H=.39).

9. Three test items constituted a Judaism knowledge scale: date of Israel's foundation, meaning of "anti-Semitism," and meaning of "Zionism." The three items formed a strong Mokken scale (H=.56).

10. The general attitudes were measured using the following scales.

— *Confidence in people.* Agreement with these three statements: "Most people are to be trusted," "Most people want to help others," and "Most people try to be honest" (summation scale).

— *Intolerance toward others.* Agreement with these four items: "I would disapprove of a friend favoring removal of immigrant workers' children from schools," "smashing up a clubhouse for the fun of it," "calling a Black person names because of his color," "disliking Jews," or "shoplifting" (weak Mokken scale, H =.37).

— *Intolerance of deviant behavior.* Agreement with these three statements: "I would disapprove of a friend using heroin," "caught joyriding," or "being homosexual" (weak Mokken scale H=.35).

— *Acceptance of authority.* Five-item scale showing respondents to favor strong police action against crime, severe punishment of criminals, teachers taking sides with the school board in case of conflicts, and disciplined attitude toward superiors (moderately strong Mokken scale H=.39).

— *Liberalism.* Five-item scale (out of the same 15 mentioned above) showing respondents to agree with these statements: "People who disagree with me should be free to speak out," "Everybody should be free to say or write what he wants," "All citizens have equal rights," "People should be free to become a teacher regardless of their political conviction," and "Holland should accept all people driven out of their own country" (summation scale).

— *Resistance to minority oppression.* Three items showing respondents to agree with violent resistance if (1) One stood to lose all his belongings, (2) One lived on the minimum level of subsistence, and (3) One suffered discrimination because of color (summation scale).

A quite different study of Holocaust *is reported here from Austria by Peter Diem. Using independent samples in four waves—one before* Holocaust *and three after, the last wave conducted five months following the broadcast—Dr. Diem finds little long-term cognitive change among Austrian adults in response to* Holocaust. *(In a fifth wave of interviewing— conducted in August 1980, after the article published here went to press—Dr. Diem says he found evidence "that the originally quite marginal cognitive effects increased over time.") In conjunction with survey research, extensive content analyses of other response to the program were conducted. A majority of editorials and columns were favorable to the* Holocaust *broadcast; letters to the editor and phone calls and mail to the Austrian Radio (ORF) were less likely to be favorable. The more spontaneous (the earlier in the series) the viewer response, the less likely was the respondent to be sympathetic to the broadcast. Dr. Diem is a media researcher at Austrian Radio and is a lecturer in the Media Studies Institute at the University of Vienna.*

34

"HOLOCAUST" AND THE AUSTRIAN VIEWER

Peter Diem

THE TELEVISION SERIES 'Holocaust' was broadcast in the Federal Republic of Germany on the third channel at the end of January 1979. The four episodes[1] were each watched by between a fourth and a third of the population; 48% saw at least one episode. In Austria the series went out on the second channel from 1-4 March 1979. The individual episodes achieved viewing figures of between 40 and 50%; 61% of Austrians over 14 saw at least one episode. These high audience figures for 'Holocaust' in Austria are all the more remarkable in that all four parts were scheduled against very popular light entertainment programmes on the first channel, TV 1 (including 'The Wencke Myhre Show' and Rudi Carrell's 'Non-stop'). As a result of the considerable response to the series in the Federal Republic of Germany, Österreichischer Rundfunk (ORF) had decided to conduct an extensive research programme to obtain an accurate analysis of the impact of the series in Austria.

The 'Holocaust' research programme consisted of:

1   A *lightning telephone survey* on the day following the broadcast of the final part, in order to obtain an approximate idea of the audience figures for 'Holocaust' and what people thought of it.

2   An accurate determination of the audience figures by means of a *public opinion poll (Infratest)* conducted *before, during,* and *after* the broadcasts, with additional questions to measure the effects on the public.

3   The evaluation of the *telephone calls* to the ORF during and immediately after the broadcast.

4   The evaluation of the *correspondence* received by the ORF in connection with the series.

5   An analysis of the trend and content of the considerable response elicited by the broadcast in the *print media* (articles, reviews, readers' letters).

6   *Post-measurements* in the context of later representative surveys. Using the same questions as in the *Infratest,* the idea was to check whether the media event 'Holocaust' had been capable or not of a long-lasting impact on the population.

---

[1] Consistent with German practice, the series was shown in double-length episodes. *Ed.*

From Peter Diem, "'Holocaust' and the Austrian Viewer," EBU-Review 31, 1 (1980) 35-40. Copyright 1980 by EBU-Review. Reprinted by permission.

The lightning telephone survey

In order to obtain an initial estimate of audience figures and appreciation, a lightning telephone survey was carried out by a consortium of Fessel : Gfk and Ifes on the day following the last episode of 'Holocaust', i.e. 5 March 1979. Altogether, 377 Austrians aged from 16 to 70, representative of the corresponding population group (in absolute figures, 4,916,000 Austrians), were interviewed.

The *cumulative audience* was 59%, and 28% had seen all four parts. The series was positively rated by 87% of all 'Holocaust' viewers, the average index being 2.25 (on a scale ranging from 1 'liked it very much' to 5 'didn't like it at all').

Assessment according to characteristics was predominantly positive: 92% described the programme as 'believable', 85% as 'tense', 79% as 'really gripping', 73% as 'necessary', 68%, after all, as 'objective' and 65% as 'historically interesting'. At the same time there were clear signs of the younger generation taking more interest in contemporary history. The appreciation figures given by the under-40s were better in all dimensions than those given by the over-40s.

Audience survey

The Fessel ÷ Gfk and Ifes institutes carried out an audience survey for the ORF in the form of a representative fixed-date interview covering the four days *before* 'Holocaust', the event itself (five days) and the four days *following* the broadcasting of the series (13 report days altogether). Austrians over 14 were questioned. On each survey day, 200 interviews were conducted, so that 800 *pre*-programme and 800 *post*-programme interviews were available for measurements of Austrians' attitudes to the National-Socialist era.

The programme was rated on the *Infratest* survey index, a six-point scale from 'very good' to 'very poor', the most favourable value being 5.0.

The survey confirmed the results of the telephone operation. As many as 61% of Austrians aged 14 or over (3,500,000) had seen at least one episode; almost exactly a quarter (26% or 1,500,00) had watched all four parts. There was an unmistakable correlation between audience figures, age, income, and size of locality. The highest figures were achieved in Vienna, among the under-19s and in families having net monthly incomes in excess of 17,000 schillings. In contrast, the lowest audience figures for the series were found in localities of under 2,000 inhabitants, among the over-50s, and among people

having a net monthly household income of less than 5,000 schillings.

As regards occupational categories, it was mainly schoolchildren, self-employed persons, and the professional classes that were most likely to watch the programme, while farmers and pensioners showed least interest.

Regionally, interest was greatest in Vienna and southern Austria, and least in Upper Austria and Salzburg (apparently the series had already been extensively viewed on German television in these two federal provinces). The appreciation figures for 'Holocaust' improved from episode to episode, the average reaction index being 3.91; 90.3% of respondents expressed a positive opinion on 'Holocaust'.

The—competing—light entertainment programme on TV 1 mainly attracted the interest of older viewers. See the following table.

The 'Holocaust' day compared on the two television channels			
(Viewers aged 14 or over)			
Broadcast date/title	*absolute*	%	*reaction index*
Wednesday 28.2, 20.00 hours			
TV 1 Carnival	1,666,000	29	3.0
TV 2 Final solution	892,000	15	4.0
	2,558,000	44	
Thursday 1.3, 20.00 hours			
TV 1 Adoptions	731,000	13	4.1
TV 2 Holocaust 1	3,025,000	52	3.5
	3,756,000	65	
Friday 2.3, 20.15			
TV 1 The Wencke Myhre Show	831,000	14	4.3
TV 2 Holocaust 2	2,860,000	49	3.7
	3,691,000	63	
Saturday 3.3, 20.15			
TV 1 Non-stop (Am laufenden Band)	1,681,000	29	3.6
TV 2 Holocaust 3	2,212,000	38	3.9
	3,893,000	67	
Sunday 4.3, 20.15			
TV 1 The Great Race	915,000	16	3.5
TV 2 Holocaust 4	2,540,000	44	4.1
TV 2 Club 2, 22.00 hours	483,000	8	4.4
	3,938,000	68	

According to the above figures, from Thursday 1 March to Sunday 4 March 1979 almost exactly two-thirds of the nation watched television in the evening—truly a 'media event'.

Broken down per channel, the maximum figures ('viewed at all') for 1975/1978 were 63% on average for TV 1, and 18% on average for TV 2. Therefore, despite strong competition, 'Holocaust' was able to 'reverse' the channels.

The overall reaction remained 75% positive when individual dimensions of the series were examined. Here the youngest population group gave a distinctly better verdict than the oldest. Altogether, 'Holocaust' came across outstandingly well, both as regards content and in television terms, the programme being described as 'believable' by 89% of respondents, as 'interesting' by 70%, as 'objective' by 60%; only by 13% was the series felt to be melodramatic and over-sentimental, which had been one of the main criticisms in the prior discussion in the print media.

Exactly half of the respondents indicated that 'Holocaust' was a current topic of conversation for them. Younger people, in particular, spoke a great deal about the series.

Analysis of the telephone calls

It was known, from the experience of the ORF's audience relations service, that a telephone response to the *content* of a programme normally turns out to be negative. This holds especially for the first—and most spontaneous—calls. The hypothesis on which the analysis was based, i.e. that television broadcasts which take existing social prejudices as their themes initially result in a spontaneous protest by the highly prejudiced (the 'parade-ground effect') which dies down in the course of the broadcast and gives way to a calmer, more positive assessment by the less-prejudiced viewers, was wholly confirmed in the case of 'Holocaust'.

With 8,227 calls about 'Holocaust' the spontaneous response was almost twice as high—in relation to the population—as in the Federal Republic of Germany. The time trend was clearly in favour of the positive calls: for the documentary 'Final Solution' on 28 February, 40% positive and 44% negative calls were counted; for the fourth part of 'Holocaust' there were 58% positive and 30% negative calls. Altogether, the spontaneous telephone response, with 49% positive and 39% negative attitudes to 'Holocaust', was distinctly more positive than for comparable earlier programmes.

Male callers were over-represented by about a fifth. Women reacted much more positively than men on the telephone; the positive attitude to 'Holocaust' diminished with increasing age, but rose again in the population group aged over 60 (which includes a higher proportion of women).

Qualitative individual results in the spontaneous response

'Manifest antisemitism' dimension

Manifest antisemitism (8%) was to be noted more among *male callers* (men 10%, women 5%). This attitude was found chiefly among callers from Voralberg, Carinthia, and Styria.

'Latent antisemitism' dimension

Altogether, latent antisemitism was found among 11% of callers. In this respect, callers were uniformly distributed among the various federal provinces. This dimension was especially frequently in evidence in the case of *pensioners* (possibly expellees?), with 14%, and farmers, with 17% (in a small basic population class!).

'Manifest antifascism' dimension

This dimension occurred most frequently among the over-60s (9%—the average was 4%).

Criticism of presentation

This was found chiefly among the *self-employed* and among *students* (21% and 20% respectively, as against 16% on average). It was also frequently made by persons who stated that they themselves had direct experience (as victims); they frequently said, too, that the reality had been much worse.

Emotional effect

On average, 7% of callers mentioned the emotional effect. The figures were appreciably higher in the case of *house-*

wives (12%); they seem to have been most strongly affected emotionally by the programmes.

Requests for repeats; programming policy

A desire to have the programme repeated was expressed by an average of 9% of callers. It was found chiefly among *younger people* (13% of the under-25s and 12% of the under-40s, as against only 7% of the over-40s). It was also frequently expressed by *students* (11%). Comments on programming policy were made by 5% of callers (8% in the case of workers).

Correspondence received by ORF

Altogether, ORF received 529 letters on the subject of 'Holocaust'. The trend of the attitudes expressed in the letters corresponded to the results of the telephone evaluation, but detailed examination revealed that the letter-writers exhibited a higher degree of antisemitism than the callers. Women accounted for 36% of the mail, and men for 54%. Here, too, the women's reactions were distinctly more positive than the men's. On a regional basis, however, the figures are markedly skew compared with the telephone calls; the largest proportion of negative mail was received from the provinces of Salzburg und Upper Austria.

The time trend in the basic attitude expressed tallied with that of the telephone calls; before 1 March 19% of letters were positive and 59% negative, and after 1 March 51% positive and 39% negative letters were recorded. There was a strikingly high proportion of irrational communications.

Analysis of the press coverage of 'Holocaust'

Of a total of 1,099 newspaper articles on 'Holocaust' published in the period from 17 January to 2 April 1979, 22% appeared in the party press of the SPÖ (Social Democrats), 9% in the party press of ÖVP (Christian Democrats), and 4% in Church newspapers; 65% of the articles were printed in independent press vehicles or those belonging to other groups, such as the KPÖ (Communists).

Readers' letters accounted for 46% of all items ; 12% were editorials and columnists' articles.

Of this total, 49% expressed a positive attitude to 'Holocaust', 14% were negative, and 9% were ambivalent.

The *editorials and columnists' articles* in the newspapers were more positive than the attitude of the population (82% approval, 4% rejection as against 76% approval and 18% rejection).

The SPÖ press most clearly approved of 'Holocaust'; approval in the *Church media* was almost as great, while the least positive attitude was expressed by the *ÖVP media*.

Comparison of readers' letters in the three groupings shows that letters to SPÖ and Church press vehicles were likewise more positive than letters to ÖVP media. The tabloids *Kronen-Zeitung* and *Kurier* came respectively slightly below and above the average appraisal index as regards content. The major provincial papers had below-average figures, as did all ÖVP vehicles.

Comparison of results overall			
	Positive	*negative*	*index*
	%	%	
Editorials, columns	82	4	2,050.0
Population (*Infratest*)	76	18	422.2
Readers' letters	57	27	211.1
Telephone calls to ORF	49	39	125.6
Mail to ORF	47	38	123.7

The most positive reaction to 'Holocaust' was noted in the *editorials and columns* in the press coverage of the programme.

With 82% positive statements, they come above the *Infratest results* which showed 76% of positive basic attitudes in the total population.

The opinions expressed in readers' letters were positive in 57% of cases. The lowest percentages of positive basic attitudes were seen in *telephone calls* (49%) and *mail* (47%) to the ORF.

From this may be derived the logical statement that *the response to the media event 'Holocaust' was proportionately worse, the more spontaneous the reaction.*

A clear idea of the distribution of the attitude patterns in 'published opinion' is given by the following *comparison* between statements in columnists' pieces, newspaper articles, readers' letters, and mail received by ORF.

	Editorials, columns	News-paper articles overall	Readers' letters	ORF mail
	%	%	%	%
Antisemitism	0 ⎫	3 ⎫	6 ⎫	13 ⎫
Counter-version	8 ⎬ 10	11 ⎬ 19	18 ⎬ 34	20 ⎬ 48
Dismissal of facts	2 ⎭	5 ⎭	10 ⎭	15 ⎭
Antifascism	1	1	1	9
Topical relevance	44	44	33	34
References to contemporary history	24	16	19	33
Creation of awareness	51	27	30	*
	n = 131	n = 1,099	n = 505	n = 529

* The 'creation of awareness' category was not determined in any comparable form in letters to the ORF. The categories under which the telephone calls about 'Holocaust' were evaluated were not directly comparable with the above categories.

The attitude breakdown in the 'general opinion' (which can be measured demoscopically and, taken together with the 'published opinion', goes to make up the total phenomenon of 'public opinion') was *three-quarters in favour* and *one-fifth against*, during the period the programme was broadcast.

The *short-term impact* of 'Holocaust' indicated attitude changes in about 5% of Austrians (300,000), who appeared *more informed* and *less prejudiced* immediately after the programme.

The long-term effect of 'Holocaust' on the attitude of the Austrians to the persecution of the Jews

In order to establish whether the effect of the television series 'Holocaust' on the Austrian population's attitude to the mass murders of the Jews as measured immediately after the broadcast was maintained, three relevant points were covered again in representative surveys in July and August.

While shortly after the series was broadcast distinctly more Austrians were of the opinion that millions of Jews were murdered under the Nazi regime, the enlightenment effect diminished again in the long run. Nonetheless, a larger proportion of the population than before the broadcasts now considers the mass killings to be proved. Hence *a definite, if slight, long-term effect of the film as regards the historical truth of the extermination of the Jews exists.*

Five months after the broadcasting of 'Holocaust', the number of those who considered the mass killings to be *unproved* rose once more to the level of immediately before the programme. Those 'brought round' by the series and the response to it (5%) have either returned to their original convictions or now dare to express them again, as 'Holocaust' has ceased to be a matter of public discussion.

Attitude to the fact of the mass killings				
Given statement	Before the 'Holo-caust' broad-casts	After the 'Holo-caust' broad-casts	July 1979	August 1979
In the National-Socialist period, millions of Jews were killed	72% →	81% ←	76% ↖	75%
The mass extermination of the Jews by National-Socialism is unproved	16%	11%	16%	15%
	n = 800	n = 800	n = 1,000	n = 1,600

Ways of coming to terms with the past				
Given statement	Before the 'Holo-caust' broad-casts	After the 'Holo-caust' broad-casts	July 1979	August 1979
We should let the matter rest at last	47%	42%	48% ↖	49%
It is important to be aware of what happened	48% →	55% ←	46% ↖	47%
	n = 800	n = 800	n = 1,000	n = 1,600

The desire 'to hear nothing more of all that' seems to have been reinforced in the long term. It is possible that some degree of 'overload' produced by the television programmes broadcast in this period ('Holocaust' and the extensive discussions on it, Syberberg's *Hitler*, 'Club 2' on this topic, documentaries on the attempted assassination of Hitler and on the beginning of the Second World War) played a part, so that the emotional effect felt immediately after the programmes—55% expressed the view that people must be made aware of what happened so that nothing of the kind could ever occur again—had to give way to the endeavour to suppress everything.

On the statute of limitations for war crimes

Given statement	Before the 'Holo-caust' broad-casts	After the 'Holo-caust' broad-casts	July 1979	August 1979
The matter should be closed	77%	74%	71%	≠ 75%
The matter should be kept open	17% →	24% ←	23%	≠ 20%
	n = 800	n = 800	n = 1,000	n = 1,600

The percentage of *those advocating the statute of limitations* for war crimes followed a non-standard pattern— at all events, it did not correspond to the trend of the other questions. In the end, however, the number of these people also seems to settle down to a level slightly *above* that found before the series was broadcast, but yet *below* that obtained *before* 'Holocaust'.

The figures for those *against* a time-limitation for war crimes were wholly in accordance with the general trend; they were lower than immediately after 'Holocaust', but *higher* than before the broadcasts.

If the long-term effect is analysed according to *population groups*, it is noticeable that the number of those who did not reply to the survey questions fell, especially in the younger age groups—an indication of an *increase in awareness*. On the other hand, those groups that watched 'Holocaust' least (e.g. farmers and pensioners) still exhibited a prejudice pattern at least as definite as before the broadcasts. Even major media events, in fact, are unable to change attitudes that are frequently centuries old.

Again with the qualification that the survey contains error limits that are in part greater than the measured percentage differences, it may consequently be said that even the long-term impact on the total population of a media event like 'Holocaust' is clearly minimal.

It is a legitimate hypothesis that, in the *cognitive area*, 'Holocaust' clearly achieved only a minimal (manifest) long-term effect, but that in the *emotional* area it probably produced a greater (latent) lasting impact. This could no

doubt be 'called up' if the subject became topical again. However, the series certainly brought about a sensitization of the vehicles of published opinion and of the whole area of school and national education.

Accompanying measures of the Federal Ministry for Education and Art

In view of the anticipated considerable interest of the television series, the Ministry of Education made extensive accompanying material on contemporary history and a number of official advisers on contemporary topics available to schools.

The interest in accompanying information was, however, rather slight on the whole, especially as regards the demand for advisers. Nonetheless, it was possible to initiate a pedagogical process: the great response to 'Holocaust' in all the mass media encouraged new didactic approaches in dealing with contemporary history.

Summary

The findings of the empirical social research into the subsequent effects of 'Holocaust' are both encouraging and discouraging. While full recognition must be given to the immediate impact that the 'Holocaust media event' had in Austria (high penetration, good reception in the press and the population, arousal of interest with young people and adult educationists), the question as to the *long-term effect* remains open. If, barely half a year after the broadcasts, reliable demoscopic attitude measurements showed little more than a marginal change in the distribution of prejudice and in historical knowledge among Austrians, we must then ask why even easily-digested and emotionally very positive attempts to inform on the part of the mass media do not trigger off any real (i.e. long-term effective) and profound learning processes. The wider impact of 'Holocaust' was evidently only slight.

And yet one may hope that, in more deep-seated socio-psychological areas and among not-insignificant groups, such as young people or adult educationists, the series has resulted in an increased willingness to face up to tragic periods of our own history and that the chance of coming to terms with the past is thereby improved. □

Why media campaigns fail has been the theme of much research over the years. In the last decade, improvements in theory and methodology have led to new conceptual and analytical approaches to the problems of selectivity processes and media influence. Michael A. Milburn uses the crosslag panel correlation technique and regression analysis to study the relationship between exposure to a heart disease campaign in the mass media and health knowledge and attitudes in several California communities in the early 1970s. This careful study found minimal selective exposure and a fairly strong indication that campaign media exposure increased health knowledge, resulting in attitude change. Dr. Milburn is an assistant professor of psychology at the University of Massachusetts at Boston.

35

A LONGITUDINAL TEST OF THE SELECTIVE EXPOSURE HYPOTHESIS

Michael A. Milburn

THE predominant position in the literature on the effects of mass media campaigns is that attempts at changing attitudes and behavior through the media will be unsuccessful. The argument is that it may be possible to increase knowledge, but that attitudes are highly resistant to change (Rogers, 1962, 1973), and the media's effects are severely limited by many hypothesized selective processes operating (e.g., selective exposure). An extensive review and critique of the evidence for the existence of these selective processes is presented elsewhere (Milburn, 1978).

This paper offers new evidence for the success of a media campaign. The suggestion is made that a complex relationship between selectivity effects and mass media campaign effects may be operating. The importance of supplementing a media campaign with personal contact and of working to increase knowledge prior to changing attitudes is indicated.

From Michael A. Milburn, "A Longitudinal Test of the Selective Exposure Hypothesis," *Public Opinion Quarterly* 43 (1979) 507-517. Copyright 1979 by The Trustees of Columbia University. Reprinted by permission.

The Stanford Study

The research arguing that mass media campaigns will produce no attitude or behavior change has been hampered by various methodological problems. The data used for analysis in this report, collected by the Stanford Heart Disease Prevention Project (SHDPP), a joint research program directed by Dr. John Farquhar of the Stanford Medical School, Professor Nathan Maccoby of the Stanford Department of Communication, and Dr. William Brown of the Stanford Medical School, avoids many of these problems. They conducted a major field experiment in three California communities in an attempt to reduce the risk of heart disease by disseminating information through the mass media. As a test of the major issues of the effects of mass media campaigns, this study surpasses all previous efforts in both extent of coverage and specificity of goals.

Instead of being limited in time as media campaigns in the past have been, the SHDPP campaign lasted three years. Baseline data were collected in the fall of 1972, following which the campaign began and panel data on the same individuals were collected in the fall of 1973, 1974, and 1975. Analyses of data from 1972 to 1974 are reported here.

Including adequate control groups (or any control group at all) has been a problem in past media campaigns because random assignment to exposure conditions within a community is very difficult, if not impossible. Instead of working within only one city as past campaigns have done, the SHDPP dealt with this problem by including three communities: one control community, Tracy, and two treatment communities: Gilroy, which received only the media intervention, and Watsonville, which received both the media intervention and personal instruction of a selected group of high-risk individuals. Although multiple communities in both treatment and control conditions would be preferable to single communities, the SHDPP design surpasses any previous study.

Finally, instead of working on diffuse attitudes, the SHDPP set a specific goal: reducing the risk of heart disease. Four behaviors associated with the risk of heart disease were targeted for change: encouraging people to lose weight, stop smoking, consume less cholesterol, and exercise more. The emphasis in the campaign was on skills training, so, for example, many low-cholesterol recipes were prepared and distributed through the mail, in newspaper columns, and so on.

A considerable amount of data was collected. Measures of attitudes toward physical activity, weight, diet, and smoking, as well as behavioral measures, were obtained. Attitude items included, for example, for physical activity: "Most kinds of physical activities are boring" and "I feel self-conscious when people see me exercising or playing sports"; for weight: "I should lose a few pounds" and "If I could lose weight I'd be better-looking"; and for diet: "Breakfast doesn't seem right without eggs" and "If I ate only things that are good for me, food would be boring." In addition to the attitude and behavior variable, physiological measures were taken of blood pressure and serum cholesterol levels, media campaign exposure questions were asked, health knowledge of the factors related to the risk of heart disease was assessed, and a wide range of background variables was measured.

Research Background

Many reviews of the mass media literature (e.g., Bauer, 1964; Griffiths and Knutson, 1960; Larsen, 1964) argue that media campaigns will be ineffective in changing attitudes or behavior, citing both the arguments and the evidence used by Klapper (1960). Klapper stated that the most likely effect of media campaigns will be to reinforce current attitudes rather than to change them because of three processes operating: selective exposure, selective perception, and selective retention. The hypothesis of selective exposure argues that individuals will tend to expose themselves to information with which they agree; the hypothesis of selective perception argues that even if individuals are exposed to counter-attitudinal information, the information will be distorted in such a way that the individuals will perceive it as supportive of their beliefs; and the hypothesis of selective retention argues that individuals will remember only that information which supports their current beliefs.

A review of the largely experimental literature on these three selective processes indicates fairly weak support for selective exposure and selective retention, and only moderate support for selective perception (Milburn, 1978). The evidence is by no means strong enough to conclude that, because of these processes, media campaigns will necessarily be ineffective in changing attitudes or behavior.

In an analysis of the media campaigns which Klapper cites and a review of research from more recent media campaigns (Milburn, 1978), several important observations emerge: (1) Evidence from short-term media campaigns does not address the question of the effectiveness of mass media campaigns. Simply because selective processes may operate in the short term does not mean they cannot be overcome by a longer campaign. (2) Campaigns which focus upon changing diffuse attitudes rather than on increasing knowledge and changing the specific attitudes related to important behaviors are not likely to be successful. The analysis of the Stanford data provides additional support for this argument. Finally, (3) simply because some media campaigns have been unsuccessful does not mean all campaigns must be unsuccessful. Evidence from mass media campaigns which finds no effect on attitudes and behavior supports the conclusion that it is possible to conduct an unsuccessful campaign and still find limited support for selective processes. Findings of no effect do not support the conclusion that selective effects cannot be overcome and a successful campaign conducted. Mass media interventions which fail to change the targeted attitudes and behavior are always open to the criticism that they were not conducted well enough. Mendelsohn (1973) argues that information campaigns can succeed if consideration is given not only to the interest in the campaign material of those addressed by the campaign but to their beliefs, values, and mass media habits as well; if middle-range goals are set as specific objectives; and if use is made of environmental support systems to aid the campaign.

Method of Analysis

To assess the relationship in the Stanford data between exposure to the media campaign, knowledge of factors related to heart disease, and attitudes toward the behaviors associated with the risk of heart disease, two different procedures are employed: crosslag panel correlation analysis (Kenny, 1973, 1975) and the more traditional estimation of partial regression (or path model) coefficients (Heise, 1970). These two procedures test different models of the relationships between exposure, knowledge, and attitudes and provide different perspectives on the data.

The technique of crosslagged panel correlation analysis attempts to rule out spuriousness as an explanation of the correlation between two variables, a necessary step before any causal inference can be attempted. Having found a nonzero correlation between two variables as, for example, between campaign exposure and knowledge, it may be that exposure to the campaign causes increases in knowledge. Or it may be that those individuals more knowledgeable about the risks of heart disease attend more closely to the campaign. Or it may be that some third variable is responsible for the observed correlation between the two variables. It is this third variable explanation which the crosslag technique attempts to rule out. If the explanation of spuriousness can be ruled out, then the two causal hypotheses are tested against each other; in our example: media campaign effects versus selective exposure.

It is not necessarily the case, however, that these two processes are mutually exclusive. Each may be operating to a certain extent in a media campaign. A more complex model of reciprocal causation can be estimated with the use of path model techniques. The partial regression coefficients from knowledge at Time 1 to exposure at Time 2 and from exposure at Time 1 to knowledge at Time 2 (controlling for the influences of background variables and variables' influence on themselves) estimate both the direct effect of knowledge on exposure and the effect of exposure on knowledge.

The media exposure variables used in this analysis are composite indices of the responses to several items asking whether a particular feature of the media campaign was remembered (e.g., recognition of the SHDPP logo, recollection of receiving the cookbook of low-cholesterol recipes). The length of the 1974 questionnaire was reduced from the 1973 version, so the exposure measure in 1973 was based on a larger number of items than in 1974. Because the media campaign did not begin until after the baseline data were collected in 1972, analyses involving campaign exposure measures were done only for 1973 and 1974. The knowledge variable was also an index composed of 24 questions related to the behaviors associated with the risk of heart disease (physical activity, weight, diet, and smoking). The full text of the items for both indices is reported in Milburn (1978).

The attitude measures used include composite indices of attitudes toward physical activity, weight and diet. Extensive analysis of the attitude items collected by the Stanford project has been done and is reported in Milburn (1978). The essential findings indicated that for both physical activity and weight, two attitude factors emerged representing what were labeled Specific and General attitudes. The Specific attitude factor contained items relating to the specific cues and contingencies associated with physical activity and weight behaviors, and were found to correlate highly with the measured behavior. The General attitude factor correlated close to zero. Consequently, the items from the Specific attitude factors for weight and physical activity were each summed to obtain attitude indices. This Specific-General attitude factor pattern was also found for smoking; however, the smoking items were asked only of the smokers in the study, and analyses on this domain would have necessitated excluding many subjects or using a correlation matrix with coefficients based on widely differing numbers of subjects.

For the cholesterol and diet domain, only three attitude items were asked of respondents in any year, making the attitude factor analysis done on the other domains possible, but not very informative; consequently, the three items were summed to form a scale, although the reliability was lower than the other two domains.

The most appropriate tests of the selective hypothesis would be crosslag analyses and regression analyses of attitudes and media campaign exposure. Unfortunately, because of a decision made during the progress of the study, nearly all the Specific factor attitude items for weight and physical activity were not asked in 1974, the third year of survey administration (these analyses indicating their relationship to behavior had not been done at that time). Analyses done with the available attitude items from 1973 and 1974 indicated the General factors' correlations with campaign exposure was near zero, making a test of the difference between the crosslags to indicate causal direction uninformative.

The implication of the low campaign exposure-general attitude correlations was either that there was no relationship between exposure and attitudes or that some variable was mediating between exposure and attitudes. Health knowledge appeared to be a likely mediating variable.

Crosslag and regression analyses between campaign exposure and health knowledge were done for the years 1973 and 1974 for the two treatment communities, Watsonville and Gilroy. For the general attitude and health knowledge measures, crosslag and regression analyses were done for the two treatment communities and for the control community of Tracy using data from the years 1972 and 1973. Because of the lack of appropriate 1974 attitude data, the attitude-knowledge analyses for the years 1973 and 1974 were not possible.

Results

The overall pattern of results from both the crosslag analysis and the partial regression analysis supports the inferences that exposure to the media campaign caused increases in health knowledge and that in turn these increases in health knowledge caused more positive attitudes toward physical activity and a healthy diet. There is also some minimal support for the argument that selective exposure may be operating reciprocally with media campaign effects.

The campaign exposure-health knowledge crosslag analysis indicates, particularly for Watsonville, that the model of spurious causation of the association between these two variables should be rejected. In both the treatment cities, the direction of the crosslag difference (Figure 1) supports the inference that campaign exposure caused increases in knowledge (Watsonville, $Z = 2.450$, $p < .02$; Gilroy, $Z = 1.197$, $p < .24$). The difference is much smaller, although in the same direction, for Gilroy than for Watsonville.

The partial regression analysis for exposure and knowledge evidences a very similar pattern (Table 1). Exposure had a significant effect on knowledge in Watsonville, but not in Gilroy. In both cities

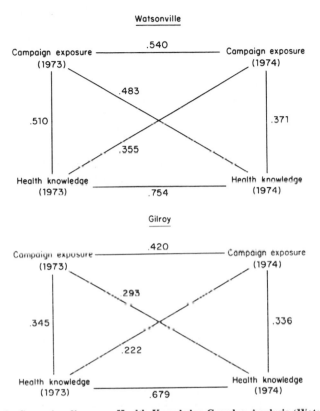

Figure 1. Campaign Exposure-Health Knowledge Crosslag Analysis (Watsonville)

the knowledge to exposure paths (representing the effect of selective exposure) do not reach standard levels of statistical significance ($p <$ .10 for both). Earlier research has indicated that significant increases in health knowledge occurred in the treatment communities and that the percentage increase was significantly different from the control community (Meyer et al., 1978), with the largest effects occurring in Watsonville. The results reported here add additional support to the

Table 1. Regression Estimates of Knowledge-Exposure and Exposure-Knowledge Effects

	Exposure-Knowledge		Knowledge-Exposure	
	(1973)	(1974)	(1973)	(1974)
Watsonville	.148*		.076	
Gilroy	.059		.090	

* ($p <$ .01).

NOTE: Regression coefficients (beta-weights) were computed controlling for the effects of age, sex, income, ethnicity, and education.

conclusion that the media campaign was effective by indicating the causal relationship between exposure and knowledge.

A potential noncausal explanation of these results arises from differences between the 1973 and 1974 exposure measures. Because fewer questions were included in the 1974 scale, it is likely to be less reliable than the 1973 measure. This lower reliability of the 1974 exposure measure may have been responsible for the crosslag difference indicating exposure causing knowledge, rather than any actual causal effect. Therefore, the 1973 index was recomputed to include the same number of items as in 1974 (eight), and the analyses were done again. Larger crosslag differences in the same direction as before were obtained.

The crosslag and partial regression analyses also indicated a link between increases in health knowledge and more positive attitudes toward health-producing behaviors. Table 2 presents the Z-tests of the differences between the knowledge and attitude crosslags for the three attitude domains of physical activity, weight, and diet for the three communities in the study. Positive differences indicate that knowledge causes a change in attitudes, and negative differences indicate that attitudes cause changes in knowledge. All these crosslag analyses were done controlling for the effects of age, sex, education, income, ethnicity, and (for Watsonville) participation in the Intensive Instruction program, as were the previous crosslag analyses.

The results are strongest for the domain of physical activity: the differences for all three communities are statistically significant, indicating that increasing knowledge causes more positive attitudes toward physical activity. The pattern of correlations for Watsonville is presented in Figure 2. The results are more equivocal for weight and diet, the only statistically significant result indicating that in Gilroy attitudes toward weight caused increasing knowledge. The results which support the conclusion that knowledge causes attitudes are most consistent for Watsonville, paralleling the finding by Meyer

Table 2. Z-Tests of Differences Between Health Knowledge and Attitude Crosslags (1972–1973)

	Watsonville (N=406)	Gilroy (N=401)	Tracy (N=374)
Physical activity	2.233*	4.583***	3.401***
Weight	1.437	−3.028**	1.097
Diet	.747	1.499	−.022

* = ($p < .05$). ** = ($p < .01$). *** = ($p < .001$).
NOTE: Positive differences indicate knowledge causing attitudes; negative differences indicate attitudes causing knowledge.

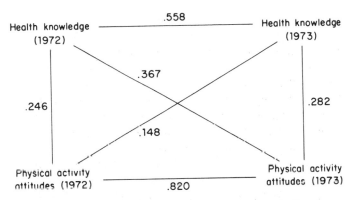

Figure 2. Health Knowledge-Physical Activity Attitude Crosslag

et al. (1978) that the greatest increases in health knowledge occurred in this community.

The partial regression results parallel the pattern of cross-lag differences very closely (Table 3). The paths from knowledge to attitudes toward physical activity are significant in all three cities, and only in Watsonville is there a significant (though smaller) path from physical activity attitudes to knowledge. For diet there are statistically significant paths from knowledge to attitudes in the treatment cities of Watsonville and Gilroy and nonsignificant paths from attitudes toward diet to health knowledge in all the cities. Attitudes toward weight show the same anomalous result of a significant negative relationship from attitudes to knowledge. Generally, the paths

Table 3. Regression Estimates of Knowledge-Attitude and Attitude-Knowledge Effects

	Attitude-Knowledge		Knowledge-Attitude	
	(1972)	(1973)	(1972)	(1973)
Watsonville				
Physical activity	.112*		.248*	
Weight	.035		−.063	
Diet	.054		.172*	
Gilroy				
Physical activity	.040		.219*	
Weight	−.117*		.067	
Diet	.012		.100*	
Tracy				
Physical activity	.008		.201*	
Weight	−.003		−.036	
Diet	.055		.058	

* ($p < .01$).

NOTE: Regression coefficients (beta-weights) were computed controlling for the effects of age, sex, income, ethnicity, education.

estimating the causal impact of attitudes on knowledge are nonsignificant, while increases in knowledge do appear to have an impact on attitudes.

A problem with the interpretation of crosslag results involves the assumption that the causal structure between variables remains the same over time (Kenny, 1975: 890–91). An implication of this assumption is that the synchronous correlations should be equal. This assumption appears to be met with respect to attitudes and knowledge, but it is not so clearly met with respect to exposure and knowledge. A reliability-ratio correction procedure for violations of this assumption, available when three or more variables are measured in a panel study, has been proposed by Kenny (1975) and was applied to these data. This procedure overcorrected the differences in the synchronous correlations and produced larger differences than before, reflecting the recurring problem of several unreliably measured variables in the 1974 survey administration.

The most reliably measured variable, attitudes toward physical activity, shows the effect of knowledge on attitudes most strongly. Coupled with the finding that exposure to the media campaign is associated with increasing knowledge, this finding provides support for the effectiveness of the media campaign. Only minimal support was found for the hypothesized operation of selective exposure.

Discussion

The relevant literature suggests that conclusions about the ineffectiveness of media campaigns in changing attitudes may be unwarranted. Further, the results presented in this paper support a model of media campaign effectiveness: Exposure to the campaign increased knowledge, which in turn resulted in attitude change. However, this conclusion cannot be stated without qualification.

The attitude-knowledge crosslag analysis was done for the years 1972–1973, while the exposure-knowledge analysis was done for the years 1973–1974. It is possible that the attitude-knowledge relationship changes from one year to the next, though why it would is not clear. Given the limitations of the data collected, it is not possible to answer this question.

In addition, the strength of the exposure-knowledge association in Watsonville compared to the much weaker effect in Gilroy cannot be overlooked. It may be that without introducing some personal contact programs into a community to supplement a media campaign (as was done in Watsonville), it is difficult to overpower any selective processes. However, whatever selective exposure effects may have operated in this campaign, the procedures used here were unable to detect the significance of their influence.

References

Bauer, R.
    1964 "The obstinate audience: the influence process from the point of view of social communication." American Psychologist 19:319–328.
Griffiths, W., and Knutson, A. L.
    1960 "The role of the mass media in public health." American Journal of Public Health, 50:515–23.
Heise, D.
    1970 "Causal inference from panel data." Pp. 3–27 in E. F. Borgatta and G. Bohrnstedt (eds.), Sociological Methodology 1970, San Francisco: Jossey Bass.
Kenny, D. A.
    1973 Cross-lagged and synchronous common factors in panel data." In A. S. Goldberger and O. D. Duncan (eds.), Structural Equation Models in the Social Sciences, New York: Seminar Press.
    1975 Cross-lagged panel correlation: a test for spuriousness." Psychological Bulletin 82:887–903.
    1979 Correlation and Causality. New York: Wiley.
Klapper, J. T.
    1960 The Effects of Mass Media. Glencoe: The Free Press.
Larson, O. N.
    1964 "Social effects of mass communication." In R. E. L. Faris (ed.) Handbook of Modern Sociology. Chicago: Rand McNally.
Mendelsohn, H.
    1973 "Some reasons why information campaigns can succeed." Public Opinion Quarterly 37:50–61.
Meyer, A. J., J. D. Nash, A. L. McAlister, N. Maccoby, and J. W. Farquhar
    1978 "Skills training in a cardiovascular health education campaign." Unpublished manuscript, Stanford University.
Milburn, M. A.
    1978 "Process analysis of mass media campaign effects." Unpublished Ph.D. dissertation, Harvard University.
Rogers, E. M.
    1962 Diffusion of Innovations. New York: The Free Press.
    1973 "Mass media and interpersonal communication." In I. Pool and W. Schramm et al. (eds.), Handbook of Communication. Chicago: Rand McNally.

PART VII

INTERNATIONAL AND
COMPARATIVE RESEARCH

With increasing exchange and collaboration among communication
scholars across the continents, true comparative research seems to be
emerging. Cooperation between American and Japanese scholars is already
underway, as evidenced in the work of this section.

The *Johoka Shakai*, or informationalized societies, approach to communi
cation research that is dominant in Japan is explained in Japanese work
comparing information flow in major industrialized nations. Using standardized measures of aggregate data, the Japanese research hints at major
breakthroughs in charting the effects of communication technology. Several
American scholars scrutinize the Japanese research and say that both
nationalities will benefit from further collaboration.

Another approach, cultural indicators analysis, has been nurtured in
Sweden over the last decade. A major report of Swedish mass communications as cultural indicators since 1945 is presented here. The report is
valuable as both a vision of the potential of cultural indicator methods and as
a summary of a massive quantity of data, which unfold in both expected and
unexpected patterns.

Two unusual pieces conclude Part VII. A most resourceful analysis of the
structure and functions of China's mass media system suggests a role of
increasing importance for the mass media in modern China. Finally, an
analysis of Western and Eastern European press coverage of Poland—a
country which has seized the limelight in world media in 1980—submits
some universals and dissimilarities in news values among the world's press.

Two striking factors mark the symposium of articles that follow about the Johoka Shakai, *or informationalized societies, approach to communication research. First, the articles represent an exciting, new direction in comparative communication research. Second, the work is evidence of emerging cooperative work between Japanese and American scholars. These papers emerged from the joint Japan-U.S.A. 1980 conference at the University of Washington on "Comparing Information Societies: Directions for Research," hosted by Alex Edelstein, professor and director of the International Communication Center at the University of Washington. In his introductory essay, Dr. Edelstein argues for major redefinition of communication research that alters the meaning of* mass *(the term would mean interacting collectivities) and* public opinion *(shifted to mean essentially communication). Furthermore, the approach would be fundamentally comparative, using a common* informationalized societies *approach.*

36

INFORMATION SOCIETIES
An Introduction

Alex S. Edelstein

At a computer and telecommunications conference in Tokyo in June of 1978, I suggested that the new field of computer-telecommunications was coming hard upon our limited success in dealing with communication and mass communication and that the time was not too far distant when our major research foci would be on the convergence of these three fields of study.[1]

I proposed as a part of the outlook for mass communications six probable changes in points of view:

1. Mass communication would undergo changes that would shift the emphasis from "mass" to communication and telecommunication. "Mass" would be redefined to describe interacting collectivities rather than individuals unconnected in time and space.

2. We would become much more concerned with how members of the society were communicating among themselves than how they were interacting with institutionalized media. Public opinion would be re-evaluated as an essentially communication concept.

3. Cognitive and affective processes would be reviewed in terms of the new technologies and modified communicative acts. There would be new ways of looking at these familiar concepts.

4. The enormous growth in communication of all kinds would hasten our emergence from the status of a derivative field in social science to a disciplinary and multi-field focus on communication, mass communication, and telecommunication.

From Alex S. Edelstein, "Information Societies: An Introduction," presented at the Japan-U.S.A. Conference on "Comparing Information Societies, Directions for Research" at the University of Washington in 1980.

5. Because of the vast societal changes that would be implied by developments in telecommunications, there would need be an increasing collaboration among managers and operators of mass communication, government, citizens and the academy.

6. We would come to a fuller realization of the value of comparative research as means of clarifying concepts, developing observational techniques and illuminating both the commonness and uniqueness of communication in societies. As post-industrial societies witnessed enormous growth in knowledge industries and in the use of electronic means for gathering and transmitting information and entertainment, there would be strong impulses to learn from one another through comparative studies.

In "The *Johoka Shakai* Approach to the Study of Information Societies," Professor Ito pulls together the several studies being done which compare Japan and the United States with post-industrial societies in the U.K. and Western Europe. Professor Ito's paper is particularly valuable for its description of the profound considerations involved in the conceptualization of comparative studies, particularly that of achieving conceptual equivalence along important dimensions so that related variables can be observed.

The most important step in achieving conceptual equivalence in the comparative application of the Johoka Shakai approach was the realization that economic values in all societies have both functional and informational values, and that the ratio varies from one society to another. Thus societies can be arrayed along this single dimension.

A second major problem of conceptual equivalence arose with respect to being able to sum information values across media. This was a difficult measurement problem, as Professor Ito points out, but it was an even greater conceptual problem. To sum across media, all media and forms of expression had to be made equivalent on some dimension. That was achieved ultimately by reducing each form of expression to a unit of analysis that could be converted into a measure of words per unit. That was a breathtaking conceptual leap, as Professor Ito pointed out so persuasively.

This measure of equivalence will become acknowledged as an intellectual tour de force when the conceptual fruits of it are more fully realized; that is, as we begin to identify the many related or concomitant variables that illustrate the responses of different cultures to informationalization, answering for us those persistent questions about the worldwide impact of new communication technologies and telecommunication systems. Is it, for an example, quite possible that numerous cultures are actually highly resistant to the attributed effects of various technologies and will assimilate communications innovations with little real impact upon valued ways of life?

Some of the social implications of informationalization can be anticipated by such conceptualization and measurement, Professor Bowes points out. He cites the work of Tomita to show that the impact of information production is related to information consumption. Tomita concluded that this produced information overload, but others see it as evidence of opportunities for individuals for increased selectivity, and indeed, as a response to increasing selectivity. Bowes cites the work of a Japanese scholar to the effect that Japan's rapid industrialization and informationalization led it to an economic "structural depression." Information was seen as both a product of the economy and as a means of boosting the economy. This had a special meaning for Japan in its energy crisis because it realized that information, and information machines, required less energy to produce than was required for the production of other commodities.

But what are the socio-cultural implications? Professor Harsel sees manifold social and cultural urgencies. He regrets that the observations of informationalization have not dwelled on cultural processes, and he asks for comparative analysis to make us more aware of how these processes develop and affect societies of all kinds and at all stages of economic development. He asks, as an example, if the meaning of information, itself, might not be undergoing change because of technological innovation, the emerging definition tending to be that which is subject to efficient coding, indexing, storage, access and retrieval. Dr. Harsel suggests that there is evidence already of seemingly contradictory changes in the lives of individuals in Information Societies, there being coexistent tendencies toward greater participation and increased privatization. These behaviors may not exist because of informationalization; rather, informationalization may be a response to these tendencies.

Such questions, a few among many, may be those to which we communication, mass communication, and telecommunication researchers will apply ourselves for several generations to come.

NOTE

[1] *Report of the International Investigatory Conference on Communications Policy,* June, 3, 1978, Tokyo.

"A breathtaking conceptual leap": that is how Alex Edelstein describes the development of the Johoka Index *and information flow census used in comparative studies as reported in the following article by Youichi Ito, associate professor at Keio University's Institute for Communication Research. The Johoka Index consists of amount of information, distribution of media, quality of information, and an information expenditure ratio. Dr. Ito concisely describes several studies using the new measures, both in single nation and comparative studies, and argues that the Japanese approach will lead to a more solid foundation for a macro theory of communication.*

37

THE *"JOHOKA SHAKAI"* APPROACH TO THE STUDY OF COMMUNICATION IN JAPAN

Youichi Ito

Introduction

Communication policies have become a popular topic for both research and discussion in recent years. It is unclear, however, how the growing international attention to this topic fits into the conventional approach to communication research. At this time, much of the discussion of communication policy has been from legal or administrative viewpoints. This is to be expected, of course, but it seems unusual that there is so little discussion of communication policy from a unique communication viewpoint. After all, there are macro-economic theories behind national economic policies. Should there not also be macro-communication theories behind national communication policies? Fortunately, such theories appear to be developing in America, Japan, Europe and other parts of the world.

This paper is concerned with one particular set of theories created in the last fifteen years by Japanese communication scholars. Called the *johoka shakai* approach, these theories and models attempt to describe and predict some of the unique macro-communication aspects of information in modern society. In Japanese, *johoka* means "informationalization" or "informationalized" and *shakai* means "society". Thus, *johoka shakai* means literally "informationalized society". This term was coined in Japan in 1966 or 1967 and was meant to be closely analogous to *kogyoka shakai* or "industrial society".[1]

Johoka shakai can be best understood in the context of the popular concept "industrial society". Several different definitions have been suggested for *johoka* and *johoka shakai*, but they will be defined here as follows. *Johoka shakai* refers

* A part of this study was made possible by the grant extended to the writer by the East-West Communication Institute, the East-West Center in Honolulu, Hawaii. Grateful acknowledgement is made for the varied aid provided by Director Jack Lyle, Dr. Syed Rahim and other staff members of the East-West Communication Institute.

From Youichi Ito, "The *'Johoka Shakai'* Approach to the Study of Communication in Japan," *Keio Communication Review* 1 (March 1980) 13-40. Copyright 1980 by Keio University. Reprinted by permission.

to a society characterized by abundant information in terms of both stock and flow, quick and efficient distribution and transformation of information, and easy and inexpensive access of information for all members of society. *Johoka* also implies a process of social change approaching the state of *johoka shakai*. The relationship between *johoka* and *johoka shakai* is the same as that of *kogyoka* (industrialization) and *kogyoka shakai* (industrial society). The following sections review how the concept has been used in Japanese articles and books.

The Development of the *Johoka Shakai* Approach

In January 1963, Tadao Umesao of Kyoto University published an article entitled "*Joho Sangyo Ron* (On Information Industries)" in *Hoso Asahi* (Asahi Broadcasting), that had a strong impact in Japanese intellectual and business circles.[2]

In this article, Umesao suggested classifying human industries into three categories: agricultural, material and spiritual industries. Colin Clark's earlier trichotomy of the "first" industries (agriculture, fishing, forestry), the "second" industries (manufacturing industries) and the "third" industries (service industries), is well-known. In contrast to Clark's schema, however, Umesao's classification grouped all the manufacturing and service industries related to materials and energy into the material industries, and all the manufacturing and service industries related to spiritual and other intellectual activities of man into the spiritual industries. Umesao based this classification on an analogy with biological organisms.

According to Umesao, agriculture meets the needs of digestive functions; the most fundamental function for the organism's survival. Material industries meet the needs of locomotive functions; to move, to catch and produce and thus to expand the organism's environment. Spiritual industries meet the needs of control functions; to plan, prepare and control the organism's behavior. Umesao further suggested that the degree of evolution of any biological organism could be determined by the proportion of these three kinds of organs. The most primitive animals do not have any muscles, brains or nervous systems. All they have are digestive organs. They do not have any means of independent locomotion. All that they can do is drift in water, or just sit and wait until something to eat comes close to them. The more envolved the animal becomes, the larger the proportion of muscles, brain and nerves becomes in relation to the digestive tract.

At a more complex level, Umesao compared the development of human industries to biological evolution. He proposed three developmental stages of human industries: the age of agriculture, the age of material industries and the age of spiritual industries. The age of agriculture is a time when food production occupies the largest proportion of human activities in the society. The age of material industries is the time when the mass production and mass consumption of material goods and energy and highly developed transportation systems characterize the society. Finally, the age of spiritual industries is the time when the mass production and consumption of knowledge and information, the diffusion of higher education and other intellectual and cultural activities characterize the society. According to this reasoning, the more evolved the society becomes, the larger will be its proportion of knowledge and information industries. He described the present age as the transitional period between the age of material industries and the age of spiritual industries. On the basis of his conceptualization, Umesao predicted that industries related to expansion of functions similar to those of the brain and nervous system will flourish in coming years. The present rapid growth of knowledge and service industries thus marks the dawning of the age of spiritual industries.

In America and Europe, other scholars were writing about the future of industrial society at the same time as Umesao. The concept of "post-industrial society", for example, was used for the first time at a seminar held in Boston in 1962.[3] Further articles and books by Daniel Bell, Herman Kahn, and Anthony Weiner made the term well-known and other work such as Brzezinski's concept of "technetronic era" and Peter Drucker's "age of discontinuity" contributed to a growing interest in future prediction. Unfortunately, because Umesao's paper was only published in Japanese it had little impact beyond Japanese intellectual and business circles. On the other hand, the books and articles written by Drucker, Bell, Kahn and Wiener were translated into Japanese and received wide attention.

Kenichi Kohyama, in his widely read article entitled "*Joho Shakai Ron Josetsu* (On Information Societies)" published in 1968, synthesized the American futurists' theories with those of Umesao. Kohyama suggests: "The kind of society Bell and Kahn called a post-industrial society, I would call more precisely *joho shakai* (information society)'."[4] *Joho shakai*, according to Kohyama, "refers to the society which comes after the stage of industrial society. It emerges through the information revolution occuring as a result of a certain degree of development and maturity of industrial societies. It is called *joho shakai* because this society is particularly characterized by the information revolution and other information phenomena."[5]

Yujiro Hayashi used the term "*johoka shakai* (informational society)" to mean what Kohyama called "*joho shakai* (information society.)" Hayashi's book entitled *Johoka Shakai* published in 1969 was probably the first book in the world that used the term "informational society" or a similar term as its book title.[6]

In this *Johoka Shakai*, Hayashi added a new meaning to *johoka* and *johoka shakai*. He pointed out that economic values have both a functional and an informational aspect. The "functional value" refers to what economists have traditionally called a "use value." Hayashi suggested that all other values besides functional value be considered as "informational" value. He noted that the ratio of informational value and functional value differed from one commodity (or service) to another. In commodities (or services) reflecting the user's personality or social status, such as automobiles cosmetics, clothing and accessories, for example, the ratio of informational value is high. On the other hand, in the case of less social or personal goods and services such as oil, gas, food, the ratio of functional value is higher. Hayashi suggested that *johoka shakai* is a society in which more and more goods and services are "personalized" and the ratio of informational value, in general, becomes higher.

While the works reviewed here laid the conceptual and theoretical foundation for *johoka shakai*, it soon became necessary to operationalize the degree of *johoka*.

Measurement and Comparison of *Johoka* Across Societies

If the society we now live in is in the process of metamorphosis to a *johoka shakai*, our next question should be how much our society and other similar societies have already been "informationalized". In other words, if we accept the position that *johoka shakai* is before us and we are approaching it, we would like to measure *johoka* so that we can compare different societies and compare them over time.

The first attempt of this kind was made by the Research Institute of Telecommunications and Economics (RITE) in Tokyo. RITE published reports in 1968 and 1970 in which they attempted to quantify the degree of *johoka*. In the 1968 report, they developed two new information-based indices: The "*joho keisu* or information ratio" and the *johoka* index.

The information ratio is analogous to the Engels' ratio expressed in Engels' Law. The Engels' ratio is the ratio of food expenditures to the total expenditure of a household. The information ratio defined by RITE is the ratio of the expenditure for various kinds of information-related activities to the total expenditure of a household. It is, of course, impossible to expect an item like information or communication expenses to appear in ordinary housekeeping account books. Therefore, in order to approximate such expenses, they subtracted all major expenses that were obviously not related to communication activities such as food, clothing and other costs from total household expenses and rather boldly assumed that the remainder were information related expenses. Thus, the information ratio is equal to what is left over after the subraction divided by the total expenditure of a household.

It is well-known that there is a negative correlation between the Engels' ratio and personal income. As personal income increases, the Engels' ratio decreases. People with higher incomes spend a smaller proportion of their total income on food. However, the information ratio moves in the opposite direction. Where the Engels' ratio is high, the information ratio is likely to be low. Therefore, as personal income increases, the information ratio will increase, and as personal income decreases, the information ratio will decrease.

It is also well-known that the Engels' ratio differs from one country to another or from one culture to another even if personal income levels are held constant. It is known, for example, that the propensity to spend more money for luxurious meals is stronger among Latin people than among Anglo-Saxon people. The same thing is true of the information ratio. It differs from one country to another and from one culture to another. The propensity to spend more money for information-related activities appears to be stronger in some countries or cultures than in others.

The RITE research group graphed the relationship between personal income and the information ratio in the sixteen countries shown in Figure 1. These calculations, based on data from 1966, indicate that Japan's information ratio is very high for its personal income level.[7]

The second information index, the *johoka* index, is composed of a number of factors in addition to the previously described information ratio. Originally composed of seven factors in 1968, the index was expanded in 1970 to include ten factors grouped into the following four categories:

Figure 1: Information Ratio and Per Capita Income

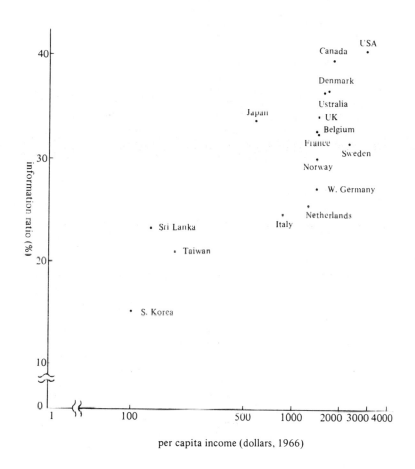

per capita income (dollars, 1966)

Research Institute of Telecommunications and Economics (1968)

A. Amount of Information
1. Telephone calls per person per year.
2. Newspaper circulation per 100 people.
3. Books published per 1,000 people.
4. Population density (a measure of interpersonal communication).
B. Distribution of communication media.
1. Telephone receivers per 100 people.
2. Radio sets per 100 households.
3. Television sets per 100 households.
C. Quality of Information Activities.
1. Proportion of service workers in total labor population.
2. Proportion of students in total appropriate age group.
D. Information Ratio
1. Information expenditures as a proportion of total expenditures.

In their first report in 1968, the RITE group compared Japan's position as a *johoka shakai* to five countries – the USA, France, Italy, West Germany and the United Kingdom – on seven of the above information factors and per capita income. To illustrate the comparison, Japan's score for each factor was divided by the corresponding mean value of the five foreign countries and multiplied by 100. The relative position of Japan versus the average of the five countries is shown in the two octagons in Figure 2. As the figure demonstrates, the Japanese had a relatively low per capita income but had higher figures for the other information factors except for book publications and proportion of service industry workers.

In the 1970 RITE report the number of factors was increased and Italy was removed from the comparison countries. Table 2 shows condensed data for each of the major categories in 1953 and 1963 with estimated figures for 1975. All numbers are reduced to a common denominator by dividing by Japan's values for 1958 and multiplying by 100. The overall *johoka* index is the mean value of the four categories. A plot of the longitudinal trends is shown in Figure 3.

The 1970 RITE report found that Japan had moved to third in the world after the United States and the United Kingdom on the index of *johoka*. The report predicted that because of the differences in the rate of growth in *Johoka* index that Japan would surpass the U.K. before 1970 to become the second most "informationalized" society in the world. As shown in Figure 3, both Japan and the United States are expected to increase their rate of *johoka* at a faster rate than the three European nations.

The 1970 RITE report also provided a more precise operational definition for the concept of a "post industrial society" According to the definition, a "post-industrial society" should satisfy the following four conditions:

1. Per capita income more than $4,000.00.
2. Number of service workers exceed 50 percent of the labor force.
3. University students exceed 50 percent of the appropriate aged population.
4. The "information ratio" is more than 35 percent.

**Figure 2: The State of Japan's *Johoka* As Compared to Other Five
Industrial Nations** (Based on 1966 Data)

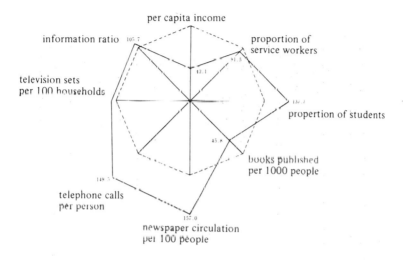

_ _ _ _   Mean value of U.S., U.K., West Germany,
           France and Italy set as 100

           Japan's score divided by the corresponding
           mean value of the five foreign countries
           and multiplied by 100

Research Institute of Telecommunications and Economics (1968)

Table 1: *Johoka* **Indices of Five Industrial Nations***

	Japan			U.S.A.			U.K.			W. Germany			France		
	1953	63	75 (Est.)	1953	63	75 (Est.)	1953	63	75 (Est.)	1953	63	75 (Est.)	1953	63	75 (Est.)
Johoka Index	75	193	379	272	370	648	133	231	312	76	160	292	88	136	249
Information Ratio	73	126	184	141	159	171	120	132	146	87	105	124	118	121	157
Quality of Information Activities	85	113	185	203	294	374	65	112	163	65	87	112	82	108	120
Amount of Information	93	108	152	96	142	232	104	118	151	59	103	119	53	54	105
Distribution of Communication Media	49	426	996	647	992	1815	243	560	815	92	344	828	101	261	615

* Condensed from Table 2-2-20 in Research Institute of Telecommunications and Economics (1970), pp. 64-65.

Figure 3: **Longitudinal Trends in** *Johoka* **Indices**
in Five Industrial Nations

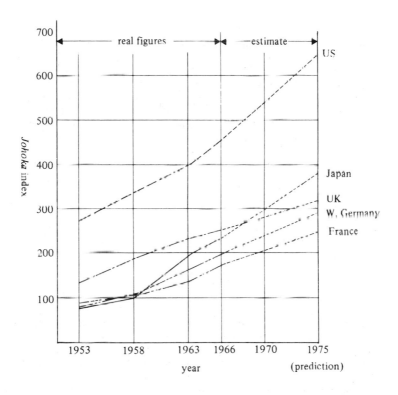

Research Institute of Telecommunications and Economics (1970), P. 63.

The report predicted that the United States would satisfy these criteria by the late 1970's. Japan would be the second country to reach this post-industrial status in the late 1980's and three Western European countries would satisfy the four conditions by the year 2000.

The operationalization of the information index provided insight into the development of the *johoka shakai* and allowed cross national comparisons to be made. In other research groups Japanese communication scholars were attempting to operationalize information in a way that would enable them to measure the flow of information *within* a *johoka shakai*.

Measuring Information Flow

At approximately the same time that RITE was comparing the *johoka* of industrialized nations, another unique research project was initiated by the *Joho Kenkyu Bukai* (Information Study Group) of the *Keizai Kikaku Kyokai* (Association for Economic Planning), a government-subsidized research organization. The report entitled *Johoka Shakai no Keisei* (The Formation of Informational Society) published in 1969 begins:

"In old times, labor force was by far the most important factor in determining the scale of a nation's economic activities. With the emergence of industrial societies, labor came to be replaced by capital. From now on, it can be said that information will play the crucial role in social and economic development. Unfortunately, it seems that no attempt has ever been made to calculate the amount of production and consumption of information. What we have attempted here, although only a first step, is to quantitatively measure the production and consumption of 'patterned' information such as language, pictures and other symbols of communication, and trace their longitudinal trends. We have also attempted to express the amount of information flow in different media by a common unit." [8]

After making a series of bold assumptions about information, they proceeded, for the first time, to measure the total amount of information produced and consumed for ten different mass and interpersonal media. The initial work of the *Association for Economic Planning* was later continued by several other research groups. In particular, the Communications Policy Division of the Ministry of Posts and Telecommunications (MPT) played an important role in further development and gave this research effort its name: The information flow census. In 1975, the MPT created a standard manual for the information flow census, and began conducting the census every year on a regular basis. Results were published in the MPT's official annual report: *Tsushin Hakusho* (White Paper on Communications).

The basic definitions, methods and assumptions of the information flow census studies are very important. To begin, information is broadly defined as any symbol, signal or image having meaning either to the sender or to the receiver. The focus of the census, however, is on information flow rather than on information *per se*. The "information flow" must satisfy three conditions. First, it must be the transfer of information from one point to another, with the two points belonging to different communication units. This condition precluded the transfer of information within the same communication unit, such as "intra-personal" communication and the flow of information within the same computer system. The second condition is that the flow must be initiated at the sender's will. This condition precludes the kind of information flow occurring when we observe the color of clouds in the western sky or other person's unintentional behavior or facial expressions. The third condition is that both the sender and the receiver must be either human or a machine working according to a human will. This condition precludes the flow of information among animals or between animals and humans.

Since the original study by the Association for Economic Planning, a distinction has been made between the amount of information supplied and the amount consumed. This distinction illustrates an important difference between the economic and communication approach to information. When used in the economic sense, supply refers to the amount of goods for sale in the market place. Consumption refers to goods purchased by consumers. If 100 newspapers are supplied to the market and are all bought in a certain period of time, then consumption will equal supply for an economist, regardless of whether anyone reads the newspapers. Economists are interested in the flow of goods and money and not in the flow of information. Because of their interest in information flow, communications scholars must define consumption differently than economists.

In the information flow census, consumption is defined not as the purchase of information but as the *perception* of information. In other words, "to consume" means, literally, "to perceive". This leads to some rather interesting conceptual notions. For example, it is possible with this definition for consumption to exceed supply. This would be impossible in economics where each unit supplied is usually only consumed once.

The supply of information is defined as the amount of information produced by the sender regardless of whether or not the information actually reaches a receiver. This definition is straightforward enough except for the case of television and radio. Researchers are faced with the choice of measuring supply at the source end or at the receiver end. If information is measured at the source, then radio and television are similar to performance media such as lectures, concerts and the theater. Thus, the amount of information measured at the source of a broadcast will be far less than books, magazines and newspapers that are produced in multiple copies. If broadcast information is measured at the receiver, one must assume that the original messages are somehow multiplied in the air and automatically delivered to each television or radio set. Here the amount of information will more clearly reflect broadcast's mass media status. RITE and MPT both settled on this latter approach.[9]

Another problem arises when measuring supply of information at the receiver end: Should the measure of information be based on the number of receiving sets or on the number of households with sets? Because of the growing number of households with multiple radio and television sets, an estimate based on the total number of sets will overestimate the amount of information flowing into a household. That is, most people with multiple sets do not often watch or listen to all their different sets at the same time. On the other hand, simply counting the number of households with a set will underestimate information flow since we also know that multiple sets are used occasionally at the same time by different members of a household. The MPT and RITE studies do not, in fact, agree on which measures to use. MPT uses the total number of sets in use and the RITE study measures households owning a radio or television set.[10]

The various media can be uniquely classified on the basis of the relationship between information supply and consumption. The researchers grouped all information sources into "personal", "mass" and "performance" media types. In personal media, the amount of supply and consumption are equal. Media such as telephone, telegraph, telex, data communication and personal letters belong to this type. With mass media, supply generally exceeds consumption. Newspapers, magazines, books, radio and television belong to this category. With performance media, the amount of supply is generally less than the amount of consumption. Lectures, music, concerts, drama, opera performances and school education belong to this type. Several media depart from their traditional classifications. Movies for example, while usually, classified as mass media are here considered performance media since their supply is generally less than consumption. Similarly, mail must be divided into personal mail, with supply equal to consumption (personal media), and advertising or "direct" mail where supply usually exceeds consumption (mass media).

As mentioned previously, the notion of supply and consumption of information produce results that are not possible in an economic sense. Because of the definition of information, when one unit of information is produced and later shared by two people, the amount of consumption becomes twice the amount of supply. In the case of a performance medium such as a lecture, when one word is spoken by a speaker to an audience of two hundred, the supply is equal to one and the consumption becomes two hundred. Although the reader may note that television is often watched by more than one person, in countries like Japan and the United States where several different programs are supplied at the same time for more than fifteen hours a day, consumption can never exceed supply.

The main purpose of the information flow census was to objectively compare supply and consumption of information using a common unit. The unit chosen for this task was the word. Now, while it is apparent that books, newspapers, lectures and discussions can be expressed in word units, pictures, film and music present a problem. Conversion is a challenging task and it is unlikely that any really satisfactory method will be achieved in the near future. A number of bold assumptions must be made, and in the end the results can only be rough approximations. The alternative is to use different units for different modes of communication; space or size for still pictures, time for music, television and movies. While such an approach seems intuitively satisfying, comparisons between media are impossible. Furthermore, it is impossible to measure media that operate in two different modes. Faced with the alternatives, the MPT research group chose to convert all media to words.

Conversion rates were developed on the basis of various empirical rationales. The average information flow for speech in the Japanese language, for example, was known to be 120 words per minute. The *kana* alphabet, which is used in Japan for telegrams, telex and data transmission translates to about 3.3 *kana* characters per word. Printed and handwritten Japanese relies on both *kana* and *kanjis* (chinese ideograms) and translates to 2.5 characters per word. These figures, based on research by the National Institute for the Study of the Japanese Language are fairly reliable. Conversion of pictures and music to words, however, is problematic.

In the information flow census, music is equated with ordinary speech. A still picture is equated to 80 words because the results of various experiments indicated that an average of 80 words could be written on a still picture and detected at a certain distance. The amount of information gained by watching images in motion was set at 800 words per minute since it was demonstrated that people usually see about ten still pictures per minute on the average. Color pictures were assumed to carry 50 percent more information than black-and-white images because about 50 percent more bandwidth was necessary to broadcast color images. Thirty-five different media were evaluated in the information flow census. Table 2 shows the conversion rates for 14 major media.

It should be obvious that serious questions can be raised about defects in these assumptions. Many people have criticized the information flow census because of the operationalization of the conversion rates.[11] The criticism is readily acknowledged and the census is still considered to be unfinished. It must be remembered that the aim was to make comparisons possible. In the following paragraphs, the results and utility of this approach should become apparent.

To create overall information supply and consumption values for the different media, the MPT researchers created 70 different equations. These equations are rather complicated but it will be useful to understand the general methods employed to arrive at final values. For personal media, supply and consumption were both set equal to the number of words flowing through each medium. For radio and television, supply was calculated by first adding the total broadcasting time of all stations and then multiplying by the number of households owning television and radio sets. These figures were then multiplied by appropriate conversion rates — 120 words-per-minute for radio, 920 for black-and-white and 1320 words for color television sets — to arrive at final values. Consumption was calculated by multiplying the average viewing and listening statistics found by audience surveys times total audience and the conversion rate. Print media supply values were calculated by simply adding from various industry figures the total number of words provided to the market. Consumption was based on readership statistics converted to word rates. Performance media supply figures were calculated from the amount of time spent for the performance multiplied by an appropriate conversion factor. Consumption statistics were calculated by multiplying supply by audience size. The results of these calculations for the 14 major media are shown in Tables 3 and 4.

With the basic figures for supply and consumption, the MPT researchers calculated a number of other measures allowing evaluation of changes in information flow. Table 5, for example, shows amount of information consumed multiplied by the distance between sender and receiver. The nature of this index will be best understood by thinking of kinds of indices often used in the field of transportation. Relative social importance, or "share" in a sense, of various different transportation media is usually expressed by the index gained by multiplying the total number of passengers, or the total weight of cargoes, by the distances of their

Table 2: The Conversion Rates for 14 Major Media*

Media	Form of Expression	Unit of Measurement	Conversion Rate (words per unit)
NTT Telephone	Voice	minute	120
Telegraph	Characters (*kana* only)	character	0.3
Privately-operated Data Communication	Characters (*kana* only)	character	0.3
Private Facsimile	Still pictures	page	80
Radio Broadcasting	Voice	minute	120
TV Broadcasting	Voice + Images in motion	minute	1320 or 920
Mail (Post Card)	Characters (*kana* & *kanji*)	character	0.4
Newspaper	Characters (*kana* & *kanji*)	character	0.4
Book	Characters (*kana* & *kanji*)	character	0.4
Music Record & Tape	Music and/or Voice	minute	120
Conversation II (outside home)	Voice + Images in motion	minute	1320
School Education	Voice + Images in motion	minute	1320
Social Education	Voice + Images in motion	minute	1320
Movie	Voice + Images in motion	minute	1320

* Condensed from Ministry of Posts and Telecommunications (1978 B), Table 1. The original table is for 35 media.

Table 3: The Supply of Information*

(All units in words)

	1960	1970	1976
NTT Telephone	2.16×10^{12}	6.62×10^{12}	7.38×10^{12}
Telegraph	6.21×10^{8}	5.08×10^{8}	3.42×10^{8}
Privately-operated Data Communication	—	5.40×10^{11}	1.45×10^{13}
Private Facsimile	1.33×10^{9}	4.08×10^{9}	3.24×10^{10}
Radio Broadcasting	8.28×10^{15}	1.09×10^{16}	2.05×10^{16}
TV Broadcasting	7.79×10^{15}	8.14×10^{16}	1.53×10^{17}
Mail (Post Card)	2.17×10^{11}	3.63×10^{11}	4.41×10^{11}
Newspaper	8.38×10^{14}	2.17×10^{15}	2.58×10^{15}
Book	1.87×10^{13}	5.53×10^{13}	8.13×10^{13}
Music Record & Tape	4.82×10^{10}	5.09×10^{11}	8.45×10^{11}
Conversation II (outside home)	7.95×10^{14}	8.22×10^{14}	8.40×10^{14}
School Education	4.04×10^{13}	3.78×10^{13}	3.93×10^{13}
Social Education	2.89×10^{12}	3.05×10^{12}	3.08×10^{12}
Movie	2.29×10^{12}	9.98×10^{11}	7.54×10^{11}

* Condensed from Ministry of Posts and Telecommunications (1978 B), Table 3-1. The original table is for 35 media.

Table 4: The Consumption of Information*

		(All units in words)	
	1960	1970	1976
NTT Telephone	2.16×10^{12}	6.62×10^{12}	7.38×10^{12}
Telegraph	6.21×10^{8}	5.03×10^{8}	3.42×10^{8}
Privately-operated Data Communication	—	5.40×10^{11}	1.45×10^{13}
Private Facsimile	1.33×10^{9}	4.08×10^{9}	3.24×10^{10}
Radio Broadcasting	3.75×10^{14}	1.02×10^{14}	1.47×10^{14}
TV Broadcasting	2.00×10^{15}	6.43×10^{15}	8.87×10^{15}
Mail (Post Card)	2.17×10^{11}	3.63×10^{11}	4.41×10^{11}
Newspaper	9.10×10^{13}	1.14×10^{14}	1.39×10^{14}
Book	2.56×10^{13}	3.01×10^{13}	3.81×10^{13}
Music Record & Tape	1.78×10^{12}	2.12×10^{13}	2.56×10^{13}
Conversation II (outside home)	1.59×10^{15}	1.64×10^{15}	1.70×10^{15}
School Education	1.65×10^{15}	2.83×10^{15}	2.56×10^{13}
Social Education	1.27×10^{14}	1.33×10^{14}	1.41×10^{15}
Movie	2.89×10^{14}	7.33×10^{13}	4.90×10^{13}

* Condensed from Ministry of Posts and Telecommunications (1978 B), Table 3-2. The original table is for 35 media.

Table 5: Consumption x Flow Distance*

(All units in word · kilometers)

	1960	1970	1976
NTT Telephone	2.16×10^{13}	1.27×10^{14}	2.10×10^{14}
Telegraph	1.86×10^{11}	1.50×10^{11}	1.03×10^{11}
Privately-operated Data Communication	–	7.56×10^{17}	3.73×10^{15}
Private Facsimile	4.92×10^{11}	1.51×10^{12}	1.12×10^{13}
Radio Broadcasting	1.54×10^{16}	4.18×10^{15}	6.07×10^{15}
TV Broadcasting	8.20×10^{16}	2.64×10^{17}	2.91×10^{17}
Mail (Post Card)	2.65×10^{13}	4.43×10^{13}	5.38×10^{13}
Newspaper	6.46×10^{15}	8.09×10^{15}	9.93×10^{15}
Book	7.81×10^{15}	9.18×10^{15}	1.15×10^{16}
Music Record & Tape	8.90×10^{10}	1.06×10^{12}	7.70×10^{15}
Conversation II (outside home)	1.50×10^{16}	1.55×10^{16}	1.68×10^{16}
School Education	4.95×10^{15}	8.49×10^{15}	8.93×10^{15}
Social Education	9.77×10^{14}	1.02×10^{15}	1.07×10^{15}
Movie	2.31×10^{15}	5.86×10^{14}	3.72×10^{14}

* Condensed from Ministry of Posts and Telecommunications (1978 B), Table 3-3. The original table is for 35 media.

travels. By the same token, the amount of information consumed multiplied by the distance between sender and receiver is an indicator of the relative importance of each communication medium in terms of dissemination and audience penetration. As we see in Table 5, television broadcasting is the most powerful medium on this index, followed by direct conversation and the other mass media. Information flow costs are indexed in Table 6. Cost refers primarily to transmission and distribution costs and does not include basic production or creative costs such as the expense of producing a television program.

A graph of the consumption x distance indices plotted against their flow costs per unit for the 14 major media for the last 15 years is shown in Figure 4. Information flow cost per unit is the information flow cost divided by information flow amount-distance (consumption x distance), which means the amount of cost necessary for transmitting and delivering one unit of information one unit of distance (Table 7). Upward movement in Figure 4 means the increase of relative social importance, or "share" in a sense, and downward movement means the opposite. Movement to the right means the increase of information flow cost per unit (to move one word one kilometer) for the medium, and movement to the left means the reduction of flow cost per unit. On the whole, left-upward movement indicates that the future of the medium is promising. Data communication and facsimile are typical examples. On the contrary, right-downward movement indicates that there may not be much future for the medium. Telegraph and movie are typical cases. Straight-upward movement such as those of television, telephone, records and tapes means that despite inflation, the flow cost per unit has been managed to keep constant, and at the same time, has gained in their social importance during the last 15 years. Straight rightward movement such as those of conversation, book, social and school education and newspaper indicates either stagnancy or no change. Speculating on the relationships shown in Figure 4, the 1978 edition of *Tsushin Hakusho* (White Paper on Communications) compiled by the Communications Policy Division of MPT gave the following analysis:

"[As seen in this Figure,] the demand for information provided by mass media, which are one-way communication, has become stagnant and the demand for information provided by personal telecommunication media, which are characterized by two-way communication, has drastically increased. This is the basic pattern in our country's *johoka* in recent years, and this trend can be seen in both business circles and private lives.

This means that our society is moving toward a new stage of *johoka shakai* in which more priority is placed on segmented, more detailed information to meet individual needs instead of conventional mass-reproduced conformed information."[12]

The information flow census is a complicated undertaking and difficult to describe in this general survey. It will be, therefore, useful to briefly summarize some of its advantages and findings. As stated earlier, the purpose of the information flow census was to calculate the amount of information in society in an objective and quantititive fashion. By using a *common unit* and by measuring *directly and objectively*, reliable data can be produced for those who must make

Table 6: Information Flow Cost*

(All units in yen)

	1960	1970	1976
NTT Telephone	1.63×10^{11}	9.68×10^{11}	2.28×10^{12}
Telegraph	2.01×10^{10}	6.29×10^{10}	1.35×10^{11}
Privately-operated Data Communication	—	1.53×10^{11}	3.02×10^{11}
Private Facsimile	2.59×10^{10}	4.53×10^{10}	3.93×10^{10}
Radio Broadcasting	7.47×10^{9}	1.31×10^{10}	3.49×10^{10}
TV Broadcasting	8.33×10^{10}	1.46×10^{10}	2.79×10^{11}
Mail (Post Card)	1.22×10^{10}	3.27×10^{10}	1.18×10^{11}
Newspaper	6.26×10^{10}	2.06×10^{11}	4.03×10^{11}
Book	7.48×10^{9}	4.03×10^{10}	1.46×10^{11}
Music Record & Tape	2.40×10^{9}	1.52×10^{10}	5.03×10^{10}
Conversation II (outside home)	1.12×10^{12}	1.92×10^{12}	4.10×10^{12}
School Education	5.64×10^{11}	2.11×10^{12}	4.85×10^{12}
Social Education	1.24×10^{11}	2.96×10^{11}	4.88×10^{11}
Movie	1.02×10^{11}	7.02×10^{10}	9.34×10^{10}

* Condensed from Ministry of Posts and Telecommunications (1978 B), Table 3-4. The original table is for 35 media.

Figure 4: Longitudinal Trends in Information Flow Amount-Distance (Consumption x Distance) and Information Flow Cost Per Unit (Flow Cost/Consumption x Distance)

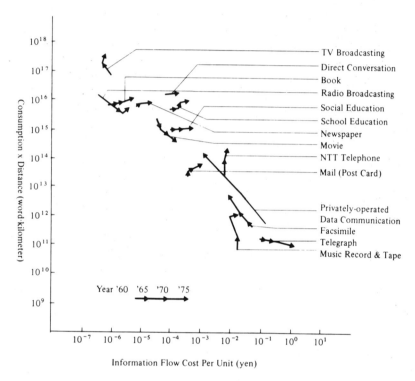

Ministry of Posts and Telecommunications (1978 B), p. 13.

Table 7: Information Flow Cost Per Unit
          (Information flow cost divided by consumption times
          flow distance)

(All units in yen)

	1960	1970	1976
NTT Telephone	7.55×10^{-1}	7.62×10^{-3}	1.09×10^{-2}
Telegraph	1.08×10^{-1}	4.19×10^{-1}	1.31×10^{0}
Privately-operated Data Communication	—	2.02×10^{0}	8.10×10^{-3}
Private Facsimile	5.26×10^{0}	3.00×10^{-2}	3.51×10^{-3}
Radio Broadcasting	4.85×10^{-7}	3.13×10^{-4}	5.75×10^{-4}
TV Broadcasting	1.02×10^{-6}	5.53×10^{-6}	9.59×10^{-5}
Mail (Post Card)	4.60×10^{-2}	7.38×10^{-2}	2.19×10^{-2}
Newspaper	9.69×10^{-4}	2.54×10^{-3}	4.08×10^{-3}
Book	9.58×10^{-5}	4.39×10^{-4}	1.27×10^{-5}
Music Record & Tape	2.70×10^{0}	1.43×10^{-2}	6.53×10^{-4}
Conversation II (outside home)	7.47×10^{-3}	1.24×10^{-4}	2.44×10^{-4}
School Education	1.14×10^{-4}	2.49×10^{-3}	5.43×10^{-3}
Social Education	1.27×10^{-3}	2.90×10^{-4}	4.56×10^{-4}
Movie	4.42×10^{-3}	1.20×10^{-4}	2.51×10^{-4}

policy decisions about media. Although there are important questions about the assumptions involved in creating various indices, the fact is that the basic equations remain the same from year to year. Thus, decision makers can obtain a reliable estimate of how the information environment is changing. This situation is not that different from the field of economic indicators where close inspection also reveals many questionable assumptions. The important point is that policy makers now have objective indices for examining change and for making intermedia comparisons. Such data can only facilitate their decisions about the allocation and development of new media systems.

The information flow census also clarifies changes in our society that were previously only thought of impressionistically or intuitively. With an objective measure of supply and consumption, for example, it is possible to estimate "information overload" in a scientifically meaningful fashion. The "information consumption rate", (consumption/supply) shown in Table 8, in fact, illustrates the relationship between the amount of information supplied and the amount of information consumed — typically, the condition thought to lead to "overload". In 1960 the rate was 40.8 percent indicating that somewhat less than half of the information supplied was being consumed. This figure dropped to 8.6 percent by 1976 showing that the objective measure of "overload" has increased nearly five fold in the last 16 years.[13]

The various indices provide insight into changes in the media marketplace as saw in Figure 4. This, of course, is most important for planners. In figure years the MPT group plans to expand the information flow census and calculate a wider variety of information statistics. Some of their plans include the following:

1. The measurement of information flow according to content. Educational materials, entertainment, news and reporting, cultural information are all possible categories.
2. The measurement of diversity. So far only the amount of information has been measured. Researchers, however, realize there is a significant difference between a society that produces ten different kinds of information versus one that produces ten copies of only one kind of information. Thus, an attempt will be made to calculate the percentage of "copied" information in the total information flow.
3. The measurement of information stock. So far only information flow has been measured. It should be possible for us to measure the amount of information stock as we did with information flow.
4. The measurement of international information flow. The census has so far been confined to domestic information flow. It is possible to measure the amount of information flow across national boundaries and thus develop an international balance sheet of information. Such data will be valuable for external cultural and information policies.

In all, the future of the information flow census looks promising. Substantial questions remain about the assumptions which underlie operationalization, but researchers are hopeful they will be resolved in coming years.

Table 8: Grand Total Data for 35 Media*

Fiscal Year	Supply (words)	Consumption (words)	Consumption rate** (%)	Consumption x Flow distance (word·km)	Average flow distance (km)
1960	1.87×10^{16}	7.63×10^{15}	40.8	1.48×10^{17}	19.4
1965	8.17×10^{16}	1.03×10^{16}	12.6	2.63×10^{17}	25.5
1970	9.63×10^{16}	1.26×10^{16}	13.1	3.25×10^{17}	25.2
1975	1.54×10^{17}	1.53×10^{16}	9.9	4.22×10^{17}	27.6
1976	1.84×10^{17}	1.58×10^{16}	8.6	3.76×10^{17}	23.8

* Condensed from Ministry of Posts and Telecommunications (1978 B), Table 2-1.
** Consumption rate = Consumption ÷ Supply

693

Concluding Remarks

To understand the future directions of the *johoka shakai* approach, it is necessary to look at the origins of communication research. The study of communication started with the study of propaganda and attitude change and was influenced by these origins for many years. In contrast, what we are calling macro-communication studies were first initiated by historians, sociologists, futurists and social critics. Innis, McLuhan, Bell, Umesao and Hayashi all made important constribtions in this are but for the most part their work was primarily intuitive and insightful and did not relate to the main stream of communication research. The attempt to bring these macro communication studies onto empirically solid ground with the *johoka shakai* approach in recent years is sure to lead to a stronger interaction with those communication researchers working in more traditional areas. By bridging the gap between intuition and empirical social science, the *johoka shakai* approach provides a more solid base for building macro communication theories and making decisions concerning communication policies.

NOTES

(1) According to Yasuda (1972), a group of communication experts who belonged to *Kagaku Gijutsu to Keizai no Kai* (A Study Group for Science, Technology and Economics) had been using the term *johoka shakai* (informational society) or *joho shakai* (information society) since 1966. T. Yasuda (1972), pp. 24-25.

(2) The fact that *Chuokoron* (Central Public Opinion), one of the most prestigious monthly opinion magazines in Japan, reprinted the article only two months later demonstrates how important the article was considered.

(3) D. Bell (1973).

(4) K. Kohyama (1968). P. 102.

(5) *Ibid.*

(6) As far as the writer knows, the first non-Japanese book that used the term "information society" or a similar term as its book title is *Information Societies: Comparing the Japanese and American Experiences* edited by Alex Edelstein, John Bowes and Sheldon Harsel. This volume collects the papers presented to the international conference held in Seattle at the University of Washington in December 1977. See Edelstein, Bowes and Harsel (1978).

(7) The following graph showing the relationship between GNP per person and
the number of telephone calls per person is consistent with the relationship
shown in Figure 1. In both figures, Japan has higher information use compared to Western nations with similar or higher levels of income.

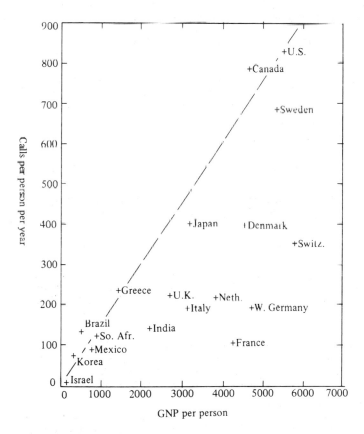

Comparison of per capita calls and GNP. (Data from *The World's Telephones;
The World Almanac, 1975.*)

Pierce (1977). p. 171.

(8) Association for Economic Planning (1969). p. 11.

(9) The Research Institute of Telecommunications and Economics (RITE) published a report in 1978 entitled *"Joho no Nagare" no Sokutei to Joho no Keizai Kohka, Shakai Kaihatsu Kohka no Sokutei* (The Measurement of the "Flow of Information" and the Measurement of Economic Effects and Social Development Effects of Information). The methods and ideas used in this RITE study were basically the same as those developed by the MPT group except for some minor technical modifications. The scale of the RITE study is more modest than the MPT's information flow census; for example, the number of media dealt with in the RITE study is only 22 compared to 35 in the MPT study. Fewer indicators are used in the RITE study than in the MPT study. Therefore, the RITE study may be said that it did not add very much to the knowledge and technique developed by the MPT study group. However, this study is valuable for its evaluation of the MPT's information flow census. The RITE researchers were much more cautious than the MPT study group. They refrained from using methods judged to be too speculative or risky. Although they did not overtly criticize the MPT group's ideas and methods, by rejecting some ideas and methods used in the information flow census, they pointed out where the problems were in the MPT group's ideas and methods. Conversely, by using and adopting ideas and methods developed by the MPT study group, they indicated which they thought valuable.

(10) From this writer's point of view, the measure based on households probably has the least distortion. People usually buy additional television and radio sets for convenience rather than for additional information. Furthermore, many new sets are acquired because they have better pictures or sound and the old set is simply not discarded. It is true that different members of the family might use different sets at the same time. This underestimate will lead to less distortion, however, than the assumption that multiple sets are on all the time. The most representative measure, of course, would be one that reflects the actual use of multiple sets.

(11) See, for example, T. Tsuneki (1980). p. 61.

(12) Ministry of Posts and Telecommunications (1978). p. 38.

(13) It is possible, on the other hand, to contend that people have come to have more choice concerning information only if the increase of information supply is accompanied by the increase of variety.

REFERENCES

Advisory Council for Industrial Structure, Information Industry Division (1969). *Joho Shori, Joho Sangyo ni Kansuru Toshin* (Report on the Policies for Data Processing and Information Industries).

American Academy of Arts and Sciences (ed.) (1967). *Toward the Year Two Thousand*. Boston: Houghton Mifflin.

Association for Economic Planning (1969). *Johoka Shakai no Keisei* (The Formation of Informational Societies).

Association for Economic Planning (1970). *Johoka Shakai no Hatten – Kokusaika Suru Joho Nettowahku* (The Development of Informational Societies – Internationalization of Information Networks)

Bell, Daniel (1973). *The Coming of Post-Industrial Society*. New York: Basic Books.

Brzezinski Z. (1970). *Between Two Ages: America's Role in the Technetronic Era.*

Drucker, Peter F. (1969). *The Age of Discontinuity*. New York: Harper & Row.

Economic Planning Agency (1969). *Keizai Hakusho* (White Paper on the Japanese Economy). English summary available.

Edelstein, Alex S., John E. Bowes and Seldon M. Harsel (1978) (Eds.). *Information Societies. Comparing the Japanese and American Experiences.* Seattle: University of Washington Press.

Hayashi, Yujiro (1969). *Johoka Shakai* (Informational Societies). Tokyo: Kodansha Gendai Shinsho.

Innis, Harold A. (1964). *The Bias of Communication.* Tront: University of Tronto Press.

Kahn, Herman and Anthony J. Wiener (1967). *The Year 2000 – A Frame work for Speculation on the Next Thirty-Three Years.*

Kohyama, Kenichi (1968). "Joho Shakai Josetsu (On Information Societies)." *Bessatsu Chuo Kohron Keiei Mondai*. Winter Edition. pp. 80-105.

Machlup, Fritz (1962). *The Production and Distribution of Knowledge in the United States*. Princeton: Princeton University Press.

McLuhan, H. Marshall (1965). *Understanding Media: The Extensions of Man*. New York: McGraw-Hill.

Ministry of Posts and Telecommunications, Communications Policy Division (1975). *Joho Ryutsu no Keiryo Shuho* (The Methods for the Measurement of Information Flow).

——————————————————————— (1978 A). *Tsushin Hakusho* (White Paper on Communications, 1978). English summary available: *Report on Present State of Communications in Japan.*

——————————————————————— (1978 B). "Information Flow Census in Japan – A Quantitative Study of Information Societies." Unpublished English paper distributed at an OECD conference.

Pierce, John R. (1977). "The Telephone and Society in the Past 100 Years," in Ithiel de Sola Pool (ed.), *The Social Impact of the Telephone*. Cambridge: The MIT Press.

Pool, Ithiel de Sola (1977). *The Social Impact of the Telephone*. Cambridge: The MIT Press.

Porat, Marc U. (1978). "Communication Policy in an Information Society." *The Bulletin of the Institute for Communication Research, Keio University*, No. 11. pp. 1-13.

Research Institute of Telecommunications and Economics (1968). *Sangyoka Igo no Shakai ni Okeru Joho to Tsushin* (Information and Communication in a Post-industrial Society).

—————————————————————————— (1970). *Sangyoka Igo no Shakai ni Okeru Denki Tsushin no Yakuwari* (The Roles of Telecommunications in a Post-industrial Society).

—————————————————————————— (1978). *"Joho no Nagare" no Sokutei to Joho no Keizai Kohka, Shakai Kaihatsu Kohka no Sokutei* (The Measurement of the "Flow of Information" and the Measurement of Economic Effects and Social Development Effects of Information). English summary available: *Information Flow in Japan*.

Takagi, Noritsune (1974). *"Joho Sangyo no Hatten* (The Development of Information Industries)," in Y. Uchikawa, K. Okabe, I. Takeuchi, A. Tsujimura (eds.), *Gendai Shakai to Komyunikeishon* (Modern Society and Communication), Vol. II, *Joho Shakai* (Information Societies). Tokyo: University of Tokyo Press. pp. 121-175.

Task Force For The Study Of Information Flow (1972). *Joho wa Bakuhatsu Shite-iruka?* (Is Information Exploding?).

Task Force For The Overall Study Of Information Flow (1973). *Joho Ryutsu no Jittai o Saguru* (The Investigatory Report on the Present State of Information Flow).

Tsuneki, Teruo (1980). *"Johoryo Sokutei ni Kansuru Ichi Kosatsu* (Measurement of the Amount of Information)." *RITE Review*, No. 4. pp. 47-67.

Umesao, Tadao (1963). *"Joho Sangyo Ron* (On Information Industries)," *Hoso Asahi*, January. pp. 4-17. Also included in *Chuokohron*, March, 1963.

Yasuda, Toshiaki (1972). *"Joho Sangyo no Enshutsushatachi* (Stage Directors of Information Industries)," in *YTV Joho Sangyo Kenkyu Gurupu* (eds.). *Joho Sangyo Monogatari*. Tokyo: Shakai Shiso Sha, Gendai Kyoyo Bunko. pp. 11-36.

A concise review of Japan's national efforts at understanding and evolving an informationalized society is presented here by John Bowes, an associate professor in the School of Communications at the University of Washington. Bowes argues that Japanese research on informationalized societies is descriptive work with aggregate data, frequently using econometric techniques. The conceptual basis for the model-building appears to be too often taken for granted and arbitrary. He sees the basic approach as an attempt to examine information as a core element of their life quality, a perspective unfamiliar to many Americans. Bowes sees the prospect of much collaboration, however, combining the American concern for the social and behavioral effects of information with the information flow approach of the Japanese. Such a collaboration might help bridge the conceptual link between information flow and life quality.

38

JAPAN'S APPROACH TO AN INFORMATION SOCIETY
A Critical Perspective

John E. Bowes

The term *Jahoka Shakai* or Information Society represents a synthesis of work by both Japanese and American scholars. The work of Americans such as Daniel Bell, Fritz Machlup, Anthony Weiner and Zbignew Brzezinski stirred Japanese interest in both future prediction and "post-industrial" society. In Japan, Tadao Umesao published *Joho Sangyo Ron* (On Information Industries) in 1963, developing "spiritual industries" as the final state of evolution in an industrial society. This end-state is characterized by the mass production and consumption of knowledge, the diffusion of higher education and expansion of cultural activities. In 1968, Kenichi Kohyama published an influential article *Joho Shakai Ron Josetsu* (On Information Societies) which sought to synthesize the work of Umesao with the Americans. In this description, as in those earlier, the *Joho Shakai* represented a mature, post-industrial society which found its wealth and culture centrally dependent on information technologies (Ito, 1980). This society differs from any preceding stage of evolution in that information is as highly valued as energy and raw materials as a basis for economic, industrial and social development (Tanaka, 1978). By the early 1970s, intellectual groundwork for "information societies" was well established, sensitizing Japanese intellectuals, business and much of the public to the value of information technologies and products as the proper path of future development.

By 1972, strong government interest in the societal influences of information industries was evident in a report of the Japanese Ministry of Posts and Telecommunication entitled, *Is Information Exploding?* (see Tanaka, 1978). Its purpose was to provide basic statistics on the production and use of information in Japan. Motivating this report was the dawning realization that information technology had shortened time and distances, and had in some cases reduced the economic gaps existing in the society. The advantages of successfully managing information resources became of great interest. Through audacious techniques of reducing all information available in the society to a single, common basis, a comparison of information production to human consumption was made. In the 10 year period from

From John E. Bowes, "Japan's Approach to an Information Society: A Critical Perspective," presented at the Japan-U.S.A. Conference on "Comparing Information Societies: Directions for Research" at the University of Washington in 1980.

1960 to 1970, for example, the government estimated that the information supply increased by 400% while consumption increased by only 140%. The Japanese public consumed 40% of information available in 1960. By 1975, this consumption rate had stabilized at a mere 10% of that made available. To the Japanese research community and the government, these data suggested a national information explosion, but one that left its consumers stunned (Tomita, 1978).

This relationship of information supply and the industry which maintains it to the citizen's capabilities to make good use of information is at the center of Japan's "information society" efforts. While such questions also provoked interest among U.S. researchers (for example, Katzman, 1975) the Japanese government and industries are unique in the importance and credence they give to information growth in planning the future of their society. In doing so, the Japanese have attempted to use national expertise in producing information technologies to answer pressing social needs and economic imperatives.

In evolving these answers, the Japanese have analyzed the power of factors responsible for their information growth. Not surprisingly, more than 70% of it could be traced to a single cause — information equipment — telephones, television receivers and computers (Tomita, 1978). Other contributors such as population growth, traditional, non-electronic information sources such as cinema, books and mail, had comparatively little impact. Industrially, the Japanese found themselves masters of producing this information equipment, but knowing comparatively little about its strong impact on their society.

From almost total destruction of Japan's telecommunication and electronics industry following World War II, the Japanese have been able to rebuild and expand information technologies and services to an extent which, based on their government statistics, places them second only to the United States. Telephone service, for example, lagged seriously behind the demand for it until 1971 when supply was for the first time in balance with demand. In 1960, residential phones numbered 2 per hundred persons. By 1977, the figure was about 75 phones per hundred. Data transmission showed an even more aggressive growth. (Nippon Telephone and Telegraph Public Corp., 1977). These domestic successes have been echoed by the dominance of Japanese consumer electronics and growing success with telecommunications equipment in international markets. But these are triumphs of mostly traditional technologies. Leadership in the manufacture of innovative computers and software systems has been vastly more difficult.

At the end of 1977, Japan had over 38,000 general purpose computers in operation with a combined value 2500 billion Yen ($12 billion) (Japan Information Processing Development Center, 1977). Compared with its successes in the consumer electronics and telecommunication industry, Japan's computer industry is in its infancy. But the Japanese government has made development of a highly competitive domestic computer industry a matter of first priority. According to the government's statement of its national computer policy:

". . . Japan's information processing industry must compete in an international arena with countries throughout the world and, in particular, must pit itself against the gigantic computer and software industries of the United States" (Japan Information Processing Development Center, 1977).

To accomplish this goal, starting in 1972, Japan has made major policy decisions which include tax and investment incentives, relaxation of monopoly regulations and other moves to assure a coordinated computer development effort among government, research institutions and industry (Walsh, 1977; *Industria*, 1978).

But more important than specific tax incentives and laws in the evolution of a Japanese information society has been the Japanese societal character which fosters consensual, cooperative effort among private industries, the government and research agencies. The avoidance of industrial strife, the orderliness and cooperation among industrial competitors, government and labor makes for strong, cost-effective production and high quality control. Clearly, this is a favorable environment for many kinds of industrial growth as witnessed by Japan's postwar ascendency in steel, shipbuilding, automobiles and heavy machinery. Why, then, has this societal advantage been focussed so intently on information?

If Japan today is on the verge of post-industrial society, it has spent the last 50 years — and especially the time since the end of WW II — in an industrial revolution. The cost to achieve industrial success has been enormous. Crowded living conditions, pollution, limited social welfare and little open space are visible indicants of single-minded devotion to production. Underlying this has been a stoic awareness among ordinary Japanese of their tenuous dependence on imported materials and the export of finished goods to world markets (Reischauer, 1977).

But cracks are appearing in this voluntary self-denial. Increasing — though by U.S. standards miniscule — levels of violent crimes, social protest, alcoholism and psychological illness signal problems. Rising energy costs and increasing restiveness by other nations against Japanese imports and trade imbalances have fueled considerable self-examination of national character and goals. As a major governmental report summarized, "Japan's economy is gasping under structural depression" (Japan Computer Usage Development Institute, 1972, p. 15).

In cooperation with leading industries, Japan's Ministry of International Trade and Industry (MITI) in 1972 formulated new policies to deal with these problems. In an ambitious *Plan for an Information Society: A National Goal Toward the Year 2000*, the MITI set forth solutions to life quality problems based on comprehensive utilization of information and information technologies (Japan Computer Usage Development Institute, 1972). The plan urged that national priority be given to knowledge-intensive, energy-economizing industry. Emphasis would be placed on such products of an R & D-intensive, high value-added quality as computers, aircraft and equipment which require highly specialized manufacturing techniques, such as telecommunications equipment and business machines. The report had considerable impact on the public imagination in Japan and aroused the ire of other nations with which Japan competes. Though the government softened its stand in the face of blunt criticism from the industrial West, there is little doubt the policy is tacitly accepted and is being implemented (Walsh, 1978).

But the social considerations of this plan are as strategic as the economic. As in many developed Western nations, considerable pressure is building among government leaders and social critics to pay better attention to the "quality of life" rather than economic success at any cost. Information industries are relatively free of pollution, require few scarce or expensive materials and provide favorable work conditions for labor. Secondly, with crowded, often dingy living conditions media content is seen as a pallative, a bright spot providing entertainment, education, culture — perhaps escape and psychological mobility. Thirdly, new media, based on computer technology is integral to this vision and involves substantial change beyond simple enhancement of traditional media:

"The information society centering around computers is different from the society characterized by projected images that are passive, sentimental and sensible such as mainly represented by TV. It is necessary to stress that the information society is an intellectual creativity society and is subjective, theoretical and objective-pursuing" (Japan Computer Usage Dev. Inst., 1972, p. 16).

These government planners caution against a status-quo, laissez-faire policy toward media growth, warning that "information pollution will spread just like industrial pollution" if planning is not oriented more to social policy, software and human use considerations than to hardware and industrialization. Part of this planning involves training the public to a computer-oriented manner of coping with the products of an information society (Japan Computer Development Institute, 1972, p. 16).

But however comforting generalities and broad plans may seem about a Japanese *Computopia*,[1] the specifics of defining "quality of life" and the informational steps necessary to attain it are elusive. In attempts to specify, the Japanese have borrowed as well as innovated in their research. They have invested heavily in new media information systems to field test the way for a better quality of life at home — and, to be sure, new products for export abroad.

The major Japanese organization concerned with the relation of information technology and the Japanese citizen is the Research Institute for Telecommunications and Economics (or RITE). It is supported jointly by the telecommunications and electronics industries, the government and by leading research universities. For several years, starting in the mid-70s, RITE has been assessing "quality of life" in Japan, using their own techniques and those developed in similar measurement efforts in the U.S. (see Takasaki, 1975). Inputs ranging from the quality of bus service to leisure and health care are considered together with such information dependent problems as newspaper delivery, insufficient mass media and the adequacy of libraries. Though much of this research is in progress, the importance of information to Japanese life quality has been shown, not surprisingly, to be considerable, impacting many other sectors of life quality such as security, education and health.

From the onset of their research, the Japanese have favored a multivariate, Forrester-style modelling approach called "Target-setting Policy Model Building." It is a method composed of: (a) models incorporating time-series analysis and projection, (b) policy and social system considerations — that is, citizen behavior and other qualitative elements are incorporated, and (c) feedback on policies from many sectors of society via a "computerization policy council" (Japan Computer Usage Devel. Inst., 1972). This research has been characterized by complex indexing of aggregate indicators (e.g. average use of media, per capita telephone use, etc.). More recently, researchers have tempered this aggregate indicators approach with direct interviews of citizens on the subject of life quality (Takasaki, 1977).

The key to Japanese research and planning rests on how to raise the utility of the information in circulation, lest "information pollution" or still greater imbalance between information production and consumption result. Information that is "polluting," versus that which isn't bears strongly on the kinds of information serving quality of life goals. Thus a major effort in current RITE research seems to build a circle of logic where characteristics of life quality and the nature of information and information media which improve it are identified.

This effort has taken several major directions:

● Conducting an "information census" and econometric analysis of the demand for information transmission (see Tomita, 1975 and Pool, 1977). The Japanese have devoted considerable attention to the flow of most forms of information transmission, ranging from television to computers, from education to postal. In doing so, they have taken on the difficult task of equating or generalizing over many different forms in terms of a common unit of message meaning. Because the engineer's solution of analyzing all information in terms of binary bits is not sensible if one is interested in transmission of meaning[1], the "word" was chosen as a basic unit. This is not perfect either, if one confronts the problem of translating moving television images to words, for example. Despite shortcomings, conversion assumptions were made and a basic index of information meaning transmission was established. A second measure, the "word-kilometer" was also established which indexed the *distance* of the transmission together with its word volume. Given two transmissions of equal length, one travelling 100 kilometers, the second just one kilometer, the transmission volume in word-kilometers is 100 time greater for the first. Cost was a third consideration: how many yen does a word kilometer cost, say, by telegraph, by books, or by radio? With these measures, the kind of media typically used for certain combinations of transmission distance and message length could be better explained and predicted. The decline in telegraph service in Japan is easily rationalized by its high cost per word-kilometer (about 1.2 cents). On the other hand, the cost of immensely popular television transmission is less than 2×10^{-5} cents per word-kilometer. However, the use of telephone in preference to the considerably cheaper mail must be considered in light of the cost of preparing the letter itself. To be sure, these measures leave much to be desired in terms of a comprehensive explanation for the use of various information forms: we send letters for their permanence and precision of meaning, television provides inexpensive entertainment, and phone calls imply informality and rapid feedback. But the measures do provide a beginning at tracking economic forces which shape and respond to policy decisions about a telecommunications future.

- Improvements on existing media systems, such as increasing the variety of television broadcast with cable distribution and origination, use of video phones, and experimenting with electronic delivery of newspapers via facsimile receivers. The assumption here seems to be that improvement in ease of access to a wider variety of information sources will be beneficial.

- Efforts to provide new systems for public information services. Much of this effort parallels efforts in other nations to provide information from centralized data bases via personal terminal equipment (e.g. "videotex" systems). The assumption made is that interactive information media will provide spot information closer to user needs in time and content. By making active search easy and the data base rich, more are inclined to do utilize information bases and the national quality of life ostensibly improves, assuming, of course, that the information aids the solution of problems and enrichment of daily life.

Three major experimental projects characterize Japan's "information society" efforts. What is common to all of them is a converging of Japan's skills in consumer electronics with a developing expertise in computer-based information technologies. Integral to this convergence is an assessment which examines life quality outcomes.

- The oldest project is the Tama New Town Coaxial Cable Information System Experiment (Tama CCIS). Begun in the mid-70s, the system was built as part of a new lower middle class apartment suburb of Tokyo. In essence, it is a greatly enhanced cable television system which field tests a variety of innovative information services and technologies. Capabilities ranging from one-way standard CATV and cable (neighborhood programs, warning systems and facsimile press) to bi-directional memo service (interconnected facsimile transmitters) and a limited audience response and video tape cassette selection system have been tried. An interem evaluation doomed such expensive and little used services as facsimile newspapers, while others (memo copy and bulletin news services, for example) have prospered (Living Visual Information System Development Assn, 1978).

- A second, more sophisticated experiment began in 1978 under the auspices of the MITI, the Japanese Ministry of International Trade and Industry. The Higashi-Ikoma Optical-Visual Information System (Hi-Ovis) is noteworthy for two major technological innovations: the use of optical fibre cable for signal transmission, and secondly — of greater significance — a large computer database accessible by householders on an individual, interactive basis via phone and home tv. The database is available both as text-on-screen and as user selected videocassettes to provide specialized programming (Visual Information System Dev. Assn., 1978).

- Finally, a third system, CAPTAIN, emphasizes personal retrieval of information from data banks at lower costs with wider access than in other systems being tested. It is perhaps the most exciting system for these reasons. By transmitting requested information over standard telephone circuits, the cost of coaxial or optic fibre networks is avoided. CAPTAIN can go anywhere within the reach of Japan's extensive telephone system. This research, as is its many counterparts in Europe (e.g. Viewdata) is being sponsored by the postal and telecommunication authorities (Tomita, 1979).

While the construction of such projects signal a certain technological success, the question is very much open as to whether they provide truly useful services able to improve effective use of Japan's information abundance. The failure of several Tama CCIS services suggest that technological cleverness is no promise of eventual cost-effective utility. The measuring of information utility to users (and thus the worth of new information technologies) confronts these Japanese researchers as well as their Western counterparts. The Japanese have attempted this kind of assessment since the late 1970s.

Early reports of RITE's research in the late 1960s consisted primarily of legal, economic or engineering research on the development of telecommunications industries. Their recent research reports show a strong increase in such titles as: "Experiment on Teleconference Communication" (Tsuneki, 1979), "Receptivity to Image Media" (Takasaki, 1979), and "Our Study of Quality of Life and Contribution of Telecommunications" (Takasaki, 1977), suggesting an increased attentiveness to basic variables of human information use.

In this effort, the Japanese have concentrated not only on "information in the narrow sense" (recall and accuracy in perceiving content), but also "emotionality" (the affective consequence of the information — Takasaki, 1979). These experiments often test combinations of program modalities (visual text, audio, motion pictures with and without sound) in terms of user response on such attributes as "brightness", "complexity" and "approachability" to better predict response to new information modalities (Tsureki, 1979).

Several of these approaches are familiar to U.S. researchers. And there has been obvious U.S. interest in the psychological and social implications of new information technologies. Innovative cable projects such as QUBE, Reading, Pa., the Knight-Ridder Viewtron experiment, and Seattle's VOXBOX have been technologically innovative and are being used for measuring social impacts (see *Intermedia*, 1979; Moss, 1978; Viewdata Corp., 1980). The nature of man-machine dialogue has been routinely examined for years (see for example, Chapanis, 1965). Many studies have argued the value and feasibility of "information utilities" (see Sackman, 1971; Englebart, 1972) Other research has focussed on broad economic questions of information in the U.S. (see Porat, 1977; Hilewick, et. al., 1978; and Fields, 1978). What then distinguishes Japanese from U.S. research?

Major differences in emphasis, scale and centralized coordination of research efforts are apparent. Too, certain efforts, such as the "information census" are unique and unparalleled in U.S. research efforts. Conceptually, the overriding difference in emphasis seems as Japanese communication scholar, Youichi Ito (1978), observed:

"The difference between conventional American communication theories and the Japanese Information Societies approach is that the former is more concerned with the social effects of content of mass communication, whereas the latter is concerned with the social effects of the amount of information flow."

This Japanese concern with amount of information flow has been strongly directed to social planning and policy making, based on a comprehensive analysis of information production and consumption in the society. Policy arguments over "information pollution," "information waste,"[3] and the social costs of "informationalization" of the society are intrinsic concerns which reflect the central role accorded to information in Japanese social planning. By contrast, U.S. efforts are typically particular to a given project of confined geographical impact or consider information in largely economic or regulatory terms when a national view is adopted.

But of obvious contrast in the other direction is the emphasis by North American scholars on "communication" — the consideration of content, shared meaning and effects of messages. Communication study historically has not been seen so much as a positive, central need of social planning as it is of an adjunct explanatory effort for advertising effectiveness, social disorder, and cultural change. It is useful to note that Japanese have no equivalent in their language for "communication." Rather, the operative term is the indigenous word *joho* (information), not the phoneticised *komyunikeishon* which is borrowed and alien (Ito, 1978).

Scale and centralized control are also obvious features of the Japanese research effort. Major investments by consortia of government agencies, industries and the research community have been made in the demonstration projects described above. A cooperative agency, RITE, has been developed to assist in conducting this research and in the training of communication scholars. There is little equivalent organizationally in the U.S.

Perhaps because it is the outgrowth of national policy development, the character of Japanese information societies has tended to be descriptive, based on aggregate data and frequently econometric in technique. Rarely are alternative conceptual models of informationalization tested for predictive power or explanatory merit. Rather, the basis for model building appears grounded in uncontested and desired national planning directions and self-described personal life goals of citizens. The problem which arises is an unreality between the concept explicated and the variables which represent it empirically. Can life quality be assessed adequately by noting bus service, telephone saturation and user satisfaction with innovative media technologies as the Japanese have done? There is an arbitrariness to these selections which, while they have the strength of plausibility, are not tested or well-justified in competition with alternate formulations.

It is apparent in comparing Japanese and U.S. research that the two have a complementary nature. The well-organized Japanese effort to examine information as a core characteristic of their society in life quality terms is a perspective unfamiliar to most U.S. researchers. Yet the problems — methodological and conceptual — of defining quality of life specific to kinds of information and the quality with which such information is communicated is perhaps where U.S. research can be of assistance. If Japanese research has been characterized by aggregate social indicators and description (e.g. "information census"), the U.S. communication scholar has done more to explain the social and behavioral effects of information (e.g. "uses and gratifications," "social in fluence," "communication accuracy").

Part of this problem is that the U.S. researcher's concerns with "communication" are not handled well by Japanese in pursuit of "information" studies. Thus different ter minology is not a mere translator's problem, it is a difference in perspective that conditions scholarship. What seems quite apparent is that both research communities have much to learn from the appreciation of the other's perspective. U.S. researchers can obtain a better appreciation of analyzing information flow and the planning such data allow on a national basis. Japanese scholars have incorporated some of the social psychological nature of U.S. communication research in their examination of information flows. Aside from general desirability of cross semination of ideas between Japan and the U.S., there are trends in both nations which argue for their attention to the research strengths of the other. Efficient use and nurturing of innovative communication / information industries in the U.S. has been a persistent policy problem which could be aided by the kind of information the Japanese are endeavoring to collect. Japan, in its pursuit of a *Johoka Shakai*, is moving to increasingly personal, interactive media. As a 1978 government *White Paper on Communication* commented:

". . . our society is moving toward a new stage of *johoka shakai* in which more priority is placed on segmented, more detailed information to meet individual needs instead of conventional mass-reproduced conformed information." (*Tsushin Hakusho*, 1978).

Japanese information research has already moved substantially from a "macroeconomic" to a "macro-communication" approach (Ito, 1980). The U.S. emphasis on individual communication and proximal social influences would seem of considerable use as research paces the increasingly individual and personal movement of information media in Japan.

For the moment, both research communities have developed research traditions that are possibly more important for the questions they raise and their complimentary perspectives than for the immediate answers obtained. Serious questions remain for Japanese researchers of the information society. The link between information technologies and life quality, they realize, must be established with greater precision and validity. Predicting the mass desirability of novel information services and terminal devices poses equally difficult questions. Policy questions concerning the operation of information centers, the cost of access and the selection of information providers will be persistent problems of operating a *johoka shakai*. What must be said for the Japanese in their struggle to define and plan an information society is that they realize the difficulty as well as the promise of of their venture. They are dealing with both in a planned and thorough manner typical of their technological successes, nurtured by an impressively strong belief that the economic and social exploitation of information is the major key to their future. What is surprising, given the scope of their activity and the value inherent in their research perspectives, is the comparatively slight awareness of their information research among the North American communication research community. As the U. S. like Japan, moves towards new, mass information technologies, Japanese efforts to plan and predict such growth should prove to be of considerable value.

NOTES

1 ''Computopia'' is a term coined by the Japanese computerization committee to describe the ultimate progression of an informationalized society, where human fulfillment is adequately served by abundant information resources and delivery systems.

2 Bit rate formulations do not work well in this context as the form of transmission for a given message affects greatly the bit rate necessary to transmit it. Telegraphic or computer transmission of a character is relatively efficient (5-8 bits). However, facsimile transmission of the same character translated into pixels might require hundreds of bits. The meaning transmitted, however, would be the same.

3 The Japanese idea of information ''waste'', as Pool (1977) points out, is somewhat peculiar in that it may merely be a reflection of increasing heterogeneity of choice and taste in information among members of a society. Ito (1980) indicates that Japanese MPT (postal & telephone) researchers are presently developing measures of redundancy to (among other things) better represent waste of information.

REFERENCES

Chapanis, Alphonse (1965). *Man-Machine Engineering*. Belmont, CA.: Wadsworth.

Edelstein, Alex, John E. Bowes and Sheldon M. Harsel (1978). *Information Societies: Comparing the Japanese and American Experiences*. (Seattle: University of Washington Press).

Englebart, Douglas C. (1972). ''On Line Team Environment: Network Information Center and Computer Augmented Team Interaction'' Publication RADC-TR-72-232, Final Report, Augmentation Research Center, Stanford Research Institutes, Menlo Park, CA.

Fields, Judith (1978). "Economic Evaluation of the Output of the Reading Interactive System". in Mitchell L. Moss (ed.), *Two Way Cable Television: An Evaluation of Community Users in Reading, Pennsylvania*. New York University.

Hilewick, Carol Lee, Edward J. Deak and Edward Heinze (1978). "Investment in Communications and Transportation: Socio- Economic Impacts on Rural Development." in Edelstein, et. al. *Information Societies, Comparing the Japanese and American Experience*, Seattle: U. Wash. Press.

Intermedia (1979) 7:3 (May). See entire issue.

Ito, Youichi (1980). "The 'Johoka Shakai' Approach to Communication Study in Japan." *Keio Communication Review 1* (No. 1), 13-40.

Ito, Youichi (1978). Report at the Final Plenary Session: Cross-Cultural Perspectives on the Concept of an Information Society in Edelstein, et. al. *Information Societies, Comparing the Japanese and American Experience*, Seattle: University of Washington Press.

Japan Computer Usage Development Institute Computerization Committee (1972). *The Plan for an Information Society: A National Goal Toward the Year 2000*. Final Report Tokyo. (reprinted in *Data Exchange*, July-August, 1973)

Japan Information Processing Development Center (1977). *Computer White Paper, 1976 Edition: A Summary of Highlights Compiled from the Japanese Original*. (Tokyo: Asahi Evening News Co.).

Katzman, N. (1974). "The Impact of Communication Technology: Promise and Prospects." *Journal of Communication 24* (No. 4), 47-58.

Living Visual Information System Development Association (1977). Tama CCIS (Coaxial Cable Information System). Technical Notes for Experimental Project. (Tokyo).

Living-Visual Information System Development Association (1977). Outline of Tama CCIS (Coaxial Cable Information System) Experiment Project, (Tokyo).

Ministry of Posts and Telecommunication (1978). *Tsushin Hakusho* (White Paper on Communications), p. 38. (quoted in Ito, 1980).

Ministry of Posts and Telecommunications (1977). Report on the Present State of Telecommunications in Japan: Fiscal 1977. (Based on Japanese language "White Paper on Communications, 1977).

Moss, Mitchell L. (1978). *Two-Way Cable Television: An Evaluation of Community Uses in Reading, PA* (vol 1). NYU Reading Consortium, Alternate Media Center, Graduate School of Public Administration, April.

Nippon Telegraph and Telephone Public Corporation (1977). *Telegraph and Telephone Service in Japan: Illustrated*. January.

Pool, Ithiel (1977-est.). Memorandum: Two Important Japanese Communications Studies. (undated internal memorandum, Department of Political Science, Massachusetts Institute of Technology).

Porat, Mark U. (1977) *The Information Economy*, Special Publication 77-12 (1) Washington D.C.: U. S. Dept. of Commerce, Office of Telecommunications.

Reischauer, Edwin O. (1977) *The Japanese*. (Tokyo: Tuttle).

Research Institute for Telecommunications and Economics (1976). *Research Report Summaries '76*. Tokyo.

Research Institute for Telecommunications and Economics (1968). *Research Report Summaries '68*. Tokyo.

Sackman, Harold (1968). *Mass Information Utilities and Social Excellence*. NY: Auerbach.

Takasaki N. and T. Ozawa (1978). *The Study of Information Flow Census*. (Tokyo: RITE).

Takasaki N. (1977) *Our Study of "Quality of Life" and Contribution of Telecommunications*. (Tokyo: RITE), November.

Takasaki, N. (1975) *Our Concept of "Quality of Life": A Tentative Study of its Thesis and Practical Application*. (Tokyo: RITE) September.

Tomita, Tetsuro (1979). "Japan: The Search for a Personal Information Medium." *Intermedia*. 7:3 (May) pp. 36-38.

Viewdata Corporation of America (1980). "Viewtron: A Service of the Future for American Homes." (pamphlet).

Visual Information System Development Association-MITI Juridical Foundation (1978). *Hi-OVIS: Optical Visual Information System*. (Tokyo).

Walsh, J. (1977) "International Trade in Electronics: U.S. - Japan Competition." *Science*, 195:4283 (18 March) pp. 1175-79.

A natural history of information, along the lines suggested in the classic work on newspapers by Robert Park, emerges from comparative research on information societies, says Sheldon Harsel in the following article. He notes that changing forms of information have produced changes in crime and deviance (for example, computer-assisted theft and fraud) and have made possible "cities of the mind." These changes highlight the need for research on the cultural meaning of such terms as data, information, knowledge, and communication. Dr. Harsel, an assistant professor in the School of Communications at the University of Washington, concludes that American scholars have much catching up to do to stay abreast of Japanese advances in the study of informationalized societies.

39

COMMUNICATION RESEARCH IN INFORMATION SOCIETIES
A Comparative View of Japan and the United States

Sheldon Harsel

Societies are identified by their institutions, artifacts, and behaviors. Thus the United States and Japan are called Information Societies because their daily life and national affairs are characterized by communication technologies, institutions, and values which are newly significant.[2] What distinguishes Information Societies from others are not merely such visible artifacts as the hardware of data manipulation and transmission. Nor are these in themselves "communication". Rather, Japan and the United States are strongly influenced or "informationalized" in social organization, culture and behavior by these artifacts.

The purpose of this paper is to identify areas of importance for communication scholarship, especially those which have concerned Japanese scholars. Its perspective is comparative, primarily because it embraces both Japan and the United States, but also because these nations are influential in the movement of others toward informationalization. Comparative communication research can help to identify the dimensions of informationalization so that the concept itself is better understood and utilized in addressing the concerns of all societies, whether informationally advanced or not.

As Bowes and Ito[3] both point out, some forms of research on informationalization have demonstrated promise; e.g. analyses of trade in information and administrative research on the development, adoption, and use of various communication devices. There are studies, as well, on the economic, technological, administrative, and regulatory aspects of information impact on the quality of life. But research on communication as "cultural process," however, is relatively unknown in the U.S.

From Sheldon Harsel, "Communication Research in Information Societies: A Comparative View of Japan and the United States," presented at the Japan-U.S.A. Conference on "Comparing Information Societies: Directions for Research" at the University of Washington in 1980.

A number of reasons can be suggested. One is that the loyalty to research traditions and attachment to academic disciplines has hindered the development of integrated studies. Another is that American communication scholars have tended to emphasize behavioral and institutional studies to the neglect of macroanalytic theory and research. A third reason is the unavailability of most of the Japanese research because of linguistic and cultural barriers. Much of the work which is in English and available represents only a narrow range of Japanese conceptualization and research.

As a result, Japanese communication scholarship is likely to be neglected or misunderstood. Even the earliest Japanese works on Information Society development drew on a century of concern with the personal, societal, and cultural functions of mass communication. Such matters as Korzybskian time-binding, education and religion as "information industries,"[4] and the meaning of the "information revolution" in the history of civilization[5] were considered.

Some of the early American interest in these efforts was expressed in a comparative framework through conferences on media, journalism, information technologies, and on Japan and America as post-industrial, knowledge-based societies. But an emphasis on institutions, economics and policy often left human communication behavior as a secondary concern. Because the characteristic behavior in Information Societies is communication, there is a need for further research and conceptualization of this sort. A few of the potentially useful directions are suggested here.

First might be matters of cultural meaning for such terms as data, knowledge, information and communication given contemporary cultural and technological change.[6] They are most useful if distinguished from each other and not used interchangeably. It is also possible that precise definitions which do exist need revision because of changes in the behaviors associated with those terms. Functionally, for example, is there a difference in what we are willing to accept as "information" — and therefore as the content of communication — based on whether it is subject to the kind of indexing, storage, and retrieval demanded by machine-based social institutions? What are the implications for legal, economic, and cultural systems? Will an emphasis on information as the focus of attention lead us back toward a transportation- or transmission-based notion of communication?

In this regard, grouping Japan and the United States together as Information Societies seems to be better supported by economic and technological indicators than by cultural or behavioral ones. Consequently, we must ask, what are the similarities which make comparison possible and what are the differences which make it productive? Does the Information Society signify nothing more than an advanced stage of industrial capitalism, as some writers have suggested, or is it a rubric to promote an insidious marketing strategy for economic and political purposes as others have said?[7]

Optimistically, does it indicate a shift from "use value" based on the physical qualities of goods to "esteem value" which is based on their informational functions, from logic to sensibility, and from a "hard" society serving primary human needs to a "soft" society serving secondary ones[8]? Does it portend a stage of material and intellectual liberation and full participation?

The problems of clarifying what is meant by information are intrinsic to its measurement, as the Japanese attempts at an information census show. Perhaps instead of trying to quantify the entire array of information potentially available within a society, we should study the information available to and / or used by the individual. From one point of view each typical person consumes, processes, or attends to approximately the same amount of information each day regardless of the potential available.

It has been several decades since Robert Park attempted a "natural history" of news and newspapers. Now there may be a need for a natural history of information. The ease and frequency with which we use the term might be keeping us from understanding it. Furthermore, the synecdoche, the rhetorical device of representing a whole (contemporary culture) by one of its parts (information), may hide more than it reveals.

There have been studies of individual behavior and capabilities such as human-machine interfaces, adoption of new technologies, patterns of use and decision-making, and the training of individuals for characteristic information society activities. But some individuals are left behind in technological development or choose to minimize their participation in it. With the informationalizing of societies, the "knowledge gap" undergoes qualitative as well as quantitative changes; e.g. individuals become handicapped by their lack of access to information, unable to participate in the communication structure and processes of their society.

It is with these sociocultural concerns that the potential for comparative and collaborative research seems to be the greatest. In both Japan and the United States "informationalization" seems to include apparently contradictory trends. One is an increase in participatory activities made possible by Information Society development. Examples include special interest and activist groups in a multitude of contexts. There are various community and neighborhood organizations, consumer and environmental groups, civil rights advocates, and strident ideological partisans throughout the political spectrum.[9]

But there also seem to be marked increases in privatization, disengagement from the public realm, and retreat into one's own sensory experience. This is not an entirely asocial phenomenon however, as often these privatized states become the organizing principles for groups. These range from the tacit recognition of like-minded individuals as fellow travelers of a lifestyle, to the more visible collectivities of cultists and splinter political cliques who function through claims of universal authority and applicability for their private, inner experience.

For this reason, the contradiction may be more apparent than real. The participatory and the privatized may be distinct and contradictory manifestations, or causes of "informationalization," or they may be complementary and interdependent. Perhaps they both demonstrate the effects of "information affluence" and "communication poverty". It is interesting that many of these developments, from recreational drug use and physical fitness to quasi-political organizations and protest movements, tend to become internationalized, possibly following patterns of mass media and information diffusion.

It might also be possible that these cultural changes are indicative of responses to *modalities* of information — nonliteral, synchronic, ideographic, affective, etc. — which are the unintended byproducts of informationalization. If so, informationalization may be accelerating what Habermas calls the "systematic distortion" of the polity through the modes of knowledge and discourse which become dominant.

Other contradictory trends seem to emerge, as well. There is cultural homogenization and the opposite movement toward fragmentation reflected in the concern of Information Society scholars with questions of community formation, interpersonal and group relations, socialization, conflict and integration, and changes in value systems.

Communities evolve through the transactions of human communication and are based on common foundations of knowledge and ways of knowing. This was noted by Dewey and later by Holzner,[10] who refers to "epistemic communities." But in the era of the Information Society the geographic community is displaced by the city, which some scholars see as being essentially an information system.[11] Informationalization transforms the epistemic communities into "cities of the mind," free of geographical restrictions but diminishing our capacity to participate in our physical communities.

Some of the Japanese attempts at community formation, such as the experiments at Tama and Higashi-Ikoma, are based on the centralization of information distribution services and the control of information content. Much less well known are the attempts to build communities on epistemic or cultural foundations and communication systems, such as the academic and research "new town" at Tsukuba.

In this same sense, the Information Society even demonstrates unique forms of crime and deviance. They include not only violation of privacy, copyright, and patent, or computer-assisted theft and fraud; but also crimes in which a major purpose is access and publicity through the communication system. Terrorism is the most dramatic example, but there have been many others, including violent attacks on media institutions and people.[12]

While much of this discussion has suggested studying the cultural effects of technology, the technologies *themselves* are cultural effects. Development of Japanese and American information technologies in response to different values and communication behaviors could be examined in such areas as banking and credit, health, employment, courtship, merchandising, child care, and so on.

One of the difficult problems of comparative research is communication itself. Since knowledge is a creation of culture, acquiring knowledge of a culture which is not one's own is at best a difficult epistemological task, and at worst approaches a logical contradiction. However, the collaborative approach allows us the opportunity to gain culturally valid knowledge from each other.

Scores of books on Information Society have been published in Japan. The implication is that Americans have some catching up to do, not only to understand Japanese society, but to learn about the potentialities and limitations of comparison processes. A scanning of just a few of the Japanese studies reveals attempts to relate the Information Society concept to the full range of human concerns.[13] One Japanese scholar called for the development of a new human science for the "information age" over a dozen years ago.[14]

These potential areas for comparative research await conceptual refinement and operationalization. But the "informationalization" of our societies does not wait. It continues at a rate and in a direction not yet known, making the research task both formidable and urgent.

NOTES

[1] A more comprehensive version of this paper was presented at the conference, "Comparing Information Societies: Directions for Research," Seattle, 1980. Japanese names are given in Western order, with surnames last. Romanization of Japanese words is by a modified version of the Hepburn system. Translations of titles, given in brackets below, are this author's.

[2] Alex Edelstein, John Bowes, and Sheldon Harsel, eds., *Information Societies: Comparing the Japanese and American Experiences* (University of Washington Press, 1978).

[3] Papers by Bowes and Ito in this volume.

[4] Tadao Umesao, "Joho Sangyo Ron" [On Information Industries], *Chuo Koron* (March, 1963), pp. 46-58

[5] Kenichi Koyama, "Joho Shakai Ron Josetsu" [Introduction to Information Society Theory], *Chuo Koron Keiei Mondai* (Winter, 1968), pp. 80-105.

[6] Cf. Lee Thayer, *Communication and Communication Systems* (Irwin, 1968), pp. 28ff.

[7] One of the earliest American expressions of skepticism is in William K. Cummings, "Japan's Educational Revolution," paper presented to the annual meeting of the Association for Asian Studies, Chicago, 1973.

[8] Yujiro Hayashi, *Johoka Shakai: Haado no Shakai Kara Sofuto no Shakai E* [Information Society: From Hard Society to Soft Society] (Kodansha, 1969).

[9] Cf. Hiroshi Akuto, *Amerika no Seiji Fudo* [American Political Climate] (Nihon Keizai Shimbunsha, 1980).

[10] Burkart Holzner, *Reality Construction in Society* (Schenkman, 1972).

[11] E.g. Melvin Webber, "Urbanization and Communications," and Richard Meier, "Urban Ecostructures in a Cybernetic Age: Responses to Communications Stress," in *Communications Technology and Social Policy: Understanding the New "Cultural Revolution"* ed. by George Gerbner, Larry Gross, and William Melody (Wiley, 1973).

[12] Cf. "Johokajidai no Horitsu Mondai" [Legal Problems of the Information Age], special issue of *Juristo* (January, 1980); also Sheldon Harsel, "Terrorism as Communication," *Progress in Communication Sciences 3* (Ablex, 1981 forthcoming).

[13] E.g. communication theory, management, urban planning, elections, consumerism, the right to know, freedom of expression, violence, youth, political consciousness and involvement, fashion, popular culture, macro- and micro-economics, developing nations, conflict, religion, social and political movements, journalism, institutional change, ideology, education, government and industry policy formation, and more. Cf. Y. Uchikawa, K. Okabe, I. Takeuchi, and A. Tsujimura, eds., *Koza: Gendai Shakai to Komyunikeishon* [Studies in Contemporary Society and Communication], 5 vols. (Tokyo University Press, 1973-74): YTV Joho Sangyo Kenkyu Gurupu [Yomiuri TV Information Industry Research Group], eds., *Nihon no Joho Sangyo* [Japan's Information Industry], 3 vols. (Simul Press, 1975): J. Sakamoto, *Chishiki Sangyo Kakumei* [Knowledge Industry Revolution] (Daiyamondo, 1968); Y. Tanaka, *Chishiki Shakai no Koso* [The Idea of the Knowledge Society] (Chuo Koronsha, 1975).

[14] Yasumasa Tanaka, *Kodo Kagaku: Joho Jidai no Ningen Kagaku* [The Science of Behavior: Human Science in the Information Age] (Chikuma Shobo, 1969) and *Komyunikeishon Kagaku* [Communication Science] (Nihon Hyoronsha, 1969).

A preview of major results of an ambitious cultural indicators project in Sweden is reported here by Karl Erik Rosengren, a sociologist at the University of Lund. Dr. Rosengren describes the theoretical development of the project, using the typology of social structure and culture he originated in the article published in Volume 1 of Mass Communication Review Yearbook, *"Mass Media and Social Change: Some Current Approaches." Data from various subsections of the project—ranging from values of freedom and equality in editorials of leading newspapers to the proportion of employed women portrayed in advertisements—are used to depict the pertinence of cultural indicators to an understanding of the development of a postwar industrial society. Most of the cultural indicators show change in expected directions, leading to speculation of their predictive value in future research. Dr. Rosengren's article is a revised version of a paper presented to the 1980 International Communication Association meeting in Acapulco, Mexico.*

40

MASS COMMUNICATIONS AS CULTURAL INDICATORS

Sweden, 1945-1975

Karl Erik Rosengren

I. THE STUDY OF CULTURAL INDICATORS

During the postwar period, Sweden—like some other countries in north-western Europe—has evolved from an incompletely industrialized society into a postindustrial one. When trying to understand and explain this postwar development, it is striking to note the decline in the sophistication of theory, methodology, and data as one moves from economic to social to cultural levels. Economic indicators have been around for centuries and have been gradually refined.

Economic indicators are indispensable; yet they do not measure important aspects of societal structure and development. As a result, social indicators have been developed, tapping important dimensions of the social reality falling outside the conceptual space delimited by the economic indicators. It is customary to distinguish between "objective" social indicators (measuring

From Karl Erik Rosengren, "Mass Communications as Cultural Indicators: Sweden, 1945-1975," original manuscript.

objective characteristics of a social structure) and "subjective" social indicators (measuring perceptions and evaluations thereof).

A striking result in recent research within the "social indicators movement" is that the relationship between objective and subjective indicators supposedly corresponding to each other is somewhat problematic. Welfare does not necessarily produce well-being—an old insight which is now being corroborated and more precisely expressed by social indicators research.

One explanation for the low or absent relationship between objective and subjective social indicators is the fact that what has sometimes been treated as a two-factor problem—objective conditions and perceptions and evaluations of these conditions—is really a three-factor problem. Perceptions and evaluations of objective social conditions are made against the background of knowledge, opinions, and values—in short, against the background of individual expectations and common culture.

The implication of the above arguments is that efforts should be directed toward the third factor influencing the relationship between objective and subjective social indicators: culture. It stands to reason that just as the scientific study of the economic aspects of society has demanded the development of economic indicators, and just as the social aspects have called for social indicators, so the serious study of culture will ultimately necessitate the systematic and sustained development of cultural indicators. Such a development—mainly methodological in its thrust—would no doubt lead to a corresponding theoretical and empirical enrichment of the study of culture, not only in the social sciences but also in the humanities (although the concept of culture as conceived here, of course, is the broad culture of the social sciences rather than the high culture or fine arts studied in the humanities). It is possible that a future development of cultural indicators studies will to some extent parallel that of the social indicators studies. Indeed, a parallelism between the two emerging fields already can be discerned.

Although the term "social indicators" was not yet in vogue then, the study of social indicators experienced a wave of interest during the 1930s (see, for example, "Recent Social Trends"). It made its breakthrough during the 1960s, followed by regular and continuing development (Bauer, 1966; Zapf, 1975; Social Indicators Research, 1975). On a smaller scale, and with some lag, the study of cultural indicators offers a parallel to this development. In the 1930s, when "Recent Social Trends" was presented, Sorokin was working on his "Social and Cultural Dynamics" (Sorokin, 1937-1941). The term "social indicators" was gradually accepted during the 1960s, and the term "cultural indicators" was introduced by Gerbner in 1969 (Gerbner, 1969). Since then, Gerbner has maintained a regular monitoring activity of American television, developing and applying a number of cultural indicators, the most widespread of which has become the "Violence Profile" (Gerbner et al., 1979). Gerbner's efforts have been widely discussed and emulated in other parts of the world (see, for instance, Wober, 1978). It would seem that the study of cultural indicators may well have a take-off stage to come, similar to that which the study of social indicators experienced during the sixties. Such a take-off stage would probably be beneficial in that it would offer an opportunity for a more concerted study of the climate of opinion, the climate of culture, the "Zeitgeist"—that is, the (more or less specific) combination of ideas, opinions, beliefs, values, and evaluations embraced by (more or less specific groups within) a given society in a given period. These are rather diffuse and imprecise but very important phenomena which over the last few decades have been the object of repeated but scattered and uncoordinated studies, with a rather low degree of cumulativity (for instance, Inglis, 1938; Davis, 1952; Funkhouser, 1973; Hubbard et al., 1975; Jones, 1976; Antunes and Hurly, 1977; Beniger, 1978).

The research program, "Cultural Indicators: The Swedish Symbol System, 1945-1975" (CISSS), is an interdisciplinary effort funded by the Bank of Sweden Tercentenary Foundation involving historians, psychologists, sociologists, political scientists, theologians, and philosophers from the universities of Lund and Stockholm. The object of the program is to construct cultural indicators for different areas of postwar Swedish society: to construct standardized instruments for measuring various aspects of the symbol system in the cultural environment conceived in a broad perspective.

Within CISSS, five independent but coordinated research projects have been working for three to four years on the task of constructing and applying a number of time series of cultural indicators in domestic politics, foreign policy debate, religion, advertising, and literature. Each of the five sub-projects is led by an experienced specialist.[1]

II. INDUSTRIAL DEVELOPMENT IN POSTWAR SWEDEN

Sweden is a fairly large country with some natural assets such as iron ore, large forests, and water power. It has a small population, about 8 million people, unevenly scattered over some 450,000 square kilometers (compared with Great Britain's 56 million and 245,000 square kilometers).[2] Two important trends in the development of the population during the postwar period are these: a slow but steady growth from 6 to 8 million people, and a proportion of people in the productive ages declining from 66 to 62 percent. The most important change in the population, however, is that it has gradually moved from the sparsely populated countryside to more densely populated townships, towns, and cities. In 1940, more than 40 percent lived in the countryside; in 1975, less than 20 percent.

In 1940, roughly one-third of the economically active population was occupied with, respectively, agriculture and forestry; industry and mining; services, communications, and administration. In 1970, the proportions were, respectively, 7, 41, and 52 percent. In these terms, Sweden was an industrialized nation until roughly between 1960 and 1965. After 1965 it gradually entered the postindustrial era.

The economic output of the differential activities more than doubled during the postwar period. In 1945, the gross domestic per capita product was some $1900, in 1975 it was about $4700 (at 1970 U.S. prices). An increasingly larger slice of this cake was used for common purposes. In 1945 about 10 percent of the GNP was used for public consumption; in 1975, 23 percent were so spent. Also, an increasing share of the yearly state budget was used for various social purposes such as state pensions and public health care (about 13 percent in 1945, about 40 percent in 1975).

An increasingly important part of the social sector of the Swedish state budget has consisted in the spending of the National Labor Market Board, intended to facilitate geographical and sector mobility in the labor force and to reduce unemployment and alleviate its effects. The budget of this agency has grown considerably and steadily over the decades, and was about 10,000 million SwCrs in 1977-1978 (8 percent of the state budget). It is one of the means by which unemployment has been kept at a fairly low level (1-2 percent of the labor force during the '60s and '70s, as opposed to 10-20 percent during the '30s).

In contrast to the increasing social sector of the state budget, a diminishing proportion of the budget has been spent on the military and civil defense of the country (a reduction from roughly 35 percent in 1945 to roughly 12 percent in 1975).

The polity allocating the various resources produced in the country has been a stable one. The country has five major political parties, the biggest being the Social Democrat Party, obtaining between 40 and 50 percent of the votes. Three "bourgeois" parties—conservatives, liberal, and "center" (formerly agrarian)—compete with each other and with the Social Democrats, while a small Communist Party (5-7 percent of the votes) usually backs up the Social Democrats. The dividing line, of course, runs between the three bourgeois parties on the one hand and the two socialist ones on the other. The balance between the two blocks has been even during most of the postwar period. The Social Democrats were in government from 1932 to 1976, most of the time alone, during the periods 1936-1945 and 1951-1957, together with one or more of the bourgeois parties. From 1976, the three bourgeois parties—for a short period the liberals alone—have formed the government.

In the bird's-eye view of Sweden given so far, we have moved from the basic levels of geography and population to the technological and economic levels, ending up with the polity. In Marxian terms, we have started at the base and moved toward the superstructure. Both these concepts are notoriously vague (Williams, 1973), but no doubt they point to something essential which other thinkers have tried to capture in other terms and concepts (for instance, Popper's first, second, and third worlds [Popper and Eccles, 1977],

Bell's (and others') economy, polity, and culture [Bell, 1976], or Boulding's economy, polity, and "integry" [Boulding, 1978]). The three levels tapped by, respectively, economic, social, and cultural indicators mark vague but important distinctions of the same type.

III. THEORETICAL BACKGROUND OF CULTURAL INDICATORS

What broad developments would we have been able to report on postwar Sweden, had cultural indicators been around to the same extent as economic or even social indicators are? Nobody knows, but there is no lack of more or less speculative, more or less well-founded hypotheses. Within CISSS, we have gradually agreed that three dimensions are probably essential in describing the development of postwar Swedish culture—that complicated web of shared, explicit, and implicit opinions and values, beliefs and evaluations, dominant and prevailing ideas embraced, defended, and attacked by different groups, strata, and classes in society.

We have provisionally labeled the three dimensions "radicalism," "internationalism," and "activism." We think that a fairly reasonable, although somewhat simplistic, hypothesis might be that along all three dimensions Sweden has shown a quasi-cyclical, curvilinear development during the postwar period. Swedish radicalism, internationalism, and activism, many observers like to think, were fairly high immediately after World War II, then declined for a decade or so, then rose again (with a peak toward the end of the sixties), and after that they seem to have been on the wane.

The three dimensions of radicalism, internationalism, and activism may be used to create a three-dimensional space, which in CISSS we like to call Goldmann's space (since Professor Kjell Goldmann, responsible for the foreign policy subproject, was the first to suggest it to the program). If we write the hypothetical, quasi-cyclical, curvilinear developments just described into Goldmann's space, we get Figure 40.1, representing an idealized descriptive model. While certainly a gross oversimplification, possibly empirically misleading and maybe even downright wrong, the figure may perhaps be useful as a heuristic tool for thinking about the development of the Swedish cultural climate during the postwar period—heuristic in the sense that it raises a number of interesting questions.[3]

The first question raised by the figure, of course, concerns the three dimensions of Goldmann's space. Within CISSS we have gradually agreed that it would be advantageous to regard the dimensions as broad umbrella concepts bringing at least some preliminary order and structure to an otherwise bewildering welter of more or less related concepts. As the work within CISSS continues, the three dimensions will, in turn, be analyzed into their various components, a development which is already under way (especially, perhaps, in the foreign policy project).

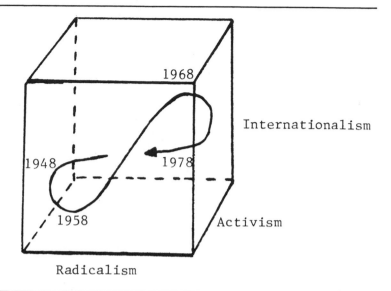

Figure 40.1: Hypothetical Development of the Swedish Cultural Climate During the Postwar
Period, in Terms of "Goldmann's Space"

Another question raised by Figure 40.1 concerns the two turns of the figure toward the end of the fifties and sixties, respectively. Were they really that parallel, each the mirror image of the other? Most Swedes would probably maintain that the changes in the late sixties were much more dramatic than those in the late fifties. Besides, it could be remarked that at the moment they happened, the changes of the late sixties were probably perceived more as a beginning than an end. Only continued and sustained work with the construction and application of cultural indicators will be able to produce meaningful answers to questions and remarks such as these.

Yet another question raised by Figure 40.1 concerns what forces may bring about a development such as the one pictured in the figure. In the next section of this paper some simple models for explaining the complex processes that must be assumed to be at work will be discussed. Before turning to that discussion, only one factor will be mentioned: the fact that Sweden is not, economically, politically, or culturally, a closed system. Many countries show a technological and economic development similar to Sweden's, and no doubt some foreign economies and technologies have been instrumental in bringing about at least certain aspects of Swedish development.

Similarly, international politics—on the European scene and in the world theatre—must have influenced the Swedish political system and probably other, less obvious aspects of Swedish culture as well (see Figure 40.2). Within the framework of CISSS, Goldmann is exploring the extent to which changes in

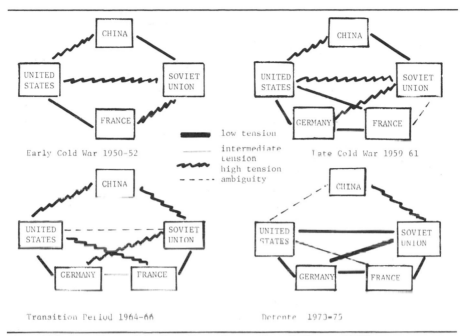

Figure 40.2: Four States of the Great Power System (from Goldmann, 1979)

Sweden's cultural climate can be explained in terms of changes in the structure of Great Power relations.

In an often-quoted letter, Engels maintained that "in the last instance" (*letzter Hand*) societal development is determined by what happens in the economic-technological base. That is Marxian materialism *in nuce*. It is often contrasted with a more Weberian idealism, maintaining, at least in principle, the possibility of an opposite influence, from the "superstructure" (for example, religion) on economic-technological developments in the base. Transposed into the conditions of modern mass communications society, the old idealism-materialism debate has sometimes focused on the more specific question of whether the mass media are "Molders or Mirrors" of societal development (see Brandner and Sistrunk, 1966). Peterson (1976), treating the related question of the relationship between social structure and culture, discussed three possibilities: Culture determines social structure (idealism); social structure determines culture (materialism); and culture and social structure are independent (autonomy). Rosengren (1980) ordered the three alternatives in a typology which called forward the obvious fourth alternative: interdependence (see Figure 40.3). In principle, the four alternatives are relevant regardless of what names are given to them or even to the two spheres whose relationship are sorted out by the typology (base and social structure, culture and superstructure, etc.).

| | | Social structure influences culture | |
		Yes	No
Culture influences social structure	Yes	Interdependence	Idealism
	No	Materialism	Autonomy

FIGURE 40.3   Four Types of Relationship between Culture and Social Structure (from Rosengren, 1980)

While in the past the debate has often moved along the axis idealism-materialism, there are signs that the other axis, interdependence-autonomy, will in the future receive increased attention (see Bell, 1976). While such debates may have—or have had—their interest, it may also be worthwhile to try another, less dogmatic and more pragmatic, approach, asking other types of questions. On the whole, questions such as "Idealism or materialism?" and "Autonomy or interdependence?" should be replaced by more straight-forward and more precise questions such as "Under what conditions do we have interdependence?" or "What type of cultural change may be regarded as autonomous?" When asking and trying to answer such questions, it is probably wise to pay special attention to two dimensions: the time per-spective and the sector of society concerned.

Economic, social, and cultural change may occur on a time-scale ranging from millennia to centuries, decades, years, or even months. It may occur in a multitude of societal sectors or subsystems. "It would be strange indeed if the relations between culture and social structure were to be the same under those very different circumstances" (Carlsson et al., 1980). When the relationship under study is no longer that between base and superstructure, but, for example, the influence of economic booms and slumps on seculari-zation as expressed in specific religious practices in a specific society of a specific time period, the general debate must be replaced by more specific theo-retical, methodological, and empirical arguments. The construction of cultural indicators of various types will have an important function in such a development.

Many questions come to mind once the problem has been reduced to these more meaningful and more manageable proportions. It would seem probable, for instance, that there exists some sort of relationship between time scale and type of change, so that changes of more basic values (see Meddin, 1975) will tend to take a longer time than changes in more ephemeral attitudes or opinions. Is there also a relationship between the time scale and the type of relationship existing between culture and social structure, so that, for instance, in the very long run (millennia) culture may determine social structure, in the long run (centuries) it could be the other way round, while in the short run (decades) the two may be interdependent, and in the very short run (years) autonomous? There is no way of answering the question at present; in any case, it would be unwise to forget the time dimension when discussing the relationship between social structure and culture.

Of course, other factors must also be heeded. To begin with, it is not uncommon to try to replace the pair of basic concepts (whether called "base-superstructure" or "social structure-culture") with a triad: economy, polity, culture (Bell, 1976), or economy, polity, "integry" (Boulding, 1978). However, this replacement, natural as it may appear, seems to entail only a differentiation of the superstructure into two components rather than adding a radically new component.

A new component, on the other hand, is the exogenous influence discussed in Section II. No doubt most societies' social structure, as well as their culture, are continuously the object of extraneous influences, and any model of the relationship between culture and social structure neglecting that influence does so at its own peril.

Another factor must not be neglected: the carriers of culture, the people populating the social structure. The most basic characteristic of people is that we are born, grow older, and die. Certainly, variations in the development of people through society and its culture must exert a decisive influence on social structure and culture (just as the people themselves are decisively shaped by their society and its culture). In combination with the phenomenon of aging, this brings us to the two time-honored, related problems of generations and Zeitgeist (or climate of opinion, climate of culture, etc.). Changes in culture imply changes of, in, and by people, which is certainly not to say that all cultural change is due to individuals alone.

In technical terms, changes in the Zeitgeist form a special case of the "cohort effect" of longitudinal studies. There are two types of cohort effects: "generation effects" (permanent effects of generation-specific experiences) and "Zeitgeist effects" (effects of systemwide changes in norms, values, beliefs, etc.; see Hofstede 1980). In reality, the two types of effects often interact. In addition, Zeitgeist effects may slowly turn into generation effects, for as a given cohort grows older, its members gradually become the only ones having experienced a certain Zeitgeist effect occurring in their youth.

This is a complicated matter, treated in sociology since Mannheim and before (for instance, see Rosenmayr and Allerbeck, 1979). In terms of an overall model, it must suffice to conclude that any model of the relationship between social structure and culture sooner or later must heed the problem of generations.

Considerations such as these led to the preliminary graphic model of the relationship between base and superstructure, social structure and culture (see Figure 40.4). The model is what could be called a "matrix model," in the sense that it could generate more specific models for more specific purposes—models in which components are added or excluded. If in some specific case, for instance, external influence is supposed to be negligible,

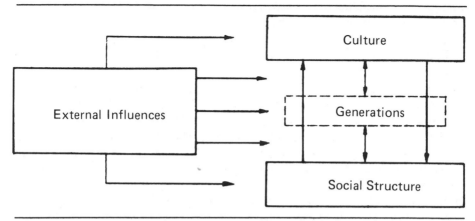

Figure 40.4: Overall Model of the Relationship Between Culture and Social Structure

obviously the arrows from the leftmost box should be deleted in that case. (A possible alternative might be that only the uppermost, or only the lowest arrow—each with its specific theoretical implications—would be deleted.) If in another specific case it appears unnecessary—or impossible—to heed the role of generations, the generation box may disappear. If in yet another case it appears necessary to differentiate between the economy, polity, and culture in a more specific sense, so be it. A hypothesis of autonomy between base and superstructure deletes the corresponding arrows. And so on.

It is possible to compare the model of Figure 40.4 with economic, social, and cultural reality; for example, in specific cases it may be perceived with the help of economic, social, and cultural indicators. A number of such comparisons having been carried out, the overall discussion of the general traits of the relationship between culture and social structure may be carried out in a more meaningful way. In Mertonian terms, such an approach equals a strategy for combining with grand theory empirical research on theories of the middle range.

As far as CISSS is concerned, one of the tasks must be to approach the question to what extent (parts of) the model in Figure 40.4 is relevant for various cultural developments in postwar Sweden.

IV. PRELIMINARY RESULTS OF
THE CULTURAL INDICATORS PROJECT

The data presented in this section come from the various subprojects within CISSS. In the domestic policy project, the values of freedom and equality as conceptualized by Rokeach and others in the same tradition (Rokeach, 1973, 1974; Feather, 1977; Rous and Lee, 1978) have been a main interest. A representative sample of editorials in five leading Swedish

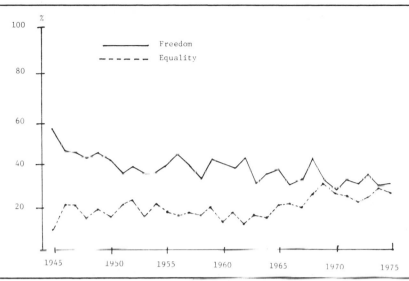

Figure 40.5: The Values of Freedom and Equality in Editorials of Five Leading Swedish Newspapers

dailies was made the object of quantitative content analysis with respect to the two concepts (Block, 1981; also see Figure 40.5). During the postwar period, the value of freedom seems to have been on the wane in Sweden; the value of equality, on the increase. In 1945, freedom dominated strongly over equality. Toward the end of the sixties and the beginning of the seventies, the two values seem to have been on a par with each other. In Rokeachean terms, this could be described as a development from a liberal political culture toward a socialist one. Developments between 1975 and 1980, again, may have changed the pattern in the direction toward a liberal culture, the gap between freedom and equality widening again.

In the foreign policy debate project, editorials from six leading dailies representing the five political parties in parliament were content analyzed with respect to the geographical area forming the subject matter of the editorial. An index varying between −1 and +1 was developed, where −1 stands for minimal, +1 for maximal orientation toward distant areas of the world (as seen from the horizon of Stockholm). The average of this index for the six newspapers is given in Figure 40.6. It shows a dramatic increase in "distant areas orientation" occurring in the early sixties (1963-1965). From 1952 to 1962, the distant areas orientation is comparatively low, while it is comparatively high from 1966 to 1975. This development could be described as an important change in the internationalism of Swedish culture. Like some other time series developed within the foreign policy project, it will be related mainly to data such as those in Figure 40.2. It will also serve as an important input to other projects within CISSS.

Figure 40.6: Distant Areas Orientation in Editorials of Six Leading Swedish Newspapers

In the project on religion, a content analysis was done of death announce-ments in Swedish dailies. (The death of most Swedes are made publicly known by such paid-for announcements, which often contain a poem or a short religious sentence.) Two samples from the Swedish daily press were drawn: one from five leading Swedish newspapers published in the three biggest cities of the country, another from the entire daily press in Sweden. In both cases the presence or absence of a religious sentence in the death announcements was noted, on the assumption that the absence or presence of such a sentence could be used as an indicator of religiousness or secularization. Figure 40.7 offers the result: a picture of increasing secularization, stronger in the cities, somewhat weaker in the rest of the country.

In the advertising project, ads in a representative sample of Swedish weeklies were content analyzed along a number of dimensions. One concerned the pronoun of address used in the ad. Swedish has two pronouns of address: "du" and "ni" (roughly comparable to the "du" and "Sie" of German, "tu" and "vous" in French). During the last decades there has been an increased tendency to use the more egalitarian "du" in cases where formerly one would have used "ni" or some equivalent. Figure 40.8 shows a dramatic shift from "ni" to "du" in the ads, starting about 1965 and probably leveling out between 1975 and 1980. (The influence from plural address, which would have demanded "ni," has been removed.) A similar shift has taken place in spoken Swedish, but it does not seem to have been given much attention in research (Paulston, 1976). The shift can be interpreted in terms of increased equality and solidarity, along the lines drawn up by Roger Brown (1965) in his fascinating chapter on the development of the European

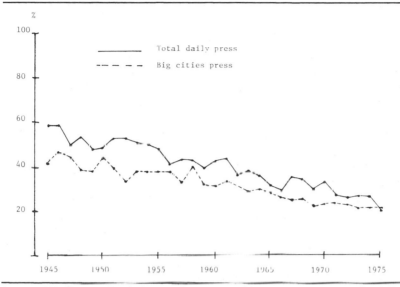

Figure 40.7: Swedish Secularization: Proportion of Death Announcements "With Sentence" Having "Religious Sentence"

pronouns of address. It is interesting to note in passing that similar shifts in the pronouns of address seem to be on their way in the other Scandinavian languages, and in French and German as well.

In the literature project, book reviews published in the daily press were content analyzed by means of a special technique (Rosengren, 1968; Rosengren and Arbelius, 1971). Reviewers of literature often mention in their reviews writers other than the one under review, and these may be regarded as expressions of associations on the part of the reviewer. All the mentions in a representative sample of literary reviews in the daily press may therefore be used to characterize the literary frame of reference of the corps of reviewers. Size and other characteristics of the literary frame of reference may be quantitatively measured. The mentions may be classified, for instance, with respect to age and language of the writer mentioned. Figure 40.9 shows the proportion of literary books published each year in Sweden having Swedish as their original language, and the proportion of Swedish mentions in a representative sample of literary reviews in six leading Swedish newspapers. It will be seen that there is a slight decline in the proportion of Swedish literary books, while the Swedish mentions show hardly any decline. On the book level, the Swedish literary system may have become somewhat more international, but that is hardly the case at the mentions level, presumably representing the frame of reference of the literary reviewers in the daily press. The international orientation of a given sector of culture may be different at different levels. It may also differ from that of another sector.

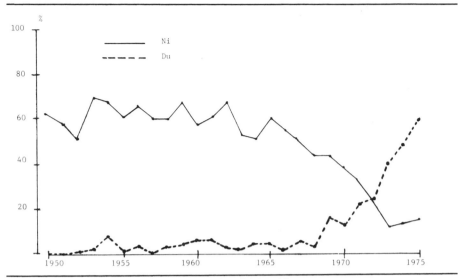

Figure 40.8: Pronouns of Address in Ads in Swedish Weeklies

V. IMPLICATIONS OF PROJECT RESULTS

The data from the five projects within CISSS presented here represent just a small sample of many time series collected within the projects. They will be theoretically and methodologically analyzed and interpreted at some length in the reports to be published from the projects. They will also be related to other time series of relevant economic and social indicators. In the final report from the research program, they will be related to each other in an attempt to create an overall picture of some aspects of the development of Swedish culture during the postwar period.

Relating the data to the idealized descriptive model in Goldmann's space, the time series presented here seem to have some bearing on the two dimensions of "radicalism" and "internationalism," while the third dimension, "activism," has not been covered. Thus, the data on equality/freedom, secularization, and pronouns of address have a bearing on the radicalism dimension, while the data on "distant areas orientation" and the literary frame of reference have a bearing on the internationalism dimension. It is obvious that something happened within Swedish culture toward the middle and end of the sixties, but the change is by no means contemporaneous for the various indicators, and it does not appear in all of them. Nor is it as smooth, of course, as the idealized descriptive model has it. The analysis of the relationship between the different types of change will form an important task in continued work in the program.

One distinction that should probably be noted in this work is the distinction between reversible and irreversible change. It is hardly probable that the shift

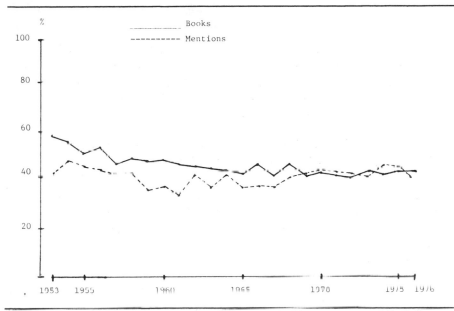

Figure 40 9· Proportion of Literary Books, and Mentions In Literary Reviews of the Daily Press Being Swedish

in the pronouns of address will be undone by a return to the former way of address; similarily, it is hardly probable that the secularization illustrated in Figure 40.7 will be followed soon by a wave of conventional religion. (Functional alternatives to religion is another matter.) On the other hand, it is conceivable that the changes in internationalism or in the stress on values such as freedom and equality may be followed by other changes which will make a future situation look pretty much the same as it did, say, in the fifties. (Indeed, in the case of the values of freedom/equality, there may well have been such a change already.) The fact, however, that some changes are irreversible raises the question whether the return of old patterns in the case of reversible changes really brings us back to a completely similar situation. Arguments such as these, of course, have a bearing on the validity of the sling in Figure 40.1.

Another distinction—which may or may not be related to the above—is the distinction between slow, gradual, quantitative changes and rather fast, almost qualitative ones. The changes in secularization and pronouns of address illustrate this distinction well. The distinction has something to do—but probably does not coincide—with the distinction between systemic changes and aggregated individual changes. Culture is a systemic phenomenon carried by groups of individuals.

A third distinction, related to the former, has to do with the variability of the curves. Some of the curves show rather high variation from year to year, while others are smoother. There is a random element involved here, no doubt, which could also be discussed in terms of the influence exerted by isolated events and individual acts by powerful agents.

Comparing the data with the explanatory model of Figure 40.4, one gets the impression that the model works pretty well (which should come as no surprise, since, being a "matrix model," it contains so many possibilities). The change in Sweden's political environments illustrated in Figure 40.2 may be meaningfully related to the shift in international orientation and probably also to the secularization process. The secularization probably has also something to do with the urbanization while the changes in the value hierarchy (freedom/equality, pronouns of address) could be related to the changes in the economy and to other data on, for example, economic (in-) equality in postwar Sweden.

A complication involved in arguments such as these is the fact that changes in the explanatory elements of Figure 40.4 may or may not coincide. The secularization of Figure 40.7, for instance, may be related to the inter-national environment described in Figure 40.2, to urbanization, and/or to generational changes having, in their turn, something to do with both. But the urbanization and the international political environment show different patterns of change. One solution of this problem may be to take variations in the time scale into consideration (see Section III). The trend in seculari-zation may be related to the urbanization trend, for instance, while the more cyclical variations in the international political situation may be responsible for corresponding deviations (residuals) from the secularization trend, possibly via variations in feelings of safety, security, and the like. Such feelings, it could be noted in passing, may be involved also in generational effects. A generation with low average education, an experience of poverty, heavy unemployment, and a world war has other needs for religion than one with high education, an experience of only little unemployment, and coming of age in a time of international détente.

Even when we limit our attention to two elements of the matrix model of Figure 40.4, however, interesting problems arise. Figure 40.10 illustrates one such problem. At first sight, it seems to demonstrate a case of autonomy between, on one hand, the symbolic environment of advertising and, on the other, social and economic realities. The proportion of economically active (gainfully employed) women has increased considerably in Sweden during the postwar period, while in the ads of the weeklies it has decreased. In this special case then, base and superstructure, social structure and culture, do not seem to have influenced each other.

But on second thought, other interpretations than that of autonomy seem possible. For instance, the message of the symbolic environment may have delayed the increase in the proportion of economically active women. The effect of culture as reflected in the ads may have been a countereffect—an interpretation made also by Lazer and Dier (1978) when confronted with

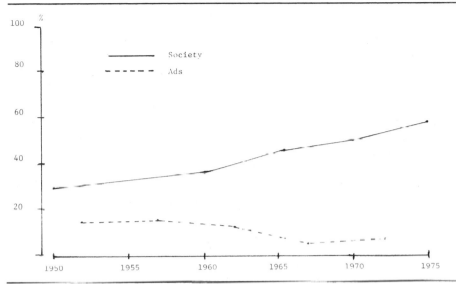

Proportion of Gainfully Employed Women in Swedish Society and in Ads in Swedish Weeklies

similar material. However, such an interpretation is hard to demonstrate empirically. To be really convincing it presupposes more data and further theoretical development. In its way, then, Figure 40.10 illustrates well how the construction and application of cultural indicators breed new problems and thus scientific development and new research.

VI. PREDICTING AND UNDERSTANDING SOCIAL CHANGE

A specific problem connected with the study of cultural indicators concerns the future. Once a set of reliable and valid cultural indicators has been developed and applied, will it be possible to use them for making predictions or forecasts? The parallel repeatedly drawn in this paper among economic, social, and cultural indicators invites the question and, in a way, also provides the answer. Economic indicators have been in existence for a long time and have gradually become embedded in a rich and sophisticated theory. This has made possible successful economic prediction and forecasting—granted that the predictions have not exactly the same character as those made by, for example, astronomers. Cultural indicators, on the other hand, are in the process of being tentatively developed. The theory supporting them is relatively underdeveloped. Given this state of affairs, it is obvious that reliable and precise predictions or forecasts made on the basis of cultural indicators will be some time in coming. However, in spite of this it is possible to discuss some relatively specific problems connected with forecasting based on cultural indicators. In such a discussion some distinctions touched upon in the previous sections will be useful.

To begin with, the nature of the forecasting will vary with the kind of relationship assumed between the components: idealism, materialism, interdependence, or autonomy (complicated by external and generational influences). In the case of autonomy, interdependence, and idealism, specific theories are needed about internal developments on the cultural level. Materialism does not need such theories to the same extent; it assumes that cultural developments are governed by developments in the socioeconomic base.

Theories about the more or less autonomous development of culture have often suggested a cyclical development pattern. Sorokin's huge scenario has this character, a cyclical succession of ideational, sensate, idealistic, and mixed systems of culture (Sorokin, 1937-1941). Using differential time perspectives in much the way discussed in Section III, Namenwirth and his associates ingeniously combine materialism with autonomy, finding in their data both long-term and short-term cycles in the American value system. The long-term cycles (some 150 years) are supposed to be due to sequential changes between four dominant clusters of Parsonian values (expressive, adaptive, instrumental, and integrative values), while the short-term cycles (some 50 years) presumably have to do with long waves of contraction and expansion in the economy (Namenwirth, 1973; Namenwirth and Bibbee, 1976).

The perspectives of Sorokin and Namenwirth are sociological. Psychologist McClelland and his associates have found cyclical patterns in the constellations of the three needs for power, affiliation, and achievement as reflected in art, literature, and so on of various cultures, and also a covariation between such cyclical patterns and secular patterns of reforms and war in English and American history—a covariation which, McClelland suggests, may be explained in either psychological, economic, or political terms (McClelland, 1975a, 1975b).

Compared with such grandiose schemes, the perspective of recent cultural indicators research in general, and that of CISSS in particular, may appear almost myopic. However, it has at least the advantage of not being confined to a single theoretical perspective. On the contrary, it tries to put various theories to as hard a test as data admit. In order ultimately to make predictions possible, a combination of research on theories of the middle range with grand theory will probably be necessary. Even then, it is highly questionable whether it will ever be possible to predict cultural change with a high degree of reliability. For one thing, the innovative element is probably too strong (assuming for a moment that the considerable methodological difficulties gradually will be overcome). But it is probably not unreasonable to assume that it will be possible to make rough forecasts about the future of a country's radicalism, internationalism, and activism (to return to the provisional terminology of Figure 40.1). Such forecasts, of course, will be the more reliable the more and the longer time-series of different cultural indicators we have available. For, after all, the only way to understand our future is first to understand our past. Cultural indicators may help us in both these tasks. That is one reason their study is so important.

NOTES

1. Dr. Eva Block and Professor Birgitta Öden (Domestic Politics), Professor Kjell Goldmann (Foreign Policy Debate), Dr. Per Block (Religion), Dr. Kjell Nowak (Advertising), Dr. Karl Erik Rosengren (Literature). This paper, of course, could not have been written without the generous help and stimulating criticism offered by everyone in the program and by many others.

2. Statistics about Sweden come from various publications of the Swedish Central Bureau of Statistics (SCB).

3. For a more detailed treatment of the many theoretical and methodological problems which can only be suggested here, the reader is referred to Rosengren et al. (1981). On culture, see, for instance, Kroeber and Kluckhohn (1952), Singer (1968), Schneider and Bonjean (1973), Bernardi (1977). On Sweden, see Castles (1978), Childs (1980), Fry (1979), Hancock and Sjoberg (1972), Koblik (1975), Korpi (1978), Lindbeck (1975), Scase (1976). Within CISSS Gunnar Andrén and Per Block are currently working on some theoretical problems connected with the concepts of base/superstructure and culture.

REFERENCES

Antunes, George E. and Patricia A. Hurly (1977) "The representation of criminal events in Houston's two daily newspapers." Journalism Quarterly 54: 756-760.

Bauer, Raymond A. [ed.] (1966) Social Indicators. Cambridge: MIT Press.

Bell, Daniel (1976) The Cultural Contradictions of Capitalism. London: Heinemann.

Beniger, James R. (1978) "Media content as social indicators. the Greenfield index of agenda setting." Communication Research 5: 437-453.

Bernardi, Bernardo [ed.] (1977) The Concept and Dynamics of Culture. The Hague and Paris: Mouton.

Block, Eva (1981) "Freedom and equality: indicators of political change in Sweden, 1945-1975," in K.E. Rosengren (ed.) Advances in Content Analysis. Beverly Hills, CA: Sage.

Boulding, Kenneth A. (1978) Ecodynamics. A New Theory of Social Evolution. Beverly Hills, CA: Sage.

Brandner, Lowell and Joan Sistrunk (1966) "The newspaper: molder or mirror of community values?" Journalism Quarterly 43: 497-504.

Brown, Roger (1968) Social Psychology. New York and London: Free Press and Collier-Macmillan.

Carlsson, Gösta, Alf Dahlberg, and Karl Erik Rosengren (1981) "Mass media content, political opinions and social change. The case of Sweden, 1967-1974," in K.E. Rosengren (ed.) Advances in Content Analysis. Beverly Hills, CA: Sage.

Castles, Francis G. (1978) The Social Democratic Image of Society. London: Routledge & Kegan Paul.

Childs, Marquis (1980) Sweden, the Middle Way on Trial. New Haven, CT: Yale University
    Press.
Davis, F. James (1952) "Crime news in Colorado newspapers." American Journal of
    Sociology 57: 325-330.
Feather, N.T. (1977) "Value importance, conservatism, and age." European Journal of Social
    Psychology 7: 241-245.
Fry, John [ed.] (1979) Limits of the Welfare State. Farnborough: Saxon House.
Funkhouser, G. Ray (1973) "The issues of the sixties: an exploratory study in the dynamics of
    public opinion." Public Opinion Quarterly 37: 62-75.
Gerbner, George (1969) "Toward 'cultural indicators': The analysis of mass mediated public
    message systems." AV Communication Review 17: 137-148.
_____ et al. (1979) "The demonstration of power: violence profile no 10." Journal of
    Communication 29: 177-196.
Goldmann, Kjell (1979) Is My Enemy's Enemy My Friend's Friend? Lund: Studentlitteratur.
Hancock, M. Donald and Gideon Sjoberg [eds.] (1972) Politics in the Post-Welfare State.
    Responses to the New Individualism. New York: London: Columbia University Press.
Hofstede, Geert (1980) Culture's Consequences: International Variations in Work-Related
    Values. Beverly Hills, CA: Sage.
Hubbard, Jeffrey C., Melvin L. DeFleur, and Lois B. DeFleur (1975) "Mass media influences
    on public conceptions of social problems." Social Problems 23: 22-34.
Inglis, Ruth A. (1938) "An objective approach to the relationship between fiction and society."
    American Sociological Review 3: 526-533.
Jones, E. Terrence (1976) "The press as metropolitan monitor." Public Opinion Quarterly 40:
    239-244.
Koblik, Steven [ed.] (1975) Sweden's Development from Poverty to Affluence. Minneapolis:
    University of Minnesota Press.
Korpi, Walter (1978) The Working Class in Welfare Capitalism. Unions and Politics in
    Sweden. London: Routledge & Kegan Paul.
Kroeber, Alfred L. and Clyde Kluckhohn (1952) Culture: A Critical Review of Concepts and
    Definitions. Peabody Museum of American Archeology and Ethnology Papers, Vol. 47, No.
    1. Cambridge, MA: Harvard University.
Lindbeck, Assar (1975) Swedish Economic Policy. London: Macmillan.
McClelland, David C. (1975a) Power. The Inner Experience. New York: Irvington.
_____(1975b) "Love and power: the psychological signals of war." Psychology Today
    (January): 45-48.
Maddison, A. (1979) "Per capita output in the long run." Kyklos 32: 412-427.
Meddin, Jay (1975) "Attitudes, values and related concepts: a system of classification." Social
    Science Quarterly 55: 889-900.
Namenwirth, J. Zvi (1973) "Wheels of time and the interdependence of value change in
    America." Journal of Interdisciplinary History 3: 649-683.
_____ and Richard C. Bibbee (1976) "Change within or of the system: an example from the
    history of American values." Quality and Quantity 10: 145-164.
Paulston, C.B. (1976) "Pronouns of address in Swedish." Language in Society 5: 359-386.
Peterson, Richard A. (1976) "The production of culture." American Behavioral Scientist 19:
    669-684.
Popper, Karl R. and John C. Eccles (1977) The Self and Its Brain. Berlin: Springer Verlag.
Recent Social Trends in the United States, I-II, 1933. New York: McGraw-Hill.
Rokeach, Milton (1973) The Nature of Human Values. New York: Free Press.
_____(1974) "Change and stability in American value systems 1968-1971." Public Opinion
    Quarterly 38: 222-238.
Rosengren, Karl Erik (1968) Sociological Aspects of the Literary System. Stockholm: Natur
    och Kultur.

_____(1980) "Mass media and social change: some current approaches," in G. C. Wilhoit and Harold de Bock (eds.) Mass Communication Review Yearbook. Beverly Hills, CA: Sage.

_____ and Bo Arbelius (1971) "Frames of reference as systems: size and other variables." General Systems 16: 205-210.

Rosengren, Karl Erik et al. (forthcoming) Cultural Indicators: The Swedish Symbol System, 1945-1975.

Rosenmayr, Leopold and Klaus Allerbeck (1979) "Social life-time of youth and historical epochs." Current Sociology 27: 59-78.

Rous, Gerald L. and Dorothy E. Lee (1978) "Freedom and equality: two values of political orientation." Journal of Communication 28: 45-51.

Scase, Richard [ed.] (1976) Readings in the Swedish Class Structure. Oxford: Pergamon.

Schneider, Louis and Charles M. Bonjean [eds.] (1973) The Idea of Culture in the Social Sciences. Cambridge: Cambridge University Press

Singer, Milton (1968) "The concept of culture." International Encyclopedia of the Social Sciences 3: 527-543.

Sorokin, P. (1937-1941) Social and Cultural Dynamics, 1-4. London: Allen & Unwin; New York: American Book Company.

Williams, Raymond (1973) "Base and superstructure in Marxist cultural theory." New Left Review 82: 3-16.

Wober, J.M. (1978) "Televised violence and paranoid perception: the view from Great Britain." Public Opinion Quarterly 42: 315-321.

Zapf, Wolfgang (1975) "Systems of social indicators: current approaches and problems." International Social Science Journal 27: 479-498.

A leading scholar of China's mass media system, Godwin C. Chu outlines and illustrates four functions of the media in China: mobilization, information, power struggle, and ideological reform. An extensive media system—comprised of the New China News Agency, the Party magazine Red Flag, *the* People's Daily *and provincial newspapers, radio, and television—carries similar official messages, supervised by the Communist Party's Central Committee (or provincial committees) through the Department of Propaganda. Prior to a year-long debate about the mass media and "truth" that began in May 1978, objective reality for Chinese media was not description of what happened, according to Chu. Instead, reality was the final outcome of an arduous process of moving through the party's "ideological lens." In July 1979, an editorial in the official* People's Daily *apparently marked the end of the debate about objectivity and signaled a move toward more factual reporting in the Chinese press. Human interest stories now appear frequently, and entertainment and feature material has returned to Chinese newspapers. Chu concludes that the mass media in post-Mao China now emphasize factual reporting to a greater extent than ideological indoctrination. This article, updated and revised especially for the* Yearbook, *is from Chu's recent book about the Chinese press. Dr. Chu is a research associate at the East-West Communication Institute of the East-West Center in Honolulu.*

41

THE CURRENT STRUCTURE AND FUNCTIONS OF CHINA'S MASS MEDIA

Godwin C. Chu

The importance of communication to building a Communist China was spelled out by the late Chairman Mao Tse-tung in a talk in 1943: "We should go to the masses and learn from them, synthesize their experience into better, articulated principles of methods, then do propaganda among the masses, and call upon them to put these principles and methods into practice so as to solve their problems and help them achieve liberation and happiness."[1] This strategy of organizing and mobilizing the people by communication has been followed since the Yenan days. By initiating a two-way communication, the Party leadership expects to learn from the masses and then reorganize their experiences into new programs of socialist reconstruction. China's mass media have played essential roles in this respect.

From Godwin C. Chu, "The Current Structure and Functions of China's Mass Media," *Moving a Mountain,* Godwin C. Chu and Francis Hsu, Eds. Copyright 1979 by the East-West Center, Honolulu, Hawaii. Reprinted by permission.

A related function of the Chinese media is to provide information that can support mass mobilization. Mao had this to say to the editorial staff of the *Shansi-Suiyuan Daily* in 1948:

> Our policy must be made known not only to the leaders and to the cadres but also to the broad masses. Questions concerning policy should as a rule be given publicity in the Party papers or periodicals. . . . Once the masses know the truth and have a common aim, they will work together with one heart. . . . The role and power of the newspapers consists in their ability to bring the Party program, the Party line, the Party's general and specific policies, its tasks and methods of work before the masses in the quickest and most extensive way.[2]

Over the last three decades, another function has become prominent. This is the use of the media as an instrument of political power struggle, a function which has been expanding with the growth of the Party but which has come to the fore more strikingly since the Cultural Revolution.

A fourth function of China's media, one that relates closely to cultural change, is what Mao called "combatting the wicked wind." It was during the Anti-Rightist movement of 1957, in the wake of the Hundred Flowers movement, that the primary objective of the media shifted from one of mobilizing for reconstruction to one of stressing the correct thinking of the people, particularly the intellectuals. There was concern that the objective of national mobilization would be seriously impaired unless the undesirable thinking was weeded out. Foreseeing such a shift, Mao came back to this theme again and again in a major policy speech in January, 1957: "By a wicked wind, we mean to say that these are not individual mistakes, but have become a general trend. Therefore we must strike it down. The way to strike it down is by reasoning. If we have persuasive power, we can knock down this wicked wind. If we don't have persuasive power, and only say nasty things, this wicked wind will keep blowing and growing."[3]

The current structure and content of China's mass media can be understood in the perspectives of these four functions: mobilization, information, power struggle, and ideological reform. The relative importance of each function has fluctuated somewhat during the last thirty years in response to the prevailing political, economic, and ideological climates. Except in the early 1950s, when the Party was able to operate with a moderate degree of unity in the first few years of the new regime, China's mass media have been inseparably involved in the internal contentions for power. This has been evident both before and after the death of Mao.

Mass mobilization for reconstruction has tended to occupy greater attention in the media when the power struggle moves toward a visible outcome and there are practical tasks to be performed. This trend can be detected during and after the Great Leap Forward, then again in the few years when Chou En-lai was picking up the pieces from the Cultural Revolution before the Chiang Ch'ing group mounted its Anti-Confucius and Anti-Lin Piao campaign, and now in the aftermath of the Gang of Four.

Providing information about Party policy, something Mao emphasized on the eve of the Communist victory, has been a function only when the media play a supportive role in either mobilization or political campaigns. The Chinese are generally told what is happening in their country when such information serves other official purposes.

The role of mass media as an instrument of ideological reform and cultural change has been emphasized since the Cultural Revolution, particularly in the few years before the death of Mao when Chiang Ch'ing was promoting her "newborn things." While there are subtle indications that the new government under Hua Kuo-feng and Teng Hsiao-p'ing is less interested, at least for the time being, in this function of the media, we should not conclude that ideological reform has been abandoned. It may someday be revived should the need ever arise again—for instance, if the current trend toward material improvement should begin to threaten the very foundation of the Chinese Communist system.

To carry out these functions, the Party leadership has developed an extensive mass communication system in which the various media —the New China News Agency (Hsinhua), the *People's Daily,* the Party magazine *Red Flag,* the provincial newspapers, radio, and television—deliver essentially the same official messages. (See the chapter by Merle Goldman for analysis of policy debates in the mass media.) They are supervised by the Department of Propaganda under the Party's Central Committee and, for the provincial media, through the Party's provincial committees. In practice, the operation of these media reflects a brand of investigative reporting with a one-sided perspective. *Red Flag* explained it this way: ". . . guided by Chairman Mao's proletarian revolutionary thinking and the various policies and directives, we must go to the masses, and carry out serious and not perfunctory investigation and research. We must grasp model materials that can point to the correct direction of a movement. Then we must use accurate, clear and vivid language to write our reports on the objective reality."[4]

This objective reality is not what is or has happened. Rather, it is the final outcome of a long and involved process by which "the rich materials we [Chinese media personnel] obtain from our senses are screened by a careful thought process, which retains the essence and leave out the unimportant, keeping the truth and eliminating the falsehood." It is meant to be a "penetrating, accurate and complete representation of objectivity" that has progressed from sensory perception to a kind of "rational perception."[5] It is a reality seen through the Party's ideological lens rather than through the uncultivated eye of the individual. The whole approach suggests a philosophy that control of information input can structure the individual's perception, which in turn can influence his values, beliefs, and behavior.

In the following pages, we briefly discuss China's major communication media.

People's Daily

The most important official newspaper in China is the *People's Daily (Jenmin Jihpao)*, voice of the Chinese Communist Party. Operated under the close supervision of the Department of Propaganda, the *People's Daily* has a large circulation, estimated in 1974 to be approximately 3.4 million copies.[6] It reaches all the agricultural production teams, some 740,000 of them, and all schools, factories, and government offices in the cities. The total number of readers reached by this official newspaper is much greater than its circulation figure would indicate because of the existence of newspaper reading groups. In each group a student or someone else reads the stories from the *People's Daily* to his illiterate neighbors. The Party's supervision over the *People's Daily* is such that major editorials have to be cleared with the highest authorities. The editorial on National Day in 1972, for instance, was approved by Chou En-lai himself.[7] All news stories, domestic and international, reflect the official stance.

The *People's Daily* appears in six full-size pages. Page 1 is for important news, mostly domestic (e.g., production campaigns), and for editorials, which appear not every day but only when important issues call for official enunciation. Pages 2 and 3 carry other domestic news and features. When there is a political campaign, such as the one criticizing Lin Piao and Confucius, long articles of criticisms are published on these two pages to signify the current ideological thinking. Letters to editors, published occasionally, appear mostly on page 3 and sometimes on page 2. Another column is called "Life of the Party," in which Party members write about their own experience in improving their ideological rectitude. The achievements of model workers, such as Iron Man Wang Ching-hsi of the Tach'ing Oilfield, and of model units, such

as the Tachai Brigade, are publicized for the whole country to emu-
late. Sometimes a particular model is given front page coverage,
such as the Hsiao Chin Chuang Brigade outside Tientsin during the
days of Chiang Ch'ing. Page 4 is usually for domestic news of a
more routine nature, as well as literary and art news. Sometimes
this page is reserved exclusively for pictures celebrating an important domestic event, such as the inauguration of Chairman Hua
Kuo-feng. Occasionally revolutionary poems and songs are reproduced. Pages 5 and 6 display foreign news. The weekly programs of
Peking Television are printed on one of these two pages, although
not regularly. So are announcements of revolutionary operas and
other entertainments.

All foreign news stories originate from the official New China
News Agency, which has correspondents in major capitals of the
world. Important domestic news stories are also released by the
agency. The *People's Daily* has correspondents all over the country
to cover local features. Occasionally, an article from a provincial
newspaper is reprinted if it is considered worthy of national attention, but no other news sources are used. Like all other newspapers
in China, the *People's Daily* carries no advertising. The post office
handles subscriptions and delivers the newspaper.

Provincial and Local Newspapers

Other than the *People's Daily,* there are some 350 provincial and
local newspapers in various provinces and municipalities. They
publish four pages a day. The *Wen Hui Pao* (Wen Hui Report) in
metropolitan Shanghai, probably one of the largest, has a circulation of 900,000 copies. Other better-known local papers include the
Kuangchow (Canton) *Daily* and *Nan Fang* (Southern) *Daily,* both
published in Canton, and the *Shensi Daily* in Sian, which distri-
butes 320,000 copies daily.[8] Unlike the *People's Daily,* which is distributed overseas as well as in China, provincial and local newspapers are not available to readers outside the country.

The reason, according to Edward Murray of the *Detroit Free
Press,* who visited China in 1972, was the nature of the local news
the provincial papers contain. Murray had this to say: "These
newspapers, we learned from interviews, not only print local news.
But they are so close to the people that news has to be factual,
which is to say, sometimes they present a much more negative picture than China wants to project to the outside world."[9] We have
recently obtained from Hong Kong one copy of the *Kuangchow
Daily* and one copy of the *Nan Fang Daily,* both dated June 1975.
Except for three brief commentaries and a few provincial news
items, however, these two newspapers are highly similar in content
to the *People's Daily.*[10]

Three brief commentaries in the *Nan Fang Daily* were selected from among those displayed in the Revolutionary Criticism Column and Blackboard Paper of Tatung Brigade in Kwangtung. They were prefaced with this editor's note:

> In the Revolutionary Criticism Column and the Blackboard Paper of Tatung Brigade there are often published brief commentaries that have a fighting spirit. Employing the teaching of Marx and Lenin and the Thought of Mao Tse-tung as their weapons, and in coordination with a realistic class struggle, these commentaries criticize various undesirable trends, rotten people and rotten behavior, in order to attack the class enemy and educate the people. We have selected three as follows.[11]

The first commentary criticized the resurgence of superstition among the peasants. The second condemned the selfish behavior of one commune member. This person, and others as well, had planted cucumbers and vegetables on a strip of land on the top of the commune's reservoir dike. When told that this practice would encourage the growth of capitalism, all of them cooperated and dug up what they had planted. But this particular commune member carried away some thirty loads of topsoil from the dike because he said he had put in chemical fertilizer. His behavior was denounced.

The third commentary was the most critical of all. It gave a rather candid account of how some members in the commune were interested in nothing but their private plots. Whenever they got together, before or after work, or after supper, they talked all the time about what vegetables to plant for the most profit, and where to sell them for the best prices. Some of them went to work on their private plots even when they should have been working for the commune. As a result, the commune's production suffered. This practice, said the commentary, must be stopped.

Interesting as these commentaries are, it must be pointed out that they did not reveal anything substantial which the *People's Daily* has not criticized from time to time. What they did contain, which is usually not found in the *People's Daily*, were factual details of the misdeeds.

Reference Information

China also has a special newspaper that is becoming more widely known to the outside world in recent years. This is *Reference Information (Ts'an-k'ao Hsiao-hsi)*. First published in the early 1950s by the New China News Agency as an internal news bulletin for high-level Party cadres, *Reference Information* expanded its circulation in 1957 from some 2,000 to more than 400,000 following a major decision by Chairman Mao.[12] The latest estimate puts the total circulation of this tabloid-size newspaper at 6 million copies, larger than the circulation of the *People's Daily*.[13] It now appears daily, usually in four pages. It contains news from around the world, both favorable and unfavorable to China, which does not appear in other newspapers in the country. Its circulation is not limited to Party members; anyone who has a cadre position can subscribe. Although the subscriber is not supposed to share this publication with nonsubscribers, including the spouse and members of the family, this rule is apparently not rigidly enforced. Accounts by former residents of China indicate that *Reference Information* is perhaps the most popular newspaper in China.

The function of *Reference Information,* according to Mao, is to provide a dose of inoculation so that the Chinese will not be totally unprepared for the realities of the world outside.

Apparently following this policy, *Reference Information,* for instance, reported on the defection of a Chinese Communist jet pilot, Lt. Liu Ch'eng-ssu, in a MIG-15 in March 1962.[14] It would be misleading, however, to assume that this publication carries anything secret about internal political affairs in China. An examination of the issue of October 9, 1972, made available to this writer by a friend, reveals that the contents of *Reference Information* are mostly reprints, without interpretation, of news and commentaries from foreign news agencies and newspapers.[15] Even though this particular issue contained nothing unfavorable to China, the news stories and commentaries it carried do present a much broader variety than those of the *People's Daily* and the provincial newspapers. The amount of international news in *Reference Information* seems to be much more than what is generally found in an average American metropolitan newspaper.

Commune Newspapers

A kind of grassroots newspaper that serves the production brigades and production teams in the communes has appeared in China since the Cultural Revolution. Sometimes called the war bulletin *(chan pao),* this is a mimeographed information sheet edited and produced by peasants in the brigade. Called *tu* (muddy) correspondents, because they have mud on their feet and calluses on their hands, they have been compared to the barefoot doctors. The Huang Lou Commune near Shanghai provided an example of how these correspondents operate.[16] In that commune there were some one hundred and fifty peasant correspondents in 1968.

Because they work on farms, "muddy" correspondents understand the problems of peasants in a way that urban reporters cannot. Most of them are sons and daughters of poor and lower-middle peasants. They usually have no training other than elementary or junior high school. More important than professional training, however, is loyalty to the Party and to Chairman Mao. A peasant correspondent must first of all be a capable and diligent worker, thus having the respect of other peasants; the ability to write well is of secondary importance.

Wen Hui Pao (Wen Hui Report) of Shanghai has reported on the style and content of the commune-level news bulletins.[17] One night a peasant correspondent at Huang Lou Commune heard over the Central People's Broadcasting Station an article from the *People's Daily* on the barefoot doctor system. Although it was already past 10 p.m., she called together the poor and lower-middle peasants in her production team to discuss the article. Afterwards, she wrote an article expressing their support to be broadcast over the commune's line-broadcasting station the following day.

In another case, several commune members were carrying topsoil for their private plots during the commune's working hours. One peasant correspondent learned about it and got someone to write a letter. He then published the letter in the production brigade's news bulletin, with an editor's note. This story was later broadcast on the commune station.

Another commune member was preparing to give a big birthday feast to celebrate the "longevity" of his grandmother according to old Chinese traditions. When a peasant correspondent learned about it, he did not write an article of criticism but instead organized the poor and lower-middle peasants of the production team to talk to this person. They finally convinced him to give up the feast and the birthday celebration.

In general, the peasant correspondents act as opinion leaders in the village, using the news bulletin to disseminate information from the national mass media and to correct what are considered to be undesirable behavioral patterns.

Tatzupao

Tatzupao, an age-old Chinese medium of communication, has now developed into a major component in China's media system. The Chinese have traditionally used wall posters for public announcements, such as the emperor's edicts, and for airing private grievances.[18] The Chinese Communists began to make effective use of this form of information dissemination as early as the Yenan days, perhaps because of the widespread use of posters in collective farms and factories in Soviet Russia shortly after the Russian revolution.[19] Those were the days when the Chinese Communists were eager to follow the Russian model.

It was during the Hundred Flowers movement and the subsequent Anti-Rightist movement that the *tatzupao* took on a new function. It became a powerful instrument of criticism and counterattack. When the Party invited Chinese intellectuals to voice their complaints in the spring of 1957, many in Peking, Shanghai, and other big cities posted lengthy criticisms. These, however, cannot compare in magnitude and vehemency with the organized *tatzupao* campaign mounted by the Party in the summer of that year to refute the rightist intellectuals.[20]

By that time, *tatzupao* had already been recognized as an effective means of mobilizing the masses for political participation. It was not until the Cultural Revolution, however, when for mcnths China was literally covered with millions of posters voicing all kinds of contentions, that *tatzupao* became widely known to the world outside. The Cultural Revolution has firmly established *tatzupao* as a major social institution in China.

The ingenious way in which the big character posters were used by the Maoist group in 1966–1967 to disrupt the channels of communication of the Liu Shao-ch'i group, to create an atmosphere of confusion and a sense of impending change, and to lend a basis of legitimacy to the power struggle has already been analyzed.[21] After the Maoist group came back to power, a halt was put to the *tatzupao* rampage. Once the Chinese got a taste of what this simple form of communication could do, however, a need grew for its continued application. In fact, since the 1975 constitution, the *tatzupao* has been recognized as a legitimate means of expression for the common people.[22]

From what we know, the ordinary people in China can put up *tatzupao* to make a complaint about the wrongdoing of lower-level cadres, or to air grievances of a minor nature. However, they must first submit the posters to the responsible local unit for approval.[23] It would be misleading to think that anybody in China can put up a *tatzupao* any time he likes.

Because of its rather surprising effects in the Cultural Revolution, the *tatzupao* has earned a permanent role in the process of China's political struggle. Opposing sides have often used the same strategy of attacking opponents in posters that are either anonymous or attributed to the study groups of some obscure units. This has been the practice both before the death of Chairman Mao, when the Chiang Ch'ing group was engaged in a power contest with Teng Hsiao-p'ing, and since the purge of the Gang of Four, as different factions jostle for authority in the new government.

Political posters of this nature often appear at odd moments in unexpected places, perhaps as a way to avoid premature confrontation. This practice, however, has made it possible for genuine critics to take advantage of the *tatzupao* as an uncensored means of attacking government policies. They can do this with temporary immunity because the local authorities are often not sure whether such attacks are part of an organized power struggle involving top-level contenders. They would thus hesitate to take punitive actions before the lines were clearly drawn.

This happened to a lengthy *tatzupao* posted in Canton in 1974 by three young intellectuals which severely criticized the Maoist policies of the Party and demanded more freedom and democracy. For days, the poster signed by Li I-che remained intact for thousands of local residents to peruse. Once the municipal authorities made sure that there was no powerful faction behind it, it was torn down. Handwritten copies of this *tatzupao* have made their way to Hong Kong, and were subsequently published by a Hong Kong periodical.[24]

Radio Broadcasting

Radio broadcasting in Communist China has come a long way from the small, antiquated transmitter which Chou En-lai brought back to Yenan from Moscow in 1940.[25] Today, nearly four decades later, radio broadcasting in China reaches all cities, more than 92 percent of the agricultural production teams (villages), and some 70 percent of the peasant homes.[26]

The development of radio broadcasting in the 1950s and the 1960s has been discussed by Frederick Yu and Alan Liu.[27] Since those days, the organizational channels for radio broadcasting have remained the same. The Central People's Broadcasting Station in Peking directs and coordinates all radio broadcasting in the provinces and large municipalities. The primary language on radio is Mandarin, but other dialects such as Cantonese, Fukien, and Hakka are used for regional broadcasts. The Central People's Broadcasting Station operates two channels, CPBS I and CPBS II, which broadcast essentially the same programs but at different hours.

The provincial and municipal stations relay a large portion of the central broadcasts and add programs of a regional nature, primarily news events in the provinces and criticisms of local deviances. Provincial broadcasts are further relayed to the counties and, subsequently, to the communes, production brigades, production teams, and individual peasant homes. Wired broadcasting is used extensively at the local level. In China, practically all places for public gatherings have installed loudspeakers, which apparently are turned on from early in the morning till closing time. By latest estimates, there were some 106,000,000 loudspeakers in China in 1975, averaging about one for every eight Chinese, young and old. The corresponding number in 1964 was 6,000,000.[28]

The radio program content is closely supervised by the Central Broadcasting Bureau, which maintains regional offices in the provinces. The bureau has four divisions: administration, technology, radio broadcasting, and television. Operating under the Office of the Premier, the bureau is not involved in actual program production but assumes the responsibility of technological improvement, personnel training, and program supervision. Major policy decisions, however, are handled by the Department of Propaganda, not by the Central Broadcasting Bureau.

A typical domestic radio broadcast begins at 4:00 a.m. for CPBS I (5:00 a.m. for CPBS II) with a brief preview of the programs for the day. There are news broadcasts, as many as ten times a day, and ideological commentaries and criticisms. There are special programs for children, for intellectual youth sent to the villages, for workers, for commune members, and for the People's Liberation Army. Special programs are featured on agricultural technology, sanitation, and physical exercise. Music, drama, art and literature, and the selected works of Marx, Lenin, and Mao Tse-tung make up the rest of the programming. The station goes off the air for about an hour in the afternoon and resumes broadcasting before 4:00 p.m. Signoff for the day comes at 1:35 a.m. for CPBS I and at 11:30 p.m. for CPBS II.

Other than relaying the central and provincial broadcasting programs, local stations at the county and commune levels carry programs of their own:[29]

1. Broadcasting of criticism sessions: The Shanghai Broadcasting Station, for instance, broadcast the sessions of criticism of antirevolutionary thinking held at the Shanghai Diesel Engine Factory in 1970.

2. Broadcast of meetings: When cadres from the counties and communes in a region meet to discuss a major problem, the meeting is sometimes broadcast live for the local audience.

3. Experience of pioneer models: The experience of model units is sometimes broadcast as a special educational program. The experiences of Tachai Brigade and Tach'ing Oilfield have been widely publicized on the radio is this manner.

4. Mobilization for production: Communes have used wired broadcasting to organize production campaigns.

Television

Television broadcasting in black and white started in Peking on September 2, 1958. Color television broadcasting is now available, but color sets are few. There are currently 37 television broadcasting stations and 120 relay stations in the country, including those in Sinkiang and Tibet.[30] In 1958, there were about 10,000 television sets in Peking. The current total has been estimated at 1,000,000 sets in the whole country.[31] Television broadcasting is centrally controlled in Peking. The Peking Television Station, which produces most programs, operates under the supervision of the Central Broadcasting Bureau. The provincial stations transmit the programs from Peking and sometimes produce programs of their own. Local programming may increase in future.

The government is planning to expand television reception. The immediate target was to reach 2,000,000 sets by 1978 so that each production brigade would have one receiving set. All factories, schools, and hospitals with more than 100 individuals would also have at least one set by the end of 1978. Eventually cable will be used to send the signals to peasant homes.[32]

Television sets in China are domestically assembled. Most sets are 9 inches, in black and white, and priced at approximately US$130. A 12-inch black and white set is sold at US$250. Sets with larger screens, 14 and 16 inches, are available, but relatively few. Reports from China in 1975 suggest that the television set factory at Shaoshan, Hunan, was capable of producing 19-inch color sets.[33]

The Peking Television Station broadcasts on two channels, channel 2 and channel 8. Both channels begin their evening broadcasts at 7:00 p.m. and sign off at 10:00 p.m. In addition, channel 2 has three morning broadcasts a week, on Tuesday, Thursday, and Sunday, from 10:00 a.m. to noon. Channel 8 has a morning broadcast only on Sunday, from 9:00 a.m. to 11:00 a.m. The evening broadcasts on both channels begin with half an hour of domestic and international news, followed by a variety of programs that are highly similar in content to the radio broadcasts.[34] There are programs on science and technology, health and sanitation, art and literature, sports and, above all, the experiences of model units whose achievements are dramatized. Almost every day there is something for children—songs, dances, and stories—to instill a revolutionary spirit in young minds. Several times a week, feature films are shown, usually after 8:00 p.m. They are generally about the unusual feats of revolutionary heroes, such as Lei Feng, a Liberation Army martyr, model communes and factories, or sent-down youths whose self-sacrificing behavior deserves praise.

The Chinese have made ingenious use of popular, traditional forms of performing art on television. For instance, *hsiang sheng* (the traditional Chinese comic duet) has been used to present a program called "Learn from Iron Man Wang Ching-hsi," an exemplary tale of a model worker at the Tach'ing Oilfield. As far as we can tell, no regular programs on television teach the works of Marx, Lenin, and Mao. (See appendix B for a listing of one week of programs on Peking Television in August 1977.)

Trends—Past and Future

One of the primary functions of China's media is to help change the behavioral patterns and ideological orientations of the Chinese people away from the confines of the past toward the new ideals of the proletariat. To achieve this objective, the media have been used to criticize, in periodical campaigns and routine reminders, the "wicked winds" mentioned previously. At the same time, in big headlines and accentuated accounts, the media feature new behavioral models and ideological commitments to teach the values of altruistic service and loyalty to the collectivity. These spell out dos and don'ts for the people of China. Any information or ideas that are contrary to the Party's ideals, whether they originate from within or without, are kept out lest the minds of the people be contaminated.

How well have the Chinese accepted this mode of communication? What has been the response of the people to this form of ideological education? No clear answers are yet available, for there are no Gallup polls in China. We may gain a circumstantial index of the impact from the way the media content is perceived by the audience. The *Takung Pao (Takung Report),* a Hong Kong newspaper that generally reflects Peking's official thinking, recently revealed some noteworthy insights.[35] Quoting an editorial in the *Liberation Army Daily* of November 14, 1977, the report said that most Chinese newspapers during the reign of the Gang of Four were filled with empty words. "In a news item of thousands of words, from the beginning to the end you could not find a single concrete example." Furthermore, said the *Takung Pao,* quoting another editorial in the *Liberation Army Daily* from the middle of October 1977, the Gang of Four created a new "eight-legged" *(pa ku)* style of fabrication: "They used false speech, fabricated events, made false reports, created false models, publicized false experiences, wrote false history, and even falsified the sayings of our revolutionary teacher," so that the credibility of China's newspapers and publications was impaired.

Another trend prevalent during that period, noted the *Takung Pao,* was wooden-headed copying. Newspapers all over the country were forced to reprint articles composed by the Gang's writers. "You take a thousand newspapers, they all have the same front page. You take a thousand publications, they all have the same tone.'' The Chinese have even concocted a popular saying: "Small newspapers copy big newspapers; big newspapers follow Liang Hsiao" *(Hsiao pao ch'ao ta pao, ta pao ch'ao Liang Hsiao).*[36] "During those days," said the *Takung Pao,* "when people read a newspaper, they only looked at the headlines. When people read a book, they only looked at the cover. Newspapers and publications were not well received by the mass of people."

The *Takung Pao* cited three letters to the editor published in Peking's *Kuangming Daily* on December 3, 1977, to point out that the practice of reprinting approved articles has not abated even though the Gang of Four has been toppled. One letter said that many professional publications were still reprinting political articles and documents from official newspapers on a massive scale, making themselves almost archives of documents.

Thus, according to the *Takung Pao,* a movement is currently afoot to reform China's newspapers and to restore the spirit which Chairman Mao encouraged during the Yenan days.

Addendum

By the summer of 1980, nearly four years after the purge of the Gang of Four, the direction of this reform began to crystallize. While the structure of the media has remained the same, there have been both continuity and change in the basic philosophy of mass communication. The mass media are still being used to organize the national efforts, to provide information in support of the mass mobilization, and to help mold a new ideology. The changes have been in the pragmatic interpretation of this philosophy and in the diminishing role of the media in class struggle.

These changes were slow and almost imperceptible at first. From October 1976, when the Gang was purged, to the spring of 1978 there was a concerted campaign in the media to condemn the Gang and its followers. Other than that, the one apparent change during that period had to do with quotations from Chairman Mao. Before his death, the upper right corner of the front page of the *People's Daily* was exclusively reserved for a daily display of his sayings, always framed in a box. This box appeared less and less frequently following his death. By the spring of 1978, this box had disappeared. In the days when Chiang Ch'ing was in power, articles in the *People's Daily* were accentuated by quotations from Mao, set in bold type. This custom was discontinued after Mao's death.

An important substantive departure from the past came in May 1978 when a public debate was initiated in the media on the criteria of truth.[37] Is truth whatever the Party leadership has said, reflecting, as it were, a personality cult? Or does truth have an empirical basis to be found in the reality of the people's experience? This debate continued for about a year. By the late spring of 1979, the outcome of this debate was no longer in doubt. Truth is not "whatever" emanates from the Party leadership, but must be grounded in an empirical validity supported by reality. As part of this debate, certain leaders in the post-Mao Party hierarchy were criticized for being "whateverists," because they had been advocating a philosophy that "whatever" the leader has said must be true, and "whatever" the leader has decided must not be changed. This philosophy has since been discarded.

The debate on truth and the resolution of the "whateverist" issue are clearly reflected in China's mass media. In July 1979, apparently marking the end of the debate, the official *People's Daily* published an editorial entitled "Defend Truthfulness and Oppose False Reporting."[38] Since the arrest of the Gang, said the editorial, many newspapers in China have made an effort to correct false reporting, but in practice, reports that are untrue or only partly true still appear in the newspapers now and then. Other cases show selective omission. The editorial gave several examples and then commented:

> These practices of false reporting and exaggeration have caused serious damage to the enterprises of our Party. They corrupt the Party's workstyle, and affect the Party's reputation. . . . We have suffered a great deal because of this.

The editorial asked the leadership cadres to be more candid and truthful.

Since then, the emphasis in the media has shifted to more factual reporting on the pressing issues of economic development in coordination with the current campaign of Four Modernizations (in agriculture, industry, science and technology, and defense) rather than political indoctrination. On January 1, 1980, the *People's Daily* was expanded from six to eight pages. A tally shows that out of 29 front-page headline news stories in January 1980, 21 (72.5 percent) were about economic development.[39] A year before, out of 27 front-page headline news stories in January 1979, only three (11 percent) were about economic development. In January 1980, 312 news stories were published on the front pages of the *People's Daily*. Of these, 173 (55.4 percent) were economic news. In January 1979, 151 news stories were published on the front pages. Only 48 (31.8 percent) of these were economic news. In an average week, the *People's Daily* now reserves nine pages for economic news, including four and a half pages on agriculture, usually on page 2, and four and a half pages on industry and commerce, usually on page 3. There has been regular coverage of science and technology.

The same statistics cited above show that the stories in the *People's Daily* are shorter. In January 1979, an average of 4.87 stories were published on the front page. In January 1980, the corresponding number was 10.1 stories.

In the ideological arena, the previous tone of extolling the radical rhetoric of class struggle has been discontinued. The new ideological hallmark is stability and unity in a socialist framework, rather than class struggle. According to an important policy speech delivered at the inauguration meeting of the newly formed Peking Journalist Association in February 1980,[40] the new tasks of China's media are to provide an ideological foundation for this unity and stability and to propagate the superiority of China's socialism. The media are considered an important weapon which Chinese journalists can use effectively to support the Party leadership in achieving these goals.

At the same time, parallel to what Mao called combating the "wicked wind," the media have launched a campaign since mid-1979 to criticize rather severely the various ills of bureaucratism that seem to stand in the way of modernization. Erroneous behavior by Party cadres is being constantly exposed. One example is the criticism of the leaders of the Tachai movement, which was once endorsed by Chairman Mao. It has now been reported that Hsiyang County, home of the famous Tachai Brigade, fabricated production figures by nearly 24 percent during the five-year period of 1973-1977 in order to maintain the myth of the Tachai model.[41]

Letters to the editor are being published in the official newspapers on a regular basis to call public attention to petty corruption and abuse of power by cadres.[42] Examples include a county cadre who used the occasion of his son's wedding to collect cash contributions and gifts, commune cadres who pocketed relief food and cloth subsidies intended for minority members, and a commune secretary who ordered the destruction of an entire crop of melons because it was not in the production plans.[43] The *People's Daily* receives an average of 2000 letters a day from its readers and has a special department for processing the audience mail. Another department makes investigations on the basis of the complaints.[44] Cases of corruption and abuse of power, when they are found true, have been publicized in the official newspapers and condemned.

Human interest stories, unknown in the Chinese media when the radical group was in control, now frequently appear, sometimes on the front page. For example, one story told how people in Shanghai breed earthworms for feeding ducks, which lay more and bigger eggs.[45] Entertainment has returned to the Chinese newspapers. China's newspapers now feature book reviews, theatre reviews, fashion, recipes, poems, essays, serialized novels, and short stories.

By the fall of 1980, an English-language daily newspaper, the first ever in China since 1949, is scheduled to be published by the People's Press. The Beijing (Peking) *Times*, as it is tentatively named, will not be an English version of the *People's Daily*; nor will it be an English-language organ of the Party, as is the Beijing (Peking) *Review*. It is primarily geared to the tourists and English-speaking population in China as well as those Chinese who can read English. The content will be half information and half entertainment. It is initially planned to be a 16-page tabloid, something like the *Christian Science Monitor*. About 25 to 30 percent of the space will be for advertising. It will be printed simultaneously in Peking, Shanghai, and Canton (or Hong Kong), and will be available for overseas subscribers. The initial issue will be 20,000 copies, to be expanded to 100,000 copies in one year.[46]

In short, the mass media in post-Mao China are primarily means of communication among the people and between the leaders and the people. It is considered an instrument for fostering unity and development rather than for waging class struggle. There is a greater emphasis on factual reporting than on ideological indoctrination. There is greater diversity in contents. Brevity and practicality take precedence over long theoretical discourse. As one editor put it, "We are released from the shackles of the Cultural Revolution. We now can write what is truth, not what someone has said."

NOTES

1. Mao Tse-tung, "Get Organized!" *Selected Works of Mao Tse-tung*, vol. 3 (Peking: Foreign Languages Press, 1966), p. 158.

2. Mao Tse-tung, "A Talk to the Editorial Staff of the *Shansi-Suiyuan Daily*," *Selected Works of Mao Tse-tung*, vol. 3 (Peking: Foreign Languages Press, 1969), p. 241.

3. Mao Tse-tung, "Talks at the Meeting of Party Secretaries of Provincial Level," *Selected Works of Mao Tse-tung*, vol. 5 (Peking: People's Publishing Press, 1977), p. 350.

4. Chiang Hung, "Strengthen the Ideological Development of the News Reporting Groups," *Red Flag*, no. 2, 1971, p. 10.

5. Ibid., p. 11.

6. Richard Dudman, "Headlines and Deadlines: Chinese Style," *Nieman Reports* (Spring and Summer 1977): 19-21.

7. Wilbur E. Elston, "In China, Newspapers Serve the Party," in *China Today* (Detroit: *Detroit News,* 1972), p. 52.

8. J. Edward Murray, "How China's Press Handles News," in *4000 Miles Across China* (Detroit: *Detroit Free Press,* 1972), p. 23.

9. Ibid.

10. The *Canton Daily* (June 12, 1975) had two stories on the front page: a telephone-broadcasting meeting among factory workers and cadres in the province to study the instructions from Chairman Mao on promoting industrial production; the visit by the president of Zambia to China. Page 2 carried an editorial supporting Chairman Mao's latest instructions and three more stories about the visit of the president of Zambia. Page 3 had three provincial news items: a feature story on ideological education for students, and two brevities. Page 4 carried mostly foreign news from the New China News Agency.

The *Nan Fang Daily* (June 13, 1975) displayed on its front page a picture of Chairman Mao greeting the president of Zambia. There was a story on how the Canton Railway Station set a record of freight transportation during the first half of the year. In another announcement, Marshal Chu Teh and Premier Chou En-lai sent a message on the Phillippine Independence Day. Page 2 carried two stories about model peasants and three brief commentaries we shall discuss. Page 3 had four stories about revolutionary operas. Page 4 had mostly foreign news from New China News Agency dispatches, in addition to reproduced posters about the first Chinese National Games.

11. *Nan Fang Jihpao* [Southern Daily], June 13, 1975.

12. Mao Tse-tung, "Talks at the Meeting of Party Secretaries of Provincial Level," *Selected Works,* vol. 5 (Peking: People's Publishing Press, 1977), p. 349. The immunizing function of what Mao called "negative materials" was discussed recently in the official press. See Hsiao Kui, "Negative Materials and Smallpox Vaccine," *People's Daily,* August 14, 1977.

13. Emmett Dedmon, *China Journal* (Chicago: Rand McNally, 1973), p. 140. Also Chang Kuo-hsin, "World News Read Only by China's Selected Few," *IPI* [International Press Institute] *Report 25* (February 1976): 1-2.

14. "A Journalist and His Paper," in Francis Harper, ed., *Out of China: A Collection of Interviews with Refugees from China* (Hong Kong: Dragonfly Books, 1964), pp. 222-225.

15. On Page 1, the major story was ABC's commentary on Deputy Foreign Minister Chiao Kuan-hua's address at the United Nations. Another leading story summarized a feature from *Tokyo Shimbun* on American and Russian reactions to the reduction of tension in Asia. A report in *Yumiori Shimbun* on normalization of relations with China and on Japan's territorial claims with Soviet Russia was also reproduced. The other three pages carried news, all from foreign sources, about: a visit by a Polish Delegation to France and the signing of an economic pact between the two countries, Brezhnev's impending visit to the United States, the conclusion of a visit to Russia by the Malaysian prime minister, Egyptian Prime Minister Sadat's interview on the Lebanon incident, Yemen's criticism of Sadat, a statement by the Indian defense minister on India's military deployment in the Himalayan region, a story in the *Washington Daily News* on China's relations with Latin America, and a train accident in Mexico. Interestingly, this particular issue carried four items on page 4 about scientific development in the United States and Soviet Russia.

16. "Peasant Correspondents of Huang Lou Commune," *Wen Hui Pao* [Wen Hui Report], December 24, 1968.

17. Ibid.

18. For a brief discussion of the traditional use of posters in China, see Godwin C. Chu, '*Tatzepao,*' in *Radical Change through Communication in Mao's China* (Honolulu: The University Press of Hawaii, 1977), pp. 232-238; also Barry M. Broman, "*Tatzepao:* Medium of Conflict in China's Cultural Revolution," *Journalism Quarterly* 46 (Spring 1969): 100.

19. See David Jim-tat Poon, "*Tatzepao:* Its History and Significance as a Communication Medium," in Godwin C. Chu, ed., *Popular Media in China: Shaping New Cultural Patterns,* (Honolulu: The University Press of Hawaii, 1978), pp. 184-221.

20. See Godwin C. Chu, "Communication and Conflict Resolution," in *Radical Change,* pp. 215-252.

21. See Broman, "*Tatzepao*"; also Godwin C. Chu, Philip H. Cheng, and Leonard Chu, *The Roles of Tatzepao in the Cultural Revolution* (Carbondale, Ill.: Southern Illinois University, 1972).

22. "Constitution of the People's Republic of China," article no. 13, *People's Daily,* January 20, 1975.

23. See Poon, "*Tatzepao.*"

24. The *tatzupao,* signed by Li I-che, was posted in a public street in Canton in November 1974 and was addressed to Chairman Mao and the Fourth National People's Congress. Its preface and text, about 23,000 words long, were later carried in full in *Ming Pao Monthly* (Hong Kong) 10 (December 1975): 53-60. Li I-che, in reality, was three persons: *Li* Cheng-tien, a 1966 graduate from the Canton Art Institute, Chen *I*-yang, and Huang Hsi-*che,* both offspring of Party cadres. All active Red Guards during the Cultural Revolution, they criticized the Party for what they considered to be major shortcomings of the Chinese Communist system. For a brief summary of their criticisms, see "Lee's *Tatzepao:* To Mao with Dissent," *The Asian Messenger,* Spring 1976, p. 27.

25. Hu Shou-heng, "A Current Analysis of Broadcasting and Television in Communist China," in *Pao Hsüeh* [Studies of Journalism] 5 (June 1977): 121-122.

26. *Peking Review* 18 (1975): 30.

27. See Frederick T. C. Yu, *Mass Persuasion in Communist China* (New York: Praeger, 1964); and Alan P. L. Liu, *Communications and National Integration in Communist China* (Berkeley: University of California Press, 1971).

28. Ming Ch'en, "Broadcasting Network in Rural China Since the Cultural Revolution," *Ming Pao Monthly,* no. 121, 1976, pp. 93-100.

29. Ibid.

30. Huai Yu, "Television Broadcasting in Communist China," in *Studies on Chinese Communism* (March 15, 1977): 73-78.

31. Ibid., p. 75.

32. Ibid.

33. Leonard Chu, "Television Broadcasting in China," *Ming Pao* [Ming Report] (Hong Kong), April 26, 1977.

34. We shall briefly describe one newscast, on August 14, 1977, from Peking Television Station. The program started with a preview of the news items for the evening. The first, lasting seven minutes, was a report on recent developments in Wenchou, Chekiang Province. Factory workers and peasants were shown to be raising their hands to denounce the Gang of Four and working hard to rebuild Wenchou from the destruction suffered under the Gang of Four's reign. The female announcer, who did not appear, emphasized that the people of Wenchou were carrying on the reconstruction following the instructions of the late Chairman Mao. The camera showed an ironworks, a china factory, and an embroidery shop. Men and women were shown busy at work, much like those pictured in *China Reconstructs,* an official Chinese pictorial for overseas distribution. Next was brief (one and a half

minutes) coverage of a salt field near Canton, where production had gone up. For the next three and a half minutes, Vice Premier Li Hsien-nien was shown greeting the prime minister from Sao Tome. Pictured were the handshaking at the Peking airport, the reception line showing each of the dignitaries present, and the dinner party, at which Li was shown making a speech; a female voice narrated. After that, Vice Premier Chi Teng-k'ui bid his welcome to a visiting group from Japan, with handshaking and a reception line.

The domestic portion of the newscast was concluded by a 6-minute report on the resurrection of a Hopeh vernacular stage show, "A Commonplace Post," which had been killed by the Gang of Four. The report began with a criticism of the Gang of Four and then proceeded to show how the actors and actresses were rehearsing for their new performance. It was a story about a young worker who did not like to carry human manure but wanted to be a truck driver in the city. His Party secretary, an old worker, eventually convinced him that he could make a contribution to the revolution even in his commonplace post as a manure collector.

International news (10 minutes) began with the introduction of the Japanese edition of volume 5 of Chairman Mao's selected works in Japan. Japanese visitors were shown buying the book at a trade fair. This was followed by a brief report on the West African economic conference in the capital of Togo, and exchange of visits by presidents and premiers in Africa and Latin America. The international news for that day included a horsemanship event in Europe and an international track meet. These events occurred in July. The weather in Peking ended the news program.

While it would be difficult to generalize from the news program of one day, several characteristics may be noted. No one talks on television in the entire news program. Everything is voiced over by the female announcer, who remains anonymous and does not appear during the program. Timeliness seems to be of no particular consequence, as most of the domestic events reported that day took place during the previous month. The leading news item, on Wenchou, was not about a particular event. None of the news reports presented any details. There were no commercials.

35. The following is based upon Chai Chi, "Newspapers in China Are Undergoing a Major Reform," *Takung Pao* (Hong Kong), December 7, 1977.

36. Liang Hsiao, apparently a pseudonym, is pronounced the same way as "two schools" in Chinese. It is generally assumed that "Liang Hsiao" referred to the team of theoretical writers from Peking University and Tsing Hua University that wrote important articles for Chiang Ch'ing and her followers prior to the death of Chairman Mao.

37. Guan Zaihan, an editor of the Beijing (Peking) *Review,* considered this debate to be the most important landmark in China's new journalism. "New Journalism in China," talk given by Guan at the East-West Center on July 16, 1980.

38. "Defend Truthfulness, Oppose False Reporting," editorial, *People's Daily,* July 24, 1979.

39. The tally was made by a Chinese editor to mark the expansion of the *People's Daily.* See Hsu Chan-kui, "Front-page Highlights," in *Xinwen Zhanxian* (Journalism Battlefront), No. 3, March 1980, pp. 28-29.

40. See Hu Chiao-mu, "Talk at the Inauguration Meeting of the Peking Journalist Association," February 6, 1980, in *Xinwen Zhanxian,* No. 4, April 1980, pp. 2-9. These remarks are attributed to Vice Premier Teng Hsiao-ping.

41. "Hsiyang County Falsified Production Figures by 270,000,000 Catties in Five-year Period," *People's Daily,* July 7, 1980; also "A Lesson to Those Who Lied," editorial, *People's Daily,* July 8, 1980.

42. For an analysis of the letters, see Godwin C. Chu and Leonard L. Chu, "Letters to the Editor They Write in China," *East-West Perspectives*, Vol. 1, No. 1, Summer 1979, pp. 2-7.

43. "How a Criticism Letter Was Handled," *People's Daily*, May 15, 1979. Lo Hsiu-hsing, "May the Leadership Send Somebody to the Miao District," *People's Daily*, July 18, 1978. "What Does the Destruction of Melons Mean?" *People's Daily*, July 27, 1979.

44. Guan Zaihan, "New Journalism in China."

45. Hsu Chan-kui, "Front-page Highlights."

46. Guan Zaihan, "New Journalism in China."

The Press Research Center in Cracow, Poland, has for several years conducted comparative analyses of socialist and nonsocialist newspapers with the objective of relating comparative press philosophies to the realities of press performance. Under the direction of Walery Pisarek, these studies provide a unique view of selected prestige newspapers of East and West. In the article that follows, Dr. Pisarek presents data showing that socialist and nonsocialist newspapers concentrate heavily on coverage of political leadership in foreign news about Poland, an important nation within the East bloc. Beyond that point, dramatic differences emerge. The Western papers studied gave considerable visibility to church leaders and to opposition-dissenting leadership in Poland. No coverage on those topics appeared in the socialist press. This paper was first presented at the May 1980 World Communications Conference at the Annenberg School in Philadelphia. Dr. Pisarek is director of the Press Research Center.

42

HEROES OF FOREIGN NEWS

A Polish Perspective on Newsmakers in Socialist and Nonsocialist Newspapers

Walery Pisarek

"Heroes" of the foreign news are those Polish people whose names appear in foreign news published in newspapers. Thus, they are not people who achieve heroic deeds but simply people doing things or affected by events covered by newspapers. We could here equally well use other terms like newsmakers, characters, or actors who are the subjects of the stories published in selected "prestige" newspapers of France, the Federal Republic of Germany, Russia, Czechoslovakia, and the German Democratic Republic.

The importance of this content analysis is twofold: First, it can be treated not only as an analysis of press coverage of Poland but as an example of foreign press coverage of actors from a typical socialist country. Second— and it should be emphasized—the study compares socialist and nonsocialist countries.[1]

The logic of this study is quite simple. For obvious reasons, every newspaper has to select people deserving to become the object of public

From Walery Pisarek, "Heroes of Foreign News: A Polish Perspective on Newsmakers in Socialist and Nonsocialist Newspapers," original manuscript.

interest. Who and how often certain actors are covered in a given newspaper may be treated as the simplest indicator of its editorial policy. Briefly, tell me about whom a newspaper most often writes and I will be able to tell you what is its political and ideological profile and what type of journalism it represents.

RELATED STUDIES

Many comparative studies have also been conducted on newspapers from selected countries in order to find out international differences in the content of communication.[2] A classical study of 17 dailies made by J. Kayser (1953) under the auspices of UNESCO is usually given as a typical example of this kind of analysis. A few years ago Gerbner and Marvanyi (1977) published an excellent report on the analysis of the content of foreign news. They showed how the presses of various countries distort the image of the world. This line of communication research has been carried out on an international scale by a large project on "cultural indicators" (Gerbner, 1969; Gerbner and Gross, 1976) and the "images of foreign countries" project sponsored by UNESCO and conducted by IAMCR (Nordenstreng and Salomaa, 1978).

Research on images of the world and racial or national stereotypes existing in consciousness of different societies[3] has probably an even longer tradition. Linguistic means used in the press and strengthening or forming stereotypes have been studied (Merrill, 1965). Finally, attempts were made to collate "media coverage" and media images of the nationalities and particular personalities with their social stereotypes (Halloran, 1974).

The conviction that newspapers published in socialist countries are diametrically opposed to those published in developed capitalist countries is quite common both in the East and the West. This belief, in my opinion, has been based on the knowledge of the two opposing press doctrines rather than on actual study of newspaper content.

PURPOSE OF THE STUDY

This study has been part of a series of comparative content analyses of the press of the developed capitalist countries and socialist countries. Such analyses have been carried out for several years in the Press Research Centre in Cracow either under my supervision or by myself personally.[4] In this study the press from socialist countries was represented by *Neues Deutschland* (*ND*) of the German Democratic Republic, *Pravda* of the USSR, and *Rude Pravo* (*RP*) of Czechoslovakia. The capitalist press were *Le Monde* of France, *Frankfurter Allgemeine Zeitung* (*FAZ*) of the Federal Republic of Germany, and *International Herald Tribune* (*IHT*) of the United States.[5]

The analysis covered all the issues from January 1 to December 31, 1978.

Each appearance of a Polish actor's name in a newspaper was counted. If a Polish name was mentioned in a story two, three, or four times, it was counted two, three, or four times, respectively. Coding was done by two experienced research assistants of the Press Research Centre in Cracow. There was more than 90 percent agreement between the coders on choice and classifications of names, indicating high reliability.

RESULTS

In a broad sense, both Western and Eastern newspapers exhibit a number of common features: political and economic news is the largest category of their editorial content; foreign affairs coverage is dominated by the foreign news abroad; and the geopolitical distribution of foreign coverage seems to be governed according to similar principles. Most news attention was devoted to the world powers the United States and the USSR—and to those countries which are in particularly close cooperation with the mother country of the newspaper in question. Thus, Britain's *The Times* devoted most of its space to Western Europe and the United States; *Pravda* of the Soviet Union focused on European socialist countries; the *International Herald Tribune* concentrated on Western Europe; the Polish press looked to the USSR, the United States, Western Europe, and other socialist countries.

Using more detailed categories in the content analysis, we discover basic differences existing between newspapers from different countries. They differ in amount of space devoted to political and economic news and in their attitudes toward the same events. They use different sources of information and differ in amount of space devoted to smaller countries. For example, comparison of Polish and Soviet newspapers on one hand and West German ones on the other shows that words denoting work, organization, nationalism, planning, and important social and economic trends dominate in Polish and Soviet newspapers. Words meaning money, government, company, market, and the unusual and exceptional dominate in the West German newspapers.

The results of comparative analyses of topics, geopolitical distribution, and words frequency in the press from various countries warrant the formulation of the following hypothesis concerning the structure of the population of actors in various newspapers: the most frequently mentioned actors of foreign news in various newspapers are either the same or they represent the same positions in social structures. The second—regarding the frequency of occurrence—category of actors of foreign news includes people the interest in whom distinguishes newspapers of socialist countries from capitalist newspapers. Finally, the third category includes those people the interest in whom is characteristic for particular newspapers or particular countries.

Using this model, let us look at the list of Polish actors of foreign news in three newspapers published in three socialist countries and three newspapers published in three capitalist countries.

The number of Polish actors[6] of foreign news mentioned in these newspapers differs. Among the three socialist newspapers, Polish citizens were mentioned relatively most frequently in *Neues Deutschland* and least often in *Pravda;* among Western newspapers, Poles were reported most frequently in *Le Monde* and least frequently in *IHT.* On one hand, we find that in general the socialist press is more interested in Poles than the Western press; however, newspapers of the two big powers (*Pravda* and *IHT*) are less interested in Poles than were the newspapers from the other countries.

All Polish actors were classified into six broad position categories: (1) government-party-administration, (2) science-art-media, (3) church-religion, (4) opposition-dissent, (5) history, and (6) ordinary people-citizens. Category 1 (government-party-administration) is the most numerous in *Pravda;* category 2 (science-culture-media) in *ND, RP, Le Monde,* and *FAZ;* whereas category 4 (opposition-dissent) is most visible, in *IHT.* Strikingly, categories 3 (church-religion) and 4 (opposition-dissent) are not news makers in the socialist press.

More interesting results can be obtained when, instead of comparing the number of various persons (types), we compare the frequency of their occurrence (tokens) in particular newspapers. In any case, the results confirm the hypothesis that each of the examined newspapers writes most often about the people who represent government, party, and administration (see Table 42.1). The second place on the hierarchy in all European newspapers belongs to the category of the representatives of science, culture, and mass media; the second place in *IHT* is the category of representatives of opposition and dissent. The third place in socialist newspapers belongs to ordinary Polish people (category 4) who are never mentioned in foreign news of the Western press. In West European presses the third and the fourth places are occupied by representatives of opposition, dissent, and church (absent in the socialist press) in the newspaper—representatives of science, culture, and mass media.

In all six newspapers, actors of foreign news are almost exclusively men. Mentions about women do not exceed one percent.

In all six newspapers E. Gierek, the former First Secretary of the Polish United Workers Party, was most visible (see Figure 42.1). But the second most visible newsmaker exemplifies the major difference between socialist and Western newspapers. In the socialist newspapers this second place has been taken up by M. Hermaszewski, a Polish astronaut whose name has never been mentioned in the Western newspapers. The Western newspapers give the second place to S. Wyszynski, Polish Prelate, who is not mentioned in any of the lists of the three socialist newspapers. The third place on the lists

TABLE 42.1 Percentage of Polish Actors of Foreign News in 6 Newspapers According to Their Area of Presented Activity, 1978, by Type and Token

Categories of presented activity	ND		PRAVDA		RP		LE MONDE		FAZ		IHT	
	Types N=246	Tokens N=945	Types N=158	Tokens N=666	Types N=206	Tokens N=752	Types N=77	Tokens N=320	Types N=69	Token N=381	Types N=57	Tokens N=204
I Government-party-central administration	28	62	46	78	36	66	34	54	31	50	14	49
II Church-religion	—	—	—	—	—	—	1	8	1	16	4	13
III Culture-science-media	56	28	32	14	46	23	37	21	43	23	5	4
IV Opposition-dissent	—	—	—	—	—	—	23	13	16	9	73	32
V History	6	3	6	3	7	5	5	4	9	2	4	2
VI Ordinary people-unknown persons	10	7	16	5	11	6	—	—	—	—	—	—

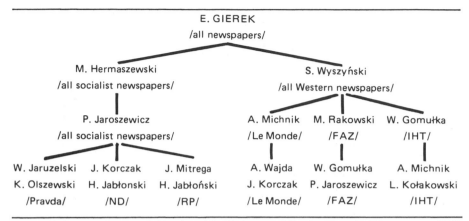

Figure 42.1: Most Frequently Mentioned Polish Actors of Foreign News in 6 Newspapers, 1978

of the three socialist newspapers is taken up by P. Jaroszewicz, then Prime Minister of Poland, who can be found in further positions on the lists of the Western newspapers. In the Western newspapers the third place falls to different persons: in *Le Monde,* to A. Michnik, representative of the Polish dissidents; in *FAZ,* to the journalist M. Rakowski, the editor-in-chief of the weekly "Polityka"; in *IHT,* to W. Gomułka, the former First Secretary of the Polish United Workers Party, presented in the newspaper as an alternative for the present party leadership. It should be stressed that Michnik, Gomułka, and Rakowski, who placed so high on the lists of the Western newspapers, cannot be found on the lists of the socialist newspapers. The fourth and fifth places are occupied by different people in each of the newspapers: in *ND,* by J. Korczak (a writer killed by Nazis during World War II) and H. Jablonski (president of State Council); in *RP,* by J. Mitrega (Polish ambassador in Prague) and H. Jablonski; in *Pravda,* by W. Jaruzelski (minister) and K. Olszewski (then Polish ambassador in Moscow); in *Le Monde,* by A. Wajda (film director) and J. Korczak; in *FAZ,* by W. Gomułka and P. Jaroszewicz; in *IHT,* by A. Michnik and L. Kolaskowski (Polish emigre).

Thus, the comparison of only the five most frequently appearing names in the analyzed newspapers suggests these similarities and differences:

— All newspapers write most frequently about the people holding the most important political position in the state (E. Gierek).

— Newspapers from socialist countries act in unison presenting people personifying common achievements of these countries (M. Hermaszewski).

— Newspapers from capitalist countries present in unison people holding key positions in the institutions which, from the editorial point of view, can form the basis for ideological or political opposition (S. Wyszynski).

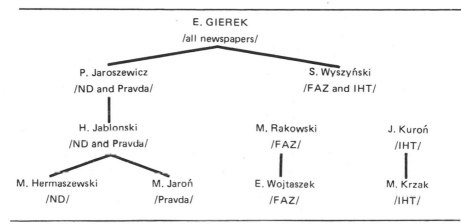

Figure 42.2: Most Frequently Mentioned Polish Actors of Foreign News in 4 Newspapers, 1979

— Newspapers from socialist countries are more unanimous concerning the selection of the "newsmakers" than newspapers of capitalist countries (the third place on the lists of all socialist newspapers takes up P. Jaroszewicz, whereas on the lists of Western newspapers there are three different persons).
— The West European newspapers bear more resemblance to socialist news-papers than the American newspaper (the name of J. Korczak belongs to the five most frequently mentioned in *ND* and *Le Monde,* and the name of P. Jaroszewicz can be found in all socialist newspapers and *FAZ*).[7]

The above conclusions were verified in a separate analysis of the actors of foreign news in *ND, Pravda, FAZ* and *IHT* throughout the year 1979. All odd issues of the above-mentioned newspapers were used as a sample (see Figure 42.2).

In the context of these results a question may be asked about the foreign newsmakers from Czechoslovakia, France, the FRG, the GDR, the United States, and the USSR as presented in the Polish newspaper *Trybuna Ludu* (*TL*). The analysis of the actors from these countries mentioned in *Trybuna Ludu* was based on the same methodological principles and took into account the same periods of time as the analyses of Polish actors mentioned in *ND, Pravda, RP, FAZ, Le Monde,* and *IHT.* The results show that the actors from the USSR and the United States were mentioned in *TL* much more often than actors from Czechoslovakia, France, the FRG, and the GDR. As a general rule, each of the six countries was represented in *TL* most often by the chief executive, president, prime minister, or first secretary of the ruling party. Editorial interest of *TL* regarding each of the countries concentrates, first of all, on the leaders of state administration or of the party hierarchy. The second—regarding quantitative force—category of foreign actors in *TL* includes, in the case of the three socialist countries and the United States, representatives of the world of science, culture, and mass media; in the case of France, representatives of the parliamentary opposition; and the FRG, war criminals. The analysis of *TL* suggests that Polish press treatment of Americans, Frenchmen, and Germans from the FRG is more similar to the way the Poles are treated in *ND, Pravda,* and *RP* than portrayal of the Poles in *FAZ, Le Monde,* and *IHT.*

CONCLUSION

An analysis of the actors of foreign news in selected socialist and capitalist newspapers suggests that the probability of writing about people who are citizens of a foreign country increases if

— the country where the newspaper is printed and homeland of the actor have common goals and cooperate;

— there is a conflict of interest between the country of the newspaper and the native country of the actor;

— the behavior of the actor conforms to the stereotypes which are regarded as socially or ideologically desirable by the newspaper;

— information on an actor turns out to be cognitively or instrumentally useful for the would-be readers of the newspaper;

— the actor's behavior has been of great value as far as "human interest" is concerned.

Citizens of large countries which play an important international role have a greater chance to become actors of news in foreign newspapers. Overwhelmingly, though, the real heroes of foreign news in the influential press all over the world are the political leaders from particular countries. On the other hand, from the comparison of mechanisms of selection of foreign actors in socialist and Western newspapers, one can draw a conclusion which can be expressed in a humorous way: If you want to become an actor of foreign news in the socialist press, try to take a leading position in the government or the party; if you want the Western press to write about you, become a dissident.

Although this analysis was conducted from the Polish point of view, its results seem to question whether the present strategy (conscious or unconscious) of choice and presentation of the actors of foreign news conforms to the needs of the peaceful coexistence on a global scale in the 1980s. Moreover, there are many indications that the revealed tendencies will not be halted but will increase in the coming decade. Would it be so that the international information contributes to the deepening divisions of the world?

NOTES

1. As P.H. Tannenbaum wrote in his comment on the World Communications Symposium held in Philadelphia in 1977, "it would be useful not to forget that we still live in an era where information/communication systems are intimately connected with political considerations."

2. After World War II the first wave of the studies of this kind has been documented in the articles published in *Public Opinion Quarterly* (Kriesberg, 1946; Dalin, 1947; Bassow, 1948).

3. A large international bibliography referring to this subject is given by Quasthoff (1973).

4. The results of the analyses have been shown by Pisarek (1977) and Lewartowska (1978, 1980).

5. All these newspapers can be considered as "prestige newspapers" according to the terminology by I. de Sola Pool. Traditionally, in comparative analyses *Le Monde* and *FAZ* have been regarded as "prestige newspapers" in France and the FRG, respectively. In the socialist countries newspapers of the central committees of the ruling parties usually function as prestige newspapers. *ND, Pravda,* and *RP* are the organs of central committees of the SED, the Communist Party of the USSR, and the Communist Party of Czechoslovakia, respectively. *IHT* was chosen as a representative of American newspapers because of the fact that by reason of the place of its publication it is more Europe-oriented than other newspapers from the United States.

6. When collecting the material the most frequently mentioned Pole in the press of the majority of countries in 1978 and 1979, Pope John Paul II, was not taken under consideration. Press interest in his person results from the fact that he is the head of the Roman-Catholic Church, and as such this interest has no national basis.

7. Extension of the analysis up to 20 names of the Poles most frequently mentioned in the six newspapers confirms the above results. Two names—Gierek and Jaroszewicz—appear in all lists. The three socialist lists give six further names: Hermaszewski, Jabloński, Jaruszelski, Wojtaszek, Frelek, Kopernik. Western lists include, apart from Gierek and Jaroszewicz, only four common names: Wyszyński, Michnik, Gomulka, Rakowski. *Le Monde* has, apart from Gierek and Jaroszewicz, only one common name with *Pravda* and one with *ND. FAZ* has two common names with *Pravda* and one with *ND. IHT* has only one common name, apart from Gierek and Jaroszewicz, with socialist newspapers: Wojtaszek.

REFERENCES

BASSOW, W. (1948) "Izvestia looks inside USA." Public Opinion Quarterly 12:430-439.
DALIN, A. (1947) "America through Soviet eyes." Public Opinion Quarterly 11:26-39.
GERBNER, G. (1969) "Towards 'cultural indicators': the analysis of mass mediated message systems." AV Communication Review 17:137-148.
_____ and L. GROSS (1976) "Living with television: the violence profile." Journal of Communication 26:173-199.
_____ and G. MARVANYI (1977) "The many worlds of the world's press." Journal of Communication 27:52-66.
HALLORAN, J.D. [ed.] (1974) "Race as news." Paris: UNESCO.
KAYSER, J. (1953) "One-week's news: comparative study of 17 major dailies for a seven-day period." Paris: UNESCO
KRIESBERG, M. (1946) "Soviet news in the New York *Times.*" Public Opinion Quarterly, 10:540-564.
LEWARTOWSKA, Z. (1978) "Prasowy obraz krajów a rzeczywistość" (Images of Countries Presented in the Press and the Reality). Zeszyty Prasoznawcze 19:25-44.
_____ (1980) "Polska w gazetach centralnych krajów sasiednich" (Images of Poland as presented in main newspapers in neighboring countries). Zeszyty Prasoznawcze 21:19-34.
MERRILL, J.C. (1965) "How *Time* stereotyped three U.S. presidents." Journalism Quarterly 42:563-570.
NORDENSTRENG, K. and M. SALOMAA (1978) "Studying the image of foreign countries as portrayed by the mass media: a progress report." Prepared for the scientific conference of the IAMCR, September 4-9, Warsaw.

PISAREK, W. (1977) "Deistvitelnost i yazyk pressy" (Reality as reflected in newspaper's language). Vestnik Moskovskogo Universiteta—Zhurnalistika, No. 5:52-56.

QUASTHOFF, U. (1973) "Soziales vorurteil und kommunikation." Athenaum Fischer, Frankfurt a/M.